C++

Object-Oriented Data Structures

Saumyendra Sengupta
Carl Phillip Korobkin

C++

Object-Oriented Data Structures

With 165 Illustrations

Diskette Included

Springer

Saumyendra Sengupta
Carl Phillip Korobkin
Silicon Graphics Corporation
2011 N. Shoreline Blvd.
Mountain View, CA 94039-7311

Cover photograph of the Temple of the Concordia, Agrigento, Italy.
Courtesy of David Viaggi, U.S.A.

Library of Congress Cataloging-in-Publication Data
Saumyendra, Sengupta.
    C++, object-oriented data structures / Saumyendra Senguta, Carl
Phillip Korobkin.
        p.   cm.
    Includes bibliographical references and index.
    ISBN 0-387-94194-0
    1. C++ (Computer program language) 2. Object-oriented programming
(Computer science) 3. Data structures (Computer science)
I. Korobkin, Carl Phillip. II. Title.
QA76.73.C153S28   1994
005.7'3—dc20   93-40950

Printed on acid-free paper

Production managed by Laura Carlson; manufacturing supervised by Vincent Scelta.
Photocomposed copy prepared from the authors' LaTeX files.
Printed and bound by R.R. Donnelley & Sons, Harrisonburg, VA.
Printed in the United States of America.

9 8 7 6 5 4

ISBN 0-387-94194-0 Springer-Verlag New York Berlin Heidelberg
ISBN 3-540-94194-0 Springer-Verlag Berlin Heidelberg New York SPIN 10544949

with heartfelt love and deep admiration for
my mother,
Prativa Sengupta,
my father,
Santosh Kumar Sengupta,
and my grandparents

dedicated to the hard work and sacrifice
of my grandparents,
Samuel and Frances Harrisburg
William and Frieda Korobkin

Preface

This book provides a broad coverage of fundamental and advanced concepts of data structures and algorithms. The material presented includes a treatment of elementary data structures such as arrays, lists, stacks, and trees, as well as newer structures that have emerged to support the processing of multidimensional or spatial data files. These newer structures and algorithms have received increasing attention in recent years in conjunction with the rapid growth in computer-aided design, computer graphics, and related fields in which multidimensional data structures are of great interest.

Our main objective is to mesh the underlying concepts with application examples that are of practical use and are timely in their implementations. To this end, we have used mainly the Abstract Data Structure (or Abstract Data Type (ADT)) approach to define structures for data and operations. Object-oriented programming (OOP) methodologies are employed to implement these ADT concepts. In OOP, data and operations for an ADT are combined into a single entity (object). ADTs are used to specifiy the objects—arrays, stacks, queues, trees, and graphs. OOP allows the programmer to more closely mimic the real-world applications. This OOP is more structured and modular than previous attempts. OOP has become de facto state-of-the-art in the 1990s.

We use the C++ programming language throughout this book. C++ is an extension of the popular C programming language and has gained considerable popularity within the software engineering community. For our purposes, C++ provides facilities for data abstraction and object-oriented programming while retaining the convenient notation and flexibility of C.

Each abstract data type introduced contains useful information from concept to application. Throughout this book, structures and algorithms are accompanied with compilable C++ OOP implementations as well as performance analysis information, providing a means to make practical comparisons and application decisions. The implementations presented make heavy use of pointers and dynamic memory allocation, although static array implementations are also presented. All implementations are compilable using either the Borland International C++ (.cpp) or AT&T C++ (.c++) compilers.

The last chapters of this book contain state-of-the-art applications in the C++ programming language. For the sake of clarity, completeness, and usability, every C++ program for the examples and applications given contains a `main()` test driver and sample output run.

Coverage of the basic data types and structured data types in C++ is provided. A brief reference for the C++ language and the standard string manipulation library are contained in appendices A and B. We do, however, assume that the reader is familiar with the C++ programming language.

This book is intended as a text for an undergraduate course in Data Structures and Advanced Programming in C++, as well as a working reference for software professionals.

Organization of the Book

Each chapter is organized by section. Major sections contain discussion, illustrative examples, and full C++ implementations.

Chapter 1 *Concepts of Function-Oriented and Object-Oriented Data Structures* is an overview of key concepts and terminologies for traditional and OOP structures and methodologies.

Chapter 2 *Pointers, Structures, Classes, Functions, Overloaded Functions, and Overloaded Operators in C++* presents a review of the major concepts in the C++ programming language.

Chapter 3 *Arrays and Strings* introduces the concepts of ADT arrays and strings, array and string objects, and their object-oriented implementations.

Chapter 4 *Recursion* is a treatment of the concepts and applications of recursive techniques.

Chapter 5 *Lists* is an introduction to ADT lists, list objects, and their object-oriented implementations using arrays and pointers.

Chapter 6 *Stacks and Queues* presents the concepts of ADT stacks and queues, stack and queue objects, and their object-oriented implementations.

Chapter 7 *Sorting and Searching* is a presentation of comparative-based and digital-based techniques for sorting and searching.

Chapter 8 *Trees and Tries* introduces the topics of ADT tree and trie structures, tree objects, and their object-oriented applications.

Chapter 9 *Multidimensional Search Trees and Search Tries* expands the

ADT tree and trie concepts to the object-oriented applications of multidimensional data.

Chapter 10 *Graphs and Digraphs* presents the ADT graph structures, graph objects, and their object-oriented applications.

Chapter 11 *An Object-Oriented Database with B-Trees* is an example of a common application of the ADT B-Tree.

Chapter 12 *Image Processing, Computer Graphics, and CAD* shows the application of the ADT multidimensional search trees and tries to problems in visual processing, VLSI design, ray tracing, and hidden surface removal.

Appendix A *C++ Fundamentals* is a high-level overview of the C++ language.

Appendix B *Assorted Library Functions for Handling Strings* contains some useful C++ library functions for processing strings.

Appendix C *Example Databases* contains several simple databases used throughout the text.

Production Notes

This book was produced from camera-ready (typeset and illustrated) copy provided by the authors. The entire book was typeset and illustrated with a variety of tools running on Silicon Graphics Iris Indigo and Personal Iris workstations. These tools include the TEX and LATEX typesetting programs, and the Iris Showcase and Adobe Illustrator illustration packages.

The cover image, the Temple of Concordia, was reprinted with permission granted to the authors by David Viaggi, U.S.A.

About the Code

All example programs in this book were compiled and tested using the AT&T C++ 3.0 compiler under the Silicon Graphics IRIX operating system (based on AT&T UNIX System V) and using the Borland Turbo C++ 3.1 compiler under IBM PC/MS-DOS. The AT&T C++ 3.0 compiler is not backwardly compatible with its earlier versions (such as 2.0 and 1.0). Therefore, the code presented in this book is not compilable with these earlier compiler releases. Some codes that are compilable using the AT&T C++ 3.0 compiler are not compilable using the the Borland Turbo C++

3.1 compiler because some "scoping rules" required by the AT&T C++ 3.0 are not recognized by the Borland Turbo C++ 3.1. In addition, the authors cannot guarantee that the code is compilable (without modification) with future compiler releases.

The authors have attempted to provide code free of errors. Each program has been compiled, executed, and examined for bugs. We are confident that the product is of a high quality, but cannot be responsible for errors that may be discovered.

Trademark Recognition

There are a number of names used throughout the book that are recognized trademarks:

AdobeIllustrator is a trademark of Adobe Systems, Inc.
C++ 3.0 is a trademark of AT&T Corporation.
IBM PC is a trademark of IBM Corporation.
IRIX is a trademark of Silicon Graphics Computer Systems, Inc.
Iris ImageVision is a trademark of Silicon Graphics, Inc.
Iris Indigo is a trademark of Silicon Graphics Computer Systems, Inc.
Iris Showcase is a trademark of Silicon Graphics Computer Systems, Inc.
MS-DOS is a trademark of MicroSoft Corporation.
Personal Iris is a trademark of Silicon Graphics Computer Systems, Inc.
Turbo C++ is a trademark of Borland International.
UNIX System V is a trademark of AT&T Corporation.

Acknowledgments

We have been fortunate by the active interest shown by our students, colleagues, and associates in the creation of this book.

At Silicon Graphics: Marc Hannah and Jim Winget provided valuable discussions, resources, and support early on. Derrick Burns and Mark Segal reviewed the text at many stages during its development and contributed invaluably to this work — they also taught us the art of TeXand LaTeX, with which we typeset this book. Tom Davis, David Fenstemaker, Efi Fogel, Andrew Grant, and Andrew Harvey served as reviewers and contributed many excellent comments and suggestions. Christine Butler moved (and climbed) mountains.

At San Jose State University, Professor Vinh Phat reviewed the text and contributed many useful comments. We are also grateful to the numerous students for their efforts.

Jack Menedez, Frank Kretz, Vasudha Bhaskara, and Jose Oliva made several contributions to the material.

We are especially greatful to Martin Gilchrist, Laura Carlson, Karen Kosztolnyik, Andrea Arnold, and David Shapiro, our editors at Springer-Verlag New York, and other staff members for their patience and dedicated efforts throughout the publication process.

A special thanks goes to Amy and Nate Smith at *SGI Yarmouth* (Maine) who made their home and their Indigo available for some "out of town" work on the manuscript.

While many people have supported our efforts, no one has given more of themselves than our families.

Thanks to the Sengupta family: my mother Prativa, brothers Saurendra and Nityananda, sisters Bani, Arati, Subhra, and Snigha, wife Juthika, daughters Lopamudra, Ballori, and Kasturi, and my father-in-law Dina Bandhu Roy. *(S.S.)*

Thanks to the Korobkin and Harrisburg families for their unwavering support, especially my parents Shirley and Harvey and brothers Paul and Steve. *(C.K.)*

S. Sengupta
C. Korobkin
December 1993

Contents

1

Concepts of Function-Oriented and Object-Oriented Data Structures

The processing of information transcends almost all activities of daily life. Whether it is the functioning of the human body or the functioning of a major corporation, the need to represent, store, delete, transform, retrieve, and transfer information is ever present at varying levels of abstraction.

The digital computer aids in the processing of all this information. Fundamental to processing data and solving problems with a computer is the necessity of

- an underlying *data structure* for representing the data, and

- a method or *algorithm* for how to process it.

The discipline of computer science is the study of data, data structures, and algorithms, and the application of the digital computer for such activities. The study of data structures is really the study of algorithms and vice versa. To impose an organization on a set of data is to imply a method for processing the data; to impose a method on processing a set of data is to imply a structure for representing the data. These concepts go hand-in-hand.

1.1 Data Types, Data Objects, and Related Terminologies

The term *data type* refers to the basic kinds of data that variables may contain, as specified by the chosen programming language. The C++ programming language provides for the direct specification of both simple unstructured data types, such as int, float, and char, as well as structured data types, such as an array or struct. These are *built-in* data structures available as a primitive call in the language. An array type, formally introduced in Chapter 3, specifies a fixed number of *data items* or *elements* that are of the same type and are stored contiguously in memory. Given an index into the structure, any Array element can be accessed in constant time.

In keeping with the notion that data types may be comprised of a mixture of unstructured and structured types, we refer to data types as *data objects*. Our baseline definition of a data structure is restated in terms of this simple abstraction.

Definition 1.1 *A data structure is an ordered collection of data objects and a set of operations on these objects.*

Again, using the *Array* as an example, we can interchangeably speak of data items, data elements, and data objects and be referring to the same entity.

For the array structure the sequential organization of the data objects is implicit since the data is automatically assigned into contiguous memory locations. In subsequent chapters, structures will be introduced in which the data objects are explicitly *linked* to each other. In such cases, the data objects are bundled with link-related information to form *nodes*. For now, we will assume that nodes always contain data and link information. In Chapter 7, we will broaden this definition and show that this is not necessarily the case.

Information processing applications are fundamentally concerned with the organization of groups of mutually related data. The term *database* is used to refer to such an organization or structure (as well as the computer hardware it is processed on and the programs that manipulate it). The groups of related data are commonly called *records*. The individual data items or components of a record are its *attributes*. Atomic database operations typically involve the sorting and searching of records based on selected attributes of the records called *keys*. For example, each record of a employee database might contain the attributes name, date of hire, and title. If this collection of records is searched for a record (or number of records) matching a given name, the name attribute is considered the search key or *target of the search*.

In this book, we consider structures processed on a single key as well as more advanced structures processed on multiple keys. The former case is commonly referred to as *primary-key processing* while the latter is denoted as *multi-key processing* or *secondary-key processing*.

The database model intuitively fits into our abstract definition of a data structure, where data records are the data objects. As will be shown in Chapter 2, the C++ struct type (record in Pascal) conveniently supports this organizational paradigm.

1.2   Definition of Abstract Data Structures

The concept of an *abstract data type* (*ADT*) or *abstract data structure* was first introduced by Liskov and Ziles [LZ74] as means of providing for data security.

Definition 1.2 *An* ADT *is a collection of data and a set of allowed operations (actions) that are used to define and manipulate the data.*

The collection of data elements of an ADT is referred to as the *data abstraction*, while the set of allowed operations is known as the *program abstraction*. The ADT concept combines the data and program abstraction together. An ADT is specified by:

- a unique type name,

- a set of values of some sort, and

- a set of operations that act on that data type.

The data type may be as simple as built-in types such as `int`, `char`, and `float`, or more complex user-defined types. The ADT concept is fundamental to the data structures introduced and implemented throughout this text. The main features of an ADT are:

- The internal representation of a data type can be changed without changing the operations that are used by external programs or functions to abstract the data. Data abstraction methods remain unchanged.

- An ADT is viewed as a single entity.

- Unessential data in an ADT is concealed from any program that is not entitled to access that data.

As an example of a "built-in" ADT, consider the C++ integer type `int`. One may write programs that use the integer operations +, -, *, %, and / without having any rights to change the internal representation of `int` in the host computer system. That is, the implementor has an outside concept of `int` without knowing or needing to know the details of its internal implementation.

As an example of a user-defined abstract data type, consider an ADT *closed interval* $[a, b]$. An ADT closed interval is a data structure that contains an ordered pair of real numbers a and b, $a \leq b$, and a set of operations on these pairs of numbers. The number a is called the *left end point* and the number b is called the *right end point*. Typical interval operations include creating or allocating an interval, initializing an interval, deleting an interval, adding two intervals, subtracting two intervals, multiplying two intervals, dividing two intervals, finding the union of two intervals, finding the intersection of two intervals, and printing an interval. The ADT interval has three parts: (1) type name `INTERVAL`, (2) data a, b of type `float`, and (3) operations such as add and subtract. The reader is referred to the work of Moore [Moo66].

Shown below are two representations of ADT interval numbers and arithmetic processing of them. The first representation employs an `Array` construct and the second employs a `struct` construct. A more complete implementation of ADT interval numbers is provided in **Code 1.1**.

```
//  Method I. Define interval number using
//             '[]' for array construct
typedef  float       DATA_TYPE;
typedef  DATA_TYPE INTERVAL[2];
typedef  INTERVAL  *INTERVAL_PTR;

DATA_TYPE lft_end_pt (INTERVAL_PTR A)
{
    return (*A);
}
DATA_TYPE rgt_end_pt (INTERVAL_PTR A)
{
    return (*(++A));
}

//  Method II. Define interval number using
//              'struct' construct
typedef struct INTERVAL
{
    DATA_TYPE   lft_end_pt;
    DATA_TYPE   rgt_end_pt;
} *INTERVAL_PTR;

DATA_TYPE lft_end_pt (INTERVAL_PTR A)
{
    return (A->lft_end_pt);
}
DATA_TYPE rgt_end_pt (INTERVAL_PTR A)
{
    return (A->rgt_end_pt);
}
```

Though the internal representation of the interval number differs between the two implementations, the data abstraction procedures, such as `lft_end_pt()` and `rgt_end_pt()`, are unchanged. The view of the ADT interval numbers to the outside world remains the same.

1.3   Object-Oriented Design and the ADT

An *object-oriented design* (*OOD*) is one based on the ADT abstraction concepts. A straightforward way of understanding the principles of object-oriented design is to differentiate it from the more traditional *function-oriented design* (*FOD*).

Property 1.1 *An object-oriented design treats a software system as a group of interacting objects rather than a set of interacting functions, as in a function-oriented design.*

An *object-oriented program* (*OOP*) is an implementation of an object-oriented design. Alternately stated, object-oriented programming methodologies are employed to implement the ADT concepts. In OOP, data and operations for an ADT are combined into a single entity, called an *object*. Object-oriented programming languages such as C++, Smalltalk, and Object Pascal directly support the object paradigm and simplify the implementation of an OOD. In C++ , the `class` construct is used to implement an ADT and thereby defines a type of an object.

Object-oriented programming is more structured and modular than function-oriented programming, yielding programs that are easily maintained, resilient, and powerful. OOP allows the programmer to more closely mimic real-world situations. Stroustrup [Str89] justifies this.

In this section, we examine and contrast the basic concepts of traditional function-oriented and object-oriented programming. A short preview of an OOP in C++ is included. In succeeding chapters, a wide assortment of data structures are presented as objects and implemented as OOPs. For a detailed discussion of OOD and OOP concepts, the reader is referred to the works of Booch [Boo91] and Meyer [Mey88], and Lafore [Laf91], respectively.

1.3.1 FUNCTION-ORIENTED DATA STRUCTURES

Function-oriented data structures are built on the concept of a collection of defined data variables and the operations allowed on them without regard to data hiding and protection. Function-oriented programming methods are based on a scheme of

- defining data requirements,

- constructing a data structure, and

- writing a set of functions to process the data.

Traditional programming languages such as C, ALGOL, and Pascal emphasize data representation and the use of fundamental data types. We see such data structure as the array (a unit of adjacent, dissimilar data types implying similar memory space usage) and the record (a unit of adjacent, dissimilar memory spaces) derived from the fundamental data types. With this approach, user-defined data types with data hiding is ignored.

Consider again the ADT interval example to illustrate the concepts of function-oriented data structures. If the data a (`lft_end pt`) and b (`rgt_end_pt`) of the ADT interval $[a, b]$ are implemented using a `struct`

INTERVAL of floats, the traditional programming approach defines the
interval data structure and a set of functions in a header file:

```
//   interval.h
//
struct   INTERVAL   {
    float   lft_end_pt,   // Left end point "a"
            rgt_end_pt;   // Right end point "b"
};
void init_interv (INTERVAL *A, float new_lft,
                    float  new_rgt);
INTERVAL   add_interv (INTERVAL A, INTERVAL B);
INTERVAL   sub_interv (INTERVAL A, INTERVAL B);
void       print_interv (INTERVAL A, char * hdr);
```

The corresponding functions are contained in a C++ source file:

```
//   interval.c++
//
void  init_interv (INTERVAL *A, float new_lft,
                    float new_rgt)
{
    A->lft_end_pt = new_lft;
    A->rgt_end_pt = new_rgt;
}

INTERVAL  add_interv (INTERVAL A, INTERVAL B)
{
    //  etc.....;
}
```

This traditional data structure and programming method has a serious deficiency in protecting data from possible misuse. In the above illustration, the data members, lft_end_pt and rgt_end_pt in the data
structure INTERVAL are publicly accessible (by default, they both have
public access specifiers in C++). These members are not concealed from
the functions and programs that may inadvertently corrupt them. This
deficiency will be resolved in an object-oriented data structure and programming method.

1.3.2   OBJECT-ORIENTED DATA STRUCTURES

Since an ADT is viewed as a type for an object, and object-oriented design
(OOD) decomposes most real-world applications as a collection of cooperating objects, it follows that an ADT (and thereby an object-oriented data
structure) is an integral feature of OOD. When an OOD is implemented by
a program in some OOD supporting language, such as C++ the program
is called an object-oriented program (OOP). An OOP employs classes and
objects. The basic features of an OOD include the following:

- Abstract Data Typing

  An ADT specifies the data and operations of an object, and is implemented by the C++ class construct.

- Data Abstraction

  Data abstraction provides a concept of an object and an interface to an object's data without involving the details of the implementation of the data. As stated by Booch [Boo91], "An abstraction denotes the essential characteristics of an object that distinguish it from all other kinds of objects and thus provide crisply defined conceptual boundaries, relative to the perspective of the viewer."

- Encapsulation and Data-hiding

  Encapsulation conceals (hides) the implementation details of the data and methods (see Methods below) of an object from its user program or function. This provides protection of the object's information (data and methods) from unauthorized users. Thus, abstraction complements encapsulation.

- Modularity

  Modularity is a means of decomposing an application into a collection of cooperating objects. As Booch [Boo91] says, "The principles of abstraction, encapsulation, and modularity are synergistic. An object provides a crisp boundary around a single abstraction, and both encapsulation and modularity provide barriers around this abstraction." By modularity, the logically related abstractions are compacted.

- Classes

  Classes define types or templates of objects. The type concept is derived from ADT. A class is derived from an ADT in addition to protection of data and operations. The classes are templates that describe the data structure and the valid actions that act on the data.

- Identification of Objects and Classes

  An object is an *instance* of a class; it has a unique variable name. It is identified by its behavior and state. A common class is used to define the behavior and structure of objects of the same type.

- Methods

  Valid actions are implemented with member functions of the class that defines an object. Such member functions are called *methods* (or operations or actions). Methods are used to send messages to an object that can only act upon the message.

- Hierarchy and Inheritance

  A problem is divided into a collection of objects or classes. A collection of classes exhibits an *inheritance hierarchy* as one class *derives from* another (inherits members) in a hierarchical fashion. The root class of an inheritance hierarchy is the *base class*. The base class establishes common data members and member functions for all classes. Classes that inherit members from the base class are *subclasses* or *derived classes* of the root base class. These derived classes extend the base class capability to provide their own specific functionality and/or implementation of the base class functionality. Inheritance allows the sharing of data and methods between classes with levels of abstraction.

- Message Passing Between Objects

  Objects are independent of each other. An object of the same or different class can send a message to any object, and the object receiving the message can only act upon that message. A message may contain a request for action such as to create an object, initialize an object, print internal data items in an object, etc. In OOP terminology, one would request a "String" object as initialization, as opposed to a statement of the form "call function `string_init()`".

- Polymorphism and Dynamic Binding

  Polymorphism means that a single method name can be used for the different operations on derived classes (subclasses). Since the specific operation called depends on the class of the object the message is being sent to, the address of the operation is not known until runtime. The address is dynamically attached, a process referred to as *dynamic binding* or *late binding*. Polymorphism and dynamic binding are implemented using C++ `virtual` functions, and `overloaded` functions and operators. A more detailed discussion is presented in Chapter 2.

1.3.3 A UNIFIED APPROACH

The purpose of a good object-oriented design is to present the user with a rich set of extensible, interchangeable, and reusable components upon which a software system may be built. In such an environment, objects may be viewed as *off-the-shelf* modules; an OOP is a network of such objects, plugged into each other and communicating by message passing through their specified public interfaces. Encapsulation hides the data structure and algorithms associated with an object from the user. Thus, in an object-oriented design, the user is more concerned with *what* an object does rather than *how* it does it.

A traditional function-oriented design presents a complementary approach to object-oriented design. In a function-oriented design, the basic module is a function and not an abstract data entity. In such an environment, the user is typically involved with what a function does *and* how it does it.

In any design, however, be it function-oriented or object-oriented, the implementor or user is usually concerned with the performance of the software system. To this end, a discussion of pertinent space and time tradeoff issues enters into the design considerations. Data structures and their associated algorithms are thus characterized by their efficiencies under varying application conditions. Thus, in an object-oriented design, one may be concerned with not only *what* an object does but *how well* it does it.

In this book, a unified approach to the subjects of traditional function-oriented data structures and object-oriented data structures is presented. Throughout this book, classical data structures – such as lists, stacks, queues, trees, and graphs – are presented. Each data structure is given as a C++ object in the form of a base class. For each base class, various implementations are discussed, with the notion that one implementation may be better suited than another for a given application. These data structures are then implemented as a set of subclasses, from which the application programmer may choose the one which best meets the performance characteristics required by the application.

To illustrate the concepts in abstract terms, consider an application that involves the painting of a house interior and the need to employ a painter. In selecting the painter most appropriate for the job, we may consider various qualifications, such as whether the painter specializes in interiors, exteriors, or both, how fast the painter works, and how much the work would cost. In our search we find three qualified painters. Two of them specialize in interiors—one is faster than the other but charges considerably more for the job. The third painter is a general painter (does interiors as well as exteriors), is priced between the others, but is really slow.

If we think of these painters as objects, we can illustrate their use in terms of a base class and a set of derived subclasses, as follows:

- Abstract Base Class

  The *abstract base class* contains a common set of interfaces to be shared by all the subclasses that *derive from it*. The subclasses that derive from the abstract base class *inherit only interface and not implementation*. The abstract base class defines a common framework for all implementations of the class in terms of a list of methods (actions) as virtual functions.

  For our housepainter example we define the abstract base class HousePainter. This base class defines the interface of a set of generic painter operations that are common to all painters of this class.

```
class HousePainter {

    // list of methods
    // (e.g., scrape, sand, mask, paint interior, clean)
};
```

- Derived Classes

  A *derived class* or *subclass* implements the common interfaces specified by the base class. It may also extend the functionality of the base
  class by defining and implementing additional members required for
  its specific needs. *The implementation of the derived class charac-
  terizes the performance of the object.* Derived classes are alternately
  referred to as *implementation specific classes*. It is implementor's responsibility to provide a set of uniform interfaces which match the
  base class such that the application programmer may plug in one implementation specific class or another without changing their code.

  In our example, there are three derived classes:
  Fast_Interior_Painter and Faster_Interior_Painter are
  the interior specialists, while General_Painter is the interior-
  exterior painter. All three know how to paint interiors as part of the
  interface defined by the abstract base class. The General_Painter,
  however, extends this functionality by providing an exterior painting
  capability. All three derive from the HousePainter base class.

  ```
  class Fast_Interior_Painter : public HousePainter { //..};
  class Faster_Interior_Painter : public HousePainter { //..};
  class General_Painter : public HousePainter { //..};
  ```

- Instantiation

  A *derived object* is an instantiation of a derived class and is the top
  level of object abstraction. It is an object whose methods are given
  by the base class and whose features and performance are attributed
  to the plugged-in implementation specific class. As such, it is also referred to as an *implementation specific object*. Application programmers may simply attach their programs to an implementation specific
  object.

  In our example, we decide that the lower cost interior specialist
  (Fast_Interior_Painter) best suits our requirements. The following instantiation creates a HousePainter_Object:

  ```
  Fast_Interior_Painter HousePainter_Object;
  ```

Figure 1.1 shows the inheritance hierarchy of the abstract base class and
its derived subclasses for the housepainter example.

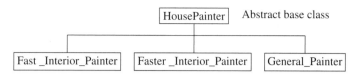

FIGURE 1.1. Inheritance hierarchy for HousePainter class.

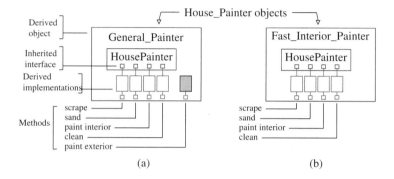

FIGURE 1.2. Objects derived from HousePainter base class.

The process of creating an instanced HousePainter_Object is illustrated in Figure 1.2. Two cases are depicted, one in which the object is an instance of the General_Painter derived class, Figure 1.2(a), and the other as an instance of the Fast_Interior_Painter derived class, as shown in Figure 1.2(b). In both cases, the objects contain the House_Painter abstract base class and inherit its *scrape, sand, paint interior,* and *clean* methods as interface. Each provides its version of an implementation of these methods. In the case of the General_Painter derived class, though, we see that the *paint exterior* method is defined and implemented but is not inherited from the base class. The interface provided by the abstract base class is extended by the General_Painter class, giving the object additional functionality. This additional functionality is depicted by the solid shaded box in Figure 1.2(a).

1.3.4 STEPS FOR DERIVING AN OBJECT-ORIENTED DESIGN

Some key steps in deriving an OOD for a given problem are:

Step 1. Partitioning

Divide the problem into a set of objects. Identify each object by its data and related operations (ADT).

Step 2. Sharing

Determine commonality between objects and hierarchy of classes.

Step 3. Encapsulation Determine levels of protection for data and operations in each object.

Step 4. Inheritance Determine the protection levels for data and operations in the base class(es) that are inherited by subclasses.

Step 5. Polymorphism and Dynamic Binding

Determine which methods in the base class(es) will have the same interface names across subclass(es) but may need to act differently in different subclass(es).

Step 6. Refinement

Repeat the above five steps in an iterative manner until a design is reached for an initial implementation.

1.4   Implementing an OOP in C++

In the software engineering community, the C++ programming language has emerged as a de facto state-of-the-art language for writing OOP. C++ provides the following unique features suitable for object-oriented programming:

- Classes for defining templates

- Single and multiple inheritance; hierarchy of classes and derived classes

- Member functions of a class that are methods

- Protection of data and function members of a class using the `private` and `protected` keywords

- Special functions: Constructor and Destructor

- Inline functions of a class

- Friend functions and classes that support inheritance

- Virtual functions of a class that support polymorphism

- Overloaded functions that support polymorphism

- Overloaded operators that support polymorphism

- Dynamic memory management using the `new` and `delete` operators

- Stream Input/Output operators

When implementing an object-oriented program in C++ the following points must be kept in mind:

- Use an object-oriented design (OOD) approach, where data and functions are identified as an object. An *object* is an abstract data structure (ADT) that contains data and operations that process the data. The object name is an user-defined type. A variable of that type is an instance of that object.

- Data abstraction and encapsulation are implemented using the C++ `class` construct. The C++ `class` construct defines a type for objects. It groups data and operations into a single entity and provides support for data-hiding using the keywords `private` and `protected`. It supports data abstraction through `public` implementation operations.

- Inheritance is implemented using the C++ `class`, `friend`, and ":" operator for a well-organized and modularized hierarchy of classes and subclasses.

- Polymorphism is implemented using C++ `virtual` functions, and `overloaded` functions and operators.

- Methods are `public` functions, and C++ special functions, called constructors and destructors.

- Variables defined locally within a class are accessible to any members of the same class with read and write permissions.

- Identify global objects and variables that can be used to define a base class. Subclasses will be built from the base class.

The key features of C++ are summarized in Table 1.1. Although C++ retains some of the characteristics of C, and early versions of C++ were a front end translator of C++ code to standard C, C++ provides the means of organizing data structures in an elegant way suitable for object-oriented programming. Table 1.2 compares terminologies used in function-oriented and object-oriented programming.

Since this book is intended as a study of data structures and algorithms, their presentation as objects, and their implementation in C++, it is assumed that the reader is familiar with C++. Nevertheless, a review of the major concepts of C++ is presented in the next two chapters. For those

OOP Features	Implemented Using C++ Features
Objects	⟨class_name⟩ ⟨object_variable⟩;
Data-hiding and Abstraction	class ⟨ class_name ⟩ ... ; with private and protected access specifiers in class.
Methods	Functions for valid operations, and constructor and destructor.
Message Passing	public declaration for methods in class construct.
Inheritance	friend class and function, and : for derived classes.
Polymorphism	virtual function; overloaded functions and operators.

TABLE 1.1. Useful C++ features for implementing OOP.

Function-Oriented Programming (C)	OOP (C++)
User-defined types	Classes
Variables	Objects
Structure members	Instance variables
Functions	Methods
Function call	Message passing

TABLE 1.2. Equivalent terminologies used in Function-Oriented programming and OOP.

who are completely unfamiliar with C++ or desire a more thorough review or reference, Stroustrup [Str89] provides one of the many comprehensive treatments of the subject.

1.4.1 A SHORT PREVIEW OF OBJECT-ORIENTED PROGRAMMING

The interval data structure introduced earlier is revisited here in a preview object-oriented programming.

A class is defined with two parts: A private or protected section holding data and operations that can only be used internally, and a public section that holds the interface operations. In other words, the definition of a class comprises the following:

• The name of the class.

- The internal representation of data structure, storage.

- The internal implementation of the interface.

- The external operations for accessing and manipulating the instances of the class.

A class uses an ADT. The elements belonging to the set of objects described by the class are called instances of the class. Keeping the OOP characteristics (object, class, data-hiding, methods, etc.) in mind, we present the following OOP **Code 1.1** for the interval object $[a, b]$, $a \le b$, a and b being real numbers. For interval objects, we defined an `Interval` class, overloaded constructor `Interval()`, overloaded operator `+()` function, and one more method. Notice that hiding the data `lft_end_pt` and `rgt_end_pt` is accomplished by declaring these `private` within the class construct of an `Interval` object.

Code 1.1

```
//   Program:   interval.c++
//   Purpose:
//      Object-oriented implementation of ADT interval
//      numbers, [a, b], where a \le b.
//
#include <stdio.h>

// Define an "Interval" class
class Interval {
  private:
      //  Declare data as \keyword{private} for hiding
      float  lft_end_pt,  // Left end point "a"
             rgt_end_pt;  // Right end point "a"

  //  Declare methods as \keyword{public}
  public:
    Interval(float new_lft, float new_rgt);  // Constructor
    Interval(float new_lft_rgt);  // Constructor for
                                  // degenerate Interval
                                  // object
    friend Interval operator+(Interval A, Interval B);
    void   print_interval(char *hdr);
};

//   Interval(): First Constructor function.
//      Construct and initialize an "Interval" object
//      using two input values.
//
Interval::Interval (float new_lft, float new_rgt)
{
    lft_end_pt = new_lft;
```

```
        rgt_end_pt = new_rgt;
}


//   Interval():  Overloaded constructor function.
//      Construct and initialize an "Interval"
//      degenerate object using one input value.
//
Interval::Interval (float new_lft_rgt)
{
    lft_end_pt = new_lft_rgt;
    rgt_end_pt = new_lft_rgt;
}


//   Overloaded operator+():
//      Add two "Interval" objects and return an
//      "Interval" object.
//
Interval   operator+ (Interval A, Interval B)
{
    return (Interval(A.lft_end_pt + B.lft_end_pt,
                     A.rgt_end_pt + B.rgt_end_pt));
}


//   print_interval():
//      Print an "Interval" object
//
void Interval::print_interval(char *hdr)
{
    printf("    Interval %s is: [ %f, %f] \n",
            hdr, lft_end_pt, rgt_end_pt);
}


//   main():  Test driver for OOP Intervals
void   main(void)
{
    //   Declare "intrvl_obj1" and "intrvl_obj2"
    //   of the "Interval" class
    Interval   intrvl_obj1( -2, 4),   // Interval A
               intrvl_obj2(  6, 9);   // Interval B
    printf("\n == OOP IMPLEMENTATION %s == \n",
            "OF INTERVAL NUMBERS");
    intrvl_obj1.print_interval("A");
    intrvl_obj2.print_interval("B");
    (intrvl_obj1 + intrvl_obj2).print_interval(
                                    "A + B");
}
```

Code 1.1 produces the following output:

```
    == OOP IMPLEMENTATION OF INTERVAL NUMBERS ==
    Interval A is: [ -2.000000, 4.000000]
```

```
Interval B is: [ 6.000000, 9.000000]
Interval A + B is: [ 4.000000, 13.000000]
```

1.5   Example Databases

To aid in the illustration of the topics presented in this book, we have created two example databases. These databases are used by a majority of the sample programs in the chapters that follow. By employing the same sets of data from one example to the next, the various data structuring techniques and implementations presented are more readily contrasted.

The first database, referred to as the PEOPLE database, is a collection of records involving information about a group of individuals and their membership in an organization. Each record of a person contains six attributes: name, age, income, occupation of member, the member identification number, and the years that the member has belonged in the organization. As a matter of implementation, three versions of the PEOPLE database are presented, each differing by the number of attributes of the record that are encoded as keys: thus people_1d, people_2d, and people_3d correspond to records containing one, two, and three keys, respectively.

The second database, referred to as the GEOMETRY database, is a collection of records involving colored points in space. There are two versions, geometry_2d and geometry_3d. For geometry_2d, each record is a point in a two-dimensional space; each contains two keys, coordinate x and coordinate y, plus the attributes of color and label. For geometry_3d, each record is a point in a three-dimensional space; each contains three keys, coordinate x coordinate y, and coordinate z, plus additional attributes of color and label. Figure 1.3 illustrates the format of these records. The complete databases are presented in Appendix C.

1.6   Big Oh Notation

To choose an efficient data structure for an application, we employ a tool, called $O(n)$ (Big Oh), to measure the performance of data structures operations. The notation $O(n)$ means "On the Order of n." For example, $O(n^3)$ means on the order of n-cube or proportional to n-cube.

Given two mathematical functions $u(n)$ and $v(n)$, n being an integer, $u(n) = O(v(n))$ if for some positive constants p and q

$$u(n) \leq pv(n) \quad \text{for all values of } n \geq q$$
$$\text{(i.e., for all sufficiently large } n)$$

This means that $u(n)$ is of order $v(n)$, or $u(n)$ will grow no faster than

Member id
Name
Occupation
Age
Income
Years Member

(a) people_1d

Age
Income
Member id
Name
Occupation
Years Member

(b) people_2d

Age
Income
Years Member
Member id
Name
Occupation

(c) people_3d

Coordinate x
Coordinate y
Color
Label

(d) geometry_2d

Coordinate x
Coordinate y
Coordinate z
Color
Label

(e) geometry_3d

FIGURE 1.3. The PEOPLE and GEOMETRY databases.

$v(n)$. For example, given $u(n) = 100n^3 + 20000n^2 - 5$

$$u(n) = O(v(n)) \quad where \quad v(n) = n^3$$

Note that $v(n)$ is the dominant term with the highest power. Though for large values of n, the second term of $u(n)$ with coefficient 20000 may be considerably high, it is ignored in $O(v(n))$. This is the drawback of the Big Oh notation. We call $O(n)$ the *linear*, $O(n^2)$ the *quadratic*, $O(n^3)$ the *cubic*, $O(a^n)$ the *exponential* for some constant a, and $O(\log n)$ the *logarithmic* functions of n. Some examples of the Big Oh notation are shown in the table on page 19.

Note that given two algorithms for a problem of size n, with computing times $u(n) = O(n^2)$ and $v(n) = O(\log_2 n)$, the algorithm with logarithmic time is more efficient than the other because the growth rate of the logarithmic function $v(n)$ is much slower than the quadratic function $u(n)$ as n grows.

1.7   Exercises

1. For the interval object in **Code 1.1**, implement and test public methods for (a) subtracting two interval objects, and (b) multiplying

$u(n)$	$v(n)$	$u(n) = O(v(n))$
199	1	$O(1)$
$-230n$	n	$O(n)$
$n^9 + 500{,}000n^8 + 900{,}000$	n^9	$O(n^9)$
$(n^3 + 2)\log n$	$(n^3)\log n$	$O(n^3 \log n)$

two interval objects. For example, for $X = [a, b]$ and $Y = [c, d]$, $X - Y = [a - c, b - d]$, and $X \times Y = [min\{a \times c, a \times d, b \times c, b \times d\}, max\{a \times c, a \times d, b \times c, b \times d\}]$.

2. Design a string object. Identify the object by its data and allowed operations. Use the `class` construct to implement the object type that combines data and operations into a single entity. Write and test functions implementing some operations in C++.

3. Use the object-oriented design approach for a set object. Identify the object by its data and allowed operations (e.g., union). Use the `class` construct to implement the object type that combines data and operations into a single entity. Write and test functions implementing some operations in C++.

4. Use the object-oriented design approach for an ADT polynomial in two variables. Identify the object by its data and allowed operations. Use the `class` construct to implement the object type that combines data and operations into a single entity. Write and test functions implementing addition and printing operations in C++. (Hint: Use an array.)

5. Use the object-oriented design approach for ADT rational numbers. For two integers a and b (b not being zero), a/b is a rational number. Identify the object by its data and allowed operations. Use the `class` construct to implement the object type that combines data and operations into a single entity. Write and test functions implementing some operations in C++.

6. Use the object-oriented design approach for ADT vectors. A vector of dimension n is an array of n real numbers. Identify the object by its data and allowed operations. Use the `class` construct to implement the object type that combines data and operations into a single entity. Write and test functions implementing some operations in C++.

7. Use the object-oriented design approach for ADT matrix numbers. A two-dimensional array denoted by $[c_{i,j}]$, $c_{i,j}$ being real numbers, $0 \leq i \leq p - 1$, and $0 \leq j \leq q - 1$, is called a matrix with p rows and q columns. Identify the object by its data and allowed operations.

Use the `class` construct to implement the object type that combines data and operations into a single entity. Write functions implementing some operations including equality of two matrices.

8. Use the object-oriented design approach for ADT complex numbers. A real number tuple (a, b) of the form $a + bi$, a and b being real numbers, is called a complex number. The number a is the real part, and b is the imaginary part of the complex number. Identify the object by its data and allowed operations. Use the `class` construct to implement the object type that combines data and operations into a single entity. Write and test functions implementing some operations in C++.

9. Use the object-oriented design approach for an ADT file. A file is a logical entity that represents a named portion of information (program source, text and/or binary data). For example, in the PC-DOS operating system on an IBM PC or compatible systems, files with unique names "Example1.txt" and "Example2.txt" are stored on a disk; "COPY Example1.txt Example2.txt" copies one file to the other. Identify the object by its data and allowed operations. Use the `class` construct to implement the object type that combines data and operations into a single entity. Show several examples of user-typed commands that implement some of these operations within a commonly used operating system such as MS-DOS or UNIX.

2

Pointers, Structures, Classes, Functions, Overloaded Functions, and Overloaded Operators in C++

The primary goal of this book is to develop and implement object-oriented programs in C++ for complex data structures such as arrays, strings, lists, stacks, queues, trees, and graphs. These implementations rely heavily on the concepts of pointers, structures, classes, functions, overloaded functions, and overloaded operators. While it is assumed that the reader has a working knowledge of the C and C++ programming languages, a discussion of some of the key concepts used extensively throughout this text is presented here as a review. The reader is referred to AT&T manuals [ATT89] and [ATT91], Weiskamp [WF90].

2.1 C++ Pointers

Before or during the execution of a program, its code, data, and variables are loaded in main memory with relocatable addresses. With assembly language programming, *pointers* were primarily utilized to directly or indirectly access a program's code, data, and variables. As more sophisticated programming techniques evolved, such low level support was inherited by higher level languages such as C, C++, and Pascal.

A pointer is a variable that contains the address (i.e., the location in main memory) of another variable, a function, or the address of a pointer that points to a variable. For example, consider the following statements:

```
int *ptr, a = 7, b = -2;    // Statement 1
ptr = &a;                   // Statement 2
ptr = &b;                   // Statement 3
```

Statement 1 declares that `ptr2` is a pointer to any variable of type `int` using the operator `*`; `ptr` does not have any value yet. From Statement 2, the address of the integer type variable `a` is assigned to the pointer variable `ptr`, and `*ptr` is the actual content (7) of that memory location. From Statement 3, `ptr` contains the address of another variable b, which is of

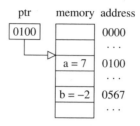

FIGURE 2.1. Pointer concept.

type `int`. Figure 2.1 illustrates this concept after Statement 1 is executed. After the execution of Statement 3, `ptr = 0567`.

Applications of pointers include:

- Passing variables, arrays, functions, strings, and structures as function arguments.

- Returning structured variables from functions.

- Swapping variables without physically moving them.

- Establishing links between data elements or objects for such complex data structures as linked lists, stacks, queues, trees and tries, and graphs.

- Supporting dynamic allocation and deallocation of memory segments.

As in assembly language, the automatic-increment and automatic-decrement capabilities of pointers are accomplished in C++ with the operators `++` and `--`, respectively. Table 2.1 summarizes the C++ operators for pointers.

As an example of the use of pointers, the concept of a *pointer to a pointer variable* is shown below in **Code 2.1**.

Code 2.1

```
//   Program:   ptr_ptr.c++
//   Purpose:   To demonstrate the use of a
//              pointer to a pointer
//
#include <stdio.h>
void main(void)
```

C++ Operator		Description
DATA_TYPE	*	Pointer declaration for a pointer to a variable of type DATA_TYPE.
DATA_TYPE	**	Pointer declaration for pointer to a pointer that points to a variable of type DATA_TYPE.
	&	Receive address of the variable.
	=	The pointer is assigned the address of variable.
	*	Content of location pointed to by the pointer.
	++	Increase the value of the pointer by adding the size of DATA_TYPE.
	--	Decrease the value of the pointer by adding the size of DATA_TYPE.
	+= n	Increase the value of the pointer by adding n times the size of DATA_TYPE.
	-= n	Decrease the value of the pointer by adding n times the size of DATA_TYPE.

TABLE 2.1. C++ pointer operators.

```
{
    int    a = 5,
         *a_ptr,          // Pointer to variable a
        **a_ptr_ptr;      // Pointer to pointer a_ptr

    printf("\n ** Demo of pointer to a pointer ** \n");
    printf(" a = %d                   Address of a = %u \n",
           a, &a );
    a_ptr = &a;           // Assigned address of a
    printf(" *a_ptr = %d    %s = %u %s = %u \n",
           *a_ptr, "        Content of a_ptr", a_ptr,
      "\n                   Address of a_ptr", &a_ptr);
    a_ptr_ptr = &a_ptr;  // Assigned address of a_ptr
    printf(" **a_ptr_ptr = %d    %s = %u \n",
       **a_ptr_ptr, "Content of a_ptr_ptr", a_ptr_ptr);
}
```

Code 2.1 for pointer to a pointer produces this output on an IBM PC/386 system:

```
        ** Demo of Pointer to pointer **
        a = 5                 Address of a = 65524
        *a_ptr = 5            Content of a_ptr = 65524
                              Address of a_ptr = 65522
        **a_ptr_ptr = 5    Content of a_ptr_ptr = 65522
```

2.1.1 C++ POINTER ARITHMETIC AND OPERATIONS

Arithmetic operations on pointers is a key feature in C++. The operators
++ and -- are useful for pointer arithmetic. For the statement

```
DATA_TYPE *ptr;
```

Table 2.2 summarizes the use of these operators for referencing the contents
pointed to by ptr.

The key difference between the number arithmetic and pointer arithmetic
is shown below:

```
float x, *x_ptr;

x++;       // Statement 1, x = x + 1
x_ptr++;   // Statement 2, x_ptr = x_ptr + sizeof(float)
```

Statement 1 is a numeric arithmetic operation that increments the float
data variable x by one. On the other hand, Statement 2 is a pointer arithmetic operation, where the pointer variable x_ptr is incremented to the
next memory location, an increment equal to the size of a float variable.

A further example of pointer arithmetic is provided below in **Code 2.2**.
The interested reader is referred to Holub [Hol87] for an expanded discussion of pointers.

2.1.2 CALL-BY-REFERENCE USING POINTERS AS FUNCTION ARGUMENTS

In C++, the *call-by-value* method is used to pass the actual values of
variables to functions as arguments. This means that the values can be
used, but cannot be changed. In order to change the variable within the
function, the pointer to the variable (i.e., address/reference to the variable)
is passed as an argument of the function. This is referred to as the *call-by-
reference* method. For example:

```
void interchange (int *a, int *b)
{
    int swap_area = *a;  // content of 'a' is copied
    // Replace actual content of 'a' by content of 'b'
    *a = *b;
    // Replace actual content of 'b' by content of 'a'
    *b = swap_area;
}
```

is called as

```
interchange (&a, &b)
```

This means that the addresses of a and b are passed to the function
interchange().

Pointer arithmetic	Description
`ptr++`	`ptr = ptr + sizeof(DATA_TYPE);` Use the original value of `ptr` and then `ptr` is incremented after statement execution.
`++ptr`	`ptr = ptr + sizeof(DATA_TYPE);` Original `ptr` is incremented before the execution of statement.
`ptr--`	`ptr = ptr - sizeof(DATA_TYPE);` Use the original value of `ptr` and then `ptr` is decremented after statement execution.
`--ptr`	`ptr = ptr - sizeof(DATA_TYPE);` Original `ptr` is decremented before the execution of statement.
`*ptr++ == *(ptr++)`	Retrieve the content of the location pointed to by `ptr`, and then increment `ptr`.
`*++ptr == *(++ptr)`	Increment `ptr` and then retrieve the content of the new location pointed to by `ptr`.
`(*ptr)++`	Increment content of the location pointed to by `ptr`. For pointer-type content, use pointer arithmetic, else use standard arithmetic.
`++*ptr == ++(*ptr)`	Increment the content of the location pointed to by `ptr` depending upon the type of this content.
`*++ptr == *(++ptr)`	Increment `ptr`, then retrieve the content of the new location pointed to by `ptr`.
`--*ptr == --(*ptr)`	Decrement content of the location pointed to by `ptr` depending upon the type of this content.
`*ptr-- == *(ptr--)`	Retrieve the content of the location pointed to by `ptr`, and then decrement `ptr`.
`*--ptr == *(--ptr)`	Decrement `ptr`, then retrieve the content of the new location pointed to by `ptr`.
`(*ptr)--`	Retrieve content `*ptr` of the location pointed to by `ptr`, then decrement the content of that location; `ptr` is not changed.

TABLE 2.2. Pointer arithmetic and referencing.

2.1.3 POINTERS AS RETURN VALUES OF FUNCTIONS

Using a pointer as a return value facilitates the access of the memory location pointed to by that pointer. Its use is found when dealing with structured data (e.g., arrays, structures, and unions) that are defined outside
the function. For example:

```
typedef  <DATA_TYPE> *PTR_TYPE;
PTR_TYPE  function ()
{
    PTR_TYPE  a_ptr;
    // ...
    return (a_ptr);
}
```

2.2 Structures in C++

A collection of unlimited data elements that are related and are of different
types is known as a *structure*. The data elements are referred to as the
components or *members* of the structure. The structure type is a built-in
data structure in C++ and is implemented by the keyword struct; its
counterpart is a *record* and the keyword record in the Pascal language.
The struct construct is a fundamental building block for more complex
data structures. The types of its members may be the C++ built-in basic
types, such as int, char, float, struct, union, or user-defined data
types.

2.2.1 DEFINING A STRUCTURE

The syntax in declaring a structure type variable is given in many forms.
One form is:

```
struct  <struct_name>  {
    <type_of_mem1>        name_of_mem1;
    <type_of_mem2>        name_of_mem2;
                . . .
    <type_of_memN>        name_of_memN;
    <diff_struct_name>    struct_var;
    <union_name>          union_var;
    <same_struct_name>    *struct_ptr;
    <return_type>     <function_name>(
        <arg_type> <arg>,  ..., <arg_type> <arg>);

} struct_var_1, *ptr = &struct_var_1;
```

Note that the use of `typedef` is not required for the `struct` construct in C++. However, `typedef` can be used to simultaneously define the type of a pointer to this structure. This declaration of `struct` does five things:

- Allocates memory space for the identifier `struct_var_1`.

- Assigns the address of the variable to the pointer `ptr`.

- Recursively defines the structure by including the pointer variable `struct_ptr` for the same structure.

- Allows nesting of structures within a structure (i.e., structure of structures)

- Allows nesting of union within a structure (i.e., structure of union)

For example, in a `people_1d` database management system, the information for a member includes the member's identification, name, occupation, age, yearly gross salary, and the number of years of membership. Though these components are of different types, they can be combined into a single entity using the `struct` construct. For example, the record for the people database `people_1d` is defined as follows:

```
typedef int      Keytype;
typedef int      Nodetype;
typedef int      dummytype;
typedef char     *Name;

struct DataObject {
    Keytype key;            // member id
    Name    name;           // name
    char    *occupation;    // occupation
    int     age;            // age
    int     income;         // yearly gross / $1000
    int     years;          // number years member
};
```

2.2.2 POINTERS TO STRUCTURES

When a pointer is used to hold the address of a structure variable, the syntax is:

<struct_name>   *<struct_ptr_name>;

It is assigned to hold the address of a structure of the same type using the & operator. The syntax is:

<struct_ptr_name> = &<struct_var_name>;

After this assignment statement, the pointer `struct_ptr_name` can be used to reference any member of `struct_var_name`. Without this assignment, any such reference will cause a *memory fault* during the execution of a program. For example:

```
DataObject record_of_mem1, *mem_ptr;
mem_ptr = &record_of_mem1;
```

2.2.3   ACCESSING STRUCTURES

There are two C++ operators available for accessing the individual members of a structure:

- Operator . (period)

- Operator -> (dash followed by a greater than)

The structure member syntaxes are:

```
<struct_var_name>.<mem_name>
<struct_ptr_name>-><mem_name>
*<struct_ptr_name>.<mem_name>
```

For example:

```
DataObject record_of_mem1, *mem_ptr;

// Initialize values to the fields
record_of_mem1.key = 16;              // ...(1)
record_of_mem1.name = "Bob";
record_of_mem1.occupation = "engineer";
record_of_mem1.age = 29;
record_of_mem1.income = 57;
record_of_mem1.years = 3;

// Assign address of "record_of_mem1" to "mem_ptr"
// Now, "mem_ptr" is a pointer to the structure.
mem_ptr = &record_of_mem1;

// Alternative approach using "->" operator
mem_ptr->key = 16;  // equivalent to (1)

//   OR
(*mem_ptr).key = 16;  // equivalent to (1)
```

2.2.4   INITIALIZING STRUCTURES

Initializing a structure requires three key items:

- Only `static` and `extern` storage classes can be used.

- The data types and the order of member names in the structure definition must be strictly followed in order to assign values.

- It is permissible to assign values to `auto` members.

For example:

```
static DataObject record_of_mem1 = {
          16,              // key
          "Bob",           // name
          "engineer",      // occupation
          29,              // age
          57,              // income
          3                // years
};
```

The following example **Code 2.2** demonstrates the use of structures and pointer arithmetic.

Code 2.2

```
//   Program:  ptrarith.c++
//   Purpose:  To demonstrate the simple uses
//              of struct & pointer arithmetic.
//
#include <stdio.h>
void main(void)
{
    static struct arith  {
       float    a, b, c;
    } X = { 10, 5, -20 };   // Values assigned
    //
    //   Declare pointer variable *ptr_a to hold
    //   the address of a float type variable
    float *ptr_a;

    printf("\n ** Demo of Pointer Arithmetic ** \n");
    printf(" %s \n       a = %f  b = %f  c = %f \n",
         " Without using pointer arithmetic:",
           X.a, X.b, X.c);
    //   Because the components of a 'struct' are of
    //   the same type and are sequentially stored in
    //   memory, for this example the pointer arithmetic
    //   can be used after assigning ptr_a
    //   to the first component of the X structure.
    ptr_a   = &X.a;    // Assign address of "a"
    printf(" %s \n       a = %f  ",
         " Using pointer arithmetic:", *ptr_a);
    printf("b = %f   ", *(++ptr_a));
    printf("c = %f  \n", *++ptr_a);
 }
```

Code 2.2 produces this output:

```
** Demo of Pointer Arithmetic **
Without using pointer arithmetic:
     a = 10.000000   b = 5.000000   c = -20.000000
Using pointer arithmetic:
     a = 10.000000   b = 5.000000   c = -20.000000
```

2.2.5   STRUCTURE AS A FUNCTION ARGUMENT AND RETURN VALUE

In C++, a structure can be used as an argument to a function. Like call-by-value for variables, copies of values of the components are passed to a function. A structure can also be returned from a function to the caller. For example:

```
struct  INTERVAL {
    float   lft_end_pt,
            rgt_end_pt;
};

INTERVAL   add_interv (INTERVAL A,  INTERVAL B)
{
    INTERVAL   sum;

    sum.lft_end_pt = A.lft_end_pt + B.lft_end_pt;
    sum.rgt_end_pt = A.rgt_end_pt + B.rgt_end_pt;
    return (sum);
}
```

2.2.6   POINTER TO A STRUCTURE AS A FUNCTION ARGUMENT

In the previous section, passing a structure variable as an argument was shown. In this scheme — since copies of the structure fields are used — these fields cannot be modified within the function. If there is a need to modify or interchange the original values of the fields, it requires passing a pointer to a structure. When using pointers, structure variables are not automatically given memory space; it requires the use of the new operator for memory allocation. For example:

```
typedef struct  INTERVAL {
    float   lft_end_pt,
            rgt_end_pt;
} *INTERVAL_PTR;
```

```
INTERVAL_PTR  add_interv (INTERVAL_PTR A,  INTERVAL_PTR B)
{
    INTERVAL_PTR  sum;

    sum = new INTERVAL;

    sum->lft_end_pt = A->lft_end_pt + B->lft_end_pt;
    sum->rgt_end_pt = A->rgt_end_pt + B->rgt_end_pt;
    return (sum);
}
```

2.2.7 ARRAYS OF STRUCTURES

In database applications we need to deal with a collection of records that are structures. Such a collection can be organized as an array of records (structures) of the same type. The syntax for declaring and allocating an array of structures is:

```
struct <struct_name>  <array>[<size>];
```

For example, for the `people_1d` database with 10 members as shown in Appendix C,

```
struct DataObject {
    Keytype key;        // member id
    char *name;         // name
    char *occupation;   // occupation
    int  age;           // age
    int  income;        // yearly gross / $1000
    int  years;         // number years member
} people_db[10];        // an array of 10 members
```

a field, `age`, of the third structured data element in `people_db[]`, is accessed as

```
people_db[2].age
```

2.3 Unions

A *union* can be viewed as a structure except that it can be of a variable size and different type member fields. The size must be sufficiently large to hold any member field at any time. The advantage of using a union variable is to allow its members to share the same memory area. Like structures, a union can contain structures, unions, and functions. Its member fields cannot be `static` and are `publicly` accessible. The syntax for defining a union construct is:

```
union   <name_of_union>   {
    <type_of_mem1>   <name_of_mem1>;
        . . .
    <type_of_memN>   <name_of_memN>;
    <struct_name>   <struct_var>;
    <union_name>    <union_var>;
    <return_type>   <function_name>(
        <arg_type> <arg>, ..., <arg_type> <arg>);
}   <name_of_union_var>,
    *<name_of_union_var_ptr>;
```

The syntax for accessing the member fields of a union variable directly by name is

name_of_union_var.name_of_mem

while access indirectly by a pointer to the union is given by

name_of_union_var_ptr->name_of_mem.

For example:

```
union   demo {
    int     a;
    char    *b;
    float   add (float c,  float d);
} xx, *xx_ptr;

xx.a = 3;
xx_ptr.a = 5;
```

2.4   C++ Class

The *class* construct is a fundamental and powerful keyword in C++. It is significantly useful in OOP as it is used to combine the data and operations of an ADT structure into a single entity. The class construct differs from the conventional C language `struct` construct in that, for OOP, it provides support for data hiding, abstraction and encapsulation, public interface functions (methods) for message passing between objects, single and multiple inheritances, and polymorphism. In OOP terminology, it defines a type (template) of object. The syntax of the `class` construct is:

```
class   <class_type_name>   {
    private:
            <type> <data_members>;
            <implementation_operations>;   // methods
            <List of "friend" classes>;
            <List of "friend" functions>;
```

```
    protected:
        <type> <data_members>;
        <implementation_operations>;   // methods
    public:
        <type> <data_members>;
        <implementation_operations>;   // methods
};
```

The keyword typedef is not required since a class name is a type of name. The keywords private, protected, and public are used to specify the three levels of access protection for hiding data and function members internal to the class:

- private means that this member can only be accessed by the member functions and friends of this class. The member functions and friends of this class can always read or write private data members. The private member is not accessible to the outside world (that is, outside of this class).

- protected (read/write for data members only) means that this member can only be accessed by the member functions and friends of this class and member functions and friends derived from this class. It is not accessible to the outside world (that is, outside of this class).

- public means that this member can be accessed by any function in the outside world. The public implementation-operations (also called functions or methods) are interfaces to the outside world so that any function, in OOP terminology, can send messages to an object of this class through these interface functions.

The data members are always read/write. A member function can be *inline*, which means the member function can be defined within the body of the class construct. The keyword inline is used for short functions, and for efficient storage like the register keyword. A class is an abstract data type. It specifies how objects of its type behave, are created and deleted, and are accessed.

An example of a Stack-type class is as follows:

```
class  Stack  {
    int  *stk;    // Stack::stk is private by default
private:
    int  size;    // Stack::size is private
protected:
    int  *top;    // Stack::top is protected
public:
    int  top_of_stack;    // Stack::top_of_stack is public
    // Special "public" function "constructor"
    Stack(int sz)  { top = stk = new int[size=sz]; }
    // Special "public" function "destructor"
```

```
~Stack()   { delete []stk; }
// Other "public" functions (methods)
inline void push(int data) { *top++ = data; }
inline int  pop(void)    { return *--top; }
int          retrieve_top(void);
};
```

In the example code, above, the data elements in the Stack-type object
are integers.

2.4.1 Defining a Member Function of a Class Outside Its Scope

A member function of a class is defined using the : : scoping operator; the
syntax is:

```
<return value> <class_type_name> :: <member_function>
 (<arg type> <argument>, ..., <arg type> <argument>)
```

Note that the types of the member-function arguments must exactly match
with the types declared in the class definition of class_type_name.

For example, instead of defining the inline member function pop()
inside the body of Stack class, we can alternatively define it outside of
the body as follows:

```
inline  int Stack::pop(void)
{
    return (* --top);
}
//  Define member function retrieve_top(), which is not
//  defined inside the body of Stack class.
int  Stack::retrieve_top(void)
{
    return (*top);
}
```

2.4.2 Defining an Object of a Class

We define an instance of a class (interchangeably used with object) of a
predefined class type using the following syntax:

```
<class_type_name>   <object>;
```

Two objects of the same Stack class given above can be defined and
initialized in main(), as shown in **Code 2.3**.

Code 2.3

```
//  This is a test driver for the Stack class
#ifdef  MSDOS
```

```
#include   "ex2_3.cpp"
#else
#include   "ex2_3.c++"
#endif

void main(void)
{
     //  Declare and initialize two objects "stack_obj1" and
     //  "stack_obj2" of the same type: "Stack" class.
     Stack   stack_obj1(1024);
     Stack   stack_obj2(512);
     //  Define a pointer "stk_ptr" to an object of
     //  "Stack" class
     Stack   *stk_ptr;

     //  Connect "stk_ptr" to the object "stack_obj2"
     stk_ptr = &stack_obj2;

     //  Send a message ("push -20 in stack") to "stack_obj1"
     stack_obj1.push( -21 );

     //  Send a message ("push 11 in stack") to "stack_obj2"
     stk_ptr->push( 11 );
}
```

Note that the objects stack_obj1 and stack_obj2 of the same Stack class have their own copies of data and function members.

2.4.3   ACCESSING A MEMBER OF A CLASS

There are two ways we can access a member of a class similar to accessing members of a struct or union construct. A data or function member of the class construct is accessed using the . (period) operator in the following manner:

```
<class_object>.<data member>
<class_object>.<function member>
```

When a pointer to an object of a class is used, the -> operator is used to access data or function members of the class. The syntax is:

```
<class_object_pointer>-><data member>
<class_object_pointer>-><function member>
```

Accessing of a member function push() of the objects stack_obj1 and stack_obj2 is stated as:

```
stack_obj1.push(-21);

stk_ptr->push(11);
```

Another example of the class construct and referencing the members using a pointer is illustrated below in **Code 2.4**.

Code 2.4

```
//   Program:  point.c++
//   Purpose:
//      To demonstrate the uses of class, and
//      pointer to class object, and special function
//      constructor.
//
#include <stdio.h>
#include <math.h>    //  For 'sqrt()' function

typedef  int  COORD;
// Define a "Point" class
class Point {
  private:
    COORD   x,  y;  // x- & y-coordinates
  public:
    Point( COORD x_new, COORD y_new);
    //  To provide "READ-ONLY" access
    inline COORD get_x() { return x; }
    inline COORD get_y() { return y; }
    float find_dist (Point A, Point B);
};

//  Point():
//     Special function: constructor and initializer
//
Point::Point(COORD x_new, COORD y_new)
{
    x = x_new;
    y = y_new;
}

//  find_dist():
//     Compute distance between two point objects
//
float  Point::find_dist(Point A, Point B)
{
    float  dist_sqrd = (B.y - A.y) * (B.y - A.y) +
                       (B.x - A.x) * (B.x - A.x);
    return (sqrt(dist_sqrd));
}

//  main(): Main test driver
//
void  main(void)
{
    //  Declare and initialize two "Point" type
    //  objects.
```

```
Point   A_pt_obj( 4, 3), B_pt_obj( 0, -1);
Point *A_ptr = &A_pt_obj,
       *B_ptr = &B_pt_obj;

printf("\n ** Demo of Class, and Pointer %s \n",
       "to Class Objects **");
printf(" Point object A = ( %d, %d ) \n",
       A_ptr->get_x(), A_ptr->get_y());
printf(" Point object B = ( %d, %d ) \n",
       B_ptr->get_x(), B_ptr->get_y() );
printf(" Distance between A and B is: %f \n",
       A_ptr->find_dist(A_pt_obj, B_pt_obj));
}
```

Code 2.4 for the `Point class` construct produces this output:

```
** Demo of Class, and Pointer to Class Objects **
Point object A = ( 4, 3 )
Point object B = ( 0, -1 )
Distance between A and B is: 5.656854
```

2.4.4   FRIEND OF A CLASS AND INHERITANCE

In OOP, sometimes functions of one class need to access all private and protected data and function members of another class. To allow inheritance of such an access privilege, the `friend` keyword is only used in the helper class. The syntax is:

```
class   <helper_class_name>   {
  private:
    <data_members>;
    <function_members>;
    friend class  <friend_class_name>;
    friend <type> <friend_function_name>
               ( <arg_type> <arg> );
  public:  // ...
};
```

All member functions of the `friend_class_name` class and the friend function `friend_function_name` can have read/write access of data members and access of function members of the `helper_class_name` class. This friendship is inherited. It is not transitive and inherited, so a friend of the `friend_class_name` cannot inherit the privilege to access private data and function members of the `helper_class_name` class; the friendship is a privilege, and it is not transferable. Only the helper_class_name class can declare who can be its friend. Friends are privileged classes or functions. A friend is not a member of the helper class.

To illustrate the use of the friend keyword, we define a singly linked list of integer objects with access protection. For a detailed description of a singly linked list, see Chapter 5.

```
class  Slist_Node_Object  {
  private:
    int                data;
    Slist_Node_Object  *next;
    friend class   Singly_Linked_List;
};
//  Now define its "friend" class
class  Singly_Linked_List  {
  private:
    Slist_Node_Object  *head_ptr;
    void init_list();
  public:
    Singly_Linked_List();    // Constructor
    ~Singly_Linked_List();   // Destructor
    void append_node_obj();
    void prepend_node_obj();
    //  define more methods ...
};
```

All the member functions of the Singly_Linked_List class are friends of the Slist_Node_Object class. These member functions have read and write access privileges of data and *next that are members of the helper Slist_Node_Object class.

2.4.5 DERIVED CLASS AND MULTIPLE INHERITANCE

In OOP, sometimes we need to construct new classes that inherit data and functions from one or more previously declared classes. These new classes are called derived (or sub) classes. By deriving new classes from already defined classes, we can build well-organized hierarchies of classes. The syntax of deriving a new class from a base class uses the : operator as follows:

```
class <base_class> {
    private:
            // "private" members of base class
    protected:
            // "protected" members of base class
    public:
            // "public" members of base class
        virtual <type> <function>(<arg_type> <arg>);
};
```

```
class <derived_class>:<access_specifier> <base_class>{
   private:
             // "private" members of derived class
   protected:
             // "protected" members of derived class
   public:
             // "public" members of derived class
};
```

If the `access_specifier` is `private` in the derived class definition, the `protected` and `public` members of the base class are made `private` members of the derived class. If the `access_specifier` is `public` in the derived class definition, the `protected` and `public` members of the base class are made `public` members of the derived class. Private members of the base class are still not accessible to the function members of the derived class unless the `friend` keyword is used in the base class for a specific function.

When a subclass is derived from two or more previously defined base classes `base1_class` and `base2_class`, it is a case of multiple inheritance. The syntax is:

```
class <derived_class> :
        <access_specifier> <base1_class>,
        <access_specifier> <base2_class> {
   private:
             // "private" members of derived class
   protected:
             // "protected" members of derived class
   public:
             // "public" members of derived class
};
```

Multiple inheritance is the ability of a derived class to have multiple parent classes. To illustrate the concepts of derived class and multiple inheritance, consider the following code segment in which we define two base classes, `base1` and `base2`, and a derived class `derived`:

```
// Define "base1" class
class base1 {
  private:
    int a;
  protected:
    int b;
  public:
    int c;
    int f();
};
// Define "base2" class
```

```
class  base2  {
  private:
    int  d;
  protected:
    int  e;
  public:
    int  g;
    int  f();
};

//  Define "derived" class based on the
//  "base1" and "base2" classes
class  derived : public base1, private base2  {
  private:
    int  x;
  protected:
    int  base1::c;  // redefine access to "base1::c"
  public:
    int  y;
    int  z();
};
```

The members b, c, and f() of the base1 class are inherited, but b and f() are public and base1::c is protected in the derived class. The members e, g, and f() are private in the derived class derived. The private members a and d of the base1 and base2 classes, respectively, are not inherited to the derived class. Notice that ambiguity in referencing the inherited function f() occurs since f() is found in both of the base classes. To resolve the ambiguity in such a case of multiple inheritance, use the base class name base1::f() or base2::f() as follows:

```
int  derived::z()
{
  return ( y + base1::f() );
}
```

2.4.6 NESTED CLASS

Like the conventional struct construct, the class constructs may be nested, one class being declared within another. For example, for a singly linked list,

```
class  slist  {       // "slist" is outer class
  private:
   node_obj  *head_ptr;
   class node_obj  {  //  "node_obj" is inner class
     private:
       int            data;
       node_obj  *next;
     public:
       node_obj *set_next (node_obj *new_next);
     };
```

```
    public:
      slist();     // Constructor
      ~slist();    // Destructor
      //  define more methods ...
    };
```

2.5 Functions in C++

In C++, there are two categories of functions with regard to the `class` construct,

- the member function, and

- the nonmember function.

The C++ functions that fall into these two categories are listed below in Table 2.3. The C++ keywords `inline`, `friend`, `virtual`, `overload`, and `operator` are used as attributes of the functions listed in Table 2.4. The applicable usage of these attributes for a class member and nonmember function is listed Table 2.4.

Both the class member function and the nonmember function can be defined with the `inline` attribute. Note that the `overload` keyword is not used in C++ 2.0 or above; the overload function can simply be defined without the `overload` keyword.

2.5.1 SPECIAL FUNCTIONS: CONSTRUCTORS

Constructors are special functions in C++. They are member functions of a class, and widely used in OOP. The constructors have the following features:

- The name of a constructor must be the same as the class name.

Class Member Functions	Class Nonmember Functions
Constructors	Standard functions
Destructions	Friend functions
Implementation	Operator functions
operations (methods)	
Operator function	
Constant function	
Static functions	

TABLE 2.3. Class member and nonmember functions.

Attributes	Class Member Function	Class Nonmember Function
inline	Yes	Yes
friend	No	Yes
virtual	Yes	No
overload	Yes	Yes
operator	Yes	Yes

TABLE 2.4. Attributes for class member and nonmember functions.

- They cannot have any return type, not even `void`, but can have arguments.

- They are used to construct an object.

- They can initialize an object.

- They are automatically and implicitly called when an object of a class is declared.

In **Code 2.3**, the statement

```
Stack   stack_obj1(1024);
```

implicitly calls the constructor `Stack()` that dynamically allocates memory storage and initializes the `stack_obj1` object of the `Stack` type.

2.5.2   SPECIAL FUNCTIONS: DESTRUCTORS

Destructors are special functions in C++. They are member functions of a class, and are widely used in OOP. The destructors have the following features:

- The name of a destructor must be the same as the class name preceded by ~.

- They cannot have any return type and arguments.

- They are used to destroy or deallocate the memory space of an object by using the `delete` operator.

- They are automatically and implicitly called when an object of a class is deleted or the program is exited.

- They can be declared `virtual`.

In the last code segment of Section 2.4, `~Stack()` is the destructor for the `Stack` class, and calls

```
delete   []stk;
```

2.6 Polymorphism, Virtual Functions, and Inheritance

In OOP, polymorphism is an important concept, and an action that is implemented by a method. In OOP, polymorphism means that a method with the same name in a hierarchy of base classes and derived classes acts differently appropriate to the class or subclass. Such a method is called a virtual function. That is, a virtual function is used to implement different behaviors or actions appropriate to the class or subclass in which it is defined. In C++, a virtual function is declared by using the `virtual` keyword, only in the base class:

```
virtual <type> <function>( <argument_type> <argu-
                           ment> );
```

The virtual function must be defined in the base class, but its definition or purpose can be changed in any subsequent derived class. C++ internally uses special pointers to implement virtual functions.

2.6.1 FRIEND FUNCTIONS AND INHERITANCE

In OOP, sometimes a nonmember function needs to inherit the access privilege of any data or function members of another class (e.g., `class A`). In order to grant access permission, we declare this nonmember function as a `friend` of this class `A` by using the `friend` keyword. For syntax, see Section 2.4.4.

2.6.2 OVERLOADING AND POLYMORPHISM

To achieve polymorphism (a state of assuming different forms of actions) for OOP in C++, we can use overloaded functions and operators.

2.6.3 OVERLOADED FUNCTIONS

Functions that have the same name, but that implement many different actions, are called *overloaded functions*. Most of the time the choice of which function to use will be determined by the number and the type of the function's argument list (called *signature*); this is how the ambiguity of having the same function name is resolved. In C++, an overloaded function must be declared with `overload` keyword before it is defined. For example:

```
overload  add;   // Must be first declaration in C++ 1.0.
                 // Not needed in C++ 2.0 or later.

int   add( int, int );     // Is called when args are integers
float add( float *, float *); // Is called when args are
                              // pointers to floats
```

2.6.4 OVERLOADED OPERATORS

An overloaded operator is loaded with different meanings and actions depending on its operands. An overloaded operator must match the C++ built-in operators op and their meanings. It is defined as an operator function with the `operator` keyword. The syntax of defining an overloaded function is:

```
<return type> operator<op> ( <type> <arg1>, ...,
                            <type> <argN> )
```

The key points in creating an overloaded operator are:

- For maintainability of program, overloaded operators may carry the same meanings as their C++ built-in counterparts.

- C++ built-in operators cannot be combined to create new overloaded operators.

- The precedence of the new overloaded operators must remain unchanged as their C++ built-in counterparts.

- For binary overloaded operators, one of the operands must be an object of the user-defined class, or the overloaded operators must be friends of the class.

In **Code 2.5**, the operator + may be defined for `Complex`-type numbers as follows:

```
Complex operator+ (Complex A, Complex B)
{
    // ...
}
```

The operator + is then overloaded with different meanings: one for the addition of `Complex`-type numbers, and the other for the standard C++ built-in meaning. Notice that the overloaded operator functions for +, -, *, and / operators are defined as `friends` of the `Complex` class in **Code 2.5**.

2.7 Dangling Pointers and Memory Leaks

A C++ program may dynamically allocate memory space for data objects (ADTs) using the built-in functions `malloc()`, `calloc()`, `realloc()` or the new operator, and deallocate these run-time resources via the C++ `free()` function or `delete` operator.

From the computer system's point of view, memory resources are managed through a *free list* mechanism. When a program dynamically requests memory space, if the requested amount of memory space (in bytes) is available in the free list, the memory manager of the operating system will assign and allocate at least the requested amount of memory space from the *heap* to the C++ program. When the program specifies that previously allocated memory resources are to be freed, the operating system will return these resources to the free list.

While the operating system is keeping track of the overall memory resources, it is the program that is making the requests and thus it is the program that has direct control. As such, it is possible that ill-conceived programs may improperly allocate and deallocate memory, precipitating serious system problems. Two of the most common such problems are identified as *dangling pointers* and *memory leaks*.

2.7.1 DANGLING POINTERS

To illustrate the concept of a dangling pointer, consider the following code segment:

```
DATA_OBJECT  *ptr_1, *ptr_2;   // Statement 1
ptr_1 = new DATA_OBJECT;       // Statement 2
ptr_1->data = 'A';             // Statement 3
ptr_2 = ptr_1;                 // Statement 4
delete   ptr_2;                // Statement 5
ptr_1->data = 'B';             // Statement 6
```

In this code segment, Statement 1 allocates two ptrs, ptr_1 and ptr_2, to a data type DATA_OBJECT. Statement 2 subsequently allocates memory space for the DATA_OBJECT and assigns it to ptr_1. Statement 3 assigns 'A' as the data of this DATA_OBJECT while Statement 4 equates ptr_2 with ptr_1. At this point, both pointers hold the base address of the same DATA_OBJECT, as shown in Figure 2.2(a). Subsequently, Statement 5 frees the DATA_OBJECT memory space, leaving ptr_1 a dangling pointer, as it references a deallocated resource, as shown by the shaded box in Figure 2.2(b). Further operations on ptr_1, as suggested by Statement 6, result in a programming error.

2.7.2 MEMORY LEAKS

A memory leak (also referred to as *garbage*) is the most serious and frequent programming error when using C++ classes. Consider the following code segment as an illustration of the problem:

```
OBJECT  example_obj;                             // Statement 1
example_obj.ptr = example_obj.create("FOO"); // Statement 2
example_obj.ptr = NULL;                          // Statement 3
```

Statement 1 creates an example_object as an instance of an OBJECT class. Statement 2 creates some internal data structures for the object

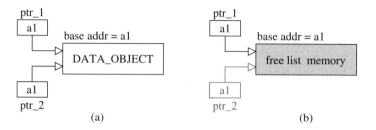

FIGURE 2.2. Dangling pointer.

`example_object`, allocating memory for these structures as required. Figure 2.3(a) depicts the memory allocation at this point. Statement 3 subsequently sets the pointer to these memory resources to NULL, thus rendering them inaccessible to the program. However, these resources were never explicitly freed. Thus, Statement 3 creates a memory leak or garbage — *there is a chunk of memory allocated to the program which is not used, not accessible by any other user's program, and not returned to the free list.* Figure 2.3(b) depicts the memory leak problem by showing the allocated memory as garbage in the shaded box.

Left unchecked, a memory leak problem may eventually put the computer system in a state of slow response, as usable memory resources are diminished, or eventually hang (deadlock) the system, as usable memory resources are fully depleted.

It is difficult to trace and debug the cause of a memory leak problem. It then becomes the memory manager's task to automatically cope with the memory leak problem and efficiently manage the free list. Some reasonable solutions for managing the memory leak problem are as follows:

- The program that caused the memory leak is stopped so that all memory spaces allocated to this program will be automatically freed and returned to the system's free list. The program may be restarted, but if the amount of memory leakage is significant, the program should be run only for a predetermined period.

- Two other automatic solutions are to apply the techniques of *counted pointers* and *automatic garbage collection*. These methods are discussed in Chapter 5 where a more detailed treatment of memory management is presented.

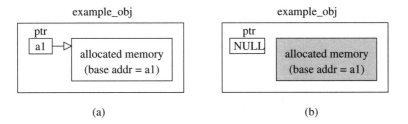

FIGURE 2.3. Memory leak.

2.8 OOP Application: Complex Numbers

While C++ does not provide a built-in type for the complex numbers, a complex number may be viewed as a structured pair (a, b) data object. We define a Complex type class and the overloaded operators +, −, *, and / as friends of the Complex class. These concepts are demonstated in **Code 2.5**.

Code 2.5

```
//   Program:   complex.c++
//   Purpose:   Object-Oriented Implementation of
//              Complex numbers objects "a + bi".
//              Use "Operator Overloading" method.
//
#include <stdio.h>
#include <stdlib.h>
typedef   float        DATA_TYPE;

//   Define a class "Complex" for complex number
//   objects "a + bi"
class   Complex {
  private:
    DATA_TYPE   real;   // Real part "a"
    DATA_TYPE   imag;   // Imaginary part "b"
  public:
    Complex( DATA_TYPE new_re, DATA_TYPE new_im );

    friend Complex   operator+ (Complex A, Complex B);
    friend Complex   operator- (Complex A, Complex B);
    friend Complex   operator* (Complex A, Complex B);
    friend Complex   operator/ (Complex A, Complex B);
    friend Complex   operator- (Complex A);
    friend void      print_complex ( Complex A,
                     char   *Complex_var_name );
};
```

```cpp
//   Complex():
//      Constructor and initializer
//
Complex::Complex( DATA_TYPE new_re,
                  DATA_TYPE new_im )
{
    real = new_re;
    imag = new_im;
}

//   Overloaded Complex operator: " + "
//    Performs addition of "Complex" objects A + B
//    and returns Complex-type object.
//
Complex operator+ ( Complex  A, Complex  B )
{
   return Complex( A.real + B.real,
                   A.imag + B.imag );
}

//   Complex unary Operator "-"   for -A
//     Negate A and return Complex
//     For A = ( A_Real, A_imag),
//        - A = ( - A_Real, - A_imag )
//
Complex operator- ( Complex  A )
{
   return Complex( - A.real, - A.imag );
}

//   Complex binary Operator  "-" for A - B
//    A - B = ( A_Real - B_Real, A_imag - B_imag )
//      where  A = ( A_Real, A_imag )
//        and   B = ( B_Real, B_imag )
//
Complex  operator- ( Complex A, Complex B )
{
   return Complex( A.real - B.real,
                   A.imag - B.imag );
}

//   Overloaded Complex operator: " * "
//    Performs A * B and returns Complex
//    A * B = ( A_Real * B_Real - A_imag * B_imag,
//              A_Real * B_imag + A_imag * B_Real )
//
Complex operator* (Complex A, Complex B)
{
   return Complex( A.real * B.real - A.imag * B.imag,
                   A.real * B.imag + A.imag * B.real );
}

//   Overloaded Complex operator: " / "
//    Performs A / B and returns Complex
```

```
//
Complex  operator/ (Complex A, Complex B)
{
    DATA_TYPE    temp1, temp2, temp3;

    // Is the divisor  B = 0 ?
    if (B.real != 0 && B.imag != 0) {
       //  Divisor complex number B is non-zero
       temp1 = A.real * B.real + A.imag * B.imag;
       temp2 = A.imag * B.real - A.real * B.imag;
       temp3 = B.real * B.real + B.imag * B.imag;
       return Complex( temp1/temp3, temp2/temp3 );
     }
     else {
       printf("\n complex_div: ERROR: Division by %s \n",
              "a Complex number ZERO is not allowed ");
       exit(-1);
     }
}

//  print_complex() : Print a complex object
//
void  print_complex (Complex  A,
                     char    *Complex_var_name)
{
    printf(" Complex %s = %10.3f +  %10.3f * i \n",
           Complex_var_name, A.real, A.imag );
}

// main():
//   OBJECT-ORIENTED IMPLEMENTATION of Complex
//   number objects.
//
void  main(void)
{
    //  Declare and initialize "C_obj" and
    //  "D_obj" of the "Complex" class
    Complex  C_obj(10.0, 12.0),
             D_obj(-5.0, 15.0);

    printf("\n ** OOP IMPLEMENTATION %s \n\n",
           "OF COMPLEX NUMBER OBJECTS **");
    print_complex (C_obj, "C    ");
    print_complex (D_obj, "D    ");
    print_complex (C_obj + D_obj, "C + D");
    print_complex (C_obj - D_obj, "C - D");
    print_complex (C_obj * D_obj, "C * D");
    print_complex (C_obj / D_obj, "C / D");
    print_complex (- C_obj, "- C  ");
}
```

Here is the output of **Code 2.5**:

```
** OOP IMPLEMENTATION OF COMPLEX NUMBER OBJECTS **

Complex C     =      10.000 +       12.000 * i
Complex D     =      -5.000 +       15.000 * i
Complex C + D =       5.000 +       27.000 * i
Complex C - D =      15.000 +       -3.000 * i
Complex C * D =    -230.000 +       90.000 * i
Complex C / D =       0.520 +       -0.840 * i
Complex - C   =     -10.000 +      -12.000 * i
```

2.9 Exercises

1. Write a derived class `Rectangle` from the base class `Point` defined in **Code 2.4**. Write a constructor and a member function of the `Rectangle` class that determines the area of a rectangular object. Include a print function and a test driver.

2. Write a derived class `Circle` from the base class `Point` defined in **Code 2.4**. Write a constructor and a member function `area()` of the `Circle` class that determines the area of a circular object. Include a print function and a test driver.

3. Write a derived class `Cylinder` from the base class `Circle` defined in **Code 2.4**. Write a constructor and a member function `area()` of the `Cylinder` class that determines the area of a cylindrical object. Note the usage of the function name `area()` is the same as that in the `Circle` class. Include a print function and a test driver.

4. Write a `Calculator` class that embodies memory as data and the following operations as methods: (i) Constructor, (ii) Destructor, (iii) Add two integers and return the result, (iv) Subtract two integers and return the result, (v) Multiply two integers and return the result, (vi) Add an integer to memory, store the result in memory and return the result, (vii) Clear memory, and (viii) Recall memory.

3

Arrays and Strings

The *array* and *string* data structures are essential components of all high level programming languages. This chapter discusses their fundamentals and presents them as abstract data types. Array objects and string objects are defined and implemented using OOPs. An OOP people database is presented as an object-oriented application of these objects.

3.1 Array Objects

Definition 3.1 *An ADT array is a data structure that contains a set of data elements of the same type, a set of indices, and a set of operations that are used for defining, manipulating, and abstracting these data elements.*

An *array object* is one specified by an ADT array. A set of possible methods on an array object is shown in Table 3.1. Such methods characterize the array object. The elements of the array are as abstract as possible and can be accessed at random by index.

Example Array Object Methods
Instantiate and initialize an array object.
Destroy an array object.
Build an array object from a given set of data.
Store an element in an array object.
Retrieve an element from an array object.
Insert an element before a specified element.
Insert an element after a specified element.
Delete an element from an array object.
Update an element in an array object.
Search for an element in an array object.
Sort data elements in an array object.
Print elements in an array object.

TABLE 3.1.

The indices are determined by the dimensions of the array. The dimensionality directs the implementation of an array object.

FIGURE 3.1. Array base class methods.

As identified by Definition 3.1, an array object is an instance of some derived *implementation specific* class. For the examples in this chapter, we define a *base* class `Array` from which all array classes derive. The `Array` class is defined in `bc_array.h` as follows:

```
// Program:  bc_array.h
// Purpose:  Define base class "Array" for array objects.

extern class Derived_Ary;
// "Derived_Ary" may be a template for a 1- or 2- or
// multi-dimensional array objects.
class  Array {
  //  Declare member functions for matrix
  //  operations as public interfaces
  public:
    virtual void       store(DATA_TYPE data) = 0;
    virtual DATA_TYPE  retrieve(void) = 0;
    friend Derived_Ary operator+ (Derived_Ary A, Derived_Ary B);
    friend Derived_Ary operator- (Derived_Ary A, Derived_Ary B);
    friend Derived_Ary operator* (Derived_Ary A, Derived_Ary B);
    Derived_Ary operator= (Derived_Ary A);
    friend void print_array(Derived_Ary A, char *header);
};
```

Figure 3.1 depicts the base `Array` object and its members. For reasons of convention and efficiency, overloaded operators are defined as `friends` of the `Derived_Ary` class. The `Derived_Ary` class is an implementation specific class derived from the base class `Array`, and may be a template for one-, two-, or multidimensional array objects. `Derived_Ary` is implemented separately in **Code 3.1** for the one-dimensional array object and in **Code 3.2** for the two-dimensional array object. Since `store()` and `retrieve()` use the array object's index or indices, they are implementation specific. However, they could have been declared as `public` members only in the derived class `Derived_Ary`.

3.2   One-Dimensional Arrays

In this section the basic concepts and ADT definitions are first discussed and then the OOP implementation of one-dimensional arrays is presented.

3.2.1   DECLARATION OF ARRAYS IN C++

An array is a sequential form of the same data type objects. The array is identified by a *name* and an *index* and is of fixed size. The syntax for declaring an array is:

```
<data_type>   <array_name>[<size>];
```

For example, the statement int array[4];, declares an array named array whose data elements are of integer type. The structure array has four elements, array[0], array[1], array[2], and array[3]. The array index ranges from 0 to 3. The memory layout for array is linear and contiguous. That is, memory location array[0] is adjacent to array[1]. The memory layout of an array is shown in Figure 3.2.

3.2.2   STORING AND RETRIEVING AN ELEMENT IN AN ARRAY

Array elements may be randomly accessed. The two ways of accessing array elements are by

- array name and index, and

- a pointer to an array.

The syntax for accessing an array element by name and index is

```
<array_name>[index]
```

For example, the third element in the array array is accessed by array[2]. A value, new_value, may be stored into and retrieved from array[2] with the statements:

```
array[2] = new_value; // store
get_value = array[2]; // retrieve
```

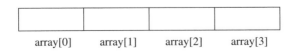

FIGURE 3.2. Memory layout of an array.

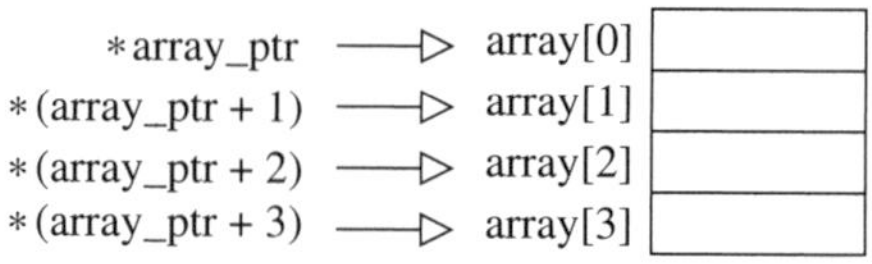

$$
\begin{array}{ll}
*\text{array\_ptr} & \longrightarrow \text{array}[0] \\
*(\text{array\_ptr} + 1) & \longrightarrow \text{array}[1] \\
*(\text{array\_ptr} + 2) & \longrightarrow \text{array}[2] \\
*(\text{array\_ptr} + 3) & \longrightarrow \text{array}[3]
\end{array}
$$

FIGURE 3.3. Pointer to an array.

When a pointer to an array is used, the syntax is:

```
<data_type>  <array_name>[<size>];
<data_type> *<array_pointer> = &<array_name>[0];
```

For the array `array[]` in Figure 3.2, declare:

```
int  *array_ptr = &array[0];
```

Then `array_ptr` points to the array elements as shown in Figure 3.3. The numbers 1, 2, 3 are used in conjunction with the size of the data type (e.g., 4 for `int`s). In this case, storing and retrieving values to and from `array[2]` is accomplished by pointer and not by index:

```
*(array_ptr + 2) = new_value;    // Store
get_value = * (array_ptr + 2);   // Retrieve
```

3.2.3 INITIALIZING AN ARRAY

An array may be initialized at its declaration using the `static` keyword. For example,

```
static int array[] = { -2, 1, -20, 9 };
```

declares an array named `array` with elements 0 through 4 of value -2, 1, -20, and 9, respectively. When a pointer, such as `array_ptr`, is used, initializing the array `array` is accomplished by storing a value in each element as follows:

```
*array_ptr        = -2;
*(array_ptr + 1) =   1;
*(array_ptr + 2) = -20;
*(array_ptr + 3) =   9;
```

3.2.4 ONE-DIMENSIONAL ARRAY ADDRESS TRANSLATION

The concept of *address translation* is the relationship between the base memory address of an array and the address of its data elements. It is very useful for pointer and object-oriented implementations of arrays. The formula is:

$$Address\ of\ array[i] = base\ address + i * sizeof(int)$$
$$= \&array[0] + i * element\ size$$

3.2.5 ARRAY AS FUNCTION ARGUMENTS

Since an array name is itself the base address of an array, we pass the array name as a function argument. The array elements are directly accessed by the function. The syntax of function declaration is:

```
<return_type> <function>(<data_type> <array_name>,...)
```

This method is used in the sorting and searching examples in Chapter 7. For example, for the array

```
static int array[] = { -2, 1, -20, 9 };
```

the array name `array` is used to define the function `Bubble_Sort()` as shown below:

```
void  Bubble_Sort (int array)
{
    // ...
}
```

3.2.6 ONE-DIMENSIONAL ARRAY OBJECT

Definition 3.2 *An ADT one-dimensional array is a data structure that contains a set of data elements, a single index for each a element (to access the element) such that contiguous indices access contiguous elements, and a set of operations on these elements.*

The elements are as abstract as possible and can be accessed at random. First, we consider some of these operations in the case of the indexed implementation. This ADT definition specifies a one-dimensional object. The type of this object is defined by the `Array` class shown in Section 3.2.7.

Allocating an array object is accomplished by the `new` operator or its declaration in C++. For example, `int array[4];` automatically allocates memory spaces for four integer-type elements.

An array object is automatically destructed at the program exit or using the `delete` operator explicitly.

The *initialize* operation is discussed in Section 3.2.3. When using an index, the code is:

```
typedef  int    DATA_TYPE;
void init_ary (DATA_TYPE   array[])
{
    int   index,
    size = sizeof(array)/sizeof(DATA_TYPE);
    for (index = 0; index < size; index++)
        array[index] = 0;
}
```

When a pointer `array_ptr` to an array is used, the code for initializing a one-dimensional array is:

```
void init_ary (DATA_TYPE   array[])
{
    int   index,
    size = sizeof(array)/sizeof(DATA_TYPE);
    register DATA_TYPE *array_ptr = &array[0];
    for (index = size; --index >= 0; *array_ptr++ = 0);
}
```

The *store* (or *put*) and *retrieve* (or *get*) operations, as discussed in Section 3.2.2, are implemented as follows:

```
array[2]  = new_value;  // Store "new_value"
get_value = array[2];   // Get value from array[2]
```

The *retrieve* operation does not destroy the element to be retrieved. This operation may fail in the following cases:

- When the specified array index, say k, is less than 0, or greater than the array size.

- When the specified array index, say k, is within the valid range, but the element `array[k]` is not defined.

Since other operations primarily depend on the store and retrieve operations, these operations do not need to be discussed. The focus is primarily on its OOP implementation shown in **Code 3.1**.

3.2.7 OOP for One-Dimensional Array

For an OOP implementation, the one-dimensional array object is identified by an ADT one-dimensional array, which is derived from the array object's abstract base class `Array` and is implemented by the `Derived_Ary` class. To ensure data-hiding, encapsulation, message-passing for an OOP, the `Derived_Ary` class, defined in `class_Array_def.h` of **Code 3.1**, is:

```
typedef   int  DATA_TYPE;
#include  "bc_array.h"     // For base class "Array"

//  Define a class "Derived_Ary"
```

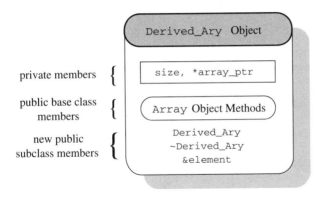

private members {

public base class members {

new public subclass members {

FIGURE 3.4. Derived_Ary object

```
class  Derived_Ary : private Array {
  private:
    int        size;       // Number of elements
    DATA_TYPE  *array_ptr; // Pointer to data area

  //  Declare member functions for Derived_Ary
  //  operations as public interfaces
  public:
    Derived_Ary(int sz);   // Constructor
    ~Derived_Ary();        // Destructor
    DATA_TYPE  &element(int index);
    void       store(DATA_TYPE data);
    DATA_TYPE  retrieve(void);
    friend Derived_Ary operator+(Derived_Ary A, Derived_Ary B);
    friend void print_array(Derived_Ary A, char *header);
};
```

The `Derived_Ary` class, shown in Figure 3.4, defines a type for one-dimensional array objects, e.g., A_obj,B_obj. The members `size`, and `array_ptr` are declared `private` for data-hiding and protection from corruption. The member functions `Derived_Ary()`,`~Derived_Ary()`, `element()`,`store()` and `retrieve()` are declared `public`; these are interfaces to the outside world in order to facilitate message passing between an `Array`-type object and any other type of object. `Print_array()` and the overloaded operator `+()` are declared `friends` of the `Derived_Ary` class.

To allow reusability of the `Derived_Ary` class, DATA_TYPE is defined outside the `Array` class. In C++ 3.0, this is not necessary, and can be achieved by using the `template` keyword as follows:

```
template<class DATA_TYPE> class Derived_Ary :
          private Array {
  private:
```

```
    int         size;
    DATA_TYPE   *array_ptr;
  public:
    Derived_Ary(int sz);
    ~Derived_Ary();
    DATA_TYPE   &element(int index);
    void        store(DATA_TYPE data);
    DATA_TYPE   retrieve(void);
    friend Derived_Ary operator+(Derived_Ary A,  Derived_Ary B);
    friend void print_array(Derived_Ary A,  char *header);
};
```

This `Derived_Ary` class defines an array object of elements of an arbitrary type, and template member functions. This class would produce array objects with size 10 and data of any type:

```
Derived_Ary<int>     int_ary_obj(10);
Derived_Ary<char>    char_ary_obj(10);
Derived_Ary<float>   float_ary_obj(10);
```

Caution must be taken in the `print_array()` function to deal with possible values of DATA_TYPE. For more information, see [Str91].

`Derived_Ary()`, with the same name as the type `Derived_Ary`, is called the constructor. It initializes the dimension size. It also dynamically allocates memory spaces for DATA_TYPE elements of the `Derived_Ary` type object by using the new operator:

```
array_ptr = new DATA_TYPE[size];
```

The constructor is automatically called when the two class objects `A_obj` and `B_obj` are instantiated in `main()`.

`~Derived_Ary()`, is the destructor function. It destroys the allocated memory space for the `Derived_Ary` type objects `A_obj` and `B_obj`, by using the `delete` operator:

```
delete []array_ptr;
```

It is implicitly called when the objects are destroyed or at the program exit in `main()`.

The operation `&element()` is a `public` member function of the class `Derived_Ary`. It performs both storing and retrieving operations for an element `array_ptr[index]` of an object, e.g., `A_obj`, in the class `Derived_Ary`. It is used as follows:

```
A_obj.element(0) = 2;            // Store
get_value = A_obj.element(0);    // Retrieve
```

The key operations `store()` and `retrieve()` are made `public` members of the `Derived_Ary` class. These functions ask the user for the array index and subsequently call `&element()`.

The operator +() is an overloaded operator function. It is a declared friend of the Derived_Ary class so that it is allowed to access the data and function members of the Derived_Ary class. It carries the same meaning as the standard + operator, but it adds two Derived_Ary type objects and a Derived_Ary type object. Its usage is as follows:

```
Derived_Ary  A_obj(2),  B_obj(2),  C_obj(2);
C_obj = A_obj + B_obj;
```

Print_array() is declared a friend of the Derived_Ary class. It prints all elements of a Derived_Ary type object, say A_obj, by calling A_obj.element().

Main() is the test driver for OOP implementation of a one-dimensional array. It instantiates two Derived_Ary-type objects A_obj and B_obj of dimension two. It passes the messages such as "store data" to the these objects using element(). It calls the overloaded operator +() function, and then calls print_array() to print the objects of type Derived_Ary.

The complete code and output are given below as **Code 3.1**.

Code 3.1

```cpp
// Program: 1dim_ary.c++
// Purpose:
//    Object-Oriented Implementation of a
//    one-dimensional array. Implement "Constructor",
//    and "Destructor", and  "store", "retrieve",
//    "print" operations.

#include  <stdio.h>
#include  <iostream.h>
#include  "class_Array_def.h"  // For "Array" class
// Derived_Ary():
//    Initialize the dimension, and allocate
//    memory space for an object of "Derived_Ary" class
//
Derived_Ary::Derived_Ary(int sz)
{
    // Initialize dimension of object of "Derived_Ary" class
    size  = sz;
    // Allocate memory space
    array_ptr = new  DATA_TYPE[size];
}

// ~Derived_Ary():
//    Delete memory space for a "Derived_Ary" object
//
Derived_Ary::~Derived_Ary()
{
    delete  [] array_ptr;
}
```

```
// element():
//    Store and retrieve an element A[i]
//    of an object in "Derived_Ary" class
//    Usages:
//      To store: A.element(index) = new_value;
//      To retrieve: value = A.element(index);
//
DATA_TYPE & Derived_Ary::element(int index)
{
    return (array_ptr [index]);
}


void Derived_Ary::store(DATA_TYPE data)
{
    int index = 0;
    printf("\nTo store, enter array index: ");
    cin >> index;
    element(index) = data;
}


DATA_TYPE Derived_Ary::retrieve(void)
{
    int index = 0;
    printf("\nTo retrieve, enter array index: ");
    cin >> index;
    return (element(index));
}


// Derived_Ary Overloaded Operator: "+"
//    Add two one-dimensional array objects
//    A (m) & B (m)
//    and return a "Derived_Ary" object C (m).
//    Usage: C = A + B;
//
Derived_Ary operator+ (Derived_Ary A, Derived_Ary B)
{
    // Declare a temporary array  for result
    Derived_Ary  tmp(A.size);

    for (int i = 0; i < A.size; i++)
        tmp.element(i) = A.element(i) + B.element(i);
    return (tmp);
}


// print_array():
//    Print a "Derived_Ary" object A (m) with a header.
//
void print_array(Derived_Ary  A, char *hdr)
{
    printf("\n *** Following Array: %s \n\n", hdr);
    for (int i = 0; i < A.size; i++)
        printf(" %5d ", A.element(i));
    printf("\n");
```

```
}

// main():
//    Driver to test OBJECT-ORIENTED
//    IMPLEMENTATION of an One-Dimensional array
//
void  main(void)
{
    // Declare and allocate memory space for two
    // objects "A_obj", "B_obj" in "Derived_Ary" class
    Derived_Ary  A_obj(2), B_obj(2);

    // Initialize Derived_Ary objects A_obj and B_obj
    A_obj.element(0) = 2;  A_obj.element(1) = 4;
    B_obj.element(0) = 8;  B_obj.element(1) = 3;
    printf("\n == OOP IMPLEMENTATION %s == ",
            "OF ONE-DIMENSIONAL ARRAY");
    print_array(A_obj, "A");
    print_array(B_obj, "B");
    print_array(A_obj + B_obj, "A + B");
}
```

Here is the output of **Code 3.1**:

```
== OOP IMPLEMENTATION OF ONE-DIMENSIONAL ARRAY ==
*** Following Array: A

    2              4

*** Following Array: B

    8              3

*** Following Array: A + B

    10             7
```

3.3 Two-Dimensional Arrays

Though C++ does not provide any built-in type for multidimensional arrays, such arrays can be built by adding multiple bracket [] pairs to the array variable name. For the two-dimensional and three-dimensional arrays, two bracket pairs and three bracket pairs, respectively, are used.

This section discusses basic concepts, the ADT definition and an OOP implementation. Like one-dimensional arrays, multidimensional arrays have a fixed size, which cannot be dynamically changed during the program execution.

The two-dimensional array, also called a *matrix*, is comprised of *rows* and *columns*. Every data element of a two-dimensional array has two indices: the first index indicates the row number (the first dimension), and the second index indicates the column number (the second dimension). In a mathematical representation, the two-dimensional p-by-q array M[] [] with p-rows and q-columns has the following rectangular form:

$$
M = \begin{bmatrix}
M[0][0] & M[0][0] & \cdots\cdots & M[0][q-1] \\
M[1][0] & M[0][0] & \cdots\cdots & M[1][q-1] \\
\vdots & \vdots & & \\
M[p-1][0] & M[p-1][1] & \cdots\cdots & M[p-1][q-1]
\end{bmatrix}
\begin{array}{l}
\text{(row 0)} \\
\text{(row 1)} \\
\\
\text{(row p-1)}
\end{array}
$$

column 0   column 1   column q–1

For a data element M[i] [j], the row index ranges from 0 to $(p-1)$, and the column index ranges from 0 to $(q-1)$. The total number of elements in the matrix M is $p \times q$.

3.3.1 C++ DECLARATION OF TWO-DIMENSIONAL ARRAYS

A two-dimensional array is a sequential form of the same data type objects. It is identified by a name and two indices. The sizes of row and column dimensions are fixed. The syntax for declaring a two-dimensional array is:

```
<data_type>   <marray_name>[<row_size>][<col_size>];
```

For example, int   mAry[2][3]; declares a two-dimensional array, mAry with two rows and three columns. Its data elements are of integer type. It has six elements: mAry[0][0],mAry[0][1],mAry[0][2],mAry[1][0], mAry[1][1], and mAry[1][2]. This declaration automatically allocates memory space for the six elements, and in the linear memory it stores the first row followed by the second row. The linear memory layout for the array mAry[2][3] is contiguous and is shown as array[2][3] in Figure 3.5.

3.3.2 STORING AND RETRIEVING AN ELEMENT IN A TWO-DIMENSIONAL ARRAY

Two-dimensional array elements can be randomly accessed. The two ways of accessing elements of a two-dimensional array are by

array[0][0]   array[0][1]   array[0][2]   array[1][0]   array[1][1]   array[1][2]

FIGURE 3.5. Memory layout of a two-dimensional 2x3 array.

- array name and two indices, and

- using a pointer to an array.

An element of a two-dimensional array is accessed by using the array name and two indices:

<marray_name>[row_index][col_index]

For example, the element at the (1,2) position in the two-dimensional array mAry is accessed by mAry[1][2].

A value new_value is stored into and retrieved from mAry[1][2] by:

```
mAry[1][2] = new_value;   // Store
get_value = mAry[1][2];   // Retrieve
```

To use a pointer to a two-dimensional array, the syntax is:

```
<data_type>   <marray_name>[<row_size>][<col_size>];
<data_type> *<marray_pointer> = &<marray_name>[0][0];
```

For the two-dimensional array mAry[][] in Figure 3.5, declare:

```
int   *mary_ptr = &mAry[0][0];
```

Then the pointer mary_ptr points to the array elements as shown in Figure 3.6. The numbers 0, 1, and 2 are used in conjunction with the size of the data type (e.g., 4 bytes for ints). In this case, storing and retrieving values for mAry[1][2] are done using pointers instead of using array indices:

```
*( *(mary_ptr + 1) + 2) = new_value;   // Store
get_value = *( *(mary_ptr + 1) + 2);   // Retrieve
```

Note the key relationship between the index and the pointer representation is:

```
( *(mary_ptr + i) + j) == A[i][j].
```

```
* ( * (mary_ptr + 0) + 0) ——▷ mAry[0][0]
* ( * (mary_ptr + 0) + 1) ——▷ mAry[0][1]
* ( * (mary_ptr + 0) + 2) ——▷ mAry[0][2]
* ( * (mary_ptr + 1) + 0) ——▷ mAry[1][0]
* ( * (mary_ptr + 1) + 1) ——▷ mAry[1][1]
* ( * (mary_ptr + 1) + 2) ——▷ mAry[1][2]
```

FIGURE 3.6. Pointer to a two-dimensional array.

3.3.3 INITIALIZING A TWO-DIMENSIONAL ARRAY

Initializing a two-dimensional array can be done at the declaration using the `static` keyword. For example:

```
static int mAry[2][3] = { {-2, 1, -20},    // Row 0
                          { 2, 0,   9} }; // Row 1
```

When a single pointer, e.g., `mary_ptr` is used, initializing the two-dimensional array `mAry` is done by the following statements similar to storing:

```
*mary_ptr = -2;              // mAry[0][0] = -2
*( *(mary_ptr + 0) + 1) = 1;  // mAry[0][1] =  1
  .
  .
  .

*( *(mary_ptr + 1) + 2) = 9;  // mAry[1][2] =  9
```

Alternatively, an array of pointers to each row may be used for accessing the two-dimensional arrays.

3.3.4 TRANSLATING ADDRESS OF TWO-DIMENSIONAL ARRAY ELEMENTS

This concept is very useful for pointer and object-oriented implementations of arrays. This is the relationship between the base memory address and the memory address of its elements. The formula is:

$$
\begin{aligned}
Address\ of\ mAry[i][j] &= base\ address + offset \\
&= \&mAry[0][0] + \\
&\quad (i\ *\ n\_cols + j) * sizeof(DATA\_TYPE)
\end{aligned}
$$

where `n_cols` is a number of columns, `DATA_TYPE` is the user-defined data type for elements, and `mAry` is the name of a two-dimensional array.

3.3.5 TWO-DIMENSIONAL ARRAYS AS FUNCTION ARGUMENTS

Since the array name is the base address of a two-dimensional array, the array name is passed as a function argument. The array elements are directly accessed by the function. The exact dimension of the column must be passed, whereas the row dimension is optional. The syntax of function declaration that uses a two-dimensional array as a formal argument is:

```
<return_type> <function>( <data_type>
                        <marray_name>[][<col_size>], ...)
```

For example, mAry[][3], an array with three columns, is passed to define the following function:

```
typedef    int DATA_TYPE;
DATA_TYPE  sum(DATA_TYPE mAry[][3], int n_rows)
{
    // ...
}
```

3.3.6 TWO-DIMENSIONAL ARRAY OBJECT

Definition 3.3 *An ADT two-dimensional array is a data structure that contains a set of data elements, a row index and a column index for each element (to access the element) such that contiguous row indices access contiguous row elements and contiguous column indices access contiguous column elements, and a set of operations on these elements.*

The elements are as abstract as possible, and can be accessed at random using two indices. A two-dimensional array object is specified by its ADT definition, and is instantiated by its declaration in C++. For example: int mAry[2][3]; automatically allocates memory spaces for six integer-type elements.

In the case of fixed memory allocation, a two-dimensional array object is automatically deleted at the program exit. In the case of dynamic memory allocation (using pointers), a destructor must be defined to deallocate memory space.

As discussed in Section 3.3.3, the *initialize* operation uses the row and column indices — row_inx and col_inx as follows:

```
typedef  int    DATA_TYPE;
DATA_TYPE       mAry[n_rows][n_cols];
void init_mary (DATA_TYPE   mAry)
{
  int row_inx, col_inx;
  for (row_inx = 0; row_inx < n_rows; row_inx++)
    for (col_inx = 0; col_inx < n_cols; col_inx++)
      mAry[row_inx][col_inx] = 0;
}
```

When a pointer `marray_ptr` to a two-dimensional array is used, the pointer arithmetic takes advantage of the contiguous memory locations of the two-dimensional array. The code for initializing it is as follows:

```
void init_mary (DATA_TYPE mAry)
{
  int   index,  size = n_rows * n_cols;
  register DATA_TYPE *marray_ptr = &mAry[0][0];

  for (index = size; --index >= 0; *marray_ptr++ = 0);
}
```

The store and retrieve operations, as discussed in Section 3.3.2, are done by:

```
mAry[1][2] = new_value;  // Store "new_value"
get_value  = mAry[1][2]; // Get value from mAry[1][2]
```

The retrieve operation does not destroy the element. This operation may fail in the following cases:

- When the specified array indices, say i and j, are less than 0, or greater than the row and column sizes.

- When the specified array indices, say i and j, are within the valid range, but the element `mAry[i][j]` is not defined.

Since other operations primarily depend upon the store and retrieve operations, these operations need no discussion.

3.3.7   OOP Two-Dimensional Array

For an OOP implementation, an ADT two-dimensional array (matrix) specifies an object. To attain data-hiding and encapsulation, a `Derived_Ary` class defined in `class_Derived_Ary_def.h` of **Code 3.2**, is:

```
typedef   int  DATA_TYPE;
#include   "bc_array.h"   // For base class "Array"

//  Define a class "Derived_Ary" for two-dimensional
//  array (Matrix) derived from the base class.
class  Derived_Ary : private Array {
  private:
    int          n_rows,     // Number of rows
                 n_cols;     // Number of columns
    DATA_TYPE    *mary_ptr;  // Pointer to data area
  //  Declare member functions for matrix
  //  operations as public interfaces
  public:
    Derived_Ary(int rows, int cols);  // Constructor
    ~Derived_Ary(void);               // Destructor
```

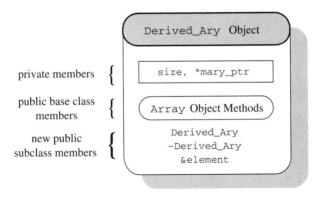

FIGURE 3.7. Derived_Ary object.

```
DATA_TYPE     &element( int i, int j);
void          store(DATA_TYPE data);
DATA_TYPE     retrieve(void);
friend Derived_Ary operator+ (Derived_Ary A, Derived_Ary B);
friend Derived_Ary operator- (Derived_Ary A, Derived_Ary B);
friend Derived_Ary operator* (Derived_Ary A, Derived_Ary B);
Derived_Ary  operator= (Derived_Ary A);
friend void  print_array(Derived_Ary A, char *header);
};
```

The Derived_Ary class defines a type for two-dimensional array (matrix) objects, shown in Figure 3.7 encompassing both data and operations. The members DATA_TYPE, n_rows, n_cols, and mary_ptr are private for data-hiding and protection from corruption. The pointer mary_ptr points to the object's data area. The members Derived_Ary(), ~Derived_Ary(), &element(), store(), retrieve() and the friend overloaded operators +, -, *, = for Derived_Ary objects, are public; these are interfaces to the outside world in order to facilitate message passing between Derived_Ary-type object and any object.

Derived_Ary(), with the same name as the type Derived_Ary, is the constructor. It initializes the dimension variables n_rows and n_cols. Using the new operator, it dynamically allocates memory space for n_rows * n_cols number of DATA_TYPE elements for a Derived_Ary type object as follows:

```
mary_ptr = new DATA_TYPE[ n_rows * n_cols ];
```

It is called automatically when Derived_Ary-type object A_obj with two rows and two columns is instantiated:

```
Derived_Ary  A_obj(2, 2);
```

~Derived_Ary(), the destructor, destroys all n_rows * n_cols elements of a Derived_Ary-type object by using the delete operator. The data area being pointed to by mary_ptr, it does:

```
delete [] mary_ptr;
```

The C++ compiler automatically determines the size of the array. This function is implicitly called at the program exit.

The operation, &element(), performs both the store and retrieve operations by using C++ specific feature &. To store a new value, new_value at the position [i, j], use element(i, j). To retrieve a value, use the same function as

```
get_value = element(i, j);  // Retrieve
```

Like their one-dimensional counterparts, the operations store() and retrieve ask user for inputting row and column numbers and subsequently call &element().

The + operator is defined as an overloaded operator for Derived_Ary-type objects. It is a friend of the Derived_Ary class so that it accesses all the private members of the class. It calls Derived_Ary() and element() functions, performs addition of two Derived_Ary-type objects, and returns the result as a Derived_Ary-type object. Its usage is A_obj + B_obj.

The – operator is defined as an overloaded operator for Derived_Ary-type objects. It is a friend of the Derived_Ary class so that it accesses all the private members of the class. It calls Derived_Ary() and element() functions, performs subtraction of two Derived_Ary-type objects, and returns the result as a Derived_Ary-type object. Its usage is A_obj – B_obj.

The * operator is defined as an overloaded operator for Derived_Ary-type objects. It is a friend of the Derived_Ary class so that it accesses all the private members of the class. It calls Derived_Ary() and element() functions, performs multiplication of two Derived_Ary-type objects, and returns the result as a Derived_Ary-type object. Its usage is A_obj * B_obj.

The = operator is defined as an overloaded operator for Derived_Ary-type objects. It is a public member of the Derived_Ary class so that it is accessible outside of this class. It calls Derived_Ary() and element() functions, assigns one Derived_Ary-type object to another, and returns the result as a Derived_Ary-type object. Its usage is B_obj = A_obj.

Print_array() is declared a friend of the Derived_Ary class. It calls element() to retrieve Derived_Ary-type object's data elements, and prints them.

Main() is the test driver for OOP implementation of the two-dimensional array. It instantiates two objects A and B of type Derived_Ary by implicitly calling Derived_Ary(). Since main() is not a member of the

Derived_Ary class, it sends messages to the objects A and B through the public interface routines. The messages include storing values, adding, subtracting, multiplying, assigning, and printing objects.

The complete code and the output are in **Code 3.2**.

Code 3.2

```
// Program: 2dim_ary.c++
//
// Purpose:
//    Object-Oriented Implementation of a two-dimensional
//    array (matrix). Implement "store", "retrieve",
//    matrix "addition", "subtraction", "multiplication"
//    "assignment" as "Overloaded Operators".

#include  <stdio.h>
#include  <iostream.h>
#include  "class_Derived_Ary_def.h"

//    Define a class "Derived_Ary" for two-dimensional
//    array (Matrix) derived from the base class.
class  Derived_Ary : private Array {
  private:
     int          n_rows,      // Number of rows
                  n_cols;      // Number of columns
     DATA_TYPE    *mary_ptr;   // Pointer to data area

  //  Declare member functions for matrix
  //  operations as public interfaces
  public:
     Derived_Ary(int rows, int cols);  // Constructor
     ~Derived_Ary(void);               // Destructor
     DATA_TYPE    &element( int i, int j);
     void         store(DATA_TYPE data);
     DATA_TYPE    retrieve(void);
     friend Derived_Ary operator+ (Derived_Ary A, Derived_Ary B);
     friend Derived_Ary operator- (Derived_Ary A, Derived_Ary B);
     friend Derived_Ary operator* (Derived_Ary A, Derived_Ary B);
     Derived_Ary  operator= (Derived_Ary A);
     friend void  print_array(Derived_Ary A, char *header);
};

// Derived_Ary():
//    Initialize the dimension, and allocate
//    memory space for an object of "Derived_Ary" class
//
Derived_Ary::Derived_Ary(int rows, int cols)
{
   // Initialize dimensions of the array object.
   n_rows = rows;
   n_cols = cols;
   // Allocate memory space
```

```
      mary_ptr = new DATA_TYPE[n_rows * n_cols];
}


// ~Derived_Ary():
//    Delete memory space for an object of "Derived_Ary"
//    class.
//
Derived_Ary::~Derived_Ary(void)
{
    delete  [] mary_ptr;
}


// element():
//    Store and retrieve an element A[i][j]
//    of an object in "Derived_Ary" class
//    Usages:
//      To store: A.element(i,j) = new_value;
//      To retrieve: value = A.element(i,j);
//
DATA_TYPE & Derived_Ary::element(int i, int j)
{
    return (mary_ptr [i * n_cols + j]);
}


void Derived_Ary::store(DATA_TYPE data)
{
    int row_index = 0, col_index = 0;
    printf("\nTo store, enter array row index: ");
    cin >> row_index;
    printf("\nTo store, enter array column index: ");
    cin >> col_index;
    element(row_index, col_index) = data;
}


DATA_TYPE Derived_Ary::retrieve(void)
{
    int row_index = 0, col_index = 0;
    printf("\nTo retrieve, enter array row index: ");
    cin >> row_index;
    printf("\nTo retrieve, enter array column index: ");
    cin >> col_index;
    return (element(row_index, col_index));
}


// Derived_Ary Overloaded Operator: "+"
//    Add two matrices A (m x n) & B (m x n)
//    and return a "Derived_Ary" object C (m x n).
//    Usage: C = A + B;
//
Derived_Ary  operator+ (Derived_Ary A, Derived_Ary B)
{
    int  i, // Used for row index, e.g. A[i][j]
         j; // Used for col index, e.g. A[i][j]
    // Declare a temporary matrix for result
```

```
   Derived_Ary tmp( A.n_rows, A.n_cols);

   for (i = 0; i < A.n_rows; i++)
     for (j = 0; j < A.n_cols; j++)
       tmp.element(i,j) = A.element(i, j) + B.element(i, j);
   return (tmp);
}

// Derived_Ary Overloaded Operator: "-"
//   Subtract two matrix objects A (m x n) &
//   B (m x n) and return a "Derived_Ary" object
//   C (m x n).
//   Usage: C = A - B;
//
Derived_Ary  operator- (Derived_Ary A, Derived_Ary B)
{
   int  i, // Used for row index, e.g. A[i][j]
        j; // Used for col index, e.g. A[i][j]
   // Declare a temporary matrix for result
   Derived_Ary tmp( A.n_rows, A.n_cols);

   for (i = 0; i < A.n_rows; i++)
     for (j = 0; j < A.n_cols; j++)
       tmp.element(i,j) = A.element(i, j) - B.element(i, j);
   return (tmp);
}

// Derived_Ary Overloaded Operator: "*"
//   Multiply two matrices A (m x n) & B (n x p)
//   and return a "Derived_Ary" object C (mxp).
//   Usage: C = A * B;
//
Derived_Ary  operator* (Derived_Ary A, Derived_Ary B)
{
   int  i, // Used for row index, e.g. A[i][j]
        j; // Used for col index, e.g. A[i][j]
   DATA_TYPE  sum;
   // Allocate a temporary matrix for result
   Derived_Ary tmp( A.n_rows, B.n_cols);

   for (i = 0; i < A.n_rows; i++) {
     for (j = 0; j < B.n_cols; j++) {
       sum = 0;
       for (int k = 0; k < A.n_cols; k++)
           sum += A.element(i, k) * B.element(k, j);
       tmp.element(i,j) = sum;
     }
   }
   return (tmp);
}

// Derived_Ary Overloaded Operator: "="
//   Assign one matrix object A (m x n)
//   a matrix object B (m x n)
```

```
//   Usage: B = A;
//
Derived_Ary  Derived_Ary::operator= (Derived_Ary A)
{
   int  i, // Used for row index, e.g. A[i][j]
        j; // Used for col index, e.g. A[i][j]

   // Allocate a temporary matrix for result
   Derived_Ary tmp( A.n_rows, A.n_cols);

   for (i = 0; i < A.n_rows; i++)
     for (j = 0; j < A.n_cols; j++)
       tmp.element(i, j) = A.element(i, j);
   return (tmp);
}


// print_array():
//   Print a matrix object A (m x n) with a
//   header.
//
void print_array (Derived_Ary A, char *hdr)
{
   int  i, // Used for row index, e.g. A[i][j]
        j; // Used for col index, e.g. A[i][j]
   // Declare a temporary matrix to store result
   Derived_Ary tmp(A.n_rows, A.n_cols);

   printf("\n *** Two-dimensional array (matrix): %s \n\n",
          hdr);
   printf("      ");
   for (j = 0; j < A.n_cols; j++)
     printf("  col %d", j);
   printf("\n\n");   // Skip a line
   for (i = 0; i < A.n_rows; i++) {
     printf("row %d ", i);
     for (j = 0; j < A.n_cols; j++)
       printf(" %5d ", A.element(i, j));
     // Print a new line after a row
     printf("\n");
   }
}


// main():
//   Driver to test OBJECT-ORIENTED
//   IMPLEMENTATION of a two-dimensional object.
//
void  main(void)
{
   // Instantiate two objects "A_obj" & "B_obj"
   // in "Derived_Ary" class
   Derived_Ary A_obj(2, 2), B_obj(2, 2);

   // Initialize Derived_Ary objects A_obj and B_obj
   A_obj.element(0,0) = 2; A_obj.element(0,1) = 4;
```

```
    A_obj.element(1,0) = 5; A_obj.element(1,1) = 6;
    B_obj.element(0,0) = 8; B_obj.element(0,1) = 3;
    B_obj.element(1,0) = 7; B_obj.element(1,1) = 1;
    printf("\n OOP IMPLEMENTATION OF %s",
       "TWO-DIMENSIONAL ARRAY OBJECT");
    print_array(A_obj, "A");
    print_array(B_obj, "B");
    print_array(A_obj + B_obj, "A + B");
    print_array(A_obj - B_obj, "A - B");
    print_array(A_obj * B_obj, "A * B");
    B_obj = A_obj;
    print_array(B_obj, "B = A");
}
```

Here is the output of **Code 3.2**:

```
OOP IMPLEMENTATION OF TWO-DIMENSIONAL ARRAY OBJECT
*** Two-dimensional array (matrix): A

        col 0    col 1

row 0      2        4
row 1      5        6

*** Two-dimensional array (matrix): B

        col 0    col 1

row 0      8        3
row 1      7        1

*** Two-dimensional array (matrix): A + B

        col 0    col 1

row 0     10        7
row 1     12        7

*** Two-dimensional array (matrix): A - B

        col 0    col 1

row 0     -6        1
row 1     -2        5

*** Two-dimensional array (matrix): A * B

        col 0    col 1

row 0     44       10
row 1     82       21
```

```
*** Two-dimensional array (matrix): B = A

        col 0    col 1

row 0      8        3
row 1      7        1
```

3.4 Strings

A *character string* is an array of characters. An n-character string is a one-dimensional array of $(n+1)$ characters, with a terminating NULL character, denoted as \0. At program compilation, C++ pads the string with the null character so that it can find the end of the string. To avoid an out-of-range condition, programs must check for the NULL character.

3.4.1 IMPLEMENTING STRINGS USING ARRAYS AND POINTERS

A string can be implemented as

- a fixed array of characters using the built-in array construct, or

- a dynamically linked sequence of characters using pointers.

When the string is implemented as an array of characters, it is of a fixed length. An array-based string is declared in one of two ways. In the first style of declaration, the entire string is presented verbatim in double quotes; the compiler automatically sizes the array to accommodate the number of quoted characters plus the null character (which it adds to the end). For example, the character array str is assigned the string String and allocated a fixed size of 7 chars with the statement

```
static char  str[] = "String";  // String constant
```

The second style of declaration involves specifying the string as a sequence of individual characters, each encased in single quotes:

```
static char str[] = {'S','t','r','i','n','g','\0'};
```

In this form, the termination sequence \0 must be explicitly added. The size of the resulting array is the same as it is for the other method. The address of the string array, &str[0], is the base address, which is used for pointers to the string.

An array-based string may be printed with the statement

```
printf("%s", str);
```

where `str` is the name of the string.

It is not possible to initialize an array-based string of `auto` storage class. Figure 3.9 depicts the memory layout of an array-based string. **Code 3.3** shows a simple example of an array-based string; it calculates the length of a given string.

Code 3.3

```
//
// Program:   ary_strng.c++
// Purpose:
//   When a string is implemented as an array of
//   characters, i.e., it is of fixed length, the
//   length of the array-based string is calculated.
//
#include <stdio.h>
void main(void)
{
    static char str[] = "String"; // Initialize string

    //  '\0' indicates end of the string; it is
    //  not a part of the string. The length is
    //  calculated by counting characters in it.

    for (int i = 0, char_count = 0; str[i] != '\0';
            i++)
        ++char_count; // Increment counter by 1
    printf(" **  An Array Based String ** \n");
    printf("\n For the string: %s", str);
    printf("\n The length is:   %d\n", char_count);
}
```

Code 3.3 produces this output:

```
**   An Array Based String **

For the string: String
The length is:   6
```

The second method for implementing strings uses pointers. A pointer-based string is declared as:

```
char *str_ptr = "String";
char *s = str_ptr;
```

The character pointers `str_ptr` and `s` both point to the same string, `String`. A pointer-based string is printed by the statement:

'S'	't'	'r'	'i'	'n'	'g'	'\0'

s   s+1   s+2   s+3   s+4   s+5   s+6

FIGURE 3.8. Accessing a pointer-based string.

```
printf("%s", str_ptr);
```

In the case of a pointer-based representation of a string, pointer arithmetic is conveniently used to manipulate and traverse the string. In Figure 3.8, s points to the first character S of the string, `*s = 'S'`; s++ (i.e., s is incremented by 1) points to the next character t, `*(s + 1) = 't'`. This pointer arithmetic process may be continued to access and traverse the string until the end of the string, `\0`, is encountered.

An OOP for a pointer-based string is given as **Code 3.4**. What sets the pointer-based version of the array apart from the array-based version is its use of memory space. An array-based string is allocated a fixed amount of memory space at its declaration; this is potentially wasteful. On the other hand, no fixed memory space is allocated for a pointer-based string; it is of variable length and is dynamically stored in memory.

3.4.2   ARRAY OF ARRAY-BASED STRINGS

When a string is represented by an array of characters, an array of such strings is a two-dimensional array of characters, the row dimension being the number of strings, and the column dimension being the maximum string length (i.e., the maximum number of characters among the strings).

In C++, the declaration of an array of strings, for example menu[][], is:

```
char   menu[ARY_SIZE][MAX_STR_LENGTH];
```

where ARY_SIZE is the maximum number of menu items, and each menu item is a string of maximum length, MAX_STR_LENGTH. The memory spaces of ARY_SIZE × MAX_STR_LENGTH number of bytes are automatically allocated by this declaration. The characters or substring beyond the MAX_STR_LENGTH will be automatically truncated.

Initializing an array of strings is done at the declaration, as shown below.

```
const int ARY_SIZE       = 5;
const int MAX_STR_LENGTH = 26;
static char menu[ARY_SIZE][MAX_STR_LENGTH] = {
    "Add a member record",
    "Remove a member record",
    "Change a member record",
    "Show a member record",
```

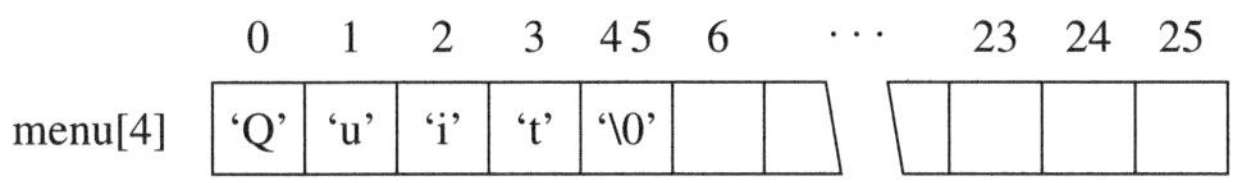

FIGURE 3.9. Memory layout for an array-based string.

```
    "Quit"
};
```

The menu[4][0-25] is stored in the memory as in Figure 3.9.

Note that in Figure 3.9, 21 more bytes are allocated and not used for the Quit menu item. This is the main drawback of an array of array-based strings.

This code shows how to print a menu string for an array of strings:

```
// print_menu():  Print a menu string
//
print_str_ary (char menu[][26], int index)
{
    printf("%s \n ", menu[index]);
}
```

3.4.3   ARRAY OF POINTERS TO STRINGS

As discussed earlier, an array of array-based strings has the drawbacks of memory waste and the truncation of a string's characters. Both of these drawbacks are resolved by an array of pointers to strings. An array of pointers to strings holds strings that are of variable lengths and are defined by character-type pointers. The size of the array is the maximum number of pointer-based strings.

An array of pointers to strings, say menu_ptr, is declared and initialized in the following manner:

```
static char *menu_ptr[ARY_SIZE] = {
    "Add a member record",
    "Remove a member record",
    "Change a member record",
    "Show a member record",
    "Quit"
};
```

The string content Quit is represented by a pointer *menu_ptr[4], which is stored in the memory as shown in Figure 3.10.

For an array of pointers to strings, each element of the array holds the address of a string. For example:

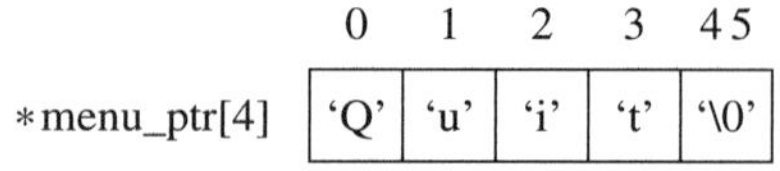

	0	1	2	3	4	5
*menu_ptr[4]	'Q'	'u'	'i'	't'	'\0'	

FIGURE 3.10. Memory layout for a pointer-based string.

menu_ptr[0] ==   address of "Add a member record"
menu_ptr[1] ==   address of "Remove a member record"
menu_ptr[2] ==   address of "Change a member record"
menu_ptr[3] ==   address of "Show a member record"
menu_ptr[4] ==   address of "Quit"

The following code shows how to print a menu string, an array of pointers to each menu item:

```
//
// print_str_ptr():
//   Print a variable length string, strings
//   are stored in an array.
//
void print_str_ptr (char *menu_ptr[], int index)
{
    printf(" %s \n", menu_ptr[index]);
}
```

3.4.4 STRING OBJECT AND ITS OOP IMPLEMENTATION

A *string object* is specified by an ADT string. An ADT string is a data structure that contains a sequence of characters as data, and the associated operations to process the data. Some operations for an ADT string are shown in bc_strng.h. The OOP implementation of string objects whose data are of variable length is shown in **Code 3.4**. For string objects, an abstract base class String shown in Figure 3.11 is defined in bc_strng.h:

```
// Program:  bc_strng.h

extern class Derived_String;
//  Define base class "String" for "String" objects
class  String {
  public:
    virtual int     get_length (void) = 0;
    virtual Derived_String parse_str_obj(Derived_String Delim)=0;

    // Declare Overloaded Operators for "String"
    virtual void    operator=(Derived_String A) = 0;
    friend  Derived_String operator+(Derived_String A,
```

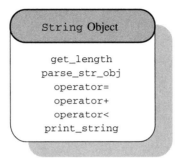

FIGURE 3.11. String base class methods.

```
                                    Derived_String B);
    friend   int   operator<( Derived_String A, Derived_String B);
    friend   void print_string(char *hdr);
};
```

`Derived_String` may be a template for array-based (i.e., fixed-length) or pointer-based (i.e., variable-length) string objects.

When the string is of a fixed length `STR_SIZE`, that is, data of the string is maintained as an array `str_data_ptr[STR_SIZE]` of characters, the array-based string object is defined by the `Derived_String` class, derived from the base class `String`, as follows:

```
//   Define class "Derived_String" derived from "String"
class   Derived_String : private String {
  private:
    int    STR_SIZE;            // Array str_data_ptr[STR_SIZE]
    char   *str_data_ptr;       // of fixed length STR_SIZE
  public:
    Derived_String(char *str, int size);  //  Constructor
    ~Derived_String();          //  Destructor
    int     get_length (void);
    Derived_String  parse_str_obj(Derived_String Delim);

    // Declare Overloaded Operators for "String"
    void    operator=( Derived_String A);
    friend  Derived_String operator+
                          (Derived_String A, Derived_String B);
    friend  int operator<( Derived_String A, Derived_String B);
    void    print_string(char *hdr);
};
```

The complete OOP implementation for an array-based string is left as Exercise 3-3.

An OOP implementation of string objects whose data are of variable length is shown in **Code 3.4**. This string object is depicted in Figure 3.12.

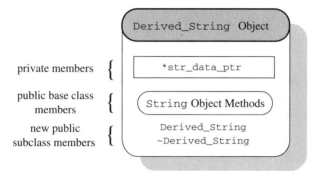

FIGURE 3.12. Derived_String object

Code 3.4

```
//   Program:  string.c++
//   Purpose:
//     OBJECT-ORIENTED IMPLEMENTATION OF VARIABLE-
//     LENGTH (POINTER-BASED) STRING OBJECTS USING
//     OVERLOADED Operators "+", "<", "="
//
#include  <stdio.h>
#include  <stdlib.h>
#include  <ctype.h>
#include  <string.h>     // For strdup(), strcpy()
#include  "bc_strng.h"   // For base class "String"

//  Define class "Derived_String" derived from "String"
class  Derived_String : private String {
  private:
    char  *str_data_ptr;          // variable length
  public:
    Derived_String(char *str);   //   Constructor
    ~Derived_String();            //   Destructor
    int    get_length (void);
    Derived_String  parse_str_obj(Derived_String Delim);

    // Declare Overloaded Operators for "String"
    void    operator=( Derived_String A);
    friend  Derived_String operator+
                          (Derived_String A, Derived_String B);
    friend  int operator<( Derived_String A, Derived_String B);
    void    print_string(char *hdr);
};

//   Derived_String():
//     Allocate and initialize str_data_ptr
```

```
//
Derived_String::Derived_String(char *str)
{
    str_data_ptr = strdup(str);
}

// ~Derived_String():
//    De-allocate and free up memory space
//
Derived_String::~Derived_String()
{
    delete  str_data_ptr;
}

// get_length():
//    Get the length of the string object A.
//    '\0' is not included in the length.
int  Derived_String::get_length(void)
{
    for (int i = 0, str_length = 0;
            str_data_ptr[i] != '\0'; i++)
        str_length++;  // Increment "str_length"
    return (str_length);
}

//  parse_str_obj():
//      Parses a "String" type object upto the
//      delimiter (end mark), and returns the
//      parsed "Derived_String" type object.
//
Derived_String
Derived_String::parse_str_obj(Derived_String Delim)
{
    Derived_String output_obj(""); // To store "output" string
    char  *input_str   = str_data_ptr,
           *delimiter    = Delim.str_data_ptr,
           *output_str   = output_obj.str_data_ptr;

    while ((*input_str != *delimiter) &&
            *input_str != '\0')
            *output_str++ = *input_str++;
    *output_str = '\0';
    return (output_obj);
}

//  "String" Overloaded Assignment Operator: "="
//    Usage:   Derived_String A, B;
//             B = A;
//
void  Derived_String::operator= (Derived_String A)
{
    strcpy(str_data_ptr, A.str_data_ptr);
}
```

```
//   "String" Overloaded Operator: "+"
//     Join two strings together by
//     adding str2 after str1 object.
//     Usage:  Derived_String  str1, str2, str3;
//             str3 = str1 + str2;
//
Derived_String
operator+ (Derived_String str1, Derived_String str2)
{
  //  Declare the resulting "Derived_String" object
  Derived_String   sum_obj(" ");  // initialized blank

  char *str1_data_ptr = str1.str_data_ptr;
  char *str2_data_ptr = str2.str_data_ptr;
  char *sum_data_ptr  = sum_obj.str_data_ptr;

  //  The data of the first Derived_String object
  //  is copied into data of "sum_obj" string.
  while (*str1_data_ptr != '\0')
        *sum_data_ptr++ = *str1_data_ptr++;

  //  add a space between str1 & str2 objects
  *sum_data_ptr++ = ' ';
  //  now the second Derived_String object is copied.
  while (*str2_data_ptr != '\0')
        *sum_data_ptr++ = *str2_data_ptr++;

  //  put '\0' to indicate end of string.
  *sum_data_ptr = '\0';
  return (sum_obj);
}


//   "String" Overloaded Operator: "<"
//
//     Returns
//       -1 if numerical value of str1 object is  < str2
//        0 if     "        "      "  "       "      "     =  "
//        1 if     "        "      "  "       "      "     >  "
//
//   "str_data_ptr" members of the two "String" objects
//   "str1", "str2" are compared.
//
int
operator< (Derived_String str1_obj, Derived_String str2_obj)
{
  // ASCII str1 & str2 are coverted into floating
  // point values.
  float str1_value = atof(str1_obj.str_data_ptr);
  float str2_value = atof(str2_obj.str_data_ptr);
  if (str1_value < str2_value)
        return (-1);
  else if (str1_value > str2_value)
        return (1);
  else            //  str1_value = str2_value
```

```
            return (0);
}

//  print_string():
//     Print the data of a "String" object
//
void  Derived_String::print_string(char *hdr)
{
  printf("\n %s: \n     %s \n", hdr, str_data_ptr);
}

//
//  main():
//     Object-Oriented Implementation of ADT Derived_String
void    main(void)
{
    //  Declare and initialize "Derived_String" class'
    //  objects "str_obj1", "str_obj2"
    Derived_String    str_obj1("Object-Oriented");
    Derived_String    str_obj2("Strings");

    printf("\n ** OOP IMPLEMENTATION %s %s %s \n",
           "OF STRING OBJECTS","\n     USING",
           "POINTERS **");
    str_obj1.print_string("String object 1 is");
    str_obj2.print_string("String object 2 is");
    //  Test overloaded "String" operators: +, <, =
    (str_obj1 + str_obj2).print_string(
                 "Concatenated string is");
    if ((str_obj1 < str_obj2) == 1)
      printf("\n String1 is greater than String2 \n");
    str_obj1 = str_obj2;
    str_obj1.print_string(
      "After assigning String2 to String1");
}
```

Code 3.4 for an OOP implementation of pointer-based string objects yields this output:

```
** OOP IMPLEMENTATION OF STRING OBJECTS
   USING POINTERS **

String object 1 is:
   Object-Oriented

String object 2 is:
   Strings

Concatenated string is:
   Object-Oriented Strings
```

```
After assigning String2 to String1:
   Strings
```

3.5   OOP Application: An Object-Oriented Database

In this section an OOP for the `people_1d` database from Appendix C is implemented. In this implementation, the underlying data structure is an array. That is, the database is processed as an array of `people_1d` records.

Keeping OOP characteristics of object identification, data-hiding, message-passing, and inheritance in mind, a class `People_Database` is defined in Appendix C. A people database object is identified by `DataObject` as its data. The `DataObject` contains the fields shown below.

The people database is maintained as an array of `DataObject` type people records. The size of the array is `db_size`, and the pointer to the array is `*people_db`. The other data variables are `total_members` and `index`. All these data members except `db_size` are declared `private` for data-hiding. `db_size` is declared `protected` so that it is accessible to any class derived from the `People` class. The `People` class is derived from the `People_Database` class. The operations for the people database object are:

- Adding a member record

- Removing a member record

- Modifying a member record

- Displaying a member record

These methods are declared `public` in the `People` class to facilitate message passing between a `People`-type object and an object of any other

Member id	integer
Name	character string
Occupation	character string
Age	integer
Income	integer
Years Member	integer

type. The constructor People() dynamically allocates a People-type object. The destructor ~People() deallocates the memory space for an object of type People.

For the user interface, a People_Menu class is derived from the base class People. All of the member functions show_menu() and do_menu() of the People_Menu class inherit the access privilege of data and member functions of the base class People. The special functions People_Menu() and ~People_Menu() are the constructor and destructor functions for People_Menu-type objects, respectively. People_Menu() initializes a People_Menu object, and it automatically calls People() constructor, which allocates memory space for an array and sets the input value to db_size.

Main() is the test driver. The difficulty in this implementation arises from name and occupation fields that are of variable lengths. This requires allocation of memory space as shown in read_str_input(). The code and output are given in **Code 3.5**.

Code 3.5

```
// Program:   peopl_ary.c++
// Purpose:
//    This shows how to use
//       1. "struct", "class" constructs,
//          derived class, and strings
//       2. an array of "struct"s data.
//    This is for a "Database of people" who are
//    members in an organization; attributes are either
//    keyed data or other data. In terms of 1D database:
//       The MEMBERSHIP NUMBER is THE key.
//    Two records with the same member number.   This
//    would represent an error in the database
//    (like two people having the same social security
//    number) but is useful to show that structures
//    handle duplicate keys properly.
//
//    To compile on MSDOS using Turbo C++:
//        TCC -DMSDOS PEOPL_DB.CPP
//
#include   <stdio.h>
#include   <stdlib.h>  // for 'exit()', atoi()
#include   <string.h>
#include   <iostream.h>
#ifdef   MSDOS
#include   <conio.h>
#include   "peopl_1d.cpp"
#else
#include   "peopl_1d.c++"  // Database in Appendix C
#endif

// Define "People" class derived from the
```

```
//   "People_Database" class
class  People: private  People_Database {
  private:
    int      total_members,
             curr_last;
  protected:
    int      db_size;
  public:
    People(int size);   //  Constructor
    int      search_member (Keytype srch_key);
    void     read_str_input (char **str);
    void     add_member(void);
    void     remove_member(void);
    void     change_member_record(void);
    void     wait_for_any_key(void);
    void     show_member_record(void);
    void     exit_people_db(void);
};

//   Define "People_Menu" class that uses all the
//   components and functions of the base class
//   "People".
class  People_Menu : private People {
  private:
    char *title,        *menu_item1, *menu_item2,
         *menu_item3, *menu_item4, *menu_item5;
  public:
    People_Menu(int db_sz);     // Constructor
    ~People_Menu();    // Destructor
    void     display_menu_title(char *title);
    void     show_menu(void);
    void     do_menu(void);
};

//   People():
//     Construct and initialize people
//     database object
//
People::People(int size) : People_Database(size)
{
    People_Database::build_initial_db();
    curr_last    = 9;
    total_members = 10;
}

//   search_member():
//     Search for people from people_db
//     people number as key. If it is not found,
//     return an invalid array index, -1.
//
int  People::search_member(Keytype srch_key)
{
    int  i;
```

```
   if (total_members >= 0) {  // database nonempty
     for (i = 0; i < total_members; i++)
        if (srch_key == people_db[i].key)
           return (i);
   }
   // Search fails. People record is not found
   return (-1);
}


//  read_str_input():
//    Get a character string from console.
//
void  People::read_str_input (char **str)
{
  char  *input_str = new char [81];

  gets (input_str);
  if (input_str[0] != '\0') {
    // Allocate memory for variable string
    *str = new char [strlen(input_str) + 1];
    strcpy (*str, input_str);
  }
  delete  input_str;
}


//  add_member():
//    Add a new member in the people_db database.
//    It does not allow duplicate records. Two
//    members with the same id are not allowed.
//
void  People::add_member(void)
{
   Keytype    member_id;
   int        i;

   //  Check whether maximum database size reached
   if (total_members == db_size) {
      printf("\n add_member: Array Database Full. \n");
      return;
   }
   printf("\n Enter Member's Id <integer>: ");
#ifndef MSDOS
   fflush (stdout);
#endif
   cin >> member_id;
   printf("\n Please wait_for_any_key. Checking %s \n",
     "whether \n same member id already exists ...");
   if ((i = search_member(member_id)) != -1) {
      if (total_members != 0) { // nonempty database
         printf("\n add_member: Same member %s \n",
                "id already exists.");
         return;
      }
   }
```

```
    // Increase curr_last by 1
    people_db[++curr_last].key = member_id;
    printf(" Enter Member's Name:        ");
    read_str_input (&people_db[curr_last].name);
    printf(" Enter Member's Occupation: ");
    read_str_input (&people_db[curr_last].occupation);
    printf(" Enter Member's Age <integer>: ");
    scanf("%d", &people_db[curr_last].age);
    printf(" Enter Member's Income <integer x $1000>: ");
    scanf("%d", &people_db[curr_last].income);
    printf(" Enter Member's Years <integer>: ");
    scanf("%d", &people_db[curr_last].years);

    total_members = curr_last + 1;
}

//  wait_for_any_key():  Pause screen
//
void  People::wait_for_any_key(void)
{
    printf("\n\n Press y to return to main menu ... ");
#ifdef  MSDOS
    while (getch() != 'y')
#else
    while (getc(stdin) != 'y')
#endif
    ;
}

//  remove_member():
//     Remove a member from people_db database object
//
void  People::remove_member(void)
{
    printf(" Remove menu is not implemented.");
    wait_for_any_key();
}

//  change_member_record():
//     Change people record in people_db database.
//
void  People::change_member_record(void)
{
    printf(" Change menu is not implemented.");
    wait_for_any_key();
}

//  show_member_record():
//     Search a member by member's id (key),
//     and if successful, show that member's
//     record from an object in "People_Database".
//
void  People::show_member_record(void)
{
```

```
   int       db_index;
   Keytype   key;
   char      input_buff[81];

   printf("\n Enter Member's Id: ");
#ifndef MSDOS
   fflush (stdout);
#endif
   cin >> key;
   db_index = search_member(key);

   if (db_index == -1) {
      printf("\n Error: %s ",
             "Member is not in Database.");
      wait_for_any_key();
      return;
   }
   // Now display complete info for the people
   printf("\n Member's Number:      %d",
          people_db[db_index].key);
   printf("\n Member's Name:        %s",
          people_db[db_index].name);
   printf("\n Member's Occupation:  %s",
          people_db[db_index].occupation);
   printf("\n Member's Age:         %d",
          people_db[db_index].age);
   printf("\n Yearly Income:        $%d",
          people_db[db_index].income * 1000);
   printf("\n Year's of Membership: %d",
          people_db[db_index].years);
   wait_for_any_key();
}

// exit_people_db(): Exit from database program
//
void  People::exit_people_db(void)
{
   printf("\n Exiting from %s \n",
          "People DataBase ...");
   exit(0);
}

// People_Menu():
//   Construct and initialize people menu
//   object. Also call base class constructor
//   with the exact argument "db_size".
//
People_Menu::People_Menu(int db_size)
           : People(db_size)
{
   title = "\n\n          PEOPLE ORGANIZATION \
                 \n     People DataBase MAIN MENU\n";
   // Initialize the menu items for user interface
   menu_item1 = "\n Add a member              ..  a";
```

```
   menu_item2 = "\n Remove a member         ..  r";
   menu_item3 = "\n Change a member record  ..  c";
   menu_item4 = "\n Show a member record    ..  s";
   menu_item5 = "\n Exit from database      ..  e";
}

//   ~People_Menu():
//      Destructor
//
People_Menu::~People_Menu()
{
   delete title;        delete menu_item1;
   delete menu_item2;   delete menu_item3;
   delete menu_item4;   delete menu_item5;
}

//   display_menu_title():  Print header of a menu
void  People_Menu::display_menu_title (char *title)
{
   printf("\n\n    ========================== \n");
   printf("    *   PEOPLE %s MENU \n", title);
   printf("    ========================== \n");
}

//   show_menu():
//      Show menu items as the user interface
//      for People Database
//
void  People_Menu::show_menu(void)
{
   printf ("%s %s %s %s %s %s",
      title,             // Main menu title
      menu_item1,        // Menu: ADD people
      menu_item2,        // Menu: REMOVE people
      menu_item3,        // Menu: CHANGE
      menu_item4,        // Menu: SHOW
      menu_item5);       // Menu: EXIT
}

//   do_menu():
//      Get the correct choice number from 1 to 5.
//      Transfer control to the corresponding function.
void  People_Menu::do_menu(void)
{
   char  selection;

   printf("\n\n Select menu (a, r, c, s, e): ");
#ifdef  MSDOS
   switch (getch()) {
#else
   fflush(stdout);
   cin >> selection;
   switch (selection) {
#endif
```

```
    case 'a':
    case 'A':
        //  Add a people record in people_db
        display_menu_title("ADD");
        People::add_member();
        break;
    case 'r':
    case 'R':
        //  Remove people record in people_db
        display_menu_title("REMOVE");
        People::remove_member();
        break;
    case 'c':
    case 'C':
        //  Change people record in people_db
        display_menu_title("CHANGE");
        People::change_member_record();
        break;
    case 's':
    case 'S':
        //  Find people record in people_db & show.
        display_menu_title("SHOW");
        People::show_member_record();
        break;
    case 'e':
    case 'E':
        //  Exit from database people_db
        People::exit_people_db();
        break;
    default:
        printf("\n Unknown choice !!! \n");
        People::wait_for_any_key();
        break;
    }
}

//   main():
//      Test driver for OBJECT-ORIENTED people_1d
//      DATABASE
//
void  main(void)
{
    //  Define an object "pmenu_obj" of "People_Menu",
    //  which will initialize "People_Database" and
    //  "People" type objects with size 50.
    People_Menu  pmenu_obj(50);
    int          REPEATED = 1;

    setbuf(stdin, NULL);
    while (REPEATED) {  // infinite loop until "e"
      pmenu_obj.show_menu();
      pmenu_obj.do_menu();
    }
```

```
    }
```

Code 3.5 for an OOP implementation of `people_1d` database produces this output:

```
    PEOPLE ORGANIZATION
People DataBase MAIN MENU

Add a member              ..   a
Remove a member           ..   r
Change a member record    ..   c
Show a member record      ..   s
Exit from database        ..   e

Select menu (a, r, c, s, e): a


============================
*   PEOPLE ADD MENU
============================

Enter Member's Id <integer>: 23
Please wait_for_any_key. Checking whether
same member id already exists ...
Enter Member's Name:    Joe Barish
Enter Member's Occupation: Marketing Engineer
Enter Member's Age <integer>: 34
Enter Member's Income <integer x $1000>: 56
Enter Member's Years <integer>: 5


    PEOPLE ORGANIZATION
People DataBase MAIN MENU

Add a member              ..   a
Remove a member           ..   r
Change a member record    ..   c
Show a member record      ..   s
Exit from database        ..   e

Select menu (a, r, c, s, e): s


============================
*   PEOPLE SHOW MENU
============================

Enter Member's Id: 23
Member's Number:     23
Member's Name:       Joe Barish
Member's Occupation:Marketing Engineer
Member's Age:        34
Yearly Income:       $56000
Year's of Membership: 5
```

```
Press y to return to main menu ... y


    PEOPLE ORGANIZATION
People DataBase MAIN MENU

Add a member                .. a
Remove a member             .. r
Change a member record  ..  c
Show a member record    ..  s
Exit from database          .. e

Select menu (a, r, c, s, e): r

==========================
*   PEOPLE REMOVE MENU
==========================
Remove menu is not implemented.

Press y to return to main menu ... y


    PEOPLE ORGANIZATION
People DataBase MAIN MENU

Add a member                .. a
Remove a member             .. r
Change a member record  ..  c
Show a member record    ..  s
Exit from database          .. e

Select menu (a, r, c, s, e): c

==========================
*   PEOPLE CHANGE MENU
==========================
Change menu is not implemented.

Press y to return to main menu ... y


    PEOPLE ORGANIZATION
People DataBase MAIN MENU

Add a member                .. a
Remove a member             .. r
Change a member record  ..  c
Show a member record    ..  s
Exit from database          .. e

Select menu (a, r, c, s, e): s

==========================
*   PEOPLE SHOW MENU
```

```
============================

Enter Member's Id: 63
Member's Number:      63
Member's Name:        Peter
Member's Occupation:sales
Member's Age:         51
Yearly Income:        $95000
Year's of Membership: 1


Press y to return to main menu ... y


    PEOPLE ORGANIZATION
People DataBase MAIN MENU

Add a member            ..  a
Remove a member         ..  r
Change a member record  ..  c
Show a member record    ..  s
Exit from database      ..  e

Select menu (a, r, c, s, e): e
Exiting from People DataBase ...
```

3.6   Exercises

1. For the OOP implementation of an ADT one-dimensional array in **Code 3.1**, write the overloaded operator functions

    (a) - ( ) to subtract one `Array` type object from another.

    (b) = ( ) to assign one `Array` type object to another.

    (c) * ( ) for the vector product of two `Array` type objects.

2. For the OOP implementation of a variable-length string (i.e., pointer version) in **Code 3.4**, write the overloaded operator -() for subtracting (removing) one `String` type object from another on the condition that there is a complete match of the specified string in the target string.

3. Write an OOP for a fixed-length string (i.e., array version) that includes a test driver `main()` and the overloaded operators

    (a) + ( ) to append one string object to another.

    (b) - ( ) to subtract one string object from another.

    (c) * ( ) for appending one string object to another.

    (d) > ( ) for appending one string object to another.

(e) = ( ) for assigning one string object to another.

4. Write an OOP to read ten variable-length strings from a file and print those strings with lengths of greater than 66 characters into another file.

5. Write an OOP that reads a string from the user keyboard, counts the number of words in the string, and prints the string and the count.

6. The graphical form of the well-known *Pascal's Triangle* is shown below. Each row begins and ends with 1.

```
            1
         1     1
      1     2     1
   1     3     3     1
1     4     6     4     1
```

Write an OOP that implements and displays the graphical form of Pascal's triangle.

7. (Sengupta and Edwards [SE91]) Write an OOP for a string parser. Given a file of input strings, the parser should search each string for braces, parentheses, brackets, and quotes, finding the matching member of the pairs (a) left and right braces, (b) left and right parentheses, (c) left and right brackets, and (d) double quotes. The number of occurrences of the matching member may be more than one, and must be reported. The parser should indicate the location of invalid syntax. The following C++ syntax should be followed:

- For every open (left) brace, parenthesis, bracket, or quote, there should be a matching close (right). The number of opens should equal the number of closes.

- Before the innermost open brace, parenthesis, or bracket close, others cannot be closed. For example, { { [}] } , ( ], and {) are invalid.

- Braces cannot be nested inside parentheses or brackets. For example, ([ ] { ( ) }) is invalid.

- After an open quote, any character can follow any other character until the close quote. For example, "xyz{]{]]]]]" is valid.

- Quotes cannot be nested. For example, "xyz ("abc") " is considered to be two strings, "xyz (" and ") ".

8. Write an OOP that reads an array-based string, reverses the string, and prints the original and reversed strings.

9. For the pointer-based String class in **Code 3.4**, implement and test the C++ standard operators for strings: [], ==, !=, the input operator >>, the output operator <<.

10. Given a file containing a set of names in the format (first, middle, last), write an OOP that reads these names, lexically arranges them in ascending order by the last name, and prints the ordered names into another file in the format (last, first, middle).

11. For the OOP of the people_1d database in **Code 3.5**, write the public member function remove_member() of the People class, which removes a people record from the People type object.

12. For the OOP implementation of the people_1d database in **Code 3.5**, write a public member function change_member_record() of the People class, which changes a member's record in the People type object. For each field of the record, it displays the current values within a bracket, and gets the new value. If a return is entered, the current value stays. Otherwise, the new values are entered into the record.

13. Write an OOP for a simple word processor containing the following features:

   - *Character Insertion*: Allow the user to move the cursor to the desired position and type characters until the ESC key is used.
   - *Character Deletion*: Allow the user to move the cursor to the desired character position and type
     (a) the x key to delete the character at the current cursor position.
     (b) <number>x key to delete the succeeding characters of the specified number starting from the current cursor position.
   - *Printing*: Print the original and new (or modified) strings.

4

Recursion

The concept of *recursion* is central to the disciplines of computer science and mathematics. Proper application of recursive programming techniques can give way to elegant, compact, and readily maintainable programs. A characteristic situation where recursive programming techniques are useful involves applications for which solutions can be devised as a process of dividing the given problem into a series of smaller and similar subproblems, each requiring the same procedural steps and stopping criterion. Recursive techniques are not always applicable or may be too costly to consider — in such situations, *iterative* (nonrecursive) solutions are best.

This chapter discusses the basic concepts of recursion, how it works, the concepts of the C++ *run-time stack*, as well as the space and time trade-offs associated with recursive implementations. As evidence of its general applicability, recursive programming techniques are to be found throughout the remaining chapters of this book.

4.1 Concept of Recursion

Definition 4.1 *A function is said to be recursive if it is defined in terms of itself. Similarly, a program is said to be recursive if it calls itself.*

There are two main types of recursion to be considered. With *direct recursion*, procedures may call themselves before they are completed. That is, a direct recursive function will call itself from within its own body. The function, factorial_n_recur(), given in **Code 4.1** below, is an example of a direct recursive function. With *indirect recursion*, procedures may call other procedures that in turn invoke the procedure that called them. For example, a function f() calls a function g(), which calls a function h(), which in turn calls the original calling function f().

Recursive functions are powerful. They are compact in their representation, as compared to their nonrecursive (iterative) counterparts. However, this does not necessarily come without a price. A major potential drawback of recursive implementations is that many levels of recursion (repeated calls for the same types of tasks) can consume excessive memory space and computing time.

4.2   Divide-and-Conquer and Recursion

Intimately related to recursion is the *divide-and-conquer* approach to problem solving. A divide-and-conquer strategy is used in devising a recursive function for a given problem.

The principal methodology of divide-and-conquer is to repeatedly split or *divide* a given problem into a number of smaller or simpler subproblems until these subproblems are *conquered*; the solution of the individual subproblems merges to a solution of the whole problem. Each division of the problem is a recursive call, and recursion continues until a *terminating condition* is reached — that is, when a solvable subproblem is encountered. The existence of a terminating condition, also referred to as the *anchor* of a recursive function, is an absolute requirement, as the recursive process cannot continue forever. A given problem is conquered when all recursive calls successfully terminate.

In a typical divide-and-conquer scheme, the given problem is divided approximately in half at each stage. A recursive program implementing such a divide-and-conquer strategy would contain two recursive calls, each handling about half of the given input data.

4.3   Recursive and Nonrecursive Functions in C++

We now discuss how to derive a recursive function for a given application, say $n!$ (factorial of n), n being a nonnegative integer.

$$n! = n * (n-1) * (n-2) * \ldots * 3 * 2 * 1.$$

The first step in the derivation is to identify the terminating condition. Since by definition,

$$0! = 1, 1! = 1$$

these are the termination conditions.

Next, consider a simple case and redefine it in terms of its previous case, using inductive steps to deduce generality. For example:

$$
\begin{aligned}
n &= 2, & 2! &= 2 * 1 = 2 * 1! \\
n &= 3, & 3! &= 3 * 2 * 1 = 3 * (2 * 1) = 3 * 2! \\
n &= m, & m! &= m * (m-1) * \ldots * 2 * 1 \\
n &= m+1, & (m+1)! &= (m+1) * m * (m-1) * \ldots * 2 * 1 \\
& & &= (m+1) * (m * (m-1) * \ldots * 2 * 1) \\
& & &= (m+1) * m!
\end{aligned}
$$

Since the same relation is true for $n = 1$ and $n = m+1$, given $n!$ for $n = m$, by induction, the recursive function is deduced as:

$$n! = n * (n - 1)!$$

Thus, the recursive definition of $n!$ is:

$$n! = \begin{cases} 1 & \text{for } n = 0 \text{ or } 1 \text{ (terminating condition)} \\ n * (n - 1)! & \text{for } n = 2, 3, \ldots \end{cases}$$

The key steps in deriving a recursive definition (function) are summarized as follows:

Step 1. Consider a simple case for the given problem.

Step 2. Identify a terminating condition for recursive calls. If a terminating condition cannot be identified, recursion cannot be used. Otherwise, continue to Step 3.

Step 3. Consider the next higher form of the problem, and redefine it in terms of the value(s) returned by its previous form of the problem.

Step 4. The redefined form specifies the recursion.

The recursive function `factorial_n_recur()` and the iterative function `factorial_n_iter()` of **Code 4.1** implement $n!$. We find that for `factorial_n_recur()`, the recursive calls terminate when $n = 0$ or 1. The execution trace for `factorial_n_recur()` with n = 6 is:

```
factorial_n_recur(6)                                       1st call
 = 6 * factorial_n_recur(5)                                2nd call
 = 6 * (5 * factorial_n_recur(4))                          3rd call
 = 6 * (5 * (4 * factorial_n_recur(3)))                    4th call
 = 6 * (5 * (4 * (3 * factorial_n_recur(2))))              5th call
 = 6 * (5 * (4 * (3 * (2 * factorial_n_recur(1))))) 6th call
 = 6 * (5 * (4 * (3 * (2 * 1))))                    /\
 = 6 * (5 * (4 * (3 * 2)))              terminating condition
 = 6 * (5 * (4 * 6))
 = 6 * (5 * 24)
 = 6 * 120
 = 720
```

At the sixth recursive call, a terminating condition is encountered and executed, and the value 1 is returned to the previous recursive function call. The returned value 1 is used to multiply with 2, and the computed value 2 is returned to the previous recursive function call. By backtracking recursive calls in this manner, all recursive function calls are executed, and the final value of **720** is returned.

An alternative way of viewing a trace of a recursive function is in the form of an *execution binary tree*. This is illustrated in Figure 4.1 for a

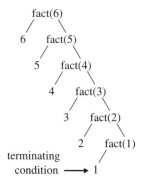

FIGURE 4.1. Execution binary tree.

factorial function `fact(n)`. The tree structure depicts the hierarchy of successively spawned recursive calls, in much the same way as a family history tree depicts the hierarchy of spawned generations of family members. Tree structures are the subject of Chapter 8.

Proper execution of a recursive function requires that a return-address and some return value be stored at each stage of recursion. This storage is typically handled by the *call stack* of the system; the call stack is a portion of system memory specially reserved for storing automatic variables, parameters to functions, return values, and return addresses. The call stack and its relationship to recursive program execution is the subject of Section 4.4 below.

Code 4.1

```
//  Program:   factorial_n_recur.c++
//  Purpose:   Compute n! (factorial of integer n)
//             n! = n * (n-1) * (n-2) * ... * 2 * 1
//
#include  <stdio.h>
#include  <stdlib.h>

int  factorial_n_recur (int n)
{
   if (n < 0) {
      printf("\n factorial_n_recur: %s %d \n"
             "Invalid n =", n);
      exit (0);
   }
   if (n == 1)
      return (1);   // anchor case
   return (n * factorial_n_recur (n - 1));
}
```

```
int   factorial_n_iter (int n)
{
    int   fact = 1;

    if (n < 0) {
        printf("\n factorial_n_iter: %s %d \n",
               "Invalid n =", n);
        exit (0);
    }
    if (n == 1)
        return (1);
    while (n > 1)
        fact *= n--;   // fact = fact * n--
    return (fact);
}

void main(void)
{
    int   n = 5;
    printf ("\n ** FACTORIAL n! ** \n");
    printf ("\n Recursive Version: %d! = %d \n",
                    n, factorial_n_recur(n));
    printf (" Iterative Version: %d! = %d \n",
                    n, factorial_n_iter(n));
}
```

Code 4.1 for recursive and iterative (nonrecursive) implementations of factorial function for $n = 5$ produces this output:

```
** FACTORIAL n!  **

Recursive Version: 5! = 120
Iterative Version: 5! = 120
```

A second example of recursion deals with the power function. That any number A is raised to the power B, B being a nonnegative integer, is denoted by A^B and is defined by:

$$power(A, B) = \begin{cases} undefined & \text{if } A = 0,\ B = 0 \\ 0 & \text{if } A = 0,\ B \neq 0 \\ 1 & \text{if } A \neq 0,\ B = 0 \\ A^B & \text{if } A \neq 0,\ B \neq 0 \end{cases}$$

From the definition, two termination conditions are identified by $(A = 0, B \neq 0)$, and $(A \neq 0, B = 0)$. One of these two stopping conditions will terminate the recursive calls. The recursive definition for the power function is:

$$power(A, B) \quad = \quad A^B$$
$$= \quad A^1 * A^{B-1}$$
$$= \quad A * power(A, (B-1)), \; if B > 1$$

In **Code 4.2**, the direct recursive function, `power_recur()`, and its nonrecursive counterpart, `power_recur()`, are given. Shown below is the sequence of recursive calls for `power_recur(3, 4)`. Note that the termination for this sequence of direct recursive calls is reached for the values of $A = 3$ and $B = 0$.

```
power_recur(3, 4)                                  1st call
  = 3 * power_recur(3, 4 - 1)                       2nd call
  = 3 * (3 * power_recur(3, 2))                     3rd call
  = 3 * (3 * (3 * power_recur(3,1)))               4th call
  = 3 * (3 * (3 * (3 * power_recur(3,0))))         5th call
  = 3 * (3 * (3 * (3 * 1)))              /\
  = 3 * (3 * (3 * 3))                terminating condition
  = 3 * (3 * 9)
  = 3 * 27
  = 81
```

Code 4.2

```
//
//  Program:  power.c++
//  Purpose:
//     Raise integer 'a' to the power 'b', i.e., a^b.
//        (i)  Recursive implementation
//        (ii) Nonrecursive (iterative ) implementation.
//
#include  <stdio.h>
#include  <stdlib.h>

//  Recursive version
int  power_recur (int a, int b)
{
     if ((a == 0) && (b == 0)) {
         printf ("\n power_recur: Undefined 0^0 \n");
         exit (0);
     }
     if (a == 0)
         return (0);
     if ((a != 0) && (b == 0))
         return (1);
     if (b > 0)
         return (a * power_recur (a, b - 1));
}
```

```
//   Nonrecursive or iterative version
int   power_iter (int a, int b)
{
      int   repeated_product = 1;

      if ((a == 0) && (b == 0)) {
          printf ("\n power_recur: Undefined 0^0 \n");
          exit (0);
      }
      if (a == 0)
          return (0);
      if ((a !=0) && (b == 0))
          return (1);
      while (b > 0) {
          repeated_product *= a;
          b--;
      }
}

void  main(void)
{
      int a = 3, b = 4;

      printf ("\n ** POWER FUNCTION: A^B ** \n");
      printf ("\n Recursive version: %d^%d = %d \n",
                  a, b, power_recur (a, b));
      printf (" Iterative version: %d^%d = %d \n",
                  a, b, power_iter (a, b));
}
```

Code 4.2 for recursive and iterative (nonrecursive) implementations of power function (3 raised to the power 4) produces this output:

```
** POWER FUNCTION: A^B **

Recursive version: 3^4 = 81
Iterative version: 3^4 = 81
```

4.4   Recursion and Trace of C++ Stack

To fully understand recursion and to help assess whether a recursive implementation is suitable for a given problem, one must understand how state values are kept and how they are retrieved during the execution of a recursive function.

During execution of a recursive function, the C++ compiler will automatically *push* (store) the state variables (local variables, the parameter values, the value returned, and the return address) onto a memory space called the *run-time stack* (see Chapter 6 for a more detailed discussion of the *stack* structure). As each recursive call causes the push of such a stack frame, the stack may grow very large if there are many recursive calls. Once a recursive call reaches its terminating condition, the compiler starts to *pop* (retrieve) values and return addresses from the stack until the first return address is popped. Note that in addition to the overhead of stack space utilization with the growth of the stack, the associated push and pop operations are themselves time-consuming. In totality, a very deep recursive call can cause very slow performance of the computer system.

As an example, consider a trace of the run-time stack for the recursive function power_recur(a, b) of **Code 4.2**. For the sake of convenience, let a = 3 and b = 2. In main(), power_recur(3,2) is the first call and its address is assumed to be Z. Initially, the stack is empty:

Empty stack

At the first call, the run-time stack contains the stack frame, which consists of the returned value (not yet known), a value of 3 for a, a value of 2 for b, and the return address Z:

1st call frame	Z	returned addr
	2	'b'
	3	'a'
	?	returned val

Call power_recur(3,2)

The state of the C++ stack after the second call power_recur(3,1) is:

2nd call frame	Z	returned addr
	1	'b'
	3	'a'
	?	returned val
1st call frame	Z	returned addr
	2	'b'
	3	'a'
	?	returned val

Call power_recur(3,1)

The third recursive call, `power_recur(3,0)`, encounters the stopping condition for any further recursive calls:

3rd call frame	Z	STOPPING CONDITION
	0	
	3	
	1	returned val
2nd call frame	Z	returned addr
	1	'b'
	3	'a'
	?	returned val
1st call frame	Z	returned addr
	2	'b'
	3	'a'
	?	returned val

Call power_recur(3,0)

Backtracking now begins, popping the run-time stack for the process until the stack is empty:

2nd call frame	Z	returned addr
	1	'b'
	3	'a'
	3	returned val
1st call frame	Z	returned addr
	2	'b'
	3	'a'
	?	returned val

After 1st return of power_recur(3,0)

1st call frame	Z
	2
	3
	9

After 2nd return of power_recur(3, 1)

Empty stack after 3rd return of power_recur(3, 2)

When the C++ stack for the recursive function `power_recur(3,2)` is empty the value returned to `main()` is 9.

Note that the C++ stack of this example could grow larger in size if a larger value of b was considered. This would require the consumption of more stack space and more time for pushes and pops.

4.5   OOP Application: The Towers of Hanoi

The game problem *Towers of Hanoi* is a famous application of recursion. As the underlying story goes, three priests in the Temple of Brahma were given three needles and asked to move 64 golden disks from one needle to another. They were to do this in such a way that only one disk would be moved at a time and no disk would ever rest on a smaller one. The world would be destroyed by the time they were to complete their tasks. The problem is restated below.

The Towers of Hanoi Problem

Given three poles (needles), move a tower of N disks from one pole, the *start* pole, to another pole, the *finish* pole, with the added conditions that

- only the start pole contains all of the disks (see Figure 4.2),

- only one disk may be moved at a time, and

- no disk ever rests on a smaller one.

In Figure 4.2, the disks on pole 1 will be moved to pole 2, using pole 3 as the temporary working storage, while adhering to the previously stated conditions. The moves are to be recursively performed until the start pole is empty and the finish pole has all the disks in the prescribed order.

Initially, pole 1 has five disks and poles 2 and 3 are empty. Note that the smallest disk and the largest disk are at the top and the bottom of pole 1, respectively. It is easy to move the smallest disk from one pole to another. The complex part is that, for a pole of height N, the disk at the bottom of the pole is not accessible until all the previous $(N-1)$ smaller disks are moved somewhere and placed subject to the third condition.

The divide-and-conquer approach will be used to solve this problem. We proceed by breaking up the whole problem into a set of three smaller subproblems, identified as the *one-disk*, *two-disk*, and *three-disk* problems. In doing so, similar steps used in solving these subproblems are identified.

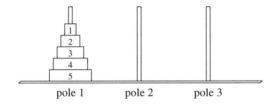

FIGURE 4.2. The Towers of Hanoi with three poles.

This approach leads us to identify the terminating condition and the same set of steps for the recursive process that will be used to solve the N disk version of the Towers of Hanoi problem.

One-Disk Version of the Towers of Hanoi

> Given three poles and one disk on pole 1, move the disk from the start pole (pole 1) to the finish pole (pole 2). The problem is solved.
>
> *The terminating condition of recursion is the one-disk version, which requires only one move.*

Two-Disk Version of the Towers of Hanoi

> Given three poles and two disks on pole 1, the objective is to move all disks from the start pole (pole 1) to the finish pole (pole 2), using pole 3 as the temporary pole. The steps are:
>
> Step 1. Move the smaller disk (i.e., the disk at the top) from pole 1 to pole 3.
>
> Step 2. (Pole 1 has only the largest disk, and all the smaller disks are moved to the temporary pole, pole 3.) Move the larger disk from pole 1 to the finish pole (pole 2).
>
> Step 3. Move the smaller disk from pole 3 to the finish pole (pole 2), and place it on top of the largest disk, which is on pole 2.
>
> Step 4. The start pole (pole 1) is now empty and the finish pole (pole 2) has all the disks in the desired order. The problem is solved.

Three-Disk Version of the Towers of Hanoi

> Given three poles and three disks on pole 1, the objective is to move all disks from the start pole (pole 1) to the finish pole (pole 2), using the pole 3 as the temporary pole. For convenience, we assign the numbers 1 through 3 to the disks, corresponding to the smaller through the larger disk, respectively. That is, disk 1 is the smallest, disk 3 is the largest, and disk 2 is in between. The steps for solving the three-disk version of the Towers of Hanoi problem are:

Step 1. Move disk 1 (i.e., the smallest disk at the top) from the start pole (pole 1) to the finish pole (pole 2).

Step 2. Move the larger disk (disk 2) from the start pole to the temporary pole (pole 3).

Step 3. Move disk 1 from the finish pole to the temporary pole (pole 3).

Step 4. Pole 1 has only the largest disk (disk 3), and both of the smaller disks are moved to the temporary pole, pole 3. Move the largest disk (disk 3) from pole 1 to the finish pole (pole 2).

Step 5. Move the smallest disk (disk 1) from the temporary pole (pole 3) to the start pole (pole 1).

Step 6. Move the smaller disk (disk 2) from the temporary pole (pole 3) to the finish pole (pole 2), and place it on top of the largest disk (disk 3) on the finish pole.

Step 7. Move the smallest disk (disk 1) from the start pole (pole 1) to the finish pole (pole 2).

Step 8. The start pole (pole 1) is empty, and the finish pole (pole 2) has all the disks in the desired order. The problem is solved.

Alternatively, the three-disk version of the Towers of Hanoi problem can be viewed in terms of the two-disk version. To move the whole pile to pole 2, move the $(N-1)$ stack for $N = 3$ to pole 3, move the largest disk to pole 2, and then move the stack on top of it. In this way, the problem is stated in terms of divide-and-conquer and reduces the complexity of the size-N problem to a problem of size $N-1$.

An analysis of the solutions for one-disk, two-disk, and three-disk versions shows that all the disks, except for the largest disk on the start pole, must be moved to the temporary pole before the largest disk is moved from the start pole to the finish pole.

An OOP implementation of the Towers of Hanoi problem with three poles and N disks is presented as **Code 4.3**. For the current example, we consider the five-disk problem; that is, we have set $N = 5$. To illustrate the actual workings of this code, Figure 4.3 provides a graphical trace of some of the intermediate disk moves involved, starting with the first disk moved.

The object `hanoi_obj` is identified of type `Towers_of_Hanoi`. The data elements of `hanoi_obj` are maximum disks, three poles, pole number, an array of disks associated with each pole, and the height of each pole with disks (rings). The operations for this object are implemented with the methods

- `Towers_of_Hanoi()`, `~Towers_of_Hanoi()`,

- build_and_init_poles(),

- move_disk(),

- solve1_hanoi(), solve_hanoi(),

- draw_pole(), and

- get_max_disks().

In the header file def_class_Towers_of_Hanoi.h we define a class Towers_of_Hanoi as follows:

```
class  Towers_of_Hanoi {
  private:
    typedef  int  POLE_NO;
    typedef  int  DISK_NO;
    typedef  int  POLE_HEIGHT;
    int  MAX_DISKS;
    int  MAX_HEIGHT;  // max = MAX_DISKS
    int  MAX_DISK_NO;

    typedef struct POLE_WITH_DISKS {
       // DISK_NO  DISK_ARRAY[MAX_HEIGHT];
       DISK_NO  *DISK_ARRAY;
       DISK_NO  ring_height;
       POLE_NO  pole_no;
    } *POLE_PTR;
    POLE_PTR  pole_1_ptr, pole_2_ptr, pole_3_ptr;
  public:
    POLE_WITH_DISKS pole_1,  // start pole
                    pole_2,  // finish pole
                    pole_3;  // temporary pole
    Towers_of_Hanoi(int max_disks);
    ~Towers_of_Hanoi();
    void  build_and_init_poles(void);
    void  move_disk(POLE_PTR from, POLE_PTR to);
    void  solve1_hanoi(DISK_NO no_of_disks,
            POLE_PTR start_pole,
            POLE_PTR finish_pole,
            POLE_PTR temp_pole);
    void  solve_hanoi(int no_of_disks);
    void  draw_pole (POLE_WITH_DISKS  pole);
    int  get_max_disks() { return MAX_DISKS; }
};
```

The space DISK_ARRAY[] is dynamically allocated when the input MAX_DISKS is given, allowing this implementation to support any specified number of disks on three poles. However, the current implementation of draw_pole() only allows for the display of the five disks specific to the five-disk version of the Towers of Hanoi problem. Modification of this implementation to allow for the display of any specifiable number of disks is left as an exercise. The methods of **Code 4.3** are now briefly discussed.

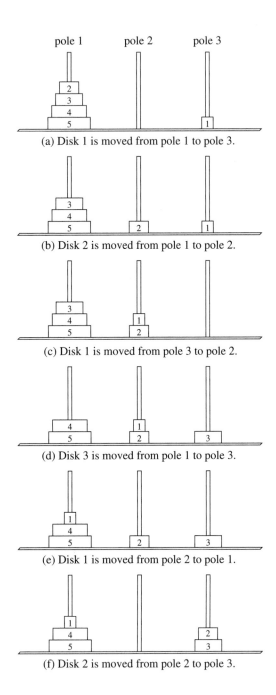

(a) Disk 1 is moved from pole 1 to pole 3.

(b) Disk 2 is moved from pole 1 to pole 2.

(c) Disk 1 is moved from pole 3 to pole 2.

(d) Disk 3 is moved from pole 1 to pole 3.

(e) Disk 1 is moved from pole 2 to pole 1.

(f) Disk 2 is moved from pole 2 to pole 3.

FIGURE 4.3. Trace of the Towers of Hanoi with three poles. (*Continued on next page*)

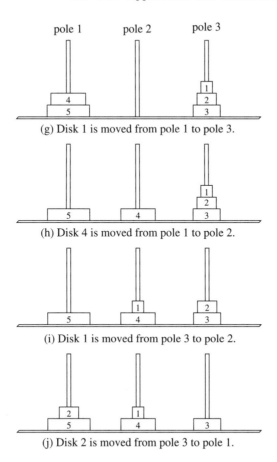

(g) Disk 1 is moved from pole 1 to pole 3.

(h) Disk 4 is moved from pole 1 to pole 2.

(i) Disk 1 is moved from pole 3 to pole 2.

(j) Disk 2 is moved from pole 3 to pole 1.

FIGURE 4.3. *Continued.*

Towers_of_Hanoi() is a publicly accessible member function of the Towers_of_Hanoi class. As it accepts the input max_disks, it sets MAX_DISKS. Using the new operator, it dynamically allocates three arrays DISK_ARRAY[] of type DISK_NO for the three poles pole_1, pole_2, and pole_3.

~Towers_of_Hanoi() is also a publicly accessible member function of the Towers_of_Hanoi class. This member function is a destructor for an object of type Towers_of_Hanoi. It dynamically deallocates memory space for the three disk arrays DISK_ARRAY[].

Build_and_init_poles() is a publicly accessible member function of the Towers_of_Hanoi class. It builds disk numbers for pole_1 and initializes disk numbers for pole_2 and pole_3. It also initializes the fields ring_height and pole_no of each pole structure. The three pointers pole_1_ptr, pole_2_ptr, and pole_3_ptr, of type POLE_PTR, are also set to the addresses of pole_1, pole_2, and pole_3, respectively.

Move_disk() is a public member function of the Towers_of_Hanoi class. It accepts arguments from_pole and to_pole of type POLE_PTR. It actually moves a disk from from_pole to to_pole. The function lifts the disk at the current ring_height position in from_pole, and drops (adds) that disk to to_pole. After the move, the function appropriately adjusts the ring heights and disk arrays for both poles. It is called by solve1_hanoi(). When it is called the first time, from_pole and to_pole are respectively pole_1 and pole_3. When it is called the second time, from_pole and to_pole are respectively pole_3 and pole_2.

As a public member function of the Towers_of_Hanoi class, the recursive function Solve1_hanoi() accepts the arguments no_of_disks, start_pole, finish_pole, and temp_pole. Its recursion terminates when
no_of_disks > 0. This function initiates the actual move of disks from start_pole to finish_pole by twice calling move_disk(). During each recursive call, it also prints "Move disk from pole to pole" with disk and pole numbers.

Solve_hanoi(), called in main(), is a public member function of the Towers_of_Hanoi class. It accepts one argument, no_of_disks, and calls solve1_hanoi() with pole_1 as start_pole, and pole_3 as finish_pole. It subsequently calls solve1_hanoi() with pole_3 as start_pole, and pole_2 as finish_pole.

Draw_pole() is a public member function of the Towers_of_Hanoi class. It accepts one argument, pole, of type POLE_WITH_DISKS. It initializes a picture of a pole with five disks. Then it graphically displays the picture of the specified pole with disks.

Main() is the test driver for an OOP implementation of Towers of Hanoi problem with three poles. It instantiates an object hanoi_obj for five disks, numbered from 1 to 5. It passes messages to hanoi_obj through this object's public methods build_and_init_poles(), solve_hanoi(), and draw_pole().

Code 4.3

```
// Program:  hanoi.c++
// Purpose:
//   Object-Oriented implementation of
//   Towers of Hanoi problem for N disks using
//   recursion.  Show consecutive positions of
//   disks on three columns to move a tower from
//   one column to another in such a manner that
//   no disk rests on a smaller one.
//
#include  <stdio.h>
#include  <stdlib.h>

class  Towers_of_Hanoi {
  private:
    typedef  int  POLE_NO;
    typedef  int  DISK_NO;
    typedef  int  POLE_HEIGHT;

    int  MAX_DISKS;
    int  MAX_HEIGHT;  // max = MAX_DISKS
    int  MAX_DISK_NO;

    typedef struct POLE_WITH_DISKS {
        // DISK_NO  DISK_ARRAY[MAX_HEIGHT];
        DISK_NO  *DISK_ARRAY;
        // DISK_NO  disk_no;
        DISK_NO  ring_height;
        POLE_NO  pole_no;
    } *POLE_PTR;

    POLE_PTR  pole_1_ptr, pole_2_ptr, pole_3_ptr;

  public:
    POLE_WITH_DISKS pole_1,  // start pole
                    pole_2,  // finish pole
                    pole_3;  // temporary pole
    Towers_of_Hanoi(int max_disks);
    ~Towers_of_Hanoi();

    void  build_and_init_poles(void);
    void  move_disk (POLE_PTR from, POLE_PTR to);
    void  solve1_hanoi (DISK_NO no_of_disks,
            POLE_PTR start_pole,
            POLE_PTR finish_pole,
            POLE_PTR temp_pole);
    void  solve_hanoi(int no_of_disks);
    void  draw_pole (POLE_WITH_DISKS  pole);
    int   get_max_disks() { return MAX_DISKS; }
};

// ---  Implement methods for "Towers_of_Hanoi" class
```

```
//  Constructor for "Towers_of_Hanoi" class
Towers_of_Hanoi::Towers_of_Hanoi(int max_disks)
{
   MAX_DISKS   = max_disks;
   MAX_DISK_NO = MAX_DISKS - 1;
   MAX_HEIGHT  = MAX_DISKS;

   pole_1.DISK_ARRAY = new DISK_NO [MAX_DISKS];
   pole_2.DISK_ARRAY = new DISK_NO [MAX_DISKS];
   pole_3.DISK_ARRAY = new DISK_NO [MAX_DISKS];
}

//  Destructor for "Towers_of_Hanoi" class
Towers_of_Hanoi::~Towers_of_Hanoi()
{
   delete pole_1.DISK_ARRAY;
   delete pole_2.DISK_ARRAY;
   delete pole_3.DISK_ARRAY;
}

// build_and_init_poles():
//   Build and initialize three poles with disks.
//
void Towers_of_Hanoi::build_and_init_poles(void)
{
  for (int i = 0; i < MAX_DISKS; i++ ) {
  //   pole_1.DISK_ARRAY = ({ 0, 1, 2, 3, 4, 5}, 5};
  //   Bottom (i.e., largest) disk = DISK_ARRAY[MAX_DISKS - 1]
  //   Top (i.e., smallest) disk = DISK_ARRAY[0]
    pole_1.DISK_ARRAY[i] = MAX_DISKS - i;
    pole_2.DISK_ARRAY[i] = 0;
    pole_3.DISK_ARRAY[i] = 0;
  }
  pole_1.ring_height = MAX_DISKS - 1;
  pole_1.pole_no = 1;
  pole_2.ring_height = 0;
  pole_2.pole_no = 2;
  pole_3.ring_height = 0;
  pole_3.pole_no = 3;

  //  Set up the pointers to poles' data structures
  pole_1_ptr = &pole_1;
  pole_2_ptr = &pole_2;
  pole_3_ptr = &pole_3;
}

//
// move_disk():
//   Move disks from one pole "from_pole" to another
//   pole "to_pole".  This is the heart of
//   "Towers of Hanoi" problem.
//
void  Towers_of_Hanoi::move_disk (POLE_PTR from_pole,
                                  POLE_PTR to_pole)
```

```
{
   DISK_NO         disk_no;

   disk_no = from_pole->DISK_ARRAY[from_pole->ring_height];

   // --- Begin "Lift disk (ring)" from "from_pole"
   POLE_HEIGHT  old_height = from_pole->ring_height;

   from_pole->DISK_ARRAY[old_height] = 0; // Lifted
   from_pole->ring_height = old_height - 1;

   // --- End of "lift disk (ring)"

   // --- Begin "Drop disk (ring)" on "to_pole"
   POLE_HEIGHT  new_height = to_pole->ring_height + 1;

   to_pole->ring_height = new_height;
   to_pole->DISK_ARRAY[new_height] = disk_no;  // Dropped

   // --- End   "Drop disk (ring)"
}

// solve1_hanoi():
//   Recursive function that calls move_disk()
//   to move disks from "start_pole" to
//   "finish_pole" using temporary pole "temp_pole".
//
void  Towers_of_Hanoi::solve1_hanoi (DISK_NO no_of_disks,
       POLE_PTR start_pole, POLE_PTR finish_pole,
       POLE_PTR temp_pole)
{
   if (no_of_disks > 0) {
      solve1_hanoi (no_of_disks - 1, start_pole,
                    temp_pole, finish_pole);
      move_disk (start_pole, finish_pole);
      printf("\n Move disk %d from %s %d to %s %d",
        no_of_disks, "pole", start_pole->pole_no,
        "pole", finish_pole->pole_no);
      solve1_hanoi (no_of_disks - 1, temp_pole,
                    finish_pole, start_pole);
   }
}

// solve_hanoi():
//   Calls solve1_hanoi() twice which call move_disk()
//   that moves disks from one pole to another.
//
void  Towers_of_Hanoi::solve_hanoi (int no_of_disks)
{
   solve1_hanoi (no_of_disks, pole_1_ptr, pole_3_ptr,
                                  pole_2_ptr);
   solve1_hanoi (no_of_disks, pole_3_ptr, pole_2_ptr,
                                  pole_1_ptr);
}
```

```cpp
//  draw_pole():
//    Graphically display picture of a pole with disks.
//
void Towers_of_Hanoi::draw_pole (POLE_WITH_DISKS  pole)
{
    static char *pole_picture[] =
      {"                    ",
       "                    ",
       "          --        ",
       "         01       ",
       "         ----       ",
       "         02       ",
       "         ------       ",
       "        03      ",
       "        --------      ",
       "       04      ",
       "       ----------    ",
       "      05     ",
       "      -----------   " };

    printf("\n");

    for (int i = MAX_DISKS - 1; i > 0; i--) {
        DISK_NO disk_no = pole.DISK_ARRAY[i];

        switch(disk_no) {
          case 0:
                printf("%s\n%s\n",
                    pole_picture[0], pole_picture[1]);
                break;
          case 1:
                printf("%s\n%s\n%s\n%s\n",
                    pole_picture[0], pole_picture[1],
                    pole_picture[2], pole_picture[3]);
                break;
          case 2:
                printf("%s\n%s\n",
                    pole_picture[4], pole_picture[5]);
                break;
          case 3:
                printf("%s\n%s\n",
                    pole_picture[6], pole_picture[7]);
                break;
          case 4:
                printf("%s\n%s\n",
                    pole_picture[8], pole_picture[9]);
                break;
          case 5:
                printf("%s\n%s\n",
                    pole_picture[10], pole_picture[11]);
                break;
        }
    }
}
```

```
    printf(" =============== %s %d\n\n",
           " \n       Pole", pole.pole_no);
}

//  main(): Test driver for OOP implementation of a
//          "Towers of Hanoi" with 3 poles.
//
void main(void)
{
    // Declare a "Towers_of_Hanoi" type object
    // with 5 disks; MAX_DISKS = 6
    Towers_of_Hanoi  hanoi_obj(6);
    Towers_of_Hanoi::DISK_NO
      max_disk_no = hanoi_obj.get_max_disks() - 1;

    printf("\n ** OOP IMPLEMENTATION OF %s  **\n %s \n",
      "TOWERS OF HANOI", "              USING RECURSION");
    hanoi_obj.build_and_init_poles();
    printf("\n\n ** States of Poles before moves **\n");
    hanoi_obj.draw_pole(hanoi_obj.pole_1);
    hanoi_obj.draw_pole(hanoi_obj.pole_2);
    hanoi_obj.solve_hanoi (max_disk_no);
    printf("\n\n ** States of Poles after moves **\n");
    hanoi_obj.draw_pole(hanoi_obj.pole_1);
    hanoi_obj.draw_pole(hanoi_obj.pole_2);
}
```

Code 4.3, an OOP of the Towers of Hanoi with three poles and five disks, yields this output:

```
    **  OOP IMPLEMENTATION OF TOWERS OF HANOI   **
                     USING RECURSION


    **  States of Poles before moves **

             !!
             !!
             --
           !01!
           ----
          ! 02 !
          ------
         !  03  !
         --------
        !   04   !
        ----------
       !    05    !
      ===============
             Pole 1
```

```
              !!
              !!
              !!
              !!
              !!
              !!
              !!
              !!
              !!
              !!
        ===============
            Pole 2
```

```
Move disk 1 from pole 1 to pole 3
Move disk 2 from pole 1 to pole 2
Move disk 1 from pole 3 to pole 2
Move disk 3 from pole 1 to pole 3
Move disk 1 from pole 2 to pole 1
Move disk 2 from pole 2 to pole 3
Move disk 1 from pole 1 to pole 3
Move disk 4 from pole 1 to pole 2
Move disk 1 from pole 3 to pole 2
Move disk 2 from pole 3 to pole 1
Move disk 1 from pole 2 to pole 1
Move disk 3 from pole 3 to pole 2
Move disk 1 from pole 1 to pole 3
Move disk 2 from pole 1 to pole 2
Move disk 1 from pole 3 to pole 2
Move disk 5 from pole 1 to pole 3
Move disk 1 from pole 2 to pole 1
Move disk 2 from pole 2 to pole 3
Move disk 1 from pole 1 to pole 3
Move disk 3 from pole 2 to pole 1
Move disk 1 from pole 3 to pole 2
Move disk 2 from pole 3 to pole 1
Move disk 1 from pole 2 to pole 1
Move disk 4 from pole 2 to pole 3
Move disk 1 from pole 1 to pole 3
Move disk 2 from pole 1 to pole 2
Move disk 1 from pole 3 to pole 2
Move disk 3 from pole 1 to pole 3
Move disk 1 from pole 2 to pole 1
Move disk 2 from pole 2 to pole 3
Move disk 1 from pole 1 to pole 3
Move disk 1 from pole 3 to pole 2
Move disk 2 from pole 3 to pole 1
Move disk 1 from pole 2 to pole 1
Move disk 3 from pole 3 to pole 2
Move disk 1 from pole 1 to pole 3
Move disk 2 from pole 1 to pole 2
Move disk 1 from pole 3 to pole 2
Move disk 4 from pole 3 to pole 1
```

```
Move disk 1 from pole 2 to pole 1
Move disk 2 from pole 2 to pole 3
Move disk 1 from pole 1 to pole 3
Move disk 3 from pole 2 to pole 1
Move disk 1 from pole 3 to pole 2
Move disk 2 from pole 3 to pole 1
Move disk 1 from pole 2 to pole 1
Move disk 5 from pole 3 to pole 2
Move disk 1 from pole 1 to pole 3
Move disk 2 from pole 1 to pole 2
Move disk 1 from pole 3 to pole 2
Move disk 3 from pole 1 to pole 3
Move disk 1 from pole 2 to pole 1
Move disk 2 from pole 2 to pole 3
Move disk 1 from pole 1 to pole 3
Move disk 4 from pole 1 to pole 2
Move disk 1 from pole 3 to pole 2
Move disk 2 from pole 3 to pole 1
Move disk 1 from pole 2 to pole 1
Move disk 3 from pole 3 to pole 2
Move disk 1 from pole 1 to pole 3
Move disk 2 from pole 1 to pole 2
Move disk 1 from pole 3 to pole 2
```

```
        ** States of Poles after moves **

            !!
            !!
            !!
            !!
            !!
            !!
            !!
            !!
            !!
            !!
=================
        Pole 1

            !!
            !!
            --
           !01!
           ----
          ! 02 !
          ------
         !  03  !
         --------
        !   04   !
        ----------
       !    05    !
=================
         Pole 2
```

Notice that initially `Pole 1` has five disks and `Pole 2` has none, and after the program executes, disks were moved from `Pole 1` to `Pole 2`. Finally, `Pole 1` has no disks and `Pole 2` has all five of them.

4.6   OOP Application: Nonattacking N-Queens

The famous nonattacking N-Queens chessboard game is another good example of an application that is very nicely handled with recursion. The successive movement of queens on a chessboard demonstrates the backtracking property of recursion.

The Nonattacking N-Queens Problem

Given a variable size chessboard (two-dimensional array), the objective of the game is to move the queens such that the final configuration has no queen attacking another (in vertical and horizontal position). The movement of the queens follows the rules of the conventional game of chess. The chessboard is square and its dimensions on a side is equal to N, the number of queens placed within the board array.

Code 4.4 is an OOP implementation for the N-Queens game. An object `EightQueens` is identified whose data area is the BOARD_SIZE by BOARD_SIZE (e.g., 8×8) chessboard for $N = 8$. However, the implementation is very general because it is not specific to an 8×8 chessboard. The input for BOARD_SIZE can be any positive integer and the program will dynamically allocate the chessboard based on this specification. The chessboard data is implemented by a BOARD_SIZE by BOARD_SIZE array:

```
        int   chessboard[BOARD_SIZE][BOARD_SIZE];
    where
```

$$chessboard[i][j] = \begin{cases} TRUE & \text{if a queen is on this square of board} \\ FALSE & \text{otherwise} \end{cases}$$

A template for the `EightQueens` object is now defined by the `Queens` class in the header file `def_class_Queens.h`:

```
class Queens {
   private:          // For hiding these data
      int       BOARD_SIZE;   // same as N
      int       *chessboard;
      void      init_chessboard(void);
      int       is_safe_to_move(void);

   // Declare the "public" interface routines
```

```
public:
  Queens(int bd_size);      //  Constructor
  ~Queens();                //  Destructor
  int  add_nonattacking_queen(int position);
  void display_chessboard(void);
};
```

The data BOARD_SIZE, *chessboard and init_chessboard() are declared private for data-hiding, and the methods are declared public for passing messages between Queens type object and any other object.

Queens() constructs a Queens-type object. It sets BOARD_SIZE to the input value. Memory space for chessboard of size BOARD_SIZE x BOARD_SIZE is allocated by using the new operator. The chessboard is initialized by calling Init_chessboard().

~Queens() frees up the BOARD_SIZE x BOARD_SIZE memory space by using the delete operator.

Init_chessboard() is not a publicly accessible member function of the Queens class. It initializes the chessboard by setting FALSE to each square location.

Is_safe_to_move() is not a publicly accessible member function of the Queens class. It returns TRUE if it is safe to move a queen to any one of the surrounding squares in the current configuration of the chessboard. This means that there is no queen object (identified by FALSE value) in one of these surrounding squares. Starting from the square chessboard[0][0], it tests TRUE value for each chessboard square that is (1) on a vertical axis, (2) on a horizontal axis, (3) on the southeast diagonal axis, (4) on the northwest diagonal axis, (5) on the northeast diagonal axis, or (6) on the southwest diagonal axis. It returns FALSE if it is not safe to move in these directions.

Add_nonattacking_queen() is a publicly accessible member function of the Queens class. It is implemented as a recursive function. It adds a nonattacking queen object in the current configuration of the chessboard. It calls is_safe_to_move() to check whether to safely move a queen object in the current board. Add_nonattacking_queen() returns TRUE if it is possible to add queen objects in rows position through BOARD_SIZE without attacking queen objects. It returns FALSE if there is no solution.

Display_chessboard() is a publicly accessible member function of the Queens class. It displays the chessboard. It displays Q for queen objects in the square location of the chessboard. Absence of a queen object in a square is left blank.

Main() is the test driver for OOP implementation of N nonattacking queens. It declares EightQ object of type Queens for $N = 8$ by implicitly calling the constructor Queens(). Since main() is not a member of the Queens class, it sends messages to EightQ object through the public interface routines. The messages include adding a nonattacking queen object to the chessboard, the first queen's starting from position [0,0], and a request to display the chessboard.

Any number of queens is supported. For example, a 12-Queens problem is implemented by declaring Queen Twelve_queen_obj(12) in main().

Code 4.4

```
//
//  Program:   queens.c++
//  Purpose:   OBJECT-ORIENTED IMPLEMENTATION OF
//             THE FAMOUS EIGHT-QUEENS PROBLEM
//
#include <stdio.h>
const int TRUE  = 1;
const int FALSE = 0;
//  Define a "Queens" class
#include "def_class_Queens.h"

//  Queens():
//    Initialize the dimension and allocate
//    memory space for the square chessboard.
Queens::Queens(int bd_size)
{
    BOARD_SIZE = bd_size;
    chessboard = new int [BOARD_SIZE * BOARD_SIZE];
    init_chessboard();
}

//  ~Queens():
//    Deallocate memory space for the chessboard.
Queens::~Queens(void)
{
    delete  [] chessboard;
}

//   init_chessboard():
//      Initialize chessboard[BOARD_SIZE][BOARD_SIZE]
//
void Queens::init_chessboard(void)
{
    for (int i = 0; i < BOARD_SIZE; i++)
        for (int j = 0; j < BOARD_SIZE; j++)
            // chessboard[i][j] = FALSE;
            chessboard[i * BOARD_SIZE + j] = FALSE;
}

int Queens::is_safe_to_move(void)
{
    // Check for attack (i.e., presence of any queen,
    // identified by TRUE location value) at each
    // queen/TRUE location.
    //
    for (int i = 0; i < BOARD_SIZE; i++)
```

```
    for (int j = 0; j < BOARD_SIZE; j++)
       // if (chessboard[i][j] == TRUE)
       if (chessboard[i * BOARD_SIZE + j] == TRUE) {
         // Check for attack on vertical axis
         for (int k = 0; k < BOARD_SIZE; k++)
            if ((chessboard[k * BOARD_SIZE + j] == TRUE)
                && k != i)
               return (FALSE);

         // Check for attack on horizontal axis
         for (int l = 0; l < BOARD_SIZE; l++)
            if ((chessboard[i * BOARD_SIZE + l] == TRUE)
                && l != j)
               return (FALSE);

        //Check for attack on south east diagonal axis
        for (k = i + 1, l = j + 1;
             k < BOARD_SIZE && l < BOARD_SIZE; k++, l++)
           if (chessboard[k * BOARD_SIZE + l] == TRUE)
               return (FALSE);

        //Check for attack on north west diagonal axis
        for (k = i - 1, l = j - 1;
             k >= 0 && l >= 0; k--, l--)
          if (chessboard[k * BOARD_SIZE + l] == TRUE)
               return (FALSE);

        //Check for attack on south west diagonal axis
        for (k = i + 1, l = j - 1;
             k < BOARD_SIZE && l >= 0; k++, l--)
          if (chessboard[k * BOARD_SIZE + l] == TRUE)
               return (FALSE);

        //Check for attack on north east diagonal axis
        for (k = i - 1, l = j + 1;
             k >= 0 && l < BOARD_SIZE; k--, l++)
           if (chessboard[k * BOARD_SIZE + l] == TRUE)
               return (FALSE);
       } // -- end of "if (chessboard[i ..."
    return (TRUE);
}

//  add_nonattacking_queen():
//    Add nonattacking queens in a chessboard
//    of size BOARD_SIZE x BOARD_SIZE.
//    (Implemented using Recursion.)
//
int Queens::add_nonattacking_queen (int position)
{
   int  outcome = FALSE;
   for (int k = 0; k < BOARD_SIZE && outcome == FALSE;
         k++) {
      if (position >= BOARD_SIZE)
         return (TRUE);
```

```
      else {
        //  Add a queen in chessboard[position][k]
        chessboard[position * BOARD_SIZE + k] = TRUE;
        if (
          (add_nonattacking_queen(position + 1) == TRUE)
          && (is_safe_to_move() == TRUE))
            outcome = TRUE;
        else
          //  Remove queen from chessboard[position][k]
          chessboard[position * BOARD_SIZE + k] = FALSE;
      }
    }
    return (outcome);
}


//  display_chessboard():
//    Display the N x N chessboard showing
//    the positions of N queens, N = 8.
//
void Queens::display_chessboard (void)
{
    for (int i = 0; i < BOARD_SIZE; i++) {
        int        printQ_flag = 0;
        printf("-------------------------------\n");
        for (int j = 0; j < BOARD_SIZE; j++) {
            //  if ( chessboard[i][j] == TRUE )
            if (chessboard[i * BOARD_SIZE + j] == TRUE) {
              if ((j == 0 && printQ_flag == 0)
                  (printQ_flag != 0))
                  printf("! Q ");
              else
                  printf(" Q ");
              printQ_flag = 1;
            }
            else {
              if (printQ_flag == 1) {
                  printf("!    !");
                  printQ_flag = 0;
              }
              else if (j == 0)
                  printf("!    !");
              else
                  printf("    !");
            }
        }
        if (printQ_flag == 1)
            printf("!");
        printf("\n");
    }
    printf("-------------------------------\n");
}


//  main():
//    Test driver for Object-Oriented Eight
```

```
//     Queens problem
//
void main(void)
{
    //   Declare and initialize an object "EightQ"
    //   of the "Queens" class; set BOARD_SIZE to 8.
    Queens      EightQ(8);

    printf("\n **  OOP IMPLEMENTATION %s ** %s\n",
            "OF EIGHT QUEENS",
            "\n               USING RECURSION\n");
    // First queen is assumed at position [0,0]
    // of chessboard. The outcome varies depending
    // on this starting position.
    if (EightQ.add_nonattacking_queen(0) == TRUE)
      EightQ.display_chessboard();
    else
      printf("\n Failed to place Queens.\n");
}
```

Code 4.4 yields this output:

```
**  OOP IMPLEMENTATION OF EIGHT QUEENS **
              USING RECURSION

----------------------------------
! Q !   !   !   !   !   !   !   !
----------------------------------
!   !   !   ! Q !   !   !   !
----------------------------------
!   !   !   !   !   !   ! Q !
----------------------------------
!   !   !   !   ! Q !   !   !
----------------------------------
!   ! Q !   !   !   !   !   !
----------------------------------
!   !   !   !   !   ! Q !   !
----------------------------------
! Q !   !   !   !   !   !   !
----------------------------------
!   !   ! Q !   !   !   !   !
----------------------------------
```

4.7   Key Points for Using Recursion

Though recursion is a powerful and elegant way of programming, it is important to note its uses and abuses as a caution. The key points for using recursion are:

- Some problems, such as the Towers of Hanoi, are recursive by nature and thus are prime candidates for recursive implementations. They could, however, be implemented nonrecursively, but with much greater programming complexity in some cases.

- Recursion increases program readability and maintainability, as compared to nonrecursive (iterative) counterparts.

- *Recursion is not for all problems.* Since recursion can require excessive stack space and time for recursive calls, recursion should be judiciously used.

- Recursion should not be used unless a terminating condition is well defined. A terminating condition prevents recursive calls from executing in an endless (infinite) loop.

- Recursion should be used for those problems that can be defined in terms of a simpler and smaller form of itself and with a well-defined terminating condition.

- Recursion can be replaced by iteration and a stack.

4.8   Exercises

1. Given the recursive definition of the *Ackerman's function* for two nonnegative integers, m and n, by the formula:

$$Acker(m, n) = \begin{cases} n + 1 & \text{if } m = 0, n \geq 0 \\ Acker \ (m - 1, \ n) & \text{if } n = 0 \\ Acker \ (m - 1, \ Acker \ (m, \ n - 1)) & \text{otherwise} \end{cases}$$

(a) Calculate the following Ackerman values:

```
Acker(0, 0), Acker(7, 0), Acker(3, 2), Acker(4, 4)
```

(b) Identify the terminating condition and show the traces of recursive calls for each function in Exercise 4-1(a). (c) For each Ackerman function in Exercise 4-1(b), show the contents and trace of C++ stack for all recursive calls. (d) Implement and test the recursive Ackerman's function.

2. Implement and test a recursive function to compute an arithmetic progression for n integers:

$$1 + 2 + 3 + ... + (n - 1) + n$$

3. Implement and test a recursive function for the high-order *Bessel function*, which is used for evaluating an integral with variable x. The recursive definition of Bessel function of order n is

$$J_n(x) = 2(n-1)/x J_{n-1}(x) - J_{n-2}(x), \; n \geq 2$$

The mathematics library `math.h` provides J_0 and J_1 , which are `j0(double)` and `j1(double)`, respectively. Test with input values (i) $x = 20$, $n = 13$, (ii) $x = 15.5$, $n = 9$.

4. Implement and test a recursive function for a palindrome. A palindrome is an alphanumeric string such that the string reads the same in a forward and backward direction. For example, the string "MOM" is a palindrome, but "12345321" is not.

5. Implement and test a recursive function for computing the greatest common divisor $GCD(m, n)$, where m and n are positive integers. The recursive definition of $GCD(m, n)$ is:

$$GCD(m,n) = \begin{cases} m & \text{if } n = 0 \\ n & \text{if remainder } m\%n = 0 \\ \text{GCD(n, remainder)} & \text{if } n \neq 0 \end{cases}$$

6. Modify and test `power_recur(a, b)` in **Code 4.2**, so that it can accept any integer values of a and b.

7. Given the recursive definition of binomial coefficient `C(m, n)` for two positive integers, $m \geq 0, n \geq 0$,

$$C(m,n) = \begin{cases} 1 & \text{if } n = 0 \text{ or } m = n \\ \text{C(m - 1, n - 1) + C(m - 1, n)} & \text{otherwise} \end{cases}$$

(a) Implement and test a recursive function `C(m, n)` for binomial coefficients for two positive integers m and n. You must check and report invalid values. (b) Implement and test a nonrecursive version of `C(m, n)`. You must check and report invalid values, and must not use an array or a stack.

8. *Fibonacci numbers* are useful to demonstrate the performance problem in recursion. Fibonacci numbers are

$$0, 1, 1, 2, 3, 5, 8, 13, 21, 34, 55, 89, \ldots$$

The recursive definition of Fibonacci numbers $Fib(n)$, n being a nonnegative integer, is

$$Fib(0) = 1, Fib(1) = 1, Fib(n) = Fib(n-2) + Fib(n-1), n \geq 2$$

(a) Implement and test a recursive function for Fibonacci numbers with $n = 8$, and calculate the number of recursive calls. (b) Implement and test a recursive function for Fibonacci numbers with $n = 28$, and calculate the number of recursive calls. (c) Write traces of recursive Fibonacci function calls for $n = 8$. (d) Write the recursion tree for Fibonacci function calls for (i) $n = 5$, (ii) $n = 8$. (e) Implement and test an iterative version of the Fibonacci function for calculating the nth Fibonacci number. (f) Devise, implement, and test a faster and modified form of the recurrence relation for computing Fibonacci numbers.

9. Implement and test a recursive function for the *continued fraction* of the form:

$$1 + \cfrac{1}{1 + \cfrac{1}{1 + \cdots}}$$

If S_n means the nth partial sum, then the recursive definition of the continued fraction is

$S_1 = 1$, $S_n = 1 + 1/S_{n-1}$ for $n > 1$, n being a positive integer.

10. Implement and test an OOP that reads data for a determinant from a user's terminal and calculates a determinant of an $n \times n$ matrix using a recursive function. Conceptually, the recursive definition of a determinant for an 3×3 matrix is:

$$\begin{vmatrix} a & b & c \\ d & e & f \\ g & h & i \end{vmatrix} = a * \begin{vmatrix} e & f \\ h & i \end{vmatrix} - b * \begin{vmatrix} d & f \\ g & i \end{vmatrix} + c * \begin{vmatrix} d & e \\ g & h \end{vmatrix}$$

$$\begin{vmatrix} e & f \\ h & i \end{vmatrix} = e * |\, i\,| - f * |\, h\,| \quad \text{(determinant for 2x2 matrix)}$$

$$|\, i\,| = i, \quad |\, h\,| = h \quad \text{(determinant for 1x1 matrix)}$$

11. (a) Modify and test **Code 4.3** for the Towers of Hanoi with 15 disks. This requires modification of draw_pole(). (Hint: In main(), instantiate: Towers_of_Hanoi hanoi_obj(16);) (b) Modify and test draw_pole() in **Code 4.3** so that it prints three poles side by side as shown in Figure 4.2.

12. (a) Devise an algorithm for the Towers of Hanoi with four poles. (b) Write and test an OOP for the Towers of Hanoi with four poles.

13. Modify and test **Code 4.4** for twelve nonattacking queens problem. (Hint: In main(), Queens Twelve_queens_obj(12);.)

14. Modify and test `add_nonattacking_queen()` in **Code 4.4** so that the first queen can be placed in any row and any column position of the chessboard.

15. Write an OOP for parsing pointer-based strings. To do this, you first define a `String` class. The parsing function must be recursive and a `public` member function of the `String` class. The program reads strings from a file until the end of file is reached. The parser scans and reports the total number of occurrences of each string for any of these matching pairs in the string:

    (a) a pair of left "(" and right ")" parentheses
    (b) a pair of left "{" and right "}" braces
    (c) a pair of left "[" and right "]" brackets
    (d) a pair of left "/*" and right "*/"

16. *Maze Problem Project*: Write and test an OOP for an $n \times n$ *maze problem* using recursion. A maze problem demonstrates the concept of *backtracking and tracing*. An $n \times n$ maze is a confusing intricate network of passages and is created when an $n \times n$ matrix is divided into a set of cells (squares), some of them being blocked. The problem is that a rat is set free inside the maze and is searching for a path to exit the maze. While moving through the unblocked (unused or blank) cells in any direction inside the maze, the rat may encounter a blocked cell (B) that is not a through street. It backtracks to find another way and will not come back to the same blocked path. The intricacy lies in finding a path from start (S) to finish (F) in the maze. Create the maze object for $n = 5$ and print the path, if any, from the start cell (denoted by $(0,0)$) to the finish cell (denoted by $(4,4)$).

	0	1	2	3	4
0	S	B		B	
1		B			
2				B	
3	B	B		B	
4			B		F

17. Redo Exercise 4-16 for a 7×7 maze object. Construct a maze to test your program.

5

Lists

An *ordered* or *linear list* is a collection of data elements organized and accessed in an *explicit* sequential fashion. It is a fundamental structure upon which a wide variety of more complex data structures are built.

A list is similar to an array in that both structures store collections of data elements in a sequential manner. In an array, however, the sequential organization of the elements is *implicit* to the position which elements occupy in the array. Thus, an array representation is equivalent to an ordered list if the order of the elements in the array, stored in consecutive memory locations (consecutive indexes), happens to correspond to the desired sequential order of the elements of the list. When an ordered list is directly represented in an array memory, there exists a one-to-one mapping between the order of the list elements and contiguous array locations — for a given element in the list, the *next* element of the list (if it exists) resides in the next incrementally (or decrementally) indexed array location.

A *linked* ordered list, or *linked list*, is a linear list for which the data elements are not necessarily organized with such an implicit sequential memory mapping. In a linked list, a data element in sequence is accessed by an index or pointer to it. As the data elements of a linked list are visited in a contiguous manner, the memory locations corresponding to the elements need not be contiguous. This is in contrast to the array, where sequential access implies indexing contiguous memory locations.

Since its size is fixed at declaration, an array representation of a list is of limited use in applications where the number of data elements is initially not known, and the number grows and shrinks in size during the execution of the application. Additionally, an array is not flexible enough to allow for elements to be rearranged efficiently. These are two major areas where linked lists hold a distinct advantage.

Linked lists are useful in applications where there is a direct sequential ordering of the data elements, access of elements is not at random, dynamic memory allocation and deallocation of data elements are frequently needed, data elements need not be stored in contiguous memory locations, and sequential access to data elements in a forward and/or backward direction is desired.

5.1   List Objects

A generic list data structure is defined in terms of the predecessor-successor relationships of the data elements contained by the structure.

Definition 5.1 *A* list *is an ordered sequential collection of data elements of the same type with a predecessor-successor relationship such that:*

> *(i) A data element with one successor and no predecessor is called the first or* head *data element in the list.*
>
> *(ii) A data element with one predecessor and no successor is called the last or* tail *data element in the list.*
>
> *(iii) Any intermediate data element has both a predecessor and and a successor.*
>
> *(iv) Any intermediate data element in a list is accessed by traversing the list from the first element to the last, or from the last element to the first.*

A list object is specified by an ADT list, a data structure that contains a set of sequential data elements and a set of generalized methods (operations) used for defining, manipulating, and abstracting these data elements. While the internal representation of the data elements may change, the actions on them will not. This is the basis and convenience of abstract data typing. A subset of possible methods on a list object is shown in Table 5.1.

Example List Object Methods

Construct a list object.
Build a list object from a given set of data.
Destroy (delete) a list object.
Check to see if a list object is empty.
Add a data element after a given data element.
Add a data element before a given data element.
Search for a data element by a single key value.
Search for the successor (predecessor) of an element (single key).
Delete a data element identified by a single search key value.
Get a specified attribute using a single search key.
Modify specified attribute using a single search key.
Sort a list object into a specified order using a single search key.
Display (print) a list object.
Get the total number of data elements in a list object.

TABLE 5.1.

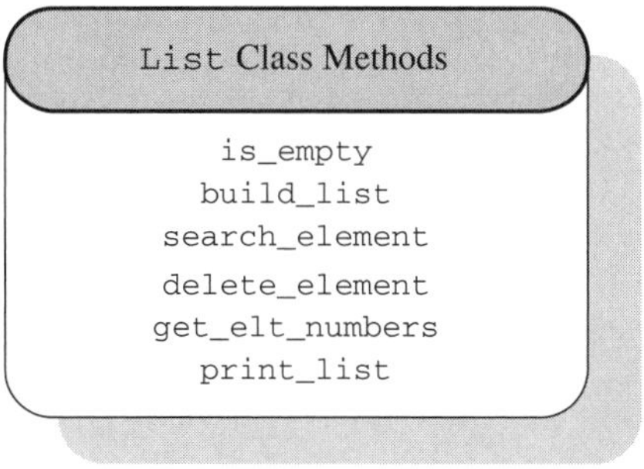

FIGURE 5.1. Public methods for the list class.

A list object is an instance of a derived *implementation specific* class. The *base* class, from which the list object is derived, is implementation unspecific; it provides a set of uniform methods (actions or interfaces) for a list object, which are implemented in the derived class. For the current discussion, a base class List is defined in the file bc_list.h:

```
//  Program: bc_list.h (Abstract Base class for List object)

class List {
  public:
    virtual BOOLEAN is_empty() = 0;
    virtual void    build_list (DATA_TYPE *A) = 0;
    virtual void    search_element (DATA_TYPE srch_key) = 0;
    virtual void    delete_element (DATA_TYPE target_key) = 0;
    virtual int     get_elt_numbers(void) = 0;
    virtual void    print_list(char *hdr) = 0;
};
```

Figure 5.1 shows the List object and its members. The names and arguments for the methods in the base class List and in the derived class must exactly match each other.

An implementation specific class is created from the abstract base class with a statement of the form:

```
class <implementation_specific_class>:public List{
    //  ...
};
```

A list object list_obj is created by instancing a selected implementation specific class:

```
<implementation_specific_class>  list_obj;
```

5.2   Implementation Specific Linked List Classes

Several OOP implementations for a list object are presented as implementation specific classes.

The lists presented in this chapter fall into one of four structural categories:

- *Singly linked list* — each node (element) contains a single link that connects the node to its successor node. The list is efficient at *forward* traversals.

- *Doubly linked list* — each node contains two links, one to its predecessor node and the other to its successor node. The list is efficient at *forward* as well as *backward* traversal.

- *Singly linked circular list* — a singly linked list for which the last element (tail) is linked to the first element (head) such that the list may be traversed in a circular (ring) fashion.

- *Doubly linked circular list* — a doubly linked list for which the last element is linked to the first and vice versa. As such, the list may be traversed in a circular (ring) fashion in both a *forward* and *backward* direction.

For each of these four types of list structures, one may choose either an array-based implementation or a pointer-based implementation. Fundamentally, these implementations differ in the way memory is allocated for the data elements, how the elements are linked together, and how they are accessed. More specifically, the implementations presented here are categorized as either

- those that employ fixed array memory allocation, or

- those that employ dynamic memory allocation and pointers.

5.3   Array-Based Linked Lists

Linked lists that are implemented using fixed-size array memory typically exist in two varieties, distinguished by the manner in which the elements are stored in the array:

- *Sequential element storage* — predecessor and/or successor links are *implicit* to the array structure.

- *Nonsequential element storage* — predecessor and/or successor links are *explicit* to the array structure, specified in terms of array indexes.

LIST

list[0]	elem_1
list[1]	elem_2
	$\vdots$
list[i−1]	elem_i−1
list[i]	elem_i
list[i+1]	elem_i+1
	$\vdots$
list[LAST]	last_element
	$\vdots$
list[LIST_SIZE−1]	

FIGURE 5.2. Array-based list with data elements stored sequentially.

In the sequential storage scheme, the elements of an ordered list are arranged in the exact consecutive order as the locations of the array. A key feature of this sequential storage scheme is that *the predecessor and successor indexes of each data element need not be stored as a part of the data record for each element*. These indexes are *implicit* since the list elements are stored in successive elements of the array. Traversing such a list amounts to sequentially indexing the array structure. However, if elements are to be inserted into or deleted from the list, the existing elements must be shifted around. This process is not efficient.

Consider a list array, list[], of size LIST_SIZE. The maximum number of elements that may be stored in this list corresponds to LIST_SIZE. The successor and predecessor of each element, if either or both exist, is easily referenced in terms of the index of the array. Figure 5.2 illustrates this list using sequential element storage. The following items characterize the predecessor-successor relationship of the data elements:

- list[0] has no predecessor; its successor is list[1].

- list[LIST_SIZE-1] has no successor; its predecessor is list[LIST_SIZE-2].

- For any i, 1 <= i <= LIST_SIZE-1, list[i] has predecessor list[i-1], and successor list[i+1].

A nonsequential storage scheme, on the other hand, relies on explicit storage of predecessor and successor indexes. Insert and delete operations are more efficient in this case, as elements need not be moved. The link indexes are updated instead. This scheme requires additional memory for each element.

For example, the predecessor and successor for any element, say x, in a list array `list2[]`, may be stored anywhere in the array as long as their indexes are kept relative to x. Since this is true for all elements in `list2[]`, each data element is viewed as a record of the form:

P[0]	P[1]	P[2]		P[n−1]	P[n]
P_0	P_1	P_2	...	P_{n-1}	P_n

To implement the nonsequential format, each element may be implemented with the `struct` construct:

```
struct  LIST_ELEMENT {
     DATA_TYPE   1st_data;
     INDEX       predecessor;
     INDEX       successor;
};
LIST_ELEMENT  *list;
```

For both array-based schemes, sequential and nonsequential, the number of elements in the list is limited to the fixed size of the array.

The OOP implementation of an array-based list using the nonsequential scheme is left as an exercise. In the next section, we consider the fixed-size list using implicit links.

5.3.1 OOP for Array-Based Linked Lists with Implicit Links

An OOP implementation in C++ of an array list employing the sequential storage strategy depicted in Figure 5.2 is presented as **Code 5.1**. The implementation specific class, `Ary_List`, is contained in the header file `class_Ary_List_def.h`:

```
class Ary_List : public List {
  private:
     DATA_TYPE *list;
     int  LIST_SIZE;
     int  LAST;  // Counter for last element in list
     int  search_element1(DATA_TYPE srch_key);

     //  Declare interface routines as "public"
  public:
     Ary_List (int list_sz);
     ~Ary_List();
     BOOLEAN is_empty() { return (LAST == NIL);}
     BOOLEAN chk_full_list() {return (LAST == LIST_SIZE - 1);}
     void    build_list (DATA_TYPE *);
```

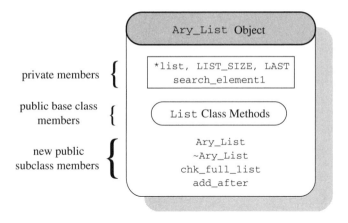

FIGURE 5.3. Ary-List object.

```
        void     search_element (DATA_TYPE srch_key);
        void     add_after (DATA_TYPE elt_after,
                            DATA_TYPE new_elt);
        void     delete_element (DATA_TYPE target_key);
        int      get_elt_numbers(void);
        void     print_list (char *hdr);
    };
```

The `Ary_List` class is derived from the base class `List`. It contains an array size `LIST_SIZE`, data stored in an array, and a set of operations derived from the `List` class as well as methods specific to the array implementation. Its members `list`, `LIST_SIZE`, and `LAST` are declared `private` so that these members are not accessible to the outside of this class, and thereby these are protected from corruption caused by any unauthorized function. The interface routines that are members of the same class `Ary_List` are authorized to manipulate these private data. These interface routines are declared `public` so that any function that is not a member of the `Ary_List` class can send messages to `Ary_List`-type objects by calling these public routines. Note that `DATA_TYPE` could have been made a `private` member of `Ary_List` class to achieve tighter protection. Figure 5.3 depicts an array-based list object.

Class `Ary_List` defines a type of array-based list objects. An object `alist_obj`, an instance of `Ary_List` is declared in `main()` for a list of seven elements as follows:

```
    Ary_List alist_obj(7);
```

5.3.2   ADDING AN ELEMENT AFTER A GIVEN ELEMENT

For the array-based list, a new element new_elt is added after a given element, after_elt using the following steps:

Algorithm: Add an Element After Another

Step 1. Search for after_elt in list[]. If search is not successful, return; otherwise, assume i is the array index for elt_after, i.e., list[i] = elt_after, and proceed to Step 2.

Step 2. Check whether the list is full. If it is full, return; otherwise proceed to Step 3.

Step 3. Make space for new_elt; move list[LAST], ..., list[i] downward to respectively list[LAST+1], ..., list[i + 1].

Step 4. Insert new_elt: list[i + 1] = new_elt.

Step 5. Increment LAST counter: LAST = LAST + 1.

   In **Code 5.1**, the public member function add_after() of the class Ary_List implements this algorithm. It calls search_element1(), a private member function of the Ary_List class. Note that a similar function for inserting before a given element can be written; this is left as an exercise.

5.3.3   DELETING AN ELEMENT FROM AN ARRAY LIST

For the array-based list, a specified element target_elt is deleted using the following steps:

Algorithm: Delete an Element

Step 1. Search for target_elt in list[]. If search is not successful, return; otherwise, assume i is the array index for target_elt, i.e., list[i] = target_elt, and proceed to Step 2.

Step 2. Overwrite list[i] by its successor list[i + 1] in the following manner: move up the list elements list[i + 1], ..., list[LAST] to respectively list[i], ..., list[LAST - 1].

Step 3. Decrement LAST counter: LAST = LAST - 1.

   The implementation of this deletion process is left as an exercise.

Code 5.1

```
//
//   Code 5.1
//   Program:  Ary_List.c++
//   Purpose:  Object-Oriented implementation of
//             an array list of character data.
//
#include <stdio.h>
typedef    int    BOOLEAN;
typedef    char   DATA_TYPE;  // Element's data type
const      int NIL  = -1;     // For no next or prev
extern     LIST_PTR;
#include   "bc_list.h"        // For base class
//  Define class "Ary_List" for array list
//  with the abstract base class "List"
#include   "class_Ary_List_def.h"

//   Ary_List():
//     Constructor for array based list
//
Ary_List::Ary_List (int list_sz)
{
    // Allocate memory space for array list[list_sz]
    list = new DATA_TYPE[LIST_SIZE = list_sz];
    LAST = NIL;
}

//    ~Ary_List():
//      Destructor for array based list
//
Ary_List::~Ary_List ()
{
   delete []list;
}

//   build_list():
//     Build the initial list object from a given string.
//
void  Ary_List::build_list (DATA_TYPE *string)
{
   while (*string != '\0')
      list[++LAST] = *string++;
}

//   search_element1():
//     Find an element specified by its srch_key
//     in an array based list. Return the index
//     of array list if found; otherwise NIL.
//
int  Ary_List::search_element1(DATA_TYPE  srch_key)
{
   for (int j = 0; j <= LAST; j++)
      if (srch_key == list[j])
```

```
            return (j); // Return index of the element
        printf("\n Element %c not found\n", srch_key);
        return (NIL);
    }

    void Ary_List::search_element(DATA_TYPE  srch_key)
    {
        if (search_element1(srch_key) != NIL)
            printf("\n Element is found in list \n");
    }

    //  add_after():
    //    Insert an element after the specified
    //    element in the array based list
    //
    void Ary_List::add_after (DATA_TYPE  after_elt,
                              DATA_TYPE  new_elt)
    {
        // search for 'after_elt'
        int i = search_element1 (after_elt);
        if (i != NIL) {  // 'after_elt' is in list[]
            if (chk_full_list())
                return;    // List is full
            // Make room for new element
            for (int j = LAST; j > i; j--)
                list[j + 1] = list[j];
            // Insert 'new_elt' in list[i + 1]
            list[i + 1] = new_elt;
            // Increment LAST for one additional element
            LAST++;
        }
    }

    void Ary_List::delete_element (DATA_TYPE target_key)
    {
        printf("\n delete_element: Exercise !! \n");
    }

    int Ary_List::get_elt_numbers(void)
    {
        printf("\n get_elt_numbers: Exercise !! \n");
        return (0);  // To avoid compilation error
    }

    //  print_list ():
    //    Print a header and elements list[0],
    //    ..., list[LAST] in the list object.
    //
    void Ary_List::print_list (char *hdr)
    {
        if (!is_empty()) {
            printf(" List %s is:  ", hdr);
            for (int j = 0; j <= LAST; ++j)
                printf(" %c ", list[j]);
```

```
        printf("\n");
    }
    else
        printf("\n List is empty \n");
}

//  main():
/      Test driver for Object-Oriented
/      implementation of an ADT array list
//
void main(void)
{
    // Declare an object of the "Ary_List" class
    // and set the size of array to 7
    Ary_List  alist_obj(7);

    printf("\n** OOP IMPLEMENTATION %s \n",
           "OF AN ARRAY LIST **");
    alist_obj.build_list ("BALORI");
    alist_obj.print_list ("before inserting \'L\'");
    alist_obj.add_after ('L', 'L');
    alist_obj.print_list ("after inserting \'L\' ");
}
```

Code 5.1 for an OOP implementation of an array-based list object produces this output:

```
** OOP IMPLEMENTATION OF AN ARRAY LIST **
  List before inserting 'L' is:    B  A  L  O  R  I
  List after inserting 'L'  is:    B  A  L  L  O  R  I
```

The array-based list implemented in **Code 5.1** has a couple of general deficiencies. First, the list implements a sequential element storage scheme, and as such, its insertion and deletion procedures require a physical movement of the data elements. This process is inefficient.

Second, as with any array implementation, the size of the array is fixed. In **Code 5.1** the object `alist_obj` is declared with the size of its data area, which is initialized to 7. This limits the list in two ways:

- The growth of the list object cannot exceed the initially declared and allocated size of the array.

- Memory space is wasted if the list does not fully occupy the allocated space.

5.4   Pointer-Based Linked Lists

In this and subsequent sections, we implement pointer-based lists employing C++ pointers to establish the links between data elements. In general, these implementations are identified as those that

- employ dynamic memory allocation, and

- have explicitly specified predecessor and/or successor links using pointer variables.

In a pointer-based scheme the size of the list may shrink and grow as required. Elements are dynamically allocated from memory and linked to successor and (or) predecessor elements by explicitly containing the addresses of such elements.

In Figure 5.4 four linked lists are depicted. These lists are either singly or doubly linked and differ in their use of head and tail pointers (head_ptr and tail_ptr). Figure 5.4(a) shows a singly linked list with a head pointer and no tail pointer while Figure 5.4(b) shows a singly linked list with both head and tail pointers present. Doubly linked lists, one with a head pointer only and another with both head and tail pointers, are depicted in Figure 5.4(c) and Figure 5.4(d), respectively.

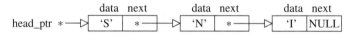

(a) Singly linked list with head pointer

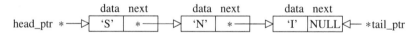

(b) Singly linked list with head and tail pointers

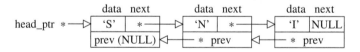

(c) Doubly linked list with head pointer

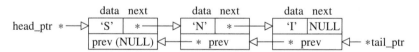

(d) Doubly linked list with head and tail pointers

FIGURE 5.4. Pointer-based linked lists.

For the singly linked lists depicted in Figure 5.4 we find that each data element contains two fields, the data contained in the node, labeled data, and the pointer to the successor element of the current element, labeled next. The elements of the doubly linked lists contain the same fields plus an additional pointer to the predecessor element of the current element, labeled prev.

Notice that for all the linked lists depicted in Figure 5.4, the element with a data field 'I' and a next field with a value of NULL is called the last element. Thus, the end of a singly or doubly linked list is determined by the NULL value of the next field of an element in the list. It follows that an empty list contains NULL values for head_ptr and tail_ptr.

For circularly linked lists, the concept of a tail (or last) data element does not apply. For these types of linked lists it is appropriate to speak of a head pointer only. These structures will be considered in a later section.

5.4.1 NON-OOP IMPLEMENTATION OF THE SINGLY LINKED LIST

In the following, a simple non-OOP implementation of a singly linked list object is given. This simple approach will provide motivation for using an OOP approach.

For the singly linked list in Figure 5.4(a), a data element is defined by the following structure:

```
typedef int     DATA_TYPE;
typedef struct SLIST_ELEMENT {
    DATA_TYPE      data;
    SLIST_ELEMENT  *next;
} *LIST_PTR;
```

For simplicity, there are three data elements elem_1 (first element), elem_2, and elem_3 (last element) of type SLIST_ELEMENT, head_ptr of type LIST_PTR pointing to the first element elem_1. As shown below in **Code 5.2**, the singly linked list is formed by making elem_2 the successor of elem_1, and elem_3 the successor of elem_2. This sort of chaining is done by manually using the single link variable next. The printing of the first element is done using head_ptr, and the next two successive elements are printed using the links head_ptr->next and head_ptr->next->next.

Code 5.2

```
//  Program:  simple_slist.c++
//  Purpose:  Implementation of a singly linked list
//            by simply linking its each element
//            (character-type data) using pointers.
```

```
//
#include  <stdio.h>
typedef int DATA_TYPE;  // Data type for list's element
typedef struct SLIST_ELEMENT {
    DATA_TYPE       data;
    SLIST_ELEMENT   *next;
} *LIST_PTR;

void main(void)
{
    // Declare and initialize elements
    static SLIST_ELEMENT  elem_1 = { 1, NULL},
                          elem_2 = {-3, NULL},
                          elem_3 = {10, NULL};
    LIST_PTR  head_ptr = &elem_1;

    // Form the singly linked list by making
    // 'elem_2' the successor of 'elem_1', &
    // 'elem_3' the successor of 'elem_2'. This is
    // done by using the single link variable, 'next'.

    elem_1.next = &elem_2;
    elem_2.next = &elem_3;

    // Print the singly linked list
    printf("\n ** A Simple Singly Linked List **\n");
    printf("\n The list is: ");
    while (head_ptr != NULL) {
       printf(" %d -> ", head_ptr->data);
       head_ptr = head_ptr->next;
    }
    printf("NULL \n");
}
```

Code 5.2 for a simple singly linked list produces this output:

```
** A Simple Singly Linked List **

The list is:  1 ->  -3 ->  10 -> NULL
```

The deficiencies of the above simple approach in **Code 5.2** are:

- It does not conceal data, next, and head_ptr.

- It is not designed to handle a large number of the list's data elements.

- It does not have a capability of dynamically increasing and decreasing the number of data elements in the list.

To conceal the data elements and compact the data elements and operations into a single entity, an OOP approach is required. Dynamic list sizing can be accomplished with the dynamic memory allocation and deallocation techniques in C++. In particular, one may employ the `new` operator or `malloc()` call for allocating memory space, and the `delete` operator or `free()` call for deallocating memory space. For example,

```
LIST_PTR elem_1_ptr = new SLIST_ELEMENT;
elem_1_ptr->data = 1;
elem_1_ptr->next = NULL;
delete elem_1_ptr;
```

As pointed out in Chapter 2, the use of the dynamic memory allocation may lead to a problem with memory leaks. This possibility is well noted and resolved in the OOP approach shown below in **Code 5.3**.

5.4.2 OOP IMPLEMENTATION OF THE SINGLY LINKED LIST

As discussed above, the member fields of the `SLIST_ELEMENT`-type data structure are not hidden from users or client programs. In the OOP implementation, the data-hiding is performed by using the C++ `class` construct. From the ADT definition of list, the `Singly_Linked_List`-type object is identified. This list object contains list elements as data and ADT list operations as methods. Each list element contains a data field, and a link field. Then, in C++ the singly linked list object is defined by the following `Singly_Linked_List` class in the header file `slist.h`:

```
class  Singly_Linked_List : public List {
  private:
    typedef struct SLIST_ELEMENT {
        DATA_TYPE       data;
        SLIST_ELEMENT  *next;
    } *LIST_PTR;
    LIST_PTR  head_ptr; // Ptr to first element in list
    void      init_slist() { head_ptr = NULL;}};
  protected:
    LIST_PTR  search_element1(LIST_PTR, DATA_TYPE);
    LIST_PTR  search_previous(LIST_PTR, DATA_TYPE);
    LIST_PTR  get_head(void) { return head_ptr; }
    BOOLEAN   is_sublist_empty(LIST_PTR lst_ptr);
// Declare the interface routines as "public"
  public:
    Singly_Linked_List() { init_slist(); }
    ~Singly_Linked_List();

    BOOLEAN   is_empty() {return (head_ptr == NULL);}
    void      build_list (DATA_TYPE *A);
    void      search_element (DATA_TYPE srch_key);
    void      add_after (DATA_TYPE elt_after,
```

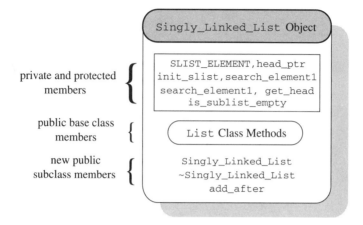

FIGURE 5.5. Singly_Linked_List object.

```
                         DATA_TYPE new_elt);
    void     delete_element (DATA_TYPE target_key);
    int      get_elt_numbers(void);
    void     print_list(char *hdr);
};
```

The data members data, next, and head_ptr, and the member function init_slist() of the class Singly_Linked_List are declared private so that these members are made hidden and are not accessible to the outside of this class, and thereby these are protected from corruption caused by any unauthorized function or client program. (These members could have been declared protected to allow access to any derived class of the class Singly_Linked_List.) Since an improper call of init_slist() is unsafe and may cause a memory leak, init_slist() is not public. Search_element1(), search_previous() are declared protected members for any subclass of the Singly_Linked_List class. The interface routines of this class, are authorized to manipulate these private data. These interface routines are declared public so that any client function, which is not a member of the Singly_Linked_List class, can send messages to Singly_Linked_List-type objects by calling these public routines. The inline member function get_head() is defined to allow read-only access of the private data member head_ptr. Note that to allow reusability of the Singly_Linked_List class, the template keyword (in C++ 3.0) may be used for respecifying DATA_TYPE (see Chapter 2). Figure 5.5 depicts a Singly_Linked_List-type object.

Class Singly_Linked_List defines a type of singly linked list objects. An object slist_obj of this type is declared in main() as follows:

```
Singly_Linked_List slist_obj;
```

In the next sections, we discuss some of the algorithms that may be employed to implement the interface routines (methods) of this class.

5.4.3 BUILDING A SINGLY LINKED LIST

An algorithm for building a singly linked list object from a given string is outlined with the steps below:

Algorithm: Build a Singly Linked List

Step 1. Declare the data type SLIST_ELEMENT, and the head_ptr, and new_ptr of type LIST_PTR.

Step 2. Allocate memory for a new element of type SLIST_ELEMENT using the new operator; the address of the new element is new_ptr.

Step 3. Iteratively create the first (head) element and the successive elements of the singly linked list object in steps 3.1 and 3.4.

Step 3.1. new_ptr->data = string_data;

new_ptr->next = NULL;

Step 3.2. If the singly linked list object does not have any elements (i.e., head_ptr is NULL), do:

head_ptr = new_ptr; tmp_ptr = new_ptr;

Step 3.3. Using the new operator, allocate memory spaces for the next elements pointed to by new_ptr. Connect it with its previous element by the following statements:

tmp_ptr->next = new_ptr;

tmp_ptr = tmp_ptr->next;

Step 4. Repeat until there is no more input for the element.

These steps are implemented by the nonrecursive function build_list() in **Code 5.3**. The last element in the singly linked list object has a NULL value for next pointer because it does not have any successor.

5.4.4 INSERTING AN ELEMENT IN A SINGLY LINKED LIST

The algorithm employed for adding or inserting an element in a singly linked list varies depending on where the incoming element is to be inserted. The location for insertion can be:

- the head (first) element,

- the tail (last) element,

- before a specified element, or

- after a specified element.

Adding an element at the head of the list is a subcase of adding an element before a specified one. Likewise, adding an element at the tail of the list is a subcase of adding one after another. To add an element after another efficiently, a pointer to the last element, `tail_ptr`, needs to be added and maintained in `build_slist()`.

The operation of adding one element before another specified element is shown in Figure 5.6. The intent is to add an element 'N' before the first encountered element containing the data 'I'. Figure 5.6(b) shows how the links are adjusted to make the new element a member of the list. Figure 5.4(a) is the final form of the singly linked list after this operation. The steps are outlined as follows:

Algorithm: Add an Element Before Another

Step 1. Test to see if the singly linked list is empty; if yes, return. Otherwise, go to Step 2.

Step 2. Call `search_element1()` to find the given element (e.g., 'I') that is first encountered in the singly linked list. If it is found, assume that `element_ptr` of type `LIST_PTR` points to the given element, and go to Step 3. If it is not found, return.

Step 3. Using the `new` operator, get the address of memory space for the new element, which is set to `new_ptr`, i.e., `new_ptr =` address of memory space for new element.

Step 4. If the given element (e.g., 'I') is the first element in the list (i.e., `element_ptr == head_ptr`), make the new element the first element in the following steps:

Step 4.1. `new_ptr->next = element_ptr;`

Step 4.2. `head_ptr = new_ptr;`

Step 4.3. `return;`

Step 5. Calling `search_previous()`, find the previous element (e.g., 'S') of the given element (e.g., 'I'), which is pointed to by `previous_ptr`.

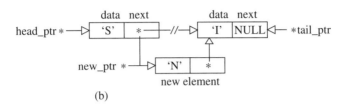

(a)

(b)

FIGURE 5.6. (a) Singly linked list before adding 'N' before 'I'. (b) Adjusting links during addition of 'N' before 'I'.

Step 6. Add the element between elements 'S' and 'I' by adjusting the next link field for the element 'S':

Step 6.1. `new_ptr->next  = element_ptr;`

Step 6.2. `previous_ptr->next = new_ptr;`

Step 6.3. `return;`

Of note is the fact that these steps do not require any physical movement of the elements. Instead, links are adjusted, as in steps 4 and 6. As pointed out earlier, this is a major advantage of the pointer-based list implementations.

The above steps for inserting an element before another specified element may be easily modified for inserting an element after a specified element. In the latter case, steps 4 and 5, the process of searching for the previous element of a given element, would not be necessary.

The actual implementations of the "add-before" and "add-after" algorithms are left as exercises for the reader.

5.4.5 Deleting an Element in a Singly Linked List

The process of deleting a specified element from a singly linked list is straightforward and is illustrated in Figure 5.7. For this example, the element with the data 'I' is to be deleted. Figure 5.7(a) shows the initial state of the list. In Figure 5.7(b) the link to the element containing 'I' is broken and the element is deleted using the `delete` operator. In **Code**

5.3, `delete_element()` implements the deletion algorithm for which the steps are outlined as follows:

Algorithm: Delete an Element

Step 1. If the singly linked list object is empty, return.

Step 2. Check to see if the element to be deleted (e.g., with value 'I'), is the first one in the list object. If it is, delete it and make its successor the first element in the list. Do:

`element_ptr = head_ptr->next; delete head_ptr;`

`head_ptr = element_ptr; return;`

Otherwise, go to Step 3.

Step 3. Search for the element specified by its search key (e.g., value 'I') in the singly linked list object. If the element to be deleted is found, assume `element_ptr` points to this element, and perform steps 4 through 6; otherwise, return with a message.

Step 4. Search for the predecessor of the element to be deleted pointed to by `element_ptr`. If the search succeeds, `previous_ptr` points to the previous element (e.g., with value 'N'), and perform steps 5 and 6. Otherwise, return.

Step 5. Make the successor of 'I' (element with 'G' and pointed to by `element_ptr->next`) the successor of 'I's previous element (element with 'N' and pointed to by `previous_ptr`), that is,

`previous_ptr->next = element_ptr->next;`

Step 6. Free the memory space allocated to the element to be deleted (e.g., element with value 'I'):

`delete element_ptr;`

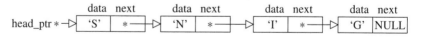

(a) Singly linked list before deleting 'I'.

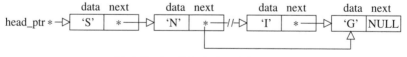

(b) Adjusting links before deleting 'I'.

FIGURE 5.7. Deleting an element from a singly linked list.

5.4.6 METHODS OF THE Singly_Linked_List CLASS

The following functions are all public (i.e., publicly accessible) member functions (interface routines or methods) of the Singly_Linked_List class. These are interface routines to the outside client programs including main(). These routines allow nonmember functions to pass messages (e.g., requests for actions) to the slist_obj object of Singly_Linked_List class. All the member fields are accessible to the member functions of the same Singly_Linked_List class. Consequently it is not necessary to pass the data members data, next, and head_ptr as arguments of these member functions.

Singly_Linked_List(), the constructor and public member function of the Singly_Linked_List class, is automatically called when a class instance (interchangeably used with object or instance) slist_obj of type Singly_Linked_List is declared in main(), and constructed. It calls init_slist() to initialize the object.

~Singly_Linked_List(), the destructor and public member function of the Singly_Linked_List class, is implicitly called in main() before the program exits. It is iteratively implemented. It destroys the entire singly linked list object. First, it calls is_sublist_empty() to check whether the list object pointed to by tmp_ptr (= head_ptr) is empty. For an empty singly linked list object, it sets head_ptr to NULL and returns. For a nonempty list object, the pointer to the successor of the current element pointed to by tmp_ptr is saved in next_ptr, and then frees up the memory space of the current element. It linearly traverses the singly linked list object using the next pointer, and deallocates the memory space by calling the delete operator:

```
delete tmp_ptr;
```

Init_slist() initializes an object of the Singly_Linked_List class. It sets head_ptr to NULL.

Is_empty(), a public member function of Singly_Linked_List class, tests whether an object (e.g., slist_obj) of this class is empty. It returns 1 if head_ptr has the NULL value; otherwise, it returns 0.

Build_list(), an iterative function and a public member function of the Singly_Linked_List, expects an address of a string A. It builds a Singly_Linked_List-type object (e.g., slist_obj) with characters of an array A as data elements. For each character in A, the new operator is used to allocate the memory space of SLIST_ELEMENT type element, pointed to by new_ptr, and new_ptr->data is set to the character. The single link (pointer) field, next of type LIST_PTR, is used to connect the successive elements of the list object. The next field of the last element in the list object has a NULL value because it does not have any successor.

Singly_Linked_List class's public member search_element() calls search_element1(), which is a protected member function of the `Singly_Linked_List` class. It is called by `delete_element()`. The recursive function `search_element1()` has two arguments, the list pointer of type `LIST_PTR`, and `search_key` of type `DATA_TYPE`. It searches for a list element specified by a single search key, `search_key`. It first calls `is_sublist_empty()`. If the list object is empty or no match is found, it prints a message "Element is not found in list." For a nonempty list, it starts the search from the first element, and compares the given `search_key` with the element's key value. If there is a match, it returns a pointer of type `LIST_PTR`; otherwise, it linearly (straight line manner) moves to the next element (successor) using the `next` pointer field, and repeats the comparison process. This repeating process ends if a match or the last element is reached. For its algorithm, see Chapter 7.

`Search_previous()` is a protected member function of the class `Singly_Linked_List`. It is called by `delete_element()` and is implemented as a recursive function. It has two arguments, the list pointer `1st_ptr` of type `LIST_PTR`, and `search_key` of type `DATA_TYPE`. This function searches for the predecessor of a given list element specified by one search key, `search_key`. It successively compares `search_key` with the data value of the next element using `1st_ptr->next`. If there is a match, it returns `1st_ptr`, which points to the previous element of the element with given `search_key`; otherwise, it prints an error message "Previous element is not found in list" and returns `NULL`.

`Delete_element()` is a public member of `Singly_Linked_List` class. If the element to be deleted is the first one in the list object, the function makes its successor the head of the list, and deletes the given element. Otherwise, it calls `search_element1()` to find the given element specified by `search_key`. If the given element is found, it is pointed to by `element_ptr`. The function then calls `search_previous()` which returns `previous_ptr`, a pointer to the predecessor of the given element. It sets `previous_ptr->next` to `element_ptr->next`, and thus breaks the link to the given element (pointed to by `element_ptr`). It then frees up the memory space held by the target element using the `delete` operator.

`Get_elt_numbers()`, a public member of `Singly_Linked_List` class, is an iterative function. When the `Singly_Linked_List`-type object is empty, it returns zero. It returns total number of `SLIST_ELEMENT`-type objects in the singly linked list object.

`Print_list()` is an iterative and a public member function of the `Singly_Linked_List` class. It displays a `Singly_Linked_List`-type object by linearly traversing the list from the first element to the last. The list traversal is aided by the `next` pointer field of each element, which provides connection between successive elements.

`Get_head()`, a protected member function of `Singly_Linked_List` class, provides "read-only" access of private data member `head_ptr` to any class derived from the `Singly_Linked_List` class.

Main(), a client function of the Singly_Linked_List class, instantiates this class's object slist_obj. It calls slist_obj.build_list() to create the slist_obj object from the given string "SNIGDHA". It calls slist_obj.print_list(), slist_obj.delete_element() and slist_obj.get_elt_numbers(). In this manner, main() sends requests for such actions as creating, printing, deleting a specified element, and counting total number of elements, to the object slist_obj. The program's memory is freed by delete str and ~Singly_Linked_List().

Code 5.3

```
//
//   Program:   slist.c++
//   Purpose:   Object-oriented implementation of a singly linked
//              list with a simple data of 'char' type.
//
#include <stdio.h>
typedef    int   BOOLEAN;
typedef    char DATA_TYPE;
#include   "bc_list.h"   // For base class
//   Define a singly linked list type class
//   "Singly_Linked_List" with base class "List"
#include   "slist.h"
//
//   ~Singly_Linked_List():
//      Delete entire singly linked list object and free
//      up its memory spaces (Iterative implementation).
//
Singly_Linked_List::~Singly_Linked_List(void)
{
    LIST_PTR   next_ptr, // pointer to next element
               tmp_ptr;

    tmp_ptr = head_ptr;
    while  (!is_sublist_empty(tmp_ptr)) {
       // Save pointer to next element
       next_ptr = tmp_ptr->next;
       delete tmp_ptr;      // Dispose of its space
       tmp_ptr = next_ptr;
    }
    // Assure 'head_ptr' is not a "dangling pointer"
    head_ptr = NULL;
}

BOOLEAN Singly_Linked_List::is_sublist_empty(
                          LIST_PTR lst_ptr)
{
    return (lst_ptr == NULL);
}

//
```

```
//   build_list():
//      Build a singly linked list object from a
//      given string of variable length.
//      (Iterative implementation)
//
void Singly_Linked_List::build_list(DATA_TYPE *str)
{
    LIST_PTR tmp_ptr, new_ptr;

    while (*str != '\0') {
        new_ptr       =   new SLIST_ELEMENT;
        new_ptr->data =   *str++ ;
        new_ptr->next =   NULL;
        if (head_ptr == NULL) {
            head_ptr = new_ptr;
            tmp_ptr = new_ptr;
        }
        else {
            tmp_ptr->next =   new_ptr;
            tmp_ptr = tmp_ptr->next;
        }
    }
}


//   search_element1():
//      Search for an element identified by its key
//      'search_key' (search data) in a list object,
//      pointed to by 'lst_ptr'. Return the pointer
//      if found; otherwise return NULL.
//      (Recursive method)
//
Singly_Linked_List::LIST_PTR
Singly_Linked_List::search_element1(
            LIST_PTR lst_ptr, DATA_TYPE search_key)
{
    if (!is_sublist_empty(lst_ptr)) {
        if (search_key == lst_ptr->data)
            return (lst_ptr);
        search_element1 (lst_ptr->next, search_key);
    }
    else {
      printf("\n search_element: %s \n",
             "Element is not found in list");
      return (NULL);
    }
}

void
Singly_Linked_List::search_element(DATA_TYPE search_key)
{
    if (search_element1 (head_ptr, search_key) != NULL)
      printf("\n Element is found %s \n",
             "in singly linked list");
}
```

```
//   search_previous():
//     Search for an element in a singly linked
//     list object given its data as key 'search_key',
//     and return a pointer to the previous element
//     (predecessor) if found. Return NULL if the
//     given data element is not found or the first
//     element in the list. (Recursive method)
//
Singly_Linked_List::LIST_PTR
Singly_Linked_List::search_previous (LIST_PTR lst_ptr,
                                     DATA_TYPE search_key)
{
    if (lst_ptr != NULL) {
      if (search_key == lst_ptr->next->data)
        return (lst_ptr);
      search_previous (lst_ptr->next, search_key);
    }
    else {
      printf("\n search_previous: Previous %s \n",
             "element is not found in list");
      return (NULL);
    }
}

//   delete_element():
//     Delete an element in a singly linked list
//     object given its data as the search key.
//
void
Singly_Linked_List::delete_element(DATA_TYPE search_key)
{
      LIST_PTR   element_ptr, previous_ptr;

      // Check to see if the given element is the
      // first one in the list object.
      if ((head_ptr != NULL) &&
          (head_ptr->data == search_key)) {
        element_ptr = head_ptr->next;
        delete head_ptr;
        head_ptr = element_ptr;
      }
      if ((element_ptr = search_element1 (head_ptr,
                          search_key)) != NULL) {
        previous_ptr = search_previous (head_ptr,
                                        search_key);
        previous_ptr->next = element_ptr->next;
        delete element_ptr;
      }
}

//   get_elt_numbers():
//     Get elements in a singly linked list object.
//     (Non-recursive, that is, iterative procedure)
```

```
//
int Singly_Linked_List::get_elt_numbers(void)
{
    LIST_PTR  tmp_ptr = head_ptr;
    int      element_numbers = 0;

    while (tmp_ptr != NULL) {
        ++element_numbers;
        tmp_ptr = tmp_ptr->next;
    }
    return (element_numbers);
}

//  print_list():
//     Print the elements of a singly linked list
//     object starting from head elem to tail.
//
void Singly_Linked_List::print_list(char *hdr)
{
    LIST_PTR  tmp_ptr = head_ptr;

    printf("\n List %s is:\n  ", hdr);
    while (tmp_ptr != NULL) {
        printf("%c -> ", tmp_ptr->data);
        tmp_ptr = tmp_ptr->next;
    }
    printf("NULL \n");
}

//  main():
//     Test driver for OOP IMPLEMENTATION
//     OF SINGLY LINKED LIST
//
void main(void)
{
    Singly_Linked_List  slist_obj;
    char *str = "SNIGDHA";        // Input string

    printf("\n ** OOP IMPLEMENTATION %s \n",
            "OF SINGLY LINKED LIST ** " );
    slist_obj.build_list (str);
    slist_obj.print_list("");
    printf(" %s in this list object is: %d \n",
      "Number of elements", slist_obj.get_elt_numbers());
    slist_obj.delete_element ('D');
    slist_obj.print_list("after deleting \'D\'");
    printf(" %s in this list object is: %d \n",
      "Number of elements", slist_obj.get_elt_numbers());
    delete str;
}
```

Code 5.3 for a singly linked list object yields this output:

```
** OOP IMPLEMENTATION OF SINGLY LINKED LIST **

List  is:
 S -> N -> I -> G -> D -> H -> A -> NULL
Number of elements in this list object is: 7

List after deleting 'D' is:
 S -> N -> I -> G -> H -> A -> NULL
Number of elements in this list object is: 6
```

Although the above OOP implementation of a list object using a singly linked list data structure displays the advantage of dynamic memory allocation of the list elements, the following deficiencies still exist:

- The list traversal is linear. That is, one may only start from the head of the list, and move forward only one element at a time using the link field next.

- Random access to any list element except the first (pointed to by head_ptr) and the last (pointed to by tail_ptr, if used) is not possible.

- Search for any intermediate element must always start from the head of the list.

- The insert and delete operations are complex and time-consuming.

- In the worst-case performance, for a singly linked list object containing n data elements, it takes $O(n)$ time to search for an element in the list object. This makes singly linked list access inefficient.

- While taking advantage of dynamic memory allocation, programming errors such as dangling pointers and memory leaks may occur.

5.4.7 OOP IMPLEMENTATION OF THE DOUBLY LINKED LIST

From Figure 5.4(d), a doubly linked list object contains a set of data elements, head_ptr, and tail_ptr; each data element is a data structure that contains a data field, data, and two link fields, next (a pointer to the successor) and prev (a pointer to the predecessor). Thus, an element in a doubly linked list is a record of the form:

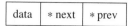

data	* next	* prev

In the following, a simple approach is used to implement a doubly linked
list object. This simple approach will motivate us to use an OOP approach
for the same. The two pointer fields, next and prev, are useful in traversing the doubly linked list in the forward direction (i.e., from the head to
tail) and in the backward direction (i.e., from the tail to head). The change
of direction of the traversal from any intermediate element is also possible.

In an OOP, a doubly linked list object has element objects defined by
DLIST_ELEMENT class:

```
typedef char    DATA_TYPE;
class DLIST_ELEMENT {
  private:
    DATA_TYPE data;
    DLIST_ELEMENT   *next,
                    *prev;
    //  Declare "Doubly_Linked_List" class
    //  as a "friend" of this class.
    friend   class Doubly_Linked_List;
  public:
    //  For read-only access to others
    DLIST_ELEMENT   *get_next() {return next;};
    DLIST_ELEMENT   *get_prev() {return prev;};
};
typedef  DLIST_ELEMENT *LIST_PTR;
```

The pointers to the next and previous element objects in a doubly linked
list object are respectively next and prev of type LIST_PTR. In the
DLIST_ELEMENT class, private is used to hide the data members data,
next, and prev from any unauthorized access. Doubly_Linked_List
class (shown below) needs to share these data members as resources, therefore it is declared as a friend of the DLIST_ELEMENT class and as a subclass
of the abstract base class List. This means that any member function of
Doubly_Linked_List class inherits the privilege to access and manipulate these data members. Doubly_Linked_List class is defined in the
header file dlist.h.

```
class  Doubly_Linked_List : public List {
  private:
    LIST_PTR head_ptr,
             tail_ptr;
    void     init_dlist(void);
    LIST_PTR search_elt_obj (LIST_PTR, DATA_TYPE);
    BOOLEAN  chk_empty_dlist (LIST_PTR);
    void     print_dlist_obj_forward(void);
  //  Declare its member functions as public interfaces
```

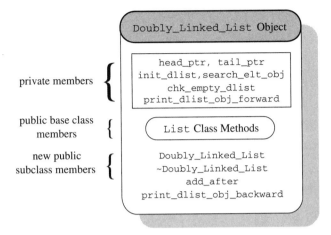

FIGURE 5.8. Doubly_Linked_List object.

```
//  so that outside world including main() can send
//  messages to objects of "Doubly_Linked_List" class.
public:
   Doubly_Linked_List() {init_dlist();}
   ~Doubly_Linked_List();
   BOOLEAN is_empty() {return (head_ptr == NULL);}
   void build_list (DATA_TYPE *);
   void search_element (DATA_TYPE srch_key);
   void delete_element (DATA_TYPE target_key);
   void add_after (DATA_TYPE elt_after, DATA_TYPE new_elt);
   int  get_elt_numbers(void);
   void print_list(char *hdr)
        { printf("\n List %s is:\n  ", hdr);
          print_dlist_obj_forward();}
   void print_dlist_obj_backward(void);
};
```

The DLIST_ELEMENT class represents the element objects in the doubly
linked list, and the Doubly_Linked_List class represents the doubly
linked list objects. The head_ptr and tail_ptr are private members.
These pointers respectively point to the first and the last element objects
in the Doubly_Linked_List type object. This object is shown in Figure
5.8.

The last element in a doubly linked list is identified by the NULL value
of next pointer field.

For an empty doubly linked list object, head_ptr and tail_ptr have
NULL values. When Doubly_Linked_List-type list object dlist_obj
has two DLIST_ELEMENT-type objects, the two classes are related as shown
in Figure 5.9.

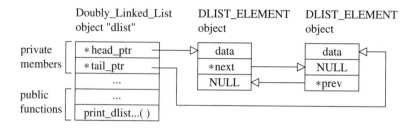

FIGURE 5.9. A doubly linked list object with two element objects.

5.4.8   ADDING AN ELEMENT IN A DOUBLY LINKED LIST

As with a singly linked list object, adding (inserting) a new element object in a doubly linked list is divided into four groups. These are

- at the head,

- at the tail,

- before a specified element, and

- after a specified element.

Note that the last last two groups are subcases of the first two.

The operation of adding a new element after an existing specified element is illustrated in Figure 5.10. In this example, an element with data 'N' is to be added after the first encountered element with data 'S'. Figure 5.10(a) shows the list prior to the insertion while Figure 5.10(b) shows how the links are adjusted to make the new element a member of the list. Figure 5.4(d), previously shown, is the final form of the doubly linked list after this operation.

Figure 5.10(a) shows that the element with 'S' has its successor element with 'I', and the element with 'I' has the predecessor element with 'S'. The new element with 'N' is pointed to by new_ptr. Figure 5.10(b) shows the new element with 'I' becomes the successor of the element with 'S' and the predecessor of the element with 'I'. This is done by adjusting the two pointer fields next and prev of the three elements with 'S', 'N', and 'I'.

Algorithm: Add an Element After Another

Step 1. Test to see if the doubly linked list is empty; if yes, return. Otherwise, go to Step 2.

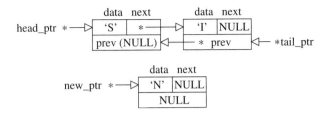

(a) Doubly linked list before adding 'N' after 'S'.

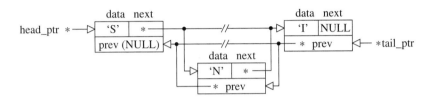

(b) Adjusting links during addition of 'N' after 'S'.

FIGURE 5.10. Adding an element in a doubly linked list.

Step 2. Call `search_element()` to find the given element (e.g., 'S') that is first encountered in the doubly linked list. If it is found, assume that `element_ptr` of type `LIST_PTR` points to the given element, and go to Step 3. If it is not found, return.

Step 3. Using the `new` operator, get the address of memory space for new element of type `DLIST_ELEMENT`, which is set to `new_ptr`; `new_ptr` = address of memory space for new element.

Step 4. Connect the new element (pointed to by `new_ptr`) to the doubly linked list by adjusting the link fields `next` and `prev` for the new element, the given element, and its successor. Perform 4.1 through 4.4 in the following order:

Step 4.1. `new_ptr->next = element_ptr->next;`

Step 4.2. `new_ptr->prev = element_ptr;`

Step 4.3. `element_ptr->next->prev = new_ptr;`

Step 4.4. `element_ptr->next = new_ptr;`

Step 5. `return;`

Notice that the `next` and `prev` links are simply adjusted in Step 4. Thus adding a new element with the aid of pointers did not require any

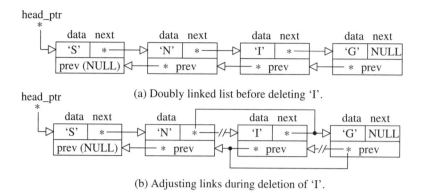

(a) Doubly linked list before deleting 'I'.

(b) Adjusting links during deletion of 'I'.

FIGURE 5.11. Deleting an element from a doubly linked list.

physical movement of any elements in the doubly linked list. Because of the back-link `prev`, there is no need of finding the previous element even for the "add-before" operation in a doubly linked list. The codes for both the "add-after" and "add-before" operations on a doubly linked list object are left as exercises.

5.4.9 DELETING AN ELEMENT IN A DOUBLY LINKED LIST

To illustrate the operation of deleting a given element in the doubly linked list, Figure 5.11(a) shows an element with key value 'I' to be deleted. Figure 5.11(b) shows how the links are adjusted to make the next element of 'I' as the next element of 'N', which is the previous element of the element to be deleted. Here follows the algorithm for deleting an element in a doubly linked list object.

Algorithm: Delete an Element

Step 1. If the doubly linked list object is empty, return.

Step 2. Search for the element specified by its search key (e.g., value 'I') in the doubly linked list object. If the element to be deleted is found, assume `search_ptr` points to this element, and perform steps 3 through 6; otherwise, return with a status message.

Step 3. Check to see if the element to be deleted (e.g., with value 'I'), is the first one in the list object. If it is, delete the first element, and make its successor the first element in the list. Set `tmp_ptr = head_ptr->next;` If there is only one element, set `tail_ptr = NULL` (so that `tail_ptr` is not a "dangling pointer"). Otherwise, `delete head_ptr;`

```
head_ptr = tmp_ptr; head_ptr->prev = NULL;
return;
```

Step 4. Check to see if the element to be deleted (e.g., with value 'I'), is the last one in the list object. If it is, delete the last element, and make its predecessor the last (tail) element of the list. Do:

```
tail_ptr = search_ptr->prev;
tail_ptr->next = NULL; delete search_ptr;
return;
```

Step 5. Now the element to be deleted (pointed to by `search_ptr`) is between the head and the tail elements of the doubly linked list. Drop the link to the target element, and then adjust the links of its next (pointed to by `search_ptr->next`) and previous (pointed to by `search_ptr->prev`) elements to retain the doubly linked list structure.

```
search_ptr->prev->next = search_ptr->next;
search_ptr->next->prev = search_ptr->prev;
```

Step 6. Free the memory space of the element to be deleted (e.g., element with value 'I'): `delete search_ptr; return;`

In Figure 5.11(b), the links to the element with key value 'I' are broken, and then the element is deleted using the `delete` operator. In **Code 5.4**, `delete_elt_obj()` implements this algorithm.

5.4.10 METHODS OF THE Doubly_Linked_List CLASS

The following functions are all member functions (some of them being `public` interface routines) of `Doubly_Linked_List` class. These are interface routines to the outside world including `main()`. These routines allow nonmember functions to pass messages (e.g., requests for actions) to `dlist_obj` object of `Doubly_Linked_List` class. All the member fields are accessible to the member functions of the same `Doubly_Linked_List` class. Therefore, it is not necessary to pass these member fields, `head_ptr` and `tail_ptr`, as arguments of the member functions. Since the class `Doubly_Linked_List` is a `friend` of the `DLIST_ELEMENT` class, its member functions do not require the passing of the data members `data`, `next`, and `prev` of `DLIST_ELEMENT` class as arguments. arguments

   `Doubly_Linked_List()`, the constructor and `public` member function of `Doubly_Linked_List` class, is implicitly called when this class's object `dlist_obj` is instantiated. It calls `init_dlist()`.

   `~Doubly_Linked_List()`, a `public` member function of the class `Doubly_Linked_List`, is implicitly called in `main()` before the program exits. It is iteratively implemented. It destroys the entire doubly linked list object. First, it calls `chk_empty_dlist()` to check whether the list object pointed to by `tmp_ptr` (= `head_ptr`) is empty. For an empty doubly linked list object, it sets `head_ptr` to `NULL` and returns. For a nonempty list object, the pointer to the successor of the current element pointed to by `head_ptr` is saved in `tmp_ptr`. It traverses the doubly linked list object using the forward link pointer `next`, and deallocates the memory space by using the `delete` operator.

`Init_dlist()` initializes an object of `Doubly_Linked_List` class. It sets `head_ptr` to `NULL`. It is made `private` to disallow possible misuse that may cause memory leak.

`Chk_empty_dlist()`, a `private` member of `Doubly_Linked_List` class, compares `lst_ptr` with `NULL`. It returns 1 if list object is empty, and 0 otherwise.

`Build_list()`, a `public` member of `Doubly_Linked_List` class, is an iterative function. An address of a string is passed to this function. Like its counterpart in `Singly_Linked_List` class, it iteratively builds a doubly linked list object `dlist_obj` with character data from a string. The only additional work is properly setting up `prev` pointer field of each `DLIST_ELEMENT`-type object.

`Search_element()` is a `public` member of `Doubly_Linked_List` class. It calls `search_elt_obj()` and if successful, it displays a message "Element is found in doubly linked list object."

`Search_elt_obj()`, a `private` member of `Doubly_Linked_List` class, is a recursive function. It has two arguments, the list pointer `lst_ptr` of type `LIST_PTR`, and `search_key` of type `DATA_TYPE`. It performs like `search_element1()` in **Code 5.3**. It directly calls itself until a match of the target key or the end of list is reached.

`Delete_element()` is a `public` member of `Doubly_Linked_List` class. It calls `search_elt_obj()` to find the given element object specified by `search_key`. If the given element object is not found, it displays a message and returns. Otherwise, the element object is found in the doubly linked list object, and is pointed to by `search_ptr`. It considers three cases for the element object to be deleted at the (1) head of the list, (2) tail of the list, (3) intermediate position. In either of these positions, it efficiently uses the back link `prev` to break the link to the given element object and maintains the list object. Finally, it frees up the memory space held by the given element using the `delete` operator.

`Get_elt_numbers()` and `Print_list()` are `public` member functions of the `Doubly_Linked_List` class. Both perform exactly the same operations as their counterparts in the `Singly_Linked_List` class of **Code 5.3**.

`Print_dlist_obj_backward()`, a `public` member function of the `Doubly_Linked_List` class, is an iterative function. It displays this class's object by linearly traversing the list from the last element object

(pointed to by `tail_ptr`) to the first element. The list traversal is aided
by the `prev` pointer field of each element object, which provided a backward reference to an element object's predecessor. Without any performance loss, the backward printing is possible due to the previous pointer,
the unique feature of a doubly linked list object. However, this could have
been achieved with a great deal of effort for a singly linked list object.

`Get_next()` and `get_prev()` are `public` member functions of the
`DLIST_ELEMENT` class. These provide a "read-only" access of the `private`
data members, `next` and `prev`, to the outside world.

`Main()`, a client function of the `Doubly_Linked_List` class, instantiates this class's object `dlist_obj`

$$\text{Doubly\_Linked\_List} \quad \text{dlist\_obj;}$$

To `dlist_obj`, `main()` sends requests for such actions as building,
printing forward and backward, deleting a specified element respectively
through `dlist_obj` object's methods `build_list()`, `print_list()`,
`print_dlist_obj_backward()` and `delete_element()`. Program's
memory is cleaned up by `delete   str` and `~Doubly_Linked_List()`.

Code 5.4

```
// Program:  dlist.c++
// Purpose:  OOP implementation of a doubly
//           linked list (dllist). Used
//           data type 'char' for testing.
#include <stdio.h>
typedef int     BOOLEAN;
typedef char    DATA_TYPE;
#include "bc_list.h"   // For base class "List"

typedef class DLIST_ELEMENT {
  private:
    DATA_TYPE       data;
    DLIST_ELEMENT   *next,
                    *prev;

    //  Declare "Doubly_Linked_List" class as
    //  a "friend" of this class.
    friend   class Doubly_Linked_List;
  public:
    // For read-only access to others
    DLIST_ELEMENT   *get_next() { return next; };
    DLIST_ELEMENT   *get_prev() { return prev; };
} *LIST_PTR;

#include "dlist.h"  // For "Doubly_Linked_List"

//  ~Doubly_Linked_List():
//      Delete entire doubly linked list object and free
```

```
//      up its memory spaces (Iterative implementation).
//
Doubly_Linked_List::~Doubly_Linked_List(void)
{
    LIST_PTR tmp_ptr;

    while (!chk_empty_dlist(head_ptr)) {
        //  Save pointer to next element
        tmp_ptr = head_ptr->next;
        delete head_ptr;  // Free up memory space
        head_ptr = tmp_ptr;
    }
    head_ptr = NULL;
}

//  init_dlist():
//     Initialize "Doubly_Linked_List"-type object.
void Doubly_Linked_List::init_dlist(void)
{
    head_ptr = tail_ptr = NULL;
}

BOOLEAN Doubly_Linked_List::chk_empty_dlist(
                             LIST_PTR lst_ptr)
{
    return (lst_ptr == NULL);
}

//   build_list():
//     Build a doubly linked list object
//     from an input string of variable length.
//
void Doubly_Linked_List::build_list(DATA_TYPE *str)
{
    LIST_PTR tmp_ptr, new_ptr;

    while (*str != '\0') {
        new_ptr       =  new DLIST_ELEMENT;
        new_ptr->data =  *str++;
        new_ptr->next =  NULL;

        if (head_ptr == NULL) {
            new_ptr->prev = NULL;
            head_ptr      = new_ptr;
            tmp_ptr   = new_ptr;
        }
        else {
            tmp_ptr->next =  new_ptr;
            new_ptr->prev =  tmp_ptr;
            tmp_ptr = tmp_ptr->next;
        }
        tail_ptr = new_ptr;
    }
}
```

```
//  search_elt_obj():
//    Search for an element with its key value in
//    a list object. Return the pointer if found;
//    otherwise NULL. (Recursive procedure)
//
LIST_PTR Doubly_Linked_List::search_elt_obj(
            LIST_PTR lst_ptr, DATA_TYPE search_key)
{
    if (!chk_empty_dlist(lst_ptr)) {
        if (search_key == lst_ptr->data)
            return (lst_ptr);
        search_elt_obj (lst_ptr->next, search_key);
    }
    else {
      printf("\n search_elt_obj: %s \n",
             "Element is not found");
      return (NULL);
    }
}

void Doubly_Linked_List::search_element(DATA_TYPE search_key)
{
    if (search_elt_obj(head_ptr, search_key) != NULL)
       printf("\n Element is found %s \n",
              "in doubly linked list object.");
}

//  delete_element():
//    Delete a specified DLIST_ELEMENT object
//
void Doubly_Linked_List::delete_element(DATA_TYPE element_key)
{
    LIST_PTR   lst_ptr = head_ptr,
                 search_ptr, tmp_ptr;

    //  Search for the object to be deleted
    search_ptr = search_elt_obj(lst_ptr, element_key);
    if (search_ptr == NULL) { // object is not found
       printf("\n delete_element: Object to be %s \n",
              "deleted is not found");
       return;
    }
    //  DLIST_ELEMENT class object is found.
    //  Is the object to be deleted the head of the list?
    if (search_ptr == head_ptr) {
       tmp_ptr = head_ptr->next;
       if (tail_ptr == head_ptr)
          tail_ptr = tmp_ptr;
       delete head_ptr;             //  Free up memory
       head_ptr = tmp_ptr;
       head_ptr->prev = NULL;
       return;
     }
```

```
        //   Is the object to be deleted the tail of the list?
        if (search_ptr == tail_ptr) {
          tail_ptr = search_ptr->prev;
          tail_ptr->next = NULL;
          delete search_ptr;          //  Free up memory
          return;
        }
        //
        //   The object to be deleted is between the head and
        //   the tail of the list. Drop the link to target
        //   object, and then adjust the links of the next
        //   and previous objects.
        //
        search_ptr->prev->next = search_ptr->next;
        search_ptr->next->prev = search_ptr->prev;
        delete search_ptr;
}


//   get_elt_numbers():
//     Count DLIST_ELEMENT class objects in a
//     "Doubly_Linked_List" type object
//     (Iterative procedure)
//
int Doubly_Linked_List::get_elt_numbers(void)
{
    LIST_PTR  lst_ptr = head_ptr;
    int    obj_numbers = 0;

    while (lst_ptr != NULL) {
        ++obj_numbers;
        lst_ptr = lst_ptr->next;
     }
     return(obj_numbers);
}


//   print_dlist_obj_forward():
//     Nonrecursively print the "Doubly_Linked_List"-
//     type object in the forward (from first element
//     to last) direction only.
//
void Doubly_Linked_List::print_dlist_obj_forward(void)
{
    LIST_PTR  lst_ptr = head_ptr;

    while (lst_ptr != NULL) {
        printf("%c <-> ", lst_ptr->data);
        lst_ptr = lst_ptr->next;
    }
    printf("NULL\n"); // NULL means last elt of list
}


//   print_dlist_obj_backward():
//     Nonrecursively print the "Doubly_Linked_List"-
//     type object in the reverse (from last to first)
```

```
//     direction only.
//
void Doubly_Linked_List::print_dlist_obj_backward(void)
{
     LIST_PTR   lst_ptr = tail_ptr;

     while (lst_ptr != NULL) {
         printf("%c <-> ", lst_ptr->data);
         lst_ptr = lst_ptr->prev;
     }
     printf("NULL\n"); // NULL means last elt of list
}

//  main():
//    Test driver for OBJECT-ORIENTED IMPLEMENTATION
//    OF A LIST OBJECT USING DOUBLY LINKED LIST.
//
void main(void)
{
    Doubly_Linked_List  dlist_obj;
    char    *str = "LOPAMUDRA";        // Input string

    printf("\n ** OOP IMPLEMENTATION OF %s \n",
           "DOUBLY LINKED LIST ** " );

    // Since main() is not a member of "Doubly_Linked_List"
    // class, it calls the interface routines, the
    // components of the "dlist_obj" object for sending
    // messages to the object "dlist_obj".
    dlist_obj.build_list (str);
    dlist_obj.print_list("(forward)");
    printf("\n The list object (backward) is:\n  ");
    dlist_obj.print_dlist_obj_backward();
    printf(" %s in this list object is: %d \n",
      "Number of elements", dlist_obj.get_elt_numbers());
    dlist_obj.delete_element ('R');
    dlist_obj.print_list("after deleting \'R\'");
    printf(" %s in this list object is: %d \n",
      "Number of elements", dlist_obj.get_elt_numbers());
    delete  str;
}
```

Code 5.4 produces this output:

```
** OOP IMPLEMENTATION OF DOUBLY LINKED LIST **

List (forward) is:
 L <-> O <-> P <-> A <-> M <-> U <-> D <-> R <-> A <-> NULL

The list object (backward) is:
 A <-> R <-> D <-> U <-> M <-> A <-> P <-> O <-> L <-> NULL
```

```
Number of elements in this list object is: 9

List after deleting 'R' is:
 L <-> O <-> P <-> A <-> M <-> U <-> D <-> A <-> NULL
Number of elements in this list object is: 8
```

5.5   Circular List Objects

Circular lists are useful for applications such as those that require a message queuing system, read/write (R/W) or input/output (I/O) buffer management, or fixed size files for recording activity logs. In the area of computer networks, the terms *circular list* and *ring* are used interchangeably. The ring configuration of a computer network, in which multiple computers are connected through cables or wires, makes heavy use of the circular list concept. In Chapter 6, an array-based circular list will be employed to implement circular queues.

A circular list object is specified by an ADT circular list, which is a special case of an ADT list. An ADT circular list is a list structure such that every element within it contains an address of its successor element. A circular list does not have any first or last element.

In terms of implementation, the data elements of a circular list object can be stored in an array or as a series of singly or doubly linked nodes. Thus, a circular list has three categories of implementation:

- Array-based circular list

- Singly linked circular list

- Doubly linked circular list

A singly linked circular list is shown in Figure 5.12, and a doubly linked circular list is shown later in Figure 5.14.

Irrespective of its implementation, a circular list does not have any first or last element. Since accessing the circular list requires an address of the

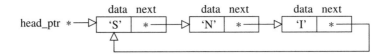

FIGURE 5.12. A singly linked circular list.

starting element, it will use `circ_array[0]` (in case of an array implementation) or `head_ptr` (in case of a singly or doubly linked list implementation) for the starting element. A tail pointer, `tail_ptr`, is not
needed for a circular list. The elements in a circular list may *wrap around*
the data storage area – an array or a linked list.

When implementing a circular list object, the following key issues and
considerations are generally applicable:

- An entire circular list can be traversed using only one pointer
  (e.g. , `head_ptr`).

- It is important to check for a *wraparound* condition. For example, if
  we start the circular list traversal using `head_ptr`, which may be
  pointing to any element, say *E*, the traversal must terminate when
  we come back to this initial position *E*.

- Checking for the *wraparound* condition eliminates a possible infinite
  loop situation.

- When the `head_ptr` is `NULL` or self-pointing, the circular list is
  empty.

5.5.1 OOP IMPLEMENTATION OF SINGLY LINKED CIRCULAR LISTS

In an object-oriented approach, an ADT singly linked circular list specifies
an object of the `Circ_Linked_List` class, which is derived from the
abstract base class `List`, and which encapsulates `data` and `next` pointer
for each element, and the allowed operations. It is in `cirlist.h`.

```
class  Circ_Linked_List : public List {
  private:
    typedef struct  CLIST_ELEMENT {
        DATA_TYPE        data;
        CLIST_ELEMENT  *next;
    } *LIST_PTR;

    LIST_PTR  head_ptr;
    void  init_clist(void) { head_ptr = NULL; }
  protected:
    LIST_PTR  search_element1(LIST_PTR,
                             DATA_TYPE);
    LIST_PTR  search_previous(DATA_TYPE search_key);
  //  Declare its member functions as public
  public:
    Circ_Linked_List() { init_clist(); }
    ~Circ_Linked_List();
    BOOLEAN  is_empty(void);
    void       build_list(DATA_TYPE *);
    void       search_element(DATA_TYPE);
```

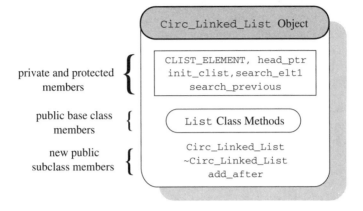

FIGURE 5.13. Circ_Linked_List object.

```
    void      delete_element(DATA_TYPE);
    void      add_after(DATA_TYPE elt_after,
                        DATA_TYPE new_elt);
    int       get_elt_numbers(void);
    void      print_list(char *hdr);
};
```

Figure 5.13 depicts a `Circ_Linked_List` object. **Code 5.5** shows an object-oriented implementation of some operations that are necessary to work with a singly linked circular list.

5.5.2 METHODS OF THE Circ_Linked_List CLASS

The methods of the `Circ_Linked_List` class are described below. Some of them are publicly accessible interface routines to client programs and the world outside of this class. Since these methods are allowed to access and manipulate the data members of the same class per scoping rules of C++, it is not necessary to pass these member fields, `data`, `next`, and `head_ptr` as arguments to these methods.

`Circ_Linked_List()`, constructor and a `public` member function of the `Circ_Linked_List` class, instantiates a singly linked circular list object (e.g., `clist_obj`). It calls `init_clist()`.

`~Circ_Linked_List()`, a `public` member of `Circ_Linked_List` class, is implicitly called in `main()` before the program exits. It is iteratively implemented. It destroys the entire singly linked circular list object. First, it calls `is_empty()` to check whether the list object pointed to by `tmp_ptr` (= `head_ptr`) is empty. For an empty singly linked circular list object, it returns. For a nonempty list object, the pointer to the successor of the current element pointed to by next_ptr, is saved in next_ptr. It traverses the singly linked circular list object using the next pointer, and deallocates the memory space by calling the delete operator:

```
delete next_ptr;
```

Init_clist() initializes an object (e.g., clist_obj) of the class Circ_Linked_List. It sets head_ptr to NULL. Its private attribute prevents its misuse from causing a memory leak.

Is_empty(), a public member function of the Circ_Linked_List class, tests whether an object (e.g, clist_obj) of this class is empty. It returns TRUE if head_ptr has a NULL value; otherwise, it returns FALSE.

Build_list() is a public member function of Circ_Linked_List class. It is an iterative function. It accepts an address of a string. It builds a Circ_Linked_List type object (e.g., clist_obj) of characters using the input string. For each character as data in CLIST_ELEMENT element, the new operator is used to allocate the memory space, pointed to by new_ptr, and new_ptr->data is set to the character. The single pointer field, next of type LIST_PTR, is used to connect the successive elements of the list object. The next field of the element with the last character is set to head_ptr in order to connect the last element to the first one.

Search_element() is a publicly accessible member function of the Circ_Linked_List class. It calls the recursive and protected member function
search_element1().

Search_element1() has two arguments, a pointer of type LIST_PTR, and a single search key search_key of type DATA_TYPE. It searches for a list element specified by search_key. It is similar to its counterpart of the Singly_Linked_List class in **Code 5.3** except that it checks the "wraparound" condition to determine the starting element.

Delete_element(), a publicly accessible member function of the class Circ_Linked_List, deletes an element specified by search_key. It is similar to delete_element() of the Singly_Linked_List class in **Code 5.3** except that it checks the "wraparound" condition to determine the starting element.

Add_after() is a publicly accessible member function of the class Circ_Linked_List. It calls search_element() to search for an element with search_key. If it is found, the given element is pointed to by elem_ptr. Using the new operator, it allocates memory space for the new element pointed to by new_ptr. The new_ptr->data is set to given_data. Then the function connects the new element into the circular list using the pointer field new_ptr->next. It assures circular connection of the elements.

Get_elt_numbers() is a publicly accessible member function of the Circ_Linked_List class. It is implemented as an iterative function using a for loop. If the list object is empty, it returns zero. It returns the total number of CLIST_ELEMENT-type objects in the singly linked circular list object.

Print_list(), a public member function of Circ_Linked_List class, is similar to print_list() of the Singly_Linked_List class in **Code 5.3** with the exception of the "wraparound" check.

Main(), a client function, instantiates clist_obj which is an object of the Circ_Linked_List class:

Circ_Linked_List clist_obj;

For a string "PRATIVA" pointed to by str, main() sends messages to the object clist_obj through this object's methods build_list(), delete_element(), add_after(), and print_list() for their associated actions. At the program exit, memory is cleaned up by delete str and the implicit call of ~Circ_Linked_List().

Code 5.5

```
//  Program:  cirlist.c++
//  Purpose:
/       Object-oriented implementation of a
/       singly linked circular list; assumed
/       'char' type data for each element.
//
#include <stdio.h>
typedef   int     BOOLEAN;
typedef   char    DATA_TYPE;
#include "bc_list.h"  // For base class "List"
#include "cirlist.h"  // For derived class
                         // "Circ_Linked_List"
// ~Circ_Linked_List():
//     Destroy the entire singly linked circular
//     list object. This destructor function is auto-
//     matically called before exiting program.
//
Circ_Linked_List::~Circ_Linked_List()
{
  LIST_PTR   tmp_ptr, next_ptr;

  if (!is_empty()) {
    // To stop 'for' loop, do "wrap around" check
    for (tmp_ptr = head_ptr;
         tmp_ptr->next != head_ptr; // "wrap around" check
         tmp_ptr = tmp_ptr->next) {
      next_ptr = tmp_ptr;
      delete  next_ptr;   // free up memory space
    }
    head_ptr = NULL;
  }
}
```

```
// is_empty():
//   Check empty status of a singly
//   linked circular list object.
//
BOOLEAN Circ_Linked_List::is_empty(void)
{
  return (head_ptr == NULL);
}

// build_list():
//     Build a singly linked circular list object
//     from an input string of variable length.
//     (Iterative implementation)
//
void Circ_Linked_List::build_list(DATA_TYPE *str)
{
  LIST_PTR   tmp_ptr, new_ptr;

  while (*str != '\0') {  // string end
    new_ptr = new  CLIST_ELEMENT;
    new_ptr->data = *str++;
    new_ptr->next = NULL;

    if (head_ptr == NULL) {
      head_ptr = new_ptr;
      tmp_ptr  = new_ptr;
    }
    else {
      tmp_ptr->next = new_ptr;
      tmp_ptr = tmp_ptr->next;
    }
  }
  // Join the last element with the head
  tmp_ptr->next = head_ptr;
}

// search_element1():
//   Search for an element given by its key
//   'search_key' in a singly linked circular
//   list object, pointed to by 'head_ptr'.
//   Return the pointer if the element is
//   found; otherwise return NULL.
//   (Recursive implementation)
//
Circ_Linked_List::LIST_PTR
Circ_Linked_List::search_element1(
      LIST_PTR lst_ptr, DATA_TYPE search_key)
{
  if (!is_empty() &&
      (lst_ptr->next != head_ptr)) {
    if (search_key == lst_ptr->data)
      return (lst_ptr);
    search_element1 (lst_ptr->next, search_key);
```

```
    }
    else {
      printf("\n search_element: %s \n",
              "Element is not found in list");
      return (NULL);
    }
}

void Circ_Linked_List::search_element(DATA_TYPE search_key)
{
    if (search_element1(head_ptr, search_key) != NULL)
        printf ("\n Element is found in circular list. \n");
}

// search_previous():
//   Search for an element in a singly linked
//   circular list object given its data
//   'search_key'. If match is found, it returns
//   a pointer to previous element. Otherwise, it
//   returns NULL. (Iterative method)
//
Circ_Linked_List::LIST_PTR
Circ_Linked_List::search_previous(DATA_TYPE search_key)
{
  LIST_PTR  tmp_ptr = head_ptr;

  if (is_empty())
      return (NULL);
  // Test "wrap around" condition
  while (tmp_ptr->next != head_ptr) {
    if (tmp_ptr->next->data == search_key)
        return (tmp_ptr);
    tmp_ptr = tmp_ptr->next;
  }
  if (tmp_ptr->next->data == search_key)
      return (tmp_ptr);
  else
      return (NULL);
}

// delete_element():
//   Delete an element in a singly linked
//   circular list object given its data
//   'search_key' as the search key.
//
void  Circ_Linked_List::delete_element(
                          DATA_TYPE search_key)
{
  LIST_PTR  elem_ptr, prev_ptr;

  if (is_empty())
    return;
  // Check to see if the given element is the
  // first one in the circular list object.
```

```
  if ((head_ptr != NULL) &&
      (head_ptr->data == search_key)) {
         elem_ptr = head_ptr->next;
         delete head_ptr;
         head_ptr = elem_ptr;
   }
   if ((elem_ptr = search_element1 (head_ptr,
                      search_key)) != NULL) {
     prev_ptr = search_previous (search_key);
     prev_ptr->next = elem_ptr->next;
     delete elem_ptr;
   }
}

// add_after():
//  Add a new element (given its 'given_data')
//  after a given element ('search_key') in a
//  singly linked circular list object.
//
void  Circ_Linked_List::add_after(
      DATA_TYPE search_key, DATA_TYPE given_data)
{
  LIST_PTR  new_ptr, elem_ptr;

  if ((elem_ptr = search_element1 (head_ptr,
                                 search_key))
         != NULL) {
    new_ptr = new  CLIST_ELEMENT;
    new_ptr->data  = given_data;
    new_ptr->next  = elem_ptr->next;
    elem_ptr->next = new_ptr;
  }
}

// get_elt_numbers():
//  Get the number of elements in a
//  singly linked circular list object.
//  (Iterative or nonrecursive method)
//
int Circ_Linked_List::get_elt_numbers(void)
{
  int element_numbers = 0;

  if (head_ptr == NULL)
    return (0);
  for (LIST_PTR  tmp_ptr = head_ptr;
       tmp_ptr->next != head_ptr;
       tmp_ptr = tmp_ptr->next)
    ++element_numbers;
  return (++element_numbers);
}

// print_list():
//  Print the elements of a singly linked
```

```
//  circular list object starting from head
//  element to the previous element of head.
//
void    Circ_Linked_List::print_list (char *hdr)
{
    printf("\n The singly linked %s %s is:\n      ",
           "circular list", hdr);
    if (head_ptr == NULL) {
      printf ("\n List is empty! \n");
      return;
    }
    // Test "wrap around" condition
    for (LIST_PTR  tmp_ptr = head_ptr;
         tmp_ptr->next != head_ptr;
         tmp_ptr = tmp_ptr->next)
      printf ("%c -> ", tmp_ptr->data);
    printf ("%c -> head \n", tmp_ptr->data);
}

//  main( ):
//   OBJECT-ORIENTED Implementation of a list
//   object using a Singly Linked Circular List.
//
void  main(void)
{
  // Declare an object "clist_obj" pertaining
  // to the class "Circ_Linked_List"
  Circ_Linked_List  clist_obj;
  char *str = "PRATIVA"; // Input string

  printf("\n ** OOP IMPLEMENTATION %s \n",
         "OF SINGLY LINKED CIRCULAR LIST **");
  clist_obj.build_list (str);
  clist_obj.print_list("object");
  printf(" %s in this list object is: %d \n",
    "Number of elements", clist_obj.get_elt_numbers());
  clist_obj.delete_element ('V');
  clist_obj.print_list("after deleting V");
  printf(" %s in this list object is: %d \n",
    "Number of elements", clist_obj.get_elt_numbers());
  clist_obj.add_after ('I', 'V');
  clist_obj.print_list("after adding V after I");
  printf(" %s in this list object is: %d \n",
    "Number of elements", clist_obj.get_elt_numbers());
  delete str;
}
```

Code 5.5 produces this output:

```
** OOP IMPLEMENTATION OF SINGLY LINKED CIRCULAR LIST **
```

```
The singly linked circular list object is:
    P -> R -> A -> T -> I -> V -> A -> head
Number of elements in this list object is: 7

The singly linked circular list after deleting V is:
    P -> R -> A -> T -> I -> A -> head
Number of elements in this list object is: 6

The singly linked circular list after adding V after I is:
    P -> R -> A -> T -> I -> V -> A -> head
Number of elements in this list object is: 7
```

5.5.3 DOUBLY LINKED CIRCULAR LIST AND ITS OOP IMPLEMENTATION

A doubly linked circular list is shown in Figure 5.14. Each element contains two pointer fields, next and prev, and a data field data. Any one element, say 'S', can be considered as the first element pointed to by head_ptr and by the pointer field next of the element 'I'. The element 'I' is pointed to by the pointer field prev of the element 'S'. The "circular connection" between the elements are defined in this manner. An OOP implementation of a doubly linked circular list is similar to that of a doubly linked list (see **Code 5.4**) with additions of logic for *circular connection*. It is left as an exercise.

5.6 Performance Analyses of List Operations

In this chapter, several implementations of the list object are discussed using: (1) array list, (2) singly linked list, (3) doubly linked list, (4) singly linked circular list, and (5) doubly linked circular list. Uses of these data structures depend on the applications and the operations required to perform in these applications. Thus, for the selection of an appropriate and efficient form of list data structure for a list, it is important to know at least

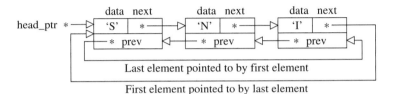

FIGURE 5.14. A doubly linked circular list.

List Structure	Worst-case performance of		
	Search (random)	Delete (random)	Insert after a random element
Array-based	$O(n)$	$O(n)$	Between $O(1)$ and $O(n)$
Singly linked	$O(n)$	$O(n)$	Between $O(1)$ and $O(n)$
Doubly linked	$O(n)$	$O(n)$	Between $O(1)$ and $O(n)$
Singly linked circular	$O(n)$	$O(n)$	Between $O(1)$ and $O(n)$
Doubly linked circular	$O(n)$	$O(n)$	Between $O(1)$ and $O(n)$

TABLE 5.2. Performance of list operations.

the comparative-based worst-case performance of some key list operations such as search and delete. The worst case occurs when the data element to be searched or deleted is not in the list or is at the end of the list. Consider n data elements in the list object. Table 5.2 shows the worst-case performances of some operations for the lists.

To delete a data element specified by its index from an array list object will require only one comparison. When the data element to be deleted is only specified by the key, the delete operation requires a search process, and the search does n number of comparisons when the target data element is not in the array list. So, the worst-case performances for the search and delete operations in an array list of size n are $O(n)$. The insert-after (add-after) operation inserts a new element after a specified data element, and thus requires a search for the specified data element, which has worst-case performance $O(n)$.

5.7   OOP Application: Polynomial Objects in Single Variable

5.7.1   CONCEPT OF A POLYNOMIAL IN SINGLE VARIABLE

A real polynomial $P(x)$ in a single variable of degree n or less is algebraically represented by the expression

$$P(x) = P_n x^n + P_{n-1} x^{n-1} + ... + P_1 x^1 + P_0$$

Example Polynomial Object Methods

Read the terms (coefficients and powers of x) of a polynomial.
Construct a polynomial.
Delete a polynomial.
Insert a polynomial term.
Add two polynomials.
Subtract two polynomials.
Multiply two polynomials.
Divide two polynomials.
Evaluate a polynomial for a given value of x.
Print a polynomial.

TABLE 5.3.

where x is the single variable, and P_n, P_{n-1}, ..., P_0 are coefficients and real numbers. $P(x)$ is of degree n if P_n is not zero. Each *term*, also called *element*, of $P(x)$ is, for example, $P_i x^i$ $(i = n, n-1, ..., 3, 2, 1, 0)$, and contains a coefficient and a power of x. Addition of two polynomials is done as follows:

$$
\begin{aligned}
P(x) &= 30x^3 + 20x^2 + 5 \\
Q(x) &= 20x^2 + 10x^1 \\
P(x) + Q(x) &= 30x^3 + 40x^2 + 10x^1 + 5
\end{aligned}
$$

Note that like terms (i.e., terms with the same powers of x) are added.

5.7.2 POLYNOMIAL OBJECTS

A polynomial is a collection of many (poly) terms that are data. A polynomial object is specified by an ADT polynomial. An ADT polynomial in a single variable, for example x, is a collection of a set of terms (elements) and a set of such methods such as those given in Table 5.3.

5.7.3 OBJECT-ORIENTED DESIGN AND IMPLEMENTATION FOR POLYNOMIALS

The object-oriented design (OOD) for single variable polynomials identifies the polynomial object, which is specified by the definition of ADT polynomials. The methods are operations identified by the definition of ADT polynomials in Section 5.7.2. The data contained in a polynomial object entail the coefficient and power of x of each term (element). To structure the collection of such data, we may use an array or a linked list. For a polynomial with $(n + 1)$ terms, we use an array of $(n + 1)$ elements. Each element is considered as a record:

```
typedef  double  DATA_TYPE;
struct    POLY_ELEMENT {
   DATA_TYPE  coefficient;
};
typedef POLY_ELEMENT POLY_ARY[DEGREE + 1];
POLY_ARY  p;
```

where DEGREE is the degree of the polynomial. Note that a polynomial of degree n has at most $(n + 1)$ terms (elements). POLY_ELEMENT does not need to have a field for the power of x, because the array index can be used to correspond to the power. A POLY_ARY-type polynomial p of degree n and with coefficients P_0 , P_1 , P_2 , ..., P_{n-1}, P_n is shown in Figure 5.15.

An OOP implementation using an array is left as an exercise.

When a singly linked list is used to organize data elements of a single variable polynomial, the polynomial of degree n and with coefficients P_0, P_1, P_2, ..., P_{n-1}, P_n is represented by Figure 5.16. Here, each term (element) is a structure of type POLY_ELEMENT:

```
struct   POLY_ELEMENT {
    DATA_TYPE        coefficient;
    unsigned  int  power_of_x;
    POLY_ELEMENT    *next;
};
```

Now for an OOP implementation of a polynomial, it is necessary to hide POLY_ELEMENT-type terms (elements) from the outside world, and also to provide public methods as interfaces (message-passing media) for the outside world. This is accomplished by defining a class Polynomial in class_poly_def.h as follows:

```
class Polynomial {
private:
   typedef struct  POLY_ELEMENT {
       DATA_TYPE        coefficient;
       unsigned int  power_of_x;
       POLY_ELEMENT  *next;
   } *POLY_PTR;
```

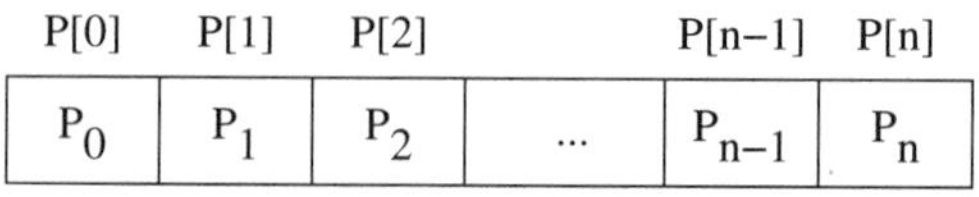

P[0]	P[1]	P[2]		P[n−1]	P[n]
P_0	P_1	P_2	...	P_{n-1}	P_n

FIGURE 5.15. Polynomial representation using an array.

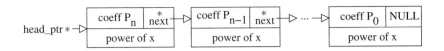

FIGURE 5.16. Polynomial representation using a singly linked list.

```
  POLY_PTR   head_ptr;
  void       inline poly_obj_init () { head_ptr = NULL; };
  POLY_PTR   allocate_poly_element(POLY_ELEMENT new_element);
  POLY_PTR   link_poly_element (POLY_PTR head_ptr,
  POLY_ELEMENT new_element, enum type_def type);
  POLY_PTR   read_poly_obj (int poly_number);
  void       key_to_continue (void);
public:
  Polynomial () { poly_obj_init(); } // Constructor
  ~Polynomial ();   // Destructor

  void       build_poly_obj (int poly_num)
               { head_ptr = read_poly_obj(poly_num); }
  void       print_poly_obj (POLY_PTR head_ptr);
  POLY_PTR   get_poly_head() { return head_ptr; };

  friend Polynomial operator+ (Polynomial poly_obj1,
                        Polynomial poly_obj2);
  friend Polynomial operator- (Polynomial poly_obj1,
                        Polynomial poly_obj2);
  friend Polynomial operator* (Polynomial poly_obj1,
                        Polynomial poly_obj2);
  friend Polynomial operator/ (Polynomial poly_obj1,
                        Polynomial poly_obj2);
  friend void  display_poly (Polynomial poly_obj1,
      Polynomial poly_obj2, Polynomial poly_obj_sum);
  float  evaluate_poly_obj (float x_value);
};
```

The `Polynomial` class defines a type for single-variable polynomial objects encompassing both data elements (terms and `head_ptr`) and operations (methods). These methods are now described and later implemented in **Code 5.6**.

The operation `Polynomial()` is called the constructor. Using the new operator, it constructs an object (e.g., `poly_1_obj`) of type `Polynomial`. It calls `poly_obj_init()`. It is called in `main()`.

`~Polynomial()` is called the destructor. It destroys a `Polynomial` type object by iteratively freeing up the memory spaces of POLY_ELEMENT-type elements for that object. Since the POLY_ELEMENT-type elements are structured as a singly linked list, `~Polynomial()` uses while loop for iteration, and linearly advances one element at a time and frees up its memory space using the delete operator. The iteration stops when it reaches the end of the list, i.e., the value of next pointer is NULL. At the program exit in main(), ~Polynomial() is implicitly called to destroy the Polynomial type objects, poly_obj1, poly_obj2, and poly_obj_sum.

The operation poly_obj_init() of type void is a private member function of the Polynomial class. It initializes the Polynomial-type object by setting its data pointer, head_ptr, to NULL. To ensure protection of internal data, it is made private. poly_obj_init() is called by the constructor.

The operation allocate_poly_element() of type POLY_PTR is a private member function of the Polynomial class because it is not necessary as a public interface routine. It dynamically allocates memory space for a POLY_ELEMENT-type element of a Polynomial-type object. It uses the new operator and sets the fields, coefficient and power_of_x to the given values. It returns a POLY_PTR-type pointer.

The operation print_poly_obj() of type void is a public member function of the Polynomial class. It prints a Polynomial-type object in an algebraic form with terms from the highest to the lowest power of x. It is recursively called to print the nonzero coefficient and power of x for each element of a Polynomial-type object, until the end of the singly linked list of elements is reached.

Link_poly_element() of type POLY_PTR is a private member function of the Polynomial class. It expects head_ptr, new_element of type POLY_ELEMENT, and type of ADD or REPLACE as arguments. It inserts a polynomial element into a singly linked list of polynomial elements (terms). The element is inserted in order of declining power of x. REPLACE or ADD is passed to the function to indicate whether a duplicate element should replace the original, or if it should be added to the original. A new root (head) pointer is returned to the calling function.

The operation read_poly_obj() of type POLY_PTR is a private member function of the Polynomial class. It reads the coefficient and power of x for a term (element) of a polynomial object from the operator via keyboard input one element at a time. A number for the polynomial object is passed to the function. The head pointer head_ptr of the polynomial object is returned to the calling function.

The overloaded operator + is not a public member function of the Polynomial class. It is a friend of the Polynomial class so that it accesses all the private members of the class. It accepts two Polynomial-type objects poly_obj1 and poly_obj2 as arguments. Poly_obj1 is added to the sum polynomial object, poly_obj_sum. Using the method of adding "like-terms" (i.e., the terms with the same power of x), it adds poly_obj2 to the sum polynomial object, and returns a Polynomial-type object poly_obj_sum.

Display_poly() of type void is not a member function but a friend function of the Polynomial class. It displays the three Polynomial-type objects, poly_obj1, poly_obj2, and poly_obj_sum in their algebraic forms by calling the method print_poly().

Main() is the test driver for OOP implementation of single-variable polynomials. It instantiates three objects, poly_obj1, poly_obj2, and poly_obj_sum, all of type Polynomial, by implicitly calling the constructor Polynomial(). Since main() is not a member of Polynomial class, it sends messages to these objects through the public interface routines. The messages include reading terms (elements) for the objects, adding two Polynomial-type objects (poly_obj1 and poly_obj2), and displaying all three objects.

Code 5.6

```
//  Program:  polynoml.c++
//  Purpose:
//    Object-oriented implementation of ADT polynomials
//    in single variable using singly linked list of
//    terms (elements).
//
#include  <stdio.h>
#include  <stdlib.h>
#ifdef  MSDOS
#include  <conio.h>
#define  CLRSCR()  (clrscr())
#else
#define  CLRSCR()  (system("clear"))
#endif

typedef  double  DATA_TYPE;  // for coefficient
const int FOREVER = 1;
// "type_def" is used by link_poly_element()
enum  type_def { REPLACE, ADD };

#include "class_poly_def.h"  // For "Polynomial" class

Polynomial::~Polynomial ()    // Destructor
{
    POLY_PTR  current_ptr = head_ptr, next_elt_ptr;

    while  (current_ptr != NULL) {
        next_elt_ptr = current_ptr->next;
        delete  current_ptr;
        current_ptr = next_elt_ptr;
    }
}

//  allocate_poly_element():
```

```
//    Allocate memory space and return a pointer to the
//    allocated memory for a new polynomial element. The
//    element is initialized with new data passed to the
//    function.
Polynomial::POLY_PTR
Polynomial::allocate_poly_element(POLY_ELEMENT new_element)
{
    POLY_PTR  new_poly_elt_ptr = new POLY_ELEMENT;
    if (new_poly_elt_ptr == NULL) {
      printf ("\nERROR: System memory is not available \n");
      exit (-1);
    }

    //   Initialize element
    new_poly_elt_ptr->coefficient = new_element.coefficient;
    new_poly_elt_ptr->power_of_x  = new_element.power_of_x;
    new_poly_elt_ptr->next = NULL;
    return (new_poly_elt_ptr);
}


//   read_poly_obj ():
//    Read the coefficient and power of x for a term
//    (element) of a polynomial from the operator via
//    keyboard input one element at a time. The head
//    pointer of the polynomial is returned to the
//    calling function.
//
Polynomial::POLY_PTR Polynomial::read_poly_obj(int number)
{
    POLY_ELEMENT  new_element;
    char          buffer[25];

    if (head_ptr != NULL)
      return (head_ptr);  // polynomial is already defined
    while (FOREVER) {
      CLRSCR ();   // in conio.h
      printf ("\n OOP for Single Variable Polynomials");
      printf ("\n------------------------------------\n");
      printf ("\n Current Polynomial Object %d is: \n\n",
              number);
      print_poly_obj (head_ptr);  // print current polynomial
      printf ("\n\n == Enter Polynomial Term ==");
      printf ("\n Enter Coefficient and Power of X %s",
              "for each Term.");
      printf ("\n Polynomial Terms will be %s",
              "automatically ordered.");
      printf ("\n New coefficient will replace %s",
              "old for like powers of X.");
      printf ("\n Zero coefficient will erase %s",
              "old for like powers of X.");
      printf ("\n <ENTER> with no Value at %s\n",
              "Coefficient Prompt when Finished");
      printf ("===================================%s",
              "=====================");
```

```
        printf ("\nCoefficient:  ");
        gets (buffer);  // get coefficient of X
        if (buffer[0] == '\0')
          return (head_ptr);
        new_element.coefficient = atof (buffer);
        printf ("Power of X :  ");
        gets (buffer);  // get power of X
        new_element.power_of_x = atoi (buffer);
        head_ptr = link_poly_element(head_ptr,
                              new_element, REPLACE);
    }
}


//  print_poly_obj():
//    Print polynomial of single variable. It is
//    recursively called to print each element
//    until the end of polynomial is reached.
//
void Polynomial::print_poly_obj(POLY_PTR head_ptr)
{
    if (head_ptr == NULL)
      return;   // end of polynomial
    if (head_ptr->coefficient != 0) { // non-zero term
      //  print coefficient of x
      printf ("%.2f", head_ptr->coefficient);
      if (head_ptr->power_of_x > 0) {
        printf ("x");
        if (head_ptr->power_of_x > 1)
          //  print power of x
          printf ("^%d", head_ptr->power_of_x);
      }
    }
    if (head_ptr->next == NULL)
      return;   // end of polynomial
    else {
      // The next term is a non-zero one
      if (head_ptr->next->coefficient != 0)
        printf (" + ");
      print_poly_obj(head_ptr->next); // print next term
    }
}


//  link_poly_element():
//    Insert a polynomial element into a singly linked
//    list of polynomial elements (terms). The element
//    is inserted in order of declining power of x.
//    "REPLACE" or "ADD" is passed to the function to
//    indicate a duplicate element should replace the
//    original, or if it should be added to the original.
//    A new root (head) pointer is returned to the caller.
//
Polynomial::POLY_PTR
Polynomial::link_poly_element (POLY_PTR  head_ptr,
            POLY_ELEMENT new_element, enum type_def type)
```

```
{
    POLY_PTR  new_poly_elt_ptr, previous_ptr,
              current_ptr = head_ptr;

  new_poly_elt_ptr = allocate_poly_element (new_element);

    //  insert new element at the head of the list
    //  if the singly linked list is empty.
    if (head_ptr == NULL) {
      head_ptr = new_poly_elt_ptr;
      return (head_ptr);
    }

    //  locate power of x that element should precede in list
    while ((new_poly_elt_ptr->power_of_x <
            current_ptr->power_of_x) &&
            current_ptr->next != NULL) {
      previous_ptr = current_ptr;
      current_ptr  = current_ptr->next;
    }

    //  if power of x is less than all elements,
    //  insert the new element at the tail end
    if (new_poly_elt_ptr->power_of_x <
        current_ptr->power_of_x) {
      current_ptr->next = new_poly_elt_ptr;
      return (head_ptr);
    }

    //  if power of x is greater than current element
    if (new_poly_elt_ptr->power_of_x >
        current_ptr->power_of_x) {
      //  if power of x is greater than all elements,
      //  insert the new element at the head (start).
      if (current_ptr == head_ptr) {
        new_poly_elt_ptr->next = current_ptr;
        return (new_poly_elt_ptr);
      }

    else {    // insert before current element
       previous_ptr->next = new_poly_elt_ptr;
       new_poly_elt_ptr->next = current_ptr;
       return (head_ptr);
    }
  }

else {  // power of x is equal to current element
  if (type == REPLACE)
     //  replace coefficient with new value
    current_ptr->coefficient = new_poly_elt_ptr->coefficient;
  else  // type == ADD, add new value to coefficient
    current_ptr->coefficient += new_poly_elt_ptr->coefficient;
  delete  new_poly_elt_ptr;
  return (head_ptr);
```

```
        }
}

//  operator+ ():
//     Add two polynomials, each of which is structured as
//     a singly linked list of terms (elements). The head
//     pointers, head_ptr_1 and head_ptr_2, for the two
//     polynomials to be added are passed to the function.
//     A pointer to the resulting (sum) polynomial is
//     returned to the calling function. It is not a member
//     function but a "friend" of the class "Polynomial".
//     Usage:  poly_obj_sum = poly_obj1 + ploy_obj2;
//
Polynomial operator+ (Polynomial poly_obj1,
                      Polynomial poly_obj2)
{
    Polynomial poly_obj_sum;
    Polynomial::POLY_PTR
              head_ptr_1   = poly_obj1.head_ptr,
              head_ptr_2   = poly_obj2.head_ptr,
              head_ptr_sum = NULL,
              current_ptr;

    current_ptr = head_ptr_1;

    while (current_ptr != NULL) {
      //  Add polynomial 1 to sum polynomial,
      //  which is NULL.
      head_ptr_sum = poly_obj1.link_poly_element
                         (head_ptr_sum, *current_ptr, ADD);
      current_ptr = current_ptr->next;
    }

    current_ptr = head_ptr_2;
    while (current_ptr != NULL) {
      //  Add polynomial 2 to sum polynomial,
      //  which is polynomial 1.
      head_ptr_sum = poly_obj2.link_poly_element
                         (head_ptr_sum, *current_ptr, ADD);
      current_ptr = current_ptr->next;
    }

    poly_obj_sum.head_ptr = head_ptr_sum;
    return (poly_obj_sum);
}

//  operator- (): Subtract 'poly_obj2' from 'poly_obj1'
Polynomial operator- (Polynomial poly_obj1,
                      Polynomial poly_obj2)
{
    //  Left as an exercise
    Polynomial sub;
    return (sub);  // To avoid compilation error
}
```

```cpp
//   operator* (): Multiply 'poly_obj2' with 'poly_obj1'
Polynomial operator* (Polynomial poly_obj1,
                           Polynomial poly_obj2)
{
    //   Left as an exercise
    Polynomial mult;
    return (mult);   // To avoid compilation error
}


//   operator/ (): Divide 'poly_obj1' by 'poly_obj2'
Polynomial operator/ (Polynomial poly_obj1,
                           Polynomial poly_obj2)
{
    //   Left as an exercise
    Polynomial divide;
    return (divide); // To avoid compilation error
}

//   evaluate_poly_obj():
//     Evaluate a single-variable polynomial object
//     for a given x, x_value.
//
float  Polynomial::evaluate_poly_obj (float x_value)
{
    float  result;
    //   Left as an exercise; Use Horner's rule
    return (result);
}

//   key_to_continue():
//     Wait for any key to be pressed to continue.
//
void  Polynomial::key_to_continue (void)
{
    printf ("\nPress any key to continue!");
#ifdef  MSDOS
    if (getch () == 0) // read extended ASCII code
        getch ();
#else
    getchar ();
#endif
}


//   display_poly():
//     Display polynomial numbers 1 &2, polynomial sum
//
void display_poly (Polynomial poly_obj1,
        Polynomial poly_obj2, Polynomial poly_obj_sum)
{
    CLRSCR ();
    printf ("\n OOP for Single Variable Polynomials");
    printf ("\n-----------------------------------\n");
    printf ("\nPolynomial Object 1: \n\n");
```

```
      //   Print Polynomial object 1
      poly_obj1.print_poly_obj(poly_obj1.head_ptr);
      printf ("\n\nPolynomial Object 2: \n\n");
      //   Print Polynomial object 2
      poly_obj2.print_poly_obj(poly_obj2.head_ptr);
      printf ("\n\nSum of Polynomial Object 1 %s: \n\n",
            "and Polynomial Object 2");
      //   Print Polynomial object "Polynomial sum"
      poly_obj_sum.print_poly_obj(poly_obj_sum.head_ptr);
      printf ("\n");
      poly_obj1.key_to_continue ();
}

//   main():   Test driver for OOP implementation of
//             ADT polynomials in single variable
//
void   main (void)
{
   //   Declare objects, "poly_obj1", "poly_obj2",
   //   "poly_obj_sum" as instances of "Polynomial" class
   Polynomial  poly_obj1, poly_obj2, poly_obj_sum;

   poly_obj1.build_poly_obj (1);
   poly_obj2.build_poly_obj (2);
   poly_obj_sum = poly_obj1 + poly_obj2;
   display_poly (poly_obj1, poly_obj2,
                   poly_obj_sum);
   CLRSCR ();   // Clear screen
}
```

Code 5.6 for single-variable polynomial objects yields this output:

```
 OOP for Single Variable Polynomials
 ------------------------------------

 Current Polynomial Object 1 is:



 == Enter Polynomial Term ==
 Enter Coefficient and Power of X for each Term.
 Polynomial Terms will be automatically ordered.
 New coefficient will replace old for like powers of X.
 Zero coefficient will erase old for like powers of X.
 <ENTER> with no Value at Coefficient Prompt when Finished
 ============================================================
 Coefficient:  20
 Power of X :  2

 OOP for Single Variable Polynomials
 ------------------------------------
```

Current Polynomial Object 1 is:

20.00x^2

  == Enter Polynomial Term ==
  Enter Coefficient and Power of X for each Term.
  Polynomial Terms will be automatically ordered.
  New coefficient will replace old for like powers of X.
  Zero coefficient will erase old for like powers of X.
  <ENTER> with no Value at Coefficient Prompt when Finished
  ==
  Coefficient: 10
  Power of X : 1

  OOP for Single Variable Polynomials

  Current Polynomial Object 1 is:

20.00x^2 + 10.00x

  == Enter Polynomial Term ==
  Enter Coefficient and Power of X for each Term.
  Polynomial Terms will be automatically ordered.
  New coefficient will replace old for like powers of X.
  Zero coefficient will erase old for like powers of X.
  <ENTER> with no Value at Coefficient Prompt when Finished
  ==
  Coefficient: ENTER

  OOP for Single Variable Polynomials

  Current Polynomial Object 2 is:

  == Enter Polynomial Term ==
  Enter Coefficient and Power of X for each Term.
  Polynomial Terms will be automatically ordered.
  New coefficient will replace old for like powers of X.
  Zero coefficient will erase old for like powers of X.
  <ENTER> with no Value at Coefficient Prompt when Finished
  ==
  Coefficient: 10
  Power of X : 1

  OOP for Single Variable Polynomials

  Current Polynomial Object 2 is:

10.00x

```
== Enter Polynomial Term ==
Enter Coefficient and Power of X for each Term.
Polynomial Terms will be automatically ordered.
New coefficient will replace old for like powers of X.
Zero coefficient will erase old for like powers of X.
<ENTER> with no Value at Coefficient Prompt when Finished
============================================================
Coefficient:   5
Power of X :   0


 OOP for Single Variable Polynomials
 ------------------------------------


 Current Polynomial Object 2 is:

10.00x + 5.00

 == Enter Polynomial Term ==
 Enter Coefficient and Power of X for each Term.
 Polynomial Terms will be automatically ordered.
 New coefficient will replace old for like powers of X.
 Zero coefficient will erase old for like powers of X.
 <ENTER> with no Value at Coefficient Prompt when Finished
 ============================================================
Coefficient:   ENTER

 OOP for Single Variable Polynomials
 ------------------------------------


Polynomial Object 1:

20.00x^2 + 10.00x

Polynomial Object 2:

10.00x + 5.00

Sum of Polynomial Object 1 and Polynomial Object 2:
20.00x^2 + 20.00x + 5.00

Press any key to continue!
```

5.8 OOP Application: Memory Management

As discussed in Chapter 2, two common programming errors associated with data structure implementations making use of dynamic memory allocation are *dangling pointers* and *memory leaks*.

It is shown here how a doubly linked list object may be applied to the task of dynamic system memory management for the purpose of avoiding memory leaks. In particular, we illustrate a *free list* data structure as a circular doubly linked list. We then show how to manage such a free list using the techniques of *counted pointers* and *automatic garbage collection*.

5.8.1   THE FREE LIST

The *main memory* or *primary memory* of a computer system is an expensive resource. Its management is one of the most important and difficult tasks of an operating system.

In a multiprogramming computing environment, several processes (i.e., programs in execution) may request main memory space, and are subsequently fetched from the secondary memory (such as disk, tape, and drum) into this memory. While concurrently residing in the memory they may request more space. Any given process will release the occupied memory space upon completion of execution. To synchronize these dynamic activities and maintain an efficient use of memory, the memory manager of a typical operating system will employ the following three management strategies:

- Fetching program and data from disk into primary memory by:
  - Demand fetching, or
  - Anticipatory fetching.

- Allocation or placement by:
  - First-fit,
  - Best-fit, and
  - Worst-fit.

- Deallocation and replacement by releasing the memory space after it is no longer required.

To accomplish these management activities, the memory manager keeps a database in the form of a list of free partitions known as the *free list*. A free list contains information such as the starting address, size, and type of an unallocated memory partition (*block* or *segment*).

There are several methods of organizing the free list. One way is to use a doubly linked list. The doubly linked structure facilitates quick insertion, deletion, search, and combining of two adjacent (neighboring) partitions. Combining two or more adjacent partitions (also called *coalescing*), is useful to create a larger free partition, and is performed by well-known *boundary tag method*. In this method, two boundary tags (USED or FREE) are added to each partition. A doubly linked list of free partitions using boundary tags is shown in Figure 5.17.

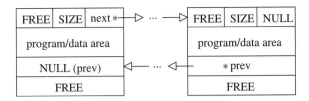

FIGURE 5.17. Free list with boundary tags.

The general structures for the allocated and free partitions (blocks) are shown in Figure 5.18. In our approach, the free memory segments (blocks) are maintained as a doubly linked list as shown in Figure 5.19.

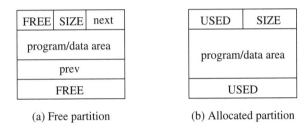

(a) Free partition   (b) Allocated partition

FIGURE 5.18. Structures for free and allocated partitions.

For an OOP implementation of a free list in this approach, a free list object is a data structure that contains each structure for a free partition as a doubly linked list, and operations (add memory block to free list, remove a block from free list, and so on) as methods. A class `Free_List` is used in **Code 5.7** and defined in `class_Free_List_def.h` as follows:

```
class Free_List {
  private:
    // Define Structure for Memory Segment
    typedef struct MEM_SEG {
    char   *addr;   // char-type pointer to Start address
    int    size;    // Size of the memory segment
    STATUS status;  // Status of the memory segment
    int    btype;   // Type: CODE, PRIVATE, SHARED
    int    refcnt;  // Reference Count : incremented when
                    // referenced by a process.
    MEM_SEG *next,// Pointer to the Next memory structure
                // in order to form a doubly linked list
            *prev;
    } *FREE_MEM_LIST_PTR;
```

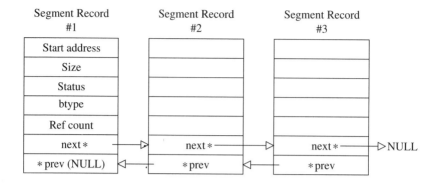

FIGURE 5.19. Free list as a doubly linked list.

```
int   max_avail;
int   *mem_pool;  // an array of free memory segments
FREE_MEM_LIST_PTR   FRL_head_ptr,
                    FRL_tail_ptr,
                    block_ptr;
   void init_FrList(); // Initialize free list
   void set_mem_defaults (FREE_MEM_LIST_PTR ptr,
                       int size);
   FREE_MEM_LIST_PTR memory_status(int size);
public:
   Free_List() { init_FrList(); }  // Constructor
   ~Free_List();                   // Destructor
   void build_FrList();
   void add_blk_to_FrList(FREE_MEM_LIST_PTR blk);
   char *get_mem_block(int, int);
   char *allocate_mem_block(PCB_LIST_PTR pid,
                        int block_type);
   void dump_mem(PCB_LIST_PTR pid);
   void release_mem_block(PCB_LIST_PTR pid);
   FREE_MEM_LIST_PTR   merge_mem_blocks(
   FREE_MEM_LIST_PTR block1, FREE_MEM_LIST_PTR block2);
   FREE_MEM_LIST_PTR   collect_garbage();
};
```

An ADT free list is used to identify the object of type `Free_List`. Each free segment is of type `MEM_SEG` that contains all fields shown in Figure 5.19. `PCB_LIST_PTR` is a type pointer for process control block structure `PCB_S` that defines the singly linked list data structure for a process.

The methods for the `Free_List` class are implemented in C++ and are completely shown in **Code 5.7**. Some of these are described below.

`Get_mem_block()` is a `public` member function of the `Free_List` class. It performs as follows. When all blocks of the free list have been allocated, it returns an overflow condition and the requesting process must go to sleep at this condition, and wake it up when available. Otherwise, get_mem_block() allocates a block using the *best fit* allocation policy, and returns its character-type pointer location. It expects two inputs, block_size and block_type. The algorithm for get_mem_block() is:

```
BEGIN
  ptr = head of MEMORY Structure;
  if (size > the maximum allowable block)
     return (address 0);
  while (not at end of the free list)
  BEGIN
    if (ptr->size just fits the block_size)
    BEGIN
       if (block is free or can be shared)
          return (location of block);
       else ptr = next element in list;
    END
    else ptr = next element in list;
  END
  If (reached this point)
     set overflow flag & return(address 0);
END
```

Allocate_mem_block() is a public member function of the class Free_List. It expects a pointer pid of type PCB_LIST_PTR, and an integer argument block_type. Its algorithm is:

```
allocate_mem_block(pid, block_type)

BEGIN
  Call get_mem_block() to allocate a block.
  If (return address 0) exit this procedure now.
  Allocate block for the process.
  Appropriately set characteristics for the allocated block.
  Increment process size according to allocated block.
  Update the MEMORY Structure and the PROCESS Structure.
  Return (the location of the allocate block).
END
```

Release_mem_block() is a public member function of the class Free_List. It expects a pointer pid of type PCB_LIST_PTR. Its algorithm is:

```
release_mem_block(pid)

BEGIN
  ptr = head of MEMORY Structure;
  while (ptr->size not equal to process memory limits)
          ptr = next element;

  Decrement reference counter of the block by 1;
```

```
  if (reference count equals zero)
  BEGIN
    first, to dump the memory, and to clear
    the memory, it calls dump_mem(), which
    calls memory_status();
    set free status of block to true;
    set locked status of block to false;
    set modified status of block to false;
    set in demand status of block to false;
  END
  Otherwise, simply return because the block
  has been referenced by other process(es).
END
```

It does not put the released block back into the free list.

Build_FrList() is a public member function of the Free_List class. It simulates operating system's free memory list by building a doubly linked list of 10 blocks of memory, of sizes:

118, 200, 256, 526, 300, 500, 400, 420, 800, 320 in bytes.

It calls set_mem_defaults(), and also sets max_avail to the maximum available block size. Its algorithm is:

```
build_FrList()

BEGIN
  Allocate memory for head of MEMORY Structure;
  for (i <= 10)
  BEGIN
    allocate a block in real, physical memory;
    insert the free block in the MEMORY structure;
    set FRL_head_ptr, and FRL_tail_ptr.
  END
END
```

Code 5.7

```
// Program:   free_list.c++
// Purpose:
//   Form a data structure a list of free blocks
//   as a doubly linked list, and manage this free
//   list. (Object-Oriented simulation program)
//
#include <stdio.h>
#include <stdlib.h>
#ifdef  MSDOS
#include <alloc.h>
#else
#include <malloc.h>
#endif
```

```
typedef   int   BOOLEAN;
typedef   int   PROCESS_ID;
const     int   TRUE    = 1;
const     int   FALSE   = 0;
const     int   CODE    = 0; // Block type to hold
                             //   program's CODE
const     int   SHARED  = 1; // SHARED block type
const     int   PRIVATE = 2; // Block type to hold
                             //   PRIVATE data/text
const     int   STACK   = 3; // Block type to hold
                             //   program's STACK.

struct STATUS {              // Status structure for each block
    BOOLEAN isfree;          // Block Is FREE
    BOOLEAN islocked;        // Block Is LOCKED
    BOOLEAN isindemand;      // Block Is In Demand
    BOOLEAN ismodified;      // Block Is Modified (Written into)
};
struct dosregs {     // Intel 8086 Registers to be
                     //   accessible under DOS BIOS
    unsigned int ax, bx, cx, dx, di, si;
    unsigned int cs, ds, es, ss;
    unsigned int sp, bp;
    unsigned int cflags, flags;
};
// Structure for Process Control Block (PCB)
typedef struct PCB_S {
    PROCESS_ID id;  // Process ID
    int     state;  // Process State: READY, RUN, SLEEP
    char    *base;  // Base address of the memory segment
                    // in which it is loaded
    int     limit;  // Limit of the segment
    int     size;   // Size  of the segment
    dosregs regs;   // Process registers
    PCB_S   *next;  // Pointer to the Next PCB Structure
                    // in order to form a Singly Linked List
} *PCB_LIST_PTR;

#include "class_Free_List_def.h" // For "Free_List" class

Free_List::~Free_List()
{
    // Left as an exercise
}

// init_FrList(): Initialize a free list object.
void Free_List::init_FrList()
{
   FRL_head_ptr = NULL;
   FRL_tail_ptr = NULL;
   // Assign sizes of initial 10 free blocks.
   static int mem[] = {118, 200, 256, 300,
                  320, 400, 420, 500, 526, 800, 0};
```

```
      mem_pool = mem;
}

void Free_List::set_mem_defaults (
      FREE_MEM_LIST_PTR ptr, int size)
{
   ptr->size = size;
   ptr->status.isfree     = TRUE;
   ptr->status.islocked   = FALSE;
   ptr->status.isindemand = FALSE;
   ptr->status.ismodified = FALSE;
   ptr->refcnt = 0;
 } // end of memdefaults()

// =========================================
//  build_FrList():
//    Build a doubly linked free list from an
//    initial set of free mem blocks.
// =========================================
void Free_List::build_FrList(void)
{
   int *pool = mem_pool;  // initial memory pool

   FREE_MEM_LIST_PTR  new_ptr = new MEM_SEG;
   if (new_ptr == NULL)
       exit (1);
   new_ptr->addr = (char *)calloc(*pool,
                                  sizeof(char));
   new_ptr->next = NULL;
   new_ptr->prev = NULL;
   max_avail = *pool;  // assign maximum available memory

   if (FRL_head_ptr == NULL)  // Free list is empty
       FRL_head_ptr = new_ptr;
   FRL_tail_ptr = FRL_head_ptr;
   set_mem_defaults (FRL_tail_ptr, *pool);
   for (++pool; *pool; ++pool) {
      if ((FRL_tail_ptr->next = new MEM_SEG) == NULL)
          exit (1);
      FRL_tail_ptr->next->prev = FRL_tail_ptr;
      FRL_tail_ptr = FRL_tail_ptr->next;
      if ((FRL_tail_ptr->addr = (char *)calloc(*pool,
                            sizeof(char))) == NULL)
        exit(1);

      // Calculate maximum available size of a block
      max_avail = (max_avail > *pool) ? max_avail : *pool;
      set_mem_defaults(FRL_tail_ptr, *pool);

   } // end of for()
   FRL_tail_ptr->next = NULL;  // end of free list
} // end of build_FrList()

Free_List::FREE_MEM_LIST_PTR
```

```
Free_List::memory_status(int size)
{
    FREE_MEM_LIST_PTR ptr = FRL_head_ptr;

    while ((ptr->size < size) && ptr)
        ptr = ptr->next;
    return (ptr);
} // end of memory_status()

//
//  dump_mem(): Display free list
//
void  Free_List::dump_mem(PCB_LIST_PTR pid)
{
    FREE_MEM_LIST_PTR ptr;
    char *addr, *stop;

    ptr = memory_status(pid->limit);
    // point to physical memory location
    addr = ptr->addr;
    // stop at end of physical block memory
    stop = addr + ptr->size;
    while (addr < stop)
        *addr++ = '\0';     // clear memory
    // Exercise: Now, add this in the free list.
} //     end of dump_mem()

// ==========================================
//  release_mem_block():
//    Release memory block if no other process
//    is referencing it.
// ==========================================
void Free_List::release_mem_block(PCB_LIST_PTR pid)
{
    FREE_MEM_LIST_PTR ptr = FRL_head_ptr;

    while ((ptr->size < pid->limit) && ptr)
        ptr = ptr->next;
    if (ptr->refcnt)
        --ptr->refcnt;
    if (!ptr->refcnt) {
        dump_mem(pid); // release memory held by process
        // Reset status flags
        ptr->status.isfree = TRUE;
        ptr->status.islocked = FALSE;
        ptr->status.isindemand = FALSE;
        ptr->status.ismodified = FALSE;
    }
} // end of release_mem_block()

// ==========================================
//  get_mem_block():
//    Get a block from the free list, that
//    satisfies the "Best Fit" alloc policy.
```

```
// ==========================================
char *Free_List::get_mem_block(int block_size,
                               int btype)
{
    FREE_MEM_LIST_PTR  block_ptr;
    int overflow = FALSE;  // assume no overflow condition

    // first check if block can be allocated
    if (block_size > max_avail)
       return (NULL);  // if size too large, exit

  FREE_MEM_LIST_PTR ptr = FRL_head_ptr;
  while (ptr) {
    if (ptr->size >= block_size) {
      if ((ptr->status.isfree)
          (ptr->btype == SHARED && btype == SHARED)) {
         // save memory location in the linked list
         block_ptr = ptr;
         // return location of real memory
         return (ptr->addr);
      }
    }
    ptr = ptr->next;
  }
  overflow = TRUE;  // overflow condition
  return (NULL);    // can't allocate enough memory
 } // end of get_mem_block()

// ==========================================
//  allocate_mem_block():
//    Use "Best Fit" method to allocate a free
//    memory from the free list to a process.
// ==========================================
//
char *Free_List::allocate_mem_block(PCB_LIST_PTR pid,
                                    int block_type)
{
  char *location;

  // try to allocate memory for process
  if ((location = get_mem_block(pid->size,
                     block_type)) == NULL)
        return (NULL);
  if (block_ptr->status.isfree
      block_type == SHARED) {
    if (location != pid->base)
       ++block_ptr->refcnt;
    block_ptr->status.isfree = FALSE;
  }
  if (block_type == STACK   block_type == CODE)
    block_ptr->status.islocked = TRUE;
  if (block_ptr->refcnt > 1)
    block_ptr->status.isindemand = TRUE;
  pid->limit = block_ptr->size;
```

```
    block_ptr->btype = block_type;
    return (location);
  } // end of allocate_mem_block()

//
//  main():  Test driver for OOP implementation
//               of memory management for free list.
//
void main(void)
{
    Free_List   free_list_obj;

    free_list_obj.build_FrList();
}
```

5.8.2   FREE LIST MANAGEMENT BY COUNTED POINTERS

One approach to dealing with the problem of memory leaks is the *counted pointers* technique. The counted pointers method automatically facilitates dynamic management of the free list by maintaining a count of how many pointers refer (or point to) an object or element.

The counted pointers technique is straightforward:

Counted Pointers Technique

For a given element there is an associated *reference count*:

- The reference count is *incremented* whenever a new pointer points to that element.

- The reference count is *decremented* whenever a pointer ceases to point that element.

- An element is *deleted* when its associated reference count becomes zero.

The advantage of the counted pointers method is that it is possible to preserve efficiency for objects and elements. The disadvantages are:

- The program must use special pointers and referencing techniques (e.g., overloaded operators *, &, ->, ( ), and [ ]) for those objects or elements managed by the counted pointers method.

- The program must use special forms of the C++ operators new and delete (i.e., the overloaded versions of new, delete). When overloaded, delete operator decrements the reference count, and deletes the element if the reference count becomes zero.

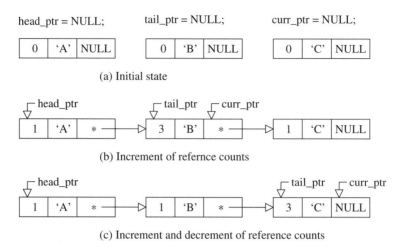

(a) Initial state

(b) Increment of refernce counts

(c) Increment and decrement of reference counts

FIGURE 5.20. Counted pointers for a singly linked list.

- In the case of cyclic pointers, the reference count for an object or element will never be zero, and that object or element will never be freed.

To illustrate the counted pointers method for a singly linked list, an additional field `reference_count` is added for each element.

Figure 5.20(a) shows zero reference count for each element. In Figure 5.20(b), reference counts for the elements with 'A', 'B', and 'C' are respectively 1, 3, and 1. In Figure 5.20(c), the counted pointers `tail_ptr` and `curr_ptr` now point to the element with 'C'; its associated reference count is increased by two, and the associated reference count for 'B' is decreased by two. This means that using one counted pointer to another requires decreasing the reference count for the old element and increasing the reference count for the new element. A simple OOP code and output for a singly linked list using counted pointer are given in **Code 5.8**. It would have been ideal and efficient by implementing the reference operators `*`, `&`, `->`, `()`, `[]`, and `delete` as overloaded operators incorporating pointer reference counts. This is left as an exercise.

Code 5.8

```
//  Program:  count_ptr_singly_lnk_lst.c++
//  Purpose:
//    Objected-Oriented counted pointer version of singly
//    linked list. This is to manage "memory leaks."
//
#include  <stdio.h>
typedef char          DATA_TYPE;
typedef unsigned int  UINT;

class Count_Ptr_Singly_Linked_List {
  private:
    typedef struct SLIST_ELEMENT_CP {
        UINT              ref_count;
        DATA_TYPE         data;
        SLIST_ELEMENT_CP  *next;
    } *SLIST_CNT_PTR;
    SLIST_CNT_PTR  head_ptr, tail_ptr, curr_ptr;
    void  init_slist_CP (void);
  public:
    Count_Ptr_Singly_Linked_List () { init_slist_CP();}
    ~Count_Ptr_Singly_Linked_List ();
    void  print_ref_count (SLIST_CNT_PTR elem_ptr,
                             char *hdr);
    UINT  incr_count (SLIST_CNT_PTR  elem_ptr);
    UINT  decr_count (SLIST_CNT_PTR  elem_ptr);
    void  set_address (SLIST_CNT_PTR  given_elem_ptr,
                         SLIST_CNT_PTR  *to_elem_ptr);
    void  demo_counted_ptr (void);
};

Count_Ptr_Singly_Linked_List::~Count_Ptr_Singly_Linked_List ()
{
   // Left as an exercise
}

void Count_Ptr_Singly_Linked_List::init_slist_CP (void)
{
   head_ptr = tail_ptr = curr_ptr = NULL;
}

UINT Count_Ptr_Singly_Linked_List::incr_count
                         (SLIST_CNT_PTR elem_ptr)
{
   UINT count = (elem_ptr->ref_count)++;
   return (count);
}

UINT Count_Ptr_Singly_Linked_List::decr_count
                         (SLIST_CNT_PTR elem_ptr)
{
   if (elem_ptr != NULL) {
      UINT count = (elem_ptr->ref_count)--;
```

```
        if ((count + 1) == 0) delete elem_ptr;
        return (count);
    }
    return (0);
}

void Count_Ptr_Singly_Linked_List::set_address (
 SLIST_CNT_PTR given_elem_ptr, SLIST_CNT_PTR *to_elem_ptr)
{
    // Decrement the referenece counter for the element
    // it was previously pointing to
    decr_count (*to_elem_ptr);
    *to_elem_ptr = given_elem_ptr;
    // Increment the referenece counter for the element
    // it is currently pointing to
    incr_count (*to_elem_ptr);
}

void Count_Ptr_Singly_Linked_List::print_ref_count
                    (SLIST_CNT_PTR elem_ptr, char *hdr)
{
    printf (" %s ref count is: %d \n", hdr,
            elem_ptr->ref_count);
}

void Count_Ptr_Singly_Linked_List::demo_counted_ptr
                                    (void)
{
    static SLIST_ELEMENT_CP  elem_1 = {0, 'A', NULL},
                             elem_2 = {0, 'B', NULL},
                             elem_3 = {0, 'C', NULL};
    printf("\n** Counted Pointer Version %s \n\n",
            "of a Singly Linked List **");
    set_address (&elem_1, &head_ptr);
    set_address (&elem_1, &tail_ptr);
    set_address (&elem_1, &curr_ptr);
    print_ref_count (head_ptr, "Initially, element 1's");

    //  Assign address of elem_2; ref cnt = 2
    set_address (&elem_2, &elem_1.next);
    set_address (&elem_2, &curr_ptr);
    set_address (&elem_2, &tail_ptr);

    print_ref_count (head_ptr,
      "After assigning curr & tail to elt 2, elt 1's");
    print_ref_count (curr_ptr, "Element 2's");

    //  Assign address of elem_3
    set_address (&elem_3, &elem_2.next);
    set_address (&elem_3, &curr_ptr);
    set_address (&elem_3, &tail_ptr);

    print_ref_count (head_ptr->next,
      "After assigning curr & tail to elt 3, elt 2's");
```

```
      print_ref_count (curr_ptr, "Element 3's");
}

//  main(): Test driver for OOP imlementation of
//          singly linked list using counted pointer
//
void main (void)
{
    Count_Ptr_Singly_Linked_List count_slist;

    count_slist.demo_counted_ptr();
}
```

Code 5.8 for an OOP implementation of a singly linked list using counted pointers produces this output:

```
** Counted Pointer Version of a Singly Linked List **

Initially, element 1's ref count is: 3
After assigning curr & tail to elt 2, elt 1's ref count is: 1
Element 2's ref count is: 3
After assigning curr & tail to elt 3, elt 2's ref count is: 1
Element 3's ref count is: 3
```

5.8.3   FREE LIST MANAGEMENT BY GARBAGE COLLECTION

Automatic garbage (memory leak) collection is accomplished by a runtime program, called *garbage collector* (or *compaction*), which will be automatically executed when a program requests a piece of memory, often called *partition* or *block* (e.g., 512 bytes) and the system's free list does not have enough free memory space to match the request. The objective of the garbage collector is to reclaim all garbages in main memory (i.e., memory pieces/blocks that are allocated to but not used by programs, and not accessible to any user's programs) and to return them to the system's free list. The garbage collection and management of free lists are important tasks of the operating system's memory manager. We now discuss garbage collection methods including coalescing and compaction. In the next section, we discuss organizing the free list by a structure (a doubly linked list, a max heap or a min heap), which is mainly influenced by the placement (or "allocation") method of the memory manager. (For the max and mean heaps, see Chapter 7.)

Garbage Collection Technique

The garbage collection method consists of the following steps:

Step 1. *Marking*: Identify and mark all "active" (allocated and used) objects and memory spaces. Identify and mark all "inactive" (allocated but not used) (i.e, garbage) objects and memory spaces.

Step 2. *Collecting*: Collect or reclaim all inactive (unused and inaccessible) memory spaces and return them to the free list.

Step 3. *Coalescing*: Coalesce or merge two adjacent (contiguous) free memory spaces to one larger free memory space.

Step 4. *Compacting*: If any free memory space in the free list is not large enough to satisfy any program's request for memory, perform compaction. That is, move all used (active) memory spaces (partitions/blocks) to one end of memory in order to yield one large hole (free space).

The disadvantages of the compaction step include stopping execution of all processes, using some stack space for garbage collector, and taking time for the careful adjustment/assignment of previous pointers to the newly configured memory's used (active) blocks.

There are several versions of the marking algorithm by which garbage collection algorithms differ. Since C++ is designed to be both downward compatible with C and efficient, C++ does not provide any automatic garbage collection facilities (programs). Some automatic garbage collection versions of `malloc()` are developed by Boehm and Weiser [BW88]. The basic principles used by their marking algorithms are almost the same. Due to the limited scope of this book, the reader is referred to [BW88] for further discussion on the automatic garbage collection.

5.9   Summary

The main points for list objects are summarized below:

- Due to various implementations, list objects are categorized into (1) array-based list, (2) singly linked list, (3) doubly linked list, (4) singly linked circular list, and (5) doubly linked circular list.

- The worst-case performances of the insert, delete, and search operations for these lists with n data elements are $O(n)$.

- The array-based list is fixed in size; it cannot dynamically grow or shrink in size. The insert and delete operations are not efficient because these operations may require physical movement of data elements. It does allow for random access of data elements using the array index. Memory space may be wasted if there are not enough data elements in the array.

- The singly linked list can dynamically grow or shrink in size. The insert before and delete operations are complex because there are no back links to predecessor elements.

- The doubly linked list can dynamically grow or shrink in size. The insert before and delete operations are simple and efficient because there is a back link to predecessor elements. This implementation of the List object is the most commonly applied.

- Traversal of singly and doubly lists starts only from the head of the list and is performed sequentially.

- Only one pointer is necessary for the traversal of a singly or a doubly linked circular list.

- The selection of a list implementation is highly influenced by the operations and the static or dynamic storage requirement of the application.

- One or combinations of these list data structures are used to develop such complex data structures as stacks, queues, trees, tries, and graphs.

- Due to dynamic memory allocation used in implementing the List objects, two common memory management errors are dangling pointers and memory leaks, which are handled by counted pointers and garbage collection techniques.

5.10   Exercises

1. For an array-based OOP implementation of a list object in **Code 5.1**, write tests and methods to implement the following public member functions of the Ary_List class:

   (a) get_element() to get an element (must check if there is any data in that location). (b) put_element() to update/modify a given element in an array list object. (c) add_before() to add a new element before a given element in an array list object.

2. For the OOP implementation of a singly linked list in **Code 5.3**, write tests and `public` member functions of the `Singly_Linked_List` class to implement the following actions:

(a) Add a new element after a given element in a singly linked list object. (b) Add a new element before a given element in a singly linked list object. (c) Modify a given element with a new data in a list object; one must find the given element first. (d) Get information of an element specified by its key in a singly linked list object; one must find the given element first.

3. Write a test driver and an OOP to reverse a singly linked list object using three list pointers. Implementation using `while` loop for n elements yields performance $O(n)$, $n >= 1$.

4. Write a test driver and an OOP to merge two singly linked list objects. Display the two input list objects, and the merged list object. [Note: When multiple objects of the same class type are created, each object gets its own copy of the `private` and `public` data members.]

5. Write a test driver and an OOP for the `Triangle` class using a singly linked list.

6. Write a test driver and an OOP for the `Right_Angle_Triangle` class using a singly linked list.

7. Write a test driver and an OOP for the `Circle` class using a singly linked list.

8. Write a test driver and an OOP for the `Rectangle` class using a singly linked list.

9. Write a test driver and an OOP for the `Square` class using a singly linked list.

10. To draw the shape of a rectangular object, write a `public` member function of the `Rectangle` class. This requires redefining the `Rectangle` class in Exercise 5-8.

11. Write a test driver and an OOP for the `Hexagon` class using a singly linked list.

12. Write a test driver and an OOP for the `Polygon` class using a singly linked list.

13. For the singly linked list based OOP of a single-variable polynomial of degree n in **Code 5.6**, write test drivers and the `friend` methods of the `Polynomial` class.

(a) operator- () that subtracts two Polynomial-type objects.
(b) operator* () that multiplies two Polynomial-type objects.
(c) operator/ () that divides one Polynomial-type object by another Polynomial-type object. (d) evaluate_poly_obj() that evaluates a Polynomial-type object for a given real number (use Horner's method for rewriting the terms of the polynomial.) (e) Print the results in the symbolic form.

14. An algebraic expression $P(x, y)$ of the form

$$P(x, y) = P_m x^m + P_{m-1} x^{m-1} y + \ldots + P_1 x y^{n-1} + P_0 y^n$$

is a polynomial in two variables x and y, m and n being degrees of x and y. Write a test driver and an OOP using a doubly linked list for a two-variable polynomial with the following actions:

(a) Add two polynomial objects. (b) Subtract two polynomial objects. (c) Multiply two polynomial objects. (d) Divide one polynomial object by another polynomial object. (e) Evaluate a polynomial object for a given real number. (f) Display a polynomial object as an algebraic expression.

15. For the OOP implementation of a doubly linked list in **Code 5.4**, write tests and public member functions of Doubly_Linked_List class to implement the following actions:

(a) Add a new element after a given element in a doubly linked list object. (b) Add a new element before a given element in a doubly linked list object. (c) Modify a given element with a new data in a list object; one must find the given element first. (d) Get information of an element specified by its key in a doubly linked list object; one must find the given element first. (e) Search for a specified element in the backward direction.

16. Write a test driver and an OOP to merge two doubly linked list objects. Display the two input list objects, and the merged list object.

17. Write a test driver and an OOP for the Triangle class using a doubly linked list.

18. Write a test driver and an OOP for the Right_Angle_Triangle class using a doubly linked list.

19. Write a test driver and an OOP for the Circle class using a doubly linked list.

20. Write a test driver and an OOP for the Rectangle class using a doubly linked list.

21. To draw the shape of a rectangular object, write a `public` member function of the `Rectangle` class. This requires redefining the `Rectangle` class in Exercise 5-20.

22. Write a test driver and an OOP for the `Square` class using a doubly linked list.

23. Write a test driver and an OOP for the `Hexagon` class using a doubly linked list.

24. Write a test driver and an OOP for the `Polygon` class using a doubly linked list.

25. For the OOP implementation of a singly linked circular list object, write tests and `public` member functions of `Circ_Linked_List` class in **Code 5.5** that implement the following actions:

    (a) Add a new element before a given element in a singly linked circular list object. (b) Modify a given element with a new data in a list object; one must find the given element first. (c) Get information of an element specified by its key in a singly linked circular list object; one must find the given element first.

26. For an OOP implementation of a doubly linked circular list, write and test `public` member functions of `Circ_Doubly_Linked_List` class that implement the following actions:

    (a) Constructor. (b) Destructor. (c) Build a `Circ_Doubly_Linked`-type object from a given set of integer data elements. (d) Check whether a `Circ_Doubly_Linked`-type object is empty. (e) Search for an element given by its key in a doubly linked circular list object. (f) Add a new element after a given element in a doubly linked circular list object. (g) Get information of an element specified by its key in a doubly linked circular list object; one must find the given element first.

27. Write a `public` member function of the `Circ_Doubly_Linked` class that searches for the predecessor of an element with its key value in a doubly linked circular list object. One must include a test driver.

28. Write a `public` member function of the `Circ_Doubly_Linked` class that deletes an element given by its key from a doubly linked circular list object. One must include a test driver.

29. Write a `public` member function of the `Circ_Doubly_Linked` class that adds a new element after a given element in a doubly linked circular list object. One must include a test driver.

30. Write a `public` member function of the `Circ_Doubly_Linked` class that modifies an element in a doubly linked circular list object. One must include a test driver.

31. Write a `public` member function of the `Circ_Doubly_Linked` class that calculates the length of a circular list object. One must include a test driver.

32. Write a test driver and an OOP to merge two doubly linked circular list objects. Display the two input list objects and the merged list object. [Note: When multiple objects of the same class type are created, each object gets its own copy of the `private` and `public` data members.]

33. Write a test driver and an OOP for the `Triangle` class using a singly linked circular list.

34. Write a test driver and an OOP for the `Right_Angle_Triangle` class using a singly linked circular list.

35. Write a test driver and an OOP for the `Circle` class using a singly linked circular list.

36. Write a test driver and an OOP for the `Rectangle` class using a singly linked circular list.

37. Write a test driver and an OOP for the `Square` class using a singly linked circular list.

38. To draw the shape of a rectangular object, write a `public` member function of the `Rectangle` class. This requires redefining the `Rectangle` class in Exercise 5-36.

39. Write a test driver and an OOP for the `Hexagon` class using a singly linked circular list.

40. Write an OOP for the `Polygon` class using a singly circular linked list. Implementation must include a test driver and the `public` interface functions.

41. Write a test driver and an OOP to merge two doubly linked circular list objects. Display the two input list objects, and the merged list object. [Note: When multiple objects of the same class type are created, each object gets its own copy of the `private` and `public` data members.]

42. Write a test driver and an OOP for the `Triangle` class using a doubly linked circular list.

43. Write a test driver and an OOP for the `Right_Angle_Triangle` class using a doubly linked circular list.

44. Write a test driver and an OOP for the `Circle` class using a doubly linked circular list.

45. Write a test driver and an OOP for the `Rectangle` class using a doubly linked circular list.

46. Write a test driver and an OOP for the `Square` class using a doubly linked circular list.

47. To draw the shape of a rectangular object, write a `public` member function of the `Rectangle` class. This requires redefining the `Rectangle` class in Exercise 5-36.

48. Write a test driver and an OOP for the `Hexagon` class using a doubly linked circular list.

49. Write a test driver and an OOP for the `Polygon` class using a doubly linked circular list.

50. For the counted pointer version of a singly linked list, rewrite the OOP in **Code 5.8** by implementing the reference operators `*`, `&`,`->`, `()`, `[]`, and `delete` as overloaded operators.

51. In **Code 5.7** for the OOP implementation of free lists, write the test driver and the following `public` member functions:

    (a) `~Free_List()`

    (b) `void add_blk_to_FrList(FREE_MEM_LIST_PTR blk)`

    (c) `FREE_MEM_LIST_PTR   merge_mem_blocks(`
    `FREE_MEM_LIST_PTR block1,FREE_MEM_LIST_PTR block2)`

    (d) `FREE_MEM_LIST_PTR   collect_garbage()`.

52. *Programming Project*: An $m \times n$ sparse matrix is a rectangular array with m rows and n columns and most of its elements are zero. If a sparse matrix is treated like a regular matrix, memory spaces would be allocated for zero elements; this is clearly a waste and an inefficient use of memory. For OOP implementation of a sparse matrix, use a doubly linked circular list data structure.

    (a) Using a diagram, show a sparse matrix object where elements are stored in doubly linked circular lists. (b) Define a `Sparse_Matrix` class for sparse matrix objects. (c) Write test drivers and `public` member functions as methods of the `Sparse_Matrix` class for the following operations: (i) Construct a sparse matrix object. (ii) Destroy a sparse matrix object. (iii) Initialize a sparse matrix object. (iv) Add two sparse matrix objects. (v) Subtract two sparse matrix objects. (vi) Multiply two sparse matrix objects. (vii) Print a sparse matrix object in a rectangular form. Hint: Keep one m-dimensional array of pointers to row elements and one n-dimensional array of pointers to column elements; each element of a sparse matrix has the data structure:

elem_value	row index	column index
index of next non−zero row		index of next non−zero column

6

Stacks and Queues

Recall from the previous chapter that for an ordered list object, a data element may be inserted into and deleted from any specified position in the list structure. That is, a general list object provides for random access of its data elements. This flexibility, however, is realized at the expense of having to either explicitly rearrange the data elements or maintain a potentially complicated data linking structure.

For many applications, the flexibility provided by a general list object is unnecessary and inefficient. For example, many situations arise where a list data object, which solely provides for efficient access operations to the *last* data element inserted in the object, is best suited.

In general, one may find that a specialized or *restricted access* version of a particular general data object is appropriate. A restricted access version of the general object provides for

- a simpler user-interface, as only a restricted set of methods (operations) are supported, and thus

- simpler implementations.

Two of the most fundamental and generally applicable restricted access data objects in the study of computer science are the *stack* object and the *queue* object. Both are specialized versions of the general list object. Neither are built-in data types in C++ language. The ADT stack and queue objects are the topic of this chapter.

Applications of stacks are found in such areas as compilers (Reverse Polish Notation, parsers, recursion), operating systems (push directory, pop directory), hypertext applications (stack of card objects), and window management (push window and pop window). Applications of queues include such areas as operating systems (process queues, message queues, disk, tape, and printer scheduling), computer networks, and general scheduling applications.

6.1 Stack Objects

The stack data structure is the most commonly occurring restricted access data structure. The primary reason for this, as we shall see, is the intimate relationship between its operations and the process of recursion.

Definition 6.1 *A* stack *(pushdown stack) is an ordered list in which all insertions and deletions are made at one end, called the* top *of the stack. The other (fixed) end is referred to as the* bottom *of the stack. A stack supports two primary operations:*

(i) push — *insertion into the top of the stack.*
(ii) pop — *deletion (retrieval) from the top of the stack.*

This description of the stack implies that the first element inserted is the last to be removed and the last element inserted is the first removed. As such, stacks are also referred to as *Last In First Out (LIFO)* lists. A *stack object* is specified by an ADT stack which has two parts:

- a collection of data elements that adhere to the LIFO policy, and

- a collection of some generalized operations on the data elements.

The collection of data elements is the data abstraction while the collection of operations is the program abstraction. An ADT stack allows programmers to program with an abstract concept of the data element in the stack. The tools they have include the types of data elements, the ADT stack, and the set of outside interface routines. A set of example methods for a stack object is given in Table 6.1.

A stack with no elements on it has zero size. A stack grows in size from the bottom element on up as elements are pushed onto it and decreases in size from the top element on down as elements are popped off of it.

Example Stack Object Methods

Construct and initialize a stack object.
Destroy a stack object.
Check if a stack object is empty.
Check if an (array-based) stack object is full.
Build a stack object from a given set of data.
Add *push* a data element in a stack object.
Delete *pop* a data element from a stack object.
Get any attribute of the top-of-stack element.
Modify any attribute of the top-of-stack element.
Display (print) a stack object.
Get the total number of data elements.

TABLE 6.1.

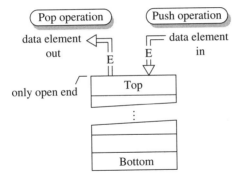

FIGURE 6.1. A stack and its push/pop operations.

For a stack of fixed size n, only n successive push operations are valid. Any push operations beyond the size of the stack will fail, a condition commonly referred to as *stack overflow*. When a stack object is empty, that is, when it has no data elements, further pop operations will fail. Such a state is referred to as *stack underflow*. Figure 6.1 depicts a stack object with the push and pop operations.

A stack structure is analogous to a pile (stack) of cards. Placing (pushing) a new card in this stack means laying the new card on the card currently at the top of the pile. Removing (popping) a card from the pile means taking out the card currently at the top of the pile, making the card immediately below it the new card at the top of the pile.

A stack object can be implemented in two ways, differing by the way the data elements are organized:

- The data elements of the stack are stored in an array structure.

- The data elements of the stack are stored in a singly or doubly linked list structure.

In the following subsections, both of these approaches are presented. The choice between an array-based stack or a linked list-based stack object is highly influenced by the number of data elements, fixed or variable.

An abstract base class Stack is defined in the file bc_stack.h:

```
// Program: bc_stack.h  (Base class for Stack object)

class Stack {
  public:
    virtual BOOLEAN   is_empty() = 0;
    virtual void      build_stack(DATA_TYPE *A) = 0;
    virtual void      push(DATA_TYPE new_data) = 0;
    virtual DATA_TYPE pop(void) = 0;
```

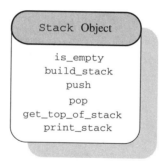

FIGURE 6.2. Public methods for the Stack class.

```
    virtual DATA_TYPE get_top_of_stack(void) = 0;
    virtual void      print_stack(void) = 0;
};
```

The names and arguments for the methods in the abstract base class Stack and in the derived (implementation specific) class must exactly match each other as the base class Stack provides a minimal common framework of behavior of a stack object.

```
class <implementation_specific_class>:public Stack{

   //  ...
};
```

A stack object, stack_obj, is depicted in Figure 6.2 and is created by instancing a selected implementation specific class:

```
<implementation_specific_class>  stack_obj;
```

A stack object is an instance of a derived class. From the user's perspective, the base class (i.e., Stack), from which the stack object is derived, is not implementation specific; it provides a uniform set of methods (behavior) for a stack object, which is implemented in the derived class. The derived classes that are implementation specific are discussed later with the issues surrounding their implementations. The names chosen for the derived classes are intended to reflect their implementations. Since the base class Stack defines a common framework of behavior for stack objects, the names for the methods in the implementation specific class exactly match the associated names in the base class Stack. This approach of using derived class based on the abstract base class allows "interchangeable implementations without considerable recompilation after change" (refer to Stroustrup [Str91]).

For example, when the data of a stack object are structured as an array, the implementation specific class `Ary_Stack` is derived from the abstract base stack class `Stack` as follows:

```
class Ary_Stack : public Stack {

    // ...
};
```

A stack object with array size 10 is instantiated by this statement:

```
Ary_Stack   stack_obj(10);
```

Several OOP implementations for a stack object are presented as implementation specific classes. Fundamentally, these implementations differ in the way memory is allocated for the data elements and the way in which the elements are linked together. More specifically, implementations of a stack object are categorized as

- those that employ fixed array memory allocation
  - the previously and the currently pushed data elements are stored in the array structure, or
  - links between the previously and the currently pushed data elements explicitly specified in terms of array indexes, or
- those that employ dynamic memory allocation and have
  - links between the previously and the currently pushed data elements explicitly specified as pointers.

6.1.1 OOP ARRAY IMPLEMENTATION OF A STACK OBJECT

The data of a stack object is internally implemented by an array, say `stack[]` of maximum size `STK_SIZ`. An index of the array `stack[]` denotes the location of a data element in the stack. Since a stack has only one open end, either `stack[0]` or `stack[STK_SIZ - 1]` may be assumed to be the closed end through which data elements cannot be pushed onto or popped out of the stack. When `stack[0]` is assumed to be the closed end of the array stack, the stack grows upward from `stack[0]` to `stack[STK_SIZ-1]`, and the `top_of_stack` index is initially -1 and grows from 0 to (`STK_SIZ - 1`) (this is implemented in **Code 6.1**). When `stack[STK_SIZ - 1]` is assumed to be the closed end of the array stack, the stack grows downward from `stack[STK_SIZ - 1]` to `stack[0]`, and the `top_of_stack` index is initially `STK_SIZ` and decreases from `STK_SIZ` to 0. In order to satisfy *LIFO* policy in a stack, one must use only the `top_of_stack` index to access a data element in a stack.

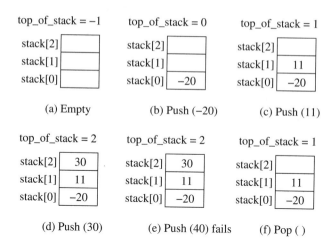

FIGURE 6.3. An array-based stack.

To illustrate an array-based stack, the array `stack[STK_SIZ]` with `STK_SIZ = 3`, is used for storing integer data elements in the stack. Figure 6.3 demonstrates the step-by-step building of an array-based stack of fixed sized three. Initially, for the empty stack, `top_of_stack = -1`.

If data of a stack object are of type `char` and are represented by an array, the array-based character stack object is defined by the `Ary_Stack` class, derived from the base class `Stack`, contained in the header file `Ary_Stak.h`:

```
class  Ary_Stack : public Stack {
  private:
    void        init_stack();
  protected:
    // stack is defined as an array of size STK_SIZ
    DATA_TYPE   *stack;
    int         STK_SIZ;
    int         top_of_stack;

  // Declare Stack's member functions as public to
  // allow access of the ADT stack operations
  public:
    Ary_Stack(int stk_siz);
    ~Ary_Stack();

    BOOLEAN     is_empty() {return top_of_stack == -1;}
    void        push (DATA_TYPE new_data);
    DATA_TYPE   pop (void);
    void        build_stack (DATA_TYPE *str);
    DATA_TYPE   get_top_of_stack (void);
```

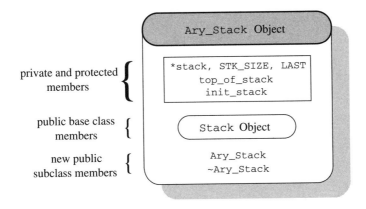

FIGURE 6.4. Ary_Stack object.

```
    void        print_stack (void);
};
```

The members `stack[]` and `top_of_stack` of the `Ary_Stack` class
are declared `protected` so that these members are not accessible to
the outside of this class except the derived classes (see RPN class in this
chapter), and thereby these are protected from corruption caused by any
unauthorized user or application. The interface routines, `Ary_Stack()`,
`is_empty()`, ..., `print_stack()`, are member functions of the same
class `Ary_Stack`, and therefore are authorized to manipulate these protected data, defined locally within the same class. These interface routines are declared `public` so that any function that is not a member of
the `Ary_Stack` class, can send messages to `Ary_Stack`-type objects, as
shown in Figure 6.4, by calling these public routines. As shown in Chapter 3, the `template` keyword may be used to define the `Stack` class of
elements of an arbitrary type:

```
template<class DATA_TYPE> class Ary_Stack {

    // Same members and declarations as above.
};
```

An array-based stack object `ary_stk_obj` with size 8 is declared in
main() of **Code 6.1** as:

```
Stack  ary_stk_obj(8);
```

The member functions of the `Ary_Stack` class are interfaces to the outside world, including `main()`. These routines allow nonmember functions
to pass messages (e.g., requests for actions) to `ary_stk_obj` object of

Ary_Stack class. Thus multiple objects of Ary_Stack type or any other type can communicate between them through these interface routines; this is one of the important aspects of an OOP. It is not necessary to pass the member fields stack[] and top_of_stack as the arguments of these member functions.

The public member function, is_empty() of the Ary_Stack class, checks whether an array stack object is empty. If it is empty, it returns 1, otherwise it returns 0.

The private member function, init_stack() of the Ary_Stack class, initializes and clears this class's object by setting top_of_stack to an invalid array index -1. It sets all slots in the array stack[] to null values. It assumes that the array stack object will grow from 0 to (STK_SIZ - 1). It is called by the constructor, Ary_Stack().

The public member function, push() of the Ary_Stack class is shown in **Code 6.1**, and implements the push operation on an array stack object. Push() adds a new data element new_data in a stack object. The algorithm for the push() operation is given below.

Algorithm: Stack Push

Step 1. Test to see if the stack object is full. If it is so, display an error message "Stack Overflow" and stop the program. If the stack object is not full, go to Step 2.

Step 2. Increase array index counter top_of_stack by 1:

```
++top_of_stack;
```

Step 3. Put the new data element new_data at the top of the array-based stack object:

```
stack[top_of_stack] = new_data;
```

The public member function pop() of the Ary_Stack class, as shown in **Code 6.1**, implements the pop operation on an array stack object. Pop() removes the data element at the top of a stack object, and returns the data of type DATA_TYPE to the calling function. The algorithm for the pop() operation is given below.

Algorithm: Stack Pop

Step 1. Test to see if the stack object is empty. If it is empty, pop() displays an error message "Stack Underflow" and stops the program. If it is not empty, go to Step 2.

Step 2. Remove the data element at the top of the array-based stack object and place it in popped_data.

```
popped_data = stack[top_of_stack];
```

Step 3. Decrease `top_of_stack` by 1. This effectively makes the successor of the old top-of-stack data element the new top-of-stack data element.

Step 4. Return `popped_data` to the calling function.

The `public` member function `build_stack()`, of the `Ary_Stack` class as shown in **Code 6.1**, builds an `Ary_Stack`-type array object (e.g., `ary_stk_obj`) from a given string of characters. It repeatedly calls `push()` to push character data into `stack[]` until the end of the input string is encountered. The first character data pushed on the stack object is at the bottom of the stack object.

The `public` member function `get_top_of_stack()`, of the class `Ary_Stack` as shown in **Code 6.1**, returns a copy of the data element at the top of the array stack object. It does not destroy that element. If the stack object is empty, it prints an error message "No Element in Stack," and returns.

The `public` member function `print_stack()`, of the `Ary_Stack` class as shown in **Code 6.1**, prints all the data elements of the array stack object in a `for` loop. It does not destroy the elements of the stack object. If the stack object is empty, it displays an error message and returns.

`Main()` in **Code 6.1** is the test driver for the OOP implementation of the array stack. It is not a member function of the `Ary_Stack` class, so it cannot directly call the interface functions of the `Ary_Stack` class. Conventionally, it instantiates an `ary_stk_obj` object with array-size 8. `Main()` sends requests for actions (create, and print) to `ary_stk_obj` through this object's methods `build_stack()` and `print_stack()`.

For a detailed object-oriented implementation of these operations and output for an array-based stack object in C++, see **Code 6.1**.

The first and major drawback of the array-based stack implementation is that the stack size is fixed at the run time. This stack cannot dynamically grow or shrink in size. Second, there is a possibility of allocating more memory space for the array than the actual usage; the unused memory space cannot be released during the program's run time. Both drawbacks are resolved by the singly or doubly linked implementation of the stack (to be discussed in Section 6.1.2).

Code 6.1

```
//   Program: Ary_Stak.c++
//   Purpose:
//     Object-oriented implementation of a
//     stack; its data are stored in an array
//     stack[STK_SIZ]. "top_of_stack" is an array
//     index from 0 to STK_SIZ - 1, and set to -1.
//     Stack grows from "stack[0]" to "stack[STK_SIZ-1]".
//
```

```c
#include <stdio.h>
#include <stdlib.h>
typedef  int   BOOLEAN;
typedef  char  DATA_TYPE;
#include "bc_stack.h"   // For base class "Stack"
#include "Ary_Stak.h"    // For derived class "Ary_Stack"

// Implement methods for the "Ary_Stack" class

Ary_Stack::Ary_Stack(int stk_siz)  // Constructor
{
    // Allocate an array "stack[STK_SIZ] to store
    // stack's data
    stack = new  DATA_TYPE[STK_SIZ = stk_siz];
    init_stack();
}

Ary_Stack::~Ary_Stack()  // Destructor
{
    delete []stack;
}

// init_stack():
//   Initialize stack's data area by putting
//   null values; also set "top_of_stack" to -1.
//
void  Ary_Stack::init_stack (void)
{
    top_of_stack = -1;  // Invalid array index
    for (int j = 0; j < STK_SIZ; j++)
      stack[j] = '\0';
}

// push():
//   Add a new element with data "new_data" in
//   an array based stack. The new element
//   becomes the new top element in the stack.
//
void  Ary_Stack::push (DATA_TYPE new_data)
{
    // Check whether stack is full
    if (top_of_stack == STK_SIZ - 1) {
        printf("\n push: Stack Overflow!!\n");
        exit (1);
    }
    ++top_of_stack;
    stack[top_of_stack] = new_data;
}

// pop():
//   Remove and return the current element at the
//   top of the stack. Its successor is made the
//   new top element in the stack.
//
```

```
DATA_TYPE  Ary_Stack::pop (void)
{
   DATA_TYPE  popped_data;

   if (is_empty()) {
      printf("\n pop: Stack Underflow. \n");
      exit (2);
   }
   else { // At least one element in stack
      popped_data = stack[top_of_stack];
      // Decrement the counter "top_of_stack" by 1.
      --top_of_stack;
      return (popped_data);
   }
}

// build_stack ():
//    Build an array based stack from
//    a given string of characters.
//
void  Ary_Stack::build_stack (DATA_TYPE str[])
{
   if (str[0] == '\0')
      printf("\n build_stack: Empty string.\n");
   else
      //  Since 'str[0]' is first pushed into the
      //  array stack, it is at its bottom.
      for (int j = 0; str[j] != '\0'; ++j)
         push (str[j]);
}

// get_top_of_stack():
//    Get the element at the top of array stack.
//    It does delete the element from stack.
//
DATA_TYPE  Ary_Stack::get_top_of_stack (void)
{
   if (is_empty())
      printf("\n get_top_of_stack: %s \n",
             "No Element in Stack.");
   else
      return (stack[top_of_stack]);
}

// print_stack():
//    Print the elements (data) in an array stack;
//    The element at "top of the stack" is
//    printed first, and the element at
//    "bottom of the stack" is printed last.
//
void  Ary_Stack::print_stack (void)
{
   if (!is_empty ()) {
      for (int i = top_of_stack; i >= 0; i--)
```

```
            printf(" %c ", stack[i]);
         printf("\n   \^ \n");
         printf("  !___  Top of this stack object\n");
      }
      else
         printf("\n No Element in Stack.\n");
   }


   // main():
   //   Test driver for Object-Oriented implementation
   //   of a stack object with data as an array.
   //
   void main (void)
   {
      // Declare and define size "8" of an object
      // "ary_stk_obj" belonging to class "Ary_Stack"
      Ary_Stack  ary_stk_obj(8);
      static char *str = "SAUREN";

      printf("\n ** OOP IMPLEMENTATION OF %s ** \n",
             "ARRAY STACK");
      printf("\n Stack representation of \"%s\" is:  \n ",
             str);
      ary_stk_obj.build_stack (str);
      ary_stk_obj.print_stack();
      delete  str;
   }
```

Code 6.1 for an OOP implementation of an array-based stack object produces this output:

```
** OOP IMPLEMENTATION OF ARRAY STACK **

Stack representation of "SAUREN" is:
 N   E   R   U   A   S
 ^
 !___  Top of this stack object
```

6.1.2 OOP IMPLEMENTATION OF A STACK USING LINKED LISTS

The previous section showed that an array-based implementation of a stack object is efficient but it is not flexible primarily due to the fixed size of the array. To alleviate this deficiency of limited data space, the stack object's data may be internally implemented as a singly or doubly linked list. The linked lists use pointers (links) to connect the stack's data element to its next (successor) element. An array-based stack has a maximum limitation imposed by the size of the array. For a singly or doubly linked list based

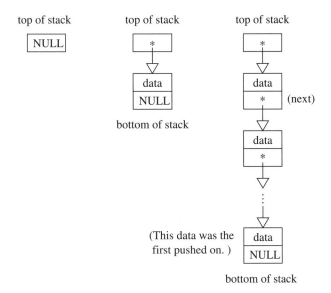

(a) Empty stack   (b) Single element stack   (c) Multiple element stack

FIGURE 6.5. The structure of a singly linked stack.

stack object, the lower limit is the NULL pointer field of the data element at the bottom of the stack, and the upper limit is the available system's memory space. Figure 6.5 shows step-by-step development and a typical structure of a singly linked stack.

Figure 6.6 shows states of a singly linked list based stack, before and after two successive push operations and one pop operation. For an empty stack, the pointer top_of_stack = NULL.

When a stack object's data elements are structured as a singly linked list, and its data elements data of type char, pointer field next of type STACK_PTR, and top_of_stack need to be protected, the Lnk_Stack class in the header file Lnk_Stak.h for an OOP implementation is derived from the base stack class Stack that is in bc_stack.h:

```
class  Lnk_Stack : public Stack {
  private:
    typedef struct STACK_ELEMENT {
      DATA_TYPE      data;
      STACK_ELEMENT  *next;
    } *STACK_PTR;
    STACK_ELEMENT *top_of_stack;
    void  init_stack() {top_of_stack = NULL;}
    void  clear_stack(void);
```

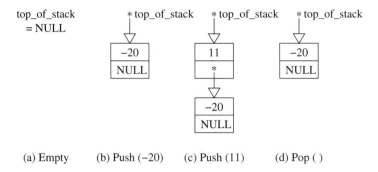

(a) Empty   (b) Push (−20)   (c) Push (11)   (d) Pop ( )

FIGURE 6.6. Push and Pop operations on a singly linked stack.

```
//  Declare Stack's member functions as "public"
//  to allow access of the stack operations
public:
  Lnk_Stack();        // Constructor
  ~Lnk_Stack();       // Destructor
  BOOLEAN    is_empty() {return top_of_stack == NULL;}
  void       build_stack(DATA_TYPE *str);
  void       push(DATA_TYPE  new_data);
  DATA_TYPE  pop(void);
  DATA_TYPE  get_top_of_stack(void);
  void       print_stack(void);
};
```

For an OOP implementation of the stack as a singly linked list, the class Lnk_Stack defines a type of this stack object. Lnk_stk_obj is a stack object of this type and is a data structure in which the data objects of type STACK_ELEMENT are maintained as a singly linked list and the actions that operate on them are locally defined. It is instantiated in main() as:

```
  Lnk_Stack lnk_stk_obj;
```

The data fields data, next, top_of_stack and the member functions init_stack() and clear_stack are hidden to the outside of this Lnk_Stack class, and are considered local variables to all the member functions of the same class Lnk_Stack. Clear_stack is declared for protected access to avoid possible memory leak caused by unauthorized user application. The member fields, next and top_of_stack, are respectively pointers to the next and the top elements, both of type STACK_ELE\-MENT, in a Lnk_Stack-type object shown in Figure 6.7. The interface routines define the behavior of a stack object. These are declared public so that multiple objects of Lnk_Stack or an object of any other class can communicate with the lnk_stk_obj object through these routines.

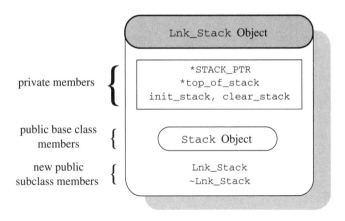

FIGURE 6.7. Lnk_Stack class.

Lnk_Stack(), with the same name as the type Lnk_Stack, is the constructor for a stack object. It is automatically called when a class variable of type Lnk_Stack is declared and allocated. It calls init_stack() to initialize the object.

~Stack(), the destructor, must not have any argument and any return value. It is implicitly called in main() before the program exits. It destroys an object of the Lnk_Stack class by destroying the entire singly linked list of STACK_ELT objects. It calls clear_stack().

The private member function clear_stack(), of the Lnk_Stack class as in **Code 6.2**, clears the entire singly linked stack object. It calls pop() repeatedly to free up the memory space until the stack object is empty.

The inline and public member function is_empty(), of the class Lnk_Stack as in **Code 6.2**, checks whether a Lnk_Stack-type object (e.g., lnk_stk_obj) is empty. If the object is empty (that is, it does not have any STACK_ELT-type objects), the function returns 1. Otherwise, it returns 0.

The inline and private member function, init_stack() of the Lnk_Stack class as in **Code 6.2**, initializes a Lnk_Stack-type object (e.g., lnk_stk_obj) by setting its data field top_of_stack to NULL.

The public member function push(), of the Lnk_Stack class as in **Code 6.2**, implements the push operation for a singly linked stack object (e.g., lnk_stk_obj). It expects one argument, new_data. It allocates the memory space for a STACK_ELEMENT-type element object as follows:

```
new_ptr = new  STACK_ELEMENT;
```

Push() sets the new element's data field, data, to new_data. It makes the current top element object the successor of the new element object, and the new element object the top of the stack object; these two actions are accomplished by the adjustments of pointer fields. The data field top_of_stack of the stack object now points to the new element object. The stack elements are randomly stored in memory, in contrast to the sequential implementation of a stack. The advantage of this implementation is that it allows the stack object to dynamically grow or shrink as needed during the execution of the program. One disadvantage is that in addition to the stack data element, space for a pointer (in the case of a singly linked list; two pointers in the case of a doubly linked list) is needed.

The public member function pop(), of the Lnk_Stack class as in **Code 6.2**, implements the pop operation for a singly linked stack object (e.g., lnk_stk_obj). It pops (removes) the top element object of the stack object and uses the delete operator that returns the memory space allocated to the stack object's currently popped element to the system memory heap.

The public member function get_top_of_stack(), of the class Lnk_Stack as shown in **Code 6.2**, calls is_empty(). If the singly linked stack object is empty, the function prints an error message "No Element in Stack" and returns. If the stack object is not empty, the function returns the data field data of the top element object without destroying it.

The public member function print_stack(), of the Lnk_Stack class as in **Code 6.2**, calls is_empty(). If the singly linked stack object is empty, the function prints a message "No Element in Stack" and returns. For a nonempty stack object, the function prints the data field element of each STACK_ELEMENT-type object from the top to the bottom element object of the stack object. It does not destroy the stack object.

The public member function build_stack(), of the Lnk_Stack class as in **Code 6.2**, builds a Lnk_Stack-type singly linked stack object from a string of characters. It repeatedly calls push() to add character data at the front of the singly linked list of STACK_ELEMENT-type objects until the end of the input string is encountered.

Main() instantiates a lnk_stk_obj object of the Lnk_Stack class. It calls this object's methods build_stack(), and print_stack() to send requests for actions (build a stack from a given string "SAUREN", and print the stack data, respectively) to the object lnk_stk_obj. At the program exit, ~Stack() implicitly releases allocated memory spaces.

Code 6.2.

```
//  Program: Lnk_Stak.c++
//  Purpose:
//     OBJECT-ORIENTED IMPLEMENTATION OF A
```

```
//     STACK; Its data of type 'char' are
//     stored in a singly linked list.
//
#include <stdio.h>
#include <stdlib.h>
typedef  int   BOOLEAN;
typedef  char  DATA_TYPE;
#include "bc_stack.h"  // For base class "Stack"
#include "Lnk_Stak.h"  // For derived class "Lnk_Stack"

// ---- Implement methods for "Lnk_Stack" class  ---
// clear_stack():
//   Takes out all datas in the stack
//   calling 'pop()' that frees spaces.
//
void  Lnk_Stack::clear_stack(void)
{
   while (!is_empty())
      pop();
}

// Lnk_Stack():
//   Construct a Stack object by initializing it.
//
Lnk_Stack::Lnk_Stack()
{
   init_stack();
}

// ~Lnk_Stack():
//   Destroys an object of class "Stack"
//
Lnk_Stack::~Lnk_Stack()
{
   clear_stack();
}

// push():
//   Add a new element with data 'new_data' to
//   a singly linked stack. This is added at the
//   front of the linked list, and becomes the
//   element at the top of singly linked stack.
//
void  Lnk_Stack::push(DATA_TYPE  new_data)
{
   // Allocate memory space using the operator 'new'
   STACK_PTR  new_ptr = new  STACK_ELEMENT;
   // Add the new data element to the top of stack
   new_ptr->data = new_data;
   new_ptr->next = top_of_stack;
   // Current element at the top of the linked
   // stack is made successor of the new element
   // pointed to by 'new_ptr'
   top_of_stack = new_ptr;
```

```
}

// pop():
//  Remove and return the current element at
//  the top of the singly linked stack pointed
//  to by 'top_of_stack'. Its successor is
//  made the new top element in the stack.
//  Release memory space for this popped element.
//
DATA_TYPE   Lnk_Stack::pop(void)
{
    STACK_PTR tmp_ptr = top_of_stack;

    if (is_empty()) {
       printf("\n pop: Stack Underflow.\n");
       exit(1);
    }
    else {  //  At least one element in stack
       DATA_TYPE  popped_data = top_of_stack->data;
       // Top of the stack now points to next elt
       top_of_stack = top_of_stack->next;
       delete    tmp_ptr;   //  Free up memory space
       return(popped_data);
    }
}

// build_stack():
//   Build a singly linked stack from a given
//   string of characters.
//
void  Lnk_Stack::build_stack(DATA_TYPE str[])
{
    if (str[0] == '\0')    // End of string
       printf("\n build_stack: Empty string.\n");
    else
       for (int j = 0; str[j] != '\0'; ++j)
           push(str[j]);
}

// get_top_of_stack():
//   Get the element at the top of singly linked
//   stack. It does delete the element from stack.
//
DATA_TYPE   Lnk_Stack::get_top_of_stack(void)
{
    if (!is_empty())
       return(top_of_stack->data);
    else
       printf("\n get_top_of_stack: %s \n",
              "No Element in Stack.");
}

// print_stack():
//   Print stack (iterative method)
```

```
//
void  Lnk_Stack::print_stack(void)
{
    if (!is_empty()) {
        for (STACK_PTR tmp_ptr = top_of_stack;
             tmp_ptr != NULL; tmp_ptr = tmp_ptr->next)
        printf(" %c -> ", tmp_ptr->data);
        printf("NULL\n  \^");
        printf("\n  !___  Top of this stack object \n");
    }
    else
        printf("\n No Element in Stack.\n");
}

// main():
//   OBJECT-ORIENTED IMPLEMENTATION OF A STACK
//   with data being stored in a singly linked list.
//
void main(void)
{
    // Declare an object "lnk_stk_obj" belonging
    // to class "Lnk_Stack"
    Lnk_Stack  lnk_stk_obj;
    static char str[] = "SAUREN";

    printf("\n ** OOP IMPLEMENTATION OF %s ** \n",
           "SINGLY LINKED STACK");
    printf("\n Stack representation of \"%s\" is:  \n ",
           str);
    lnk_stk_obj.build_stack(str);
    lnk_stk_obj.print_stack();
    delete  []str;
}
```

Code 6.2 for an OOP implementation of a stack object using a singly linked list produces this output:

```
** OOP IMPLEMENTATION OF SINGLY LINKED STACK **

Stack representation of "SAUREN" is:
 N -> E -> R -> U -> A -> S -> NULL
 ^
 !___  Top of this stack object
```

6.1.3 PERFORMANCE ANALYSES OF STACK OPERATIONS

This chapter so far discussed two forms of the stack data structure: (1) array stack and (2) singly linked stack. The stack data structure is useful for the applications that require the push and pop operations in *LIFO* manner. The random search and delete operations do not apply to a stack data structure. If an application requires the random search and delete operations, the stack data structure is not appropriate for that application. Table 6.2 shows worst-case performances of operations for stack objects with any number of elements.

The stack data structure is not efficient and recommended for applications that frequently require random search and delete. A stack structure is useful and efficient when dealing with the data element at the top of the stack.

6.2 Double Stack Objects

Consider the problem of implementing two stacks within the confines of a small amount of fixed memory. This brings forth the concept of a double stack. A *double stack object* is specified by an ADT double stack. An ADT double stack is a data structure having two parts:

- A collection of data elements of the same type contained in two array stacks that simultaneously reside in the same array memory. They have top of stack indexes top_of_stack1 and top_of_stack2.

- A set of operations on the data elements and the two array stacks.

An array-based double stack is depicted in Figure 6.8. Since two stacks reside in the same array there is a distinct possibility of collision of the individual stacks, resulting in corruption of each other's data. A few key guidelines can help manage the array-based implementation:

- One stack may grow faster than the second stack does. This may corrupt and overwrite the data for the second stack, a problem that can be avoided by adding a boundary check in the push operation.

Stack structure	Worst-case performance of Push	Worst-case performance of Pop
Array-based stack	$O(1)$	$O(1)$
Singly linked stack	$O(1)$	$O(1)$

TABLE 6.2. Worst-case performance of stack operations.

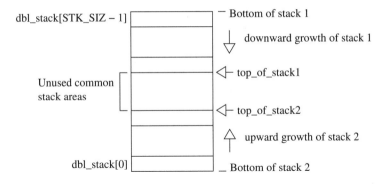

FIGURE 6.8. Two simultaneous stacks in one array.

- During the push operation, if it found that the top of stack index for one stack is crossing over the other's top of stack, the push operation must be blocked. A message, such as, "Stack number:stack overflow" might be useful feedback for the user. Push operations may be resumed after the other stack releases space by performing one or more pop operations.

- Checking boundary is useful for the most operations. This is done by testing

```
(top_of_stack1 - 1) == top_of_stack2
(top_of_stack2 + 1) == top_of_stack1
```

The OOP implementation of a double stack object is left as an exercise.

6.3   OOP Application: Reverse Polish Notation Using Stacks

Stacks are useful in processing arithmetic expressions. In writing arithmetic expressions, there are three types of notations employed:

- *Infix* $(1 + 3) + 7$

- *Postfix* $1\ 3 + 7 +$

- *Prefix* $+1\ 3 + 7$

With infix notation, the most common, parentheses are used to identify operator binding and precedence. However, with the postfix and prefix notations there is no need of such parentheses.

Postfix notation is also commonly referred to as *Reverse Polish Notation* (RPN). In many applications (e.g., calculators, compilers), infix expressions are translated into a postfix expression using a stack, and then the postfix expression is evaluated using a stack of operands.

6.3.1   POSTFIX EVALUATION

As an illustration of RPN expression evaluation, consider the expression

$$11\ 3\ +\ 20\ -$$

which has the value -6. Postfix (RPN) evaluation utilizes a stack of integer or floating point operands. It assumes a valid RPN expression is a sequence of operands and operators comprised of the characters '0', '1', ..., '9', '+', '-', '*', '/'. The given RPN is parsed from left to right until the end of expression (EOE) is reached. Figure 6.9 traces the steps involved, showing the expression, the current action, and the state of the stack at each stage. As one can see, the stack contains at most two operands at any given time. When an operator is encountered, the operands are popped from the stack, the current expression is evaluated, and the intermediate result is pushed back on to the stack. This process continues until the expression is empty, at which time the final result is popped from the stack.

Algorithm: Postfix (RPN) Evaluation

Step 1. Allocate memory space for input and working buffers to store RPN.

Step 2. Initialize the operand stack.

Step 3. Get a valid RPN expression from the user's terminal. (Note: Validity of RPN is not checked here.)

Step 4. Until the end of the RPN expression, continue parsing the RPN from left to right and evaluate doing the steps 4.1 through 4.3.4:

Step 4.1. If it is a blank, ignore it.

Step 4.2. If an operand is read in ASCII form, it is converted into a floating point number, and then is pushed onto the operand stack.

Step 4.3. If an operator (opr) is read, to apply the operator to the two top operands perform the following:

Step 4.3.1. Pop the operand stack for the right operand and save it as op2.

RPN expression	Action	Stack
11 3 + 20 – EOE	Initial state	empty
3 + 20 – EOE	Read 11 and push onto stack	11
+ 20 – EOE	Read 3 and push onto stack	3 11
20 – EOE	Read + and pop 3 and 11, perform 11 + 3 and push 14	14
– EOE	Read 20 and push onto stack	20 14
– EOE	Read – and pop 20 and 14, perform 14 – 20 and push –6	–6
EOE	Expression empty	–6
	Pop the stack, result is –6	empty

FIGURE 6.9. Trace of RPN expression evaluation.

Step 4.3.2. Pop the operand stack for the left operand, and save it as op1 (it is a serious error if pop fails in case of a binary operator).

Step 4.3.3. Evaluate the operation: op1 opr op2.

Step 4.3.4. The result of the operation is pushed onto the operand stack.

Step 5. The entire RPN is parsed, and the operand stack has only one value.

Step 6. Pop the stack to get the result of the RPN expression.

Step 7. Delete the operand stack as it is no longer needed.

Step 8. Delete memory spaces for the input and working buffers.

Code 6.3

```
// Program:   Eval_RPN.c++
// Purpose:
//   Evaluate RPN (the postfix expression) and
//   return the result using an OOP approach.
//
#include <stdio.h>
```

```
#include <stdlib.h>
#include <math.h>
//
//  For Class "Lnk_Stack", its member functions
//  pop(), push(), modify Code 6.2 (Lnk_Stak.c++):
//      (i)  typedef float DATA_TYPE;
//      (ii) remove main()
//
#ifdef  MSDOS
#include    "Lnk_Stak.cpp"
#else
#include    "Lnk_Stak.c++"
#endif
const    int BLANK = ' ';   // blank space
typedef int BOOLEAN;

//  Define class RPN (Reverse Polish Notation expression).
//  It uses the class "Stack" as the base class in order
//  to use the Stack functions.

class RPN : public Lnk_Stack {
    int    BUFF_SIZE;
    char   *in_buff;
    char   *work_buff; // for holding numbers

  public:
    RPN (int buff_sz);  // Constructor
    ~RPN();                  // Destructor
    BOOLEAN      chk_if_number (char);
    DATA_TYPE    get_value_of_RPN (char *rpn_expr);
    void   get_rpn (void);
    void   eval_rpn_and_print (void);
};

//  RPN(): Constructor for an object of RPN class
//
RPN::RPN(int buff_sz) : Lnk_Stack ()
{
    BUFF_SIZE = buff_sz;
    in_buff   = new char[BUFF_SIZE + 1];
    work_buff = new char[BUFF_SIZE + 1];
}

RPN::~RPN()    // Destructor
{
    delete []in_buff;
    delete []work_buff;
}

// chk_if_number():
//    Ascertain if an input is a decimal point
//    or a decimal digit between 0 and 9.
//
BOOLEAN RPN::chk_if_number(char ch)
```

```
{
   return ((ch == '.')   (ch >= '0' && ch <= '9'));
}

// get_value_of_RPN():
//   Determine value of an RPN (postfix expression
//   only in digits). The result is returned. It
//   assumes the given string input is a valid RPN;
//   it does not check the validity of the string.
//
DATA_TYPE RPN::get_value_of_RPN (char *rpn_ptr)
{
   DATA_TYPE   op1, op2;
   char        *work_buff_ptr;

   while (*rpn_ptr != '\0') {  // not end of string
      // ignore blank spaces
      if (*rpn_ptr != BLANK) {
         if (chk_if_number (*rpn_ptr)) {
            //
            //   Get each number in RPN string;
            //   ignore blank; set up working
            //   buffer as a copy of input RPN.
            work_buff_ptr = &work_buff[0];
            while (chk_if_number (*rpn_ptr) &&
                              *rpn_ptr != '\0')
               *work_buff_ptr++ = *rpn_ptr++;

            *work_buff_ptr = '\0';
            //
            //   ASCII data is coverted into floating point
            //   number and pushed into the stack object.
            //
            push (atof (work_buff));
         }
         else {
            // Two operands for a binary operator
            // are stored in stack object. Get them
            // by two successive "pop" operations.

            op2 = pop();
            op1 = pop();
            switch (*rpn_ptr++) {
               case '+':
                  push (op1 + op2);
                  break;
               case '-':
                  push (op1 - op2);
                  break;
               case '*':
                  push (op1 * op2);
                  break;
               case '/':
                  if (op2 != 0)
```

```
                        push (op1 / op2);
                    else {
                        printf ("\n get_value_of_RPN: %s \n",
                          "Division by zero!!");
                        exit (1);
                    }
                    break;
                default:
                    printf ("\n Unknown operator \n");
                    exit (2);
            } //  End of "switch (*rpn_ptr++)"
        }
    }
    else
        ++rpn_ptr;

    }  //  End of "while (*rpn_ptr != '\0')"
    //  Result in top of the stack object is
    //  retrieved using "pop" operation
    return (pop ());
}

//  get_rpn ():
//     Get RPN input from user's keyboard
//
void  RPN::get_rpn (void)
{
    printf ("\n ** OOP FOR RPN EVALUATION ** \n");
    printf ("\n Please enter a valid %s %s \n ",
            "RPN expression", "(e.g., 6 3 +):");
    gets (in_buff);
}


void  RPN::eval_rpn_and_print (void)
{
    get_rpn ();
    printf ("\n The value of %s: \n %s \n is: %7.2f\n",
            "given RPN expression", in_buff,
            get_value_of_RPN (in_buff));
}

//  main (): Test driver for OOP for "RPN evaluation"
void  main(void)
{
    // An object in the class RPN that initializes
    // size of the base class "Lnk_Stack"'s stack
    // object that holds the operands.
    RPN  rpn_obj(80);  // An object in the class RPN

    rpn_obj.eval_rpn_and_print ();
}
```

The OOP for RPN in **Code 6.3** produces this output:

```
** OOP FOR RPN EVALUATION **

Please enter a valid RPN expression (e.g., 6 3 +):
11 3 + 20 -

The value of given RPN expression:
11 3 + 20 -
is:    -6.00
```

Note that in this OOP example of RPN evaluation, resource sharing between the two classes Lnk_Stack and RPN is accomplished by deriving RPN class from the public Lnk_Stack class. In C++, this is performed by using the : operator.

```
class RPN : public Lnk_Stack
```

An object rpn_obj of type RPN with its buffer size 80 is instantiated by this statement:

```
RPN     rpn_obj(80);
```

6.3.2 INFIX TO RPN TRANSLATION

As mentioned above, infix evaluation is more complex than postfix and prefix evaluation due to the presence of parentheses. One useful approach to infix evaluation is to first convert the expression to an RPN (postfix) expression. Infix expressions involving parentheses and the arithmetic operators +, -, *, and / are considered.

The presence of parentheses in the infix expression stresses on binding. This means that all the operations within the parentheses must be executed before any operations outside the parentheses. When a part or full infix expression does not have parentheses, *priority* or *precedence* of the arithmetic operators must be defined and used to perform the arithmetic operations. The priority values for the operators will impact the translation process. For example, the coverted RPN expression for the infix expression (a + b) - c is

$$a \ b \ + \ c \ -.$$

Table 6.3 provides an example set of priority levels for a set of operators.

Operator	Priority level
(	0 (highest)
+, −	1
*, /	2 (lowest)

TABLE 6.3. Priority levels for operators.

Algorithm: Translating Infix to RPN

Step 1. Allocate memory spaces for input infix expression, output postfix (RPN) expression.

Step 2. Allocate and initialize a stack of operator – characters: (, +, −, *, and /.

Step 3. Define priority levels as shown in Table 6.3.

Step 4. Parse the input infix expression from left to right, get opr_tkn (a token, separated by blank spaces), and do the steps 4.1 through 4.5.2. until the end of the infix expression.

Step 4.1. If the token opr_tkn is a blank space, ignore it and continue reading the next token.

Step 4.2. If the token opr_tkn is a left parenthesis, push it onto the operator stack.

Step 4.3. If opr_tkn is an operand, put it to the RPN.

Step 4.4. If the token opr_tkn is an operator (+, −, *, or /), compare it with the operator on top of the stack:

Step 4.4.1. Pop the stack, and call it old_opr_tkn

Step 4.4.2. If the priority level of opr_tkn (the token just read from the infix expression) is less than or equal to the priority level of old_opr_tkn, put a blank space followed by old_opr_tkn in the RPN expression. Otherwise, do Step 4.4.3.

Step 4.4.3. Push old_opr_tkn back onto the operator stack.

Step 4.4.4. Repeat steps 4.4.1 through 4.4.3 until the stack is empty.

Step 4.4.5. If the stack is empty, push opr_tkn onto the stack.

Step 4.5. If the token `opr_tkn` is a right parenthesis, continue popping the operator stack and doing steps 4.5.1 and 4.5.2 until
the left parenthesis in the operator stack is encountered:

Step 4.5.1. Put a blank space in the RPN expression.

Step 4.5.2. Put the popped operator in the RPN expression.

Step 5. At the completion of parsing (when the end of the infix expression is reached), continue popping the operator stack and
putting the remaining just-popped operators in the RPN expression with a preceding blank space until the operator stack
becomes empty.

Step 6. To indicate end of string, put a null character in the final RPN
expression.

Step 7. Print the input infix expression and the output RPN expression.

Step 8. Release allocated memory spaces for the infix and RPN expressions, and the operator stack.

The above algorithm is implemented by `Translate_infix_to_RPN()`
in **Code 6.4**. Note that the order of the operands remain unchanged in the
RPN since they are put directly into the RPN. An operator, with priority
higher than that of the operator at the top of the stack, is pushed onto the
operator stack. To illustrate this translation algorithm, Figure 6.10 shows
the states of infix expression, the operand stack, and RPN expression during the process.

Code 6.4

```
//   Program:   Infix_To_RPN.c++
//   Purpose:
//     Convert an Infix expression to the RPN
//     (postfix) form using an OOP approach.
//   NOTE:
//     Include Code 6.1 without main() in order to use
//     "Ary_Stack" Class, and its member functions
//     "push()"and "pop()". The type of data is "char".
//
#ifdef   MSDOS
#include "Ary_Stak.cpp"
#else
#include "Ary_Stak.c++"
#endif
const int   BLANK = ' ';

//   Define class RPN (Reverse Polish Notation
//   expression). It uses the class "Ary_Stack"
```

Input Infix	Stack	Output RPN
23 – (14 / 77) *9	empty	empty
– (14 / 77) * 9	empty	23
(14 / 77) * 9	–	23
14 / 77) * 9	– (	23
14 / 77) * 9	– (	23 14
/ 77) * 9	– (/	23 14
/ 77) * 9	– (/	23 14 77
(14 / 77) * 9	–	23 14 77 /
14 / 77) * 9	– *	23 14 77 /
14 / 77) * 9	– *	23 14 77 / 9
(14 / 77) * 9	–	23 14 77 / 9 *
– (14 / 77) * 9	empty	23 14 77 / 9 * –

FIGURE 6.10. Infix to RPN translation.

```
//   as the base class in order to inherit the
//   privilege of using the "Ary_Stack"s data
//   and methods.

class RPN : public Ary_Stack {
  private:
    int     BUFF_SIZE;
    char    *exprsn;  // char exprsn[BUFF_SIZE]
    char    *input_buffer;
    char    *output_buffer;
    typedef char *EXPRSN_PTR;
    typedef char Token;
    enum    priority {PRIORITY_0, PRIORITY_1, PRIORITY_2};

  public:
    RPN (int buff_sz);
    ~RPN();
    int   get_priority (char  oper);
    void  Translate_infix_to_RPN
             (EXPRSN_PTR infix_expr,
              EXPRSN_PTR rpn_expr);
    void  get_infix_expr (void);
    void  convert_infix_to_rpn_and_print (void);
};
```

```
//  RPN():
//   Constructor for RPN, a derived class
//   of "Ary_Stack" class. Note that base class
//   "Ary_Stack" is initialized simultaneously.
//
RPN::RPN (int buff_sz) : Ary_Stack (buff_sz)
{
    exprsn         = new char [BUFF_SIZE = buff_sz];
    input_buffer  = new char [BUFF_SIZE + 1];
    output_buffer = new char [BUFF_SIZE + 1];
}

RPN::~RPN()      // Destructor
{
    delete  [] exprsn;
    delete  [] input_buffer;
    delete  [] output_buffer;
}

// get_priority(): Get the priority of operators
//
int   RPN::get_priority (char oper)
{
    switch (oper) {
        case '(': return PRIORITY_0;  // highest
        case '+':
        case '-': return PRIORITY_1;
        case '*':
        case '/': return PRIORITY_2;  // lowest
    }
}

// Translate_infix_to_RPN():
//   Convert an Infix expression to a
//   Postfix expression (RPN).
//
void RPN::Translate_infix_to_RPN
        (EXPRSN_PTR infix_expr, EXPRSN_PTR rpn_expr)
{
    Token   opr_tkn, old_opr_tkn;

    //  The operator stack is initialized to store
    //  tokens (operators and operands).
    //  Tokens are separated by a blank space(s).

    while ((opr_tkn = *infix_expr++) != '\0') {
      if (opr_tkn == BLANK)
         continue;
      else
       switch (opr_tkn) {
         case '(':
            push (opr_tkn);
            break;
```

```
        case ')':
          while ((old_opr_tkn = pop()) != '(') {
              *rpn_expr++ = BLANK;
              *rpn_expr++ = old_opr_tkn;
          }
          break;
        case '+':
        case '-':
        case '*':
        case '/':
          while (!is_empty()) {
            old_opr_tkn = pop();
            if (get_priority (opr_tkn) <=
                       get_priority (old_opr_tkn)) {
              *rpn_expr++ = BLANK;
              *rpn_expr++ = old_opr_tkn;
            }
            else {
              push (old_opr_tkn);
              break;
            }
          }
          push (opr_tkn);
          *rpn_expr++ = BLANK;
          break;
        default:
          *rpn_expr++ = opr_tkn;
          break;
      }   //  end of switch
    }         //  end of while
    while (!is_empty()) {
      *rpn_expr++ = BLANK;
      *rpn_expr++ = pop();
    }
    *rpn_expr = '\0';
  }


  //  get_infix_expr ():
  //     Get a valid infix expression from user's
  //     terminal (keyboard)
  //
  void  RPN::get_infix_expr (void)
  {
      printf ("\n\n For conversion into RPN, %s %s \n ",
          "please enter a",
          "\n valid infix expression (e.g., 6 + 3):");
  #ifndef MSDOS
      fflush(stdin);  // Flush input buffer
  #endif
      gets (input_buffer);
  }


  void  RPN::convert_infix_to_rpn_and_print (void)
  {
```

```
    char   answer;
    do {
      get_infix_expr ();

      Translate_infix_to_RPN (input_buffer,
                                  output_buffer);
      printf ("\n\n %s: \n %s \n %s is: \n %s \n",
            "For the given infix expression",
            input_buffer,
            "the translated RPN expression",
            output_buffer);
      printf("\n Any more infix expression (y/n)? ");
    } while (((answer = getchar()) == 'Y')
           (answer == 'y'));
}

//  main():  Test driver for "Infix to Postfix"
//            conversion OOP.
void  main(void)
{
    RPN rpn_obj(128); // An object in the class "RPN"

    printf("\n ** OOP FOR INFIX TO RPN CONVERSION **");
    rpn_obj.convert_infix_to_rpn_and_print();
}
```

Code 6.4 produces the following output:

```
** OOP FOR INFIX TO RPN CONVERSION **

For conversion into RPN, please enter a
valid infix expression (e.g., 6 + 3):
23 - (14/77) * 9


For the given infix expression:
23 - (14/77) * 9
the translated RPN expression is:
23 14 77 / 9 * -

Any more infix expression (y/n)? y


For conversion into RPN, please enter a
valid infix expression (e.g., 6 + 3):
((A - C) + (B - D)) * (E + F)

For the given infix expression:
((A - C) + (B - D)) * (E + F)
the translated RPN expression is:
A C - B D - + E F + *
```

```
Any more infix expression (y/n)? y


For conversion into RPN, please enter a
valid infix expression (e.g., 6 + 3):
2 * (A + B) / (C + 4 * D)

For the given infix expression:
2 * (A + B) / (C + 4 * D)
the translated RPN expression is:
2 A B + * C 4 D * + /

Any more infix expression (y/n)? n
```

Notice that the RPN class is defined as a derived class of the `Ary_Stack` class using `:`. Thus the RPN class members inherit the privilege of accessing the `protected` and `public` data fields and methods of the `Ary_Stack` class. This is one characteristic of an OOP. Further, the behavior of an RPN object is tightly encapsulated by implementing its `private` data and `public` methods `RPN()`, `~RPN()`, `priority()`, `infix_to_RPN()`, `get_infix_expr()`, and `convert_infix_to_rpn_and_print()`.

6.4   Queue Objects

The second most common restricted access structure is the queue.

Definition 6.2 *A queue is an ordered list in which all insertions are made at one end, called the tail or rear of the queue, while all deletions are made at the other end, called the head or front of the queue. A queue supports two primary operations:*

(i) Enqueue — insertion into the front of the queue.
(ii) Dequeue — deletion (retrieval) from the rear of the queue.

This description of the queue implies that the first element inserted is the first to be removed and the last element inserted is the last removed. As such, queues are also referred to as *First In First Out (FIFO) lists.* This is in contrast to the LIFO operation of a stack.

The implementation of a queue object is more complex than that of a stack object — a stack object has only one end for the entry and exit of data elements while a queue object has two separate ends.

A *queue object* is specified by an ADT queue. An ADT queue is a data structure that contains a collection of data elements that follow FIFO policy, and a collection of some generalized operations. A set of example methods for a queue object is given in Table 6.4.

Example Queue Object Methods

Construct and initialize a queue object.
Destroy (delete) a queue object.
Check if a queue object is empty.
Check if a queue object is full.
Build a queue object from a given set of data.
Enqueue (add) a data element in a queue object.
Dequeue (delete) a data element from a queue object.
Print a queue object.

TABLE 6.4.

The data elements in a queue object are of complex or simple data types. A queue object is a data structure that encapsulates data fields and this set of operations.

There are two other versions of a queue object:

- a *dequeue* (or *double-ended queue*)

- a *priority queue*.

In a *dequeue*, both front and rear ends are used for adding and deleting a data element in the queue. In a *priority queue* (see Exercise 6-22), the data insertion and deletion operations do not follow the FIFO policy; these operations are influenced by a special value, called the *priority*, associated with each element. Implementations of these special queues are left as exercises.

The data structures used to store the data elements of a queue are (1) array, (2) singly linked list or doubly linked list, or (3) array, or singly or doubly linked circular list. A queue object is a circular queue object when a circular list is used to implement its data elements.

A queue object is an instance of a derived *implementation specific* class. The *base* class, from which the queue object is derived, is implementation unspecific; it provides a set of uniform methods (actions or interfaces or behavior) for a queue object, which are implemented in the derived class. For the current discussion, an abstract base class Queue is defined in the file bc_queue.h. The corresponding base class object is depicted in Figure 6.11.

```
// Program: bc_queue.h (Base class for Queue object)

class Queue {
  public:
    virtual BOOLEAN   is_que_empty (void) = 0;
    virtual BOOLEAN   is_que_full  (void) = 0;
    virtual void      build_que (DATA_TYPE str[]) = 0;
    virtual void      add_que (DATA_TYPE) = 0;
```

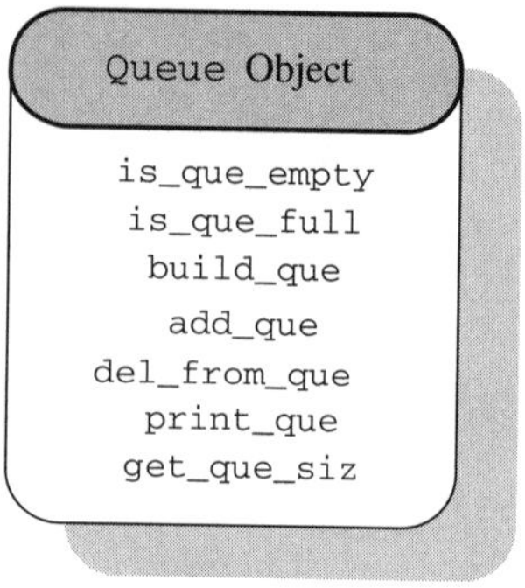

FIGURE 6.11. Base class for the queue object.

```
    virtual DATA_TYPE del_from_que (void) = 0;
    virtual void      print_que (void) = 0;
    virtual int       get_que_siz(void) = 0;
};
```

The names and arguments for the methods in the base class Queue and in the derived class must exactly match each other.

```
class <implementation_specific_class>:public Queue{

    //  ...
};
```

A queue object, queue_obj, is created by instancing a selected implementation specific class:

```
<implementation_specific_class>  queue_obj;
```

For example, when the data of a queue object are organized as an array, the derived queue class Ary_Queue is defined as:

```
class Ary_Queue : public Queue {

    // ...
};
```

A queue object, queue_obj with array-size 10, is created by the statement:

```
Ary_Queue  queue_obj(10);
```

6.5   Implementation Specific Queue Classes

Several OOP implementations for a queue object are presented as implementation specific classes. Fundamentally, these implementations differ in the way memory is allocated for the data elements and how the elements are linked together. More specifically, implementations are categorized as

- those that employ fixed array memory allocation and have

  - predecessor and/or successor links implicit to the array structure, or
  - predecessor and/or successor links explicitly specified in terms of array indexes, or

- those that employ dynamic memory allocation and have

  - predecessor and/or successor links explicitly specified as pointers.

6.5.1   OOP IMPLEMENTATION OF A QUEUE USING ARRAY

In this implementation approach, the data elements of a queue object are stored in an array queue[n] of size n = QUEUE_SIZ, and the two array indexes front_of_queue and rear_of_queue are used to respectively access the data elements at the front and at the rear of the queue. These array indexes range from 0 to (QUEUE_SIZ - 1), where queue[0] is assumed to be the front of the queue. Figure 6.12 shows an array-based queue. Then, front_of_queue = 0, and rear_of_queue ranges from 0 to (QUEUE_SIZ - 1). For an empty queue, front_of_queue = 0, and rear_of_queue = -1.

To illustrate, two successive add operations are performed with data 9 and 7, followed by one deletion operation. Figure 6.13 shows the states of the array-based queue. The front of the queue is assumed to be fixed at zero, and the array index rear_of_queue changes, which requires upward physical shifts of the data elements from queue[QUEUE_SIZ - 1], ..., queue[1] to respectively queue[QUEUE_SIZ - 2], ..., queue[0]. This makes the implementation in **Code 6.5**, with front_of_queue fixed at zero, inefficient. Improvement of Code 6.5 is achieved by incrementing front_of_queue when a data element is removed. This alleviated the physical movement of the data elements. This is left as an exercise.

In an object-oriented implementation, an ADT queue specifies a queue object. The ADT definition of the queue helps us identify the QUEUE_SIZ, front_of_queue, rear_of_queue, and queue[] as data elements and the operations as methods for an array queue object shown in Figure 6.14. With data abstraction and encapsulation in mind, an OOP implementation in C++ of an array-based queue employing the sequential storage strategy

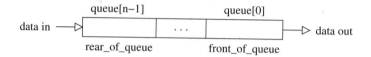

FIGURE 6.12. An array-based queue.

queue[1]	queue[0]
7	9

front_of_queue = 0
rear_of_queue = 1

(a) Array–based queue after adding 9 and 7.

queue[1]	queue[0]
	9

front_of_queue = 0
rear_of_queue = 0

(b) Array–based queue after deletion.

FIGURE 6.13. Operations on an array-based queue.

is presented as **Code 6.5.** For this implementation, the implementation specific class, `Array_Queue`, contained in the header file `Ary_Que.h`, is:

```
class  Array_Queue : public Queue {
  private:
    int    QUEUE_SIZ;
    // The array-based queue is composed of
    // queue indices, "front_of_queue" and
    // "rear_of_queue", and the stored data
    // in the array 'queue' of size QUEUE_SIZ.
    int         front_of_queue,
                rear_of_queue;
    DATA_TYPE  *queue;
    void        init_ary_que (void);

  //  Declare public interface functions
  //  that implement queue operations
  public:
    Array_Queue(int que_siz);   // Constructor
  ~ Array_Queue();              // Destructor
    BOOLEAN    is_que_empty (void);
    BOOLEAN    is_que_full   (void);
    void       add_que (DATA_TYPE);
    void       build_que (DATA_TYPE str[]);
    DATA_TYPE  del_from_que (void);
    void       print_que (void);
    inline int get_que_siz() {return(QUEUE_SIZ);}
```

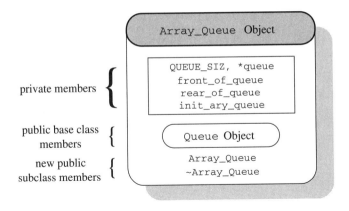

FIGURE 6.14. An Array_Queue object.

```
};
```

The Array_Queue class, derived from the base class Queue, encapsulates data and functions for an array-based queue object in a single entity. It defines a type for the array-based queue objects. An object ary_que_obj is an instance of the Array_Queue class; it is a data structure containing data fields and function members that are used to process data. The data fields QUEUE_SIZ, front_of_queue, rear_of_queue, and queue[] to hold the queue's data are declared private to this class, and so they are not accessible to the outside world (that is, outside this class Array_Queue). This is the data-hiding feature of an OOP. The member functions Array_Queue(), ..., get_que_siz() are public and valid interfaces (also called methods) to the outside world. Using these public functions, an object of the same or different type class sends messages (e.g., initialize, add, print) to an object (e.g., ary_que_obj) of the Array_Queue class. This implementation of an array-based queue object has the OOP characteristics — "class," "objects," "methods," and "messages." An array-based queue object is shown in Figure 6.14. As shown in Chapter 3, the template keyword may be used to define the Array_Queue class of elements of an arbitrary type:

```
template<class DATA_TYPE> class Array_Queue:public Queue{

    // Members and declarations are same as above.
};
```

In **Code 6.5**, the behavior of an array-based queue object with character type data is characterized by the following methods.

The `public` member functions of the `Array_Queue` class will now be described.

`Array_Queue()`, the constructor, is used to create a queue object. It is implicitly called when an instance `ary_que_obj` of type `Array_Queue` is created in `main()` by this statement:

```
Array_Queue  ary_que_obj(11);
```

`Array_Queue()` dynamically allocates memory storage for an array queue of size 11 using the `new` operator:

```
queue = new DATA_TYPE[QUEUE_SIZ = que_siz];
```

It sets QUEUE_SIZ to the desired value, e.g., 11. It calls `init_ary_que()` to initialize the queue object.

`~Array_Queue()`, the destructor, is implicitly called in `main()` before the program exits. It deallocates the memory space of the data array of size QUEUE_SIZ by the `delete` operator:

```
delete []queue;
```

`Init_ary_que()`, a `private` member function of the `Array_Queue` class, initializes the `Array_Queue`-type object (e.g., `ary_que_obj`) by setting `front_of_queue` to 0 and `rear_of_queue` to -1 (an invalid array index).

`Is_que_empty()`, a `public` member function of the `Array_Queue` class, checks whether an object of the `Array_Queue` class is empty by testing `rear_of_queue == -1`. If it is empty, it returns 1; otherwise, it returns 0.

`Add_que()`, a `public` member function of the `Array_Queue` class, implements the add (enqueue) operation on the `Array_Queue`-type object (e.g., `ary_que_obj`). The steps for `add_que()` are:

Step 1. If `rear_of_queue` is less than QUEUE_SIZ, (i.e., the array is not fully occupied), increase `rear_of_queue` by 1:

```
rear_of_queue = rear_of_queue + 1;
```

Step 2. The new element `new_data` is put in the array queue, `queue[]`:

```
queue[rear_of_queue] = new_data;
```

Step 3. If the array queue is full, display an error message "Queue Overflow" and return.

`Del_from_que()`, a `public` member function of the `Array_Queue` class, implements the delete (dequeue) operation. `Del_from_que()` performs the following steps:

Step 1. If rear_of_queue >= front_of_queue (i.e., the array queue has at least one data element), do steps 2 through 5; otherwise, go to Step 6.

Step 2. Get data from the front of the array queue:

remove_data = queue[front_of_queue];

Step 3. Move up elements queue[1],.., queue[rear_of_queue] to respectively queue[0],..,queue[rear_of_queue - 1].

Step 4. Decrease rear_of_queue by 1:

rear_of_queue = rear_of_queue - 1;

Step 5. Return remove_data.

Step 6. The array queue is empty. Display an error message "Queue Underflow" and return.

Print_que(), a public member function of the Array_Queue class, prints an array queue object from its front queue[0] to the rear of the queue, queue[rear_of_queue]. For an empty queue object, it prints a message.

Main() is not a member function of the Array_Queue class, so it cannot directly call the interface functions of the Array_Queue class. It instantiates an ary_que_obj object of the Array_Queue class, which can have at most 11 elements of type DATA_TYPE. Main() calls this object's methods build_que(), print_que(), and del_from_que() to send messages (build an array-based queue object from a string "SAUREN", print the queue object, delete the front element from the queue object) to the object ary_que_obj. At the program exit, ~Array_Queue() is implicitly called to release allocated memory spaces.

The implementation of these methods for an array-based queue object is shown in **Code 6.5**.

Code 6.5

```
// Program:  Ary_Que.c++
// Purpose:
//    OBJECT-ORIENTED IMPLEMENTATION OF A
//    QUEUE; its character type data are
//    stored in an array "queue[]". queue[0]
//    is the element at the front of queue.
//
#include <stdio.h>
typedef int    BOOLEAN;
const   int    UNDERFLOW = 1;
typedef char   DATA_TYPE;
#include "bc_queue.h" // For base class "Queue"
```

```
#include "Ary_Que.h"  // For derived class "Array_Queue"

// Implement the methods of class "Array_Queue"
//
//   Array_Queue():
//      Allocate memory space for an object in the
//      "Array_Queue" class
//
Array_Queue::Array_Queue (int que_siz)
{
    queue = new DATA_TYPE[QUEUE_SIZ = que_siz];
    init_ary_que();
}

//   ~Array_Queue():
//      Free memory for an "Array_Queue"-type object
//
Array_Queue::~Array_Queue()
{
    delete []queue; // delete array queue
}

//   init_ary_que():
//      Initialize "Array_Queue"-type object.
//
void  Array_Queue::init_ary_que(void)
{
    front_of_queue = 0;
    rear_of_queue  = -1;
}

//   is_que_empty():
//      Check whether an object of
//      "Array_Queue" class is empty
//
BOOLEAN Array_Queue::is_que_empty(void)
{
    return (rear_of_queue == -1);
}

BOOLEAN Array_Queue::is_que_full(void)
{
    return (rear_of_queue == QUEUE_SIZ);
}

//   add_que():
//      Add a new data at the rear of an object of the
//      "Array_Queue" class. If it reaches the maximum
//      capacity of the array queue object, it reports
//      an OVERFLOW error message, and returns.
//      queue[0] is always the front element.
//
void Array_Queue::add_que (DATA_TYPE new_data)
{
```

```
    if (rear_of_queue < QUEUE_SIZ)
        queue[++rear_of_queue] = new_data;
    else
        printf("\n add_que:: Queue Overflow\n");
}

// del_from_que():
//    Delete a data from the front of an object
//    of the "Array_Queue" class. If the queue
//    object is empty, it reports an UNDERFLOW
//    error by returning UNDERFLOW.
//
DATA_TYPE Array_Queue::del_from_que (void)
{
    if (rear_of_queue >= front_of_queue) {
        // Get data from the front of array queue,
        // queue[0]
        DATA_TYPE remove_data = queue[front_of_queue];
        //
        // Move up all data elements queue[1],..,
        // queue[rear_of_queue] to respectively
        // queue[0],.., queue[rear_of_queue - 1].
        //
        for (int i=front_of_queue; i<rear_of_queue; i++)
            queue[i] = queue[i + 1];
        // Decrement "rear_of_queue" by 1.
        --rear_of_queue;
        return (remove_data);
    }
    else {
        printf ("\n del_from_que:queue underflow\n");
        return (UNDERFLOW);
    }
}

// build_que ():
//    Build an array based queue from
//    a given string of characters.
//
void  Array_Queue::build_que(DATA_TYPE str[])
{
    if (str[0] == '\0')
        printf("\n build_que: Empty string.\n");
    else
        // Since 'str[0]' is first added into the
        // array queue, it is at the queue's front.
        for (int j = 0; str[j] != '\0'; ++j)
            add_que (str[j]);
}

// print_que():
//    Print the queue object from its front to rear
//
void Array_Queue::print_que(void)
```

```
{
    if (!is_que_empty())
      for (int i = 0; i <= rear_of_queue; i++)
        printf("  queue[%i] = %c\n", i, queue[i]);
    else
        printf ("\n print_que: Empty Queue.\n");
}


//  main():
//     Test driver for Object-Oriented implementation
//     of array-based queue objects.
//
void main (void)
{
    // Declare an object "ary_que_obj" of size
    // 11, belonging to "Array_Queue" class.
    Array_Queue     ary_que_obj(11);
    static char     str[] = "SAUREN";

    printf("\n ** OOP IMPLEMENTATION OF %s ** \n",
            "ARRAY QUEUE");
    printf("\n Queue representation of \"%s\" is:\n",
            str);
    ary_que_obj.build_que(str);
    ary_que_obj.print_que();
    printf("\n After one remove %s:\n",
            "operation, queue is");
    ary_que_obj.del_from_que();
    ary_que_obj.print_que();
    delete  []str;
}
```

Code 6.5 for an array-based queue object produces the following output:

```
** OOP IMPLEMENTATION OF ARRAY QUEUE **

Queue representation of "SAUREN" is:
  queue[0] = S
  queue[1] = A
  queue[2] = U
  queue[3] = R
  queue[4] = E
  queue[5] = N

After one remove operation, queue is:
  queue[0] = A
  queue[1] = U
  queue[2] = R
  queue[3] = E
  queue[4] = N
```

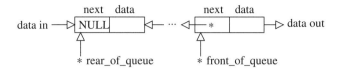

FIGURE 6.15. A singly linked queue.

The above OOP implementation of a queue using an array has the following drawbacks:

- It inherits all disadvantages of an array. Since the size of the queue is fixed at the compilation time, the queue cannot dynamically grow or shrink in size during execution time.

- It wastes memory space.

- By fixing the index of the front queue to zero, removal of a data element from the queue requires that the data elements are physically shifted in the main memory.

These drawbacks are resolved by the approach in Section 6.5.2.

6.5.2   OOP IMPLEMENTATION OF A QUEUE USING LINKED LIST

In this implementation approach, the data elements of a queue object are stored in a singly or doubly linked list. There is no limitation on the number of data elements in the queue. Two pointers `front_of_queue` and `rear_of_queue` are used to access the data elements at the front and at the rear of the queue, respectively. Figure 6.15 shows a singly linked based queue. The `front_of_queue` = NULL, and `rear_of_queue` = NULL indicate that the queue is empty. The `next` field of the element at the rear of the queue is NULL.

To illustrate, two successive add operations with data 9 and 7, followed by one deletion operation, are performed. Figure 6.16 shows the states of the singly linked queue.

For an object-oriented implementation of a queue object, the ADT definition of the queue and the singly linked queue in Figure 6.16 identify the `data`, `next`, `front_of_queue`, and `rear_of_queue` as data elements and the operations as methods for a singly linked queue object. With data abstraction and encapsulation of queue data fields and operations in mind, an OOP implementation in C++ of a singly linked list

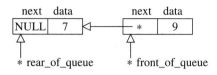

(a) Singly linked queue after addition of 9 and 7.

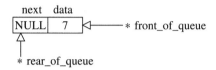

(b) Singly linked queue after deletion.

FIGURE 6.16. Operations on a singly linked queue.

based queue object employing the nonsequential storage strategy is presented as **Code 6.6**. For this implementation, the implementation specific class, `Singly_Linked_Queue`, contained in the header file `Lnk_Que.h`, is:

```
class  Singly_Linked_Queue : public Queue {
  private:
    // Singly linked queue is composed of
    // queue pointers, "front_of_queue" and
    // "rear_of_queue",and the "QUEUE_ELEMENT"
    // type data stored in a singly linked list.
    //
    typedef struct QUEUE_ELEMENT {
        DATA_TYPE        data;
        QUEUE_ELEMENT   *next;
    } *QUEUE_PTR;
    QUEUE_PTR  front_of_queue,
               rear_of_queue;
    void       init_lnk_que (void);

  //  Declare public interface functions that
  //  implement operations for a queue object.
  public:
    Singly_Linked_Queue() {init_lnk_que();}
    ~Singly_Linked_Queue();
    BOOLEAN    is_que_empty (void);
    BOOLEAN    is_que_full  (void);
    void       add_que (DATA_TYPE);
    void       build_que (DATA_TYPE str[]);
    DATA_TYPE  del_from_que (void);
    void       print_que (void);
    int        get_que_siz(void);
```

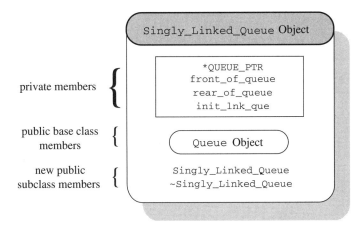

FIGURE 6.17. Singly_Linked_Queue class.

};

The Singly_Linked_Queue class is derived from the base class Queue. Figure 6.17 shows the Singly_Linked_Queue class. It defines a type of queue objects (e.g., lnk_que_obj). Such queue objects contain QUEUE_ELEMENT-type element objects that are stored in a singly linked list. These queue objects also contain the private pointer variables, front_of_queue and rear_of_queue of type QUEUE_PTR, and some operations that are used to process the queue element objects and the associated singly linked list. These operations, implemented as public functions, are interfaces to the outside world. The QUEUE_ELEMENT-type element object is composed of data, and a pointer next of type QUEUE_PTR, for forward linking to the next elements in the Singly_Linked_Queue-type queue object. Pertaining to the object lnk_que_obj, the pointer variables front_of_queue and rear_of_queue point to the front and the rear of QUEUE_ELEMENT-type element objects, respectively. When lnk_que_obj has two QUEUE_ELEMENT-type element objects, Figure 6.18 shows connection between two such objects.

In the following, the member functions of the Singly_Linked_Queue class will be described. It is not necessary to pass the member data fields data, next, front_of_queue and rear_of_queue as arguments of these member functions because these member fields are locally defined within the same class Singly_Linked_Queue.

Singly_Linked_Queue(), the constructor, is automatically called when an object (e.g., lnk_que_obj) of type Singly_Linked_Queue is instantiated by this statement:

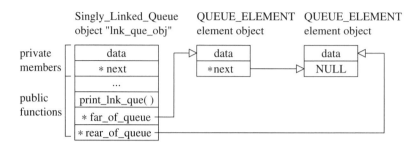

FIGURE 6.18. A singly linked queue object.

```
Singly_Linked_Queue   lnk_que_obj;
```

Singly_Linked_Queue() calls init_lnk_que() to initialize the object.

~Singly_Linked_Queue(), the destructor, destroys the entire singly linked queue object. Starting from the front of the queue object, the function traverses the queue object using the next pointer, and deallocates the memory space by using the delete operator. It is implicitly called in main().

Init_lnk_que() initializes a singly linked queue object, by setting the pointers front_of_queue and rear_of_queue to NULL. It is a private member function of the class Singly_Linked_Queue as in Code 6.6.

Is_que_empty(), a publicly accessible member function of the class Singly_Linked_Queue as in Code 6.6, checks whether a singly linked queue object is empty. If the pointer front_of_queue has a NULL value, it returns 1; otherwise, it returns 0.

Add_que(), a public member function of Singly_Linked_Queue class as in Code 6.6, enqueues a new data new_data in the singly linked queue object. It uses the new operator to dynamically allocate memory space for the QUEUE_ELEMENT-type element object to be added in the queue object (e.g., lnk_que_obj). If the queue object is empty, the new element is added at the front; otherwise, it is added at the rear of the queue.

Del_from_que(), a publicly accessible member function of the class Singly_Linked_Queue as in Code 6.6, dequeues a QUEUE_ELEMENT-type object from the singly linked queue object. The function removes the data element at the front from the queue object, and uses the delete operator to release the memory space. The successor of the old front element is made the new front element, and is now pointed to by front_of_queue. If the queue object is empty, a message "Queue Underflow" is displayed.

Main() is not a member function of the Singly_Linked_Queue class.

It instantiates a `lnk_que_obj` object of the `Singly_Linked_Queue` class. Main() passes messages to `lnk_que_obj` through this object's methods `build_que()`, `print_que()`, and `del_from_que()` for actions. At the program exit, `~Singly_Linked_Queue()` is implicitly called to release the object's allocated memory spaces for later use.

The OOP implementation of a queue object using a singly linked list has this advantage — the queue object can dynamically grow or shrink in size, if required, during the run-time. The disadvantage is the extra memory space for the single link (next) in case of a singly linked list, or double links in case of a doubly linked list.

Code 6.6 shows an OOP implementation of a singly linked queue object.

Code 6.6

```
// Program:   Lnk_Que.c++
// Purpose:
//    OBJECT-ORIENTED IMPLEMENTATION OF A
//    QUEUE; its character type data are
//    stored in a singly linked list pointed
//    to by a pointer "fornt_of_queue" of
//    type QUEUE_PTR.
//
#include <stdio.h>
const    int    UNDERFLOW = -1;
typedef  int    BOOLEAN;
typedef  char   DATA_TYPE;
#include "bc_queue.h"  // For base class "Queue"
#include "Lnk_Que.h"   // For derived class
                       // "Singly_Linked_Queue"

//   Implement methods of class "Singly_Linked_Queue"
//
//   ~Singly_Linked_Queue():
//      Deallocate memory space for an object in the
//      "Singly_Linked_Queue" class. It is automatically
//      called before the program exit in main().
//
Singly_Linked_Queue::~Singly_Linked_Queue()
{
    QUEUE_PTR  tmp_ptr;
    while (front_of_queue != NULL) {
        tmp_ptr = front_of_queue;
        front_of_queue = tmp_ptr->next;
        delete  tmp_ptr;  //  Free up memory space
    }
    init_lnk_que();
}

//   init_lnk_que():
//      Initialize "Singly_Linked_Queue" type object
//
```

```
void  Singly_Linked_Queue::init_lnk_que(void)
{
    front_of_queue = rear_of_queue  = NULL;
}

//  is_que_empty():
//    Check whether an object of
//    "Singly_Linked_Queue" class is empty
//
BOOLEAN Singly_Linked_Queue::is_que_empty(void)
{
    return (front_of_queue == NULL);
}

BOOLEAN Singly_Linked_Queue::is_que_full(void)
{
    printf("\n is_que_full: Not applicable.\n");
    return(0);
}

//  add_que():
//    Add a new data at the rear of an object
//    of the "Singly_Linked_Queue" class.
//
void Singly_Linked_Queue::add_que(DATA_TYPE new_data)
{
    QUEUE_PTR  new_ptr = new QUEUE_ELEMENT;
    new_ptr->data  = new_data;
    new_ptr->next  = NULL;

    // If the queue is empty, add it at the front
    if (is_que_empty())
       front_of_queue = new_ptr;
    else
       //
       // The queue object is not empty; add the new
       // queue item at the rear of the queue object
       //
       rear_of_queue->next = new_ptr;
    rear_of_queue = new_ptr;
}

//  del_from_que():
//    Delete a data from the front of an object
//    of the "Singly_Linked_Queue" class. If the
//    queue object is empty, it reports an error
//    message "underflow", and returns NULL.
//
DATA_TYPE Singly_Linked_Queue::del_from_que (void)
{
    if (!is_que_empty()) {
        // Get data from the front of singly linked
        // queue, pointed to by "front_of_queue".
        //
```

```
        DATA_TYPE remove_data = front_of_queue->data;

        // Make successor of old front-element
        // the new front element of the queue.
        front_of_queue = front_of_queue->next;
        return (remove_data);
    }
    else {
        printf ("\n del_from_que:queue underflow\n");
        return (UNDERFLOW);
    }
}

// build_que ():
//   Build a singly linked list based queue
//   from a given string of characters.
//
void Singly_Linked_Queue::build_que(DATA_TYPE str[])
{
    if (str[0] == '\0')
        printf("\n build_que: Empty string.\n");
    else
        // 'str[0]' being first added into the singly
        // linked queue, is at the queue's front.
        for (int j = 0; str[j] != '\0'; ++j)
            add_que (str[j]);
}

//   print_que():
//     Print the queue object from its front to rear
//
void  Singly_Linked_Queue::print_que (void)
{
    if (!is_que_empty()) {
        for (QUEUE_PTR tmp_ptr = front_of_queue;
              tmp_ptr != NULL;
              tmp_ptr = tmp_ptr->next)
            printf(" %c -> ", tmp_ptr->data);
        printf("NULL\n \^");
        printf("\n !___  Front of this queue object \n");
    }
    else
        printf ("\n print_que: Empty Queue.\n");
}

int Singly_Linked_Queue::get_que_siz(void)
{
    printf("\n get_que_siz: Exercise !!\n");
    return(0);  // To avoid compilation warning
}

//   main():
//     Test driver for OO implementation
//     of singly linked list-based queues
```

```
//
void main (void)
{
    // Declare an object "lnk_que_obj" of
    // the "Singly_Linked_Queue" class
    Singly_Linked_Queue    lnk_que_obj;
    static char    str[] = "SAUREN";

    printf("\n ** OOP IMPLEMENTATION OF %s ** \n",
            "SINGLY LINKED QUEUE");
    printf("\n Queue representation of \"%s\" is:\n",
            str);
    lnk_que_obj.build_que (str);
    lnk_que_obj.print_que();
    printf("\n After two remove %s \n",
            "operations, queue is:");
    lnk_que_obj.del_from_que();
    lnk_que_obj.del_from_que();
    lnk_que_obj.print_que();
    delete  []str;
}
```

Code 6.6 produces this output:

```
** OOP IMPLEMENTATION OF SINGLY LINKED QUEUE **

Queue representation of "SAUREN" is:
S  ->  A  ->  U  ->  R  ->  E  ->  N  -> NULL
^
!___  Front of this queue object

After two remove operations, queue is:
U  ->  R  ->  E  ->  N  -> NULL
^
!___  Front of this queue object
```

6.6   Circular Queue Objects

For array-based queue objects, it was noticed that removing a data element from the queue requires shifting of the remaining data elements. To circumvent this problem, a special and efficient form of a simple queue, called *circular queue*, may be used. A circular queue is not a circle, but a modified form of simple queue in which the rear of the queue is permitted to wrap around to the original starting location. Applications of circular queues are in the operating system (e.g., buffering for read and write I/O associated with each port, interprocess communication) and computer networking (e.g., buffering data during data exchange between two or more computers).

A *circular queue object* is specified by an ADT circular queue. An ADT circular queue is a data structure that contains a collection of data elements that follow *FIFO* policy with the rear allowed to wrap around, and a collection of some generalized operations.

Notice that the operations for an ADT circular queue are similar to those of a simple queue, but their implementations must consider "wraparound" conditions. It is also required to consider whether to "overwrite the front of queue" or not to overwrite in case of a full queue (i.e., no room for new element.) The overwrite condition arises when the rear is immediately behind the front of the circular queue.

A circular queue object can be implemented using the data structures (1) an array, (2) a singly linked circular list, and (3) a doubly linked circular list. The overwriting requirement produces two versions of each of these implementations.

The key advantage of an array-based circular queue over an array-based simple queue is that the data element can be put in any empty or unused slot of the array because the rear index is allowed to wrap around the front index of the circular queue; this alleviates the necessity of shifting data upward or downward to fill in the hole created by the dequeue operation.

6.6.1   OOP IMPLEMENTATION OF A CIRCULAR QUEUE USING ARRAY

In this array-based implementation approach, the data elements of a circular queue object are stored in an array `queue[n]` of size n = QUEUE_SIZ, and the two array indexes `front_of_queue` and `rear_of_queue` are used to access the data elements respectively at the front and at the rear of the queue. These array indexes range from 0 to (QUEUE_SIZ - 1), where `circ_queue[QUEUE_SIZ]` is initially assumed to be the front of the queue, but it changes for dequeue operation. For an empty circular queue, `front_of_queue` =QUEUE_SIZ and `rear_of_queue` =QUEUE_SIZ.

For example, Figure 6.19 shows a circular queue that is based on an array `c_queue[]` of size 7. At the initial state, `front_of_queue` = 7 and `rear_of_queue` = 7. After three remove operations, the front and the rear of the queue are changed as follows: `front_of_queue` = 3 and `rear_of_queue` = 0. The data elements `c_queue[6]`, `c_queue[5]`, `c_queue[4]` have already been removed, and are accessible and garbage. The next add operation, say with data 8, will cause the rear to wrap around the maximum range, and set `rear_of_queue` to 6; `c_queue[6]` becomes 8.

An OOP implementation of an array-based circular queue object em-

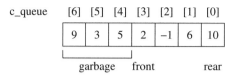

FIGURE 6.19. An array-based circular queue.

ploying the sequential storage strategy is presented as **Code 6.7**. For this implementation, the implementation specific class, `Array_Circ_Queue`, contained in the header file `Ary_Circ_Que.h` is:

```
class  Array_Circ_Queue : public Queue {
  private:
    int   QUEUE_SIZ;       // Maximum queue size
    int     front_of_queue, // or, "qhead"
            rear_of_queue;  // or, "qtail"
    DATA_TYPE *circ_queue;
    void   init_ary_circ_que (void);

  public:
    Array_Circ_Queue(int que_siz);
    ~Array_Circ_Queue();
    BOOLEAN        is_que_empty (void);
    BOOLEAN        is_que_full (void);
    void           build_que (DATA_TYPE str[]);
    void           add_que (DATA_TYPE);      // put
    DATA_TYPE      del_from_que (void);      // get
    void           print_que (void);
    inline int get_que_siz() {return (QUEUE_SIZ);}
};
```

The `Array_Circ_Queue` class is derived from the abstract base class `Queue`. It encapsulates data and functions for an array-based circular queue in a single entity. It defines a type for the array-based circular queue objects. An object `ary_circ_que_obj` of the `Array_Circ_Queue` class is a data structure containing data fields and function members that are used to process the data. The data fields `QUEUE_SIZ`, `front_of_queue`, `rear_of_queue`, and array `circ_queue[]` are declared `private` to this class, and so they are not accessible to the outside world (that is, outside the `Array_Circ_Queue` class). This is the data-hiding feature of an OOP. The member functions `Array_Circ_Queue()`, …,`get_que_siz()` are `public` interfaces to the outside world. Using these `public` functions (methods), an object of the same or different type class sends messages (e.g., add, delete, print) to an object (e.g., `ary_circ_que_obj`) of the `Array_Circ_Queue` class. This implementation of an array-based circular queue object, as shown in Figure 6.20, possesses these OOP character-

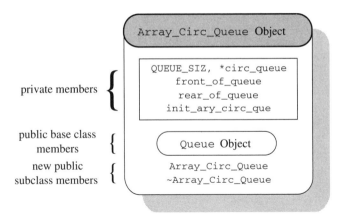

FIGURE 6.20. Array_Circ_Queue class.

istics, "classes," "objects," "methods," and "messages."

The array-based circular queue has the queue indices `front_of_queue` and `rear_of_queue` and the character type data elements stored in the array `circ_queue[]`. Because of the *circular* nature of this data structure, these two indices are carefully handled to wrap around the maximum limit `QUEUE_SIZ` of the array. During the add operation, the index `rear_of_queue` decreases starting out with (`QUEUE_SIZ - 1`), and when it reaches zero, it is reset to `QUEUE_SIZ`. In a similar manner, `front_of_queue` is handled in the delete operation.

The publicly accessible member functions of the `Array_Circ_Queue` class are now described.

`Array_Circ_Queue()` is the constructor for a circular queue object. It is implicitly called when `ary_circ_que_obj`, an object with array size 6 of type `Array_Circ_Queue`, is instantiated in `main()` as follows:

```
Array_Circ_Queue  ary_circ_que_obj(6);
```

It sets `QUEUE_SIZ` to 6, and dynamically allocates memory storage for the array `circ_queue[]` of `DATA_TYPE` by using the new operator:

```
circ_queue = new DATA_TYPE[QUEUE_SIZ];
```

`~Array_Circ_Queue()` destroys an array-based circular queue object of type `Array_Circ_Queue`. It deletes the data array `circ_queue[]` by using the `delete` operator:

```
delete []circ_queue;
```

It is implicitly called in main() before program exit.

Init_ary_circ_que() is a private member function of the class
Array_Circ_Queue. It initializes this class's object ary_circ_que_obj
by setting rear_of_queue and front_of_queue to QUEUE_SIZ.

Is_que_empty() is a publicly accessible member function of the
Array_Circ_Queue class. It checks whether an array-based circular queue
object is empty by testing:

$$rear\_of\_queue == QUEUE\_SIZ, \text{ and}$$
$$front\_of\_queue == QUEUE\_SIZ.$$

If it is empty, it returns 1; otherwise, it returns 0.

Is_que_full(), a publicly accessible member function of the class
Array_Circ_Queue, checks whether an array-based circular queue object
of Array_Circ_Queue class is full by testing:

$$rear\_of\_queue \ \ == 0 \text{ and } front\_of\_queue == QUEUE\_SIZ,$$
$$\text{or, } rear\_of\_queue \ \ == front\_of\_queue + 1.$$

The second test is required of circular nature. If the circular queue object
is full, it returns 1; otherwise, it returns 0.

Add_que() is a public member function of the Array_Circ_Queue
class. It adds a new data element new_data of type DATA_TYPE at the
rear of a circular queue object. The algorithm for this enqueue operation
is:

Step 1. It calls is_que_full(). If the array-based queue is full, it
prints a message "Queue Overflow" and returns. Otherwise, do
steps 2 through 5.

Step 2. If rear_of_queue <= 0 (i.e., it reaches the maximum array
size QUEUE_SIZ), reset it to QUEUE_SIZ to wrap around the
array's maximum size.

Step 3. It calls is_que_empty(). If the circular queue is empty, decrement front_of_queue by 1.

Step 4. Decrement rear_of_queue by 1:

rear_of_queue = rear_of_queue - 1;

Step 5. Put the new data element at the rear:

circ_queue[rear_of_queue] = new_data;

Build_que() is a publicly accessible member function of the class
Array_Circ_Queue. It builds a circular queue object from a given character string. It calls add_que() for each character data in the string in a
for loop.

Del_from_que() is a publicly accessible member function of the
Array_Circ_Queue class. It takes out the data element from the front

of an object of the `Array_Circ_Queue` class and then deletes it. If the queue object is empty, it reports "Queue Underflow" and returns "UNDER-FLOW." It has a check that handles the "wrap condition." The algorithm of the delete (dequeue) operation is:

Step 1. It calls `is_que_empty()`. If the circular queue object is empty, it prints a message "Queue Underflow" and returns. Otherwise, do steps 2 through 5.

Step 2. If `front_of_queue` < 0 (i.e., it reaches the maximum array size `QUEUE_SIZ`), reset it to `QUEUE_SIZ` to wrap around the array's maximum size. `front_of_queue = QUEUE_SIZ`

Step 3. Get the data element at the front:

`remove_data = circ_queue[front_of_queue];`

Step 4. Decrement `front_of_queue` by 1:

`front_of_queue = front_of_queue - 1;`

Step 5. Return the data: `return(remove_data);`

`Print_que()` is a public member function of `Array_Circ_Queue` class. It prints an array-based circular queue object from its front to rear. It calls `is_que_empty()`. If the queue is empty, it prints a message. Otherwise, it considers two cases due to the "circular" nature of the queue. The cases are:

- `(rear_of_queue < front_of_queue)` and `(rear_of_queue >= 0)`

- `rear_of_queue > 0` and `front_of_queue ¡= rear_of_queue`

In both cases it prints the circular queue starting from the front to the rear.

`Main()` is not a member function of the `Array_Circ_Queue` class. It instantiates an `ary_circ_que_obj` object, with data array size being 6, of the `Array_Circ_Queue` class. `Main()` sends messages (builds a circular queue object for a given character string "SAUREN", dequeues, and prints the queue object) to `ary_circ_que_obj` object through this object's methods `build_que()`, `print_que()`, and `del_from_que()`. For a clean memory management, the `~Array_Circ_Queue()`, is implicitly called at the program exit.

Code 6.7 shows an OOP implementation of an array-based circular queue.

Code 6.7

```
// Program:   Ary_Circ_Que.c++
// Purpose:
//    OBJECT-ORIENTED IMPLEMENTATION OF A
//    CIRCULAR QUEUE; its character type
//    data are stored in an array "circ_queue[]".
//    circ_queue[QUEUE_SIZ -1] is initially assumed
//    to be the element at the front of queue.
//    "Wrap around" condition is checked due to
//    circular nature. This implementation allows
//    "overwrite" if the queue is full.
//
#include <stdio.h>
const    int    UNDERFLOW = -1;
typedef  int    BOOLEAN;
typedef  char   DATA_TYPE;
#include "bc_queue.h"     // For base class "Queue"
#include "Ary_Circ_Que.h" // For derived class
                          // "Ary_Circ_Que"
//   Implement methods of class "Array_Circ_Queue"
//
//   Array_Circ_Queue():
//     Allocate memory space for an object in the
//     "Array_Circ_Queue" class
//
Array_Circ_Queue::Array_Circ_Queue (int que_siz)
{
    circ_queue = new DATA_TYPE[QUEUE_SIZ = que_siz];
    init_ary_circ_que();
}


//   ~Array_Circ_Queue():
//     Deallocate memory space for an object in the
//     "Array_Circ_Queue" class. It is automatically
//     called before the program exit in main().
//
Array_Circ_Queue::~Array_Circ_Queue()
{
  delete []circ_queue; // delete array queue
}


//   init_ary_circ_que():
//     Initialize an object of "Array_Circ_Queue" class
//     by setting both front and rear to queue max size.
//
void  Array_Circ_Queue::init_ary_circ_que (void)
{
    front_of_queue = QUEUE_SIZ;
    rear_of_queue  = QUEUE_SIZ; // Maximum size
}


//   is_que_empty():
//     Check whether an object of "Array_Circ_Queue"
```

```
//     class is empty
//
BOOLEAN Array_Circ_Queue::is_que_empty (void)
{
    return ((rear_of_queue == QUEUE_SIZ) &&
            (front_of_queue == QUEUE_SIZ));
}

// is_que_full():
//     Check whether a circular queue object of
//     "Array_Circ_Queue" class is full. (This is
//     specially needed for a circular queue.)
//
BOOLEAN Array_Circ_Queue::is_que_full (void)
{
  return ((rear_of_queue == 0) &&
          (front_of_queue == QUEUE_SIZ)
          (rear_of_queue == (front_of_queue + 1)));
}

// add_que():
//     Add a new data at the rear of an object of the
//     "Array_Circ_Queue" class. If it reaches the maximum
//     capacity of the array queue object, apply
//     "wrap condition" by resetting "rear_of_queue"
//     to QUEUE_SIZ. Otherwise, the queue is full, it
//     reports an OVERFLOW error message, and returns.
//
void Array_Circ_Queue::add_que(DATA_TYPE new_data)
{
    if (!is_que_full()) {
        // Reset "rear_of_queue" to QUEUE_SIZ for
        // "wrapping around" the array's max size
        if (rear_of_queue <= 0)
            rear_of_queue = QUEUE_SIZ;
        if (is_que_empty())
            --front_of_queue;
        circ_queue[--rear_of_queue] = new_data;
    }
    else
     printf("\n add_que: Queue Overflow\n");
}

// del_from_que():
//     Delete a data from the front of an object
//     of the "Array_Circ_Queue" class. If the
//     queue object is empty, it reports an
//     UNDERFLOW error message by returning
//     UNDERFLOW. Check for "wrap condition".
//
DATA_TYPE Array_Circ_Queue::del_from_que (void)
{
    if (!is_que_empty()) {
        if (front_of_queue < 0)
```

```
            front_of_queue = QUEUE_SIZ; // Reposition
        // Get data from the front of array queue,
        return (circ_queue[front_of_queue--]);
    }
    else {
        printf ("\n del_from_que:%s \n"
                "Queue Underflow");
        return (UNDERFLOW);
    }
}


// build_que():
//    Build an array based queue from
//    a given string of characters.
//
void Array_Circ_Queue::build_que(DATA_TYPE str[])
{
    if (str[0] == '\0')
        printf("\n build_que: Empty string.\n");
    else
        //  Since 'str[0]' is first added into the
        //  array queue, it is at the queue's front.
        for (int j = 0; str[j] != '\0'; ++j)
            add_que (str[j]);
}


//  print_que():
//    Print the queue object from its front to rear
//
void  Array_Circ_Queue::print_que (void)
{
    if (!is_que_empty()) {
        if ((rear_of_queue < front_of_queue) &&
            (rear_of_queue >= 0)) {
          printf(" c_queue[%i] = %c  <- Queue front\n",
            front_of_queue, circ_queue[front_of_queue]);
          for (int i = front_of_queue - 1;
               i >= 0; i--)
              printf(" c_queue[%i] = %c \n", i,
                        circ_queue[i]);
          for (i = QUEUE_SIZ - 1;
               i <= rear_of_queue; i--)
              printf("  queue[%i] = %c \n", i,
                        circ_queue[i]);
        }
        else
          // CASE: rear > 0 & front <= rear
          if (rear_of_queue > 0)
            printf(" c_queue[%i] = %c  <- Queue front\n",
              front_of_queue, circ_queue[front_of_queue]);
            for (int i = front_of_queue - 1;
                (i >= 0 && i <= rear_of_queue); i--)
                printf(" c_queue[%i] = %c \n", i,
                        circ_queue[i]);
```

```
    }
    else
        printf ("\n print_que: Empty Queue.\n");
}

//  main():
//      Test driver for Object-Oriented implementation
//      of array-based circular queue objects.
//
void main (void)
{
    // Declare and define size "6" of an object
    // "ary_circ_que_obj" belonging to class
    // "Array_Circ_Queue"
    Array_Circ_Queue  ary_circ_que_obj(6);
    static char       str[] = "SAUREN";

    printf("\n ** OOP IMPLEMENTATION OF %s ** \n",
            "ARRAY CIRCULAR QUEUE");
    printf("\n Queue representation of \"%s\" is:\n",
             str);
    ary_circ_que_obj.build_que (str);
    ary_circ_que_obj.print_que();
    printf("\n After adding one element, queue is:\n");
    ary_circ_que_obj.add_que ('K');
    ary_circ_que_obj.print_que();
    printf("\n After one remove %s:\n",
            "operation, queue is");
    ary_circ_que_obj.del_from_que();
    ary_circ_que_obj.print_que();
    delete  []str;
}
```

Code 6.7 produces this output:

```
** OOP IMPLEMENTATION OF ARRAY CIRCULAR QUEUE **

Queue representation of "SAUREN" is:
c_queue[5] = S  <- Queue front
c_queue[4] = A
c_queue[3] = U
c_queue[2] = R
c_queue[1] = E
c_queue[0] = N

After adding one element, queue is:
c_queue[5] = K  <- Queue front
c_queue[4] = A
c_queue[3] = U
c_queue[2] = R
c_queue[1] = E
```

```
c_queue[0] = N

After one remove operation, queue is:
c_queue[4] = A   <- Queue front
c_queue[3] = U
c_queue[2] = R
c_queue[1] = E
c_queue[0] = N
```

6.6.2 OOP Implementation of a Circular Queue Using a Linked List

The previous section showed that an array-based circular queue object is more efficient than an array-based queue, but neither queue can dynamically grow because of the array with fixed size. In some applications, this may be a critical problem. The requirement for dynamic growth and circular characteristic can be achieved by using a singly or doubly lined circular queue. A doubly linked circular queue is shown in Figure 6.21.

When a circular queue object is implemented as a singly or doubly linked list, the linked circular queue is initially assigned a size limit. During runtime, if this queue becomes full, it is possible to dynamically increase the size by double, using a function so that the circular queue will not be full. If the number of data elements in the circular queue object reaches the newly increased limit, it is possible to reuse the function for increasing the queue size.

When a circular queue is implemented using a doubly linked list, as shown in Figure 6.21, each data object is a record containing a data element of some given type, one forward link pointer (next), and one backward link pointer (prev). The OOP implementations for both singly linked and singly linked circular queue objects are left as exercises.

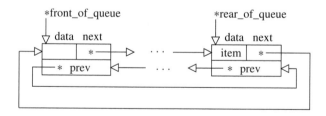

FIGURE 6.21. Doubly linked circular queue.

Queue structure	Worst-case performance of			
	Search (random)	Delete (random)	Enqueue	Dequeue
Array-based queue	$O(n)$	$O(n)$	$O(1)$	$O(1)$
Singly linked queue	$O(n)$	$O(n)$	$O(1)$	$O(1)$
Doubly linked queue	$O(n)$	$O(n)$	$O(1)$	$O(1)$
Singly linked circular queue	$O(n)$	$O(n)$	$O(1)$	$O(n)$
Doubly linked circular queue	$O(n)$	$O(n)$	$O(1)$	$O(n)$

TABLE 6.5. Performance of queue operations.

6.6.3 PERFORMANCE ANALYSES OF QUEUE OPERATIONS

In this chapter, several implementations of a queue object are discussed: (1) array queue, (2) singly linked queue, (3) doubly linked queue, (4) singly linked circular queue, and (5) doubly linked circular queue. Uses of these data structures depend on the applications and the operations required in these applications. Thus, for the selection of an appropriate and efficient form of list data structure, it is important to know at least the comparative-based worst-case performance of some such key queue operations as search and delete. The worst case occurs when the data element to be searched or deleted is not in the queue or is at the end of the queue. Consider n data elements in the queue. Table 6.5 shows the worst-case performances of operations for the queue objects.

The form of a queue data structure is such that random access of a data element is not possible. The element only at the front of queue is accessible.

The worst case for search of a random data element in a queue occurs when the target key element is at the rear of the queue, or does not exist in the queue. The search for an arbitrary element other than the one at the front of the queue is not efficient for this type of data structure. This is because a search requires n number of dequeue operations and n number of comparisons with the specified key. To restore the queue in the form previous to the search operation, one must store data elements in a temporary area, and do n number of enqueue operations. Thus, the worst-case performance for the search operation in a queue is $O(n)$.

Since the delete operation depends on the search operation, it is not efficient for deleting a specified data element that is not at the front of a queue. In this case, the worst-case performance of the delete operation is $O(n)$.

Thus, the queue data structure is not efficient and not recommended for applications that frequently require random search and delete. A queue structure is useful and efficient when dealing with the data element at the front of the queue.

6.7   OOP Application: SCAN Disk Scheduling with Priority Queues

This section demonstrates an application of queues in managing a disk subsystem resource. First shown is how such queue objects are created in this environment, and then basic concepts of data address in a disk, followed by the discussion and OOP implementation of the *SCAN algorithm* based disk scheduler.

In a multiprogrammed computing environment, multiple processes (i.e., programs in execution) simultaneously reside in main memory. Only one of them is executed by one central processing unit (CPU) at any point in time. They generate access requests for reading or writing program or data in a disk. Because these requests are generated at random and faster than the moving-head disk subsystem can process them, the requests will wait in a line, called *queue*. A disk scheduling program (or *disk scheduler*) manages this queue. Each request is identified by the address of data on the disk. Because of diversity in hardware configuration of a disk, the typical address of data on a pack of disks (called *disk drive*) is shown in Figure 6.22 where *Surface #* refers to the magnetic disk surface; *Track #* indicates the number of the track (tracks are concentric circles on the disk surface), *Sector #* is the disk's partition, and *Size* indicates the amount of requested data. The data on a disk is accessed by a fixed or moving *read-write (R/W) head*. The total time for accessing a data is the sum of track seek time, latency (disk rotational) time, and the data transmission time. The data access time plus the waiting time in the request queue is the total response time. For a fair and efficient service, the disk subsystem strives to minimize the seek time because the times for the rotation and data transfer are highly dependent on mechanical parts of the disk drive. For further information, refer to Deitel [Dei90]. It is the responsibility of the disk scheduler to optimize the data access time. The usual disk scheduling algorithms are:

- First-Come-First-Serve (*FCFS*), which inefficiently moves the R/W

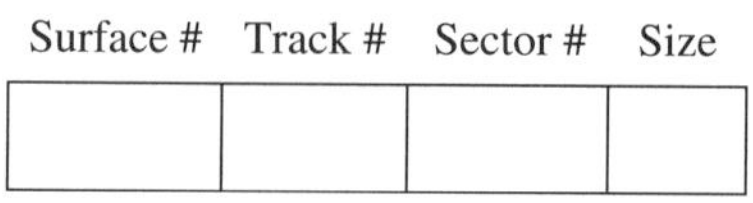

Surface #	Track #	Sector #	Size

FIGURE 6.22. Address of data in a disk drive.

head back and forth.

- Shortest Seek Time First (*SSTF*), which judiciously moves the R/W head to serve disk access requests.

- SCAN, which is an improvement over SSTF algorithm.

The OOP implementation of FCFS disk scheduling is left as an exercise. For a C implementation of the SSTF algorithm, the reader is referred to Sengupta and Edwards [SE91].

The SCAN disk scheduling is used in most applications. It alleviates the drawback of SSTF scheduling, which is the possible *indefinite wait* in the request queue. The SCAN algorithm accomplishes this by seeking the shortest distance from the current read-write (R/W) head position to all requests including those that arrived during the current sweeping direction. The SCAN disk scheduling also optimizes the movement of the R/W head.

Algorithm: SCAN Disk Scheduling

It keeps a priority process queue of disk access requests ordered by the track number. The track number associated with process is used to determine the priority value, the shortest distance between the current track and the requested tracks in the input queue.

   Step 1. For the R/W head in the current sweep, note the current track number and the movement direction (outward or inward).

   Step 2. Find a process in the input request queue with the shortest seek track-distance from the current track position in the current direction of R/W head movement. Consider all requests in the queue pending in the current direction and the requests that arrived in front of the current R/W head position after the start of this current sweep. The process just serviced is removed from the input queue.

   Step 3. Requests that arrived after the start of the current sweep and are behind the current head position are put in the input process queue; these are serviced in the next sweep.

   Step 4. Direction of sweep is changed if the last track (i.e., outermost in case of outward sweep) or the first track (i.e., innermost in case of inward sweep) is encountered, or if there are no more requests pending in the current direction.

   Step 5. Continue steps 1 through 4 until the input process queue is empty.

For an OOP implementation of SCAN disk scheduling simulation, it is necessary for queue objects to hold input and output processes and their requested track numbers. These queues and process information are considered data for the disk scheduler. It needs operations governed by the SCAN policy. In **Code 6.8**, the Disk_Sched class is defined for data hiding and encapsulation.

Disk_Sched(), the constructor, is a publicly accessible member function of the Disk_Sched class. MAX_TRACK_NOS and MAX_PROCESSES are set to given values. It then allocates memory spaces for the input priority process queue, in_process_que[], and the output queues.

~Disk_Sched() is a public member function of the Disk_Sched class. It deallocates the memory spaces for both the input and output queues.

Get_track() is a public member function of the Disk_Sched class. It generates a track number for a process using the standard random number generator, random(). The random number for a track is used to simulate the random arrival of disk access requests.

Init_process_ques() is a private member function of the class Disk_Sched. It initializes two queues. Then, it creates two processes with random track numbers by calling get_track().

Print_process_que() is a public member function of the class Disk_Sched. It prints the two array-based process queues.

Find_scan_track() is a publicly accessible member function of the Disk_Sched class. It expects the current track number and the current direction of sweep (i.e., read-write head movement). It returns the track number closest to the current track in the given direction.

Scan_disk_sched() is a publicly accessible member function of the Disk_Sched class. It simulates SCAN disk scheduling. It implements the above described SCAN disk scheduling algorithm. It continue servicing requests (identified by track number) until the input process queue is empty. It starts out with initial processes, and then creates two more processes. It prints out the input queue during each sweep. This function is the heart of this program.

Main() is the test driver for object-oriented SCAN disk scheduling simulation. Main() is not a member function of the Disk_Sched class. It declares an object scan_dsk_sched_obj of type Disk_Sched. It calls scan_dsk_sched_obj.scan_disk_sched() to pass such message as performing SCAN disk scheduling to the object scan_dsk_sched_obj.

The OOP implementation is shown in **Code 6.8**. The output shows that the arrival order of four processes is 1, 2, 3, 4. Using the SCAN disk algorithm, their disk access requests were processed in the order 1, 3, 4, and 2 as shown below.

Process Number	Track Number
1	15
3	82
4	98
2	18

Code 6.8

```
//  Program:  scan_disk_sched.c++
//  Purpose:
//    Object-Oriented implementation of a Disk
//    Scheduling Simulator that uses SCAN algorithm
//    to process requests for disk read or write.
//
//  COMMENTS:
//    1. INPUT for the program is from a random
//       number generator.
//       The process number is the order in which
//       processes arrive.
//       The track number for each process is obtained
//       from a random number generator.
//    2. Initially process queue is assumed to have a
//       certain number of processes. This is achieved
//       by calling random number generator repeatedly.
//       More processes arrive during the sweep. This is
//       achieved by calling the random number generator
//       after each request is serviced. But this is
//       called only for limited number of times,
//       depending on the value of MAX_PROCESSES.
//    3. OUTPUT is displayed after every service.
//       At the end the order in which the requests
//       are serviced is displayed.
//
//  ASSUMPTIONS:
//    1. It is assumed that the tracks are numbered from
//       1 to N from inner most track to outer most track.
//
#include <stdio.h>
#include <math.h>
#include <stdlib.h>

typedef  int  TRACK_NO;
typedef  int  PROCESS_NO;

//  Define a "Disk_Sched" class for the disk
//  scheduling objects.
//
class  Disk_Sched {
  private:
```

```
      int  MAX_TRACK_NOS;      // max tracks on a disk
      int  MAX_PROCESSES;
      int  no_of_processes;  // counter
      //
      //  Define a request queue stores process
      //  number and track number of each process.
      //
      struct PROCESS_QUE {
          PROCESS_NO   proc_id;
          TRACK_NO      track_number;
      };
      // Declare queues for "Input" & "Output" processes
      // Output process queue is maintained with order.
      //      PROCESS_QUE in_process_que[MAX_PROCESSES];
      PROCESS_QUE  *in_process_que;
      //      PROCESS_QUE out_process_que[MAX_PROCESSES];
      PROCESS_QUE  *out_process_que;
      void          init_process_ques (void);

   public:
     Disk_Sched (int max_track, int max_processes);
     ~Disk_Sched(); // Destructor
     void      print_process_que (PROCESS_QUE *que);
     TRACK_NO get_track(void);
     TRACK_NO find_scan_track(TRACK_NO curr_track,
                              int out_sweep);
     void      scan_disk_sched (void);
};


//  Define member functions for "Disk_Sched" class

Disk_Sched::Disk_Sched (int max_track,
                        int max_processes)
{
    MAX_TRACK_NOS   = max_track;
    MAX_PROCESSES   = max_processes;
    in_process_que  = new PROCESS_QUE[MAX_PROCESSES];
    out_process_que = new PROCESS_QUE[MAX_PROCESSES];
    init_process_ques();
}


Disk_Sched::~Disk_Sched ()   // Destructor
{
    delete [MAX_PROCESSES]in_process_que;
    delete [MAX_PROCESSES]out_process_que;
}


//  init_process_ques():
//    Initialize the input and output queues
//    for processes, and create 2 processes
//    with their track numbers generated by
//    a random number generator.
void Disk_Sched::init_process_ques (void)
{
```

```
    //   Initialize the process queues by
    //   putting '\0' in the places for process
    //   numbers and track numbers.
    for (int i = 0; i < MAX_TRACK_NOS; i++) {
        in_process_que[i].proc_id      = '\0';
        in_process_que[i].track_number = '\0';
        out_process_que[i].proc_id      = '\0';
        out_process_que[i].track_number = '\0';
    }
    // Initial processes 1 & 2 are created;
    // their requests for track numbers are
    // generated by a random number generator.
    for (i = 0; i < 2; i++) {
        in_process_que[i].proc_id = i + 1;
        in_process_que[i].track_number = get_track();
    }
    no_of_processes = i;
}

//   get_track(): Get a process' track
//       Get a process' new track generated by the
//       standard random number generator, random().
//
TRACK_NO   Disk_Sched::get_track (void)
{
   return (random() % MAX_TRACK_NOS);
}

//   print_process_que ():
//       Print the array-based process queue with
//       process number and track number.
//
void Disk_Sched::print_process_que(PROCESS_QUE *queue)
{
    if (queue[0].proc_id == '\0') {
        printf("\nServiced all processes; %s \n",
                "No more processes in queue.");
        return;
    }
    else {
        printf("Process#    Requested Track#\n");
        for (int j = 0; queue[j].proc_id != '\0'; j++)
            printf(" %d           %d\n",
                queue[j].proc_id, queue[j].track_number);
    }
}

//   find_scan_track ():
//       Using SCAN disk scheduling algorithm,
//       find a process in the input process queue
//       with minimum seek time from the current
//       process(track) in the preferred direction.
//   input:  The current track number and the current
//               direction of sweep (i.e., read-write head
```

```
//            movement).
//   output: The track number closest to the current
//            track in the given direction.
//
TRACK_NO   Disk_Sched::find_scan_track (
             TRACK_NO   curr_track, int out_sweep)
{
     int min_dist, dist, // dist between the current
                         //  track and the tracks requested
                         //  by the processes in the queue
         min_track = curr_track, // Track number closest
                                 //  to the current track
         min_track_number = 0;
     PROCESS_QUE   *ord_q;

     //  Get the distance from the current track
     //  and first entry in the input queue.
     //
     min_dist = curr_track - in_process_que[0].track_number;
     if (out_sweep == 1 && min_dist < '\0')
        min_dist = -min_dist;
     if (out_sweep == 1 && min_dist > '\0')
        // Assign some high value
        min_dist = MAX_TRACK_NOS + 1;
     if (out_sweep == 0 && min_dist < 0)
        // Assign large value
        min_dist = MAX_TRACK_NOS + 1;

     //  Test all processes in the input queue and
     //  find the process with minimum seek distance
     //  in the given direction from the current track.
     //
     for (int i = 1; in_process_que[i].proc_id != '\0'; i++) {
        dist = (curr_track - in_process_que[i].track_number);
        if (out_sweep == 1 && dist < 0 )
        {  //  Test if it is only in the outward
           //  direction.
           dist = - dist;
           if (dist < min_dist && min_dist != '\0') {
              min_dist = dist;
              min_track_number = i;
           }
        }
        if (out_sweep == 0 && dist > 0)
        {  //  Test if it is in the inward direction.
           if (dist < min_dist ) {
              min_dist = dist;
              min_track_number = i;
           }
        }
     }
     //  Enter in the output queue if correct
     //  process is found.
     if (min_dist != (MAX_TRACK_NOS + 1)) {
```

```
      if (out_sweep == 1)
         ord_q = out_process_que;
      else
         ord_q =  out_process_que;
      for (i = 0; ord_q[i].proc_id != '\0'; i++)
            ;
      ord_q[i].proc_id =
         in_process_que[min_track_number].proc_id;
      ord_q[i].track_number =
         in_process_que[min_track_number].track_number;
      min_track =
         in_process_que[min_track_number].track_number;
      printf("\nIn current sweep, serviced process is: ");
      printf ("%d\n",
           in_process_que[min_track_number].proc_id);
      //  The serviced process is deleted from
      //  the input queue.
      i = min_track_number;
      int j = i + 1;
      do {
         in_process_que[i].proc_id = in_process_que[j].proc_id;
         in_process_que[i].track_number =
                in_process_que[j].track_number;
         i++;
      } while (in_process_que[j++].proc_id != '\0');
      }
      return (min_track);
}


//  scan_disk_sched():
//      SCAN Disk Scheduling Simulator
//      Process number of the last request is passed
//      to indicate the current R/W head position.
//      SCAN algorithm is used to service all
//      processes in 'in_process_que[]'.
//
void Disk_Sched::scan_disk_sched (void)
{
   TRACK_NO curr_track = in_process_que[0].track_number;
   //  Track number of the last process serviced.
   //  int  prev_track = seed;
   intprev_track = 5;
   //  Track number of the previous process serviced.
   int  out_sweep = 1, i;
   //
   //  Continue servicing requests (identified
   //  by track number) until the input process
   //  queue is empty.
   //
   while (in_process_que[0].proc_id != '\0') {
     printf("\n\nThe current track is:    %d",
            curr_track);
     if (out_sweep == 1)
        printf("\nCurrent Sweep Direction: Outward\n");
```

```
        else
            printf("\nCurrent Sweep Direction: Inward\n");
            printf("Request Queue before SCAN is: \n");
        print_process_que (in_process_que);
        //
        //  Find the track with the minimum seek time
        //  from the current track in the current sweep
        //
        curr_track = find_scan_track (curr_track, out_sweep);
        if (curr_track == prev_track)
        {
            //  If there are no processes in the current
            //  direction, change the direction
            //  of motion of the read-write head.
            if (out_sweep == 1)
                out_sweep = 0;
            else
                out_sweep = 1;
            printf("There are no more requests in %s \n",
                    "the current direction.");
        }
        prev_track = curr_track;
        //  Enter new process, if any, calling random().
        if (no_of_processes < MAX_PROCESSES) {
            for (i = 0; in_process_que[i].proc_id != '\0';
                    i++)
                        ;
            in_process_que[i].proc_id = ++no_of_processes;
            in_process_que[i].track_number = get_track();
        }
        printf("Request Queue after SCAN (%s %s \n",
            "including new",
            "\nrequests arrived during the sweep) is:");
        print_process_que (in_process_que);
    } // end of 'while (in_process_que[0]...)'

    printf("\nDuring outward sweep, order of %s \n",
            "serviced processes:");
    print_process_que (out_process_que);
    printf("\nDuring inward sweep, order of %s \n",
            "serviced processes:");
    print_process_que (out_process_que);
}

//  main():
//    Main test driver for SCAN disk scheduling
//    simulation, an OBJECT-ORIENTED PROGRAM.
//
void main(void)
{
    //  Declare an object "scan_dsk_obj" of
    //  the "Disk_Sched" class;
    //      max_track = 99, max_processes = 4
    //
```

```
    Disk_Sched    scan_dsk_sched_obj (99, 4);

    printf("\n ** OBJECT-ORIENTED SCAN DISK %s",
            "SCHEDULING SIMULATION **");
    scan_dsk_sched_obj.scan_disk_sched ();
}
```

The output of **Code 6.8** is:

```
** OBJECT-ORIENTED SCAN DISK SCHEDULING SIMULATION **

The current track is:    15
Current Sweep Direction: Outward
Request Queue before SCAN is:
Process#     Requested Track#
  1               15
  2               18

In current sweep, serviced process is: 1
Request Queue after SCAN (including new
requests arrived during the sweep) is:
Process#     Requested Track#
  2               18
  3               82


The current track is:    15
Current Sweep Direction: Outward
Request Queue before SCAN is:
Process#     Requested Track#
  2               18
  3               82

In current sweep, serviced process is: 3
Request Queue after SCAN (including new
requests arrived during the sweep) is:
Process#     Requested Track#
  2               18
  4               98


The current track is:    82
Current Sweep Direction: Outward
Request Queue before SCAN is:
Process#     Requested Track#
  2               18
  4               98

In current sweep, serviced process is: 4
Request Queue after SCAN (including new
requests arrived during the sweep) is:
```

```
Process#      Requested Track#
   2              18


The current track is:     98
Current Sweep Direction: Outward
Request Queue before SCAN is:
Process#      Requested Track#
   2              18
There are no more requests in the current direction.
Request Queue after SCAN (including new
requests arrived during the sweep) is:
Process#      Requested Track#
   2              18


The current track is:     98
Current Sweep Direction: Inward
Request Queue before SCAN is:
Process#      Requested Track#
   2              18

In current sweep, serviced process is: 2
Request Queue after SCAN (including new
requests arrived during the sweep) is:

Serviced all processes; No more processes in queue.

During outward sweep, order of serviced processes:
Process#      Requested Track#
   1              15
   3              82
   4              98
   2              18

During inward sweep, order of serviced processes:
Process#      Requested Track#
   1              15
   3              82
   4              98
   2              18
```

6.8   Exercises

1. Write a test driver and a `public` member function of the array-based `Ary_Stack` class in **Code 6.1**, that modifies any field information of the data at the top of a stack object.

2. Write a test driver and a `public` member function of the singly linked `Lnk_Stack` class in **Code 6.2**, that calculates the total number of data elements in the object.

3. Write a test driver and a `public` member function of the singly linked list based `Lnk_Stack` class in **Code 6.2**, that performs reversion of a given string.

4. Write a test driver and a `public` member function of the singly linked list based `Lnk_Stack` class in **Code 6.2**, that raises a real number x to the power of an integer n, that is, x^n.

5. Write a test driver and a `public` member function of the singly linked `Lnk_Stack` class in **Code 6.2**, that tests whether a string is a palindrome (e.g., "MOM" is the same if it is read from left or from right).

6. Write a test driver and a `public` member function of the singly linked `Lnk_Stack` class in **Code 6.2**, that first checks the existence of at least three data elements in a stack object, and pops them. Its use may be found in the evaluation of binary operators in an RPN expression.

7. For double stack objects implemented using an array, write an OOP and test drivers for the following methods:

   (a) `Double_Stack()`
   (b) `~Double_Stack()`
   (c) `chk_dbl_stk_empty (stack_number)`
   (d) `chk_dbl_stk_full (stack_number)`
   (e) `build_dbl_stack(stack_number)`
   (f) `init_dbl_stack (stack_number)`
   (g) `push (new_data, stack_number)`
   (h) `pop (stack_number)`
   (i) `print_dbl_stack(stack_number)`
   (j) `check_stk_boundary()`

8. Translate each of the following infix expressions into RPN, and show the trace of stack contents:

   (a) $4 - (3 + 10) * 5$
   (b) $(AB - CD) * (E + G) - 20$
   (c) $((A * B) - (C * D)) * (E - F) / G$
   (d) $A / (B - C) + B / (C - A)$
   (e) $(A - B) + (C - D) * (E + F)$

9. Translate each of the following RPN expressions into infix:

   (a) 11 3 + 20 −

   (b) A 30 + B 20 − ∗ C 10 − /

   (c) 19 20 4 3 + 5 ∗ 6 − ∗ −

   (d) 5 25 ∗ 2 3 ∗ + 14 7 / −

   (e) A B + A B − ∗ C D + C D − ∗ +

10. Evaluate each of the RPN expressions in Exercise 6-9 and show the trace of stack contents.

11. Translate each of the infix expressions in Exercise 6-8 into prefix expressions.

12. Write and test a `public` member function of the RPN class in **Code 6.4** that checks whether the syntax of an infix expression is correct.

13. Translate each of the infix expressions in Exercise 6-8 into prefix form.

14. Translate each of the following prefix expressions to infix form:

   (a) − + A − B C D ∗ E

   (b) + A B ∗ A B

   (c) − + 2 3 A / − B C

   (d) ∗ − 7 A + B 3 − C D

   (e) / ∗ A B + 4 7

15. Translate each of the postfix expressions in Exercise 6-9 to prefix form.

16. For prefix notation, integer operands, and operators +, −, ∗, /, and %, write an OOP and test drivers for the following operations: (a) Translate from infix expression to prefix expression. (b) Evaluate prefix expressions containing integer operands. (c) Translate from postfix expression to prefix expression.

17. For postfix notation, write an OOP and test drivers for the following operations: (a) Translate from postfix expression to prefix expression. (b) Translate from prefix expression to postfix expression.

18. Implement a queue object using a doubly linked list of the queue data elements. Write an OOP and test drivers for the following actions for a doubly linked queue object: (a) Constructing and initializing a queue object. (b) Destroying (deleting) a queue object. (c) Checking to see if a queue object is empty. (d) Building a queue object from a set of data of an arbitrary type. (e) Adding a data element in a queue object. (f) Removing a data element from a queue object. (g) Displaying (printing) a queue object.

19. Implement a circular queue object using a singly linked list of the queue data elements. Write an OOP and test drivers for the following actions for a circular queue object:

    (a) Constructing and initializing a circular queue object. (b) Destroying (deleting) a circular queue object. (c) Checking to see if a circular queue object is empty. (d) Building a circular queue object from a given set of data of an arbitrary type (Hint: use `template`). (e) Adding a data element in a circular queue object. (f) Removing a data element from a circular queue object. (g) Displaying (printing) a circular queue object (must indicate the front and rear of the queue).

20. Implement a circular queue object using a doubly linked list of the queue data elements. Write an OOP and test drivers for the operations listed in Exercise 6-19.

21. Implement a *double-ended queue* (*dequeue*) object using a doubly linked list of the queue data elements. In a double-ended queue, both the enqueue and dequeue operations are permitted at either the front or the rear of the queue. Write an OOP and "menu-driven" test drivers for the doubly linked dequeue with the operations: (a) Constructing and initializing a dequeue object. (b) Destroying (deleting) a dequeue object. (c) Checking to see if a dequeue object is empty. (d) Building a dequeue object interactively. (e) Enqueuing a data element at the front of a dequeue object. (f) Enqueuing a data element at the rear of a dequeue object. (g) Dequeuing a data element from the front of a dequeue object. (h) Dequeuing a data element from the rear of a dequeue object. (i) Displaying (printing) a dequeue object (must indicate the front and rear of the queue).

22. A simple queue uses FCFS policy, which is based on the order of arrival in the queue. A *priority queue* is a special form of a simple queue, where FCFS is not used. Instead, a special value, called *priority* (or precedence factor), associated with each data element is used to determine the positioning at the front of the queue. In a "highest" priority queue, the data element with the highest priority value is taken out (i.e., serviced). In a "lowest" priority queue, the data element with the lowest priority value is taken out. In either form of a priority queue, there is an implicit ordering of the priority values. To maintain the ordering in a priority queue, use a doubly linked list. However, an efficient data structure would be a *max heap* for a highest priority queue, and a *min heap* for a lowest priority queue (to be discussed in Chapter 8). Write an OOP and a test driver for a doubly linked highest priority queue object with the actions: (a) Constructing and initializing a priority queue object. (b) Destroying (deleting) a priority queue object. (c) Checking to see if a priority queue object is empty. (d) Building a priority queue object from a given set of data.

(e) Adding a data element in a priority queue object. (f) Removing a data element with the highest priority from a priority queue object. (g) Displaying (printing) a priority object (must indicate the front and rear of the queue).

23. Redo the *Maze* problem in Exercise 4-16 using a singly linked stack object.

24. When disk scheduling uses *First-Come-First-Serve* (*FCFS*) policy, it works like a simple queue. It services requests with tracks that arrive at random on an FCFS basis. Write and test a `public` member function of the `Disk_Sched` class in **Code 6.8** that implements the FCFS policy.

7

Sorting and Searching

For a collection of data objects, we have discussed some data organizing techniques that use array, linked list, stack, queue, tree, and graph objects (to be discussed later). Such basic operations as insertion, deletion, and even searching for these objects were discussed and implemented. A wise selection of one or more such objects for an application is influenced by the efficiency of sorting or searching or both operations. In this chapter, we discuss, implement, and compare several sorting algorithms and several searching algorithms in a sorted (ordered) or unsorted (unordered) data structure. For the purpose of sorting and searching, each data object contains an uniform key (often called a *primary key*), which is used to perform these operations. The searching based on multiple (primary and secondary) keys will be discussed in Chapter 9.

Using a sorting method, a set of data elements is arranged in ascending or descending order based on the associated keys. Two major types of sorting techniques will be explored: those based on a *full comparison of key values* and those that exploit the *digital properties of the keys*. Sorting is useful in such applications as customer names, grades of students, etc. It is also useful to enhance the performance of a search process on an ordered list.

A searching method looks for specified data in an ordered or unordered set of data. When the target data are found in that set, the information of the target data is retrieved for further processing.

7.1   Sorting Methods

In this section, techniques for rearranging data objects in a sorted order will be discussed and implemented. Each data object or element is conveniently viewed as a *record* containing an identifying key value (numeric or alphabetic). A sort process on a given data set is guided by these keys and is based on one of two fundamental techniques:

- Key comparative sorts, or

- Radix (digital) sorts.

Sorting methods typically involve the two basic operations of comparing two keys and exchanging or swapping two records. Key comparative sorts follow this model; the sorting criteria (equality with the key) may be based on the numeric or alphabetic (lexicographic) value of the data objects. However, for many applications it is advantageous to exploit the digital properties of the keys. Radix sorts proceed by "comparing" the individual "bits" of a key instead of requiring full key value comparisons.

Sorting methods are categorized into several groups based upon data structures and storage requirements. The primary two categories are (1) *internal sorting methods*, that is, sorting methods that are applied to the list of data elements small enough to fit in the internal main memory; and (2) *external sorting methods*, that is, sorting methods that are applied to larger list of data elements residing in an external storage (e.g., files on a disk). The list of discussed and implemented internal sorting methods include insertion sort, selection sort, quick sort, merge sort, tree sort, heap sort, straight and exchange radix sorts, and shell sort. The merge sort as the external sort method is also discussed and implemented.

The *fundamental steps in a sort method* are:

Step 1. Set exchange = TRUE.

Step 2. Search for a minimum (maximum) data element specified by a given key in a set (collection) of data elements.

Step 3. If the exchange criterion is satisfied, exchange the data element with the other element(s) to bring it in the proper (i.e., sorted) position; and set exchange = TRUE. Otherwise,

exchange = FALSE.

Step 4. Repeat steps 2 and 3 until exchange is FALSE, i.e., there are no more exchanges.

Step 5. Arranging the given set of data elements in an ascending or descending order is now complete.

The *recursive definition of sorting methods* contains:

Step 1. Split or divide the data set into two smaller subsets, say $S1$ and $S2$.

Step 2. Recursively sort the smaller set $S1$ using a sort method.

Step 3. Recursively sort the smaller set $S2$ using a sort method.

Step 4. Merge or join the two sorted subsets $S1'$ and $S2'$ into the sorted data set S'.

Two groups for the most often used sorting methods are:

Simple Sort Methods	Advanced Sort Methods
Insertion Sort	Shell Sort
Linked List Insertion Sort	Quick Sort
Selection Sort	Merge Sort
Bubble Sort	Binary Tree Sort
	Heap Sort
	Straight Radix Sort
	Radix Exchange Sort

Merge sort and quick sort methods are also viewed as basic general types, and other methods fall into one of these two methods.

Figure 7.1 shows the selection sort and the insertion sort as special cases of quick sort and merge sort, respectively, because they split the data set by selecting or inserting one data element.

Using an object-oriented approach, a Sort class is defined below for an array-based list with integer data:

```
typedef  int DATA_TYPE;
class Sort {
  private:
  typedef    DATA_TYPE  ARY_LIST[];
  DATA_TYPE  *A;  // Array list A[]
  int        n;  // size of A
  void debug_print (int iteration, int debug, char *hdr);
  public:
  Sort (int size) {A = new DATA_TYPE[n=size];}
  ~Sort()  { delete []A; }
  void build_list (DATA_TYPE input[]);
  void print_list (void);
  void Insertion_Sort (DATA_TYPE input[]);
  void Selection_Sort (DATA_TYPE input[]);
  void Bubble_Sort (DATA_TYPE input[]);
  void Quick_Sort (DATA_TYPE input[]);
  void Merge_Sort (DATA_TYPE input[]);
  void Heap_Sort (DATA_TYPE A[]);
  void Radix_Exch_Sort (DATA_TYPE input[],
                        int  bitnum);
  void Shell_Sort (DATA_TYPE input[]);
};
```

Using the template keyword (refer to Stroustrup [Str91]), the Sort class is redefined for an array-based list of elements of an arbitrary type:

```
template<class DATA_TYPE> class Sort {
  // all members and methods are same as above.
};
```

Sorting methods are now presented, keeping their progressive performances in mind.

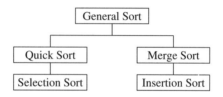

FIGURE 7.1. Overview of sort methods.

7.1.1 INSERTION SORT FOR AN ARRAY LIST

Sorting an array-based list $A[0]$, $A[1]$, ..., $A[n-1]$ of n data elements in ascending order, the data elements are used as keys for comparison. There are two versions of insertion sort method:

1. Start insertion process from the end of the array list, $A[n-1]$, and continue until the first element $A[0]$ is inserted.

2. Start insertion process from the first of the array list, $A[0]$, and continue until the last element $A[n-1]$ is inserted.

The next section shows implementation of the second version of the insertion sort method for a doubly linked list. This section describes and implements the first version of the insertion sort. The insertion sort method first orders $A[n-1]$ and $A[n-2]$ by inserting $A[n-1]$ before $A[n-2]$ if $A[n-2] > A[n-1]$. Using this ordered sublist, say $A[n-2]$ and $A[n-1]$, the method iteratively inserts the remaining data elements in the ordered sublist. After the kth iteration, $A[k]$ is inserted in its sorted position in the sorted sublist $A[k+1]$, $A[k+2]$, ..., $A[n-1]$; this yields the sublist $A[k]$, $A[k+1]$, ..., $A[n-1]$ sorted in ascending order.

The algorithm for the insertion sort method, which begins the insertion process from $A[n-2]$, is:

Step 1. If $n \leq 0$, return. Otherwise, go to Step 2.

Step 2. Set $begin = n - 2$.

Step 3. For $k = n - 2, n - 3, ..., 0$ do Step 3.1.

Step 3.1. Insert $A[k]$ in its sorted position in sorted sublist $A[k+1], A[k+2], ..., A[n-1]$ by interchanging $A[k]$ and $A[i]$ if $A[k] > A[i]$, $A[i]$ being in this sublist.

Note that the list A is now arranged in ascending order.

The steps of the insertion sort is illustrated using the following list of data elements:

$$A = \{33, 60, 5, 15, 25, 12, 45, 70, 35, 7\}$$

Here $n = 10$, $A[n-1] = 7$. Now, inserting $A[n-2] = 35$ into the sublist $A[n-1] = 7$ yields the ascending ordered sublist $A_1 = \{7, 35\}$ (see pass one in output). Then, inserting 70 in A_1 yields the ascending ordered sublist $A_2 = \{7, 35, 70\}$; the previous sorted sublist A_1 is not changed. In the third iteration, inserting 45 in A_2 yields ascending ordered sublist $A_3 = \{7, 35, 45, 70\}$. Continuing similarly until all elements are considered, the final form of the ascending ordered list is:

$$A = \{5, 7, 12, 15, 25, 33, 35, 45, 60, 70\}$$

For an OOP implementation of insertion sort, see **Code 7.1**.

Code 7.1

```
//   Program:  Insertion_Sort.c++
//   Purpose:
//      Use "insertion sort" method for sorting an
//      array list A of n elements A[0], ..., A[n-1]
//      in an ascending order.
//
#include  <stdio.h>
typedef   int         DATA_TYPE;
typedef   DATA_TYPE   ARY_LIST[];
class Sort {
  private:
    DATA_TYPE  *A;  // Array list A[]
    int        n;   // size of A
  public:
    Sort (int size) { A = new DATA_TYPE[n=size]; }
    ~Sort()   { delete []A; }
    void build_list (DATA_TYPE input[]);
    void debug_print (int iteration, int debug,
                      char *hdr);
    void Insertion_Sort (DATA_TYPE input[]);
};

void Sort::build_list(ARY_LIST input)
{
    for (int i = 0; i < n; i++)
        A[i] = input[i];
}

//   debug_print ():
//      Print the array list A[n] for each iteration
//
void Sort::debug_print(int iteration, int debug, char *hdr)
{
    if (debug == 0)
        printf("\n %s \n", hdr);
    else
```

```
      printf(" Pass #%d:", iteration + 1);
   for (int i = 0; i < n; i++)
      printf(" %d", A[i]);
   printf("\n");
}


//   Insertion_Sort():
//     Insertion sort for an array list of
//     "n" elements.
//
void Sort::Insertion_Sort(ARY_LIST input)
{
   build_list(input);   // Build array A
   debug_print (0, 0,
     "List to be sorted in ascending order:");
   //  Start inserting data element A[n-2]
   //  before or after A[n-1].
   //
   int begin = n - 2;
   for (int k = begin; k >= 0; k--) {
      int i = k + 1;
      DATA_TYPE swap_area =  A[k];

      //  Insert A[k] in its sorted position
      //  among  A[k+1], A[k+2], ..., A[n-1]
      //
      while (swap_area > A[i]) {
         A[i - 1] = A[i];
         i++;
      }
      A[i - 1] = swap_area;
      debug_print (n - 2 - k, 1, "");
   }
}


// main(): Test driver for insertion
//         sort of an array list
//
void main(void)
{
   // Declare an object of "Sort" class
   Sort insert_srt_obj (10);
   static ARY_LIST  A = {33, 60,  5, 15, 25,
                         12, 45, 70, 35, 7 };
   printf("\n **  OOP IMPLEMENTATION OF %s",
          "INSERTION SORT  **");
   insert_srt_obj.Insertion_Sort (A);
   insert_srt_obj.debug_print (0, 0,
      "List sorted using insertion sort:");
}
```

Code 7.1 produces this output:

```
**   OOP IMPLEMENTATION OF INSERTION SORT   **
List to be sorted in ascending order:
33 60 5 15 25 12 45 70 35 7
Pass #1: 33 60 5 15 25 12 45 70 7 35
Pass #2: 33 60 5 15 25 12 45 7 35 70
Pass #3: 33 60 5 15 25 12 7 35 45 70
Pass #4: 33 60 5 15 25 7 12 35 45 70
Pass #5: 33 60 5 15 7 12 25 35 45 70
Pass #6: 33 60 5 7 12 15 25 35 45 70
Pass #7: 33 60 5 7 12 15 25 35 45 70
Pass #8: 33 5 7 12 15 25 35 45 60 70
Pass #9: 5 7 12 15 25 33 35 45 60 70

List sorted using insertion sort:
5 7 12 15 25 33 35 45 60 70
```

Performance Analysis of Insertion Sort

Insertion_Sort() is a public member function of the Sort class in
Code 7.1. It implements the insertion sort method for arranging an array-
based list A of n data elements in ascending order. The function has one
outer loop for with loop index k. The inner loop specified by the while
statement depends on k and the comparative value of $A[k]$ and $A[i]$, where
$i = k + 1$ at the start. In the best case where the data elements are in
the preferred order, the while loop is not executed. In the worst case, the
while loop performs $(k+1)$ number of comparisons, where the outer loop
index k ranges from 0 to $(n-2)$. Hence, the worst-case performance of the
insertion sort is:

$$[(n-2)+1] + [(n-3)+1] + ... + [0+1]$$
$$= (n-1) + (n-2) + ... + 2 + 1$$
$$= n(n-1)/2 = O(n^2)$$

The insertion sort is simple and efficient for a small n. Its main drawback
is that it places only one data element in the sorted position at a time.

7.1.2   INSERTION SORT FOR A LINKED LIST

As for an array-based list, the insertion sort method can also be applied to
the singly or doubly linked list data structures of elements. The insertion
sort for a linked list is more efficient than that for an array-based list

because insertion of data elements is efficiently done using pointers (links) and without any physical movement of the data elements.

Since the insertion sort is primarily based on finding the smallest or largest element in the linked list and then on inserting that element in its sorted position in the linked list, the insertion operation of a linked list object will be frequently used. Because of the nonavailability of the "link to previous element," the insertion operation is very inefficient and complex in a singly linked list compared to its counterpart in a doubly linked list.

Given a set of data elements as a doubly linked list in Figure 5.10, we use an approach similar to the one used for an array-based list; begin the search and insertion process starting from the first element pointed to by head_ptr in its sorted position. In the case of an array-based list, we performed the insertion by physically shifting the data elements up or down the array. This is not required for the insertion sort on a singly or doubly linked list. As shown in Figure 5.9 for a doubly linked list, both head_ptr and tail_ptr have NULL values when the list is empty. The two pointers next and prev are modified for insertion.

Code 7.2 shows an OOP implementation of the insertion sort for a doubly linked list. In **Code 7.2**, Insert_Sort_dlist() is a public member function of the Doubly_Linked_List class. It implements the insertion sort method for arranging data elements of a doubly linked list object in ascending order.

Code 7.2

```
//  Program:   Insert_Sort_Lnk_List.c++
//  Purpose:
//     OOP implementation of insertion sort for
//     a doubly linked list.
//
#include    <stdio.h>
#include    <stdlib.h>
const int FOREVER = 1;
typedef int    DATA_TYPE;

class    Doubly_Linked_List {
  private:
    typedef struct DLIST_ELEMENT {
        DATA_TYPE          data;
        DLIST_ELEMENT      *next;
        DLIST_ELEMENT      *prev;
    } *DLLIST_PTR;
    DLLIST_PTR    head_ptr, tail_ptr, curr_ptr;
    void   init_dlist (void);

  public:
    Doubly_Linked_List () { init_dlist(); }
    ~Doubly_Linked_List () { };
```

```
    void  build_dlist (void);
    void  Insert_Sort_dlist (void);
    void  print_dlist (void);
};

void Doubly_Linked_List::init_dlist(void)
{
   head_ptr = tail_ptr = curr_ptr = NULL;
}

//  build_dlist():
//    Build a doubly linked list with input from
//    operator.
//
void   Doubly_Linked_List::build_dlist(void)
{
   DLLIST_PTR     prev_ptr = NULL,
                  new_ptr;
   char           buffer[81];

   printf ("\n ** OOP FOR INSERTION SORT OF %s \n\n",
           "A DOUBLY LINKED LIST **");
   while (FOREVER) {
     printf ("\nCreate List - %s"
             "<Return> with no Value to Quit");
     printf ("\nEnter an Integer:  ");
     gets (buffer);
     if (buffer[0] == '\0') {
       tail_ptr = curr_ptr;  // initialize tail pointer
       return;
     }
     new_ptr = new DLIST_ELEMENT;
     new_ptr->data = atoi (buffer);
     new_ptr->next = NULL;
     new_ptr->prev = NULL;
     curr_ptr = new_ptr;

     if (head_ptr == NULL)    // initialize head pointer
       head_ptr = curr_ptr;
     else {
       curr_ptr->prev = prev_ptr;   // link element
       prev_ptr->next = curr_ptr;
     }
     prev_ptr = curr_ptr;
   }
}

//  Insert_Sort_dlist():
//    Sort a doubly linked list using an insertion
//    algorithm.
//
void  Doubly_Linked_List::Insert_Sort_dlist(void)
{
```

```
      DLLIST_PTR   curr_ptr = head_ptr, search_ptr;

    while ((curr_ptr = curr_ptr->next) != NULL) {
      //  find location to insert current value after
      search_ptr = curr_ptr->prev;
      while (search_ptr != NULL &&
             curr_ptr->data < search_ptr->data)
        search_ptr = search_ptr->prev;

      //  remove current value and insert
      //  to new location if required

      if ((curr_ptr->prev != search_ptr) &&
          (search_ptr != NULL
           curr_ptr->data < head_ptr->data)) {
        //  remove current value
        curr_ptr->prev->next = curr_ptr->next;
        if (curr_ptr == tail_ptr)
          tail_ptr = curr_ptr->prev;
        else
          curr_ptr->next->prev = curr_ptr->prev;

        if (search_ptr != NULL) {
          //  insert value at new location
          curr_ptr->prev = search_ptr;
          curr_ptr->next = search_ptr->next;
          search_ptr->next->prev = curr_ptr;
          search_ptr->next = curr_ptr;
        }
        else { //  curr_ptr->data < head_ptr->data
          //  insert value at head of list
          curr_ptr->prev = NULL;
          curr_ptr->next = head_ptr;
          head_ptr->prev = curr_ptr;
          head_ptr = curr_ptr;
        }
      }
    }
}

// print_dlist():
//    Print a doubly linked list in the forward
//    direction.
//
void  Doubly_Linked_List::print_dlist (void)
{
  DLLIST_PTR  tmp_ptr = head_ptr;
  printf ("NULL <-> ");
  while (tmp_ptr != NULL) {
    printf ("%d <-> ", tmp_ptr->data);
    tmp_ptr = tmp_ptr->next;
  }
  printf ("NULL \n");
}
```

```
//  main():
//    Test driver for OOP implementation of
//    a doubly linked list with sorting.
//
void  main(void)
{
  Doubly_Linked_List  dlist_obj;

  dlist_obj.build_dlist ();
  printf ("\nDoubly Linked List Before %s \n",
          "Insertion Sort is:");
  dlist_obj.print_dlist ();
  printf ("\nDoubly Linked List After %s \n",
          "Insertion Sort is:");
  dlist_obj.Insert_Sort_dlist ();
  dlist_obj.print_dlist ();
}
```

Code 7.2 produces this output:

```
  ** OOP FOR INSERTION SORT OF A DOUBLY LINKED LIST **


Create List - <Return> with no Value to Quit
Enter an Integer:  33

Create List - <Return> with no Value to Quit
Enter an Integer:  60

Create List - <Return> with no Value to Quit
Enter an Integer:  5

Create List - <Return> with no Value to Quit
Enter an Integer:  15

Create List - <Return> with no Value to Quit
Enter an Integer:  25

Create List - <Return> with no Value to Quit
Enter an Integer:  12

Create List - <Return> with no Value to Quit
Enter an Integer:  45

Create List - <Return> with no Value to Quit
Enter an Integer:  70

Create List - <Return> with no Value to Quit
Enter an Integer:  35

Create List - <Return> with no Value to Quit
```

```
Enter an Integer:   7

Create List - <Return> with no Value to Quit
Enter an Integer:

Doubly Linked List Before Insertion Sort is:
NULL <-> 33 <-> 60 <-> 5 <-> 15 <-> 25 <-> 12 <->
         45 <-> 70 <-> 35 <-> 7 <-> NULL

Doubly Linked List After Insertion Sort is:
NULL <-> 5 <-> 7 <-> 12 <-> 15 <-> 25 <-> 33 <->
         35 <-> 45 <-> 60 <-> 70 <-> NULL
```

For convenience of display, the above two lines in the output are broken.

7.1.3 SELECTION SORT

For sorting an array-based list $A[0], A[1], ..., A[n-1]$ of n data elements in ascending order, the data elements are used as keys for comparison. The algorithm for the selection sort method is:

Step 1. If $n \leq 0$, return. Otherwise, go to Step 2.

Step 2. (*Outer loop*) For $j = 0, ..., n-1$, do steps 2.1 through 2.2.

    Step 2.1. (*Inner loop*) Find the lowest element, say $A[lower]$, among the elements $A[j+1], ..., A[n-1]$.

    Step 2.2. Place $A[lower]$ in its sorted position $A[j]$ by performing swap between them.

Note that the list A is now arranged in ascending order.

The steps of the selection sort are illustrated using the following list of data elements:

$$A = \{33, 60, 5, 15, 25, 12, 45, 70, 35, 7\}$$

For the first iteration ($j = 0$) in the outer loop of Step 2, $A[3] = 5$ is found as the lowest number, and is placed in its sorted position (denoted by the underline) by swapping it with the first element $A[0]$; list A is:

$$A = \{\underline{5}, 60, 33, 15, 25, 12, 45, 70, 35, 7\}$$

After the second iteration (j = 1), the lowest element $A[9] = 7$ among $A[1], ..., A[8]$ is swapped with $A[1]$; list A is:

$$A = \{5, \underline{7}, 33, 15, 25, 12, 45, 70, 35, 60\}$$

Similarly continuing the above process for iterations from third through ninth, the ascending ordered list A after the ninth iteration is:

$$A = \{5, 7, 12, 15, 25, 33, 35, 45, 60, 70\}$$

The deficiencies of the selection method are:

1. In each pass (iteration), only one element is placed in its proper sorted position.

2. For a list of n data elements, it does $(n - 1)$ iterations.

3. Partial or full sorted state of the list is not checked by the selection sort method.

See **Code 7.3** for an OOP implementation of the selection sort. In main(), select_srt_obj of the Sort class is declared and initialized with size 10 for the array-based list. Selection_Sort() is a public member function of the Sort class. It implements the selection sort method for arranging an array-based list in ascending order.

Code 7.3

```
//   Program:  Selection_Sort.c++
//   Purpose:
//     Use "selection sort" method for sorting an
//     array list A of n elements A[0], ..., A[n-1]
//     in ascending order.
//
#include <stdio.h>
typedef    int   DATA_TYPE;
typedef DATA_TYPE   ARY_LIST[];

class Sort {
  private:
    DATA_TYPE   *A;   // Array list A[]
    int         n;    // size of A
  public:
    Sort (int size) { A = new DATA_TYPE[n=size]; }
    ~Sort()    { delete []A; }

    void build_list (DATA_TYPE input[]);
    void debug_print (int iteration, int debug,
                      char *hdr);
    void Selection_Sort (DATA_TYPE input[]);
};

void Sort::build_list(ARY_LIST input)
{
    for (int i = 0; i < n; i++)
        A[i] = input[i];
}

//   debug_print ():
//     Print the array list A[n] for each iteration
//
```

```
void Sort::debug_print(int iteration, int debug,
      char *hdr)
{
   if (debug == 0)
      printf("\n %s \n", hdr);
   else
      printf(" Pass #%d:", iteration + 1);
   for (int i = 0; i < n; i++)
      printf(" %d", A[i]);
   printf("\n");
}


// Selection_Sort():
//    Selection sort for a "list" of "n" elements
//
void Sort::Selection_Sort(ARY_LIST input)
{
   build_list(input);  // Build array A
   debug_print (0, 0,
      "List to be sorted in ascending order:");
   if (n > 0) {
      for (int j = 0; j < n - 1; j++) {
         int lower = j;
         for (int k = j + 1; k < n; k++)
            if (A[k] < A[lower])
               lower = k;
         // Swap A[lower] & A[j]
         DATA_TYPE swap_area  = A[j];
         A[j] = A[lower];
         A[lower] = swap_area;
         debug_print (j, 1, "");
      }
   }
}

// main(): Test driver for selection
//         sort of an array list
//
void main(void)
{
   // Declare an object of "Sort" class
   Sort select_srt_obj (10);
   static ARY_LIST  A = {33, 60,  5, 15, 25,
                         12, 45, 70, 35, 7 };
   printf("\n **  OOP IMPLEMENTATION OF %s",
          "SELECTION SORT  **");
   select_srt_obj.Selection_Sort (A);
   select_srt_obj.debug_print (0, 0,
      "List sorted using selection sort:");
}
```

Code 7.3 produces this output:

```
**   OOP IMPLEMENTATION OF SELECTION SORT   **
List to be sorted in ascending order:
33 60 5 15 25 12 45 70 35 7
Pass #1: 5 60 33 15 25 12 45 70 35 7
Pass #2: 5 7 33 15 25 12 45 70 35 60
Pass #3: 5 7 12 15 25 33 45 70 35 60
Pass #4: 5 7 12 15 25 33 45 70 35 60
Pass #5: 5 7 12 15 25 33 45 70 35 60
Pass #6: 5 7 12 15 25 33 45 70 35 60
Pass #7: 5 7 12 15 25 33 35 70 45 60
Pass #8: 5 7 12 15 25 33 35 45 70 60
Pass #9: 5 7 12 15 25 33 35 45 60 70

List sorted using selection sort:
5 7 12 15 25 33 35 45 60 70
```

Performance Analysis of Selection Sort

In the outer loop with index (iteration) j, there are at most (n - j) number of comparisons, performed in the inner loop for(k = ...); the inner loop index k depends on j. Since the outer loop index j executes (n - 1) number of times, the selection sort performs the total number of comparisons:

$$(n-1) + (n-2) + ... + [n - (n-1)] = n(n-1) - [1 + 2 + ... + (n-1)] = n(n-1)/2 = n^2/2 - n/2 = O(n^2)$$

7.1.4   BUBBLE SORT

For sorting an array-based list $A[0], A[1], ..., A[n-1]$ of n data elements in ascending order, the data elements are used as keys for comparison. The algorithm for the bubble sort method is:

Step 1. Set swap_flag = TRUE.

Step 2. (*Outer loop*) For iteration = 0, ..., (n-1), and
      swap_flag == TRUE, do steps 2.1 and 2.2.

Step 2.1. Set swap_flag = FALSE.

Step 2.2. (*Inner loop*) For i = 0, ..., (n - iteration), do
      steps 2.2.1 and 2.2.2.

Step 2.2.1. Compare consecutive data elements `A[i]` and `A[i + 1]`; if they are out of the desired order (i.e., ascending order), physically swap them, and do Step 2.2.2.

Step 2.2.2. Set `swap_flag` = TRUE.

Note that no more swapping is performed. The list A is now arranged in ascending order.

One step of the bubble sort is illustrated using the following list of data elements:

$$A = \{33, 60, 5, 15, 25, 12, 45, 70, 35, 7\}$$

In the first pass, `iteration` = 0, and `swap_flag` = FALSE; the inner loop is executed as follows:

Condition	Effect of bubble sort during first pass
$33 \not> 60$	*ascending order exists; no swapping is done.*
$60 > 5$	*swap $A[1]$ and $A[2]$; swap_flag = TRUE.*
$60 > 15$	*swap $A[2]$ and $A[3]$; swap_flag = TRUE.*
$60 > 25$	*swap $A[3]$ and $A[4]$; swap_flag = TRUE.*
$60 > 12$	*swap $A[4]$ and $A[5]$; swap_flag = TRUE.*
$60 > 45$	*swap $A[5]$ and $A[6]$; swap_flag = TRUE.*
$60 \not> 70$	*ascending order exists; no swapping is done.*
$70 > 35$	*swap $A[7]$ and $A[8]$; swap_flag = TRUE.*
$70 > 7$	*swap $A[8]$ and $A[9]$; swap_flag = TRUE.*

This is the end of the first pass; the resultant array is:

$$A = \{33, 5, 15, 25, 12, 45, 60, 35, 7, 70\}$$

Note that after each pass (iteration) of the bubble sort, only one element "bubbles up" to its proper sorted position. The bubble sort method highly depends on comparing and swapping of consecutive data elements. Its performance can be greatly improved by comparing and swapping data elements that are wide apart.

Code 7.4

```
//   Program:   Bubble_Sort.c++
//   Purpose:
//      Use "Bubble sort" method for sorting an
//      array list A of n elements A[0], ..., A[n-1]
//      in ascending order.
//
#include   <stdio.h>
```

```
const int TRUE  = 1;
const int FALSE = 0;
typedef int  DATA_TYPE;
typedef DATA_TYPE  ARY_LIST[];

class Sort {
  private:
    DATA_TYPE  *A;     // Array list A[]
    int        n;      // size of A
  public:
    Sort (int size) { A = new DATA_TYPE[n=size]; }
    ~Sort()  { delete []A; }
    void build_list (DATA_TYPE input[]);
    void debug_print (int iteration, int debug, char *hdr);
    void Bubble_Sort (DATA_TYPE input[]);
};

void Sort::build_list(ARY_LIST input)
{
   for (int i = 0; i < n; i++)
       A[i] = input[i];
}

//   debug_print ():
//     Print the array list A[n] for each iteration
//
void Sort::debug_print(int iteration, int debug, char *hdr)
{
   if (debug == 0)
      printf("\n %s \n", hdr);
   else
      printf(" Pass #%d:", iteration + 1);
   for (int i = 0; i < n; i++)
      printf(" %d", A[i]);
   printf("\n");
}

//   Bubble_Sort ():
//     Bubble sort for an array list of "n" elements
//
void Sort::Bubble_Sort (ARY_LIST input)
{
    int swap_flag = TRUE;

    build_list(input);  // Build array A
    debug_print (0, 0,
        "List to be sorted in ascending order:");
    for (int iteration = 0; iteration < n &&
            swap_flag == TRUE; iteration++) {
      swap_flag = FALSE;

      for (int i = 0; i < n - iteration; i++)
         if (A[i] > A[i + 1]) {
             // Swap them
```

```
                    swap_flag = TRUE;
                    DATA_TYPE swap_area = A[i];
                    A[i] = A[i + 1];
                    A[i + 1] = swap_area;
               }
          debug_print (iteration, 1, "");
     }
}


// main(): Test driver for bubble
//         sort of an array list
//
void main(void)
{
     // Declare an object of "Sort" class
     Sort bubble_srt_obj (10);
     static ARY_LIST  A = {33, 60,  5, 15, 25,
                             12, 45, 70, 35, 7 };
     printf("\n **   OOP IMPLEMENTATION OF %s",
              "BUBBLE SORT  **");
     bubble_srt_obj.Bubble_Sort (A);
     bubble_srt_obj.debug_print (0, 0,
        "List sorted using bubble sort:");
}
```

Code 7.4 produces this output:

```
**   OOP IMPLEMENTATION OF BUBBLE SORT   **
List to be sorted in ascending order:
33 60 5 15 25 12 45 70 35 7
Pass #1: 33 5 15 25 12 45 60 35 7 70
Pass #2: 5 15 25 12 33 45 35 7 60 70
Pass #3: 5 15 12 25 33 35 7 45 60 70
Pass #4: 5 12 15 25 33 7 35 45 60 70
Pass #5: 5 12 15 25 7 33 35 45 60 70
Pass #6: 5 12 15 7 25 33 35 45 60 70
Pass #7: 5 12 7 15 25 33 35 45 60 70
Pass #8: 5 7 12 15 25 33 35 45 60 70
Pass #9: 5 7 12 15 25 33 35 45 60 70

List sorted using bubble sort:
5 7 12 15 25 33 35 45 60 70
```

Performance Analysis of Bubble Sort

Code 7.4 shows an OOP implementation of the bubble sort method for an array-based list. Bubble_Sort() is a public member function of the Sort class. It arranges n number of data elements of an array-based list

Outer loop index (iteration)	Inner loop index (i)	Number of comparisons
0	0 to $(n-1)$	$(n-1)$
1	0 to $(n-2)$	$(n-2)$
3	0 to $(n-3)$	$(n-3)$
...		
$(n-1)$	0	1

TABLE 7.1. Performance computation of bubble sort.

object bubble_srt_obj in ascending order. The output of **Code 7.4** shows that this bubble sort method took the same number of iterations (passes) as the insertion sort method did for the same set of elements.

Bubble_Sort() has one outer loop and one inner loop. The for statement implements the outer loop; the loop index (counter) iteration ranges from 0 to $(n-1)$, and the outer loop is executed until iteration reaches the maximum value $(n-1)$ and swap_flag is TRUE, or until there are no more swapping of data elements, i.e., swap_flag is FALSE. The inner loop is implemented by the for statement with the loop index i; i ranges from 0 to (n - iteration - 1), and depends on the outer loop index iteration. For each outer iteration, the inner loop makes (n - iteration) number of comparisons of data elements. In the worst case, outer loop is executed $(n-1)$ times, and the inner loop with i is executed as shown in Table 7.1.

Hence, the worst-case performance of the bubble sort, based on the number of comparisons not considering number of swaps, is:

Sum of (n - iteration) for iteration = 0, ..., (n-1)
$$= (n-1) + (n-2) + (n-3) + ... + 1 = n(n-1)/2 = O(n^2)$$

The deficiencies of the bubble sort method are:

1. In each iteration, only one element is positioned ("bubbled up") to its proper sorted position.

2. There are at most (n - iteration - 1) number of swaps (i.e., physical movement) in each execution of the inner loop; this requirement for the physical movement of data elements makes the bubble sort method inefficient particularly for complex and structured data elements.

3. It highly depends on comparing and swapping only consecutive data elements.

7.1.5   QUICKSORT

The quicksort, also called *partition exchange sort*, was invented by C.A.R. Hoare [Hoa62]. It is designed to improve and resolve the deficiencies of the selection sort described in Section 7.1.3. The quicksort with a split of one data element is called the selection sort. The quicksort is the most efficient of the internal sorting methods. Quicksort is used to sort an array-based list A of n data elements in ascending or descending order of the keys in data elements.

The quicksort is based on three main strategies: (1) *split* (divide) the array into small subarrays, (2) *sort the subarrays*, and (3) *merge (join/concatenate)* the sorted subarrays. The split divides the large array (problem) into smaller subarrays (subproblems of the original type). When these subarrays (subproblems) are ultimately sorted by recursively using the quicksort, these subarrays are called "conquered." This is why quicksort is also called the *divide-and-conquer* method. In quicksort, the split is complex and the merge is easy. The quicksort does not require any extra arrays for merging, except a single memory space for exchange. It uses the same array while dividing and merging the array.

In view of its implementation, there are two versions of quicksort: (1) the *recursive version*, and (2) the *iterative version*. Again, there are several varieties of both the recursive and iterative methods, based on how the split is performed. But in all versions of the split, the primary goal (criterion) of the *split method* is to select a data element's key and place it in its proper position, called *pivot*, say $A[k]$, such that it divides the array into two subarrays, called left and right subarrays, where each element in the left subarray is less than or equal to A[k], and each element in the right subarray is greater than $A[k]$.

This assumes the ascending order is the target. The versions and efficiencies of the split depend on the selection of the data element to be positioned as pivot.

Recursive Quicksort Algorithm

Given an array A of n data elements to be sorted in ascending order, the steps of quicksort algorithm are:

Step 1. (Split) Select a data element, position it as pivot, say $A[k]$, which divides the (sub)array into left and right (sub)subarrays satisfying the above-stated criterion. Rearrange data elements.

Step 2. Apply quicksort for the left (sub)subarray (that excludes $A[k]$).

Step 3. Apply quicksort for the right (sub)subarray (that excludes $A[k]$).

Note that the position of $A[k]$ remains unaffected in steps 2 and 3. Since the split of quicksort is complex and a primary part of quicksort, the efficiency of quicksort highly depends on an efficient split method. The steps for an efficient split method for quicksort are:

Step 1. Select the first data element's key, say Pivot, to be properly positioned as pivot. Pivot = A[First]

Step 2. Initialize two search pointers, i and j.

i = First (the first/lower index of (sub)array);

j = Last (the last/upper index of (sub)array)

Step 3. Search for a data element greater than or equal to the selected key Pivot from the left using the search pointer i. This is done by the following:

While A[i] ≤ Pivot and i < Last, continue increasing i by one. Otherwise, stop increasing i.

Step 4. Search for a data element less than or equal to the selected key Pivot from the right using the search pointer j. This is done by the following:

While A[j] ≤ Pivot and j < First, continue decreasing j by one. Otherwise, stop decreasing j.

Step 5. If i < j, interchange A[i] and A[j].

Step 6. Repeat steps 2 through 4 until i>j (i.e., the failure of Step 5).

Step 7. Interchange the selected data element Pivot and A[j].

At the end of Step 7, Pivot (i.e, A[First]) is in its sorted position. This version is implemented in **Code 7.4**.

Another version of the split method selects the middle data element of the (sub)array to be properly positioned. It is left as an exercise.

The recursive version of quicksort requires stack space. This will cause performance degradation. An alternative approach is to use the iterative version of quicksort. This avoids using system stack space and recursion by using its own stack. This stack is used for bookkeeping First and Last indexes of all (sub)arrays that must be sorted. Use a stack object described in Chapter 6. Quicksort's iterative version is left as an exercise.

Note that the quicksort splits the array into two subarrays, called *left and right subarrays* at a Pivot element, say $A[k]$, such that all the elements in the left subarray are less than $A[k]$ as well as the elements in the right subarray. $A[k]$ is in the sorted position. Also, all the elements in the right subarray are greater than $A[k]$.

The basic principles of the quicksort and the merge sort are the same, but they differ by the methods that are used to perform the split and the merge procedures.

For the convenience of illustration of the quicksort, consider an array A
of ten data elements with integer keys

$$A = \{33, 60, 5, 15, 25, 12, 45, 70, 35, 7\}$$

A[0]	A[1]	A[2]	A[3]	A[4]	A[5]	A[6]	A[7]	A[8]	A[9]
33	60	5	15	25	12	45	70	35	7
i									j
33	60	5	15	25	12	45	70	35	7
	i								j
33	7	5	15	25	12	45	70	35	60
	i								j
33	7	5	15	25	12	45	70	35	60
		i							j
33	7	5	15	25	12	45	70	35	60
			i						j
33	7	5	15	25	12	45	70	35	60
				i					j
33	7	5	15	25	12	45	70	35	60
					i				j
33	7	5	15	25	12	45	70	35	60
						i			j
33	7	5	15	25	12	45	70	35	60
						i		j	
33	7	5	15	25	12	45	70	35	60
						i	j		
33	7	5	15	25	12	45	70	35	60
						i j			
33	7	5	15	25	12	45	70	35	60
					j	i			
12	7	5	15	25	33	45	70	35	7
					j	i			

FIGURE 7.2. Trace of first pass of quicksort.

Figure 7.2 shows a trace of the first pass of quicksort, and selects the key,
$A[0] = 33$, as the Pivot for placing it in its sorted position. In Figure 7.2,
shading indicates data elements are being considered and may be swapped
at that state of A[] during the first pass.

For the Pivot=33, each state of A[] in Figure 7.2, is affected by the
values of the forward search pointer i and the backward search pointer j,
and the condition that may cause swapping. Such conditions and effects

corresponding to each state of A[] during the first pass of quicksort are noted below.

VALUES	CONDITION	QUICKSORT'S EFFECT
Pivot= 33		
First= i=0	i < Last,	Increase i by 1, j is kept
Last = j=9	A[i]=33=Pivot	fixed, swap is not needed.
i = 1	A[i]=60 >Pivot,	Stop increasing i,
j = 9	A[j]=7 <Pivot,	stop decreasing j,
	i < j	swap A[1] and A[9].
i = 1	i < Last,	Increase i by 1, j is kept
j = 9	A[1]=7 < Pivot	fixed, swapping is not needed.
i = 2	i < Last,	Increase i by 1, j is kept
j = 9	A[2]=5 < Pivot	fixed, swapping is not needed.
i = 3	i < Last,	Increase i by 1, j is kept
j = 9	A[3]=15 < Pivot	fixed, swapping is not needed.
i = 4	i < Last,	Increase i by 1, j is kept
j = 9	A[4]=25 < Pivot	fixed, swapping is not needed.
i = 5	i < Last,	Increase i by 1, j is kept
j = 9	A[5]=12 < Pivot	fixed, swapping is not needed.
i = 6	i < Last,	Stop increasing i,
j = 9	A[6]=45 > Pivot,	decrease j by 1,
	A[9]=60 > Pivot,	swapping is not needed.
	j > First	
i = 6	j > First,	Stop increasing i, decrease j
j = 8	A[8]=35 > Pivot,	by 1, swapping is not needed.
i = 6	j > First,	Stop increasing i, decrease j
j = 7	A[7]=70 > Pivot,	by 1, swapping is not needed.
i = 6	j > First,	Stop increasing i, decrease j
j = 6	A[6]=45 > Pivot,	by 1, swapping is not needed.
i = 6	j < First,	Stop increasing i and j; swap
j = 5	j crossed i,	A[First]=Pivot and A[j]=12.
i = 6	Pivot is in its	End of first pass
j = 5	sorted position	of quicksort.

In the last state of A[] of Figure 7.2, $A[5] = 33$ is in its sorted position because every data element to its right is greater than or equal to 33, and every data element to its left is less than or equal to 33. Then the selected data element $A[5] = 33$ is the pivot element that divides the array A

into two left and right subarrays $\{12, 7, 5, 15, 25\}$ and $\{45, 70, 35, 60\}$. This
is the end of the first pass of quicksort. Note that for the left subarray,
First = 0 and Last = 4, and for the right subarray, First = 6 and
Last = 9. Quick_Sort() is now applied to these subarrays in the next
pass. This process continues until all the selected elements are placed in
their proper (sorted) positions.

Code 7.5 is an OOP implementation for the quicksort.

Code 7.5

```c++
//   Program:   Quick_Sort.c++
//   Purpose:
//      Use 'Quick Sort' to arrange A[0], ..., A[n-1]
//      in an ascending order.
//
#include   <stdio.h>
typedef    int   DATA_TYPE;
class Sort {
  private:
    DATA_TYPE   *A;   // Array list A[]
    int         n;    // size of A
    int         iter;
    void qsort (int First, int Last);
  public:
    Sort (int size) {iter =0; A = new DATA_TYPE[n=size];}
    ~Sort()   { delete []A; }
    void build_list (DATA_TYPE input[]);
    void debug_print (int iteration, int debug,
                      char *hdr);
    void Quick_Sort (DATA_TYPE input[]);
};
typedef DATA_TYPE   ARY_LIST[];

void Sort::build_list(ARY_LIST input)
{
    for (int i = 0; i < n; i++)
        A[i] = input[i];
}

//   debug_print ():
//      Print the array list A[n] for each iteration
//
void Sort::debug_print(int iteration, int debug,
char *hdr)
{
    if (debug == 0)
        printf("\n %s \n", hdr);
    else
        printf(" Pass #%d:", iteration + 1);
    for (int i = 0; i < n; i++)
        printf(" %d", A[i]);
```

```
      printf("\n");
}

//  qsort(): Perform quick sort
//
void Sort::qsort (int First, int Last)
{
    if  (First < Last) {
       DATA_TYPE  Pivot = A[First];
       int        i = First;
       int        j = Last;

       while (i < j) {
           while (A[i] <= Pivot && i < Last)
               // continue increasing 'i'
               i += 1;
           while (A[j] >= Pivot && j > First)
               // continue decreasing 'i'
               j -= 1;
           if (i < j) {  // Swap the Pivots
               DATA_TYPE swap_area = A[j];
               A[j] = A[i];
               A[i] = swap_area;
           }
       }
       // Interchange A[j] & A[First]
       DATA_TYPE  swap_area = A[j];
       A[j]        = A[First];
       A[First]  = swap_area;

       debug_print (iter++, 1, "");
       qsort (First, j - 1);
       qsort (j + 1, Last);
    }
}

void Sort::Quick_Sort (ARY_LIST input)
{
    build_list(input);   // Build array A
    debug_print (0, 0,
       "List to be sorted in ascending order:");
    if (n > 0)
       qsort (0, n - 1);
}

//  main(): Test driver for QUICK SORT
//          of an array-based list
//
void main(void)
{
    // Declare an object of "Sort" class
    Sort quick_srt_obj (10);
    static ARY_LIST  A = {33, 60,  5, 15, 25,
                          12, 45, 70, 35, 7 };
```

```
printf("\n **  OOP IMPLEMENTATION OF %s",
       "QUICK SORT  **");
quick_srt_obj.Quick_Sort (A);
quick_srt_obj.debug_print (0, 0,
    "List sorted using quick sort:");
}
```

Code 7.5 produces this output for each pass:

```
**  OOP IMPLEMENTATION OF QUICK SORT  **
List to be sorted in ascending order:
33 60 5 15 25 12 45 70 35 7
Pass #1: 12 7 5 15 25 33 45 70 35 60
Pass #2: 5 7 12 15 25 33 45 70 35 60
Pass #3: 5 7 12 15 25 33 45 70 35 60
Pass #4: 5 7 12 15 25 33 45 70 35 60
Pass #5: 5 7 12 15 25 33 35 45 70 60
Pass #6: 5 7 12 15 25 33 35 45 60 70

List sorted using quick sort:
5 7 12 15 25 33 35 45 60 70
```

Performance Analysis of Quick Sort

Quick_Sort() is a publicly accessible member function of the Sort class
in **Code 7.5**. It implements the quick sort method for arranging an array-
based list of n data elements in ascending order. In the best case and on
average, quick sort is $O(nlogn)$. In the worst case, it is equivalent to the
selection sort. The worst-case performance of the quick sort is $O(n^2)$, and
is left as an exercise. Since Quick_Sort() calls the recursive function
qsort(), which is a private member function of the Sort class, its
implementation implicitly requires a stack space. In the quick sort, the
split is complex and the join (merge) is simple. For further analysis, refer
to Sedgewick [Sed77].

7.1.6   MERGE SORT

Various previously considered sorting techniques are mainly used for internal sorting, where the data elements to be sorted fit in the main memory.
When the data to be sorted reside in a file on disk and do not fit in the available memory, the *merge sort method*, well known and efficient for external
sorting, is used. The insertion sort is a merge sort of one element. Like
quicksort, the merge sort is based on *three main strategies*: (1) split the file
into small subfiles, (2) sort the subfiles, and (3) merge (join/concatenate)
the sorted subfiles. Since there are several ways of representing data in a

file or as an array, merge sort needs such work areas as subfiles or arrays of the same size. Moreover, there are several methods of splitting the data file. Yet in merge sort, the split is easy and the merge is complex. But in quicksort, the split is complex and the merge is easy. The two forms of data storing and various splitting methods yield many versions of the merge sort. Only three versions of the merge sort method are considered:

1. iterative merge sort for data in a file,

2. recursive merge sort for data in a file, and

3. linked merge sort for data in an array.

In these three versions, the objective is to arrange a set of n elements in ascending order. When data are stored in a file (array), subfiles (arrays) are created after the split.

Iterative Merge Sort Algorithm in a File

For arranging a set of n data elements in an unsorted file (UF) (n is also called the *length of the file*) in ascending order, a simple splitting method is used, which is based on grouping elements with group size 2^i for $i = 0, 1, 2, ..., log_2 n$. The steps of the iterative version of the merge sort algorithm are given below.

Step 1. Open the input data file UF for reading and writing, and two temporary subfiles, TMP_F1 and TMP_F2 for writing.

Step 2. If open is not successful, exit with an error message. Otherwise, proceed to Step 3.

Step 3. (*Split*) Copy elements of file UF one element at a time (i.e., a group of 2^0 elements) alternately to files TMP_F1 and TMP_F2.

Step 4. (*Merge*) Compare each one-element group of subfiles TMP_F1 and TMP_F2; write the minimum of the two elements first, followed by the other, back to UF.

Step 5. (*Split*) Copy elements of file UF two elements at a time (i.e., a group of 2^1 elements) alternately to files TMP_F1 and TMP_F2.

Step 6. (*Merge*) Compare each two-element group of subfiles TMP_F1 and TMP_F2; write the minimum of the two elements first, followed by the others, back to UF.

Step 7. Repeat split and merge processes similar to steps 5 and 6 with group sizes 2^i for $i = 2, 3, ..., log_2 n$.

Step 8. Now the data in the file UF are sorted in ascending order.

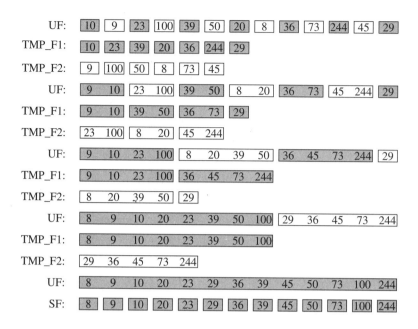

FIGURE 7.3. Iterative merge sort.

Step 9. Close the files UF, TMP_F1, and TMP_F2.

Step 10. Remove the working subfiles TMP_F1 and TMP_F2.

Note that the iterative process stops when the group size reaches n or more than n, the length of the file UF. At this stage, the data in the file UF become sorted in ascending order.

For convenience of illustration for the iterative merge sort method, consider the unsorted file UF of 13 integers (a small subset of the data file used in **Code 7.6**) shown in Figure 7.3. Figure 7.3 shows all passes of the merge sort for UF:

$$UF = \{10, 9, 23, 100, 39, 50, 20, 8, 36, 73, 244, 45, 29\}.$$

Figure 7.3 uses a shaded block to indicate grouping of elements. In the first pass of the merge sort for UF in Figure 7.3, split UF by taking every alternate element (shown with shading) one at a time, and form the temporary files $TMP\_F1 = \{10, 23, 39, 20, 36, 244, 29\}$, and $TMP\_F2 = \{9, 100, 50, 8, 73, 45\}$. Now merge TMP_F1 and TMP_F2 by comparing each one-element group (shaded within one block in TMP_F1) for the smaller element and write the merged file back into UF. That is, for 10 in TMP_F1 and 9 in TMP_F2, form the group [9, 10] since $9 < 10$, and write this group into UF. In the second pass of the merge sort, form two-element groups [9, 10], [23, 100], [39, 50], [8, 20], [36, 73], [45, 244] and [29] (shaded in Figure 7.3) of UF; split UF into TMP_F1 and TMP_F2 by taking every alternate two-element group; this yields $TMP\_F1 = \{9, 10, 39, 50, 36, 73, 29\}$, and $TMP\_F2 = \{23, 100, 8, 20, 45, 244\}$. Merge TMP_F1 and TMP_F2 by comparing each two-element group and write in UF. In the similar manner, continue successively splitting UF by taking $(2^2 =)4$-, $(2^3 =)8$- and $(2^4 =)16$-element groups (each group shown as shaded within one block in Figure 7.3) and merging the temporary files TMP_F1 and TMP_F2 until the group size $(2^4 =)16$ exceeds the size 13 of UF. As shown in Figure 7.3, the merge sort results in the sorted file (SF):

$$SF = \{8, 9, 10, 20, 23, 29, 36, 39, 45, 50, 73, 100, 244\}.$$

Note that the disadvantages of this iterative merge sort method are:

1. The method does not take advantage of the fact that parts of the file may already be in ascending order.

2. The method requires two subfiles, each of at most size n.

3. The number of elements in the subfile TMP_F1 may not be the same as that in the subfile TMP_F2, in some cases.

Code 7.6 implements the iterative version of merge sort.

Code 7.6

```
//   Program:   Merge_Sort.c++
//   Purpose:
//      Perform 'Merge Sort' on the 'n' number
//      of data elements of a list in a file.
//      The sorted file is in ascending order.
//
#include   <stdio.h>
#include   <stdlib.h>
#define    MIN(x,y)   ( (x <= y) ? x : y )
typedef    int   DATA_TYPE;
enum         STATUS   {UNSORTED, SORTED, DATA_AVAILABLE,
                       END_OF_FILE};
//   Merge_Sort():
//      Sort a file of DATA_TYPE elements. The name of
//      the file (that is to be sorted) is passed to
//      the function. Two temporary files are created
//      during sorting, and are deleted before control
//      is returned to the calling function.
//
void Merge_Sort (char *sorted_file_name)
{
   FILE            *sorted_file, *tmp_file_1, *tmp_file_2;
   enum STATUS     status = UNSORTED, status_a, status_b;
   DATA_TYPE       a, b, last = 0;
   int             file = 1;
```

```
// Open files and exit if an error occurs
if ( (sorted_file = fopen (sorted_file_name, "r+"))
        == NULL
     (tmp_file_1  = fopen ("tmp_1.fil", "w+"))
        == NULL
     (tmp_file_2  = fopen ("tmp_2.fil", "w+"))
        == NULL ) {
   printf("\nERROR: Files could not be opened!\n");
   exit(-1);
}
while (status == UNSORTED) {
  // Prepare files for unmerge pass
  rewind (sorted_file);
  fclose (tmp_file_1);
  fclose (tmp_file_2);
  remove ("tmp_1.fil");
  remove ("tmp_2.fil");
  tmp_file_1 = fopen ("tmp_1.fil", "w+");
  tmp_file_2 = fopen ("tmp_2.fil", "w+");
  while (fscanf (sorted_file, "%d", &a) != EOF) {
    if (a < last) {
      // Write to file that is not currently
      // being written
      if (file == 1)
        file = 2;
      else        // file == 2
        file = 1;
    }
    last = a;
    if (file == 1)
      fprintf (tmp_file_1, "%d ", a);
    else    // file == 2
      fprintf (tmp_file_2, "%d ", a);
  }   // End of while (fscanf...)

  // Prepare file for merge pass
  fclose (sorted_file);
  remove (sorted_file_name);
  sorted_file = fopen (sorted_file_name, "w+");
  rewind (tmp_file_1);
  rewind (tmp_file_2);
  status_a = DATA_AVAILABLE;
  status_b = DATA_AVAILABLE;
  if (fscanf (tmp_file_1, "%d", &a) == EOF) {
    status  = SORTED;
    status_a = END_OF_FILE;
  }
  if (fscanf (tmp_file_2, "%d", &b) == EOF) {
    status  = SORTED;
    status_b = END_OF_FILE;
  }
  last = MIN (a, b);
  while (status_a != END_OF_FILE &&
         status_b != END_OF_FILE) {
```

```
    if (a <= b && a >= last) {
      // Write values from first file
      fprintf (sorted_file, "%d ", a);
      last = a;
      if (fscanf (tmp_file_1, "%d", &a) == EOF)
        status_a = END_OF_FILE;
    }
    else if (b <= a && b >= last) {
      // Write values from second file
      fprintf (sorted_file, "%d ", b);
      last = b;
      if (fscanf (tmp_file_2, "%d", &b) == EOF)
        status_b = END_OF_FILE;
    }
    else if (a >= last) {
      // Write values from first file
      fprintf (sorted_file, "%d ", a);
      last = a;
      if (fscanf (tmp_file_1, "%d", &a) == EOF)
          status_a = END_OF_FILE;
    }
    else if (b >= last) {
      // Write values from second file
      fprintf (sorted_file, "%d ", b);
      last = b;
      if (fscanf (tmp_file_2, "%d", &b) == EOF)
          status_b = END_OF_FILE;
    }
    else
      last = MIN (a, b);
  } // end of while ( status_a ...)

  while (status_a != END_OF_FILE) {
    // Write remainder of first file
    fprintf (sorted_file, "%d ", a);
    if (fscanf (tmp_file_1, "%d", &a) == EOF)
        status_a = END_OF_FILE;
  }
  while (status_b != END_OF_FILE) {
    // Write remainder of second file
    fprintf (sorted_file, "%d ", b);
    if (fscanf (tmp_file_2, "%d", &b) == EOF)
        status_b = END_OF_FILE;
  }
} // end of "while (status == UNSORTED)"
// Close all files & remove temporary files
fclose (sorted_file);
fclose (tmp_file_1 );
fclose (tmp_file_2 );
remove ("tmp_1.fil");   // Clean up
remove ("tmp_2.fil");
}

// main(): Test driver for MERGE SORT
```

```
//
void main(void)
{
#ifdef DOS
    system ("copy unsorted.fil sorted.fil");
#else
    system ("cp unsorted.fil sorted.fil"); // Unix
#endif
    Merge_Sort ("sorted.fil");
}
```

Code 7.6 for merge sort uses the input file `unsorted.fil`, broken to avoid a long line:

```
10 9 23 100 39 50 20 8 36 73 244 45 29 49 50 38
266 158 148 132 89 21 65 111 211 231 157 146 176
143 36 38 51 105 207 78 87 69
```

The output file `sorted.fil` sorted by `Merge_Sort()` is shown below, broken to avoid a long line:

```
8 9 10 20 21 23 29 36 36 38 38 39 45 49 50 50
51 65 69 73 78 87 89 100 105 111 132 143 146
148 157 158 176 207 211 231 244 266
```

Recursive Merge Sort Algorithm in a File

This recursive version of the merge sort uses a simple splitting method that divides the unsorted file (UF) into two halves, almost of equal length. These two halves are called the left and right subfiles. Then these subfiles are recursively sorted in ascending or descending order. Finally, these sorted subfiles are merged together to produce the final sorted file (SF). The steps of this recursive `Merge_Sort()` for ascending order are shown below.

Step 1. Open the input data file UF for reading and writing, and two temporary subfiles, TMP_F1 and TMP_F2, for writing.

Step 2. If an open is not successful, exit with an error message. Otherwise, proceed to Step 3.

Step 3. (*Split*) Divide the length, say n, of the file UF in roughly half. Copy the left and right subfiles in TMP_F1 and TMP_F2, respectively.

Step 4. Call `Merge_Sort()` for the left (half) subfile TMP_F1.

Step 5. Call `Merge_Sort()` for the right (half) subfile TMP_F2.

Step 6. (*Merge*) Merge the two sorted subfiles TMP_F1 and TMP_F2, and write the sorted data back into UF.

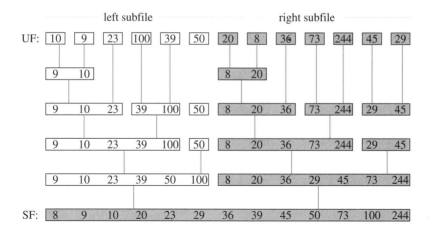

FIGURE 7.4. Merge sort example.

Step 7. Now the data in the file UF are sorted in ascending order.

Step 8. Close the files UF, TMP_F1, and TMP_F2.

Step 9. Remove the working subfiles TMP_F1 and TMP_F2.

In case of the data residing in an array, we need two arrays of sizes at most $(n/2 + 1)$ (integer). It is recommended to use quicksort for small subfiles within the Merge_Sort() for efficiency. The C++ implementation of this recursive version of the merge sort is left as an exercise.

Figure 7.4 shows all passes of the recursive merge sort. In Figure 7.4, the unsorted file UF of 13 integers is the same as the UF in Figure 7.3; SF means the sorted file, the shading differentiates between the left half and the right half subfiles, and the vertical dotted line indicates the elements or blocks being merged with ascending order. The splitting and merging of subfiles are recursively performed to yield SF.

The main drawbacks of a recursive merge sort method are that it requires:

- a stack space to implement recursion,

- two temporary subfiles,

- several passes over the elements being sorted, and

- the merging of two subfiles and thus the copying of data elements of one subfile into another.

To alleviate this unnecessary overhead of copying of subfiles as well as the requirement of the second subfile, the linked version of the merge sort is considered.

Linked Merge Sort Algorithm for an Array

The linked version of the merge sort for data in an array does not require extra space for the second array and extra effort for copying. Instead, it requires a `link` field associated with each data element. Each data element will have a key that is used for sorting. Consider an array of records, where the data record may be defined as follows.

```
typedef  int  KEY_TYPE;
typedef  struct  DATA {
   KEY_TYPE  key;
   int       link;
} ARY_LIST[SIZE];
```

If it is assumed that the data array is sorted in ascending order, the `link` field of `DATA A` contains the array index of `DATA B` that has the next higher key, i.e., `B.key > A.Key`. Using the `link` field, the algorithm alleviates swapping of data elements.

Assuming that the data elements of `ARY_LIST`-type A will be sorted in ascending order, the function for the linked version of the merge sort is of the form:

`Link_Merge_Sort (A, First, Last, Index_of_lowest_elt)`

where `A[First]` and `A[Last]` are the first and the last elements of A and inputs to `Link_Merge_Sort()`, and `Index_of_lowest_elt` is an output that is set to the index of the lowest element of the sorted array A. The steps for recursive `Link_Merge_Sort()` are:

Step 1. If `First` $\geq$ `Last`, set `Index_of_lowest_elt = First`, and return. Otherwise, do steps 2 through 6.

Step 2. Split the range in half, `Middle = (First + Last)/2` (integer).

Step 3. Do the linked version of the merge sort for the left half.

   `Link_Merge_Sort(A, First, Middle, Left_Begin)`

Step 4. Perform the linked version of the merge sort for the right half.

   `Link_Merge_Sort(A,Middle+1,Last,Right_Begin)`

Step 5. Merge the two sorted half subarrays using `Left_Begin` and `Right_Begin`. `Left_Begin` is the index of the lowest element in the left half subarray A. `Right_Begin` is the index of the lowest element in the right half subarray A. The swapping of elements is not required.

Step 6. Set `Index_of_lowest_elt` to the index of the lowest element of A.

	key	link		key	link
A[0]	33	−1	A[0]	33	8
A[1]	60	−1	A[1]	60	7
A[2]	5	−1	A[2]	5	9
A[3]	15	−1	A[3]	15	4
A[4]	25	−1	A[4]	25	0
A[5]	12	−1	A[5]	12	3
A[6]	45	−1	A[6]	45	1
A[7]	70	−1	A[7]	70	−1
A[8]	35	−1	A[8]	35	6
A[9]	7	−1	A[9]	7	5

Index_of_lowest_elt
2

(a) Initial state   (b) After completion of sort

FIGURE 7.5. Link_Merge_Sort() initial and final state.

The implementation of Link_Merge_Sort() is left as an exercise.
   The key points for Link_Merge_Sort() are:

- Its simple split method always divides the array in halves, the left half and the right half subarrays.

- Memory allocations of the left and right subarrays are not needed.

- It does not require any swapping of elements because the link field for each element is used.

- The original positions of data elements in A remain unchanged.

- It uses a recursive procedure.

- A[Index_of_lowest_elt] has the lowest key value. The next higher key value is in A[A[Index_of_lowest_elt].link].

Figure 7.5 shows the initial state and the final sorted state of the array A after using the linked version of the merge sort. That A[7].link is −1 indicates A[7] is the highest element of A.

Performance Analysis of Merge Sort

The merge sort method splits (divides) (sub)lists into halves, sorts (conquers) sublists, and joins them; this is why the merge sort is also called the *divide-and-conquer* method.

   Merge_Sort() in **Code 7.6** implements the merge sort method. It arranges n number of data elements in a file in ascending order. It does many passes (iterations) over the data elements being sorted. In the first pass ($k = 1$), it considers and joins only one file. In the second pass ($k = 2$), it splits the file into two halves, sorts them, and then joins them. In the third pass ($k = 3$), the number of subfiles being sorted and merged is 4. In the fourth pass ($k = 4$), the number of subfiles being sorted and merged is 8. In the kth pass, the number of subfiles being sorted and merged is 2^{k-1}. Since the split strategy is based on halving, there are at most $log_2 n$ (integer value) number of subfiles for the file with n data elements. Because in each pass the merge sort passes over the entire file, it performs $O(n)$ number of comparisons. Hence, considering the linear performance for merging, the worst-case performance of the merge sort is $O(nlog_2 n)$.

7.1.7 BINARY TREE SORT

For sorting an array-based list $A[0], A[1], ..., A[n-1]$ of n data elements in ascending order, the data elements are used as keys for comparison. To perform sorting of A, *binary tree sort* (or *treesort*) uses a binary search tree (*BST*) as a work area. (For discussion on BST, see Chapter 8.) It removes the BST after the list is sorted and the BST is no longer required. The algorithm for the binary tree sort method is:

Step 1. If $n \le 0$, return. Otherwise, go to Step 2.

Step 2. Declare and initialize a BST object.

Step 3. Build a BST object from the given array list A in steps 3.1 and 3.2. For each k, $k = 0, 1, ..., (n-1)$,

Step 3.1. Read $A[k]$.

Step 3.2. Insert $A[k]$ in the BST object; the values of $A[k]$ being used for key comparison and for node data.

Step 4. Using inorder traversal of the BST, get the data elements from the BST, and put them into A in steps 4.1 through 4.4.

Step 4.1. Set $k = 0$.

Step 4.2. During inorder traversal of the BST, visit a node by copying it into $A[k]$.

Step 4.3. Increment k by 1: $k = k + 1$.

Step 4.4. Repeat steps 4.2 and 4.3 until $k < n$.

Step 5. Destroy the BST by releasing the memory spaces allocated for its nodes.

Note that the list A is now arranged in ascending order.

The *drawback of the binary tree sort method* is that it requires extra memory space for storing the BST. As an application, a cross reference generator uses a BST object for alphabetically sorting tokens.

The C++ implementation and performance analysis of the binary tree sort are left as exercises.

7.1.8 HEAP SORT

In the previous sections we discussed many sorting methods. These methods, with the exception of the binary tree sort, used the array as the data structure for the data elements to be sorted. In order to arrange an array of n data elements in ascending or descending order, the heap sort requires a special form of a binary tree, called a *heap*. Thus, discussions include the basic concepts of a heap, constructing and maintaining a heap, followed by the heap sort method and the OOP implementation of a heap. Applications of heaps are found in creating and maintaining highest or lowest priority queues useful for scheduling in operating systems.

There are three main categories of a heap: (1) *max heap*, (2) *min heap*, and (3) *min-max heap*.

A heap has the following *three properties*:

1. It is complete, that is, the leaves of the tree are on at most two adjacent levels, and the leaves in the last level are in the leftmost position.

2. Each level in a heap is filled from left to right order.

3. It is partially ordered, that is, an assigned value, called a *key* of the data element stored in each node (called the *parent*), is less than or greater than or equal to the keys stored in the node's left and right children.

For further information on trees, see Chapter 8. If the key in each node is greater than or equal to the keys of its children, then that heap structure is called a *max heap*. If the key in each node is less than or equal to the keys of its children, then that heap structure is called a *min heap*. In a *min-max heap*, the one level satisfies the min heap property, and the next lower level satisfies the max heap property, alternatingly. A min-max heap is useful for double-ended priority queues. For further information, the reader is referred to Atkinson [Atk86]. Figure 7.6 shows examples of these three types of a heap for the same set of key values:

$$A = \{33, 60, 5, 15, 25, 12, 45, 70, 35, 7\}$$

Notice that in Figure 7.6(a), the root node with 70 in a max heap is the largest node (in key value) in the heap. Also Figure 7.6(b) shows that the

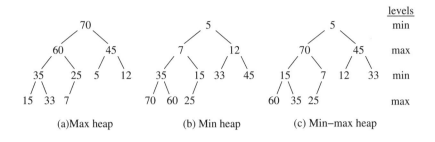

FIGURE 7.6. Three types of heaps.

root node with 5 in the min heap is the smallest node (in key value) in
the heap. The *min* and *max* levels are applicable to the min-max heap. It
is time to discuss algorithms and C++ implementations for building and
rebuilding a max heap, and sorting an array of data elements using a max
heap.

Building a Max Heap

Given an array of n data elements with the keys

$$A = \{33, 60, 5, 15, 25, 12, 45, 70, 35, 7\}$$

to be sorted in ascending order using the heap sort, a max heap is first
built as shown in Figure 7.7. Building the max heap begins by putting the
first key at the root node, adding the next two key nodes as the root node's
left and right children, adding the following four keys of A as the second
level's children (doing from left to right order, and maintaining the max
heap property), and continuing this process until all key values of A are
exhausted. All the nodes on the bottom level are leaves. Build_Heap()
builds a max heap from an array A of data elements and orders it with
each child less than or equal to its parent, using the following algorithm:

Step 1. Start with $A[0]$ as the root node of the heap.

Step 2. Now begin adding the left child of the root.

Step 3. If the last data element of A is reached, exit; else do Step 4.

Step 4. Compare each child's key with that of its parent. If the child's
key is greater, do (a) through (c): (a) swap the parent and the
child, (b) move up to the parent and its parent, (c) go back to
Step 3.

Step 5. Move to the next child and loop back to Step 3.

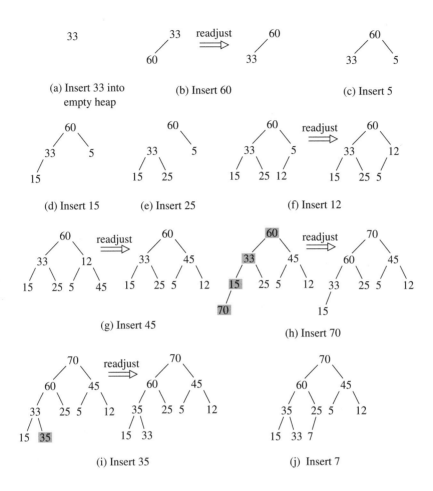

FIGURE 7.7. Creating a max heap from an array A.

At the end, the data element with the largest key will be at the root of the max heap structure. For simplicity, `ReAdjust_Heap()` is called n number of times by `Build_Heap()`. The step-by-step process of building a max heap from the above array A using the above algorithm is shown in Figure 7.7, where a shaded data element indicates that it will be swapped.

Sorting an Array of Data Elements Using a Max Heap

Once a max heap for the above array of n data elements is created, the heap is sorted by `Heap_Sort()`. Since the root of the max heap is the largest data element in its key value, it is removed from the max heap, and is stored at the bottom of the array A. As the data elements are being extracted from the max heap, the size of the max heap is reduced by one and thereby shrinks, and the size of the sorted array grows. As the maximum data element is extracted from the heap (i.e., the root of the tree), move the last data element of A (called the *promoted data element*) into the vacant root node. Then Heap_Sort() calls ReAdjust_Heap() to rebuild (also called *adjust*) a heap from the remaining data elements of A. In ReAdjust_Heap(), the promoted data element is pushed down the tree until the max heap property is satisfied again. This process is continued in Heap_Sort() until all the data elements are removed from the heap. This yields A of n data elements sorted in ascending order of the keys. The algorithm for the iterative version of Heap_Sort() is shown below.

Heap Sort Algorithm

Step 1. Initialize the heap by setting heap nodes equal to the data elements of A (in keys); it calls Init_Heap().

Step 2. Create a max heap from the n data elements of a given array A using Build_Heap().

Step 3. Extract the largest data element (i.e., root) from the heap by swapping it with the last data element of A.

Step 4. Decrease the size of the heap by one.

Step 5. Rebuild the max heap (i.e., restore the max heap property) by using ReAdjust_Heap() and putting the remaining largest data element at the root.

Step 6. Loop back to Step 3 until the max heap has only one data element, the smallest (in key value).

   $A[0], ..., A[n-1]$ are now sorted in ascending order (in their key values).

Because Heap_Sort() calls ReAdjust_Heap() to restore the max heap property (each child is smaller than its parent in key value) after the max heap is disturbed by removing the root, given below is the *algorithm for ReAdjust_Heap()*.

Step 1. Start with the root of a complete binary tree. Find the largest child (data element 1 or 2) of the root (as long as the heap has at least three data elements).

Step 2. If the child is larger than the parent (in key value), do (a) through (c): (a) swap the parent and child, (b) move to the child and find its largest child, and (c) loop back to Step 2, stopping when the leaves of the heap are reached.

Heap Sort: Pass #1

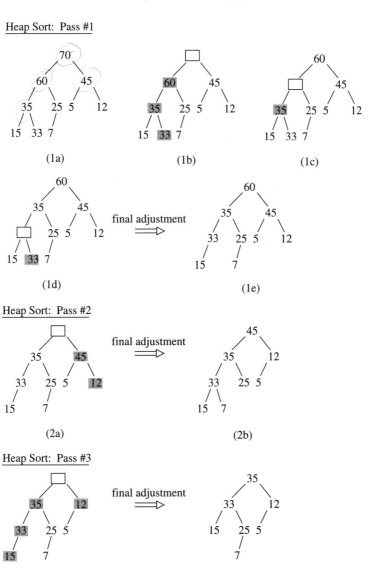

FIGURE 7.8. All passes of the heap sort. (*Continued on next page*)

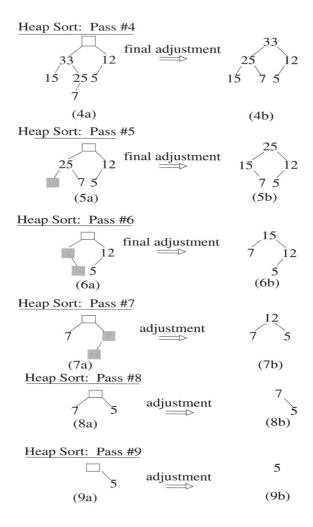

FIGURE 7.8. (*Continued.*)

Figure 7.8 illustrates all passes of Heap_Sort() using the initial max heap in Figure 7.7. In Figure 7.8, shading means data elements have been swapped, and an empty box (node) means the node is vacant and it requires an adjustment of the heap to regain the max heap property.

```
Figure 7.8    Comment/action by heap sort for ascending ordering
-----------   --------------------------------------------------------
1a            First pass starts; heap size = 10
1b            Remove root=70; Heap size=9; Sorted position: A[9]=70
1c            For the root node with 70, the node with 60 (the
              largest key among 60 and 45) is shifted to the
              vacant root node; left node is left vacant.
1d            For node with 60, the child with the largest key
              35 is shifted up the vacant node.
1e            Final adjustment of heap occurs; first pass ends.
-----------------------------------------------------------------------
2a            Remove root=60; decrement heap size; heap size=8;
              Sorted position: A[8]=60.
2b            Adjust heap; it's a max heap; end of second pass.
-----------------------------------------------------------------------
3a            Remove root=45; decrement heap size; heap size=7;
              Sorted position: A[7]=45.
3b            Nodes with 33, 33 and 15 are shifted up; it's a
              max heap; end of third pass.
-----------------------------------------------------------------------
4a            Remove root=35; decrement heap size; heap size=6;
              Sorted position: A[6]=35.
4b            Heap adjustment: nodes with 33, 25 and 7 are
              shifted up; max heap; end of fourth pass.
-----------------------------------------------------------------------
5a            Remove root=33; decrement heap size; heap size=5;
              Sorted position: A[5]=33.
5b            Heap adjustment: nodes with 25 and 15 are
              shifted up; max heap; end of fifth pass.
-----------------------------------------------------------------------
6a            Remove root=25; decrement heap size; heap size=4;
              Sorted position: A[4]=25.
6b            Heap adjustment: nodes with 15 and 7 are
              shifted up; max heap; end of sixth pass.
-----------------------------------------------------------------------
7a            Remove root=15; decrement heap size; heap size=3;
              Sorted position: A[3]=15.
7b            Heap adjustment: nodes with 12 and 5 are
              shifted up; max heap; end of seventh pass.
-----------------------------------------------------------------------
8a            Remove root=12; decrement heap size; heap size=2;
              Sorted position: A[2]=12.
8b            Heap adjustment: node with 7 is shifted up; max
              heap; end of eighth pass.
-----------------------------------------------------------------------
9a            Remove root=7; decrement heap size; heap size=1;
              Sorted position: A[1]=7.
9b            Heap adjustment: node with 5 is shifted up; max
```

```
    heap; end of ninth pass. Remove root=5;
    Sorted array A[]: 5 7 12 15 25 33 35 45 60 70
---------------------------------------------------------------
```

Notice that after the root is removed from the max heap, the heap size is decremented by one, and the vacant node, denoted by the shaded empty box, is filled in by the maximum of the root's left and right children. To preserve the max heap property, the root's maximum child's maximum child is shifted up as a ripple effect. Adjusting the heap in this way takes advantage of the max heap property of the lower levels, does not disturb too many nodes, and is efficient.

OOP Implementation of Heap and Heap Sort

For an OOP implementation, a heap object `heap_obj` is first identified, whose type is specified by an *ADT max heap*. An ADT max heap is a collection of data elements satisfying max heap properties, and a set of some operations:

Heap Object Methods

Construct and initialize a heap object using data elements of A.
Build a *max heap object* from an array A of n data elements.
Destroy a heap object and an array A.
Compare data elements.
Swap data elements.
Rebuild a max heap object.
Do a heap sort for an array A using a max heap object.
Print a max heap at each iteration of heap sort.
Print a max heap object.

The data elements may be a complex structure containing some data and a key that is used for sorting. For simplicity, each data element is assumed to contain a single key, an `int` or a `float`. The heap containing such keys may be implemented using an array or using pointers as in binary trees. For the OOP implementation, an array-based max heap is used. The pointer version of a max heap is left as an exercise. The array-based max heap ensures that the partial ordering can be maintained with a simple indexing scheme. The children of a node indexed by i are nodes indexed by $2 * i$ and $(2 * i + 1)$. The `Heap` class in **Code 7.7** defines a type for an array-based heap object. The workings of the class are hidden with private attributes to show encapsulation. The data elements to be sorted are of `int` type. **Code 7.7** shows the complete array-based OOP implementation for a heap.

Code 7.7

```
//  Program:  Heap.c++
//  Purpose:
//    Perform heap sort method to arrange
//    and modify an array of data elements
//    in an ascending order. Use an array-based
//    ADT max heap, and delete it at the end.
//
#include  <iostream.h>      // For 'cin' & 'cout'
typedef  int  DATA_TYPE;    // Also the 'key'
class Heap {
    DATA_TYPE  *heap;
    int        heap_size;
    void Init_Heap (DATA_TYPE A[]);
  public:
    Heap (int n);                        // Constructor
    ~Heap ()      { delete [] heap; }    // Destructor
    void ReAdjust_Heap (int Root, int Max_Elem);
    void Build_Heap (void);
    void Debug_Print (int pass, int reduced_heap_size);
    void Heap_Sort (DATA_TYPE A[]);
    void Print_Heap (void);
};

//  Heap():  Constructor for an object
Heap::Heap(int n)
{
    heap = new DATA_TYPE [n + 1];
    heap_size = n;
}

//  Init_Heap(): Initialize heap from the array A
void  Heap::Init_Heap(DATA_TYPE A[])
{
    for (int i = 1; i <= heap_size; i++)
       heap[i] = A[i - 1];
}

//  ReAdjust_Heap():
//    Restore the max heap properties, where the
//    parent with index 'Root=i' has left and
//    right children at '2*i' & '2*i + 1'.
//
void  Heap::ReAdjust_Heap(int Root, int Max_Elem)
{
    enum  BOOLEAN  {FALSE, TRUE};
    BOOLEAN  Finished = FALSE;
    DATA_TYPE  x = heap[Root];
    int j = 2 * Root;  // Obtain child information
    while ((j <= Max_Elem) && (!Finished)) {
        //  Find the maximum of left and right child
        if ((j < Max_Elem) && (heap[j] < heap[j + 1]))
```

```
            j++;
        //
        //  Compare the maximum child with 'x'.
        //  If 'x' is maximum, we are finished.
        //
        if (x >= heap[j])
            Finished = TRUE;
        else {
            heap[j/2] = heap[j];
            j = 2 * j;
        }
    }
    heap[j/2] = x;
}


//  Debug_Print():
//    Print each elements of the heap. A vertical bar
//    marks the end of the heap, sorted elements follow.
//
void Heap::Debug_Print(int pass, int reduced_heap_size)
{
    cout << " Pass #" << pass << ":  ";
    for (int i = 1; i <= reduced_heap_size; i++)
        cout << heap[i] << " ";
    cout << " ! ";
    for (; i <= heap_size; i++)
        cout << heap[i] << " ";
    cout << "\n";
}


//  Build_Heap():
//    Build a max heap from the given array A
//    by inserting the elements into the max
//    heap using ReAdjust_Heap().
//
void  Heap::Build_Heap(void)
{
    for (int i = heap_size/2; i > 0; i--)
        ReAdjust_Heap (i, heap_size);
}


//  Heap_Sort():
//    Perform heap sort for A and update A.
//                  (Iterative version)
//
void  Heap::Heap_Sort(DATA_TYPE A[])
{
    //  Initialize the heap with elements of
    //  the array A.
    Init_Heap (A);
    Build_Heap ();     //  Build a max heap
    //  Sort the max heap in ascending order
    for (int i = (heap_size - 1); i > 0; i--) {
        int tmp      = heap[i + 1];    // swap
```

```
        heap[i + 1] = heap[1];
        heap[1] = tmp;
        // Put root of heap in sorted position A[i]
        A[i] = heap[i + 1];
        ReAdjust_Heap (1, i);   // Rebuild max heap
#ifdef  DEBUG
        Debug_Print ((heap_size - i), i);
#endif
    }
    A[0] = heap[1];  // Put last element of heap in A
}

//  Print_Heap():  Print the result
//
void  Heap::Print_Heap(void)
{
 cout << "\n ** SORTED IN ASCENDING ORDER USING\
 HEAP SORT **\n";
 for (int i = 1; i <= heap_size; i++)
     cout << "   " << heap[i];
 cout << "\n";
}

//  main():  Test driver for OOP implementation
//           of a heap and the heap sort
//
void  main (void)
{
 int  n;
 cout << "\nEnter the number of elements\
 to be sorted: ";
 cin >> n;
 // Declare and initialize an object of "Heap" class
 Heap  heap_obj(n);
 // Array of data elements to be sorted
 static  DATA_TYPE A[] = {33, 60,  5, 15, 25,
                          12, 45, 70, 35, 7};
 cout << "Unsorted array is: \n";
 for (int i = 0; i < n; i++)
     cout << A[i] << "   ";
 cout << "\n\n";
 heap_obj.Heap_Sort (A);
 heap_obj.Print_Heap ();
 }
```

Code 7.7 for heap sort produces this output:

```
Enter the number of elements to be sorted: 10
Unsorted array is:
33  60  5  15  25  12  45  70  35  7
```

```
Pass #1:   60 35 45 33 25 12 5 15 7  ! 70
Pass #2:   45 35 12 33 25 7 5 15  ! 60 70
Pass #3:   35 33 12 15 25 7 5  ! 45 60 70
Pass #4:   33 25 12 15 5 7  ! 35 45 60 70
Pass #5:   25 15 12 7 5  ! 33 35 45 60 70
Pass #6:   15 7 12 5  ! 25 33 35 45 60 70
Pass #7:   12 7 5  ! 15 25 33 35 45 60 70
Pass #8:   7 5  ! 12 15 25 33 35 45 60 70
Pass #9:   5  ! 7 12 15 25 33 35 45 60 70

** SORTED IN ASCENDING ORDER USING HEAP SORT **
   5   7   12   15   25   33   35   45   60   70
```

Performance Analysis of Heap Sort

For n number of data elements to be sorted in ascending order, Heap_Sort() first calls Build_Heap(), whose worst-case performance is $O(n)$. Heap_Sort() is an iterative function. At each iteration within the while loop, it calls ReAdjust_Heap(), whose worst-case time complexity is proportional to the height of the complete binary tree (heap), which is $O(log_2 n)$. Since the iterative loop is executed (n - 1) times, and worst-case performance of ReAdjust_Heap() is $O(log_2 n)$, the worst-case performance for this iterative part is $O(n log_2 n)$. Hence, the total worst-case performance for the heap sort method is: $O(n) + O(n log_2 n) = O(n log_2 n)$

7.1.9 STRAIGHT RADIX SORT

Several sort methods were previously discussed for an array or a file of data elements, where the sorting is based on a single key. This key was considered and compared as one entity number or string without any regard to the key's individual digits. There are two categories of *radix sort method*: (1) *straight radix sort* and (2) *radix exchange sort*. This section discusses the radix sort method that is primarily based on taking advantage of the position of each individual digit in a key; the key may be represented in any number system. Based on a digit's position, *most-significant-digit (MSD)* or *least-significant-digit (LSD)* (to be discussed later), there are two versions of the straight radix sort (also referred to as radix sort):

1. MSD radix sort

2. LSD radix sort

The application of the radix sort is found in alphabetic ordering, and geometric and graphic fields. Before proceeding to discuss the concept and algorithm of the LSD radix sort, the concepts of LSD, MSD, and radix in some common number systems are described. The MSD version of the radix sort is left as an exercise.

Number system	Radix (base)	Possible digits
Decimal	10	0, 1, 2, 3, 4, 5, 6, 7, 8, 9
Binary	2	0, 1
Octal	8	0, 1, 2, 3, 4, 5, 6, 7
Hexadecimal	16	0, 1, 2, 3, 4, 5, 6, 7, 8, 9, A, B, C, D, E, F

TABLE 7.2. Radixes in commonly used number systems.

In any number system, numbers are represented as a string of possible digits with respect to a *radix* (commonly called *base*). Table 7.2 shows some commonly used number systems, their bases, and possible digits in those systems.

In short, for a number system with radix r, there are $(r-1)$ possible digits $0, 1, 2, ..., (r-1)$, that are used to represent any number in that system.

To describe the basic concepts of LSD and MSD, consider base conversion and the numbers with suffixes representing bases.

$$257_{10} = 2 \times 10^2 + 5 \times 10^1 + 7$$
$$257_{10} = 1 \times 16^2 + 0 \times 16^1 + 1 = (101)_{16}$$
$$257_{10} = 4 \times 8^2 + 0 \times 8^1 + 1 = (401)_8$$
$$257_{10} = (100000001)_2$$

Notice that in the decimal number system, the radix is 10, and for the decimal number 257, the digits 7, 5, and 2 are respectively in the *units*, *tens*, and *hundreds* positions. The digit 2 is the MSD, and the digit 7 is the LSD for 257. When the same decimal number 257 is represented using radix 8, the MSD is 4 and the LSD is 1.

In general, for a number system with radix (base) r, there are $(r - 1)$ possible digits $0, 1, 2, ..., (r - 1)$; the value of each digit depends on its position, and any number k of length m is represented by

$$k = d_1 d_2 ... d_m$$

where $0 \leq d_i \leq r - 1$ for $i = 1, ..., m$, d_1 being MSD, and d_m being LSD. Such a form of k is also referred to as *m-tuples* $(d_1, d_2, ..., d_m)$.

LSD Radix Sort Algorithm

In a number system with r as the radix (base), an array A of n data elements will be sorted in ascending order based on the keys in each element. For simplicity, each data element of A is assumed to contain a decimal number key k of length m. In the r-based number system, k has the *m-tuples* form as above.

The steps for LSD radix sort algorithm are:

Step 1. Allocate an array A of n data elements, each element contains a decimal number key.

Step 2. Allocate r number of queues, call them digit_queue[r] so that digit_queue[0] contains those keys whose currently considered digit (e.g., LSD) is 0.

Step 3. If the radix r is not 10, convert all data elements' keys into the r-based *m-tuples* representation.

Scan each key by its digits $d_m, d_{m-1}, ..., d_2, d_1$ first from LSD through MSD. Put the data element in the digit queue that corresponds to the currently considered digital position of the key.

Step 4. (*Outer loop*) For i=1,2,...,m, do steps 5 through 6.

Step 5. (*Inner loop 1*) For j=0,1,..., (n -1), do steps 5.1 and 5.2.

Step 5.1. For A[j], determine (extract) LSD in first pass (i = 0), digit preceding to LSD in second pass (i = 1), ..., MSD in the last pass (i = m).

x = A[j];   q_index = j-th_digit_of_x

Step 5.2. Add x=A[j] in rear of the queue, digit_queue[q_index].

Step 6. (*Inner loop 2*) For q_index = 0,1,..., (r - 1), do the following: If digit_queue[q_index] is not empty, write the digit queues into the array A sequentially, digit_queue[0] followed by digit_queue[1] followed by digit_queue[2], ...

The above LSD radix sort algorithm is so generic that it produces LSD radix sort methods for different values of the radix r as shown below.

Radix r	LSD Radix Sort
$r = 2$	LSD radix 2 sort
$r = 8$	LSD radix 8 sort
$r = 10$	LSD radix 10 sort
$r = 16$	LSD radix 16 sort
$r = 27$	LSD radix 27 sort

In the above algorithm, the length m of each decimal key determines the number of passes required. Since in an r-based number system there are r number of possible digits, it requires r number of queues digit_queue[]

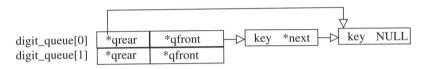

FIGURE 7.9. Digit queues for LSD radix sort for $r = 2$.

to hold each data element's key k. For each key, each digit is extracted starting from LSD (d_m), then d_{m-1}, continuing the process until the MSD d_1 is reached. In the light of implementation, it must be pointed out that some queues, `digit_queue[]`, may be empty in one pass, but may not be empty in another pass. If each digit queue is considered as an array, the total number of data elements in any queue would be at most n, the size of A. Because some array queues of size n may be empty in some passes, there would be a waste of memory space. In order to avoid the waste of memory space, the advisable approach is to implement each queue as a singly linked list as shown in Figure 7.9 for $r = 2$.

The data structure for the LSD radix sort using the singly linked queues is given below.

```
const    int   RADIX = 10;
typedef  int   KEY_TYPE;

struct   QUEUE_ELEMENT {
     KEY_TYPE         k;      //  Data element's key
     QUEUE_ELEMENT   *next;
};

struct   QUEUE {
     QUEUE_ELEMENT   *qfront;
     QUEUE_ELEMENT   *qrear;
};

QUEUE  digit_queue[RADIX];    // 'RADIX' is 'r'
```

Further C++ implementation details for the LSD radix sort is left as an exercise.

To illustrate the LSD radix sort, consider an array of ten decimal numbers with $r = 10$ as the radix.

$$A = \{33, 60, 5, 15, 25, 12, 45, 70, 35, 7\}$$

All of these numbers (keys) of A are considered to have the same length (number of decimal digits) by *prepending zeros*, if necessary. For example, 5 and 7 are respectively considered as 05 and 07, whose MSDs are zeros. Since the size of each key is 2, $m = 2$ (for Step 4), and the LSD radix algorithm will require only two passes. Because $r = 10$, there are ten possible digit values, and hence ten digit queues. Each key can now be scanned starting from LSD through MSD in each successive pass as shown below.

Pass #1 of LSD Radix Sort

Use LSD of each key to determine in which digit_queue[] the key will be added.

	qfront				qrear
digit_queue[0]	60				70
digit_queue[1]					
digit_queue[2]	12				
digit_queue[3]	33				
digit_queue[4]					
digit_queue[5]	5	15	25	45	35
digit_queue[6]					
digit_queue[7]	7				
digit_queue[8]					
digit_queue[9]					

Notice that digit_queue[5] contains 5, 15, 25, 45, and 35 because their LSDs are 5.

The ten digit queues, digit_queue[0], ..., digit_queue[9], are merged sequentially, and are written back into A[] after the first pass. The result is:

$$A = \{60, 70, 12, 33, 5, 15, 25, 45, 35, 7\}$$

Pass #2 of LSD Radix Sort

Use the digit preceding to LSD, which here happens to be MSD of each key to determine in which digit_queue[], the key will be added.

	qfront	qrear
digit_queue[0]	5	7
digit_queue[1]	12	
digit_queue[2]	25	
digit_queue[3]	33	35
digit_queue[4]	45	
digit_queue[5]		
digit_queue[6]	60	
digit_queue[7]	70	
digit_queue[8]		
digit_queue[9]		

After the merge at the end of the second pass, A is:

$$A = \{5, 7, 12, 15, 25, 33, 35, 45, 60, 70\}$$

which is sorted in ascending order.

Notice that this method does not use any other sorting method for each individual digit queue, nor any exchanging of the data elements. However, there exists another version of LSD or MSD radix sort where the insertion sort method may be used for sorting each digit queue. This is because insertion sort is efficient for almost sorted data elements.

In the case of the radix 2 number system, the keys have binary representations. Since C++ provides such low-level operations as shift and mask, it will be convenient to extract binary digits (bits) required in the radix 2 sort.

The algorithm for MSD radix sort starts sorting MSD (d_1) first and proceeds to the next MSD until LSD (d_m) is reached. The algorithm and implementation for the MSD radix sort are left as an exercise.

Performance Analysis of Straight Radix Sort

In Step 4 (the outer loop using for), the LSD or MSD radix sort algorithm performs m passes over the n data elements of A. In each pass, it executes first the inner loop n times, and the second loop r times. Hence, the total performance time is $O(m(n+r))$. In the case of the data elements' numeric keys to be sorted, the value of m depends on the radix r as well as the largest length of the key, i.e., the largest key. Different values of the radix r produce varied performance times. Radix sort is not efficient for an array that contains duplicate keys.

7.1.10   RADIX EXCHANGE SORT

In the previous section, the straight radix sort was discussed. As before, an array A of n data elements is considered whose keys are represented in a number system with radix r. The set of keys will be sorted in ascending order. The sorting strategy, called *radix exchange sort*, uses first MSD of each key's digital representation, and partitions them into r groups, because there are r possible values, $0, 1, 2, ..., (r-1)$, in an r-based number system. Then apply the same partitioning policy as the one used by straight radix sort. The steps of the radix exchange sort (also called *binary radix exchange sort*) algorithm are as follows:

Step 1. Scan from right for a key with leading 1 bit.

Step 2. Scan from left for a key with leading 0 bit.

Step 3. Exchange.

Step 4. Recurse.

The *main features of radix sorts* are:

- Keys are numbers from some restricted range of values.

- The *digital properties* of such keys are exploited.

- The key numbers are represented in a base-M system where the variable M is called the *radix*.

- The processing of keys is done on individual bits or digits (as opposed to full key processing by comparative based methods such as Quicksort/BST).

Consider two examples:

(a) 50 base-10 keys (i.e., 00 to 49) can be sorted into two partitions on the most significant digit (0-4), then each of those can be sorted on the range 0-9.

(b) 8 base-2 keys (i.e., 000 to 1000) can be sorted into two partitions on the most significant digit (0-1), then each of these partitions is sorted recursively using the next significant bit at each stage for the range (0-1).

Radix_Exch_Sort() in **Code 7.8** implements this algorithm. Some implementation notes for Radix_Exch_Sort() are as follows:

- It is similar to quicksort in the following ways: (a) scan from left (lower) to locate key with 1 for bit at level; (b) scan from right (upper) to locate key with 0 for bit at level; (c) exchange keys and continue until scan pointers cross; (d) file is partitioned in two: 0 bits and 1 bits for bit at level; (e) recursively apply this process to each partition.

- The variable bitnum keeps track of the current bit level (bit position). (a) A file can contain 2^{bitnum} keys. (b) At each recursion, the file partition is at 2^{bitnum}.

For example, suppose 3-bit keys are given to represent the base-10 numbers 0 to 8. The bit levels would be:

```
bitnum:  2  1  0              partition
         ---------------------------------
         1  0  0       2^2 = 4
         0  1  0       2^1 = 2
         0  0  0       2^0 = 1

all possible partitions are:
     1 1 1
           ------- 2^0 = 1 (bit 0)
     1 1 0
           ------- 2^1 = 2 (bit 1)
     1 0 1
           ------- 2^0 = 1 (bit 0)
     1 0 0
           -------- 2^2 = 4 (bit 2)
     0 1 1
           ------- 2^0 = 1 (bit 0)
     0 1 0
           ------- 2^1 = 2 (bit 1)
     0 0 1
           ------- 2^0 = 1 (bit 0)
```

```
               0 0 0
           -------------
      bit:   2 1 0
```

Code 7.8

```
//  Program:  radix_exch_sort.c++
//  Purpose:
//    Do 'Radix Exchange Sort' on the elements of
//    an array-based list A[0], ..., A[n-1] of
//    size n. The sorted form is in ascending order.
#include  <stdio.h>
#define    TRUE   1
#define    FALSE  0
typedef   unsigned  DATA_TYPE;
class Sort {
  private:
    DATA_TYPE  *A;  // Array list A[]
    int         n;   // size of A
    DATA_TYPE extract_bits (unsigned key,
                      int bits, int offset);
    void radix_exch_sort1 (int First,
                      int  Last, int bitnum);
  public:
    Sort (int size) { A = new DATA_TYPE[n=size]; }
    ~Sort()  { delete []A; }
    void build_list (DATA_TYPE input[]);
    void print_ary_list(int first, int last);
    void Radix_Exch_Sort (DATA_TYPE input[],
                      int  bitnum);
};
typedef DATA_TYPE  ARY_LIST[];

void Sort::build_list(ARY_LIST input)
{
    for (int i = 0; i < n; i++)
       A[i] = input[i];
}

void Sort::print_ary_list(int first, int last)
{
    for (int i = first; i <= last; i++)
       printf("%2d ", A[i]);
}

//  extract_bits():
//    Given a word of bits (key), return the
//    specified number (bits) of bits which are
//    offset by the specified number (offset) of
//    bits from the right.
//
DATA_TYPE Sort::extract_bits(unsigned key,
```

```
                              int bits, int offset)
{
    return (key >> offset) & ~(~0 << bits);
}


void Sort::radix_exch_sort1(int First,
                    int Last, int bitnum)
{
    DATA_TYPE  First_bitval, Last_bitval,
               swap_area;

    if (First < Last && bitnum >= 0) {
        int i = First;
        int j = Last;

        while (i != j) { // scanning loop
          while (TRUE) {
            First_bitval = extract_bits(A[i], 1, bitnum);
            if (First_bitval == 0 && i < j)
              i += 1;
            else break;
          }
          while (TRUE) {
            Last_bitval = extract_bits(A[j], 1, bitnum);
            if (Last_bitval != 0 && j > i)
              j -= 1;
            else break;
          }
          // Interchange First and Last elements of A
          swap_area = A[j];
          A[j] = A[i];
          A[i] = swap_area;
        }  // End of scanning loop
        if (extract_bits(A[Last], 1, bitnum) == 0)
          j += 1;
        printf(" --------------------%s\n",
               "---------------");
        printf(" bit = %d !  ", bitnum);
        print_ary_list (First, j - 1);
        printf(" ! ");
        print_ary_list (j, Last);
        printf("\n");
        radix_exch_sort1 (First, j - 1, bitnum - 1);
        radix_exch_sort1 (j, Last, bitnum - 1);
    }
}


//  radix_exch_sort():
//    RADIX EXCHANGE SORT for a list of "list_size"
//
void Sort::Radix_Exch_Sort(ARY_LIST input,int bitnum)
{
    build_list (input);
    printf ("\n List to be sorted %s:\n ",
```

```
                   "in ascending order");
        print_ary_list (0, n - 1);
        printf("\n");
        radix_exch_sort1 (0, n - 1, bitnum);
        printf ("\n List sorted using %s \n",
                "radix exchange sort:");
        print_ary_list (0, n - 1);
        printf("\n");
}

//   main(): Test driver for RADIX EXCHANGE SORT
//           for an array list of size n
//
void main(void)
{
        static ARY_LIST  A = {33, 60,  5, 15, 25,
                              12, 45, 70, 35, 7 };
        // Declare an object of "Sort" class
        Sort radix_srt_obj (10);
        printf("\n **  OOP IMPLEMENTATION OF %s",
               "RADIX EXCHANGE SORT  **");
        radix_srt_obj.Radix_Exch_Sort (A, 8);
}
```

Code 7.8 produces this output:

```
**   OOP IMPLEMENTATION OF RADIX EXCHANGE SORT   **
List to be sorted in ascending order:
33 60  5 15 25 12 45 70 35   7
----------------------------------
bit = 8 !  33 60   5 15 25 12 45 70 35   7  !
----------------------------------
bit = 7 !  33 60   5 15 25 12 45 70 35   7  !
----------------------------------
bit = 6 !  33 60   5 15 25 12 45   7 35  ! 70
----------------------------------
bit = 5 !   7 12   5 15 25   ! 60 45 33 35
----------------------------------
bit = 4 !   7 12   5 15  ! 25
----------------------------------
bit = 3 !   7  5  ! 12 15
----------------------------------
bit = 2 !   !  7  5
----------------------------------
bit = 1 !   5  !  7
----------------------------------
bit = 2 !   ! 12 15
----------------------------------
bit = 1 !  12  ! 15
----------------------------------
bit = 4 !  35 45 33  ! 60
```

```
-----------------------------------
bit = 3 !  35 33  ! 45
-----------------------------------
bit = 2 !  35 33  !
-----------------------------------
bit = 1 !  33  ! 35

List sorted using radix exchange sort:
5   7 12 15 25 33 35 45 60 70
```

The performance analysis of **Code 7.8** is left as an exercise.

7.1.11 SHELL SORT

Shell sort is an internal sorting method. It is named after its inventor, D. L. Shell [She59]. The insertion and bubble sort methods can move data elements from one position to an adjacent position. These methods cannot move elements long distances. Shell sort is designed to remedy such a deficiency. It moves data elements long distances by dividing (splitting) the array or file into subarrays or subfiles. Using an *increment* value (also called *Shell size*), say k, at start, the Shell sort divides the array into k subarrays. Then apply any sort method for these k subarrays, which is called *k-sort*. This process continues by diminishing this increment value until 1. That is why the Shell sort is also called a *diminishing increment sort*.

Shell Sort Algorithm

Given an array A of n data elements to be sorted in ascending or descending order, the Shell sort does these steps:

Step 1. Select an increment value for k (e.g., $k = n$).

Step 2. Divide A into k subarrays so that every subarray contains every kth data element of the original A.

Step 3. Apply any sorting method (e.g., insertion sort) to each of these k subarrays.

Step 4. Diminish by k specified by any formula or any sequence of decreasing integers. (The last value of k must be 1.)

Step 5. Repeat steps 2 through 4 until $k = 1$.

Step 6. The data elements in A are now sorted in ascending or descending order.

Steps 2 through 4 of the Shell sort are done iteratively. No extra spaces for the subarrays are required. The same array is used for all the iterations (passes) of the Shell sort. Thus, for an array A of 11 elements $A[0], A[1], A[2], ..., A[10]$, the *3-sort* (with $k = 3$) would be to sort the following subarrays:

$$Subarray \quad 1: \quad A[0], A[3], A[6], A[9]$$
$$Subarray \quad 2: \quad A[1], A[4], A[7], A[10]$$
$$Subarray \quad 3: \quad A[2], A[5], A[8]$$

To illustrate the Shell sort method, consider array A of 10 integer elements to be sorted in ascending order:

$$A = \{33, 60, 5, 15, 25, 12, 45, 70, 35, 7\}$$

Assume that the sequence $\{5, 3, 1\}$ for k, and the insertion sort will be used for sorting each subarray.

Pass #1 of the Shell Sort

```
A[0] A[1] A[2] A[3] A[4] A[5] A[6] A[7] A[8] A[9]
+----+----+----+----+----+----+----+----+----+----+
! 33 ! 60 ! 5  ! 15 ! 25 ! 12 ! 45 ! 70 ! 35 ! 7  !
+----+----+----+----+----+----+----+----+----+----+
```

Increment $k = 5$ yields subarrays after insertion sort:

```
Subarray 1: {A[0], A[5]} = {33, 12} == {12, 33}
Subarray 2: {A[1], A[6]} = {60, 45} == {45, 60}
Subarray 3: {A[2], A[7]} = { 5, 70} == { 5, 70}
Subarray 4: {A[3], A[8]} = {15, 35} == {15, 35}
Subarray 5: {A[4], A[9]} = {25,  7} == { 7, 25}
```

Pass #2 of the Shell Sort

```
A[0] A[1] A[2] A[3] A[4] A[5] A[6] A[7] A[8] A[9]
+----+----+----+----+----+----+----+----+----+----+
! 12 ! 45 ! 5  ! 15 ! 7  ! 33 ! 60 ! 70 ! 35 ! 25 !
+----+----+----+----+----+----+----+----+----+----+
```

Increment $k = 3$ yields subarrays after insertion sort:

```
Subarray 1: {A[0], A[3], A[8]} = {12, 15, 35} == {12, 15, 35}
Subarray 2: {A[1], A[6], A[9]} = {45, 60, 25} == {25, 45, 60}
Subarray 3: {A[2], A[5], A[8]} = { 5, 33, 35} == { 5, 33, 35}
Subarray 4: {A[4]} = {7} == {7}
```

Pass #3 of the Shell Sort

```
A[0] A[1] A[2] A[3] A[4] A[5] A[6] A[7] A[8] A[9]
+----+----+----+----+----+----+----+----+----+----+
! 12 ! 25 ! 5  ! 15 ! 7  ! 33 ! 45 ! 70 ! 35 ! 60 !
+----+----+----+----+----+----+----+----+----+----+
```

Increment $k = 1$ yields one subarray after insertion sort:

```
Subarray 1: {A[0], A[1], A[2], A[3], A[4],
             A[5], A[6], A[7], A[8], A[9]}
          == {7, 12, 15, 25, 33, 35, 45, 60, 70}
```

After the third pass of the Shell sort, A is sorted in ascending order:

$$A = \{7, 12, 15, 25, 33, 35, 45, 60, 70\}$$

Code 7.9 shows an OOP implementation of the Shell sort.

Code 7.9

```cpp
//   Program:   ShelSort.c++
//   Purpose:
//      Perform Shell sort that sorts an array
//      of n integer elements in ascending order.
//
#include <stdio.h>
typedef int DATA_TYPE;
class Sort {
  private:
    DATA_TYPE  *A;     // Array list A[]
    int        n;      // size of A
  public:
    int        iter;  // iteration
    Sort (int size) {iter = 0;A = new DATA_TYPE[n=size];}
    ~Sort()  { delete []A; }
    void build_list (DATA_TYPE input[]);
    void print_list (void);
    void Shell_Sort (DATA_TYPE input[]);
};
typedef DATA_TYPE   ARY_LIST[];

void Sort::build_list(ARY_LIST input)
{
   for (int i = 0; i < n; i++)
       A[i] = input[i];
}

void Sort::print_list(void)
{
     for (int i = 0; i < n; i++) {
        printf (" %d", A[i]);
        if (i != 0 && i % 13 == 0)
          printf ("\n"); // break line
     }
}

void  Sort::Shell_Sort(ARY_LIST input)
{
     int            i, search,
```

```
                        shell_size = n,
                        k_sort, k_sort_2, k_sort_1;

    build_list (input);
    print_list ();
    while (shell_size > 1) {
        //
        //  Find value of 'k' to break sort process into
        //  subarrays by the following rule:
        //  k_sort = (k sort - 1) * 4 - (k sort - 2) * 3
        //
        k_sort_2 = 0;
        k_sort_1 = 1;
        while ((k_sort = k_sort_1 * 4 - k_sort_2 * 3) <
                    shell_size) {
            k_sort_2 = k_sort_1;
            k_sort_1 = k_sort;
        }
        k_sort = k_sort_1;
        //  Perform insertion sort on 'k' sort subarrays
        for (i = 0; i < n; i++) {
            DATA_TYPE swap_area = A[i];
            search = i - k_sort;
            while (swap_area < A[search] && search >= 0) {
                A[search + k_sort] = A[search];
                search -= k_sort;
                iter++;
            }
            A[search + k_sort] = swap_area;
        }
        shell_size = k_sort;
    }
}

//  main(): Test driver for Shell sort.
void main(void)
{
    static DATA_TYPE A[] =
            {10, 9, 23, 100, 39, 50, 20, 8, 36,
             73, 244, 45, 29, 49, 50, 38, 266,
             158, 148, 132, 89, 21, 65, 111,
             211, 231, 157, 146, 176, 143, 36,
             38, 51, 105, 207, 78, 87, 69};
    Sort  shel_srt_obj (38);   // n = 38
    printf ("\n ** OOP IMPLEMENTATION %s ** %s",
             "OF SHELL SORT **",
       "\n\n List to be sorted in ascending order:\n");
    shel_srt_obj.Shell_Sort (A);
    printf ("\n\n List sorted using Shell sort:\n");
    shel_srt_obj.print_list ();
    printf ("\n Number of %s sort is %d \n",
             "iterations required for",
             shel_srt_obj.iter);
}
```

Code 7.9 for Shell sort produces this output:

```
** OOP IMPLEMENTATION OF SHELL SORT ** **

List to be sorted in ascending order:
10 9 23 100 39 50 20 8 36 73 244 45 29 49
50 38 266 158 148 132 89 21 65 111 211 231 157
146 176 143 36 38 51 105 207 78 87 69

List sorted using Shell sort:
8 9 10 20 21 23 29 36 36 38 38 39 45 49
50 50 51 65 69 73 78 87 89 100 105 111 132
143 146 148 157 158 176 207 211 231 244 266
Number of iterations required for sort is 83
```

Performance Analysis of Shell Sort

The calculation for performance analysis of Shell sort requires rigorous mathematical steps that are beyond the scope of this book. However, experimental results indicate that for a large n (number of data elements), the worst-case performance of Shell sort ranges between $O(n^{1.25})$ and $O(1.6n^{1.25})$. This is a remarkable improvement over the insertion sort's performance $O(n^2)$. Also, the worst-case performance of the Shell sort may be $O(n(\log n)^2)$, if a sequence of increments is properly chosen. Knuth [Knu73] has recommended a formula for choosing a sequence of diminishing increments for the Shell sort.

7.1.12 PERFORMANCE ANALYSES OF SORTING METHODS

To arrange an array-based list of n data elements (sorted; partial or random ordered), the number of comparisons performed by each sort method is noted in Table 7.3. Detailed performance analysis of each algorithm is discussed in the respective section.

For large numbers of data elements, i.e., for large n, the growth rate of $\log_2 n$ is much slower than that of n^2 or n^3. This suggests that for large n, such sort methods as quick, merge, heap, or Shell sorts are more efficient than the insertion, selection, or bubble sorts. For small n, these latter sort methods are more efficient.

Sort methods	Worst case (partial ordered)	Best case (ordered)
1. Insertion sort	$O(n^2)$	$O(n)$
2. Insertion sort (linked list)	$O(n^2)$	$O(n)$
3. Selection sort	$O(n^2)$	$O(n^2)$
4. Bubble sort	$O(n^2)$	$O(n)$
5. Quick sort	$O(n^2)$	$O(n \log_2 n)$
6. Merge sort	$O(n \log_2 n)$	$O(n \log_2 n)$
7. Heap sort	$O(n \log_2 n)$	$O(n \log_2 n)$
8. Straight radix sort	$O(m(n+r))$	
9. Shell sort	$O(n(\log_2 n)^2)$	

TABLE 7.3. Performances of sort methods.

7.2 Searching Methods

In the previous section, several sorting methods were discussed and implemented that use a single value (key) to arrange an array or a linked list in ascending or descending order. OOP implementations for several searching methods will now be discussed that look for a data element by a single (primary) key value in an unsorted or sorted array and linked list. The searching methods using more than one key (also called *multidimensional searches*) are discussed and implemented in Chapter 9.

Given a set of n data elements, all the searching methods except hash search (discussed here) are sequential; that is, the search first starts from the first data element, and linearly moves to the successive elements until the last data element or a match is encountered. The hash search, instead, uses random access technique for faster performance. Some of the search methods take advantage of sorted form to speed up.

Applications of searching are numerous, for example, database, alphabetically ordered phone book, and so on.

The two most often used groups of search methods are:

(A) Simple search methods

1. Linear search of an array

2. Linear search of a linked list

3. Linear search of an ordered array

4. Linear search of an ordered list

(B) Advanced search algorithms

1. Binary search of an ordered array

2. Interpolation search of an ordered array

3. Fibonacci search of an ordered array

4. Searching a binary search tree

5. Search using hash strategy

Using an object-oriented approach, a `Search` class is defined for an array-based list of integer data:

```
typedef    int   DATA_TYPE;
class Search {
  private:
    typedef    int   INDEX;
    typedef    DATA_TYPE  ARY_LIST[];
    DATA_TYPE  *A;  // Array list A[]
    int        n;   // size of A
  public:
    Search (int size) { A = new DATA_TYPE[n=size]; }
    ~Search()  { delete []A; }
    void  build_list (DATA_TYPE input[]);
    void  print_list (char *hdr);
    INDEX Linear_Search (DATA_TYPE srch_key);
    INDEX Linear_Search_Sorted(DATA_TYPE srch_key);
    INDEX Binary_Search (DATA_TYPE srch_key);
    INDEX Interpolation_Search(DATA_TYPE srch_key);
    INDEX Fibonacci_Search (DATA_TYPE srch_key);
};
```

Using the `template` keyword, the `Search` class is redefined for an array-based list of elements of an arbitrary type:

```
template<class DATA_TYPE> class Search {
  // all members and methods are same as above.
};
```

Search methods are now presented, keeping their progressive performances in mind.

7.2.1 LINEAR SEARCH OF AN UNSORTED ARRAY

For searching an array-based and unsorted list A of n data elements A[0], A[1], ..., A[n-1], the data elements are used as keys for comparison. The algorithm for the *sequential* or *linear search* method for a data element specified by `srch_key` in an unsorted list is:

Step 1. Set k = 0.

Step 2. Compare A[k] with `srch_key`. If it is equal, return the array index k. Otherwise, increment k by 1; k = k + 1.

Step 3. Repeat Step 2 until k < n.

Step 4. Print an error message "data is not found in list," and return an invalid index, -1.

In Step 2, srch_key is first compared with A[0]; if there is no match, it is sequentially compared with A[1], A[2], ..., A[n-1] in a linear (i.e., straight line) fashion until all elements are exhausted or a match is encountered.

Code 7.10 is an OOP for the linear search method.

Code 7.10

```
//   Program:  Linear_Search.c++
//   Purpose:
//     Using "linear (sequential) search", search
//     the unsorted array A[0], A[1], ..., A[n-1]
//     for a data element identified by its search
//     key, 'srch_key'. The array elements and the
//     'srch_key' are of same type.
//
#include   <stdio.h>
typedef    int   DATA_TYPE;
typedef    int   INDEX;
class Search {
  private:
    DATA_TYPE   *A;   // Array list A[]
    int         n;    // size of A
  public:
    Search (int size) {A = new DATA_TYPE[n=size];}
    ~Search()   { delete []A; }
    void build_list (DATA_TYPE input[]);
    void print_list (char *hdr);
    INDEX Linear_Search (DATA_TYPE srch_key);
};
typedef DATA_TYPE   ARY_LIST[];

void Search::build_list(ARY_LIST input)
{
    for (int i = 0; i < n; i++)
        A[i] = input[i];
}

void Search::print_list(char *hdr)
{
    printf("\n %s \n", hdr);
    for (int i = 0; i < n; i++)
        printf(" %d", A[i]);
    printf("\n");
}
```

```
// Linear_Search():
//    Linearly search an unsorted array-based
//    list A for a data element specified by 'srch_key'.
//    If the data element is found, it returns an array
//    index; otherwise, it returns -1, an invalid index.
//
INDEX Search::Linear_Search(DATA_TYPE srch_key)
{
    int k = 0;
    while (k < n) {
      if (A[k] == srch_key)
        // Match of 'srch_key' is found;
        // return index 'k'
          return (k);
      k++;
    }
    //  Match of "srch_key" is not found
    printf("\n Linear_Search: %d is not found %s \n",
             srch_key, "in the list");
    return (-1);
}

// main():
//   Test driver for OOP implementation of
//   linear search in an unsorted array.
//
void main(void)
{
    // Declare an object of "Search" class
    Search seq_srch_obj (10);
    static ARY_LIST  A = {33, 60,  5, 15, 25,
                           12, 45, 70, 35, 7 };
    printf("\n ** OOP IMPLEMENTATION OF LINEAR %s",
             "\n    SEARCH IN UNSORTED ARRAY **");
    seq_srch_obj.build_list (A);
    seq_srch_obj.print_list (
      "Searching for 45 in array list:");
    INDEX i = seq_srch_obj.Linear_Search (45);
    if (i != -1)
      printf("\n Search data: A[%i] = %d \n",
             i, A[i]);
}
```

An OOP for the linear search in **Code 7.10** yields this output:

```
** OOP IMPLEMENTATION OF LINEAR
   SEARCH IN UNSORTED ARRAY **
Searching for 45 in array list:
33 60 5 15 25 12 45 70 35 7

Search data: A[6] = 45
```

Performance Analysis of Linear Search

Linear_Search() is a public member function of the Search class. It implements the linear search method for a data element specified by its key srch_key in an unsorted array list A. Assume A contains n number of data elements. The best case is that srch_key is A[0]; then it requires only one comparison. Hence, the best-case performance is $O(1)$.

The worst case is that data element with srch_key is not in the array list A. The comparison within the while loop is executed n number of times. Hence, the worst-case performance of the linear search is $O(n)$. The average performance of the linear search is $O(n/2)$, i.e., $O(n)$.

7.2.2 LINEAR SEARCH OF AN UNSORTED LINKED LIST

To perform a *linear search of an unsorted singly linked list* of data elements, the data elements are used as keys for comparison. Because of the dynamic nature of a singly or doubly linked list, the number of data elements is not fixed. A singly linked list is shown in Figure 7.10. The NULL value of the last element's next field indicates the end of the list.

From Figure 7.10, it is clear that a data element is a record containing data and next fields, and is defined by SLIST_ELEMENT struct.

```
typedef  char  DATA_TYPE;
struct  SLIST_ELEMENT {
    DATA_TYPE      data;   // "key"
    SLIST_ELEMENT  *next;
};
SLIST_ELEMENT  *head_ptr;
```

The algorithm for the linear search method for a data element specified by search_key in an unsorted singly linked list is:

Step 1. Check to see if the singly linked list object is empty. If it is empty, print a message "Element is not found in the list," and return NULL. Otherwise, go to Step 2.

Step 2. If search_key is head_ptr->data, return head_ptr, which points to the first element of the list. Otherwise, do Step 3.

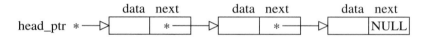

FIGURE 7.10. A singly linked list with head pointer.

Step 3. Linearly advance to the next element in the singly linked list using the link pointer next. Compare search_key with data field of the next element pointed by head_ptr->next. If equality is found, return head_ptr->next. Else, do Step 4.

Step 4. Repeat comparing srch_key with data field of the next element in a straight-line manner until an equality of keys is found or next is NULL (i.e., end of list is encountered). Return (the pointer to the searched element).

Code 7.11 shows an OOP implementation of linear search.

Code 7.11

```
//   search_element1():
//      Search for an element identified by its key
//      'search_key' (search data) in a list object,
//      pointed to by 'lst_ptr'. Return the pointer
//      if found; otherwise return NULL.
//      (Recursive method)   (See Code 5.3)
//
Singly_Linked_List::LIST_PTR
Singly_Linked_List::search_element1(
            LIST_PTR lst_ptr, DATA_TYPE search_key)
{
    if (!is_sublist_empty(lst_ptr)) {
        if (search_key == lst_ptr->data)
            return (lst_ptr);
        search_element1 (lst_ptr->next, search_key);
    }
    else {
      printf("\n search_element: %s \n",
              "Element is not found in list");
      return (NULL);
    }
}
```

search_element1() is called by search_element() that searches for key 'H', and is tested by adding following lines in main() of **Code 5.3**:

```
    LIST_PTR  srch_ptr;
    srch_ptr = slist_obj.search_element('H');
    if (srch_ptr != NULL)
       printf(" Element \"H\" is found in the list.\n");
```

Codes 5.3 and 7.11 produce this output:

```
** OOP IMPLEMENTATION OF SINGLY LINKED LIST **
```

```
List is:
  S -> N -> I -> G -> D -> H -> A -> NULL
Number of elements in this list object is: 7

The list after deleting 'D' is:
  S -> N -> I -> G -> H -> A -> NULL
Number of elements in this list object is: 6
Element "H" is found in the list.
```

Performance Analysis of Linear Search of an Unsorted Linked List

Search_element() in **Code 7.11** is a public member function of the Singly_Linked_List class in **Code 7.11**. This calls the recursive function search_element() that searches for a given list element specified by a single search key search_key. The list of n data elements are unsorted and organized as a singly linked list (it is possible to use a doubly linked list, instead) pointed to by head_ptr of type SLLIST_PTR. It first calls chk_empty_list(). If the list object is empty or no match is found, it prints a message "Element is not found in list." For a nonempty list, it starts the search from the first element, and compares the given search_key with the element's key value. If there is a match, it returns a pointer of type SLLIST_PTR; otherwise, it linearly (i.e., straight line manner) marches to the next element (successor) using the next pointer field, and repeats the comparison process until a match is encountered or the last element is reached.

The best-case performance is $O(1)$ because either the unsorted list object is empty or the target data element is at the head of the list, which requires only one comparison.

The worst-case performance of the linear search in an unsorted linked list object is $O(n)$. This is because the list object has n number of data elements, and srch_key is successively compared with the keys of all n elements; this yields n number of comparisons. Though this method is easy, it is not efficient for a large number of data elements.

7.2.3 LINEAR SEARCH OF A SORTED ARRAY

In linear search methods of unsorted arrays, computing time was wasted for failed searches. This may be improved if the array is maintained in some order, numeric or lexicographic (alphabetic). In the linear search of a sorted array, it is first checked whether the data element's key is out of range of the key values.

The goal is to search an ascending ordered array A of n data elements A[0], ..., A[n-1] for an element specified by its key srch_key; A[0] is of the highest order. The algorithm for the linear search in a sorted array is clear from its OOP in **Code 7.12**. The reader is urged to analyze the performance of this algorithm.

Code 7.12

```
//  Program:  Linear_Search_Srt.c++
//  Purpose:
//    Using "linear (sequential) search", search
//    the ascending ordered array A[0], A[1], ...,
//    A[n-1] for a data element identified by its
//    search key, 'srch_key'. The array elements
//    and the 'srch_key' are of same type.
//
#include  <stdio.h>
typedef    int    DATA_TYPE;
typedef    int    INDEX;
class Search {
  private:
    DATA_TYPE  *A;  // Array list A[]
    int        n;   // size of A
  public:
    Search (int size) { A = new DATA_TYPE[n=size]; }
    ~Search()  { delete []A; }
    void build_list (DATA_TYPE input[]);
    void print_list (char *hdr);
    INDEX Linear_Search_Sorted (DATA_TYPE srch_key);
};
typedef DATA_TYPE  ARY_LIST[];

void Search::build_list(ARY_LIST input)
{
    for (int i = 0; i < n; i++)
        A[i] = input[i];
}

void Search::print_list(char *hdr)
{
    printf("\n %s \n", hdr);
    for (int i = 0; i < n; i++)
        printf(" %d", A[i]);
    printf("\n");
}

// Linear_Search():
//    Sequential (linear) search an ascending
//    ordered array-based list A for a data
//    element specified by 'srch_key'. If the
//    data element is found, it returns an array
//    index; otherwise, it returns an invalid index -1.
//
INDEX Search::Linear_Search_Sorted(DATA_TYPE srch_key)
{
```

```
    int k = 0;
    if ((srch_key >= A[0]) && (srch_key <= A[n - 1]))
      while (k < n) {
        if (A[k] == srch_key)
          // Match of 'srch_key' is found;
          // return index 'k'
            return (k);
        k++;
      }
    //  Match of "srch_key" is not found
    printf("\n Linear_Search_Sorted: %d is %s \n",
           srch_key, "not found in the list");
    return (-1);
}

// main():
//   Test driver for OOP implementation of
//   linear search in a sorted array.
//
void main(void)
{
    // Declare an object of "Search" class
    Search seq_srch_srt_obj (10);

    static ARY_LIST  A = {5, 7, 12, 15, 25,
                          33, 35, 45, 60, 70};
    printf("\n ** OOP IMPLEMENTATION OF LINEAR %s",
           "\n    SEARCH IN SORTED ARRAY **");
    seq_srch_srt_obj.build_list (A);
    seq_srch_srt_obj.print_list (
       "Searching for 45 in array list:");
    INDEX i = seq_srch_srt_obj.Linear_Search_Sorted(75);
    if (i != -1)
      printf("\n Search data: A[%i] = %d \n", i,
             A[i]);
}
```

Code 7.12 for the linear search of a sorted list produces:

```
 ** OOP IMPLEMENTATION OF LINEAR
    SEARCH IN SORTED ARRAY **
 Searching for 45 in array list:
 5 7 12 15 25 33 35 45 60 70

Linear_Search_Sorted: 75 is not found in the list
```

7.2.4   Linear Search of a Sorted List

The drawback of the linear search of an unsorted (singly or doubly) linked list in Section 7.2.2 is that the nonexistence of the specified data element is detected after the entire list is traversed. An improvement of this is achieved by using a sorted singly or doubly linked list.

The data elements are kept in an ascending ordered linked list. Each element is of type SLIST_ELEMENT containing data as the key, and next as the pointer to the next element. The ascending order assures that the first element pointed to by head_ptr has the lowest key value. The last element pointed to by tail_ptr has the highest key value. That the linked list is empty is indicated by the NULL value of head_ptr. To search for a data element specified by the key srch_key, the algorithm for the linear search method of a sorted linked list always begins from the first element and linearly marches to the end of the list using the link next pointer.

Step 1. If (head_ptr ==NULL) OR (srch_key<head_ptr->data) OR (srch_key > tail_ptr->data) write error: "Data element is not found"; return NULL.

Step 2. Set srch_ptr = head_ptr

Step 3. Sequentially compare data elements with srch_key starting from the first element:

if (srch_ptr->data == srch_key) return srch_ptr;

(match is found)

Step 4. Else, linearly advance to the next element:

srch_ptr = srch_ptr->next;

Step 5. Repeat steps 3 and 4 until srch_ptr is NULL (i.e., tail end of the linked list is reached.)

Step 6. Write error: "Data element is not found"; return NULL.

This method assumes that the linked list is sorted; **Code 7.2** shows sorting of a doubly linked list. An OOP and analysis of searching a linked list are left as exercises.

7.2.5   Binary Search of a Sorted Array

As described earlier, the linear search for a sorted or unsorted array-based list A starts its search process from the first data element $A[0]$. The binary search method of a sorted array list is designed to greatly improve over these methods. It primarily divides the sorted array into two half-sorted subarrays (called *left* and *right* subarrays), eliminates one subarray by considering the ordering among the elements with respect to the data element being searched; it gradually reduces the size of a subarray by half, and conquers the subarrays of smaller sizes. This is the *divide-and-conquer* search method.

Given an ascending ordered array A of n number of data elements A[0], ..., A[n-1], the data element A[0] is the lowest key value, and A[n-1] is the highest key value; these two key values define the range in A. The data element to be searched for is specified by its key value, srch_key. The algorithm of the binary search of a sorted array A is:

Step 1. Set First = 0; Last = n - 1.

Step 2. If (srch_key < A[0]) OR (srch_key > A[n - 1]), the search fails; return (-1).

Step 3. While (First ≤ Last), divide the (sub)array's range (First, ..., Last) into halves, and compare in steps 3.1 through 3.4.

  Step 3.1. Split sorted (sub)array into halves:

    Middle = (First + Last)/2.

  Step 3.2. If (srch_key == A[Middle]), return Middle, which is the index of the matching data element.

  Step 3.3. If (srch_key > A[Middle]), the element is not in the left half A[First], ..., A[Middle - 1]; so eliminate this left subarray. Prepare to perform search for srch_key in the right half: First = Middle + 1 and repeat Step 3.

  Step 3.4. If srch_key < A[Middle], the specified data element is not in the right half A[Middle + 1], ..., A[Last]; so eliminate this right subarray. Set up to do search for srch_key in the left half: Last = Middle - 1 and repeat Step 3.

Step 4. Otherwise, First > Last. This means the ordered subarray in which the search is to be conducted does not have any data elements. The binary search fails; return -1, an invalid array index.

Code 7.13 is an OOP for the binary search of a sorted array.

Code 7.13

```
// Program: Binary_Search.c++
```

```
//   Purpose:
//     Using "binary search method", search the
//     ascending ordered array-based list A[0], A[1],
//     ..., A[n-1] for a data element identified by
//     its 'srch_key'. The array elements and the
//     'srch_key' are of same type.
//
#include   <stdio.h>
typedef    int   DATA_TYPE;
typedef    int   INDEX;
class Search {
  private:
    DATA_TYPE   *A;   // Array list A[]
    int           n;   // size of A
  public:
    Search (int size) {A = new DATA_TYPE[n=size];}
    ~Search()   { delete []A; }
    void build_list (DATA_TYPE input[]);
    void print_list (char *hdr);
    INDEX Binary_Search (DATA_TYPE srch_key);
};
typedef DATA_TYPE   ARY_LIST[];

void Search::build_list(ARY_LIST input)
{
    for (int i = 0; i < n; i++)
        A[i] = input[i];
}

void Search::print_list(char *hdr)
{
    printf("\n %s \n", hdr);
    for (int i = 0; i < n; i++)
        printf(" %d", A[i]);
    printf("\n");
}

// Binary_Search():
//   Binary search a sorted array-based list A
//   for a data element specified by 'srch_key'.
//   If the data element is found, it returns an
//   array index; otherwise, it returns -1, an
//   invalid index.
//
INDEX Search::Binary_Search(DATA_TYPE srch_key)
{
    int First = 0,
        Last  = n - 1,
        Middle;  // Middle element's index in (sub)array

    if ((srch_key < A[0])   (srch_key > A[n - 1]))
        return (-1);   // "srch_key" is not found
    while (First <= Last) {
      // Determine
```

```
        //    Middle = (First + Last) div 2
        Middle = (int) ((First + Last)/2
                      - (First + Last) % 2);
        if (srch_key == A[Middle])
            // Match of "srch_key" is found; return 'Middle'
            return (Middle);
        else if (srch_key > A[Middle])
            // Set First = Middle + 1; "srch_key"
            // may be in the second half of the array
            First = Middle + 1;
        else      // srch_key < A[Middle]
            // Set Last = Middle - 1; "srch_key"
            // may be in the first half of the array
            Last = Middle - 1;
    }   // End while (...)
    // Match of "srch_key" is not found
    printf("\n Binary_Search: %d is not found %s \n",
            srch_key, "in the list");
    return (-1);
}

// main():
// Test driver for OOP implementation of
// binary search in an sorted array.
//
void main(void)
{
    // Declare an object of "Search" class
    Search bin_srch_obj (10);

    static ARY_LIST  A = {5, 7, 12, 15, 25,
                          33, 35, 45, 60, 70};
    printf("\n ** OOP IMPLEMENTATION OF BINARY %s",
            "\n    SEARCH IN SORTED ARRAY **");
    bin_srch_obj.build_list (A);
    bin_srch_obj.print_list (
        "Searching for 45 in array list:");
    INDEX i = bin_srch_obj.Binary_Search (45);
    if (i != -1)
      printf("\n Search data: A[%i] = %d \n", i,
            A[i]);
}
```

Code 7.13 produces this output:

```
** OOP IMPLEMENTATION OF BINARY
   SEARCH IN SORTED ARRAY **
Searching for 45 in array list:
5 7 12 15 25 33 35 45 60 70

Search data: A[7] = 45
```

Performance Analysis of Binary Search of a Sorted Array

`Binary_Search()` is a `public` and nonrecursive member function of the `Sort` class. It primarily relies on splitting the sorted array and its subarrays into two halves; the search for `srch_key` is continued in one half subarray or the other in each iteration. The condition in the `while` statement ensures that the interval [`First, Last`] is divided into half at each iteration executed within the `while` loop. It applies the *divide-and-conquer* strategy. This splitting process reduces the search time. The singly or doubly linked list implementation and computing time for a binary search are both complex. The complexity is attributed to the random access requirement of the binary search method.

The worst-case performance of binary search is $O(\log_2 n)$, compared to the worst-case performance $O(n)$ of a linear search for an ordered array list. As the number n of data elements grows, $O(\log_2 n)$ grows less slowly than $O(n)$; thus, the binary search method is more efficient that the linear search method for a sorted array. The disadvantage is that it requires an ascending or descending ordered array based list.

The detailed analysis of this algorithm is left as an exercise.

7.2.6 INTERPOLATION SEARCH OF A SORTED ARRAY

The *interpolation search* of a sorted array is an improvement over a binary search. It is very similar to the binary search with an exception. Instead of starting from the middle of [`First, Last`], `First` $\leq$ `Last`, it starts the search process from an interpolated location that one hopes is close to the target data element.

Given an ascending ordered array A of n number of data elements `A[0]`, ..., `A[n-1]`, the data element `A[0]` is the lowest key value, and `A[n-1]` is the highest key value; these two key values define the range in A. The data element to be searched for is specified by its key value `srch_key`. The algorithm of the interpolation search of the sorted array A is similar to the binary search; the point (location) `interp_loc` it uses to divide the sorted array is calculated using an interpolation formula:

$$\texttt{interp\_loc} = \text{integer value of } (First + \tfrac{(Last-First-1)(srch\_key-A[First])}{A[Last]-A[First]})$$

Initially, `First` = 0, and `Last` = n - 1. The interpolation search is continued until `Last` - `First` $\leq$ 1. For a detailed algorithm, see its OOP implementation in **Code 7.14**.

Code 7.14

```
//  Program:  Interpolation_Search.c++
//  Purpose:
//     Using "interpolation search", search the
//     sorted array-based list A[0], A[1], ...,
//     A[n-1] for a data element identified by
//     its search key, 'srch_key'. The array
//     elements and the 'srch_key' are of same type.
//
#include  <stdio.h>
typedef    int   DATA_TYPE;
typedef    int   INDEX;
typedef    DATA_TYPE  ARY_LIST[];
class Search {
  private:
    DATA_TYPE  *A;  // Array list A[]
    int        n;   // size of A
  public:
    Search (int size) { A = new DATA_TYPE[n=size]; }
    ~Search()  { delete []A; }
    void build_list (DATA_TYPE input[]);
    void print_list (char *hdr);
    INDEX Interpolation_Search (DATA_TYPE srch_key);
};

void Search::build_list(ARY_LIST input)
{
    for (int i = 0; i < n; i++)
        A[i] = input[i];
}

void Search::print_list(char *hdr)
{
    printf("\n %s \n", hdr);
    for (int i = 0; i < n; i++)
        printf(" %d", A[i]);
    printf("\n");
}

// Interpolation_Search():
//    Interpolation search a sorted array-based list
//    A for a data element specified by 'srch_key'.
//    If the data element is found, it returns an
//    array index; otherwise, it returns -1, an
//    invalid index.
//
INDEX Search::Interpolation_Search(DATA_TYPE srch_key)
{
    INDEX  First = 0,
           Last  = n - 1,
           interp_loc;  // interpolated index
```

```
      if ((srch_key < A[0])   (srch_key > A[n - 1]))
         return (-1);   // "srch_key" is not found
      while (Last - First > 1) {
        // Calculate interpolated value
        interp_loc = First +
                           (Last - First - 1)
                         * (srch_key - A[First])
                         / (A[Last]   - A[First]);
        if (interp_loc < First   interp_loc > Last)
            return (-1);
        if (srch_key == A[interp_loc])
            //  Match of "srch_key" is found;
            //  return 'interp_loc'
            return (interp_loc);
        else if (srch_key >  A[interp_loc])
            //  Set First = interp_loc + 1; "srch_key"
            //  may be in the second part of the array
            First = interp_loc + 1;
        else      // srch_key <  A[interp_loc]
            //  Set Last = interp_loc - 1; "srch_key"
            //  may be in the first part of the array
            Last = interp_loc - 1;
      }  // End while (...)
      //  Match of "srch_key" is not found
      printf("\n Interpolation_Search: %d is %s \n",
             srch_key, "not found in the list");
      return (-1);
   }


// main():
//  Test driver for OOP implementation of
//  binary search in an sorted array.
//
void main(void)
{
   // Declare an object of "Search" class
   Search interp_srch_obj (10);

   static ARY_LIST  A = {5, 7, 12, 15, 25,
                           33, 35, 45, 60, 70};
   printf("\n ** OOP IMPLEMENTATION OF\
 INTERPOLATION %s",
           "\n     SEARCH IN SORTED ARRAY **");
   interp_srch_obj.build_list (A);
   interp_srch_obj.print_list (
      "Searching for 45 in sorted array list:");
   INDEX i = interp_srch_obj.Interpolation_Search(45);
   if (i != -1)
     printf("\n Search data: A[%i] = %d \n", i,
             A[i]);
}
```

Code 7.14 produces this output:

```
** OOP IMPLEMENTATION OF INTERPOLATION
   SEARCH IN SORTED ARRAY **
Searching for 45 in sorted array list:
5 7 12 15 25 33 35 45 60 70

Search data: A[7] = 45
```

Performance Analysis of Interpolation Search

`Interpolation_Search()` is a publicly accessible member function of the `Search` class. The `while (Last - First > 1)` loop indicates the repetition of search steps. In each step, it calculates `interp_loc`; this is more than a binary search method does.

The worst-case performance of interpolation search is $O(\log_2 \log_2 n)$. Since it requires rigorous mathematical calculation, it surpasses the scope of this book.

Since the growth of $\log_2 \log_2 n$ is much slower than $\log_2 n$ as n grows, the interpolation search of a sorted list is more efficient than the binary search for large n number of data elements. However, it is less efficient than binary search for small n.

7.2.7   FIBONACCI SEARCH OF A SORTED ARRAY

Like the interpolation search, the *Fibonacci search* of a sorted array is an improvement over the binary search method. Instead of starting the search from the middle of the array, the Fibonacci search uses Fibonacci numbers.

Fibonacci numbers are $0, 1, 1, 2, 3, 5, 8, 13, 21, 34, 55, ...$, and are given by the recursive formula:

$$Fib[0] = 0, Fib[1] = 1, Fib[k] = Fib[k-1] + Fib[k-2], k > 1$$

In a binary search, a sorted array or subarray is split into two halves by dividing its size by 2. Instead, the Fibonacci search splits a sorted array or subarray into two parts by dividing its size (a Fibonacci number) into two Fibonacci numbers. For example, a sorted array of size 55 (which is a sum of two Fibonacci numbers 21 and 34) is divided into two sorted subarrays, one of size 21 and the other of size 34. In this manner, it splits a large array into smaller subarrays.

Given an ascending ordered array A of n number of data elements `A[0]`, ..., `A[n-1]`, the data element `A[0]` is the lowest key value, and `A[n-1]` is the highest key value; these two key values define the range in A. The data element to be searched for is specified by its key value `srch_key`. For the algorithm and implementation of a Fibonacci search of A, see **Code 7.15**.

Code 7.15

```
//   Program:  Fibonacci_Search.c++
//   Purpose:
//     Using "Fibonacci search", search the sorted
//     array-based list A[0], A[1], ..., A[n-1]
//     for a data element identified by its search
//     key, 'srch_key'. The array elements and the
//     'srch_key' are of same type.
//
#include  <stdio.h>
const      int  NOT_FOUND = -1;
typedef    int  DATA_TYPE;
typedef    int  INDEX;
class Search {
  private:
    DATA_TYPE  *A;  // Array list A[]
    int        n;   // size of A
  public:
    Search (int size) {A = new DATA_TYPE[n=size];}
    ~Search()  { delete []A; }
    void build_list (DATA_TYPE input[]);
    void print_list (char *hdr);
    INDEX Fibonacci_Search (DATA_TYPE srch_key);
};
typedef DATA_TYPE  ARY_LIST[];

void Search::build_list(ARY_LIST input)
{
   for (int i = 0; i < n; i++)
       A[i] = input[i];
}

void Search::print_list(char *hdr)
{
   printf("\n %s \n", hdr);
   for (int i = 0; i < n; i++)
       printf(" %d", A[i]);
   printf("\n");
}

//  Fibonacci_Search():
//    Use a Fibonacci search to find a value in
//    an ordered list. The value, 'srch_key', to
//    search for must be passed to function. Location
//    in A containing value is returned if value
//    is found, otherwise NOT_FOUND is returned.
//
INDEX Search::Fibonacci_Search(DATA_TYPE srch_key)
{
  INDEX Fib_low = 0, Fib_high = 1,
        offset  = 0,
        location, N = n;
```

```
while (Fib_low != 1) {
  Fib_low  = 0;
  Fib_high = 1;
  while (offset + (Fib_low += Fib_high) +
              (Fib_high += Fib_low) < N - 1)
        ;
  //  location in A to check
  location = offset + Fib_low;
  if (srch_key == A[location])
    return (location);
  else if (srch_key < A[location])
    N = location;
  else    //  srch_key > A[location]
    offset = location;
}
while (offset <= N - 1) { // check remainder of A
  if (srch_key == A[offset])
    return (offset);
  ++offset;
}
//  Match of "srch_key" is not found
printf("\n Fibonacci_Search: %d is %s \n",
       srch_key, "not found in the list");
return (NOT_FOUND);
}

// main():
//  Test driver for OOP implementation of
//  binary search in an sorted array.
//
void main(void)
{
   // Declare an object of "Search" class
   Search Fib_srch_obj (10);

   static ARY_LIST  A = {5, 7, 12, 15, 25,
                         33, 35, 45, 60, 70};
   printf("\n ** OOP IMPLEMENTATION OF FIBONACCI %s",
          "\n    SEARCH IN SORTED ARRAY **");
   Fib_srch_obj.build_list (A);
   Fib_srch_obj.print_list (
      "Searching for 60 in sorted array list:");
   INDEX i = Fib_srch_obj.Fibonacci_Search (45);
   if (i != -1)
     printf("\n Search data: A[%i] = %d \n", i,
            A[i]);
}
```

Code 7.15 for a Fibonacci search produces this output:

```
** OOP IMPLEMENTATION OF FIBONACCI
   SEARCH IN SORTED ARRAY **
Searching for 60 in sorted array list:
5 7 12 15 25 33 35 45 60 70

Search data: A[7] = 45
```

The worst-case performance analysis for a Fibonacci search is left as an exercise.

7.2.8 SEARCHING A BINARY SEARCH TREE

The previously discussed search methods cannot be applied to the data structure that is a binary search tree (BST) or sorted tree (see Chapter 8). When a given set of n data elements are kept in a BST, each node, say U, contains the data element and/or a key value; the key value being used for comparison such that

1. key value of node $U \geq$ key value of its left node,

2. key value of node $U <$ key value of its right node.

This induces ascending ordering among the nodes (in inorder traversal).

Searching a BST for a given node with key srch_key, the *binary search tree method* takes advantage of the inherent ordering, and has these recursive steps:

Step 1. Test to see if the BST is empty. If it is not empty, go to Step 2. Otherwise, go to Step 5.

Step 2. If (srch_key == key value in root node of (sub)tree) report "Node is found," and return the location.

Step 3. If (srch_key < key value in root node of (sub)tree) search the left (sub)tree. Continue doing steps 3.1 and 3.2 until a match is found or the empty (sub)tree is encountered.

Step 3.1. Move to the left (sub)tree.

Step 3.2. Compare srch_key with root node of the (sub)tree (as in Step 2).

Step 4. If (srch_key < key value in root node of (sub)tree) search the left (sub)tree. Continue doing steps 4.1 and 4.2 until a match is found or the empty (sub)tree is encountered.

Step 4.1. Move to the right (sub)tree.

Step 4.2. Compare `srch_key` with root node of the (sub)tree (as in Step 2).

Step 5. Otherwise, report "Target node is not found"; return.

Since recursively searching a BST requires a stack space, the iterative version of the binary tree search method is efficient. For its algorithm, implementation, and output see **Code 7.16**.

Code 7.16

```
// search_node_in_BST():
//   Find a given node by "Key" in BST. If successful,
//   it returns the pointer that points to the node
//   with "Key"; otherwise, it returns NULL. It uses
//   preorder traversal. (Recuursive method). (See Code 8.4)
//
Binary_Search_Tree::TREE_PTR
Binary_Search_Tree::search_node_in_BST
              (TREE_PTR tree_ptr, DATA_TYPE Key)
{
   if (tree_ptr != NULL) {
      if (Key == tree_ptr->data)
         return (tree_ptr);
      else if (Key < tree_ptr->data)
         // Search for "Key" in the left subtree
         search_node_in_BST(tree_ptr->left_childptr,
                            Key);
      else    // (Key > tree_ptr->data)
         // Search for "Key" in the right subtree
         search_node_in_BST(tree_ptr->right_childptr,
                            Key);
   }
   else {
         printf("\n search_node_in_BST: Node %d %s \n",
               Key, "is not found");
         return (NULL);
   }
}

void Binary_Search_Tree::search_node(DATA_TYPE srch_key)
{
   TREE_PTR srch_ptr = NULL;
   srch_ptr = search_node_in_BST(root_ptr, srch_key);
   if (srch_ptr != NULL)
      printf("\n\n Node: %d is found in the BST\n",
            srch_ptr->data);
}
```

A binary tree search for a node with key 12 in **Code 7.16** yields:

```
OBJECT-ORIENTED IMPLEMENTATION OF BINARY SEARCH TREE

The Binary Search Tree after PostOrder traversal:
7   12   25   15   5   35   45   70   60   33

The Binary Search Tree after PreOrder traversal:
33   5   15   12   7   25   60   45   35   70

The Binary Search Tree after InOrder traversal:
5   7   12   15   25   33   35   45   60   70

Node: 12 is found in the BST
```

Performance Analysis of Searching a Binary Search Tree

`Search_node_in_BST()` in **Code 7.16** performs the search for a node specified by the key `srch_key` in a BST with n number of nodes.

The best case occurs when the BST is empty or the node with `srch_key` is at the root of BST. In either case, it requires only one comparison; the best-case performance is $O(1)$.

The worst case occurs when the target node is not in the BST or is the leaf node (at the bottom level) of the BST. Possible forms of a BST are: (1) degenerate, (2) nondegenerate or nearly balanced or balanced (see Chapter 8). Binary tree search in a degenerate BST with n nodes does $O(n)$ number of comparisons.

When the BST is balanced, the nodes are almost equally distributed in the left and right subtrees of the root node. That is, such a BST is partitioned into two equal halves by the root node. This BST has 1 node (i.e., root node) at level 1, 2 nodes at level 2, 4 nodes at level 3, and $2(\log_2(n-1))$ at level $(n-1)$. During the search for a node with `srch_key`, the BST search method searches either the left subtree or the right subtree. This yields only one comparison at any level. Since such a well-behaved BST with n nodes has $\log_2 n$ levels, there are at most $\log_2 n$ number of comparisons.

Hence, the best-case performance of searching the BST is between $O(n)$ and $O(\log_2 n)$.

7.2.9   HASH STRATEGY FOR HASH SEARCH METHOD

The discussion so far included several types of search methods for such data structures as arrays, singly or doubly linked lists, and binary trees. Keeping the advantages and disadvantages of these methods in mind, the *hash search method* is now discussed. The hash search method requires a special data structure: (1) *hash table with buckets*, or (2) *hash table with linked lists*, called *chains*. This data structure, unique to hashing, is a merger of an array-based list and linked list structures.

This section discusses the concept of hash table, hash table object, many forms of hash functions, rehashing, algorithms for overflow and collision using buckets and chaining, and hash search methods. OOP implementations for (1) hashing with buckets and (2) hashing with chaining will be presented.

Hash Tables

In hash strategy, the goal is to devise a data structure that makes random searching efficient in both performance and storage usage. In hash strategy, the data elements or the pointers to the linked lists (chains) of data elements are kept in an array-based data structure, called the *hash table*. A data element may be simple or complex, but must be *identified by a single key*, which is used for searching.

The hash table `hash_table` is divided into `HT_SIZE` number of buckets, `hash_table[0]`, ..., `hash_table[HT_SIZE - 1]`. Each bucket contains p number of *slots*, each slot being sufficiently large to hold the data elements (*records*). Since the size `HT_SIZE` of the array-based hash table is fixed, this hash strategy is also called *static hashing*. The entries in the hash table categorize the hash table into two:

1. Hash table with buckets (or *Hash table with array-based buckets*),

2. Hash table with chaining (or *Hash table with linked list-based buckets*).

These two data structures will be discussed after hash functions.

A *hash table object* is specified by an ADT hash table. An ADT hash table contains buckets with data elements as its data, and some common operations:

Hash Table Object Methods

Construct a hash table.
Destroy a hash table.
Insert a data element in a hash table identified by key.
Search a data element in a hash table identified by key.
Delete a data element in a hash table identified by key.
Retrieve a data element in a hash table identified by key.
Print a data element in a hash table identified by key.

In order to perform these operations, the hash table object is required to calculate the address (location) of the data element with a specified `key` in the hash table using some mapping function Hash(key). Such a function is called a *hash function*, which produces the desired address for the given key. The address is called the *hash value* or *hashed key*; it is the transformed value of the given key through the hash function. The hash value is the index in the array-based hash table hash_table[], and is, therefore a nonnegative integer. For the hash_table[0], ..., hash_table[HT_SIZE-1], the hash of the key ranges from 0 to (HT_SIZE - 1) and is given by

Hash(key) = Address of the data element with the key in the hash
            table hash_table[].

The implementation of a hash table uses one of the two data structuring techniques:

1. Hash table with buckets, where an array is used for the hash table and each bucket is an array of p number of slots, each slot being large enough to contain one data element (record).

2. Hash table with chaining, where an array is used for the hash table and each bucket is a singly or doubly linked list or even a tree of any variable number of slots (called *nodes*), each chain node being large enough to contain one data element (record).

In sequential (linear) searching methods, we allocate an array of size n for n data elements, and the searching is sequentially performed from first to last. In hashing strategy, the goal is to provide fast and random access of the data elements. For n data elements, the size HT_SIZE of the hash table is not the same as n; it is dependent on n as well as the type of hash function used. For some hash functions, the table size is usually chosen as a prime number of the form $4i+3$ for an integer $i = 0, 1, 2$, and so on. For generality, given a collection of n data elements, the hash_table[HT_SIZE] has $(m = $ HT_SIZE$)$ number of buckets and each bucket has p number of slots such that $n = m \times p = $ HT_SIZE $\times$ p. To illustrate, for 15 members in the People database (see Appendix C), each data element is a record with one field key as the key. If HT_SIZE = 5, then each bucket has $15/5 = 3$ slots. Thus, for the People database with 15 members, the hash table is of size 5 with 3 slots per bucket, and is shown in Figure 7.11, in which the hash value ranges from 0 to 4.

Thus, when hash strategy with buckets is used, the data elements and the hash table are defined as follows:

```
const int HT_SIZE  = 5;
const int NSLOTS   = 3;

typedef char            DATA_TYPE;
typedef unsigned short  KEY_TYPE;
struct   SLOT_ELEMENT {
    KEY_TYPE    key;    // Search key
```

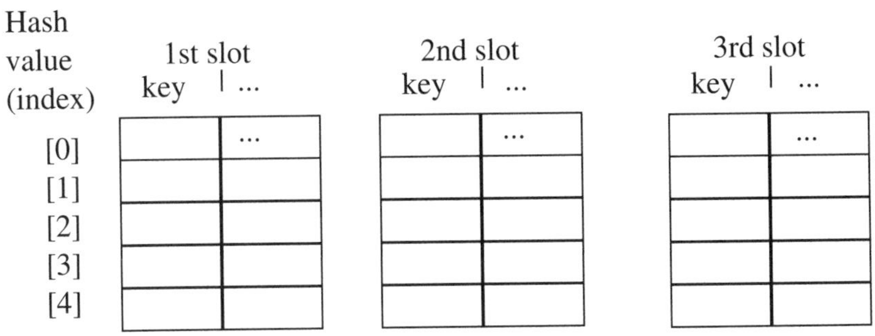

FIGURE 7.11. Hash table with five buckets and three slots per bucket.

```
    char *name;        // name
    char *occupation;  // occupation
    int  age;          // age
    int  income;       // yearly gross (x $1000)
    int  years;        // number years member
};
typedef   SLOT_ELEMENT   BUCKET[NSLOTS];
typedef   BUCKET         HASH_Table[HT_SIZE];
```

Such operations as insertion, deletion, and search of an element identified by a key in an ADT hash table are discussed later. Its OOP implementation is left as an exercise.

The other method of structuring a hash table is called *hashing with chaining* (see discussion on chaining). When hash strategy with chaining is used, the hash table is an array of head pointers to singly or doubly linked lists or trees, also called *chains* (shown later in Figure 7.14). Like bucket selection, the hashed value of a given key is computed using a hash function, and is the chain number (i.e., index) in the hash table. Since the worst-case performance of the search in a singly or doubly linked list is linear and $O(p)$ for p data elements, the efficiency of this chaining scheme depends on the uniform distribution of data elements in the chains.

For hashing with chaining, three ways to organize the hash table are:

1. Each chain as a singly linked list and the hash table as an array of pointers, each one of the pointers pointing to the head of one chain.

2. Each chain as a doubly linked list and the hash table as an array of pointers, each one of the pointers pointing to the head of one chain.

3. Each chain as a binary search tree or an AVL tree (see Chapter 8) and the hash table as an array of pointers, each one of the pointers pointing to the root of one chain.

For the first approach in hash chaining, assuming each chain as a singly linked list and hash_table as an array of pointers (each pointing to the head of one chain), the ADT chained hash structure is defined as follows:

```
typedef char              DATA_TYPE;
typedef unsigned short    KEY_TYPE;
typedef struct CHAIN_ELEMENT {
    KEY_TYPE         key;
    DATA_TYPE        data;
    CHAIN_ELEMENT    *next;
} *CHAIN_PTR;


int         HT_SIZE;  // Hash Table Size
CHAIN_PTR   **hash_table;
```

Its OOP implementation is left as an exercise. For reference, see the class Hash_Chain defined for a doubly linked chain.

For the second approach, if each chain is assumed to be a doubly linked list, each element in the chain is defined as a struct CHAIN_ELEMENT:

```
typedef struct CHAIN_ELEMENT {
    KEY_TYPE         key;
    DATA_TYPE        data;
    CHAIN_ELEMENT    *next,
                     *prev;
} *CHAIN_PTR;
int         HT_SIZE;        // Hash Table Size
CHAIN_PTR   **hash_table;
```

CHAIN_ELEMENT is later used in defining a Hash_Chain class for a complete OOP implementation.

For the third approach, if the chain is assumed to be a binary tree, struct TREE_NODE may be defined as follows:

```
typedef struct TREE_NODE {
    KEY_TYPE         key;
    DATA_TYPE        data;
    TREE_NODE        *l_node_ptr,
                     *r_node_ptr;
} *TREE_PTR;
int         HT_SIZE;
TREE_PTR   **hash_table;
```

Hash Functions

Since a hash function (or *hashing function*) is the key concept to the implementation, it is necessary to discuss the hash function. A hash function produces the hash value (address in the hash table), which is used to first insert a data element in the hash table with buckets or with chains. The hash values are the mappings of the keys as the indexes in the hash table. The generation of the hash values is important to uniformly distribute the data elements in the hash table. The uniform distribution will speed up the performance of all operations, including search, in the hash strategy.

The judicious selection of the hash function and hash table size dictates the efficiency of hash strategy. The hash table size is influenced by the hash function. For efficiency, the optimum value for a chain depth ranges from 4 to 8.

A generic hash function does not exist. However, there are several forms of hash function. An application determines the adoption of a hash function. These hash functions are discussed and implemented:

1. Modulus hash function for integers.

2. Modulus hash function for a pointer-based character string.

3. Folding hash function for integers.

4. Folding hash function for pointer-based character strings.

5. Digit analysis-based hash functions for character strings: (i) bit extraction–based hash function, (ii) digit analysis–based folding hash function for character string, (iii) multiplication-based hash function.

6. Bloom filter hash functions for rehashing.

Modulus Hash Function for Integers

The *modulus* (or *division*) *hash function* uses the *modulo* operation:

key % ¡size of hash table¿ (i.e., modulo the size of array).

Using the modulus operator %, Modulus_Hash_Func() yields the hash value for KEY_TYPE keys, which is an index in the hash_table[]. It returns one of the remainders 0, 1, ..., (HT_SIZE - 1). Its C++ code is:

```
typedef  unsigned        HASH_VALUE;
typedef  unsigned short  KEY_TYPE;

HASH_VALUE  Modulus_Hash_Func (KEY_TYPE key)
{
    return (key % HT_SIZE);
}
```

Since the index in the hash table is the hashed value and the location of the key, its type KEY_TYPE must be an unsigned integer. HASH_VALUE is also an unsigned integer. A prime number of the form $(4i + 3)$ for an integer $i = 0, 1, 2, ...$, is recommended for HT_SIZE. For example, when dealing with 3-digit integers ranging from 000 to 999, it is good to use HT_SIZE = 127.

Modulus Hash Function for a Pointer-Based Character String

Mod_Str_Hash() is useful for searching for a key, which is a pointer-based character string.

```
typedef  KEY_TYPE  *key;
HASH_VALUE  Mod_Str_Hash (KEY_TYPE key)
{
    return ( ((unsigned) key) % 0xFF);
}
```

The *modulus hash function* is found very effective. However, given a small set of integer keys, it is useful to devise a hash function that picks just one digit, say the nth one, as the hash value.

Folding Hash Function for Integers

There are two ways to accomplish folding of the integers: (1) *folding the high-order and low-order digits* or (2) *folding (swapping) the boundaries of an n-digit integer*. A folding method is known to distribute the keys well dispersed in a hash table. A *folding hash function* is a uniform hash function.

A folding hash function for integers extracts some high-order and some low-order digits of an integer key. It then puts them together to form an integer. The modulus of the new integer with respect to the hash table size is used as the hash value for the original integer key. For example, for a 8-digit integer key, the left lower half and the right upper half are extracted in the folding process as follows:

```
typedef  unsigned long int  KEY_TYPE;
HASH_VALUE  Fold_Integer_Hash (KEY_TYPE key)
{
    return ((key / 10000 + key % 10000) % HT_SIZE);
}
```

To illustrate, let key = 87629426, and HT_SIZE = 251. The hash value produced by Fold_Integer_Hash() is:

```
  (87629426/10000 + 87629426%10000) % 251
= (8762 + 9426) % 251 = 116
```

Folding Hash Function for Character Strings

This hash function is useful for applications involving symbols and names. The hash value for character strings can be computed using a folding hash function that adds ASCII values of each character and takes the modulus with respect to the hash table size. Its code is:

```
typedef  char  *KEY_TYPE;
HASH_VALUE  Fold_String_Hash (char *key)
{
    unsigned  sum_ascii_values = 0;

    while (*key != '\0')
        sum_ascii_values += *key++;
```

```
    //  take the modulus
    return (sum_ascii_values % HT_SIZE);
}
```

For example, for the string "PRATIVA" and HT_SIZE = 31, the hash value yielded by Fold_String_Hash() is:

```
  (P  + R  + A  + T  + I  + V  + A) % 31
= (80 + 82 + 65 + 84 + 73 + 86 + 65) % 31 (in ASCII value)
= 8
```

Digit Analysis–Based Hash Functions for Character Strings

The *digit analysis–based hash function* is useful in handling static files, its keys already being known. It is based on analyzing the digits of a key. In order to calculate the address (hash value) of a given key, the digit analysis decides the radix r and uses a combination of the bit (or r-based digit) patterns of the character. There are several variations of digit analysis–based hash functions. Some basic digit analysis may include any one or any combination of the following fundamental methods:

1. Extraction

2. Combination or compression

3. Multiplication

The digit analysis is based on the ASCII or bit representation. To illustrate the three methods, we consider the string based key "LOPA", and represent it as a bit string:

```
      L           O           P           A
    0x4c        0x4f        0x50        0x41      (in hex, r = 16)
  01001100    01001111    01010000    01000001  (in binary, r=2)
```

Bit Extraction–Based Hash Function

The *bit extraction–based hash function* extracts a certain number of random bits from the given character string to yield a string. The number of bits is small enough so that the hashed string is an address within the permissible index 0, ..., (HT_SIZE - 1) of the hash table. For example, bits 2, 6, 10, 14, 18, 22, 26, and 30 are extracted to form the new hashed value 00010000, which is 10 in hex. Such extraction-based hash function yields *collision*. That is, any two distinct keys, e.g., k1 and k2, will have the hashed value Hash(k1) = Hash(k2). The techniques to handle and resolve collisions are discussed later. When a collision occurs repeatedly, a family of hash functions is used; this technique is called *rehashing*. It may be worth considering all of the bits in the key.

```
MSB                                              LSB
!                                                !
01001100    01001111   01010000   01000001
  -    -       -     -      -    -     -    -
```

Digit Analysis–Based Folding Hash Function for Character String

For a character string key, the folding hash function that uses digit analysis is also known as the *compression hash function*. It uses such logical bit operations as *XOR* (exclusive or) and *AND* to produce a hash value in the hash table. For the four character string key, a simple folding hash function *XOR*ed the first and fourth characters and the second and third characters; their results are then folded to produce a hash value within the permissible index of the hash table. Its code is:

```
typedef  unsigned  HASH_VALUE;
static int HT_SIZE = 63;
typedef  char      *KEY_TYPE;  // string type

HASH_VALUE  Digit_Fold_String_Hash(char *key)
{
   HASH_VALUE
     hash = ((key[0]^key[3]) ^ (key[1]^key[2])) %
                HT_SIZE));
   return (hash);
}
```

Given the string "LOPA" and HT_SIZE = 31, the hash value yielded by Digit_Fold_String_Hash() is:

```
  ((76 ^ 65) ^ (79 ^ 80)) % 31
= ( 13 ^ 31) %  31 =  18
```

Since *XOR* is commutative, this hash function produces the same hash value for the strings "AOPL", "LPOA", "APOL". That is,

```
        Digit_Fold_String_Hash("LOPA") = 18
        Digit_Fold_String_Hash("AOPL") = 18
        Digit_Fold_String_Hash("LPOA") = 18
        Digit_Fold_String_Hash("APOL") = 18
```

Since these four character string based keys are hashed (mapped) to the same hash value, they form a *cluster*, and there is a collision. This example indicates that *clusters of keys are to be broken up.*

Multiplication-Based Hash Function

The *digit analysis hash function* is formed by using *multiplication*. For some real number R between 0.0 and 1.0 but far away from them, the hashed value for a real number key k is:

$$hash(k) = (\text{integer value of } (k * m))$$

For the multiplier m, $m = (\sqrt{5} - 1)/2$ or $m = 1 - (\sqrt{5} - 1)/2$, such a hash function hash() yields the uniform distribution.

Bloom Filter Hash Functions for Rehashing

A set of hash functions called *bloom filters* that is useful for rehashing is presented by Ramakrishna [Ram89] as follows:

$$Hash_{a,b}(key) = ((a * key + b)/q)/n$$

where q is a large prime number, n is a power of 2, and $0 < a < q$ and $0 \le b < q$.

Inserting a Key in a Hash Table with Single-Slot Bucket

Consider first the insert operation for hashing with buckets, each bucket holding single or multiple slots. For the hash strategy with chaining, the insertion of an element is discussed and implemented later (see hash table with chaining object).

To illustrate the insert operation in a hash table with a bucket that has one slot sufficiently large to hold a record, a modulus hash function is used, Hash(key) = key % 4. For a given key k, compute Hash(k), the "Hashed value" say addr_k, which is a location in the hash table hash_table[] with only one slot per bucket. Insert k in hash_table[addr_k]. Figure 7.12 illustrates this process for a key, k = 9, and the computed hash value Hash(9) = 1. Using 1 as the index in the array-based hash table, insertion of the key 9 is done by setting hash_table[1] = 9.

In a hash table with single slot bucket, two different keys may be hashed to the same hash value. That is, for two different k_1 and k_2,

$$Hash(k_1) = Hash(k_2).$$

This is called *collision*. For example, collision occurs for the keys 9 and 21, since Hash(9) = 9 % 4 = 1, and Hash(21) = 21 % 4 = 1. There are five approaches to handle collision in a hash table:

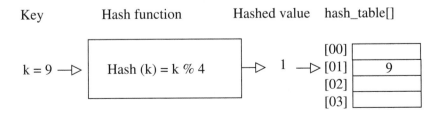

FIGURE 7.12. Insertion of a key in a hash table with buckets, one slot per bucket.

1. Hashing with single-slot buckets

2. Linear probing, or linear hash search

3. Hashing with multiple-slot buckets

4. Rehashing

5. Hashing with chaining.

Note that computing the hash value for a given key is the fundamental step in the insert, delete, search, modify, and retrieve operations in a hash table.

Collision Handling Using Hash Search with Linear Probing

As pointed out earlier, a collision may occur for inserting two different keys in a hash table with buckets, one slot per bucket. This means that the two unequal keys are hashed to the address of the same bucket in the hash table. For a hash table with single-slot buckets, the collision is handled using the *linear search method,* also called *linear probing* or *linear open addressing.* The linear probing method dictates both insertion and search. It assumes that the hash table is initialized such that an empty slot can be detected. For insertion, it first computes the hash value; if the corresponding slot in the hash table is not empty, that is, the slot is occupied by another key and the collision has occurred, it starts linear (sequential) probing for an empty slot by treating the hash table as a circular array starting from the circular index, which is initially a hashed value. It computes the next circular index (i.e., bucket address in the circular hash table) by the formula:

circular index = (circular index + hashed value) modulus (size of the hash table)

If the test of the wraparound condition shows that the circular index equals the hashed value, no empty slot (bucket) is found, the hash table is full, and the linear probing returns with failure.

Given a hash function Hash(k) for inserting a given key k in a hash table hash_table[] of single-slot buckets, the algorithm for linear probing (searching) is:

Step 1. (Assumption) Each bucket (slot) of the hash table is initialized to blank. A blank space means an empty slot.

Step 2. Compute hashed value for the given key k:

```
hashed_value = Hash(k);
circular_index = hashed_value;
```

Step 3. If hash_table[hashed_value] is empty, return the address hashed_value in the hash table. Otherwise, "collision has occurred," and go to Step 4.

Step 4. (*Collision resolution*) Treat hash_table[] as a circular array. Starting from the hash_table[hashed_value] to the hash_table[hashed_value - 1], perform search for an empty slot in a circular manner:

```
circular_index = (circular_index + hashed_value) %
                 (size_of_hash_table);
```

Step 5. Check wraparound condition for circular_index.

Step 6. If an empty slot is found, return the associated array index of hash_table[].

Step 7. If no empty slot is found, print an error message "Hash table is full" and return an invalid hash table index, -1.

Hash_Linear_Probe_and_Search() in **Code 7.17** implements this linear probing scheme. Another version of open addressing (probing) is called *quadratic probing*. It uses a quadratic formula (i.e., square of circular index in Step 4) for searching the buckets. Though linear probing successfully handles collision, it fails when the hash table is full, that is, when overflow occurs. In order to deal with this impasse, a hash table with buckets is considered, each bucket having multiple slots.

Code 7.17 shows an OOP implementation of a hash table object with single-slot hash table and linear probing.

Code 7.17

```
// Program: Hash_Bucket.c++
// Purpose:
//   OOP implementation of hash table
//   of single-slot buckets with linear
//   search (probing) for collision handling.
//
#include <stdio.h>
constint  Empty  = ' ';
typedef unsigned    KEY_TYPE;
typedef unsigned    HASH_VALUE;
typedef unsigned    HASH_INDEX;
typedef char        DATA_TYPE;
class Hash_Single_Bucket {
  private:
    typedef struct  DATA_RECORD {
          DATA_TYPE  data;
          KEY_TYPE   key;
```

```
    } SINGLE_SLOT_BUCKET;

    // SINGLE_SLOT_BUCKET  circ_hash_table[HT_SIZE];
    int   HT_SIZE;
    SINGLE_SLOT_BUCKET *circ_hash_table;
    void          Init_Hash_Tab (void);
  public:
    Hash_Single_Bucket(int table_size);
    ~Hash_Single_Bucket();
    HASH_VALUE  Hash_Function (KEY_TYPE key);
    int         Hash_Linear_Probe_and_Search
                      (KEY_TYPE srch_key);
    void        Insert_Hash_Bucket
          (KEY_TYPE new_key, DATA_TYPE new_data);
    void        Build_Single_Bucket_Hash_Table(void);
    void        Print_Hash_Table(void);
};

//  Constructor
Hash_Single_Bucket::Hash_Single_Bucket(int table_size)
{
    HT_SIZE   = table_size;
    circ_hash_table = new SINGLE_SLOT_BUCKET[HT_SIZE];
    Init_Hash_Tab();
}

//  Destructor
Hash_Single_Bucket::~Hash_Single_Bucket()
{
    delete  []circ_hash_table;
}

//  Initialize circular hash table
void Hash_Single_Bucket::Init_Hash_Tab (void)
{
    for (int i = 0; i < HT_SIZE; i++) {
        circ_hash_table[i].key  = Empty;
        circ_hash_table[i].data = Empty;
    }
}


HASH_VALUE  Hash_Single_Bucket::Hash_Function
                                (KEY_TYPE key)
{
    return (key % HT_SIZE);
}

//  Hash search with linear probing
int Hash_Single_Bucket::Hash_Linear_Probe_and_Search
                      (KEY_TYPE srch_key)
{
    //  Calculate the hashed value for "srch_key"
    int hashed_value = Hash_Function (srch_key);
    int circular_index = hashed_value;
```

```
    //  Start linear search of the hash table for
    //  an empty slot; the hash table is used as a
    //  "circular array".
    //
    while (
      (circ_hash_table[circular_index].key != Empty) &&
      (circ_hash_table[circular_index].key == srch_key)){
        // Increase the index and look for an empty slot
        circular_index = (circular_index +
                            hashed_value) % HT_SIZE;
        //  Check "wrap around condition"
        if (circular_index == hashed_value) {
          printf("\n Hash_Linear_Probe_and_Search: %s",
                "Full Hash Table\n");
          return (-1);  // Return an out of range value
        }
    }
    return (circular_index);
}  // -- End of Hash_Linear_Probe_and_Search() --

void  Hash_Single_Bucket::Insert_Hash_Bucket
        (KEY_TYPE  new_key, DATA_TYPE new_data)
{
    int  hash_index;
    hash_index = Hash_Linear_Probe_and_Search(new_key);
    if (hash_index != -1) {
        circ_hash_table[hash_index].data = new_data;
        circ_hash_table[hash_index].key  = new_key;
    }
}

void Hash_Single_Bucket::Build_Single_Bucket_Hash_Table
                                (void)
{
    Insert_Hash_Bucket (23, 'P');
    Insert_Hash_Bucket (12, 'R');
    Insert_Hash_Bucket (25, 'A');
    Insert_Hash_Bucket (28, 'T');
    Insert_Hash_Bucket (99, 'I');
    Insert_Hash_Bucket (11, 'V');
    Insert_Hash_Bucket (12, 'A');
}

void Hash_Single_Bucket::Print_Hash_Table(void)
{
    printf ("\n        OOP IMPLEMENTATION OF");
    printf ("\n   Hash Table with %s \n",
            "Single-Slot Buckets");
    for (int i = 0; i < HT_SIZE; i++)
        printf ("\n     Hash_Tabl[%d] = %c", i,
                circ_hash_table[i].data);
}
```

```
//  Test driver for OOP implementation of hash search
//  and collision handling using linear probing in
//  a hash table with single-slot buckets.
void main ()
{
    Hash_Single_Bucket ht_bucket_obj(10);

    ht_bucket_obj.Build_Single_Bucket_Hash_Table();
    ht_bucket_obj.Print_Hash_Table();
    printf ("\n");
}
```

Code 7.17 for linear probing yields this output:

```
    OOP IMPLEMENTATION OF
Hash Table with Single-Slot Buckets

  Hash_Tabl[0] =
  Hash_Tabl[1] = V
  Hash_Tabl[2] = R
  Hash_Tabl[3] = P
  Hash_Tabl[4] = A
  Hash_Tabl[5] = A
  Hash_Tabl[6] =
  Hash_Tabl[7] =
  Hash_Tabl[8] = T
  Hash_Tabl[9] = I
```

Build_Single_Bucket_Hash_Table() in **Code 7.17** shows that the two keys 12 for data 'R' and data 'A' have the same hashed value; a collision occurred in this case, and Hash_Linear_Probe_and_Search() resolves this collision. Data 'R' is in Hash_Tabl[2], and data 'A' is stored in the next available slot Hash_Tabl[4].

Collision and Overflow Handling Using Multiple-Slot Buckets

In order to handle both collision and overflow in a hash table with single-slot buckets, the bucket size is increased from 1 to m, for example. For a hash table hash_table[n] of n buckets, each bucket has m slots, and each slot is large enough to hold a record. This method is called *hashing with buckets*. This hash table can hold at most $n \times m$ records.

To illustrate the insertion, collision, and overflow, we consider a modulus hash function, Hash(k) = k % 10, a hash table hash_table[10] of ten buckets, and each bucket has three slots. Hash_table[] is an array of arrays, as shown in Figure 7.13. It may contain at most $10 \times 3 = 30$ records. Figure 7.13 shows insertion and collision of records with keys 33 and 73.

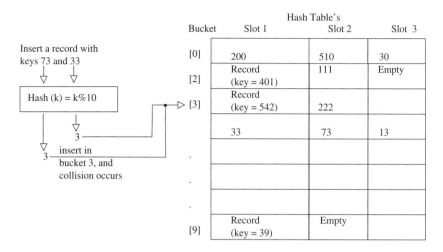

FIGURE 7.13. Inserting and handling collision in a hash table with buckets, three slots per bucket.

In Figure 7.13, the hashed value of 33 is `Hash(33)` = 33 % 10 = 3; key 33 is inserted in the first empty slot, slot number 1, in bucket 3 of the hash table. Since the hashed value of the record with key 73 is 3, the record with key 73 needs to be inserted in bucket 3. Since the hashed value of keys 33 and 73 is 3, and slot 1 of bucket 3 is occupied by the record with key 33, the collision of keys 33 and 73 occurs and is resolved by inserting 73 in the next available slot, say slot number 2, of bucket 3 of the hash table. The next record with key 13 has the hashed value 3, and is inserted in slot 3 of bucket 3. Now, if one wants to insert a record with key 43, whose hashed value is also 3, overflow occurs since bucket 3 is fully occupied. This overflow condition may be handled by the similar linear search (probe) method discussed earlier. Though the collision and overflow conditions are successfully handled so far, an impasse will be created when the 31st record needs to be inserted. This is because the hash table becomes full after the 30th record is inserted. However, if collision is too frequent, it is recommended to use *rehashing*, which defines and allows one to apply a set of hash functions. This impasse condition of overflow and collision can be successfully and efficiently handled by the *hashing with chaining* strategy.

Collision and Overflow Handling Using Hashing with Chaining

The hashing with chaining strategy requires that the data structure for the hash table is an array of pointers, with each pointer pointing to the head of a chain of records (also called *nodes*). Each chain is structured as a singly linked list. Since each is a singly linked list, each chain can dynamically grow or shrink in size, and alleviates any possibility of overflow. In this

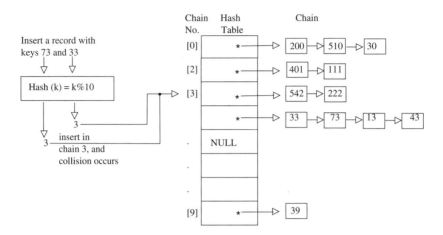

FIGURE 7.14. Inserting and handling collision in a hash table with chaining.

array of pointers based hash table, hash_table[], the hashed value of a given key is computed, and it is the index in the hash table, or the *chain number*.

To illustrate the insertion and collision in a hash table with chaining, a modulus hash function, Hash(k) = k % 10, and a hash_table[10] of 10 pointers to chains of records are considered. The hash_table[] is an array of pointers, as shown in Figure 7.14. It can contain any number of records, limited by the available memory space. Figure 7.14 shows insertion and collision of records with keys 33 and 73.

Figure 7.14 resolves collisions by hashing with chaining strategy. In Figure 7.14, a right arrow → means a link to the next record in the same chain; two records with the same hash value of their keys get into collision and are inserted into the same chain. Initially, the entries in the hash table have NULL pointer values because the chains are empty. For example, the records with keys 33, 73, and 13 have the same hashed value (chain number) 3. Inserting a record with key 43 does not cause overflow; it is simply inserted in chain number 3. One may either add the new record at the front or at the rear of the chain. In this case, the limit on the number of records per chain is imposed by the available memory space. This means overflow of chains will not occur until the computer system runs out of its available memory space.

Algorithm: Inserting a Node into a Hash Table with Chaining

This algorithm assumes that when a node specified by a key k, is inserted at the front of the singly linked list (chain), the same key k does not exist in the same chain already.

Step 1. Compute the chain number hash_index (an index of the array hash_table[]) for the specified key k using the hash function Hash(k): hash_index = Hash(k)

Step 2. Get the chain_head_ptr, the pointer to the head of the singly linked list corresponding to the hash_index. Since the list's head is stored in hash_table[hash_index],

chain_head_ptr = hash_table[hash_index];

Step 3. Get memory space for the new element pointed to by new_ptr using the new operator, and set the new element's key and data to given key and data values. If no memory space is available, exit with an error message.

Step 4. Check whether the associated list (chain) is empty by comparing chain_head_ptr with NULL. If the chain is empty, add the new node's new_ptr at the head of the chain.

hash_table[hash_index] = new_ptr; return;

Step 5. If the chain is not empty, i.e., chain_head_ptr ≠ NULL, insert the new node at the front of the list by making the node at the list's head the successor of the new node.

new_ptr->next = chain_head_ptr;

hash_table[hash_index] = new_ptr;

Insert_Hash_Chain_Node() implements this algorithm and its code is shown later. The hash strategy with chaining resolves both the overflow and collisions.

For hashing with chaining strategy, an ADT hash structure is considered, which specifies Hash_Chain type object with the following operations:

1. Constructing and initializing a Hash_Chain type object.

2. Destroying a Hash_Chain type object.

3. Inserting a record (node) in the hash table.

4. Building a chained hash table.

5. Deleting a record identified by its key from the hash table.

6. Searching for a record identified by its key in the hash table.

7. Retrieving a record identified by its key from the hash table.

Each chain is assumed to be a doubly linked list; the hash_table is an array of pointers to these lists; and the size of hash_table is defined by HTSIZE. Then for an OOP implementation of hashing with chaining, the Hash_Chain class is defined to implement the above operations as the public member functions of the Hash_Chain class.

```
#include <stdio.h>

// Define "Hash_Chain" class for Hash
// Chaining strategy
//
class Hash_Chain {
  private:
    typedef char            DATA_TYPE;
    typedef unsigned short  KEY_TYPE;
    typedef unsigned        HASH_VALUE;
    typedef struct CHAIN_ELEMENT {
       KEY_TYPE        key;
       DATA_TYPE       data;
       CHAIN_ELEMENT   *next;
       CHAIN_ELEMENT   *prev;
    } *CHAIN_PTR;
    int  HT_SIZE; // Hash Table Size
    CHAIN_ELEMENT **hash_table;
    void       Init_Hash_Chain (void);
  public:
    Hash_Chain(int table_size);
    ~Hash_Chain();

    HASH_VALUE Hash_Function (KEY_TYPE key);
    CHAIN_PTR  Create_Chain_Node (KEY_TYPE  k,
                           DATA_TYPE new_data);
    void       Insert_Hash_Chain_Node (KEY_TYPE k,
                           DATA_TYPE new_data);
    void       Create_Chained_Hash_Table (void);
    void       Delete_Hash_Chain_Node (KEY_TYPE k);
    CHAIN_PTR  Search_Hash_Chain_Node (KEY_TYPE k);
    void       Retrieve_Hash_Chain_Node(KEY_TYPE k);
};
typedef  CHAIN_ELEMENT    *CHAIN_PTR;
```

Hash_Chain(), a public member function of the Hash_Chain class, is the constructor for hash chaining strategy. It defines the type of a Hash_Chain object. It initializes the dimension HT_SIZE to table_size and allocates memory space of the chained hash table hash_table[] by using the new operator; the entries in the hash table are pointers of type CHAIN_PTR. Its code is:

```
//
// Hash_Chain():
//    Constructor for "Hash_Chain"-type object.
//
Hash_Chain::Hash_Chain (int table_size)
```

```
{
    HT_SIZE = table_size;
    hash_table = new CHAIN_PTR[HT_SIZE];
    Init_Hash_Chain();
}
```

~Hash_Chain(), a public member function of the Hash_Chain class, is the destructor of a Hash_Chain type object. It frees memory space for all chains, and the chained hash table, hash_table[] of size HTSIZE by using the delete operator. As discussed in Chapter 5, it iteratively deletes each node of each doubly linked list (chain). Its code is:

```
// ~Hash_Chain():
//    Destructor for hash chaining strategy.
//
Hash_Chain::~Hash_Chain()
{
    HASH_VALUE   chain_index;
    CHAIN_PTR    chain_head_ptr, next_ptr;

    for (chain_index = 0; chain_index < HT_SIZE;
         chain_index++) {
        // Delete each chain
        chain_head_ptr = hash_table[chain_index];
        while (chain_head_ptr != NULL) {
            next_ptr = chain_head_ptr->next;
            delete  chain_head_ptr;
            chain_head_ptr = next_ptr;
        }
    }
    // Delete the array 'hash_table[HTSIZE]'
    delete [] hash_table;
}
```

Init_Hash_Chain() is made private member function of the class Hash_Chain for protecting the Hash_Chain object. When the hash strategy with chaining is used, the hash table hash_table is an array of CHAIN_PTR type pointers to doubly linked lists, also known as *chains*. The chained hash table hash_table[] is initialized by setting each element of hash_table[] to NULL. Notice that hash_table[] does not hold the nodes of the chain. Here is the code:

```
// Init_Hash_Chain():
//    Initialize the hash table, an array of
//    CHAIN_PTR type pointers.
//
void Hash_Chain::Init_Hash_Chain (void)
{
    int j = HT_SIZE - 1;
    while (j >= 0) {
        hash_table[j] = NULL;
        j--;
    }
```

```
}
```

Hash_Function() is a public member function of the Hash_Chain class. It is a modulus hash function. It converts key using modular operation into a hashed value. Then it returns the hashed value, which is an index of the array, hash_table[]. Notice that this hash function is not different from the hash function used in the hash strategy with buckets.

```
//   Hash_Function():
//     This is a modulus hash function. As the hash
//     value, one of the remainders (0, 1, ...,
//     HT_SIZE - 1) is returned after
//     "key % HT_SIZE" is executed.
//
Hash_Chain::HASH_VALUE
Hash_Chain::Hash_Function (KEY_TYPE key)
{
    return (key % HT_SIZE);
}
```

Create_Chain_Node() is a public member function of the class Hash_Chain. It takes the two arguments new_key and new_data as inputs. It allocates memory space for the chain's node by using the new operator. If memory space is available, it sets the new node's components key to new_key, data to new_data and the pointer fields next and prev to NULL; it then returns the pointer of type CHAIN_PTR for this new node. Otherwise, it returns a NULL pointer; the calling function must check this pointer before using it. Its code is:

```
//
//   Create_Chain_Node():
//     Create a new node for the hash chain.
//     Allocate memory space.
//
Hash_Chain::CHAIN_PTR Hash_Chain::Create_Chain_Node
            (KEY_TYPE new_key, DATA_TYPE new_data)
{
    //
    //   Reserve a memory space for the new node
    //   with key 'new_key', & data 'new_data';
    //   In case of no memory space, return NULL.
    //
    CHAIN_PTR new_ptr = new CHAIN_ELEMENT;
    if (new_ptr != NULL) {
        new_ptr->key  = new_key;
        new_ptr->data = new_data;
        new_ptr->next = NULL;
        new_ptr->prev = NULL;
    }
    return (new_ptr);
}
```

Insert_Hash_Chain_Node() is a public member function of the Hash_Chain class. Its algorithm is previously presented. Here is the code for inserting an element in the hash table hash_table[] when hashing with chaining is used. Create_Chained_Hash_Table() calls it for creating a chained hash table.

```
void Hash_Chain::Insert_Hash_Chain_Node(KEY_TYPE new_key,
                                        DATA_TYPE new_data)
{
    CHAIN_PTR  chain_head_ptr, new_ptr;
    //
    //  Calculate the hash chain number in the hash
    //  table for the node with the given key 'k'.
    //

    HASH_VALUE hash_chain_no = Hash_Function (new_key);

    //  Using the hash chain number, get the pointer
    //  that points to the head of the singly linked
    //  list (chain) of hashed nodes.

    chain_head_ptr = hash_table[hash_chain_no];

    //  Reserve memory space for the new element
    new_ptr = Create_Chain_Node (new_key, new_data);
    if (new_ptr == NULL) {
      printf("\n Insert_Hash_Chain_Node: %s\n",
             "Out of memory");
      exit (-1);
    }
    //  Test to see if the associated chain is empty.
    if (chain_head_ptr != NULL)
      //
      //  The chain is not empty. Add the new node
      //  at the head of the chain.
      //
     new_ptr->next = chain_head_ptr;
    hash_table[hash_chain_no] = new_ptr;

}   //  End of Insert_Hash_Chain_Node()
```

Create_Chained_Hash_Table() is a public member function of the Hash_Chain class. It creates a chained hash table hash_table[] for a string "PRATIVA" with key values for each character. It repeatedly calls Insert_Hash_Chain_Node() to insert these characters in hash_table[]. To demonstrate, its code is written in a simple form:

```
void Hash_Chain::Create_Chained_Hash_Table (void)
{
    Insert_Hash_Chain_Node (23, 'P');
    Insert_Hash_Chain_Node (12, 'R');
    Insert_Hash_Chain_Node (25, 'A');
    Insert_Hash_Chain_Node (28, 'T');
```

```
    Insert_Hash_Chain_Node (99, 'I');
    Insert_Hash_Chain_Node (11, 'V');
    Insert_Hash_Chain_Node (12, 'A');
}
```

Delete_Hash_Chain_Node() is a public member function of the Hash_Chain class. It deletes a node specified by the key k, from a chain in the chained hash table hash_table. Search_Hash_Chain_Node() is first called, which returns a pointer srch_ptr of type CHAIN_PTR. If the node to be deleted is not found (i.e., srch_ptr == NULL), it simply returns. Otherwise, using the hash function Hash_Function(), it computes the hashed value for k, which is the hash_index, the chain index in hash_table[]. It gets the pointer to the head of the doubly linked list (chain) associated with hash_index. If the chain is nonempty and the node to be deleted is at the head of the chain, it changes the current successor of the head into the head, and deletes the space held by the target node with its key k. If the target node is between the head and the tail node of the chain, Delete_Hash_Chain_Node() establishes links between the previous (pointed to by srch_ptr->prev) and the next (pointed to by srch_ptr->next) nodes of the node to be deleted (pointed to by srch_ptr), and releases the memory space by using the delete operator. Here is the code for deleting an element specified by a key k, in the hash table when hashing with chaining is used.

```
void Hash_Chain::Delete_Hash_Chain_Node (KEY_TYPE k)
{
    CHAIN_PTR    chain_head_ptr, srch_ptr;

    // Search for target element given by key "k"
    srch_ptr = Search_Hash_Chain_Node (k);
    if (srch_ptr == NULL)   // not found
      return;
    //
    //  Calculate the hash chain number in the hash
    //  table for the node with the given key 'k'.
    //
    HASH_VALUE hash_chain_no = Hash_Function (k);

    //  Using the hash chain number, get the
    //  pointer that points to the head of singly
    //  linked list (chain) of hashed nodes.

    chain_head_ptr = hash_table[hash_chain_no];

    //  The chain is not empty. Is the node to be
    //  deleted at the head of the chain? If so,
    //  make its successor the new head, & delete it.

    if (srch_ptr == chain_head_ptr) {
     hash_table[hash_chain_no] = chain_head_ptr->next;
     delete  chain_head_ptr;
```

```
      return;
    }
    // The element to be deleted is an
    // intermediate node in the chain.
    srch_ptr->prev->next = srch_ptr->next;
    delete srch_ptr;
} //  End of Delete_Hash_Chain_Node()
```

Search_Hash_Chain_Node() is a public member function of the Hash_Chain class. For this hash search method, a new ADT structure, called a *chained hash table* hash_table[] is constructed. For hashing strategy with chaining, Search_Hash_Chain_Node() searches for a node specified by the key srch_key, in the hash table hash_table[0],..., hash_table[n-1], using the following steps:

Hash Search with Chaining Algorithm

Step 1. Calculate the hash chain number in the hash table for the node with the given key srch_key, using the modulus hash function, Hash_Function().

    hash_chain_no = Hash_Function (srch_key);

The hashed value hash_chain_no is the location of the associated chain in hash_table[], the array of pointers to chains.

Step 2. Using the hash chain number, get the pointer that points to the head of the doubly linked list (chain) of hashed nodes.

    chain_head_ptr = hash_table[hash_chain_no];

Step 3. Check to see if the associated chain is empty by comparing the chain_head_ptr with NULL. If it is empty, print a message "Empty chain" and return NULL. Otherwise, go to Step 4.

Step 4. (*Linear search step*) Compare srch_key with the key field of the first node in the chain pointed to by chain_head_ptr. If there is a match, return chain_head_ptr; else, go to Step 5 for comparing srch_key with the key field of successive nodes.

Step 5. (*Linear traversal*) Since the associated chain is a doubly linked list, do linear traversal of the chain starting from the head, chain_head_ptr, and advancing to the successive nodes using the next pointer field of chain_head_ptr.

Step 6. Repeat steps 4 and 5 until there is a match or the end of the chain is encountered.

Step 7. If the hash search fails, print a message "Element with key is not found in the chained hash table," and return NULL.

Search_Hash_Chain_Node() is a public member function of the Hash_Chain class. For the hash search using chaining, it implements the above algorithm. It assumes that multiple nodes with the same srch_key do not exist in the chain. Otherwise, it returns the pointer to the node with srch_key, encountered first. Its code is:

```
// Search_Hash_Chain_Node():
//    Implement search for hash chaining strategy.
//    If found, return a pointer of type CHAIN_PTR;
//    otherwise, return NULL.
//
Hash_Chain::CHAIN_PTR
Hash_Chain::Search_Hash_Chain_Node(KEY_TYPE srch_key)
{
    CHAIN_PTR   chain_head_ptr;

    //  Calculate the hash chain number in the hash
    //  table for the node with the given key 'srch_key'.

    HASH_VALUE hash_chain_no = Hash_Function (srch_key);

    //  Using the hash chain number, get the pointer
    //  that points to the head of the doubly linked
    //  list (chain) of hashed nodes.

    chain_head_ptr = hash_table[hash_chain_no];

    //  Test to see if the associated chain is empty?
    if (chain_head_ptr == NULL) {
      printf("\n Search_Hash_Chain_Node: Empty chain.\n");
      return (NULL);
    }
    //
    //  Doubly linked list (also called, chain)
    //  associated with this hash value is not empty.
    //  Iteratively do linear search on the chain
    //  pointed to by 'chain_head_ptr'.
    //
    while (chain_head_ptr != NULL) {
      if (chain_head_ptr->key == srch_key)
          return (chain_head_ptr);
      else
          chain_head_ptr = chain_head_ptr->next;
    }
    //  Hash search fails.
    printf("\n %s %u \n is not found in the %s \n",
        "Search_Hash_Chain_Node: Element with key",
        srch_key, "chained hash table.");
    return (NULL);
} //    End of Search_Hash_Chain_Node()
```

`Retrieve_Hash_Chain_Node()` is a public member function of the
Hash_Chain class. It retrieves a node (element) specified by its key k from
the chained hash table `hash_table[]`. `Search_Hash_Chain_Node()`
is called. If the search succeeds, it displays the key and data components
of the element. Its code is:

```
void Hash_Chain::Retrieve_Hash_Chain_Node(KEY_TYPE k)
{
   CHAIN_PTR  srch_ptr;
   if ((srch_ptr = Search_Hash_Chain_Node (k))
         != NULL) {
      printf("\n Hash chain search succeeds.");
      printf("\n Element's key  = %u",
               srch_ptr->key);
      printf("\n Element's data = %c \n",
               srch_ptr->data);
   }
}
```

Main() is the test driver for the hash strategy with chaining. Since it
is not a member of the Hash_Chain class, it declares and initializes a
Hash_Chain-type object hc_obj. Through the public member functions of hc_obj object, it passes such messages as "Create chained hash
table," "Retrieve an element (node)," and "Delete an element from the
chained hash table" to the object hc_obj. Its code is:

```
void  main(void)
{
   // Declare and initialize an object "hc_obj"
   // of "Hash_Chain" class; Hash table size = 5

   Hash_Chain hc_obj(5);

   printf("\n ** HASH SEARCH IN A HASH %s **",
            "CHAINING STRATEGY");
   hc_obj.Create_Chained_Hash_Table();
   hc_obj.Retrieve_Hash_Chain_Node (12);
   hc_obj.Retrieve_Hash_Chain_Node (44);
   hc_obj.Delete_Hash_Chain_Node (28);
   hc_obj.Retrieve_Hash_Chain_Node (28);
   hc_obj.Retrieve_Hash_Chain_Node (11);
}
```

Here is the output of the above chained hash strategy.

```
** HASH SEARCH IN A HASH CHAINING STRATEGY **
Hash chain search succeeds.
Element's key  = 12
Element's data = A

Search_Hash_Chain_Node: Element with key 44
is not found in the chained hash table.
```

```
Search_Hash_Chain_Node: Element with key 28
is not found in the chained hash table.

Hash chain search succeeds.
Element's key  = 11
Element's data = V
```

Though the hashing with chaining solves both collision and overflow, there may be a tendency of clustering of keys in some chains. Ideally, it is necessary to use a hash function that uniformly distributes keys in several chains with short depths. The uniform distribution of keys among chains saves the search time. In the worst case, all n number of records may cluster in one chain, and the search time is $O(n)$.

The main points for hashing are summarized below:

1. Hash strategy is a married form of random access in array and a sequential access in a linked list.

2. There are two types of hash strategies: (1) hashing with buckets and (2) hashing with chaining.

3. Hash search strategy requires a special ADT data structure, called a *hash table*.

4. A hash table is an array of either (a) buckets with single or multiple slots, large enough to hold the elements' records, or (b) pointers to chains that are singly or doubly linked lists of the elements' records.

5. Both the hash strategies convert the key of an element into a hashed value, the address of elements in the hash table, via the use of a hash function H().

6. Selection criteria of a hash function include (a) uniform distribution of keys in the hash table, (b) minimum number of collisions of keys, (c) efficient-handling of hash table overflow.

7. Hash search starts by translating the specified key to a hash value, which is the location in the hash table. It then performs search in the associated bucket, or in the associated chain list.

8. For a hash table with single- or multiple-slot buckets, *linear probing* and *rehashing* successfully handle collision; they fail to handle overflow.

9. Hashing with chaining successfully handles both collision and overflow.

7.2.10 PERFORMANCE ANALYSES OF SEARCHING ALGORITHMS

In previous sections, several search algorithms for an unsorted or sorted array, and for an unsorted or sorted linked list were discussed. Any one of these algorithms is not best and robust for all these data structures. For the selection of an appropriate search algorithm, the following points are generally checked:

1. The worst-case performance of search algorithm compared to the number of data elements.

2. Number of data elements, small or large.

3. Unsorted or sorted list data structure.

4. Static or dynamic list data structure.

5. Number of data elements, small or large.

6. Allowance of data element with the same key.

The worst-case performances of the search algorithms are summarized in Table 7.4.

Though it is complex to implement the search algorithms with worst-case performance $O(\log_2 \log_2 n)$ or $O(\log_2 n)$, these algorithms are more efficient than those search algorithms with performance $O(n)$ for n data elements.

7.3 Exercises

1. For an array-based list of n integer data, use the second version of insertion sort to arrange them in descending order. See Section 7.1.1.

2. Singly_Linked_List_Insertion_Sort: Given n names in a file, arrange them in lexicographically ascending order using insertion sort for a singly linked list. Store the sorted list in another file.

Search methods	Worst case (partial ordered)	Best case (ordered)
1. Linear search	$O(n)$	$O(n)$
2. Binary search	–	$O(\log_2 n)$
3. Interpolation search	–	$O(\log_2 \log_2 n)$
4. Hash search with buckets	$O(n)$	$O(1)$
5. Hash search with chaining	$O(n)$	$O(1)$

TABLE 7.4. Performances of search methods.

3. `Binary_Tree_Sort`: Given n names in a file, arrange them in lexicographically ascending order using binary sort for a singly linked list. Store the sorted list in another file.

4. Do worst-case performance analysis of a binary sort for n data elements.

5. Write a C++ program that implements iterative (nonrecursive) version of quicksort. This program arranges an array of n data elements in ascending order.

6. Write a C++ program for the recursive version of quicksort that uses the split method based on selecting the middle element of (sub)arrays. This program considers arranging an array of n data elements in descending order.

7. Write a C++ program that implements the recursive version of the merge sort. This program arranges a file of n data elements in ascending order.

8. Write a C++ program that implements the merge sort. This program arranges array of n data elements in ascending order.

9. Write a test driver and a C++ function `Link_Merge_Sort()` that implements the linked version of the merge sort.

10. Write a C++ program that implements the merge sort. This program arranges a singly linked list of n data elements in ascending order.

11. Write a C++ program that implements the recursive version of the selection sort for sorting an array of n data elements in descending order.

12. Write a C++ program for an LSD radix 2 sort that arranges an array of n decimal keys in ascending order.

13. For an MSD radix sort, write (a) a general algorithm that arranges an array of n data elements, and (b) a C++ program that implements (a).

14. Write a C++ program that alphabetically arranges a singly linked list of words using the LSD radix sort.

15. Write an OOP in C++ for a radix sort that arranges an array of n keys in ascending order using Rule 1 followed by Rule 2:

   Rule 1: apply radix sort for a given first k number of MSD.

   Rule 2: apply insertion sort for the entire array.

It should be general enough to accept a reasonable value of the radix r. Note that this approach may alleviate insignificant passes over the least-significant digits.

16. Write an OOP for arranging an array of n integer data elements in descending order using min heap sort.

17. (a) Write an OOP to search for a given key in an ascending ordered singly linked list. For algorithm, see Section 7.2.4. Also see **Code 7.2**. (b) Do a worst-case performance analysis of searching in a sorted singly linked list.

18. Do a worst-case performance analysis of the Fibonacci search in a sorted array of n elements.

19. Write a test driver and an OOP to implement a recursive version of Binary_Search() that searches a sorted array for a given key.

20. A hash table with n multiple-slot buckets is an ADT and resolves collisions. Write (a) an algorithm to implement linear probe search or bucket search for a record with key k, (b) an OOP implementing the Hash_Bucket class with public methods: (i) constructor, Hash_Bucket(); (ii) destructor, ~Hash_Bucket(); (iii) initialize the hash table with buckets; (iv) insert a key in the hash table with buckets; (v) perform linear probe search (or bucket search) for a key in the hash table with buckets; (vi) print a hash table with buckets.

21. For a set of key (k) values:

$$\{33, 60, 5, 15, 25, 12, 45, 70, 35, 7\}$$

construct a hash table with buckets for the modulus hash function Hash() and the number of slots per bucket:

(a) Hash(k) = k % 3, number of slots per bucket = 3

(b) Hash(k) = k % 5, number of slots per bucket = 4

(c) Hash(k) = k % 7, number of slots per bucket = 5

Analyze the clusters of keys in each case.

22. Redo Exercise 7-21 for hashing with chaining by disregarding the buckets with slots.

8

Trees and Tries

In the discussion of the list object in Chapter 5, it was observed that linked list representations employing pointer variables and dynamic storage allocation provide a considerable amount of flexibility over their static counterparts. Linear linked lists are useful for applications requiring fast *sequential* access to the data. However, for applications in need of a higher degree of *random* access to the data, the list object can prove to be ineffective. In this chapter, the *tree* object is introduced to fulfill such requirements.

The tree object is one of the most fundamental and universally applied concepts in computer science. Trees have many variations and implementations, and many more applications. In this chapter we develop the concepts of ADT trees and present their implementations as object-oriented programs in C++ . We concentrate on pointer-based implementations of tree structures, relying heavily on the powerful facilities of pointer variables and dynamic memory allocation, although pointer-less variations are also presented.

8.1   Fundamental Definitions and Terminology

We begin with the development of trees by introducing the basic definitions and terminology associated with this very important abstract data type.

Definition 8.1 *A tree is a nonempty and finite collection of data objects called nodes such that:*

(1) there is a single node or

(2) there is a node designated as the root connected by edges to a finite set of trees that are the offspring of the root.

A *node* is an abstract data object that contains the basic branching information of a tree and may also contain additional data attributes. Consider, for example, a tree-object based information retrieval system for the maintenance of a customer mailing list. A node in this instance might contain information (data attributes) such as the customer's name, address, and phone number. In addition to data, a node typically contains the information linking it to other nodes in the tree. This interconnectivity information forms the *edges* between nodes.

The nodes in a tree have a parent-child (predecessor-successor) relationship. Each node, with the exception of the *root* of the entire tree, has exactly one node preceding it, which is referred to as its *parent* or *ancestor*. All nodes succeeding a given node are referred to as its *children* or *descendants*. All nodes that share the same parent are *siblings*. A node that has no children (subtrees) is called a *leaf* or *terminal* and is identified as the last node in a (sub)tree. All other nodes that contain at least one child are referred to as *internal* nodes. The *degree of a node* corresponds to the number of subtrees or children of a node while the *degree of a tree* is the maximum of the degrees of its nodes. It follows that a node of degree zero is a leaf node while a tree of degree zero is a single node.

A *path* is any specifiable list of successively connected nodes in a tree. An important defining property of a tree is that there exists only one path connecting the root node to any other node in the tree. In Chapter 10, we will examine the *graph* structure for which this restriction is lifted.

The *level* of a node in a tree is equivalent to the number of ancestors for that node. Alternately, the level of a node is given as the number of nodes along the path between it and the root of the entire tree (including the root). The *height* of a tree is the maximum of the levels of the nodes. That is, the height is the length of the longest path from the root to any leaf node. The *total path length* of a tree is the sum of all lengths of all paths from the root of the tree to all the leaf nodes. This is equivalent to the sum of the levels of all the leaf nodes of the tree. The *balance* of a node in a tree is a relative measure of the number of descendants between the children of the node. The *height balance* of an entire tree is the balance among the nodes through all levels of the tree.

As an illustration of these concepts, consider the tree diagram of Figure 8.1. The nodes of this tree are labeled with the alphabetic characters A through M. Node A, the root of the entire tree, has two children, B and C. Node B, itself, is the root of one of node A's subtrees and has nodes D, E, and F as children. Node A, therefore, is the parent of node B as well as node C. Node B has one sibling, node C, while node K has three siblings. Node K, like nodes G, E, H, I, J, L, and M, is a leaf node, since it has no children. Node F is at level 2 since it has two ancestors. This number corresponds to the number of nodes encountered as one travels along the path from node F to the root node A. The height of this entire tree is 3 while the total path length is 19. The degrees of nodes A, B, and C are 2, 3 and 4, respectively. The degree of node K is zero, as it is a leaf node, while the degree of the entire tree is 4.

Tree structures are naturally recursive, as evidenced herein by the choice of definition and adopted terminology. Indeed, Definition 8.1 is recursive, as it defines a tree in terms of trees. Any node may itself be a tree (a single node) or the root of a set of trees (subtrees). In Figure 8.1, node A is found as the root of a tree that corresponds to the entire tree. Root node A is connected to a set of two trees, the roots of these trees being nodes B and

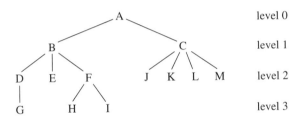

FIGURE 8.1. A tree.

C. If we follow the path from node A to node H, we find that nodes A, B, and F are all recursively roots of their corresponding subtrees. At the end of this path is the leaf node H, which, by definition, is a tree of degree zero. While a tree may be iteratively defined, the recursive representation is more elegant and convenient. Recursive implementations do, however, require the resources of a recursion stack.

An *oriented* tree is one for which the relative orientation of the nodes with respect to each other is of consideration. For the tree of Figure 8.1 it is found that node H has an ancestral lineage of nodes A, B, and F. If this tree is compared to that of Figure 8.2, it is found that node H has the same ancestry. In fact, the relative orientation of every node is both trees is the same and, as such, these two trees are considered identical as oriented trees.

When the relative ordering of the children of each node in a tree is important and explicitly assigned then a tree is said to be *ordered*. While the trees of Figures 8.1 and 8.2 are found to be identical as oriented trees, they are not the same as ordered trees. As an example of an order mismatch, consider node F: it is the second child of node B in the latter tree but is the third child of node B in the former. Ordered trees are also referred to as *plane trees*, terminology derived from the notion of embedding a tree in a plane with a specific "left-to-right" (first, second, third, ...) child ordering. This terminology is an artifact of presenting tree diagrams in a two-dimensional medium, just as the tree illustrations are provided on the planar pages of this book. This is strictly an issue of representation and one should not infer any direct spatial orientation from the depiction. In Chapter 9, this distinction will become more evident when tree structures for indexing data objects with explicit multidimensional spatial orientation are considered. In this case, nodes will have children with spatial labels such as "northwest," "northeast," "southwest," and "southeast," but will still be depicted as planar trees with a left-to-right (first, second, third, ...) labeling.

Central to the process of data structure and algorithm design are issues pertaining to implementations on a digital computer. The fundamental

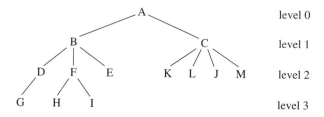

FIGURE 8.2. Another tree.

model of computer representation is one of sequential storage and execution and this in itself dictates an implicit ordering for any tree. Thus, one might view every tree as an ordered tree given these constraints. The distinction will be made that an ordered tree is one for which there is an explicit order that is relevant and this specification is dictated by the application. Unless otherwise stated, all trees presented in this book are ordered.

The trees depicted by Figures 8.1 and 8.2 are considered to be "general" trees in that any node may have any arbitrary, though finite, number of children. If the specification is made that each and every node of a tree is *required* to have a given number of children in a relative order, then the tree is a *multiway* or *M-ary tree*.

8.2   M-ary Trees

An *M-ary tree* is an ordered tree of degree M for which each node specifies an M-way branch.

Definition 8.2 *An M-ary tree is a finite collection of nodes (data objects) such that:*

> *(1) it is empty (there are no nodes, that is, NULL) or*
>
> *(2) there is a root node connected to an ordered sequence of exactly M disjoint M-ary trees.*

Figure 8.3 illustrates a 3-ary or *ternary* tree with every node possessing exactly 3 children. Larger values of M extend the branching relationship in a straightforward fashion. When M is reduced to 2, a 2-ary or *binary tree* is arrived at. This special case is the most simple M-ary tree and is one of the most important concepts we will study.

Definition 8.3 *A binary tree is a finite collection of nodes (data objects) such that:*

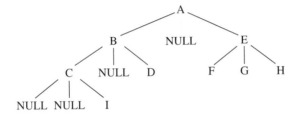

FIGURE 8.3. A 3-ary tree.

(1) there are no nodes (empty set, that is, NULL) or

(2) there is a root node connected to exactly two disjoint binary trees.

The reader should observe that the binary tree, or more generally the M-ary tree, differs from the tree given by Definition 8.1. An M-ary tree may be empty.

8.3 Traversing a Tree

To *traverse* a tree is to "visit" its nodes according to some prescribed method or order. In Chapter 5, linear list objects were traversed in a manner implicit to their definition. As the path from the head to the tail of a list is singular, we begin at the head of a list and successively make our way to the tail. With a tree, however, there is the notion of multiway branching. This means that there exists no implicit traversal mechanism, making it necessary to devise an explicit method by which all the nodes may be systematically visited.

In the next section, algorithms for the traversal of binary trees are presented. Since binary trees are the most fundamental and commonly occurring types of tree structure, these traversal methods are incurred often. For more general trees, traversal methods are derived in a similar but not necessarily direct manner.

8.3.1 TRAVERSALS OF BINARY TREES

A traversal of a binary tree entails traveling around the tree and visiting each node exactly once. The process of visiting a node involves examining key, data, or pointer items contained in the node for purposes such as comparison, replacement, sorting, deleting, or printing.

The order or sequence in which the travel is performed categorizes the traversal methods. The three most common binary tree traversal methods are

- *Preorder* or *depth-first traversal* (*NLR*),

- *Inorder* or *symmetric traversal* (*LNR*), and

- *Postorder* traversal (LRN).

These names of these traversals originate from arithmetic expressions. The alternate shorthand notations, shown in parentheses, depict the following traversal actions: "N" denotes visiting (processing) a node, "L" denotes traversing the left subtree of a node, and "R" denotes traversing the right subtree of a node. These operations are recursively applied. Thus, for example, preorder traversal is alternately referred to as NLR traversal; for a current node N, we process N, recursively traverse to the left child of N, and finally recursively traverse the right child of N. The recursive algorithms for these traversal methods are summarized as follows:

Preorder Traversal

Step 1. Process the root node. (N)

Step 2. Preorder traverse the left subtree, if any. (L)

Step 3. Preorder traverse the right subtree, if any. (R)

Inorder Traversal

Step 1. Inorder traverse the left subtree, if any. (L)

Step 2. Process the root node. (N)

Step 3. Inorder traverse the right subtree, if any. (R)

Postorder Traversal

Step 1. Postorder traverse the left subtree, if any. (L)

Step 2. Postorder traverse the right subtree, if any. (R)

Step 3. Process the root node. (N)

To illustrate these traversal methods, consider the binary tree of Figure 8.4 for the set of integers

$$\{33, 60, 5, 15, 25, 12, 45, 70, 35, 7\}.$$

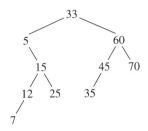

FIGURE 8.4. A binary tree.

The preorder traversal starts by first visiting the root node of the tree and printing the data attribute 33. This is followed by a preorder traversal of the left subtree, the root of which contains the data attribute 5, and a preorder traversal of the right subtree, the root of which contains the data attribute 60. For the preorder traversal of the left subtree with 5 as the root, the data 5 is printed. Since this subtree does not have a left subtree, a preorder traversal of the right subtree with 15 as the root is next, followed by a preorder traversal of the left subtree with 12 as the root, a preorder traversal of the left subtree with 7 as the root, and a preorder traversal of the right subtree with 25. So far, the preorder traversal of this binary tree prints node data in the order: 33, 5, 15, 12, 7, 25. Similarly, performing a preorder traversal of the right subtree with 60 as the root, the overall preorder traversal of the binary tree of Figure 8.4 prints the data in the order:

$$\{33, 5, 15, 12, 7, 25, 60, 45, 35, 70\}.$$

The path in Figure 8.5(c) shows that the root node with 33 is visited (printed) after the left subtree with 5 as the root is completely traveled by an inorder traversal. The inorder traversal starts by first performing an inorder traversal of the left subtree, whose root node contains 5. Then visit the root node with 33. Then proceed to do an inorder traversal of the right subtree, whose root node contains 60. For the inorder traversal of the left subtree with 5 as the root, print 5 since this subtree does not have any left subtree. Now do an inorder traversal of the right subtree with 15 as the root, an inorder traversal of the left subtree with 12 as the root, an inorder traversal of the left subtree with 7 as the root (print 7), and followed by an inorder traversal of the right subtree with 25. So far, the inorder traversal prints the nodes' data in the order: 5, 7, 12, 15, 25. Now print 33, the root of the binary tree. Similarly performing an inorder traversal of the right subtree with 60 as the root, the final inorder traversal of the binary tree of Figure 8.4 is

$$\{5, 7, 12, 15, 25, 33, 35, 45, 60, 70\}.$$

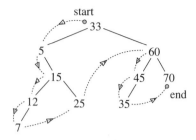

(a) Preorder traversal

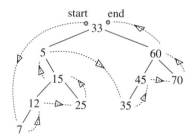

(b) Postorder traversal

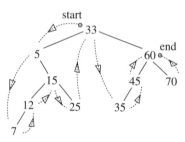

(c) Inorder traversal

FIGURE 8.5. Binary tree traversals.

For the postorder traversal, the root of the tree is visited after both the left
and the right subtrees are completely traversed. The postorder traversal
starts by first performing a postorder traversal of the left subtree, whose
root node contains 5. After the completion of the postorder traversal of
the left subtree, do a postorder traversal of the right subtree, whose root
node contains 60. Then visit the root node with 33. For the postorder
traversal of the left subtree with 5 as the root, wait to visit 5 until both
the left and right subtrees have been visited. Since this subtree does not
have any left subtree, do a postorder traversal of the right subtree with 15
as the root, a postorder traversal of the left subtree with 12 as the root,
a postorder traversal of the left subtree with 7 as the root, followed by a

postorder traversal of the right subtree with 25; visitation (i.e., printing of the root node's data for each subtree) is postponed until both the left and the right subtrees have been traversed. So far, the postorder traversal prints the nodes' data in the order: 7, 12, 25, 15, 5. Similarly, performing a postorder traversal of the right subtree with 60 as the root, the overall postorder traversal of the binary tree of Figure 8.4 is

$$\{7, 12, 25, 15, 5, 35, 45, 70, 60, 33\}.$$

The postorder, inorder, and preorder traversals for the binary tree of Figure 8.4 are diagrammed in Figure 8.5.

8.4   Tree Objects

A *tree object* is specified by an ADT tree. An *ADT tree* is defined as a data structure that has a set of node objects and a set of the generalized operations that are used for defining, manipulating, and abstracting such node objects. The data that are contained in node objects are as abstract as possible, and are abstracted (taken out) by using the specified set of operations. An example set of tree object operations is given in Table 8.1.

Example Tree Object Methods

Construct (initialize) a tree object.
Destroy (delete) a tree object.
Create a node object in a tree object.
Delete a node object in a tree object.
Check if a tree object is empty.
Build a tree object from a given set of data.
Search for a node object specified by a key.
Sort a tree object.
Add/insert a node object in a tree object.
Update a node object with new data.
Retrieve data contained in a node object.
Print a node object.
Print a tree or a subtree object.
Determine tree attributes.
Traverse a tree object.

TABLE 8.1.

In keeping with the strategy set forth in Chapter 1, we present a treatment of tree objects in terms of an abstract base class, a set of implementation specific derived classes, and derived tree objects formed by the instantiation of these derived classes.

FIGURE 8.6. Public methods for the tree class.

For a tree object, shown in Figure 8.6, incorporating a subset of the methods listed in Table 8.1, an example abstract base class `Tree` is defined in a file `bc_tree.h`:

```
class Tree {
  public:
    virtual int  is_empty() = 0;
    virtual void build_tree (DATA_TYPE *A) = 0;
    virtual void add_node (DATA_TYPE node_data) = 0;
    virtual void search_node (DATA_TYPE srch_key) = 0;
    virtual void delete_node (DATA_TYPE srch_key) = 0;
    virtual void print_tree (void) = 0;
    virtual void postorder (void) = 0;
    virtual void preorder (void) = 0;
    virtual void inorder (void) = 0;
};
```

8.5   OOP Implementation of Binary Trees

A binary tree can be implemented as either

- an array of nodes, or

- a linked list of nodes.

The data contained in a node may be of simple or structured type. The abstraction of data, and how efficiently it can be performed, significantly depends on the implementation of the tree structure and associated operations.

8.5.1   OOP IMPLEMENTATION OF A BINARY TREE USING ARRAYS

In an array implementation of a binary tree the node objects are organized as a fixed array. Each node object is built using a `struct` construct with:

- Simple or structured data.

- A left child array index `lft_index`. The left child of the node is at `binary_tree[lft_index]`.

- A right child array index `rgt_index`. The right child of the node is at `binary_tree[rgt_index]`.

Since an array is static, a binary tree implemented as an array has a fixed number of nodes. This number is equivalent to the number of elements in the array. A binary tree with the array name `binary_tree` and an array size of six is depicted below:

Array index	Node data	Left child index (lft_index)	Right child index (rgt_index)
0	M	1	2
1	A	3	LEAF
2	R	LEAF	4
3	T	LEAF	LEAF
4	Y	LEAF	LEAF
5	-	-	-

The root of the binary tree is `binary_tree[0]` while `binary_tree[3]` is a leaf node. The array has space allocation for six node objects but only five are required. Therefore, node object `binary_tree[5]` is empty and the fixed array allocation is somewhat wasteful.

Figure 8.7 shows the equivalent binary tree form of this array-based representation.

For an OOP implementation of an array-based binary tree, we can define node objects of ARY_BTREE_NODE type as data of `ary_btree_obj`, a binary tree object of the `Ary_Binary_Tree` class. This definition is established in the header file `class_Ary_Binary_Tree.h`:

```
class  Ary_Binary_Tree : public Tree {
  private:
    int     ROOT;       //  Index for the root node
    int     LEAF;       //  Indicates no child
    typedef struct  ARY_BTREE_NODE {
      int   lft_index;  // Array index for left child
      int   rgt_index;  // Array index for right child
```

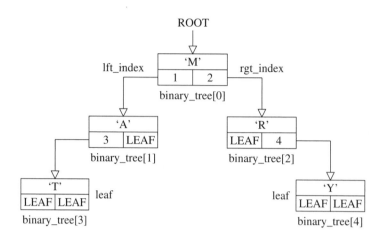

FIGURE 8.7. An array-based binary tree.

```
  DATA_TYPE   data;
  } *TREE_PTR;
  int   TREE_SIZE;
  ARY_BTREE_NODE *binary_tree;
  ARY_BTREE_NODE   create_bin_node(DATA_TYPE new_data);
public:
  Ary_Binary_Tree(int tree_size);
  ~Ary_Binary_Tree();
  BOOLEAN   is_empty (void) {return ROOT == -1;}
  void      build_tree(DATA_TYPE A[]);
  void      add_node(DATA_TYPE node_data) {};
  void      search_node(DATA_TYPE srch_key) {};
  void      delete_node(DATA_TYPE srch_key) {};
  void      print_tree(void);
};
```

The Ary_Binary_Tree class defines a template for the binary tree objects
ary_btree_obj. ARY_BTREE_NODE type node objects, TREE_SIZE, and
binary_tree are declared private for hiding the internal data representation of the tree object. Ary_Binary_Tree(), ~Ary_Binary_Tree(),
create_bin_node(), build_tree(), and print_tree() are declared
public for message-passing. Creating a node does not require the malloc
system call to allocate memory space. However, as the size of the tree is
fixed, it cannot grow its size if required during the program execution.
Code 8.1 is an OOP for an array-based binary tree object in Figure 8.8.

Code 8.1

```
// Program:  ary_btree.c++
```

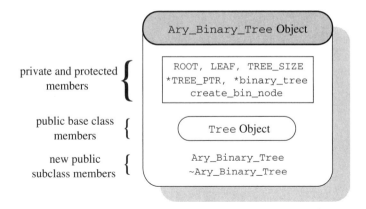

FIGURE 8.8. Ary_Binary_Tree object.

```
//   Purpose:
//     Object-oriented implementation of a binary
//     tree object when its data is an array.
//
#include   <stdio.h>
typedef    int    BOOLEAN;
typedef    char   DATA_TYPE;
#include "bc_tree.h"    // For base class "Tree"
#include "class_Ary_Binary_Tree.h"
//
//  Ary_Binary_Tree()
//   Construct an array-based binary tree
//   object, and set the dimension of tree object
//
Ary_Binary_Tree::Ary_Binary_Tree(int tree_size)
{
   TREE_SIZE   = tree_size;
   binary_tree = new   ARY_BTREE_NODE[TREE_SIZE];
   ROOT =  -1;  //  Index for the root node
   LEAF = -1;   //  Indicates no child
}

//  ~Ary_Binary_Tree()
//     Destroy an array-based binary tree object.
//
Ary_Binary_Tree::~Ary_Binary_Tree()
{
   delete  [] binary_tree;
}

// create_bin_node():
//   Create binary tree's node with 'new_data'.
```

```
//   Since an array is used, this new node's
//   memory is already allocated.
//
Ary_Binary_Tree::ARY_BTREE_NODE
Ary_Binary_Tree::create_bin_node(DATA_TYPE new_data)
{
    ARY_BTREE_NODE node;

    node.data      = new_data;
    node.lft_index = LEAF;
    node.rgt_index = LEAF;
    return (node);
}

// build_tree():
//   Build a binary tree object. It calls
//   create_bin_node() and adds the nodes
//   in the array "binary_tree" sequentially.
//   It builds a specific tree for demonstration.
void  Ary_Binary_Tree::build_tree(DATA_TYPE A[])
{
    ROOT = 0;   // Index for root node
    binary_tree[ROOT] = create_bin_node(A[0]);
    binary_tree[ROOT].lft_index = 1;
    binary_tree[ROOT].rgt_index = 2;

    binary_tree[1] = create_bin_node(A[1]);
    binary_tree[1].lft_index = 3;
    binary_tree[1].rgt_index = LEAF;

    binary_tree[2] = create_bin_node(A[2]);
    binary_tree[2].lft_index = LEAF;
    binary_tree[2].rgt_index = 4;

    binary_tree[3] = create_bin_node(A[3]);
    binary_tree[4] = create_bin_node(A[4]);

    binary_tree[TREE_SIZE - 1].lft_index = LEAF;
    binary_tree[TREE_SIZE - 1].rgt_index = LEAF;
}

//   print_tree():
//     Print a binary tree object. This assumes
//     character type data are stored in the tree.
void  Ary_Binary_Tree::print_tree(void)
{
    printf("\n Array  Node    Left Child   Right Child\n");
    printf(" index  data    index          index      \n");
    for (int i = 0; i < TREE_SIZE; i++)
      printf("\n %3d  %5c %7d %12d", i,
         binary_tree[i].data, binary_tree[i].lft_index,
         binary_tree[i].rgt_index);
    printf("\n");
}
```

```
//   main():
//      Test driver for an array-based binary tree object.
//
void   main(void)
{
      // "ary_btree_obj" is an object of size 6
      Ary_Binary_Tree      ary_btree_obj(6);
      static char str[] = "MARTY";
      printf("\n OOP Implementation %s \n",
            "of an Array-Based Binary Tree");
      ary_btree_obj.build_tree(str);
      ary_btree_obj.print_tree();
      delete  []str;   // Free up memory
}
```

Code 8.1 produces the following output. For the left or right child index, a value of −1 indicates that the corresponding child does not exist.

OOP Implementation of an Array-Based Binary Tree

Array index	Node data	Left Child index	Right Child index
0	M	1	2
1	A	3	-1
2	R	-1	4
3	T	-1	-1
4	Y	-1	-1
5		-1	-1

There are many ways of representing a binary tree using an array. In using an array representation, such binary trees inherit the disadvantages that an array possesses.

8.5.2   OOP IMPLEMENTATION OF A BINARY TREE USING POINTERS

Figure 8.9(a) presents an abstract form of an array-based binary tree in Figure 8.7. Figure 8.9(b) presents a linked list or pointer-based form of the corresponding binary tree.

In Figure 8.9(b), a node contains three fields:

- the node's data,

- left_childptr, a link to its left child, and

- right_childptr, a link to its right child.

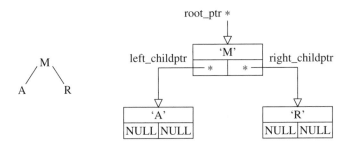

(a) Abstract binary tree   (b) Linked implementation

FIGURE 8.9. A linked binary tree.

The nodes with the character data A and R are leaf nodes and their pointers (connections) to their left and right children are NULL. The node's data may be a simple type, such as int or char, or a complex type, such as struct.

For the linked implementation of a binary tree object as shown in Figure 8.9(b), each node is of type BT_NODE.

```
typedef char DATA_TYPE;
typedef struct BT_NODE {
  DATA_TYPE    data;
  BT_NODE      *left_childptr;
  BT_NODE      *right_childptr;
} *TREE_PTR;
TREE_PTR    root_ptr;
```

The link fields, left_childptr and right_childptr, and the pointer to the root node, root_ptr, are of type TREE_PTR. The data in the root node is accessed by root_ptr, and is root_ptr->data.

In the linked implementation of a binary tree object, nodes are of type BT_NODE and are dynamically created by the new operator:

```
//  Allocate memory space for a new node in a binary
//  tree, and set its data field to 'new_data'.
//
TREE_PTR create_node_btree (DATA_TYPE   new_data)
{
  TREE_PTR   new_ptr = new BT_NODE;

  if (new_ptr != NULL) {
    new_ptr->data =  new_data;
    new_ptr->left_childptr  = NULL;
    new_ptr->right_childptr = NULL;
  }
  else
```

```
            printf ("\n create_node_btree: No memory\n");
        return (new_ptr);
    }
```

Memory space for a binary tree object node is dynamically allocated and should be freed when the node is no longer needed. For a node pointed to by bin_node_ptr, of type TREE_PTR, this is accomplished using the delete operator:

```
    void  free_node (TREE_PTR  bin_node_ptr)
    {
        delete  bin_node_ptr;
    }
```

Using an object-oriented design approach for a binary tree, the object is specified by an ADT binary tree and the methods are operations, which are directly derived from the ADT definition of the binary tree. The binary tree object is a data structure that contains the node's data and pointers to the left and right children of each node, and the operations as methods. For the OOP characteristics of data-hiding, encapsulation, and methods for message passing, the Binary_Tree class is defined in the header file class_Binary_Tree.h as follows:

```
    class Binary_Tree : public Tree {
      private:
        typedef struct BT_NODE {   //  Binary Tree Node
            DATA_TYPE   data;
            BT_NODE     *left_childptr;
            BT_NODE     *right_childptr;
        } *TREE_PTR;
        TREE_PTR  root_ptr;  // root of the binary tree
        TREE_PTR  curr_ptr;
        void      init_btree() { root_ptr = NULL;
                                 curr_ptr = NULL; }
        TREE_PTR  add_node1(TREE_PTR curr_ptr,
                        DATA_TYPE, int node_location);
        void      delete_btree (TREE_PTR tree_ptr);
        TREE_PTR  search_node1(TREE_PTR root_ptr,
                        DATA_TYPE  srch_key);
        void      Preorder1 (TREE_PTR tree_ptr);
        void      Postorder1(TREE_PTR tree_ptr);
        void      Inorder1  (TREE_PTR tree_ptr);
      public:
        Binary_Tree() { init_btree(); }
        ~Binary_Tree();
        BOOLEAN   is_empty() {return (root_ptr == NULL);}
        void      build_tree(DATA_TYPE string[]);
        void      add_node(DATA_TYPE node_data);
        void      search_node(DATA_TYPE srch_key);
        void      delete_node(DATA_TYPE srch_key) {};
        void      print_tree(void) { Inorder1(root_ptr);}
        void      Preorder(void) { Preorder1(root_ptr); }
```

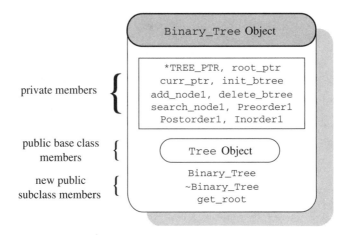

FIGURE 8.10. Binary_Tree object.

```
void       Postorder(void){ Postorder1(root_ptr);}
void       Inorder(void)  { Inorder1(root_ptr);  }
TREE_PTR  get_root(void) { return root_ptr;     }
};
```

The Binary_Tree class defines a type for btree_obj, a binary tree object encompassing both data and actions. The members DATA_TYPE, BT_NODE type structure data, and the pointers root_ptr (the pointer to the root node) and curr_ptr (the pointer to the current node) are private for data-hiding and protection from corruption. The function members Binary_Tree(),~Binary_Tree(), and is_empty() are public, meaning that these are interfaces to the outside world in order to facilitate message passing between Binary_Tree-type object and any object. The member function get_root() is made public for providing read-only access of the data member root_ptr. In the following, the methods that are defined in the Binary_Tree class are discussed. Figure 8.10 depicts a binary tree object.

For an OOP implementation of a binary tree object using linked lists (pointers), a subset of generalized actions for a binary tree object is discussed below. These are implemented as methods in the OOP **Code 8.2**.

8.5.3 METHODS OF THE Binary_Tree CLASS

Binary_Tree(), a public member function of the class Binary_Tree, is the constructor for this class's object. It constructs a binary tree object by calling init_btree(). It is automatically called when an instance (object), btree_obj, is declared in main().

~Binary_Tree(), a public member function of the Binary_Tree class, is the destructor for this class's object. It deallocates memory space for a binary tree object by calling delete_tree().

Delete_btree() of type void is a private member function of the class Binary_Tree. It is a recursive function and deletes the tree. Using postorder traversal, it visits each node, releasing the associated memory space of the node.

Is_empty() of BOOLEN type is a public member function of the class Binary_Tree. It tests to see if a binary tree object is empty. If root_ptr is NULL, it returns 1; otherwise, it returns 0.

Init_btree() of type void is a private member function of the class Binary_Tree. It initializes a binary tree object by setting root_ptr and curr_ptr to NULL. This is because the tree object is empty at the initial state. This method is made private to protect the object from its misuse that may cause "memory leak."

Add_node() of type TREE_PTR is a public member function of the class Binary_Tree. It calls add_node1() to add (insert) a new node into a binary tree object. In add_node1(), three arguments, curr_ptr of type TREE_PTR, new_data of type DATA_TYPE, and node_location of type int, are passed to this function. Using the new operator, it allocates memory space for the new node of type BT_NODE, and sets its data field to new_data, and the left and right child pointers to NULL. According to the value of node_location: ROOT, LEFT_CHILD, RIGHT_CHILD, and PARENT, it inserts the new node and returns the pointer to the new node. If it fails to insert, it deletes the allocated memory space, prints a message, and returns a NULL pointer.

Build_tree() of type void, is a public member function of the class Binary_Tree. For an input string, it repeatedly calls add_node1() to build a binary tree. While adding the nodes, it updates root_ptr and curr_ptr.

Search_node() of type TREE_PTR is a public member function of the class Binary_Tree. It calls a recursive function search_node1(). Using preorder traversal method, search_node1() searches for a node identified by its key, srch_key. If it finds a match of node data, it returns a TREE_PTR type pointer to that node. If the binary tree is empty, or no match is found, it simply returns.

Preorder() of type void is a public member function of the class Binary_Tree. It calls recursive function Preorder1(), which expects a subtree node pointer, tree_ptr, of type TREE_PTR, as an argument. It implements the preorder traversal method. It visits the root node of the subtree by printing the data contained in it. Using the pointer tree_ptr->left_childptr, it recursively traverses the subtree's left subtree. Finally, it recursively traverses the subtree's right subtree using the pointer tree_ptr->right_childptr. It simply returns to its caller if the subtree is empty. It is called with the input, root_ptr, so that the preorder traversal starts from the root of the binary tree object.

Postorder() of type void, is a public member function of the class Binary_Tree. It is similar to Preorder() except that it employs postorder traversal.

Inorder() of type void is a public member function of the class Binary_Tree. It is similar to Preorder() except that it employs inorder traversal.

Print_tree() of type void is a public member function of the class Binary_Tree. It prints data of each node in the binary tree by calling Inorder1().

Main() is the test driver for OOP implementation of the binary tree. It instantiates an object btree_obj of type Binary_Tree. Since main() is a client function of the Binary_Tree class, it sends messages to the btree_obj object through this object's publicly accessible interface routines (methods). The messages include building the binary tree object from a given string "JUTHIKA", and performing preorder, postorder, and inorder traversals. The implicit call of the object's destructor cleans up the memory space allocated by this program.

Code 8.2

```
//    Program: binary_tree.c++
//    Purpose:
//      An OBJECT-ORIENTED IMPLEMENTATION of a Binary Tree.
//      It assumes "character" type data in each node.
//
#include <stdio.h>
#include <stdlib.h>
typedef int   BOOLEAN;
     const       int   ROOT        = 0;
     const       int   LEFT_CHILD  = 1;
     const       int   RIGHT_CHILD = 2;
     const       int   PARENT      = 3;
typedef char DATA_TYPE;   // Node data type
#include "bc_tree.h"  // For base class "Tree"
// Define implementation specific class "Binary_Tree"
#include "class_Binary_Tree.h"

// delete_btree():
//   Using 'PostOrder traversal', delete or release
//   memory spaces of all nodes in a binary tree.
//
void  Binary_Tree::delete_btree (TREE_PTR tree_ptr)
{
   if (tree_ptr != NULL) {
      delete_btree (tree_ptr->left_childptr);
      delete_btree (tree_ptr->right_childptr);
      delete  tree_ptr;
   }
}
```

```
// ~Binary_Tree(): Destroy memory space for the object.
//
Binary_Tree::~Binary_Tree()
{
    delete_btree (root_ptr);
}

// add_node1():
//   Add (insert) a node with data 'new_data'
//   in a binary tree at an indicated location
//   'node_location', which is one of ROOT,
//   LEFT_CHILD, RIGHT_CHILD, and PARENT. If
//   insertion succeeds, it returns the pointer
//   to the new node. If it is unsuccessful (where
//   the node already exists with the same data),
//   it returns NULL. It assumes "character" data.
//
Binary_Tree::TREE_PTR  Binary_Tree::add_node1(
TREE_PTR curr_ptr, DATA_TYPE new_data, int node_location)
{
    TREE_PTR  new_ptr = new BT_NODE;
    new_ptr->data    = new_data;
    new_ptr->left_childptr  = NULL;
    new_ptr->right_childptr = NULL;
    switch (node_location) {
      case ROOT:
        if (root_ptr == NULL) {
            root_ptr = new_ptr;
            curr_ptr = new_ptr;
            return (new_ptr);
        }
      case LEFT_CHILD:
        if (curr_ptr->left_childptr == NULL) {
    curr_ptr->left_childptr = new_ptr;
            curr_ptr = new_ptr;
            return (new_ptr);
        }
      case RIGHT_CHILD:
        if (curr_ptr->right_childptr == NULL) {
            curr_ptr->right_childptr = new_ptr;
            curr_ptr = new_ptr;
            return (new_ptr);
        }
      case PARENT:
            // Adding a node at the parent node
            // is not allowed.
            break;
      default:
        printf("\n add_node1: Invalid node location \n");
        exit (-1);
    }
    // Adding a node into a binary tree failed.
    delete  new_ptr;
```

```
        printf("\n add_node1: Fails; Node with %c %s\n",
                new_data, "exists, or wrong location");
        return (NULL);
}

void  Binary_Tree::add_node(DATA_TYPE node_data)
{
    TREE_PTR tmp_ptr;
    int      node_loc;

    printf("\nTo add node, enter node location\n%s",
      "(ROOT=0, LEFT_CHILD=1, RIGHT_CHILD=2, PARENT=3): ");
    scanf("%d", &node_loc);
    tmp_ptr = add_node1(curr_ptr, node_data, node_loc);
    if (tmp_ptr != NULL && is_empty()) {
        root_ptr = tmp_ptr;
        curr_ptr = tmp_ptr;
    }
    else if (tmp_ptr != NULL && !is_empty())
        curr_ptr =  tmp_ptr;
}


// build_tree():
//   Build a binary tree from an input string.
//
void Binary_Tree::build_tree (DATA_TYPE string[])
{
    TREE_PTR   tmp_ptr;

    if ((tmp_ptr = add_node1(curr_ptr, 'J',
                            ROOT)) != NULL) {
        curr_ptr = tmp_ptr;
        root_ptr = tmp_ptr;
    }
    if ((tmp_ptr = add_node1(root_ptr, 'U',
                            LEFT_CHILD)) != NULL)
        curr_ptr =  tmp_ptr;
    if ((tmp_ptr = add_node1(root_ptr, 'T',
                            RIGHT_CHILD)) != NULL)
        curr_ptr =  tmp_ptr;
    if ((tmp_ptr = add_node1(curr_ptr, 'H',
                            LEFT_CHILD)) != NULL)
        curr_ptr =  tmp_ptr;
    if ((tmp_ptr = add_node1(curr_ptr, 'I',
                            RIGHT_CHILD)) != NULL)
        curr_ptr =  tmp_ptr;
    if ((tmp_ptr = add_node1(curr_ptr, 'K',
                            LEFT_CHILD)) != NULL)
        curr_ptr =  tmp_ptr;
    if ((tmp_ptr = add_node1(curr_ptr, 'A',
                            RIGHT_CHILD)) != NULL)
        curr_ptr =  tmp_ptr;
}
```

```
// search_node1():
//    Search for a node specified by 'srch_key'
//    using preorder traversal in a binary tree.
//
Binary_Tree::TREE_PTR
Binary_Tree::search_node1(TREE_PTR root_ptr,
                                DATA_TYPE  srch_key)
{
    if (root_ptr != NULL) {
        if (srch_key == root_ptr->data)
            return (root_ptr);
        search_node1(root_ptr->left_childptr, srch_key);
        search_node1(root_ptr->right_childptr, srch_key);
    }
    else
        return (NULL);
}

void  Binary_Tree::search_node(DATA_TYPE srch_key)
{
    TREE_PTR srch_ptr = search_node1(root_ptr, srch_key);
    if (srch_ptr != NULL)
        printf("\n The specified node is found in tree.\n");
    else
        printf("\n The specified node is not in tree.\n");
}

// Preorder1():
//    Traverse a binary pointed to by the tree_ptr
//    using preorder traversal (Recursive method). It
//    assumes "character" data stored in each node.
void  Binary_Tree::Preorder1 (TREE_PTR tree_ptr)
{
    if (tree_ptr != NULL) {
        // Visit root, i.e., print root's data
        printf(" %c ", tree_ptr->data);
        // Traverse its left subtree
        Preorder1(tree_ptr->left_childptr);
        // Traverse its right subtree
        Preorder1(tree_ptr->right_childptr);
    }
}

// Postorder1():
//    Traverse a binary pointed to by the
//    tree_ptr using postorder traversal.
//    (Recursive method)
void  Binary_Tree::Postorder1 (TREE_PTR tree_ptr)
{
    if (tree_ptr != NULL) {
        // Traverse its left subtree
        Postorder1(tree_ptr->left_childptr);
        // Traverse its right subtree
        Postorder1(tree_ptr->right_childptr);
```

```
            // Visit root node (i.e., print node data)
            printf(" %c ", tree_ptr->data);
        }
}


// Inorder1():
//    Traverse a binary pointed to by the
//    tree_ptr using inorder traversal.
//    (Recursive method)
void  Binary_Tree::Inorder1 (TREE_PTR tree_ptr)
{
    if (tree_ptr != NULL) {
        // Traverse its left subtree
        Inorder1(tree_ptr->left_childptr);
        // Root of the subtree, pointed to by 'tree_ptr',
        // is visited; its data is printed.
        printf(" %c ", tree_ptr->data);
        // Traverse its right subtree
        Inorder1(tree_ptr->right_childptr);
    }
}


//   main(): Test driver for an OBJECT-ORIENTED
//           IMPLEMENTATION of a Binary Tree object.
void main(void)
{
    //   Declare an instance of the Binary_Tree class
    Binary_Tree   btree_obj;

    printf("\n OBJECT-ORIENTED IMPLEMENTATION %s \n",
            "OF BINARY TREE");
    btree_obj.build_tree ("JUTHIKA");
    printf("\nBinary Tree after PreOrder traversal:\n");
    btree_obj.Preorder();
    printf("\nBinary Tree after PostOrder traversal:\n");
    btree_obj.Postorder();
    printf("\nBinary Tree after InOrder traversal:\n");
    btree_obj.Inorder();
    printf("\n");
}
```

Code 8.2 for an array-based binary tree object yields this output:

```
OBJECT-ORIENTED IMPLEMENTATION OF BINARY TREE

Binary Tree after PreOrder traversal:
 J   U   T   H   I   K   A
Binary Tree after PostOrder traversal:
 U   A   K   I   H   T   J
Binary Tree after InOrder traversal:
 U   J   H   K   A   I   T
```

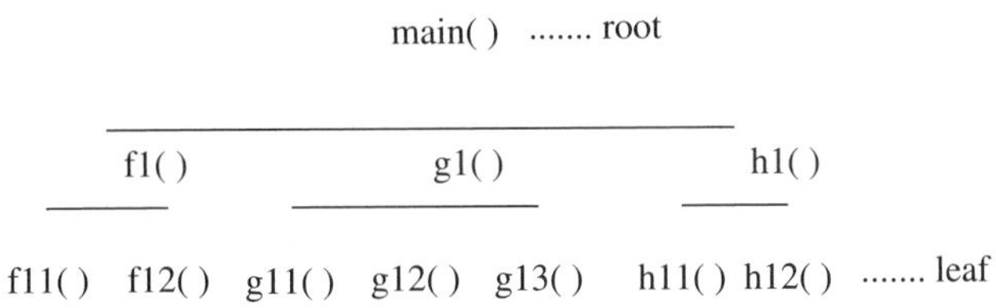

main( ) ······· root

<table>
<tr><td>f1( )</td><td>g1( )</td><td>h1( )</td></tr>
</table>

f11( )   f12( )   g11( )   g12( )   g13( )   h11( ) h12( )   ······· leaf

FIGURE 8.11. A general tree (call tree).

8.6   General Trees

The concepts of binary tree objects for which each node has a relationship with at most two child nodes were discussed in previous sections. As has been seen, the binary tree belongs to the class of M-ary trees: each node has a relationship with exactly $M = 2$ children.

The multiway tree is flexible to the extent that the number of children per node, M, is specifiable. Yet, the basic multiway tree can prove to be restrictive and impractical since

- the number of children per node is fixed in advance, and

- each node *must* have all M child fields.

In general, one might find it desirable to deal with a tree structure for which any data object may have a relationship with an arbitrary (but finite) number of child data objects. In this scenario, the number of children per node is independent between nodes and varies dynamically with the growth or decay of the overall tree. Such a tree structure is commonly known as a *general tree* or a *hierarchical tree*.

Definition 8.4 *A general tree is a tree such that:*

(1) it is empty, or

(2) it contains a root node along with a finite number of disjoint general (sub)trees.

Figure 8.11 illustrates the general tree concept taking the *call tree* of a set of functions "f1()," "g1()," "h1()." The function "f1()" calls "f11()" and "f12()"; the function "g1()" calls "g11()," "g12()," and "g13()"; the function "h1()" calls "h11()" and "h12()." The parent-child relationship is established by "who calls whom." Leaf nodes, such as the functions "f11()," "f12()," and "g11()," are those that do not call any functions.

A general tree object is specified by an ADT general tree. An ADT general tree is a data structure that contains a set of nodes satisfying Definition 8.4, and a set of operations.

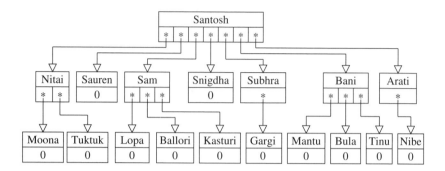

FIGURE 8.12. General tree structure for Santosh and his descendants.

Indicative of its name, the general tree is applicable to a wide and varied class of problems. Three examples are shown here to illustrate the point.

Figure 8.12 shows a general tree representation for the family tree of "Santosh" and his descendants. The main point is that parent-children relationship is distinctly defined by putting the parent, "Santosh," in the root node of level 0, and by putting all its children ("Nitai," "Sauren," and so on) in the next lower level 1. Because the nodes with data — "Nitai," "Sauren" and so on, are in the same level and have the same parent, "Santosh," they are called *siblings*. The children nodes ("Moona," "Tuktuk") of Nitai are siblings. The children nodes ("Lopa," "Ballori," "Kasturi") of "Sam" are siblings.

Figure 8.13 shows a second example of a general tree for a menu system. A general tree is used to organize a pull-down and pop-up menu system. The menu tree has main menu as the root and the submenus as the children. For example, the submenu "Windows" has the siblings "System," "Tools," and "Demos," and the children sub-submenus – "Restore," "Move," "Size," "Raise," "Lower," "Close," and "Quit," which are all leaves.

Figure 8.14 shows a third example of a general tree for a computer file system. A general tree is used to organize the hierarchical form of the file system. The root of this file system is the root directory denoted by "/" (forward slash). Its children are files and/or subdirectories contained in "/". The file "unix" and the subdirectories "etc," "bin," "debug," "lib," "stand," and "usr" are children of the root directory. These subdirectories have files and subdirectories as children. In this hierarchical file system, a directory is a parent and all files or subdirectories contained in it are its children.

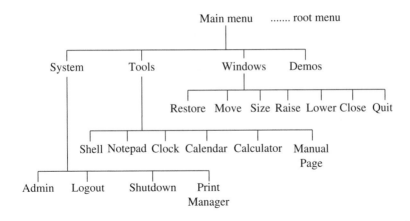

FIGURE 8.13. A general tree for a menu system.

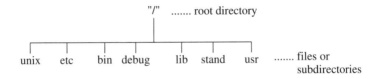

FIGURE 8.14. General tree structure for Unix file system.

8.6.1 STRATEGIES FOR REPRESENTING GENERAL TREES

There are many possible strategies for representing a general tree. Among them are those employing

- variable size nodes,

- M-ary trees, and

- binary trees.

An implementation based on variable-sized nodes can be considerably more complex than one based on fixed-size nodes. Any such implementation is not considered here.

The use of an M-ary tree is for the most part an impractical means of representing a general tree. Such an implementation requires an upper limit for the degree of the tree to be fixed in advance, limiting flexibility and ultimately leading to a lot of wasted storage space. Each and every node must contain the storage required for M child pointers, regardless of the actual number of children present at any given time. For an M-ary tree, it can be shown that the ratio of NULL to non-NULL child pointers is

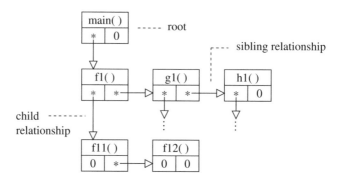

FIGURE 8.15. Binary tree implementation of a general tree with siblings.

about 2/3 for a 3-ary tree ($M = 3$) and approaches unity with increasing M.

A binary tree, on the other hand, has a NULL to non-NULL child pointer ratio of about 1/2 for large trees. This more favorable use of space is readily exploited given the realization that *any tree may be represented by a binary tree.*

8.6.2   GENERAL TREE: BINARY TREE IMPLEMENTATION

Figure 8.9 shows the abstract form of a general tree for the call tree of functions. Figure 8.15 shows its equivalent form of a general tree using child sibling relationship. It is also called binary tree or linked list implementation of a general tree. Children and siblings are both structures as a linked list. Like binary tree, each node contains a data field and two pointers: one pointer pointing to the head of the singly or doubly linked list of its children, and a second pointer pointing to the head of the singly or doubly linked list of its siblings (i.e., brothers and sisters). For example, the node containing "f1()" as data has one pointer (forward direction) pointing to the list of its siblings, "g1()" and "h1()," and a second pointer (downward direction) pointing to the list of its children functions, "f11()" and "f12()."

To avoid complexity in Figure 8.15, children of the nodes with "g1()" and "h1()" are not shown.

Figure 8.15 shows implementation of the general tree using linked lists. The siblings "f1()," "g1()," and "h1()" belong to the same array or singly or doubly linked list; "f1()" is assumed to be the first child of the root node "main()." The node containing "f1()" contains one pointer pointing to the next brother or sister, and a second pointer pointing to the singly or doubly linked list of its children function nodes, "f11()" and "f12()." **Code 8.3** implements a general tree object using this approach. Its output draws a general tree for an input string "GENERAL" showing the nodes and the list of siblings.

8.6.3 General Tree Traversal

Traversal of a general tree entails traveling around the tree and visiting each node exactly once. It is performed by traveling along the lists of siblings, and traveling downward along the lists of children. As with the binary tree traversal, the order of traveling lists of siblings and lists of children follows the preorder, postorder, and inorder traversal methods. Deleting a general tree using the postorder traversal is left as an exercise. The preorder traversal is implemented by the function gtree_preorder():

```
void gtree_preorder(TREE_PTR gtree_ptr) {
  if (gtree_ptr != NULL) {
    printf("%c ", gtree_ptr->data);
    if (gtree_ptr->sibling_listptr != NULL)
      gtree_preorder(gtree_ptr->sibling_listptr);
    if (gtree_ptr->first_childptr != NULL)
      gtree_preorder(gtree_ptr->first_childptr);
  }
}
```

8.6.4 OOP Implementation of a General Tree

Using an object-oriented design approach for a general tree, the object is specified by an ADT general tree and methods are actions, which are directly derived from the ADT definition of the general tree. To implement the OOP characteristics of data-hiding, encapsulation, and methods for message passing, the General_Tree class is defined in the header file class_General_Tree.h as follows:

```
class General_Tree : public Tree {
  private:
    typedef struct GTREE_NODE {
          DATA_TYPE      data;
          GTREE_NODE     *first_childptr;
          GTREE_NODE     *sibling_listptr;
    } *TREE_PTR;
    TREE_PTR   root_ptr;
    TREE_PTR   create_gtree_node (DATA_TYPE new_data);
    void       init_gtree (void) { root_ptr = NULL; }
    void       insert_node_in_gtree (TREE_PTR parent_ptr,
                                     DATA_TYPE new_data);
    void       gtree_preorder (TREE_PTR tree_ptr);
    void       print_gtree_sibl (TREE_PTR tree_ptr);
  public:
    General_Tree() { init_gtree(); }
    ~General_Tree();
    BOOLEAN    is_empty(void) {return(root_ptr == NULL);}
```

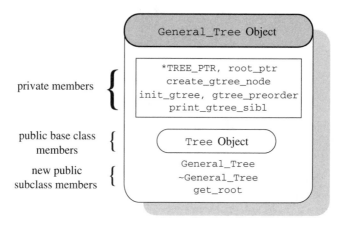

FIGURE 8.16. General tree object.

```
void       build_tree (DATA_TYPE A[]);
void       add_node(DATA_TYPE node_data)
     { insert_node_in_gtree(root_ptr, node_data); }
void       search_node(DATA_TYPE srch_key) {};
void       delete_node(DATA_TYPE srch_key) {};
void       print_tree(void)
            { printf("\n\nNODE:  CHILDREN WITH SIBLINGS");
              print_gtree_sibl(root_ptr); }
void       preorder(void)
     { printf("\nGeneral tree after PreOrder traversal:\n");
       gtree_preorder(root_ptr); }
   TREE_PTR  get_root() { return (root_ptr); }
};
```

The General_Tree class defines a type for gtree_obj, a general tree
object encompassing both data and operations. The members DATA_TYPE,
GTREE_NODE type structure data, and the pointer root_ptr (the pointer
to the root node) are private for protecting data from unauthorized
access. The function members General_Tree(), ~General_Tree(),
and insert_node_in_gtree() are public, meaning that these are
publicly accessible interfaces to the outside world in order to facilitate
message passing between General_Tree-type object and any object of
the same or different type. Get_root() is made public for providing
read-only access of the data member root_ptr. Figure 8.16 depicts a
general tree object.

8.6.5   METHODS OF THE General_Tree CLASS

The constructor General_Tree() is a public member function of the General_Tree class. It constructs an object by calling init_gtree(). It is automatically called when an object, gtree_obj, is instantiated in main().

~General_Tree(), the destructor and a public member function of the General_Tree class, deletes an object gtree_obj. Its implementation is left as an exercise.

Create_gtree_node() of type TREE_PTR is a private member function of the General_Tree class. It has one argument, new_data, of type DATA_TYPE. It allocates memory space, pointed to by new_ptr, for a node of type GTREE_NODE. The data field of this new node is set to new_data. The pointer fields first_childptr and sibling_listptr are set to NULL. It returns new_ptr.

Init_gtree() of type void is a private member function of the General_Tree class. Since a general tree object is empty at the initial state. root_ptr is set to NULL. It is made private to protect its misuse, which may cause "memory leak."

Insert_node_in_gtree() of type void, is a private member function of the General_Tree class. It inserts a new node into a general tree object. Two arguments, parent_ptr of type TREE_PTR and new_data of type DATA_TYPE, are passed to this function. If the general tree is empty, it calls create_gtree_node() and sets the root node to this new node. If the parent pointer is NULL, it prints an error message and returns. Otherwise, it calls create_gtree_node(); new_ptr points to the new node. If first_childptr of the parent node, pointed to by parent_ptr, is NULL, the new node becomes the first child of the specified parent node. If the parent node has a list of children, the function adds the new node as the sibling of the existing children. The new node is appended in this singly linked list of siblings.

Build_tree() of type void is a public member function of the General_Tree class. For an input string (e.g., "GENERAL"), it builds a general tree. It repeatedly calls insert_node_in_gtree() by passing the pointer of the parent node for the node. Build_gtree() is simple, but not robust. It is more desirable to build a general tree from a given specification that contains the nodes' data, number of children, and the data for the children. This is left as an exercise.

Preorder() of type void is a public member function of the class General_Tree. It calls gtree_preorder(), which is recursive and implements preorder traversal of a general tree object. While traversing, each node is visited and its data are printed.

Print_tree() is a public member function of the General_Tree. It calls a recursive function Print_gtree_sibl() that prints the general tree object by its node and the node's corresponding sibling list.

Main(), a client function and the test driver of the General_Tree class, instantiates this class's object gtree_obj. Main() sends messages to the gtree_obj object through the object's publicly accessible interface routines. The messages include building the general tree object from a string "GENERAL" pointed to by A, performing preorder traversal, and printing the general tree object by its node list and the list of siblings of each node. The program's allocated memory space is cleaned up by delete A and ~General_Tree().

Code 8.3

```
//  Program:   gtree.c++
//  Purpose:
//    Object-Oriented implementation of general
//    tree object for a set of characters.
//
#include  <stdio.h>
#include  <ctype.h>
typedef int    BOOLEAN;
typedef char   DATA_TYPE;
#include "bc_tree.h"  // For base class "Tree"
#include  "class_General_Tree.h"
General_Tree::~General_Tree()
{
   // Exercise: Use Postorder traversal method.
}

General_Tree::TREE_PTR
General_Tree::create_gtree_node(DATA_TYPE new_data)
{
   // Allocate memory space for a new node
   TREE_PTR  new_ptr = new GTREE_NODE;
   if (new_ptr != NULL) {
      new_ptr->data = new_data;
      new_ptr->first_childptr  = NULL;
      new_ptr->sibling_listptr = NULL;
   }
   return (new_ptr);  // NULL if alloc fails.
}

//    insert_node_in_gtree():
//    Insert a new node in a general tree.
//
void  General_Tree::insert_node_in_gtree
      (TREE_PTR  parent_ptr, DATA_TYPE new_data)
{
   // If the general tree is empty, insert it.
   if ((parent_ptr == root_ptr) && (root_ptr == NULL))
      root_ptr = create_gtree_node (new_data);
   else if (parent_ptr == NULL)
      printf ("\ninsert_node_in_gtree: Parent %s \n",
              "pointer is invalid");
```

```
    else {
      TREE_PTR new_ptr = create_gtree_node (new_data);
      if (parent_ptr->first_childptr == NULL)
        parent_ptr->first_childptr = new_ptr;
      else {
        TREE_PTR sibling_ptr = parent_ptr->first_childptr;
        //  Add at the end of the sibling list.
        while (sibling_ptr->sibling_listptr != NULL)
          // Advance to the next sibling (brother or sister)
            sibling_ptr = sibling_ptr->sibling_listptr;
        sibling_ptr->sibling_listptr = new_ptr;
      }
    }
}

void  General_Tree::build_tree (DATA_TYPE A[])
{
    //  Root = G; its children = E, N, E
    insert_node_in_gtree (root_ptr, 'G');
    insert_node_in_gtree (root_ptr, 'E');
    insert_node_in_gtree (root_ptr, 'N');
    insert_node_in_gtree (root_ptr, 'E');
    // Children of 'E' are: R, A, L
    insert_node_in_gtree (root_ptr->first_childptr, 'R');
    insert_node_in_gtree (root_ptr->first_childptr, 'A');
    insert_node_in_gtree (root_ptr->first_childptr, 'L');
}


//  gtree_preorder():
//     Perform Preorder traversal of a general tree.
//     It assumes "character" type data in each node.
void  General_Tree::gtree_preorder(TREE_PTR gtree_ptr)
{
    if (gtree_ptr != NULL) {
        printf ("%c ", gtree_ptr->data);
        if (gtree_ptr->sibling_listptr != NULL)
          gtree_preorder (gtree_ptr->sibling_listptr);
        if (gtree_ptr->first_childptr != NULL)
          gtree_preorder (gtree_ptr->first_childptr);
    }
}

//  print_gtree_sibl():
//     Print the general tree showing its
//     children siblings.
//
void General_Tree::print_gtree_sibl(TREE_PTR tree_ptr)
{
    TREE_PTR   curr_ptr = tree_ptr;
    static    int n = 0;

    if (root_ptr == NULL)
       printf ("\n General tree is empty. \n");
    while (curr_ptr != NULL) {
```

```
                    if (n > 0) {
                      if (isalnum (curr_ptr->data))
                        printf(" %c->", curr_ptr->data);
        }

                    n++;
                    print_gtree_sibl (curr_ptr->sibling_listptr);
                    if (isalnum (curr_ptr->data))
                        printf("\n %c :  ", curr_ptr->data);
                    curr_ptr = curr_ptr->first_childptr;
            }
        }

        //  main():
        //     Test driver for general tree objects
        //     (OBJECT-ORIENTED IMPLEMENTATION)
        //
        void main(void)
        {
            General_Tree  gtree_obj;

            static DATA_TYPE *A = "GENERAL";
            printf ("\n *** OOP IMPLEMENTATION OF GENERAL TREE %s",
                   "***\n        USING CHILD-SIBLING RELATIONSHIP \n");
            gtree_obj.build_tree(A);
            gtree_obj.preorder();
            gtree_obj.print_tree();
            printf("\n");
            delete A;
        }
```

Code 8.3 for general tree objects yields this output:

```
        *** OOP IMPLEMENTATION OF GENERAL TREE ***
              USING CHILD-SIBLING RELATIONSHIP

      General tree after PreOrder traversal:
      G E N E R A L

      NODE:   CHILDREN WITH SIBLINGS
      G :    E-> N-> E->
      E :
      N :
      E :    R-> A-> L->
      L :
      A :
      R :
```

8.7 Search Trees

The M-ary tree, most commonly seen in the form of a binary tree, is one of the most fundamental concepts in computer science. The binary tree finds its way into a very wide and varied range of applications. For example, the use of a binary tree is typical in an application such as an algebraic expression evaluator (see Exercise 8-66).

However, because of its generality, the ADT binary (M-ary) tree does prove to be inefficient for a broad range of applications demanding fast data search and retrieval.

An information database processing system is an example of an application in need of an underlying data structure that supports frequent data object searches, insertions, deletions, and retrieval. Here, a typical query might request the retrieval of a record matching a specified search key.

By definition, the M-ary tree is an ordered tree, so there exists a pre-scribed relative ordering among the children of the nodes of the tree. However, *there does not exist a set correspondence between the ordering of a node's children and a branch decision at a node.* In other words, there is no specification of which branch (child) to select as a result of a prescribed branch test involving the target search value (key) and a key value associated with a node. Consequently, the following major deficiencies with the basic M-ary tree are cited:

- There is no logical way of inserting a node in the tree.

- When a node is deleted from the tree, the fate of the subtree(s) hanging off the node to be deleted is not well defined.

- Searching for a node will require traversing the entire tree with worst-case time complexity of an exhaustive sequential search. $O(\log_2 n)$.

As an example, consider a binary tree consisting of numbers as depicted by Figure 8.17(a). If a query asked for the retrieval of the number 5, then an exhaustive search is imminent, since at any given node we do not know whether to look in the left subtree or the right subtree. If a request is made to delete the node containing the number 14, it is not clear what happens to the children of that node. *Does the node containing 7 or the node containing 2 replace the deleted node?*

In the following sections these issues are addressed, focusing on tree structures specifically tailored to support efficient search-related operations. Such structures, known as *search trees*, are designed to overcome the deficiencies cited above.

To introduce the search tree concept, let's look at Figure 8.17(b). This tree contains the same data (numbers) encountered in Figure 8.17(a) but they exist in an order that supports more efficient searching. What distinguishes this binary tree as a search tree is the following list of properties:

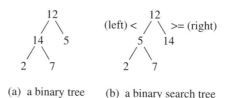

(a) a binary tree   (b) a binary search tree

FIGURE 8.17. A binary tree and a binary search tree.

- There are two children per node that are explicitly labeled *left* and *right*.

- Data objects reside in internal nodes (the numbers shown are the keys).

- A branch decision is based on a comparison test between the target search key and the key of a given node.

- All keys of value less than that of the key data at a given node are placed in the *left* subtree of the node while all keys of greater or equal value go in the *right* subtree.

In Figure 8.17(b), the number 5 resides in the left subtree of the root node since it is less in value than the number 12 associated with the root. Likewise, the number 7 is in the right subtree of its parent node, which contains the number 5, since it is of greater value. To search for the number 7, we start at the root and traverse to the left on the determination that 7 is less than 12 and then right on the determination that 7 is greater than 5. It is very important to note here that the paths leading to the nodes containing the keys 2 and 14 will never have to be visited in the search for key 7. These paths are said to be *pruned* out of the search. Even if the right subtree of the root of the tree contained a thousand nodes, none of them would ever be visited in the search for key 7. It is this pruning process that is the basis for the search tree's efficiency.

A search tree is a primary example of the divide-and-conquer strategy introduced with recursion in Chapter 4 and further discussed with sorting in Chapter 7. The principal methodology of divide-and-conquer is to split or divide a given problem into a number of smaller or simpler subproblems until these subproblems are "conquered"; the solution of the individual subproblems merges to a solution of the whole problem. Trees, by definition, represent a hierarchical recursive subdivision of a given problem. Referring again to the search for key 7 in the search tree of Figure 8.17(b), it should become evident that at each node, the search problem is divided into two subproblems. At the root node, a left traversal splits the search on all the keys in the entire tree to one on all keys of lesser value than 12, while a right traversal represents a subsearch on all keys with a value greater than or equal to 12. Since key 7 is less than 12, the "left" subproblem is selected while the "right" subproblem is pruned or rejected. This divide and-conquer strategy is recursively applied at each new node until the target of the search is acquired or the limits of the tree are reached.

In the absence of explicit branching criteria, a tree search degenerates to a linear time (sequential) search on an unordered list. Exhaustive search has the advantage of being the simplest searching method but is fundamentally inefficient. This may be acceptable for many applications. Divide-and-conquer, on the other hand, is fundamentally more efficient and algorithmicly more complex. Despite the added complexity, it is the most generally applied technique in algorithm design.

8.7.1   DATA-COMPARATIVE SEARCH TREES VERSUS RADIX SEARCH TREES

The primary purpose of a search tree is to support efficient search operations on a collection of data objects. In general, we find that searching techniques fit into one of two major categories.

Property 8.1 *There are two broad categories of search techniques: (1) those that directly organize the data objects being stored, and (2) those that organize the space, which is the domain of the objects within that space.*

A search tree may be placed in one of these two categories, depending on the method by which branch decisions are made, how the data space is partitioned, and how data objects are stored.

In the following sections, our investigation of search trees along these lines is expanded:

- All search trees that fit into Property 8.1 (1) are identified as *data-comparative* or *comparison-based* search trees.

- All search trees that fit the Property 8.1 (2) model are identified as *radix* or *digital-based search trees.*

Thus, *data-comparative search trees organize objects* while *radix search trees organize space.*

This distinction may alternately be stated in terms of how the spatial domain of the data objects is partitioned. That is, comparative-based search trees induce a partitioning of space relative to the positioning of the data objects within the space, while radix search trees induce a partitioning of space that is independent of the position of the data objects. Radix search trees (digital-based search trees) indirectly organize data objects by placing them relative to a fixed space partitioning.

8.8   Data-Comparative M-ary Search Trees

Data-comparative search trees are identified as those that rely on a full comparison between the target search key and the key contained at each node along the search path. At any node, a branching decision hinges on the result of such a comparison and some specified branching criteria. As pointed out above, a data-comparative search tree directly organizes data objects to each other. The search tree of Figure 8.17(b) is an example of such an organization. At any given node, the value of the search key of the data object being searched for is compared with the value of the search key of the data object stored at the node and a branch is taken based on the established equality criteria.

The *M-ary search tree* (*MST*) is defined by extending the recursive *M*-ary tree definition given by Definition 8.2 such that

- nodes are treated as data objects identified by key, and

- a direct relationship exists between the value of these object identifiers (keys) and the parent-child ordering of the structure.

Definition 8.5 *A M-ary search tree (MST) is an M-ary tree; it is either empty or contains a root node along with M disjoint M-ary search subtrees such that:*

> *(1) the root node (data object) contains an attribute designated as the key*

> *(2) the ordered search subtrees of the root node contain keys such that there is an explicit correspondence between the value (numeric or alphabetic) of the keys and the order of the children.*

The *binary search tree* (*BST*) is defined by applying the case of $M = 2$ to Definition 8.5. For the BST, there are only two children per node, which we label as the left child and the right child.

Definition 8.6 *A binary search tree (BST) is a binary tree; it is either empty or contains a root node along with left and right binary search subtrees such that:*

> *(1) the root node (data object) contains an attribute designated as the key*

> *(2) all nodes in the left subtree of the root contain keys of value (numerically or alphabetically) less than or equal to ($\leq$) the key of the root node*

> *(3) all nodes in the right subtree of the root contain keys of value greater than ($>$) the key of the root node.*

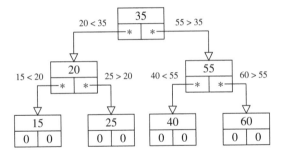

FIGURE 8.18. A binary search tree (BST).

A *BST object* is specified by an ADT BST. An *ADT BST* is a data structure that contains a set of nodes satisfying the properties in Definition 8.6, and a set of operations similar to those of an ADT binary tree. After each and every operation, the tree must remain a BST.

As an example, consider the set of integer keys

$$\{35, 20, 55, 15, 60, 25, 40\}$$

and their BST representation shown in Figure 8.18. The keys were inserted into the BST in the left-to-right order in which they are listed above. In Figure 8.18, the leaf nodes of the BST are identified as those with zero (0) valued left and right child pointers. From the "top" level (level 0), the root node contains the key value of 35. As shown, all nodes in the right subtree of this root node contain key data of value greater than 35 while all those in the left subtree contain key data of value less than 35. And at each successive level, this key value relationship with parent-child ordering is maintained.

As a comparative-based search tree, the BST of Figure 8.18 induces the data-relative key-space partitioning depicted in Figure 8.19. In this figure, the hierarchy of tree nodes is shown along with the spatial partition belonging to each node. Each node represents a splitting of a finite or semi-infinite range of the key space. For example, the node of key 25 splits the the finite range of key values bounded by 20 and 35, while the node of key 60 splits the semi-infinite range of key values bounded by 55 and heading toward positive infinity. In practice, semi-infinite or infinite regions are finite and determined by the precision of the computer.

8.8.1 INSERTING A NODE AND BUILDING A BINARY SEARCH TREE

To illustrate the process of inserting a node and building a BST, a node-by-node description of the construction of the tree of Figure 8.18 is presented

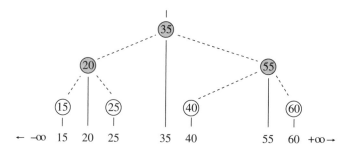

FIGURE 8.19. Data-relative space partitioning of a BST

below. At each step, the insertion keys are identified and the status of the tree is given. The tree is initially empty.

35:

Since the BST is empty, the root node is created, and the key data 35 is inserted in the new node. After the insertion of 35, the BST is shown in Figure 8.20(a).

20:

To insert 20 in this BST, we compare 20 with 35, the key data in the root node. Since 20 < 35 and the BST criterion defines the parent-child relationship to be an ascending order, the key data 20 will be inserted in the left subtree of the root node; since the left subtree of the root node with 35 is empty, the key data 20 is inserted in the left child node of the root node. After the insertion of 20, the BST is shown in Figure 8.20(b).

55:

Since BST is not empty with root node 35, and 55 > 35, and the parent-child relationship is in ascending order, and since the right child node of the root node is empty, a new node is created for this right child node of the root node; the key data 55 is inserted in this node. After the insertion of 55, the BST is in Figure 8.20(c).

15, 60, 25, 40:

Starting key comparison with the root node's key data 35, and proceeding similarly, the appropriate location of the node is found where the new node with one of these keys will be inserted. Finally, the BST is built and shown in Figure 8.18.

In **Code 8.4**, add_node() and build_tree() respectively implement the insert operation and the build operation of a BST object.

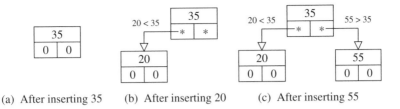

(a) After inserting 35   (b) After inserting 20   (c) After inserting 55

FIGURE 8.20. BST insert operations.

8.8.2 DELETING A NODE FROM A BST

The delete operation in a BST is not a simple process. This is because
the node to be deleted must be replaced by another of the tree and the
new tree must remain in the BST after the node is deleted from the BST.
The parent-child relationship (e.g., ascending order) must be maintained.
Assume the node to be deleted is identified by its key `delete_key`.

The algorithm of deleting a node from a BST is:

Step 1. Search the BST for the node with `delete_key`. If it is not
found, print a message and return. If it exists in the BST node,
pointed to by `target_ptr` and its parent (predecessor) node
is pointed to by `parent_ptr`, proceed to Step 2.

Step 2. Based on the location of this node with `delete_key` in the
BST, consider four cases:

Case 1. The target node, pointed to by `target_ptr`, is a
leaf node (i.e., it has no children). Set its parent's
(pointed to by `parent_ptr`) left or child pointer
to NULL.

Case 2. The target node has a left child only. If the target
node is the root node, replace the root node (pointed
to by `root_ptr`) with the target node's left child.
Otherwise, if the target node is the parent node's
left child, replace the parent node's left child with
the target node's left child; if the target node is the
parent node's right child, replace the parent node's
right child with the target node's left child.

Case 3. The target node has a right child only. As in Case
2, replace parent node's appropriate child with the
target node's right child.

Case 4. The target node has both left and right children. Replace it with the node with the largest data key, say

right_most (i.e., the right most node), in its left subtree. This maintains the ascending order property in BST because every node in the target node's right subtree is greater (in key value) than every node in its left subtree, and every node in its left subtree is less (in key value) than the right most node, right_most, which cannot have any right child. The steps for Case 4 are shown in steps 2.4.1 through 2.4.6.

Step 2.4.1. Find the right-most node and its parent.

Step 2.4.2. Delink the right-most node from its parent. If the right-most node is the left child of its parent, replace its parent's left child with its own left child. Otherwise, replace its parent's right child with its own left child.

Step 2.4.3. Insert the right-most node at the location of the target node by setting the left and right children of the right mode node to the target node's left and right children, respectively.

Step 2.4.4. If the target node is the root node, replace it with the right-most node. Otherwise, the target node is an intermediate node with nonempty children.

Step 2.4.5. If the target node is the left node of its parent, replace its parent's left child node with the right-most node. Otherwise, do step 2.4.6.

Step 2.4.6. Replace its parent's right child node with the right-most node.

Step 3. Free up memory space of the target node.

The tree now satisfies the BST properties.

To illustrate Case 4 of Step 2, consider the BST for the people database in Figure 8.18. Suppose we want to delete the node with data key 35. This node with key 35 has both left and right children. The largest data key in its left subtree is 25, which is in the right-most and leaf node. The smallest data key in its right subtree is 40, which is in the left-most and leaf node. The right-most node's key 25 is the largest of other nodes' keys 15 and 20 in the left subtree, and the smallest of all nodes' keys 55, 40, and 60 in the right subtree of the target node with 35. Replacing the node with 35 by the node with 25 still keeps both subtrees compliant with ascending ordering. Thus, after deleting the node with key 35, the BST is as shown in Figure 8.21.

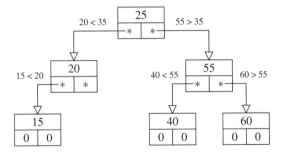

FIGURE 8.21. BST after deleting a node with key 25.

An alternative approach is to replace the target node with key 35 with its the left-most key 40 in the right subtree. The BST property still holds true.

The implementation of the delete operation is left as an exercise.

8.8.3 OOP IMPLEMENTATION OF A BINARY SEARCH TREE USING POINTERS

Using an object-oriented design approach, the BST object is specified by an ADT BST; the object's methods are directly derived from the ADT definition of the BST. The binary search tree object is a data structure that contains each node's data and pointers to the left and right children of each node, and the operations as methods. For the OOP characteristics of data-hiding, encapsulation, and methods for message passing, the Binary_Search_Tree class is defined in the header file class_Binary_Search_Tree.h as follows:

```
class Binary_Search_Tree : public Tree {
  private:
    typedef struct  BSTREE_NODE {
        DATA_TYPE       data;
        BSTREE_NODE    *left_childptr;
        BSTREE_NODE    *right_childptr;
    } *TREE_PTR;
    TREE_PTR root_ptr;    // root of the BST
    int      INPUT_SIZE;
    void     init_BSTree()    { root_ptr = NULL; }
    void     delete_BST (TREE_PTR tree_ptr);
    TREE_PTR search_node_in_BST(TREE_PTR tree_ptr,
                    DATA_TYPE srch_key);
    void     traverse_BST_Postorder(TREE_PTR tree_ptr);
    void     traverse_BST_Preorder(TREE_PTR tree_ptr);
    void     traverse_BST_Inorder(TREE_PTR tree_ptr);
  public:
```

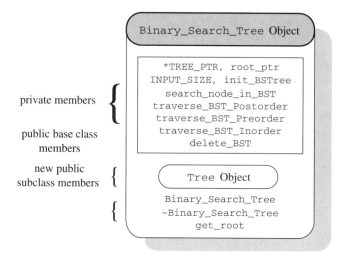

FIGURE 8.22. Binary_Search_Tree object.

```
Binary_Search_Tree(int size)
        {init_BSTree(); INPUT_SIZE = size;}
~Binary_Search_Tree();
BOOLEAN  is_empty(void) {return (root_ptr == NULL);}
void     build_tree(DATA_TYPE A[]);
void     add_node(DATA_TYPE new_data);
void     search_node(DATA_TYPE srch_key);
void     delete_node(DATA_TYPE srch_key) {};
void     print_tree(void);
void     postorder(void);
void     preorder(void);
void     inorder (void);
TREE_PTR get_root() { return root_ptr; }
};
```

The Binary_Search_Tree class defines a type for a binary search tree object, bstree_obj, encompassing both data and operations. The members DATA_TYPE, BSTREE_NODE type structure data and root_ptr (the pointer to the root node) are made private for data-hiding and protection from corruption. Binary_Search_Tree(),~Binary_Search_Tree(), and is_empty() are public member functions, which means these are interfaces to the outside world (e.g., main()) in order to facilitate message passing between Binary_Tree-type object and any other object. The member function get_root() is made public for providing read-only access of the data member root_ptr. Figure 8.22 depicts a BST object.

8.8.4 METHODS OF THE Binary_Search_Tree CLASS

Binary_Search_Tree(), a publicly accessible member function of the Binary_Search_Tree class, constructs this class's object by calling init_BSTree(). It is automatically called when an object bstree_obj is instantiated.

~Binary_Search_Tree(), a publicly accessible member function of the Binary_Search_Tree class, is the destructor for an object of this class. It deallocates memory space for a binary search tree object by calling BSTdelete_tree(). It is implicitly called at the program exit.

Is_empty() of type BOOLEAN is a public member function of the class Binary_Search_Tree. It returns 1 if a BST object is empty, and 0 otherwise.

Init_BSTree() of type void is a private member function of the Binary_Search_Tree class. It sets root_ptr to NULL in order to initialize a BST object.

Add_node() of type void is a public and nonrecursive member function of the Binary_Search_Tree class. It assumes that the data in each node are used as keys for comparison, and the BST is in ascending order if traversed in inorder mode. It takes new_data as an argument, and allocates memory space for a BST node, pointed to by new_ptr. If BST is empty, and root_ptr is set to new_ptr, then the new node is the root node, and next it will return. Otherwise, the function proceeds to search for the insertion location starting from the root node. If the node to be inserted already exists, it simply returns. If new_data is less than the data field of a subtree's root node, it traverses to this subtree's left subtree to find the target node. If new_data is greater than the data field of a subtree's root node, it traverses to this subtree's right subtree to find the target node, whose left or right child will be this new node. Assume the target node is pointed to by target_node_ptr. The new node with new_data is made left child of the target node if new_data is less than the data in the target node. The new node with new_data is made the right child of the target node if new_data is greater than the data in the target node.

Build_tree() of type void is a public member function of the Binary_Search_Tree class. It calls init_BSTree() to initialize a BST object. Given an array of n integer data elements, it calls add_node() for n times to build a BST object.

Search_node() of type BST_PTR is a public member function of the Binary_Search_Tree class. It is implemented as a recursive function. It searches a BST object for a node specified by a key, Key. It starts its preorder traversal from the root of the BST. If the Key is less than the data field of the root node of the current subtree, it continues searching its left subtree until a leaf node is encountered. If the Key is greater than the data field of the root node of the current subtree, it continues searching its right subtree until a leaf node is encountered. If Key matches the data field of the root node of the current subtree, the BST_PTR type pointer to this root node is returned. If it fails to find a match, it prints a message and returns a NULL pointer. The worst-case performance of the BST search with n nodes is between $O(n)$ and $O(\log_2 n)$. Its nonrecursive version is left as an exercise.

delete_BST() of type void is a private member function of the Binary_Search_Tree class. It is implemented as a recursive function. It does postorder traversal to free up each node in the BST object.

Preorder(), a public member function of Binary_Search_Tree class, calls the private member function traverse_BST_Preorder(), which is recursive and prints the data attribute of each node exactly once using a preorder traversal scheme.

Postorder() is a publicly accessible member function of the class Binary_Search_Tree. It prints this class's object by calling the class's private member function traverse_BST_Postorder(). Printing is done by visiting each node only once in a postorder manner.

Inorder(), a public member function of the Binary_Search_Tree class, walks through this class's object by calling the recursive function traverse_BST_Inorder(). While each node is visited in an inorder traversal manner, its data attribute is printed.

Print_tree() of type void is a public member function of the Binary_Search_Tree class. It calls traverse_BST_Inorder() to print the entire BST object in ascending order.

Main() is a test driver for OOP implementation of the binary search tree. It instantiates an object bstree_obj of Binary_Search_Tree type. Since main() is a client function of the Binary_Tree class, it sends messages to bstree_obj through the object's publicly accessible methods. Given an array A of integer keys

$$\{16, 54, 14, 63, 62, 48, 21, 53\}$$

in the people_1d database, the messages include building the search tree object for A, performing inorder, postorder, and preorder traversals, and searching for a node specified by its key. The program's memory is freed up by delete []A and the implicit call of ~Binary_Search_Tree.

Code 8.4

```
//   Program: BSTree.c++
//   Purpose:
//      OBJECT-ORIENTED IMPLEMENTATION  of a
//      Binary Search Tree for integer data.
//
#include <stdio.h>
typedef  int  BOOLEAN;
typedef  int  DATA_TYPE;   // Type of node's data
#include "bc_tree.h"  // For base class "Tree"
//  Define Binary_Search_Tree class for the BST
```

```
#include "class_Binary_Search_Tree.h"

//   ~Binary_Search_Tree():
//     Destroy memory space for an object of this class
//     It is automatically called before exit from main.
//
Binary_Search_Tree::~Binary_Search_Tree()
{
   delete_BST (root_ptr);
}

// add_node ():
//   Add (insert) a new data into BST, whose
//   root node is pointed to by 'root_ptr'. If
//   the data already exists, it is ignored.
//   (Nonrecursive Implementation )
//
void Binary_Search_Tree::add_node(DATA_TYPE new_data)
{
   TREE_PTR new_ptr, target_node_ptr;

   new_ptr = new BSTREE_NODE;
   // Add new data in the new node's data field
   new_ptr->data = new_data;
   new_ptr->left_childptr  = NULL;
   new_ptr->right_childptr = NULL;

   //  If the BST is empty, insert the new data in root
   if (root_ptr == NULL)
      root_ptr = new_ptr;

   //  Now look for the insertion location
   else  {
      TREE_PTR   tree_ptr = root_ptr;
      while (tree_ptr != NULL) {
        target_node_ptr = tree_ptr;
        if (new_data == tree_ptr->data)
           // Found same data; ignore it.
           return;
        else if (new_data < tree_ptr->data)
           // Search its left subtree for insertion location
           tree_ptr = tree_ptr->left_childptr;
        else   //  new_data > tree_ptr->data
           // Search its right subtree for insertion location
           tree_ptr = tree_ptr->right_childptr;
        }  //  end of while (tree_ptr != NULL)

      //  Now 'target_node_ptr' is the pointer to the
      //  parent of the new node. Decide where it will
      //  be inserted.
      if (new_data < target_node_ptr->data)
         target_node_ptr->left_childptr = new_ptr;
      else  // insert it as its right child
         target_node_ptr->right_childptr = new_ptr;
```

```
      }
  }

// build_tree():
//    Builds a BST from a given array of n
//    DATA_TYPE data, which are nodes' data.
//
void Binary_Search_Tree::build_tree(DATA_TYPE A[])
{
    for (int j = 0; j < INPUT_SIZE; j++)
       add_node (A[j]);
}

// search_node_in_BST():
//    Find a given node by "Key" in BST. If successful,
//    it returns the pointer that points to the node
//    with "Key"; otherwise, it returns NULL. It uses
//    preorder traversal. (Recursive method).
//
Binary_Search_Tree::TREE_PTR
Binary_Search_Tree::search_node_in_BST
               (TREE_PTR tree_ptr, DATA_TYPE Key)
{
   if (tree_ptr != NULL) {
      if (Key == tree_ptr->data)
         return (tree_ptr);
      else if (Key < tree_ptr->data)
         // Search for "Key" in the left subtree
         search_node_in_BST(tree_ptr->left_childptr,
                            Key);
      else   // (Key > tree_ptr->data)
         // Search for "Key" in the right subtree
         search_node_in_BST(tree_ptr->right_childptr,
                            Key);
   }
   else {
         printf("\n search_node_in_BST: Node %d %s \n",
                Key, "is not found");
         return (NULL);
   }
}

void Binary_Search_Tree::search_node(DATA_TYPE srch_key)
{
   TREE_PTR srch_ptr = NULL;
   srch_ptr = search_node_in_BST(root_ptr, srch_key);
   if (srch_ptr != NULL)
      printf("\n\n Node: %d is found in the BST\n",
             srch_ptr->data);
}

// delete_BST():
//    Delete entire BST. It releases all memory spaces
//    using 'PostOrder' traversal method.
```

```
//
void Binary_Search_Tree::delete_BST(TREE_PTR tree_ptr)
{
   if (tree_ptr != NULL) {
      delete_BST (tree_ptr->left_childptr);
      delete_BST (tree_ptr->right_childptr);
      delete  tree_ptr;
   }
}

// traverse_BST_Preorder():
//    Traverse BST using preorder traversal;
//    the BST is pointed to by 'tree_ptr'.
//    (Recursive method)
//
void Binary_Search_Tree::traverse_BST_Preorder
                              (TREE_PTR tree_ptr)
{
   if (tree_ptr != NULL) {
      // Root node of the subtree is visited, i.e.,
      // its data is printed.
      printf(" %d ", tree_ptr->data);
      // Traverse its left BST subtree
      traverse_BST_Preorder(tree_ptr->left_childptr);
      // Traverse its right BST subtree
      traverse_BST_Preorder(tree_ptr->right_childptr);
   }
}

void Binary_Search_Tree::preorder(void)
{
   printf("\n The Binary Search Tree after %s \n",
          "PreOrder traversal:");
   traverse_BST_Preorder(root_ptr);
}

// traverse_BST_Postorder():
//    Traverse BST using postorder traversal;
//    the BST is pointed to by 'tree_ptr'.
//    (Recursive method)
//
void Binary_Search_Tree::traverse_BST_Postorder
                              (TREE_PTR tree_ptr)
{
   if (tree_ptr != NULL) {
      // Traverse its left BST subtree
      traverse_BST_Postorder(tree_ptr->left_childptr);
      // Traverse its right BST subtree
      traverse_BST_Postorder(tree_ptr->right_childptr);
      // Root node of the subtree is visited, i.e.,
      // its data is printed.
      printf(" %d ", tree_ptr->data);
   }
}
```

```cpp
void Binary_Search_Tree::postorder(void)
{
   printf("\n The Binary Search Tree after %s \n",
          "PostOrder traversal:");
   traverse_BST_Postorder(root_ptr);
}


// traverse_BST_Inorder():
//   Traverse BST using inorder traversal;
//   the BST is pointed to by 'tree_ptr'.
//   (Recursive method)
//
void Binary_Search_Tree::traverse_BST_Inorder
                              (TREE_PTR tree_ptr)
{
   if (tree_ptr != NULL) {
      // Traverse its left BST subtree
      traverse_BST_Inorder(tree_ptr->left_childptr);
      // Root node of the subtree is visited, i.e.,
      // its data is printed.
      printf(" %d ", tree_ptr->data);
      // Traverse its right BST subtree
      traverse_BST_Inorder(tree_ptr->right_childptr);
   }
}

void Binary_Search_Tree::inorder(void)
{
   printf("\n The Binary Search Tree after %s \n",
          "InOrder traversal:");
   traverse_BST_Inorder(root_ptr);
}

// print_tree():
//   Print a BST tree using inorder traversal.
//
void Binary_Search_Tree::print_tree(void)
{
   traverse_BST_Inorder(root_ptr);
}

//  main():
//     OBJECT-ORIENTED IMPLEMENTATION of a
//     Binary Search Tree (BST)
//
void main(void)
{
   // For the following set of nodes, root = 33
   static DATA_TYPE A[8] = {16, 54, 14, 63,
                            62, 48, 21, 53};
   static int no_data = sizeof(A)/sizeof(DATA_TYPE);
   // Declare an object of Binary_Search_Tree class
   Binary_Search_Tree  bstree_obj(no_data);
```

```
      printf("\n OBJECT-ORIENTED IMPLEMENTATION %s \n",
             "OF BINARY SEARCH TREE");
      bstree_obj.build_tree(A);
      bstree_obj.postorder();
      bstree_obj.preorder();
      bstree_obj.inorder();
      bstree_obj.search_node(45);
      delete []A;
  }
```

Code 8.4 for the OOP implementation of a BST yields:

```
OBJECT-ORIENTED IMPLEMENTATION OF BINARY SEARCH TREE

The Binary Search Tree after PostOrder traversal:
14   21   53   48   62   63   54   16
The Binary Search Tree after PreOrder traversal:
16   14   54   48   21   53   63   62
The Binary Search Tree after InOrder traversal:
14   16   21   48   53   54   62   63
search_node_in_BST: Node 45 is not found
```

Notice that the inorder traversal of a BST produces an ascending ordered (sorted) form of the array.

8.8.5   BST AND QUICKSORT RELATIONSHIP

The use of a binary search tree is intimately related to that of the quicksort algorithm introduced in Section 7.1.5. The BST structure reflects the execution of Quicksort. Each node of the tree corresponds to one call to the sorting routine — each represents a data-relative comparative-based partitioning of the data space.

Property 8.2 *Binary tree searching partitions a file in exactly the same way as Quicksort.*

8.8.6   BALANCE CHARACTERISTICS OF COMPARATIVE-BASED SEARCH TREE

Since the comparative-based search tree object produces a data-relative organization, its height balance is dependent on the order in which the represented set of keys is inserted.

Property 8.3 *The shape (balance) of the ADT comparative-based search tree is extremely sensitive to the order in which the tree is built.*

As an example, consider again the BST of Figure 8.18. Note that if the insertion order of the keys is changed from

$$\{35, 20, 55, 15, 60, 25, 40\} \text{ to } \{55, 15, 35, 60, 25, 20, 40\},$$

a different BST would result. The reader should verify that this is the case (Exercise 8-16).

The main advantage of the BST over an ordinary binary tree is that it can search for and access the nodes quickly. A balanced BST of n nodes the search time $O(\log_2 n)$. However, as the BST becomes more and more unbalanced, the tree degenerates and the search time approaches a worst-case exhaustive $O(n)$. Unfortunately, the BST, in the form currently presented, has no mechanism to guarantee balance. This issue is addressed by AVL trees.

8.8.7 AVL TREES

The *AVL tree*, named after its inventors [Ade62] Adel'son-Vel'skii and Landis, was developed to deal with height imbalance in a BST. An AVL tree, also called a *height-balanced binary search tree*, can achieve a worst-case performance of $O(\log_2 n)$ for the search, retrieve, insert, and delete operations.

The AVL tree is balanced with respect to the heights of its subtrees. The relation between the height h of an AVL tree and the number n of nodes in an AVL tree is

$$n = 2^{h-1}, \text{ or } h = log_2(n+1) = O(log_2 n).$$

The *balance factor* for each node X, the root of a (sub)tree, is

$$Balance\ factor\ of\ X \quad = \quad height\ of\ right\ subtree\ of\ X \\ - height\ of\ left\ subtree\ of\ X$$

It is a characteristic of each node of an AVL tree. For any node X of an AVL tree,

$$balance\_factor(X) \quad = \quad -1, 0, +1.$$

When $balance\_factor(X) = -1$, the height of left subtree of node X is greater than that of right subtree of node X. When $balance\_factor(X) = 0$, the height of left subtree of node X equals that of right subtree of X. Finally, when $balance\_factor(X) = +1$, the height of left subtree of X is less than that of right subtree of X.

If $balance\_factor(X) = +2 \ or \ -2$, the AVL tree is unbalanced at the node X; node X is called the *pivot* node. The tree must be balanced around the pivot node using *rotation* techniques. When $balance\_factor(X) = +2$,

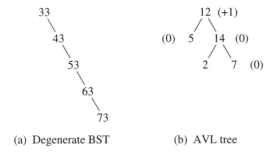

(a) Degenerate BST   (b) AVL tree

FIGURE 8.23. A degenerate BST and an AVL tree.

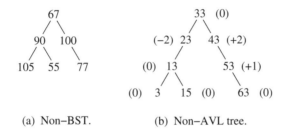

(a) Non-BST.   (b) Non-AVL tree.

FIGURE 8.24. A non-BST and non-AVL tree.

node X is *unbalanced on the right* and a left rotation is called for. When $balance\_factor(X) = -2$, to the right.

The balance of an AVL tree is checked and restored, if necessary, after each insertion and deletion of nodes. That the balance factor of a node, say X, is $+2$ or -2 after insertion or deletion, indicates the balance factor of X was $+1$ or -1 before insertion or deletion.

In an AVL tree, the data of all nodes are in ascending or descending order, and the balance factor for each node is at most one in absolute value. An AVL tree is a BST with the additional balancing requirement. For example, for a set of integers 33, 43, 53, 63, 73, a degenerate BST, and an AVL tree are shown in Figure 8.23.

In Figure 8.23(b), the balance factors for each node are shown within parentheses.

A non-AVL tree is either a non-BST or a BST but unbalanced. Figure 8.24(a) is a non-BST because its nodes do not follow any ordering. Figure 8.24(b) is a BST but not height-balanced; nodes 23 and 43 have balance factors -2 and $+2$ respectively.

8.8.8   AVL Tree Objects

An AVL tree object is specified by an ADT AVL tree. An ADT AVL tree is a data structure that contains a set of nodes and a collection of operations.

Property 8.4 *The set of nodes in an ADT AVL tree forms a binary search tree such that (1) the balance factor of the root node is at most 1, and (2) both the left and right subtrees of the root node are AVL trees by themselves.*

Since an AVL tree object is a BST object in particular, most of these operations except insert and delete are analogous to those for a BST. Though building an AVL tree uses the insert operation, we now discuss it as well as insertion, deletion, and balancing. For the sake of completeness, an OOP implementation for an AVL tree object is given in **Code 8.5**.

8.8.9   OOP Implementation of an AVL Tree Using Pointers

Using an object-oriented design approach, an AVL tree object is identified by an ADT AVL tree whose methods are directly derived from the ADT definition of the AVL tree. The AVL tree object, depicted in Figure 8.25, is a data structure that contains a node's data and pointers to the left and right children of each node, and the operations as methods. To implement the OOP characteristics of data-hiding, encapsulation, and methods for message passing, the `AVL_Tree` class is defined in the header file `class_AVL_Tree.h` as follows:

```
class AVL_Tree : public Tree {
  private:
    typedef struct AVL_NODE {
       DATA_TYPE   data;
       BALANCE     bal_fact;
       AVL_NODE    *left_childptr;
       AVL_NODE    *right_childptr;
    } *TREE_PTR;
    TREE_PTR root_ptr;
    int      INPUT_SIZE;
    int      curr_node_num;  // for printing
    int      curr_line_pos;  // for printing
    void     delete_AVL_tree(TREE_PTR tree_ptr);
    TREE_PTR create_AVL_node(DATA_TYPE new_data);
    void     rotate_right(TREE_PTR  tree_ptr);
    void     rotate_left (TREE_PTR  tree_ptr);
    void     printlevel(TREE_PTR root_ptr,
                   int level, int curr_level);
    void     show_AVL_vertically(void);
    int max(int a,int b) {
      if (a>=b) return(a); else return(b);
    }
    void     traverse_AVL_Inorder(TREE_PTR tree_ptr);
```

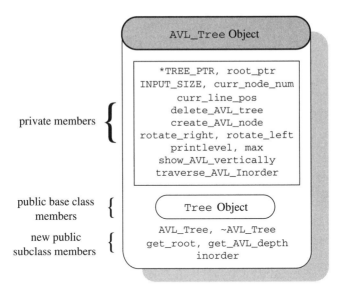

FIGURE 8.25. AVL_Tree object.

```
public:
   AVL_Tree(int size)
           { root_ptr = NULL; INPUT_SIZE = size;
             curr_node_num = curr_line_pos=0; }
   ~AVL_Tree();
   BOOLEAN is_empty() { return root_ptr == NULL; }
   void    build_tree(DATA_TYPE A[]);
   void    add_node(DATA_TYPE new_data);
   void    search_node(DATA_TYPE srch_key) {};
   void    delete_node(DATA_TYPE srch_key) {};
   void    print_tree(void)
     {AVL_Tree::show_AVL_vertically();}
   TREE_PTR get_root() { return (root_ptr); }
   int     get_AVL_depth(TREE_PTR root_ptr);
   void    inorder()
     {AVL_Tree::traverse_AVL_Inorder(root_ptr);}
};
```

The AVL_Tree class defines a type for avl_tree_obj, an AVL tree object encompassing both data and operations. The members DATA_TYPE, AVL_NODE type structure data, and the pointers root_ptr (the pointer to the root node) are private to ensure data-hiding and protection. The member functions AVL_Tree(), ~AVL_Tree(), build_tree(), and so on are public, meaning that these are interfaces to the outside world in order to facilitate message passing between AVL_Tree-type object and an object of the same or different type. The member function `get_root()` is made `public` for providing read-only access of the data member `root_ptr`. For the OOP implementation of an AVL tree object using linked list (pointers) in **Code 8.5**, the insert, delete, and rotate operations are now discussed.

8.8.10 INSERTION OF A NODE IN AN AVL TREE

Inserting a node is not done if the node already exists in the AVL tree. Inserting a new node may make an AVL tree unbalanced at any node, between the root node and the grandparent or *nearest ancestor* of the new node. Since the tree must remain balanced after insertion, the rebalancing using rotation is performed within the insert operation. After insertion, the unbalanced state of the tree occurs only when the new node is added to a subtree (e.g., left subtree) of the root whose height is already 1 more than that of the other subtree (e.g., right subtree). In an AVL tree, a new node, say P, can be inserted in the following possible locations:

- Insertion of a new node P is in the left subtree of right subtree of the grandparent node, say G.

- Insertion of a new node P is in the right subtree of right subtree of the grandparent node G.

- Insertion of a new node P is in the left subtree of left subtree of the grandparent node G.

- Insertion of a new node P is in the right subtree of left subtree of the grandparent node G.

If the balance factor of G is -1 or $+1$ before insertion, and becomes -2 or $+2$ after insertion, the tree becomes unbalanced at the grandparent node G. It requires using a single or double rotation in order to restore balance in the newly formed tree.

An AVL tree being viewed as a special form of BST, the inserting process follows the same technique as in BST and does rebalancing and adjusting balances of each node in the search path. The *search path* is the path from the root node, pointed to by `root_ptr`, to the node where the new node is inserted. The node's data are used as keys for comparison and its ordering is ascending.

8.8.11 INSERTING A NEW NODE INTO AN AVL TREE

Step 1. Allocate memory space for the new node with data, `new_data`. Assume `new_ptr` points to this memory space.

Step 2. Set the left and right link fields to `NULL`, `balance_factor` to 0, and the data field to `new_data`.

Step 3. If the AVL tree is empty, do: `root_ptr = new_ptr; return;`

Step 4. Locate the node where the new node can be inserted.

Step 5. Following ascending ordering, insert the new node.

Step 6. Recalculate the balance factor for each node in the search path from root to the new node.

Step 7. Locate the unbalanced node, if any, with balance factor $+2$ (right subtree high) or -2 (left subtree high) in the search path. Call the unbalanced node the pivot node.

Step 8. Rebalance the newly formed tree so that it satisfies the AVL property, considering four cases:

> Case 1. There is no unbalanced node in the search path. The tree is an AVL tree.
>
> Case 2. Balance factor of pivot node is $+2$, the height of the right subtree of the pivot node is 2 more than that of its left subtree; rotate left for the subtree with the pivot node as the root.
>
> Case 3. Balance factor of pivot node is -2, the height of the left subtree of the pivot node is 2 more than that of its right subtree; rotate right for the subtree with the pivot node as the root.
>
> Case 4. Balance factor of pivot node is -2, and the location of the new node may be in the left subtree of the pivot node's right subtree, or in the right subtree of the pivot node's left subtree; use double rotation in this case.

Step 9. Continue rebalancing the subtrees with nodes on the search path until the balance factors of all the nodes on the search path are -1, 0, or $+1$. Note that the newly formed tree after insertion, satisfies the AVL property.

Note that in some cases, it may be required to perform double rotation to preserve balancing. A double rotation is either a left rotation followed by a right rotation, or a right rotation followed by a left rotation.

8.8.12   INSERTING A NODE AND BUILDING AN AVL TREE

To illustrate the process of inserting a node and building an AVL tree, consider the set of ten integers

$$\{33, 60, 5, 15, 25, 12, 45, 70, 35, 7\}.$$

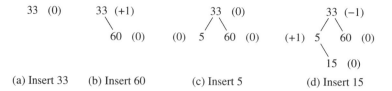

(a) Insert 33   (b) Insert 60   (c) Insert 5   (d) Insert 15

FIGURE 8.26. Insert operations on an AVL tree.

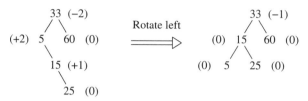

(a) Unbalanced after insertion of 25   (b) Balanced after left rotation

FIGURE 8.27. Left rotation in an AVL tree.

Initially the AVL tree is empty. Ascending ordering among these keys is used for insertion. An insertion is started as in BST. The numbers in parentheses indicate the balance factor for each node. After each insertion step, the new tree must be kept balanced in order to satisfy the AVL tree property. To do this, the balance factor for each node is recalculated only in the search path (i.e., from the root node to the new node). Note that the balance factors for other nodes and other subtrees remain unchanged.

The keys 33, 60, 5, and 15 are simply inserted. The trees in Figure 8.26 remain balanced satisfying the AVL tree property. This demonstrates Case 1 of Step 8.

Inserting the key 25 in the AVL tree shown in Figure 8.26(d) produces an unbalanced tree in Figure 8.27(a). The node with key 5 is the nearest ancestor (grandparent); its balance factor becomes −2, and so it is unbalanced. Use the node with 5 as the pivot to perform *left rotation* for rebalancing the tree. Figure 8.27(b) shows the balanced AVL tree after the left rotation around the pivot node with 5. This demonstrates Case 2 of Step 8.

Inserting the key 12 in the AVL tree shown in Figure 8.27(d) produces an unbalanced tree in Figure 8.28(a). The node with key 33 is the nearest ancestor (grandparent); its balance factor becomes −2, and so it is unbalanced with its left subtree high. Note that due to insertion of 12, the balance factors are affected for the nodes with keys 5, 15, and 33, on the search path (from the root 33 to the new node 12). Use the node with 33 as the pivot to perform *right rotation* for rebalancing the tree. Figure 8.28(b) shows the balanced AVL tree after the right rotation around the pivot node

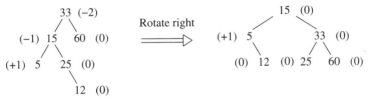

(a) Unbalanced after insertion of 12   (b) Balanced after right rotation

FIGURE 8.28. Right rotation in an AVL tree.

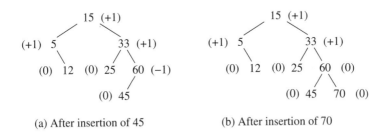

(a) After insertion of 45   (b) After insertion of 70

FIGURE 8.29. Insertion of 45 and 70 into AVL tree.

with 33. This demonstrates Case 3 of Step 8.

Inserting nodes with keys 45 and 70 do not change the AVL property for the trees in Figures 8.29(a) and 8.29(b).

Inserting a node with key 35 produces an unbalanced tree (see Figure 8.30(a)) at the pivot node with 33 and balance factor +2. To regain balance, perform double rotation (right rotation at node with 60 and then left rotation at node with 33). After double rotation, the regained AVL tree is shown in Figure 8.30(b). This demonstrates Case 4 of Step 8.

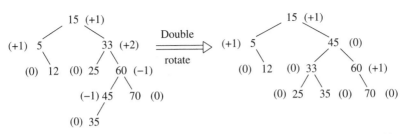

(a) Unbalanced after insertion of 35.   (b) After right rotate at 60 and left rotate at 33.

FIGURE 8.30. Balance by double rotation on AVL tree.

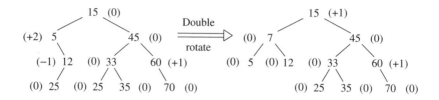

(a) Unbalanced after insertion of 7.   (b) After right rotate at 12 and left rotate at 5.

FIGURE 8.31. Another example of balance by double rotation on AVL tree.

Another example of Case 4 for Step 8 is shown in Figure 8.31. In Figure 8.31(a), the pivot node with 5 has balance factor +2. To regain balance in the tree, perform double rotation (right rotation at node with 12 and then left rotation at node with 5). After double rotation, the regained AVL tree is shown in Figure 8.31(b).

8.8.13   CREATING A NODE FOR AN AVL TREE

Creating a new node for an AVL tree involves allocating memory space for such node. Use the new operator for an AVL node of type AVL_NODE. Create_AVL_node() returns a pointer of type TREE_PTR that points to the allocated memory space of the size of AVL_NODE. It returns a NULL pointer value if there is no memory space.

```
TREE_PTR  create_AVL_node (void)
{
  TREE_PTR new_ptr = new AVL_NODE;

  if (new_ptr != NULL) {
    new_ptr->data = 0;
    new_ptr->left_childptr  = NULL;
    new_ptr->right_childptr = NULL;
  }
  else
    printf ("\n create_AVL_node: allocation failed!\n");
  return (new_ptr);
}
```

8.8.14   DELETING A NODE FROM AN AVL TREE

Deleting a node from an AVL tree is the reverse process of inserting a node into an AVL tree. If the AVL tree is empty, or the node to be deleted is not found in the AVL tree, the delete operation fails. Otherwise, since an AVL tree is a BST in particular, consider four cases as in BST:

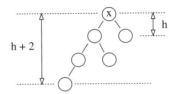

FIGURE 8.32. Unbalanced node X in a tree.

Case 1. The AVL tree is empty or the target node is not in the AVL tree.

Case 2. The target node has no children, that is, it is a leaf node.

Case 3. The target node has one child, left or right.

Case 4. The target node has two children.

For Case 1, simply report a message and return. For Cases 2, 3, and 4, proceed as follows. Release the memory space held by the target node, and recalculate the balance factors of the nodes in the search path. Rebalance if necessary, following the four cases stated in Step 8 of Section 8.8.11. Use left, or right, or double rotation to regain AVL property including the ascending or descending ordering among the keys (node's data).

The detailed algorithm and implementation are left as an exercise.

8.8.15   REGAINING BALANCE WITH ROTATION TECHNIQUES

After the insert and delete operations in an AVL tree object, the tree must remain balanced, that is, all nodes and the nodes in the search path must have balance factors $-1, 0, +1$. An unbalanced state of the tree occurs when there is at least one node with balance factor -2 or $+2$. To regain balance in the tree, it is necessary to use single or double rotation around the unbalanced node. A double rotation consists of a left rotation followed by a right rotation, or a right rotation followed by a left rotation. Figure 8.27 shows a left rotation after insertion of 25. Figure 8.28 shows a right rotation after insertion of 12. Figures 8.30 and 8.31 demonstrate two instances of double rotation after the insert operation. In short, a rotation is required when the height of the left (right) subtree of an unbalanced node is 2 more than that of the right (left) subtree. For example, Figure 8.32 shows node X is unbalanced with the balance factor -2. The height of its left subtree is $(h + 2)$ and the height of its right subtree is h.

The codes for left and right rotations are included in the insert function add_node() of **Code 8.5**. Implementations of individual functions for left and right rotations are left as exercises.

The main points for an AVL tree are summarized below.

- An AVL tree object is inherently balanced.

- Insert and delete operations must perform rebalancing the tree, if necessary.

- Balance factors of the nodes in the search path from the root to the parent node must be adjusted to satisfy the required values -1, 0, or $+1$.

- After insertion or deletion of a node, balance is regained by single or double rotations.

- Unlike BST, the AVL tree never degenerates.

- The worst-case performances for the insert, delete and search operations in an AVL tree is $O(\log_2 n)$.

Code 8.5

```
//   Program:  avl.c++
//   Purpose:
//      Object-oriented implementation of an
//      AVL tree object for integer data.
//
#include <stdio.h>
#include <stdlib.h>
#include <ctype.h>
typedef   int   BOOLEAN;
typedef   int   DATA_TYPE;
typedef   int   BALANCE;
#include   "bc_tree.h"  // For base class "Tree"
#include   "class_AVL_Tree.h"

// ~AVL_Tree():
//     This destructor deallocates memory spaces.
//
AVL_Tree::~AVL_Tree()
{
    delete_AVL_tree(root_ptr);
}

// delete_AVL_tree():
//    Deallocates the tree in the postorder
//    traversal. (Recursive implementation)
//
void AVL_Tree::delete_AVL_tree(TREE_PTR root_ptr)
{
    if (root_ptr != NULL) {
       delete_AVL_tree(root_ptr->left_childptr );
       delete_AVL_tree(root_ptr->right_childptr);
       delete root_ptr;
```

```
   }
}

// build_tree():
//   this routine will read an initialized array
//   of integers of and build an AVL tree from this array
//
void AVL_Tree::build_tree(DATA_TYPE A[])
{
   for (int i = 0; i < INPUT_SIZE; i++)
      add_node (A[i]);
}

// create_AVL_node():
//   Allocates a node  of the type AVL_NODE
//   and initializes all fields to 0 except data.
//
AVL_Tree::TREE_PTR
AVL_Tree::create_AVL_node(DATA_TYPE new_data)
{
   TREE_PTR   new_ptr;
   new_ptr = new  AVL_NODE;
   if (new_ptr != NULL) {
      new_ptr->data = new_data;
      new_ptr->left_childptr = NULL;
      new_ptr->right_childptr = NULL;
      new_ptr->bal_fact = 0;
   }
   return (new_ptr);   // NULL if alloc fails.
}

//   add_node():
//      Insert a new node into an AVL_Tree and
//      also balance the the tree if necessary.
//      The node is not inserted if it already exists.
//
void AVL_Tree::add_node(DATA_TYPE new_data)
{
   TREE_PTR
     curr_ptr = root_ptr,
     new_ptr,                             // Pointer to new node
     most_recent_ptr = root_ptr,      // Most recent node with
                                          // B.F. -1, or +1
     most_recent_child_ptr = NULL,   // Child of most recent node,
     new_root_ptr = NULL,       // New subtree root after rebalancing
     most_recents_parent_ptr = NULL, //Parent of most recent node
     parent_ptr = NULL;          // Node that new node is child of.
   int
     unbal_flag,     // Tree unbalanced after insertion
     rebal_direc;   // Rebalancing direction after insertion

   if (curr_ptr == NULL) { // AVL tree is empty
      new_ptr = create_AVL_node(new_data);
      root_ptr = new_ptr;
```

```
        }
        else {
            //
            // While locating the insertion pointer for
            // the new node, see if the node already exists.
            // While searching, keep book-keeping of the new
            // node's parent, nearest ancestor, a

            curr_ptr = root_ptr;
            while (curr_ptr != NULL) {
                if (curr_ptr->bal_fact  != 0) {
                    most_recent_ptr = curr_ptr;
                    most_recents_parent_ptr = parent_ptr;
                }
                if (new_data == curr_ptr->data)
                    return;  // Data already exists
                if (new_data < curr_ptr->data) {
                    // search for it in left subtree
                    parent_ptr = curr_ptr;
                    curr_ptr   = curr_ptr->left_childptr;
                }
                else { // if (new_data > curr_ptr->data)
                    // search for it in right subtree
                    parent_ptr = curr_ptr;
                    curr_ptr   = curr_ptr->right_childptr;
                }
            }// end of the while loop

            // Data is not found in AVL tree; create it.
            new_ptr = create_AVL_node(new_data);

            // complying with "ascending order" rule,
            // insert it as a left or right child of
            // the parent node, pointed to by 'parent_ptr'.

            // balanced as appropriate child of q
            if (new_data < parent_ptr->data)
                // insert new node as left child
                parent_ptr->left_childptr = new_ptr;
            else  // insert as a right child
                parent_ptr->right_childptr = new_ptr;

            // Now adjust balance factors of all
            // in the search path from 'root' to
            // the parent node, parent_ptr.
            // By AVL property, all nodes on the
            // search path from most recent node and
            // and parent node must have 0 balance
            // factors, and change to -1 or +1.
            // rebal_dir = -1 => new data has been
            // inserted in right subtree of most_recent_ptr.
            // rebal_dir = +1 => new data has been
            // inserted in left subtree of most_recent_ptr.
```

```
if (new_data > most_recent_ptr->data) {
   curr_ptr = most_recent_ptr->right_childptr;
   rebal_direc = -1;
}
else {
   curr_ptr = most_recent_ptr->left_childptr;
   rebal_direc = +1;
}
most_recent_child_ptr = curr_ptr;
while (curr_ptr != new_ptr)
  if (new_data > curr_ptr->data) {
     // height of right is increased by 1
     curr_ptr->bal_fact = -1;
     curr_ptr = curr_ptr->right_childptr;
}
else {
     // height of left is increased by 1
     curr_ptr->bal_fact = +1;
     curr_ptr = curr_ptr->left_childptr;
  }
  // need to check if the balance of
  // the tree is alright
  unbal_flag = 1;
  if (most_recent_ptr->bal_fact == 0) {
     // tree is not unbalanced
     most_recent_ptr->bal_fact = rebal_direc;
     unbal_flag = 0;
  }
  if ((most_recent_ptr->bal_fact +
       rebal_direc) == 0) {
      // tree is not unbalanced
     most_recent_ptr->bal_fact = 0;
     unbal_flag = 0;
  }
  if (unbal_flag == 1) {
     // Tree is unbalanced. Determine
     // rotation direction, and rotate.
     if (rebal_direc == +1 ) {
        // left subtree is imbalanced
        // Rotate left
        if (most_recent_child_ptr->bal_fact == +1) {
          most_recent_ptr->left_childptr =
            most_recent_child_ptr->right_childptr;
          most_recent_child_ptr->right_childptr =
              most_recent_ptr;
          most_recent_ptr->bal_fact = 0;
          most_recent_child_ptr->bal_fact = 0;
        }
        else {
          new_root_ptr =
              most_recent_child_ptr->right_childptr;
          most_recent_child_ptr->right_childptr =
                        new_root_ptr->left_childptr;
          most_recent_ptr->left_childptr =
```

```
                          new_root_ptr->right_childptr;
          new_root_ptr->left_childptr =
                          most_recent_child_ptr;
          new_root_ptr->right_childptr =
                          most_recent_ptr;
          switch (new_root_ptr->bal_fact) {
             case +1:
                  most_recent_ptr->bal_fact = -1;
                  most_recent_child_ptr->bal_fact = 0;
                  break;
             case -1:
                  most_recent_child_ptr->bal_fact = 1;
                  most_recent_ptr->bal_fact = 0;
                  break;
             case  0:
                  most_recent_child_ptr->bal_fact = 0;
                  most_recent_ptr->bal_fact = 0;
                  break;
          }// end of the switch statement
          new_root_ptr->bal_fact = 0;
          most_recent_child_ptr = new_root_ptr;
       }// of the else
    }// end of the if rebal_direc = -1

    else { // right subtree is unbalanced
       if (most_recent_child_ptr->bal_fact == -1) {
          most_recent_ptr->right_childptr =
             most_recent_child_ptr->left_childptr;
          most_recent_child_ptr->left_childptr =
             most_recent_ptr;
          most_recent_ptr->bal_fact = 0;
          most_recent_child_ptr->bal_fact = 0;
       }
       else {
new_root_ptr = most_recent_child_ptr->left_childptr;
          most_recent_child_ptr->left_childptr =
                          new_root_ptr->right_childptr;
          most_recent_ptr->right_childptr =
                          new_root_ptr->left_childptr;
          new_root_ptr->right_childptr =
                          most_recent_child_ptr;
         new_root_ptr->left_childptr  = most_recent_ptr;
          switch (new_root_ptr->bal_fact) {
             case -1:     // should be -1
                  most_recent_ptr->bal_fact = 1;
                  most_recent_child_ptr->bal_fact = 0;
                  break;
             case +1:     // should be +1
                most_recent_child_ptr->bal_fact = -1;
                  most_recent_ptr->bal_fact = 0;
                  break;
             case  0:
                  most_recent_child_ptr->bal_fact = 0;
                  most_recent_ptr->bal_fact = 0;
```

```
                                break;
                          }// end of the switch statement
                          new_root_ptr->bal_fact = 0;
                          most_recent_child_ptr = new_root_ptr;
                       } // of the else
                   }// end of the if rebal_direc = -1

                  if (most_recents_parent_ptr == NULL)
                     root_ptr = most_recent_child_ptr;
                  else if (most_recent_ptr ==
                              most_recents_parent_ptr->left_childptr)
                     most_recents_parent_ptr->left_childptr =
                              most_recent_child_ptr;
                  else if (most_recent_ptr ==
                        most_recents_parent_ptr->right_childptr)
                     most_recents_parent_ptr->right_childptr =
                              most_recent_child_ptr;
              } // end of if unbalanced
        }// if root_ptr not NULL
}// of the AVL insert

// traverse_AVL_Inorder():
//    Traverse AVL tree in inorder method.
//    Print data of each node.
//
void AVL_Tree::traverse_AVL_Inorder(TREE_PTR tree_ptr)
{
    if (tree_ptr != NULL) {
        // Traverse its left AVL subtree
        traverse_AVL_Inorder (tree_ptr->left_childptr);
        // Root node of the subtree is visited, i.e.,
        // its data is printed.
        printf(" %d ", tree_ptr->data);
        // Traverse its right AVL subtree
        traverse_AVL_Inorder (tree_ptr->right_childptr);
    }
}


//  get_AVL_depth():
//     Compute the depth of the AVL tree
//
int AVL_Tree::get_AVL_depth(TREE_PTR  root_ptr)
{
    int  depth_left, depth_right, retval;

    if (root_ptr == NULL )
        return (0);
    else {
        depth_left  = get_AVL_depth(root_ptr->left_childptr);
        depth_right = get_AVL_depth(root_ptr ->right_childptr);
        retval = 1 + max(depth_left, depth_right);
        return (retval);
    }
}
```

```
// printlevel():
//   Print nodes of an AVL tree by level.
//
void AVL_Tree::printlevel(TREE_PTR root_ptr,
                   int level, int curr_level)
{
    int  i, width = 80;
    int  new_width = width >> level;
    int  temp = (curr_line_pos + (2 * new_width)) % (new_width);
    int  temp2 = (2 * new_width) - temp;

    if (root_ptr == NULL) {
        if (curr_node_num == 1) {
            for (i = 1; i <= new_width - 2; i++)
                putchar(' '); // insert spaces
            curr_node_num++;
            curr_line_pos = i;
            return;
        }
        else {
            curr_node_num++;
            temp = (curr_line_pos +
                    (2 * new_width)) % (new_width);
            temp2 = (2 * new_width) - temp;
            for (i = 1; i <= temp2; i++)
                putchar(' ');
            curr_line_pos += temp2;
            return;
        }
    }
    if (curr_level == level) {
        if (curr_node_num == 1) {
            for (i = 1; i <= new_width - 2; i++)
                putchar(' '); // insert spaces
            printf("%02d", root_ptr->data);
            curr_line_pos = new_width + 1;
        }
        else {
            for (i = 1; i <= temp2; i++)
                putchar(' '); // insert spaces
            printf("%02d", root_ptr->data);
            curr_line_pos += 2;
            curr_line_pos += temp2;
        }
        curr_node_num++;
        return;
    }
    printlevel(root_ptr->left_childptr,
            level, curr_level + 1);
    printlevel(root_ptr->right_childptr,
            level, curr_level + 1);
}
```

```
//   show_AVL_vertically():
//      Prints an AVL tree in vertical form.
//
void AVL_Tree::show_AVL_vertically(void)
{
    int treedepth = get_AVL_depth(root_ptr);
    printf("\n");
    for (int i = 0; i < 33; i++)
        putchar(' ');
    printf("THE AVL TREE\n");
    for (int level = 1; level <= treedepth ;level++) {
        int curr_width = 80 >> level;
        int prev_width = 80 >> (level -1);
        curr_node_num = 1;
        curr_line_pos = 0;
        if (level != 1) {
            for (i = 1; i<= prev_width - 1; i++)
                putchar(' ');
            for (i = 0;i <= (79 - prev_width); i++) {
                if (i % (2 * prev_width) == 0)
                putchar('!');
                else
                putchar(' ');
            }
            printf("\n");
            for (i = 1 ; i <= curr_width -1; i++) {
                putchar(' ');
            }
            for (i = 0; i <= 80 - curr_width ;i++) {
                if (i < 2 * curr_width)
                    putchar('-');
                if ((i >= 2 * curr_width) && (i < 4 * curr_width))
                    putchar(' ');
                if ((i >= 4 * curr_width) && (i < 6 * curr_width))
                    putchar('-');
                if ((i >= 6 * curr_width) && (i < 8 * curr_width))
                    putchar(' ');
                if ((i >= 8 * curr_width) && (i < 10 * curr_width))
                    putchar('-');
                if ((i >= 10 * curr_width) && (i < 12 * curr_width))
                    putchar(' ');
                if ((i >=12 * curr_width) && (i < 14 * curr_width))
                    putchar('-');
                if ((i >= 14 * curr_width) && (i < 16 * curr_width))
                    putchar(' ');
            }
            printf("\n");
        }
        printlevel(root_ptr, level, 1);
        printf("\n");
    }
}

// main(): Test driver for OOP implementation
```

```
//              of an AVL tree object.
//
void main(void)
{
    // Use keys from PEOPLE_1D database in Appendix C
    static DATA_TYPE A[8] = {16, 54, 14, 63,
                              62, 48, 21, 53};
    static int no_data = sizeof(A)/sizeof(DATA_TYPE);
    AVL_Tree avl_tree_obj(no_data);

    printf("\n OBJECT-ORIENTED %s \n",
           "IMPLEMENTATION OF AVL TREE");
    avl_tree_obj.build_tree(A);
    printf("\n AVL Tree after InOrder Traversal:\n");
    avl_tree_obj.inorder();
    avl_tree_obj.print_tree();
    delete []A;
}
```

Code 8.5 for an OOP implementation of AVL tree object produces:

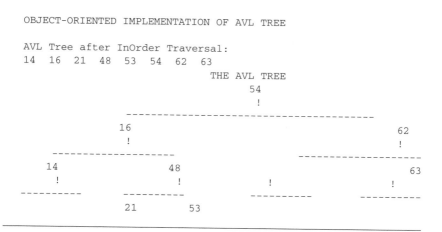

```
OBJECT-ORIENTED IMPLEMENTATION OF AVL TREE

AVL Tree after InOrder Traversal:
14   16   21   48   53   54   62   63
                              THE AVL TREE
                                   54
                                   !
```

Notice that the missing left child of node 14 causes the indentation problem in the last level. However, this problem does not occur when the left child of node 14 is not empty. This problem is left as an exercise.

8.9   Radix Search Trees

As has been seen, data-comparative search trees, such as the BST, induce a recursive hierarchical partitioning of the spatial domain of their keys. This partitioning is data object relative. Since the key space is not explicitly bounded, semi-infinite regions can exist.

In contrast, digital-based radix search trees recursively induce a fixed hierarchical partitioning of a bounded key space into a finite number of bounded subspaces. As with radix sorts in Chapter 7, keys are treated as numbers within some restricted range of values.

Branching in a digital-based tree is dependent on the digital properties of the search keys. Since our goal is to implement such structures on a digital computer, it is necessary to distinguish between keys that are numerically *discrete* versus those that are *non-discrete*.

8.9.1 DISCRETE VERSUS NON-DISCRETE KEYS

Keys are said to be discrete if the minimum separation between them is known in advance. In terms of representation on a digital computer, we consider keys to be discrete if they are integer values stored in binary and non-discrete if they are real values stored in some binary floating point format.

For a radix search tree organizing a set of discrete keys, branch decisions may be made based on an examination of the individual characters or digits of the keys. For example, with keys as binary integers and a 2-ary tree, one can examine a key one binary digit (bit) at a time to resolve 2-way branches. This extends in a straightforward manner. Again, with keys as binary integers, one can examine 2 bits at a time to resolve 4-way branches in a 4-ary tree. Alternately, keys may be interpreted as a sequence of digits or characters of any base. For example, in a 4-ary tree, we may treat keys as sequences of base-4 integers. A branch decision would entail examining one character of the key at time, where each character can be one of four values. In general, an M-way branch on a discrete key in an M-ary radix search tree can be resolved by examining c characters of the key at a time, where $M = R^c$. Here, M is the degree of the tree, R is the *radix* or base of the keys, and b is the number of characters examined. The radix R is also often referred to as the *digital cardinality* of the keys and represents the size of the alphabet of the keys.

Consider again the case of keys in a binary (2-ary) radix search tree represented as binary integers. If we specify in advance that each key has n binary digits (bits) then it follows that there may exist $N = 2^n$ distinct integer keys in the restricted range or key space of $0, 1, 2, ..., 2^{n-1}$. For example, consider keys that are 3-bit binary integers. There are 2^3 or 8 possible key values in the restricted range 0 to 7. As illustrated in Figure 8.33, the key space is hierarchically split by examination of successive bits of the keys; the leading bit splits the entire space in half, and the next bit splits that region in half, and the last bit splits that region in half. Since the keys examined are discrete, the partitioning of the key space is *implicit* to the representation of the keys. Of note is the fact that there are three levels in the hierarchy of key space partitioning in this particular example. In general, for radix search trees organizing discrete key values, there may

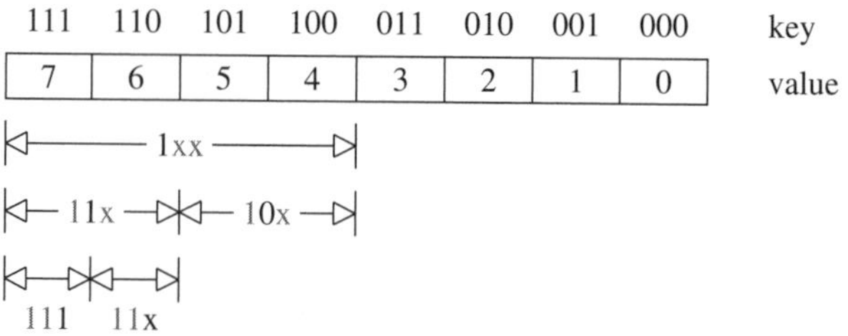

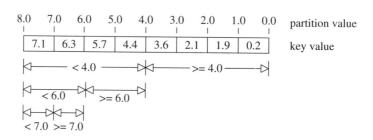

FIGURE 8.33. Partitioning of discrete keys.

FIGURE 8.34. Partitioning of non-discrete keys.

exist up to n branch levels in the tree where n is the number of characters or digits per key.

For non-discrete keys, however, the partitioning of the key space is not implicit to the representation of the keys as is the case for discrete keys. Therefore, branch decisions are not typically made by examination of individual character or digits of the keys. Instead, the radix search tree *explicitly* induces a fixed partitioning of the key space and places keys relative to such a partitioning. This is accomplished by making full key comparisons between a target key and the value of a given fixed key-space partition. Figure 8.34 illustrates this process for a set of floating-point keys in the range $0.0 \leq key \leq 8.0$.

The issues surrounding the use of a radix search tree for organizing discrete keys versus non-discrete keys are a matter of implementation; the former relies on an implicit subdivision of the key space based on individual digit or character examination, while the latter relies on an explicit subdivision of the key space based on full key comparisons. In the following sections, we consider radix search tree implementations for both discrete and non-discrete keys.

8.9.2   DIGITAL SEARCH TREES

The most simple type of radix search tree is the digital search tree. This particular structure is very similar to a comparative-based search tree except that branch decisions are digitally based. Like the M-ary comparative search tree, the M-ary digital search tree stores data objects (keys) at internal nodes as well as at leaf nodes. Searching on a digital search tree proceeds at each node by comparing the value of the target key against the value of the key stored at the node. If a branch is required, then the choice of "direction" is made based on a comparison between the value of the key-space partition that the node represents and the target search key. As noted above, the value of the key-space partition may be implicit if discrete keys are under consideration.

An M-ary digital search tree is defined in terms of discrete and non-discrete keys.

Definition 8.7 *An M-ary digital search tree is an M-ary radix tree; it is either empty or contains a root node along with an ordered sequence of M disjoint M-ary digital search subtrees such that*

> *(discrete)*
>
> *(1) the root node at level* i *contains an attribute designated as the key which is a base-M number;*
>
> *(2) the M digital search subtrees of the root, ordered from 0 to $M-1$, contain keys such that the value of their* i*th digit, also in range 0 to ($M-1$), has a unique correspondence to the order number of the subtree;*
>
> *(non-discrete)*
>
> *(1) the root node at level* i *contains an attribute designated as the key; associated with the root node are $M-1$ partition values that subdivide the key space spanned by the node into M distinct regions;*
>
> *(2) all nodes in subtree* n *($0 \le n \le M$) of the root contain keys whose value is less than that of the* n*th key-space partition value associated with the node.*

A *binary digital search tree* (*BDST*) is defined for the case of $M = 2$.

Definition 8.8 *A binary digital search tree is a binary radix tree; it is either empty or contains a root node along with left and right binary digital search subtrees such that*

(discrete)

(1) the root node at level i *contains an attribute designated as the key represented as a binary integer;*

(2) all nodes in the left subtree of the root contain keys whose i*th bit has value 0;*

(3) all nodes in the right subtree of the root contain keys whose i*th bit has value 1;*

(non-discrete)

(1) the root node at level i *contains an attribute designated as the key; associated with the root node is a partition value corresponding to the midpoint of the key space spanned at level* i*;*

(2) all nodes in the left subtree of the root contain keys whose value is less than that of the key-space partition value associated with the node;

(3) all nodes in the right subtree of the root contain keys whose value is greater than or equal to the value of the key-space partition value associated with the node.

8.9.3   OOP IMPLEMENTATION OF A BINARY DIGITAL SEARCH TREE (BDST)

A BDST of the people_1d database is shown in Figure 8.35. With the member_id data attribute as the search key, the records were inserted in the following order:

insertion order	name attribute	key (base10)	key (base2)
1	Bob	16	0x010000
2	John	54	0x100110
3	Kathy	14	0x001110
4	Peter	63	0x111111
5	Jim	62	0x101110
6	Nancy	48	0x100000
7	Paul	21	0x010101
8	Steve	53	0x100101

Code 8.6 is a pointer-based OOP implementation of an *M-ary digital search tree (MDST)*, for any $M = 2, 3, 4 \ldots$. As given, M is specified as 2, and **Code 8.6** internally creates the BDST of Figure 8.35. It implements the BDST object, bdstree_obj, for the people_1d database.

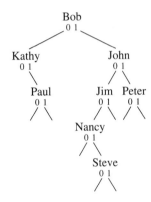

FIGURE 8.35. A BDST for the people_1d database.

Using an object-oriented design approach for a MDST, the object is identified by an ADT MDST (a data structure containing data and tree operations) and the object's methods are the operations for a MDST, which are directly derived from the ADT definition of the MDST. For $M = 2$, the MDST is a binary digital search tree (BDST). The M-ary digital search tree object is a data structure that contains node data and pointers to the M children of each node, and the operations as methods. To implement the OOP characteristics of data-hiding, encapsulation, and methods for message passing, the MDigital_Search_Tree class is defined in the header file class_MDigital_Search_Tree.h as follows:

```
class MDigital_Search_Tree : public  Tree,
                             private People_Database {
  private:
    int  MAXBITS; // Fix tree height to x-bit key
    int  NUMBITS; // examine NUMBITS bits per level
    int  LEVEL;
    int  M;        // for M-ary
    int  RADIX;    // RADIX = M;
    int  NOBJ;     // Number of input objects
    typedef struct MDSTREE_NODE {
        // define an MDST node type
        DATA_TYPE    record;
        // MDSTREE_NODE  *child_ptr[RADIX];
        MDSTREE_NODE   *child_ptr[2];
    } *TREE_PTR;
    TREE_PTR  root_ptr;
    void      init_MDSTree() { root_ptr = NULL; }
    TREE_PTR  create_MDST_node();
    unsigned  extract_bits(Keytype, int, int);
    void      add_node_into_MDST(TREE_PTR *, DATA_TYPE,
                                 int level);
    void      MDST_Postorder(TREE_PTR);
  public:
```

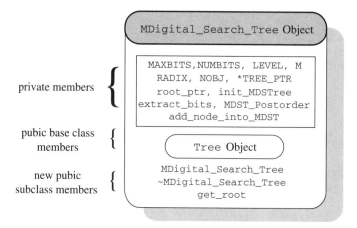

FIGURE 8.36. MDigital_Search_Tree object.

```
MDigital_Search_Tree(int M_size, int maxbits,
          int examin_bits, int level, int nobj);
~MDigital_Search_Tree();     // Destructor
BOOLEAN   is_empty(void) {return root_ptr == NULL;}
void      build_tree(DATA_TYPE *A);
void      add_node(DATA_TYPE);
void      search_node(DATA_TYPE srch_key) {};
void      delete_node(DATA_TYPE srch_key) {};
void      print_tree(void);
TREE_PTR  get_root() {return (root_ptr);}
};
```

The MDigital_Search_Tree class defines a type for an M-ary digital search tree object, mdstree_obj, encompassing both data and operations. The members DATA_TYPE, MDSTREE_NODE type structure data, and the pointer root_ptr (the pointer to the root node) are made private for data-hiding and protection from corruption. MDigital_Search_Tree(), ~MDigital_Search_Tree(), ... are public function members, which means these interfaces are accessible to the outside world (e.g., main()) in order to facilitate message passing between MDigital_Search_Tree-type object and an object of any other type. Get_root() is made public for providing read-only access of the private data member root_ptr. Figure 8.36 depicts a MDST object.

As with its comparative-based cousin (BST), there is no standard set of operations on a BDST. The operations implemented are in **Code 8.6** and parallel those listed for the BST implementation of **Code 8.4**.

Code 8.6 is flexible in that M is specifiable. As given, M is 2, resulting in a binary digital search tree. For another M, say $M = 4$, one may instantiate a 4-ary object in main() as follows:

```
MDigital_Search_Tree  bdstree_obj(4, 6, 1, 5, 10);
```

The major features of the MDST implemented in **Code 8.6** are:

- Keys are handled as discrete numbers represented as binary integers.

- Keys are examined one bit at a time to determine branch directions.
  The function extract_bits() extracts the given bit position(s)
  from the specified key.

- It is a recursive implementation.

Code 8.6

```
// Program: MDST_2bit.c++
// Purpose:
//   Object-oriented implementation of an
//   M-ARY DIGITAL SEARCH TREE (MDST)
//
//   IMPORTANT NOTES:
//    *  M-ary DST with M = 2
//         => Binary Digital Search Tree (BDST)
//    *  Keys are RADIX-2 (binary) numbers
//       represented as binary integers.
//    *  The size of the keys fixed at MAXBITS = 6 bits.
//       This yields binary integer keys in the range 0 to 64.
//    *  Examine NUMBITS = 1 bits per level
//   INPUT:
//   The PEOPLE_1D database (in order of insertion):
//
#include  <stdio.h>
#include  <stdlib.h>
#ifdef  MSDOS
#include  "peopl_db.cpp" // also defines DATA_TYPE
#else
#include  "peopl_db.c++"
#endif
typedef   int   BOOLEAN;
typedef   People_Database::DataObject DATA_TYPE;
#include  "bc_tree.h"     // for base class "Tree"
#include  "class_MDigital_Search_Tree.h"
// ---  Implement methods for MDST  --
MDigital_Search_Tree::MDigital_Search_Tree(int M_size,
  int maxbits, int examin_bits, int level, int nobj)
  : People_Database(nobj)
{
    RADIX   = M = M_size;
    MAXBITS = maxbits;
    NUMBITS = examin_bits;
    LEVEL   = level;
    NOBJ    = nobj;
    init_MDSTree();
```

```
    }

    MDigital_Search_Tree::~MDigital_Search_Tree()
    {
        //  Destructor for MDST.
        //  Left as an exercise.
    }

    // extract_bits():
    //   Given a word of bits (key), return the
    //   specified number of bits (bits) starting with
    //   the specified rightmost bit. It assumes least
    //   significant bit (rightmost) is bit number 0.
    //
    unsigned MDigital_Search_Tree::extract_bits(
                  Keytype key, int bits, int rshift)
    {
        unsigned mask = ~(~0 << bits);
        return (key >> (rshift* bits) ) & mask;
    }

    // create_MDST_node():
    //   Allocate mem space and pointer to that.
    //   Set M (radix) number of child ptrs to NULL.
    //
    MDigital_Search_Tree::TREE_PTR
    MDigital_Search_Tree::create_MDST_node()
    {
        TREE_PTR new_ptr = new MDSTREE_NODE;
        if (new_ptr == NULL) {
          printf("\n create_MDST_node: new failed\n");
          return (NULL);
        } else {
          for (int i = 0; i < RADIX; i++)
             new_ptr-> child_ptr[i] = NULL;
          return (new_ptr);
        }
    }

    // add_node_into_MDST():
    //     Insert a data object (record) into the  MDST
    //     pointed to by tree_ptr. Calls extract_bits().
    //     (Recursive implementation)
    //
    void MDigital_Search_Tree::add_node_into_MDST
      (TREE_PTR *tree_ptr, DATA_TYPE record, int level)
    {
        unsigned direction;
        TREE_PTR new_ptr;

        if (*tree_ptr == NULL) { // first node
           // create a node and place record in it
           new_ptr = create_MDST_node();
           new_ptr->record = record;
```

```
            *tree_ptr = new_ptr;
      }
      else {
        if (record.key == (*tree_ptr)->record.key) {
          return;      // key  already exists
          }
          else {
            direction = extract_bits(record.key,
                                     NUMBITS, level);
            add_node_into_MDST(
                &(*tree_ptr)->child_ptr[direction],
                record, --level);
          }
      }
}

void MDigital_Search_Tree::add_node(DATA_TYPE record)
{
    add_node_into_MDST(&root_ptr, record, LEVEL);
}

// build_tree():
//    Builds a DST from PEOPLE_1D database of
//    records (see Appendix C). It repeatedly
//    calls add_node_into_MDST(). Keys are integers.
//
void MDigital_Search_Tree::build_tree(DATA_TYPE *records)
{
    for (int i = 0; i < NOBJ; i++)
        add_node_into_MDST(&root_ptr, records[i],
                           (MAXBITS/NUMBITS) - 1);
}

// MDST_Postorder():
//    Traverse MDST using postorder traversal;
//    the MDST is pointed to by 'tree_ptr'.
//    (Recursive method).
//
void MDigital_Search_Tree::MDST_Postorder
                           (TREE_PTR tree_ptr)
{
    if (tree_ptr != NULL) {
        for (int i = 0; i < RADIX; i++)
            MDST_Postorder(tree_ptr->child_ptr[i]);
        printf(" %s ", tree_ptr->record.name);
    }
}

void MDigital_Search_Tree::print_tree(void)
{
    printf("\nThe Digital Search Tree %s:\n",
           "after PostOrder traversal");
    MDST_Postorder(root_ptr);
    printf("\n");
```

```
    }

    // main(): Test driver for a M-ARY Digital
    //         Search Tree (MDST).
    //   Here, M=2 => Binary Digital Search Tree (BDST)
    //
    void main(void)
    {
        // Declare "People_Database" object with size=10
        People_Database pdb_obj(10);
        pdb_obj.build_initial_db();
        // Declare an object of "M-ary Digital_Search_Tree"
        // class for M = 2, MAXBITS = 6, NUMBITS = 1,
        // LEVEL= MAXBITS/NUMBITS - 1.
        // NOBJ = 10 (in "People_Database" object)
        MDigital_Search_Tree  bdstree_obj(2, 6, 1, 5, 10);

        printf("\n OOP IMPLEMENTATION OF M-ARY %s \n %s \n",
               "DIGITAL SEARCH TREE, M=2",
               "         FOR PEOPLE DATABASE");
        bdstree_obj.build_tree(pdb_obj.get_db());
        bdstree_obj.print_tree();
    }
```

Code 8.6 produces the following output:

```
OOP IMPLEMENTATION OF M-ARY DIGITAL SEARCH TREE, M=2
            FOR people_1d DATABASE

The Digital Search Tree after PostOrder traversal:
Paul  Kathy  Steve  Nancy  Jim  Peter  John  Bob
```

8.9.4 RADIX SEARCH TRIES

The digital search tree is a radix tree in that it organizes the data relative to a partitioning of the key space and not relative to the data objects themselves. Unlike the comparative-based trees, the choice of branch direction is a function of the digital properties of the keys. However, like the comparative-based search trees, data objects are stored in internal nodes as well as leaf nodes. For this reason, the shape of the digital search tree is still somewhat sensitive to the order in which it is built.

In processing discrete keys on a character-wise basis, digital-based trees are capable of handling variable-length, possibly large, keys. However, as keys get large, a full key comparison at each node of the DST can become costly. One strategy for reducing or eliminating the overhead of such comparisons is not to store keys in the internal nodes at all.

Modifying the digital search tree algorithm such that

- keys are only stored in leaf nodes, and

- branching always takes place at internal nodes

leads to what is called a *trie* structure. The trie structure concept originated from the work of Fredkin [Fre60].

Definition 8.9 *A trie is an M-ary radix tree comprised of two types of nodes, internal branch nodes and external leaf nodes:*

> *(1) Branch nodes are M-place vectors whose subscripts range from 0 to* (M − 1).

> *(2) Branch nodes serve as the underlying branching structure for the data being organized — they contain no data objects.*

> *(3) Data objects (keys) are implicitly or explicitly associated with the leaf nodes.*

An ADT trie is a data structure that contains a set of nodes satisfying the properties in Definition 8.9, and a set of operations that are used to manipulate these nodes. An *M*-ary radix search trie in terms of discrete and non-discrete keys is defined.

Definition 8.10 *An M-ary radix search trie is an M-ary search tree; it is either empty or there is a root node connected to an ordered sequence of exactly M disjoint M-ary tries such that*

> *(discrete)*

> *(i) the root node is either a leaf node containing a data object (record with key), or is an internal branch node specifying an M-way branch;*

> *(2) each branch node at level* i *specifies the* ith *digit or character of the key such that no other node on the path from the root to the node specifies the same digit;*

> *(3) each branch node at level* i *has one subtrie for each of M possible values of the* ith *digit or character of the key; the records associated with the node are each placed in the subtrie with the corresponding value for that digit according to a prescribed order (i.e., a binary trie has order and assignment* left = 0 *and* right = 1*);*

> *(non-discrete)*

> *(1) the root node is either a leaf node containing a data object (record with key), or is an internal branch node specifying an M-way branch;*

> *(2) each branch node at level* i *specifies the fixed partition for the key (sub)space of the node;*

(3) each branch node at level i *has* M *possible subtries; the records (keys) associated with the node are compared with the values of the partitions and are placed in the appropriate subtrie according to a prescribed numerical relationship and order (i.e., a binary trie has order and assignment* $left \leq p$, *and* $right > p$, *for partition value* p*).*

The most simple case of a multiway radix search trie is the *binary radix search trie* (*BRST*) corresponding to $M = 2$. Assuming binary integer keys, each binary digit (bit) of a key can take on one of two values, 0 or 1. An internal branch node at level i places a key in one of two child subtries depending on the value of ith bit of the key. A node on a given level i of the trie structure represents the set of all keys that begin with the corresponding sequence of i bits.

Definition 8.11 *A binary radix search trie is a binary radix search tree; it is either empty or contains a root node along with left and right binary radix search subtries such that*

(discrete)

(1) the root node is either a leaf node containing exactly one data object (record with key), or is an internal (branch) node specifying a 2-way branch;

(2) each branch node at level i *specifies the* i*th bit of the key such that no other node on the on the path from the root to the node specifies the same bit;*

(3) each branch node at level i *has a left subtrie that corresponds to all keys associated with the node having a 0 value in the* i*th bit and a right subtrie corresponding to all keys of the node which have a 1 value in the* i*th bit;*

(non-discrete)

(1) the root node is either a leaf node containing exactly one data object (record with key), or is an internal (branch) node specifying a 2-way branch;

(2) each branch node at level i *specifies the fixed partition that splits the key (sub)space associated with the node;*

(3) each branch node at level i *has a left subtrie and a right subtrie; all keys associated with the node that have a value less than or equal to that of the split partition are placed in the left subtrie, while all those with values greater than the split partition are placed in the right.*

A diagram of the binary radix search trie for the `people_1d` database is shown in Figure 8.37. Here, the set of one-dimensional `member_id` keys

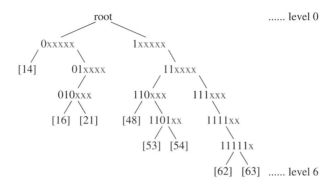

FIGURE 8.37. Binary radix search trie for people_1d database.

$$\{16, 54, 14, 63, 62, 48, 21, 53\}$$

is represented as the set of 6-bit binary integers:

$$\{010000, 110110, 001110, 111111, 111110, 110000, 010101, 110101\}.$$

The trie has six levels of branching plus the root at level 0. Starting from the root node, the most significant bit of a key encodes the branch direction to take; successive branches follow from successive bits. In the diagram the internal branch nodes are labeled according to the keys they decode. For instance, the branch node that is the left child of the root is labeled 0*****, meaning that all nodes below it contain a 0 in the most significant bit position. The five successive *'s indicate "don't cares," since these bits are decoded at their respective levels. Each key data element resides in a leaf node at the level at which it is uniquely identified. In Figure 8.37, the key data 16 (001110) is in a leaf located at level 4; it is uniquely identified by the leading sequence of bits 0100**. The key data 63 (111111), on the other hand, is located at the maximum level 6, as it takes all six bits of the key to uniquely identify it.

Operations on an ADT radix search trie are straightforward. We summarize the search and insert operations below assuming discrete keys represented as binary integers. For non-discrete keys, the procedures are the same except that a full key comparison between the target key and the value of the space partition corresponding to a node are made in place of bit comparisons.

The steps for searching a key in an ADT radix search trie are:

Step 1. Branch through the trie according the bits of the target key until a leaf node is encountered.

Step 2. Make a full key comparison between the target key and the key contained in the leaf node to determine if the value of the contained key matches that of the target.

The steps for inserting a key in an ADT radix search trie are:

Step 1. Conduct a search based on the target key.

Step 2. If a null child pointer is encountered, a leaf node is created and assigned as the child. The key data is placed here and the insertion is completed.

Step 3a. If a leaf node is encountered that contains the target key value, then we have a case of identical keys. Assuming identical keys are not allowed, the target insertion key either replaces the key at the leaf or key or is rejected. (An alternate solution for identical keys is presented in Section 8.9.10.)

Step 3b. Otherwise, if there is a key K in the encountered leaf that is not identical in value to the target key, then we must continue adding branch nodes along the branch path until a unique leaf position is found for the target key as well as the key K. The addition of branch nodes from a given node is equivalent to hierarchically subdividing the key space associated with the node down to a resolution where regions exist to uniquely contain the insertion key and the encountered key. This process is commonly referred to as *splitting*.

For discrete keys, as represented by binary integers, an alternative to the standard radix search trie is the *pure* or *complete* radix search trie. Such a structure, for the `people_1d` database, is illustrated in Figure 8.38. The pure trie differs from the standard form in that its leaf nodes always reside at the maximum level of the trie. This is in contrast to the standard trie for which leaf nodes are placed at the first instance at which the data are uniquely defined. In a pure trie, a key is located by branching on its bits or characters until the entire key has been examined and a leaf node is reached. In doing so, a complete and unique path from the root of the entire trie to the leaf will have been traversed.

The advantage of a trie in pure or complete form is that *keys need not be explicitly stored in the leaf nodes*. Since a leaf is reached only after branching through all levels, the data contained in the leaf are implicit to the path of traversal to reach it. This is in contrast to the standard implementation, where the data are only partially built into the branching structure. To illustrate this feature, consider a search for the key 54 (110110) in the trie of Figure 8.38. From the root node, we branch in the sequence right, right, left, right, right, and left. By arriving at a leaf node at level 6, we know that a key exists and its value is implicit to the traversal. The pure trie also enjoys somewhat simplified insertion, deletion, and search procedures.

The major disadvantage of the pure or complete trie is its potential of consuming a lot of storage space. With the pure trie, an internal node must

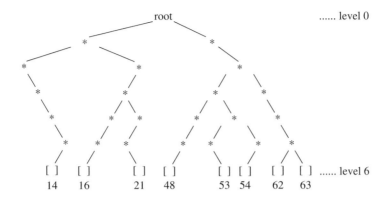

FIGURE 8.38. Pure binary radix search trie for people_1d database.

exist at every level for the entire search path of each key. As such, the use of storage space must be weighed against the simplicity of the insertion, deletion, and search algorithms and the advantage of not having to store the keys. Additionally, the use of a pure trie is not applicable to non-discrete data.

8.9.5 OOP IMPLEMENTATION OF AN M-ARY RADIX SEARCH TRIE

The 4-ary radix search trie corresponding to the data of the `people_1d` database is shown later in Figure 8.40. The keys were inserted in the order 16, 54, 14, 63, 62, 48, 21, 53 although the order is irrelevant to the final structure. The reader should be satisfied that the same trie would result from any possible insertion ordering of the keys.

A pointer-based OOP implementation of this radix search trie is presented below as **Code 8.7**. This implementation treats the keys as non-discrete floating point numbers.

Using an object-oriented design approach for an *M-ary radix search trie* (*MRST*), the MRST object is specified by an ADT MRST. The MRST object's data and methods are directly derived from the ADT MRST. For $M = 4$, MRST is a 4-ary radix search trie. The *M*-ary radix search trie object is a data structure that contains the node's data and pointers to the M children of each node, and the operations as methods. To implement the OOP characteristics of data-hiding, encapsulation, and methods for message passing, the `MRadix_Search_Trie` class is defined in the header file `class_MRadix_Search_Trie.h` as follows:

```
class MRadix_Search_Trie : public  Tree,
                  private People_Database {
```

```
    private:
      // specify bounds of key space
      float     MAX_BOUND_KEY_SPACE;
      float     MIN_BOUND_KEY_SPACE;
      int       M;    // M-ARY
      int       RADIX; // RADIX = M
      int       NOBJ;  // Number of input objects
      struct MRSTRIE_NODE {
          // define an MRST node type
          DataObject     record;
          // MRSTRIE_NODE   *child_ptr[RADIX];
          MRSTRIE_NODE    *child_ptr[4];
      };
      typedef struct MRST_dummy {
          Nodetype    type;
          int         i;
      } *TREE_PTR;

      typedef struct MRST_InternalNode {
          Nodetype    type;
          char  *name;
          //  MRST_dummy  *child[RADIX];
          MRST_dummy  *child[4];
      } *IPTR;

      typedef struct MRST_LeafNode {
          Nodetype    type;
          DataObject  record;
      } *LPTR;
      TREE_PTR  root_ptr;
      void      init_MRSTrie() { root_ptr = NULL; }
      TREE_PTR  create_MRST_node(Nodetype type);
      unsigned  find_direction(Keytype, float, float);
      int       MRST_nodetype(TREE_PTR);
      TREE_PTR  add_node_into_MRST(DataObject record,
                  TREE_PTR root_ptr, float min, float max);
      void      build_MRST(DataObject *record, int nr,
                          float min, float max);
      void      MRST_Postorder(TREE_PTR node_ptr);
    public:
      MRadix_Search_Trie(int M_size,
                float min, float max, int nobj);
      ~MRadix_Search_Trie();
      BOOLEAN   is_empty (void) {return root_ptr == NULL;}
      void      build_tree (DATA_TYPE *records);
      void      add_node(DATA_TYPE node_data);
      void      search_node(DATA_TYPE srch_key) {};
      void      delete_node(DATA_TYPE srch_key) {};
      void      print_tree(void);
      TREE_PTR  get_root() {return (root_ptr); }
      int       get_M_size() { return (M); }
};
```

The MRadix_Search_Trie class defines a type for an *M*-ary radix

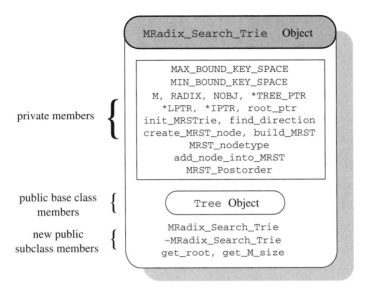

FIGURE 8.39. MRadix_Search_Trie object.

search trie object, mdstree_obj, encompassing both data and operations. The members DATA_TYPE, MRSTRIE_NODE type structure data, and the pointer root_ptr (the pointer to the root node) are made private for data-hiding and protection from corruption. MRadix_Search_Trie(), ~MRadix_Search_Trie(), add_node_into_MRST(), ... are public member functions, which means these are interfaces to the outside world (e.g., main()) in order to facilitate message passing between an object of type MRadix_Search_Trie and any other object. Get_root() is made public for providing read-only access of the data member root_ptr. Figure 8.39 depicts an MRST object. The methods for an OOP of an M-ary radix search trie object are implemented in **Code 8.7**.

However, **Code 8.7** implements an M-ary radix search trie for any $M = 2, 3, 4, ...$ In order to reuse this code, say for $M = 3$, declare a 3-ary object in main() as

```
MRadix_Search_Trie  rstrie_obj(3, 0.0, 100.0, 10);
```

For $M = 4$, **Code 8.7** implements a BDST object, rstrie_obj, for the people_1d database. From this set of keys, **Code 8.7** internally creates the 4-ary radix search trie shown in Figure 8.40. Depicted in this figure is the insertion sequence of these keys and the final resulting trie.

The major features of the MRST implemented in **Code 8.7** are:

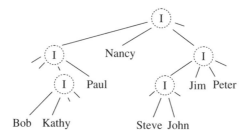

FIGURE 8.40. 4-ary radix search trie for people_1d database.

- The structure is a *standard* trie — the keys must be stored at the leaf nodes since the path from the root to each leaf is not complete.

- Keys are handled as non-discrete floating point numbers. Bit or character examinations are not done. Instead, find_direction() does a full comparison between the target keys and the values of the fixed partitions associated with the branch nodes.

- There are two distinct kinds of nodes:

    - Leaf nodes contain a type identifier and a record, but no child pointers.

    - Internal nodes contain a type identifier and M child pointers, but no record. Such an implementation requires some tricky pointer manipulation.

- It is a recursive implementation.

- Identical keys are properly handled.

Code 8.7

```
//   Program: MRST_4nondHR.c++
//   Purpose:
//     Object-oriented implementation of
//
//     M-ARY RADIX SEARCH TRIE (MRST) ( FOR M = 4)
//     for NON-DISCRETE keys.
//
#include   <stdio.h>
#ifdef   MSDOS
#include   <alloc.h>
#include   "peopl_db.cpp"   // See Appendix C
#else
#include   <malloc.h>
#include   "peopl_db.c++"
```

```
#endif
const int INTERNAL = 0;
const int LEAF     = 1;
typedefint  BOOLEAN;
typedefPeople_Database::DataObject DATA_TYPE;
#include  "bc_tree.h"    // for base class "Tree"
#include  "class_MRadix_Search_Trie.h"

//  ---  Implement methods for MRST  --
MRadix_Search_Trie::MRadix_Search_Trie(int M_size,
 float min, float max, int nobj):People_Database(M_size)
{
   M = RADIX = M_size;
   MAX_BOUND_KEY_SPACE = max;
   MIN_BOUND_KEY_SPACE = min;
   NOBJ = nobj;     // Number of objects (records)
   init_MRSTrie();
}

MRadix_Search_Trie::~MRadix_Search_Trie()
{
   // Destructor; left as an exercise.
}

// create_MRST_node():
//   Allocate mem space and pointer to that.
//
MRadix_Search_Trie::TREE_PTR
MRadix_Search_Trie::create_MRST_node(Nodetype type)
{
    TREE_PTR new_ptr;

    // Allocate memory space for the new node;
    // Return with error if no space available
    if (type == LEAF) {
        // LPTR new_ptr;
        if ((new_ptr = (TREE_PTR)malloc(
                sizeof(MRST_LeafNode))) == NULL) {
           printf("\n create_MRST_node: malloc failed\n");
           return (NULL);
        }
        ((LPTR)new_ptr)->type = type;
        return ((TREE_PTR)new_ptr);
    }
    else {
        if ((new_ptr =(TREE_PTR)malloc(
                sizeof(MRST_InternalNode)))== NULL) {
          printf("\n create_MRST_node: malloc failed\n");
          return (NULL);
        }
        ((IPTR)new_ptr)->type = type;
        return ((TREE_PTR)new_ptr);
    }
}
```

```
// add_node_into_MRST():
//   Insert a new node in M-ary Radix Search Trie.
//
MRadix_Search_Trie::TREE_PTR
MRadix_Search_Trie::add_node_into_MRST(
     DataObject record, TREE_PTR root_ptr,
     float min, float max)
{
    unsigned  d;
    float     p, dp;   // real valued
    TREE_PTR  new_ptr;

    Keytype key = record.key;
    dp = (max - min)/(float)M;
    p = min + dp;
    if (root_ptr == NULL)  {
        new_ptr = create_MRST_node(LEAF);
        ((LPTR)new_ptr)->record = record;
        return (new_ptr);
    }
    if (root_ptr->type == LEAF) { // if at a LEAF node
        //   check if key already exists in trie
        if (((LPTR)root_ptr)->record.key == key) {
            return (root_ptr);
        }
        else {
            new_ptr = create_MRST_node(INTERNAL);
            d = find_direction(
                ((LPTR)root_ptr)->record.key, p, dp);
            ((IPTR)new_ptr)->child[d] = root_ptr;
            root_ptr = add_node_into_MRST(record,
                             new_ptr, min, max);
        }
    }
    else { // else, if at an INTERNAL node
      d   = find_direction(key, p, dp);
      min += d * dp;
      max = min + dp;
      ((IPTR)root_ptr)->child[d] = add_node_into_MRST(
          record, ((IPTR)root_ptr)->child[d], min, max);
    }
    return (root_ptr);
}

void MRadix_Search_Trie::add_node(DATA_TYPE record)
{
   add_node_into_MRST(record, root_ptr,
       MIN_BOUND_KEY_SPACE, MAX_BOUND_KEY_SPACE);
}

// build_tree():
//   Creates an M-ary search trie from an array
//   of elements, calling add_node_into_MRST().
```

```
//    Elements are integers.
//    Always called with root level = 0.
//
void MRadix_Search_Trie::build_tree(DATA_TYPE *records)
{
   for (int i = 0; i < NOBJ; i++)
     root_ptr=add_node_into_MRST(records[i], root_ptr,
              MIN_BOUND_KEY_SPACE, MAX_BOUND_KEY_SPACE);
}

//  find_direction():
//    There are M intervals subdivided by (M-1)
//    partition values. Given an initial partition
//    value (p) and the distance between successive
//    partitions (dp) determine which interval the
//    given key value falls within. Intervals are
//    successively labeled 0 to M-1 (left to right).
//
unsigned MRadix_Search_Trie::find_direction(
                Keytype key, float p,  float dp)
{
    for (int i = 0; i < M-1; i++) {
        if ((float)key < p)
            return (i);
        p += dp;
    }
    return (i);
}

// MRST_Postorder():
//    Traverse the M-Ary Radix Search Trie in
//    PostOrder. Print the "names" attribute for
//    each LEAF node record. Print "I" for each
//    INTERNAL node encountered.
//    (Recursive Implementation)
//
void MRadix_Search_Trie::MRST_Postorder(
                        TREE_PTR node_ptr)
{
    if (node_ptr ==  NULL)
        return;
    if (node_ptr->type != LEAF) {
        for (int i = 0; i < RADIX; i++)
          MRST_Postorder(((IPTR)node_ptr)->child[i]);
        printf("I ");
    } else
        printf("%s  ", ((LPTR)node_ptr)->record.name);
}

void MRadix_Search_Trie::print_tree(void)
{
    printf("%d-ary radix search trie %s:\n",
      get_M_size(), "after PostOrder traversal");
    MRST_Postorder(root_ptr);
```

```
    printf("\n");
}

// main(): Test driver for an OOP of an M-ARY (M=4)
//         (i.e., 4-ARY) Radix Search Trie (MRST)
//
void main(void)
{
    // See Appendix C for "People_Database".
    // Declare "People_Database" object with size=10
    People_Database pdb_obj(10);
    pdb_obj.build_initial_db();

    // Declare an "4-ary radix search trie" object
    // of "MRadix_Search_Trie" class for M = 4,
    // MIN_BOUND_KEY_SPACE=0,MAX_BOUND_KEY_SPAC E=100,
    // NOBJ=10.
    MRadix_Search_Trie  rstrie_obj(4, 0.0, 100.0, 10);
    printf("\n OOP IMPLEMENTATION OF M-ARY %s \n %s \n",
           "RADIX SEARCH TRIE, M=4",
           "            FOR PEOPLE DATABASE\n");
    // ** Building 4-ARY Radix Search Trie
    rstrie_obj.build_tree(pdb_obj.get_db());
    rstrie_obj.print_tree();
}
```

Code 8.7 is an OOP implementation of a general M-ary radix search trie. For $M = 4$, it implements 4-ary MRST object for people database, and produces this output:

```
OOP IMPLEMENTATION OF M-ARY RADIX SEARCH TRIE, M=4
            FOR PEOPLE DATABASE

4-ary radix search trie after PostOrder traversal:
Kathy  Bob  I Paul  I Nancy  Steve  John  I Jim  Peter  I I
```

Code 8.7 shows a 4-ary non-discrete partitioning of the `people_1d` database. This code also is an example of floating point numbers where records contain 2 floating point numbers (1 key, 1 attribute) plus a name attribute.

8.9.6 BALANCE CHARACTERISTICS OF RADIX SEARCH TREES

Independent of the type of keys treated and the implementation chosen, and characteristic of the ADT radix search trees (digital search trees and radix search tries), is the property that all data objects are organized relative to a fixed space partitioning. This is in sharp contrast to the comparative-based search tree objects that rely on a data-object relative organization. This fundamental distinction differentiates the balance characteristics between these two types of trees and is a major consideration in selecting the tree object best suited to a given application.

Property 8.5 *The shape (balance) of the radix search tree object is sensitive to the digital (spatial) distribution of the inserted keys.*

Keys that are not uniformly distributed are said to be numerically *biased*. Therefore, radix search trees can degenerate in an area of the key space where the data objects are grouped or clustered together.

As a radix search tree, the height balance of the ADT digital search tree follows that of Property 8.3. At the same time, the height balance is also slightly dependent on the order in which the keys were inserted. This characteristic is a side effect of storing keys in the internal branch nodes as well as at the leaf nodes.

The ADT radix search trie, as a radix search tree, also conforms to the balance characteristics of Property 8.3. Unlike the digital search tree, however, the internal (branch) nodes of a trie carry no data and only serve to partition the bounded key space of a given data set. Each branch node specifies a fixed partition of the space independent of any of the data objects in the space. As a result, the balance of the radix search trie is fully independent of insertion order.

Property 8.6 *The shape (balance) of a radix search trie of n keys is independent of the insertion order of those n keys. A unique trie exists for any given set of distinct keys.*

With unclustered (uniformly distributed) data, radix searching methods can provide good performance without the hassle of the rebalancing schemes required with comparative-based methods.

Property 8.7 *A search or insertion in an M-ary digital search tree or radix search trie requires approximately $\log_M(N)$ comparisons on the average and b comparisons in the worst case in a tree built from N random b-bit keys.*

M-ary radix search tries can, however, be demanding of storage space. That is, the number of internal branch nodes can far exceed the total number of keys. In addition, as M gets larger, the search paths get shorter but the number of unused child pointers can increase.

Property 8.8 *A binary radix search trie built from N random b-bit keys has approximately $N/\ln 2 = 1.44N$ nodes on the average.*

Property 8.9 *For M-ary trie of N random keys, the number of used links is approximately $MN/\ln M$.*

In summary, while a comparative-based search tree is highly dependent on insertion order, the balance of a digital search tree is only slightly dependent on insertion order, and the balance of the radix search trie is fully independent of insertion order.

8.9.7   Hybrid Radix Search Tries

In dealing with M-ary radix search tries, it is important to consider space versus time efficiency issues.

With a multiway radix search trie, it is possible to realize a gain in search efficiency by increasing the degree of the trie. For example, an M-ary radix search trie can realize a 2^b factor increase in performance over its binary counterpart ($M = 2$) by examining b bits of the key at a time as opposed to one bit at a time. This speed up is at the cost of an increase in storage space overhead required to deal with $M = 2^b$ children per node. When M gets large, tries can become very inefficient in their use of storage resources, as the overhead of the child pointers at each node overwhelms that of the data stored.

Typically, tries are more efficient near the root level than at the deeper leaf levels. Branching is dense closer to the top (root) of the trie and sparse toward the bottom, where many child pointers go unused.

One may consider various hybrid schemes to address these space-time trade-off issues. A search trie implementation is possible where nodes contain smaller values of M (less child pointers) toward the bottom of the structure. Another possibility is to utilize more elementary structures, such as arrays and lists, toward the leaves. Such hybrid forms, however, can become quite complex, requiring support of several node types within the same structure.

One hybrid form of radix search trie that allows for multiple keys at the leaf nodes is referred to as a *bucket trie*. The number of keys per leaf is the *bucket capacity*. One means of implementing a bucket trie is to place a linked list at each leaf node that may be as big as the bucket capacity. When inserting a keys in such a trie, splitting does not occur until the bucket capacity at a leaf overflows. In this form, the trie may be viewed as a directory or index to a set of data buckets (lists).

In Chapter 12, an 8-ary search trie is presented that implements a bucket hybrid strategy with data buckets in the form of arrays.

8.9.8   Radix Search Tries and Radix Exchange Sorting

The execution of a radix search trie is intimately related to that of the top-down radix exchange sort introduced in Section 7.1.10. In essence, the trie structure reflects the execution of the sort. Each node of the trie corre-

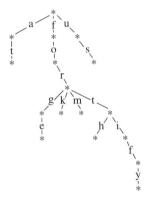

FIGURE 8.41. A simple trie word dictionary.

sponds to one call to the sorting routine — each represents a partitioning of the data space.

Property 8.10 *Binary trie searching partitions the file in exactly the same way as radix exchange sorting.*

This correspondence between the binary radix search trie is the digital analog of the relationship between the comparative-based BST and Quick-sort.

8.9.9   OOP APPLICATION: WORD DICTIONARIES USING TRIES

One common application of a radix search trie object is to the problem of word search in a dictionary of words. For keys of alphabetic words represented as sequences of characters, an M-ary radix search trie, with $M = 26$, provides a useful means of searching for a target string on a character per character basis. A basic pointer-based implementation would thus entail a 26-ary trie with each internal node containing an array of 26 child pointers. Tries, in association with this type of application, are often referred to as *lexicographic search trees*.

Figure 8.41 illustrates a simple trie word dictionary involving the words "at," "for," "forge," "fork," "form," "fort," "forth," "fortify," and "us." At each node, the branch taken is labeled as one of 26 characters in the range a through z. Each path from the root to a leaf corresponds to one word in the given represented set. Although not shown, it is assumed that each node allocates space for all 26 child pointers.

One of the most powerful aspects of the radix search trie in this capacity is its capability of *prefix search* — the process of searching and matching on partial strings or prefixes. Efficient prefix search is an important feature for word searching and spell-checking operations. If many groups of words begin with a common sequence of characters, as they do in many modern languages, then a trie organization is economical on space in the sense that common sequences "overlap" in the structure. In the trie in Figure 8.41, a search for all words beginning with the sequence "for" would yield the words "for," "forge," "fork," "form," "fort," "forth," and "fortify."

One could use any number of structures for representing word dictionaries. For example, an ADT comparative-based BST is capable of providing a lexicographic linear ordering of strings. However, as a BST, the search time on the dictionary would be proportional to a logarithm of the number of words in dictionary, whereas with the trie, the search time is only proportional to the number of characters in the words. For example, a trie can store $w = 26^4 = 456,976$ 4-bit words and locate any one of them in 4 iterations. A BST, on the other hand, would have a search performance of approximately $\log_2(w) = 5.7$ iterations.

In practice, however, the size of the words (or any search string) can become large and the number of words in the dictionary might be sparse compared to the set of all representable words. These two factors could make the BST a more favorable choice. As such, a hybrid scheme, as previously discussed in Section 8.9.4, might be considered. Here, a hybrid structure might entail a couple of 26-ary tries levels at the top, where the fanout is dense, followed by BST methods at the lower levels, where fanout is sparse.

8.9.10   PATRICIA TREES AND TRIES

The M-ary radix search tries presented previously have two fundamental drawbacks:

- discrete keys with long common prefixes lead to a considerable amount of wasted branch nodes, and

- two different types of nodes (internal and leaf) must be dealt with. Implementations that treat only one common node type for both leaf and internal branch nodes make inefficient use of storage space. Those that treat separate node types require somewhat complicated pointer manipulation (see **Code 8.7**).

The *Patricia tree*, put forth by Morrison [Mor68], provides a useful solution for these problems.

To address the situation of wasteful branch paths due to common prefixes, a Patricia tree structure places an index at each internal branch node. This index indicates which bit of the target key is to be tested for the branch decision out of the given node. Since all keys are still stored only at the leaf nodes, the structure is considered a modified binary radix search trie. The

Patricia trie, however, does not address the second problem of multiple node types.

This issue of multiple node type is addressed with a Patricia tree, a Patricia trie structure with a modification that essentially eliminates the need for leaf nodes. A Patricia tree stores keys in its internal nodes, while would-be leaf pointers point to internal node. In searching for a target key, the keys in the nodes are not used. Instead, a bit-wise radix search is performed until the "bottom" of the tree is found. A full key comparison is between the target key and the key at the internal node pointed to by the pointer at the "bottom" node. Since the keys are stored in the internal nodes, this structure is referred to as a search tree, although the search process through the structure is still a radix searching method (i.e., bit comparisons determine branching).

To insert a target key into a Patricia tree, we branch on its bits, just as is done in a binary radix search trie. This search process stops when a "bottom" node is reached. By definition, the discriminators of the nodes must decrease as the tree is traversed in increasing levels. Thus, a bottom node is reached when, in the process of the search, a branch would lead to a node with a higher discriminator than the current one. This corresponds to taking the path of an upward link (up) pointer. The target key is then compared with the key at the node at which the above search terminates. The discriminator of the target node being inserted is determined as the first bit position at which the two keys differ as the keys are scanned for common prefixes. If the discriminator of the target key is less than that of the current key, the target is inserted as the left or right child of the current key, depending on whether its discriminating bit is a one or a zero, respectively (see insertion of key 63 in example below). Otherwise, since discriminators must decrease with increasing level, the target key must be inserted between the current node and the parent of the current node (see insertion of node 14 in example below). If the discriminators of the target and the current node are the same, then the one with a one bit becomes the parent of the other (see insertion of key 54 in Exmple 8.1).

The completed Patricia trie for the `people_1d` database is shown in Figure 8.42. Its implementation is left as Exercise 8-72.

Example 8.1

The insertion process of the first three keys of the `people_1d` database is shown below. The complete set of keys is:

$$\{16, 54, 14, 63, 62, 48, 21, 53\} =$$

$$\{010000, 110110, 111111, 111110, 110000, 010101, 110101\}.$$

```
{x}       means this is an UP pointer to node x.
(a,b)     means this node contains key of value a
          and discriminates on bit b.
```

```
Action                          Comments
------                          --------
```

Insert 16:

```
        (16,5)                  This is the root node;
        /   \                   node discriminates on bit 5;
     {16}    {16}               both UP pointers are to itself.
```

Insert 54:

```
            (54,5)              Search for 54 using bit 5;
            /   \               key 54, bit 5 = "1", becomes root;
        (16,2)   {54}           key 16, bit 5 = "0", becomes left
        /   \                   child of key 54; node of key 16
     {16}   {54}                discriminates on bit 2; left UP
                                pointer to node of 16; right UP
                                pointer to node of 54.
```

Insert 14:

```
            (54,5)              Search for 14; go left; compare
            /   \               with node of 16; key 16 and 14
        (14,4)   {54}           differ at bit 4; 14 is inserted
        /   \                   between 54 and 16 since 16
     {14}   (16,2)              discriminates on bit 2; 16 becomes
            /   \               the right child of 14; 14's left UP
         {16} {54}              points to itself; 16's left UP
                                points to itself.
```

Insert 63:

```
            (54,5)              Search for 63; compare with node
            /   \               of 54; key 16 and 14 differ at bit 3;
        (14,4)   (63,3)         63 is inserted as the right child of
        /   \     /  \          54 and discriminates on bit 3.
     {14} (16,2) {54} {63}      63's left UP points to 54 while its
           /   \                right UP points to itself.
        {16} {54}
```

FIGURE 8.42. Building a Patricia tree for the people_1d database.

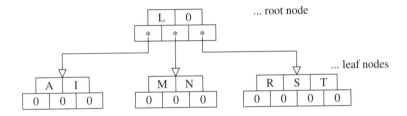

FIGURE 8.43. A B-tree of order 2.

8.10 Comparative-Based B-Trees for External Searching and Sorting

In previous sections, comparative-based search tree objects, such as the BST and AVL trees, were discussed. These structures are used for *internal* random access and searching and sorting operations. In this section, we introduce the ADT *B-tree* or *balanced sort tree*, the de facto standard for organizing large database systems and for *external* searching and sorting. By external, we mean that the records do not fit in the internal main memory, and are stored in a file on disks. IBM's Virtual Storage Access Method (VSAM) file organization uses B-tree. An OOP application of B-tree for people database is presented in Chapter 11. This database application can be modified to apply for a parts inventory control database, customer database. In a B-tree, an *order* is used to group the keys of records so that the B-tree will not grow very high; the B-tree is like a crystal. It grows from bottom (leaf) to outward and upward. The grouping of keys in each node is used to minimize the disk access time. The size of group defines the order of the B-tree. For example, for the set of keys,

$$\{L, O, R, I, N, T, A, M, S\},$$

we assume the ordering of keys in each node is alphabetically ascending; in the B-tree of order 2, each node has the maximum of $(2 \times 2) = 4$ keys and the minimum of 2 keys. For the given set, the B-tree of order 2 is shown in Figure 8.43, in which zero is used for NULL pointer values.

8.10.1 B-TREE OBJECTS

Since B-tree is used for external searching and sorting, its properties are designed to cluster the keys of data elements in a node in order to reduce the disk access. The keys are used for comparison and can be page numbers in a disk storage system. The clustering of keys in one node is done with respect to a number, N, called the *order of the B-tree*. For further information, refer to Bayer [Bay71] and [Bay72].

A B-tree object is specified by an ADT B-tree. An ADT B-tree of order N is a data structure that contains a set of nodes with some properties and some standard operations that are used to manipulate the B-tree nodes. The properties of an ADT B-tree of order N are:

- The height of a B-tree must be maintained to a minimum.

- The B-tree must remain balanced.

- The leaves of a B-tree are in the same level.

- No empty subtrees exist above the leaves of a B-tree.

- The root node may have no children if the B-tree contains only one node.

- Every node contains at least N number of keys, and at most $2N$ number of keys. A node is full if it contains $2N$ number of keys. The root node may have only one key for any order N.

- The keys in a node are maintained in ascending or descending order (lexical, numerical). Assuming ascending ordering, the left subtree of a key, say P, contains all keys that are less than the key P in the parent node; the right subtree of the key contains all keys that are greater than the key P.

- A B-tree is built by inserting keys in the leaf node. It grows upward and outward like a crystal.

- Insertion of a new data element locates a node, say X, where it is to be inserted. This is done by comparing the key, say new_key, of the new data element with the keys in the root node. If the node X has fewer than $2N$ number of keys, new_key is inserted in node X, and the ordering of keys is preserved. If the node X is full, it is split at the median N into two nodes, and the key at the median position is promoted to its parent node; if the parent node is full, the same splitting process is applied to the parent node until it reaches a nonfull node. If the node X is full and a root node, node X is split into two nodes, and another node for root is also created. The key, new_key, is inserted in the appropriate node in accordance with the ordering. The tree must remain a B-tree after insertion.

- After deletion of a key, the tree must remain a B-tree.

An example set of B-tree object's operations is implemented in **Code 11.1**.

8.10.2 Inserting a Key and Building a B-Tree

Inserting a new key in a B-tree is complex because the newly formed tree must remain a B-tree. We assume that no duplicate key is allowed, and the ordering of keys in a B-tree node is ascending. The goal is to insert a new key in a leaf node unless the leaf node is full. If the node is full, split it and move the median key to its parent. Continue this until a parent node is not full.

The insert operation for a key, say new_key, in an ADT B-tree follows this algorithm:

Step 1. Search B-tree for the new data element with new_key, which is used for comparison. If it exists in the B-tree, return. Otherwise, proceed to Step 2.

Step 2. Search B-tree for a node, pointed to by located_node_ptr where new_key is to be inserted. It starts from the root node down to the children, and compares new_key with the keys in each node.

Step 3. (Insertion process) If located_node_ptr is NULL (i.e., the tree is empty), create a node, set the number of keys to 1, and the parent pointer values of its left and right children to located_node_ptr. Now insert the new key in the node (which is both a root and a leaf node at this state), and return. Otherwise, consider two cases:

> **Case 1.** The node pointed to by located_node_ptr is not full, that is, the number of data elements (keys) in this node is less than $2N$.
>
> **Case 2.** The node pointed to by located_node_ptr is full, that is, the number of data elements (keys) in this node is $2N$.

Step 4. Based on the key value new_key, search for the "sorted position" of the new data element among the keys in the node pointed to by located_node_ptr.

Step 5. (Case 1) Insert the new data element in its "sorted position" in the node pointed to by located_node_ptr. Return.

Step 6. (Case 2) Node is full. Do steps 6.1 through 6.4.

> Step 6.1. Create a new node pointed to by new_ptr, and set its parent to the parent of the node pointed to by located_node_ptr.

Step 6.2. (Split) To split, compute the median key of the node pointed to by `located_node_ptr`. Copy all data elements with keys less than the median key into the new node. Move the data element with the median key to its parent node.

Step 6.3. If the parent is full, continue steps 6.1 and 6.2.

Step 6.4. Insert the new data element in the appropriate node and in the sorted position of that node.

To illustrate the insertion and build processes of a B-tree of order 2, let us consider the set of records with integer keys

$$\{33, 60, 5, 15, 25, 12, 45, 70, 35, 7\}.$$

For simplicity, it is assumed that each record contains one key. The ordering of keys in each node is ascending (in case of character keys, this could have been alphabetic ordering). Initially, the B-tree is empty. In the figures that follow, newly created nodes are distinguished as those that are shaded and a (0) indicates that a pointer has a NULL value.

33: Since the B-tree is empty, the root node is created, and the key 33 is inserted in the new node.

60, 5, 15: Search for these keys in the B-tree fails; they are simply inserted in this node so that they are in ascending order. The B-tree is:

5	15	33	60
0	0	0	0	0

25: The B-tree node is full as it contains 4 keys. So split the node at the median, key 15, and move it up to its parent node. Since this is the root node, create a new node as its parent node, and insert 15 in the new node. Since 25 > 15, insert it to the right half node. Then the right half node will contain {25, 33, 60}, and the left half node will contain {5} only, which violates the B-tree's order criterion (i.e., at least 2 keys per node). In order to satisfy this criterion, we denote the key 15 by moving it to the left node, and promote the key 25 to the root node so that both leaf nodes satisfy this criterion. Thus, after insertion of the key 25, the B-tree at this stage, is

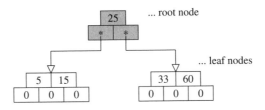

12: Search for key 12 fails; since $12 < 25$, insert it in the leaf node, the left subtree of node 25, and maintain the ascending ordering among the keys 5, 12, and 15. After insertion of the key 12, the B-tree is:

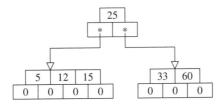

45: Search for key 45 fails; since $45 > 25$, it is simply inserted in the right subtree node of root node's key 25. The ascending ordering among 33, 60, and 45 is maintained. After insertion of key 45, the B-tree is:

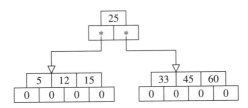

70: Search for key 70 fails; since $70 > 25$, it must be inserted in the right subtree node, which is not full. Maintain ascending ordering among 33, 45, 60, and 70. After insertion of key 70, the B-tree is:

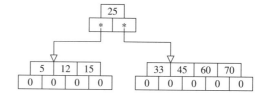

35: Search for these keys fail; since 35 > 25, it must be inserted in the right subtree node, which is full. Split this node at the median, key 45, and move it up to its parent node. Create a new node as the right subtree node of 25, which will contain 33 and the new key 35. The keys 33 and 35 in this new node maintain the ascending ordering. After the insertion of the key 35, the form of the B-tree is:

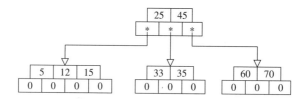

7: Search for key 70 fails; since 7 < 25, it must be inserted in the left subtree node, which is not full. Maintain ascending ordering among 5, 12, 15. and 7. After insertion of key 7, the final form of B-tree is:

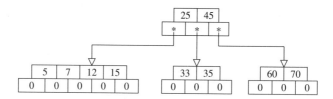

It is important to note that the insertion process maintained the height-balancing of the B-tree. Insertions of keys in a simple manner are possible because of node splitting. The node split grows the B-tree outward. The frequency of node splitting can be minimized if the number of keys in a node (i.e., the order of the B-tree) is made large. This insertion process does not allow duplicate key.

The C++ implementation of the insert and build operations for a B-tree object is presented in Chapter 11.

8.10.3   DELETING A KEY FROM A B-TREE

The delete operation in a B-tree is the reverse process of the insert operation. In a B-tree of order N, a B-tree node contains a minimum N number of data elements or keys and a maximum $2N$ number of data elements. In case of insertion, a full node (one that has overflown) is split into two B-tree nodes and the new tree is adjusted to preserve the B-tree properties. Unlike insertion, when a key, other than the root node, is deleted from a node with N keys, the node violates the B-tree property; it has a number of keys that is less than the minimum N. This condition is called *underflow*. The underflow state is resolved by borrowing one key from the parent or from the left or right neighboring nodes if they have at least $(N + 1)$ keys. Otherwise, combining the two adjacent nodes will satisfy the minimum requirement. Thus, the B-tree properties and ordering of keys are preserved after deletion.

The algorithm for deleting a data element specified by a key, `delete_key`, from a B-tree of order N is detailed as

Step 1. Search the B-tree for `delete_key`. If it is not found, print a message and return. If it exists in the node, pointed to by `located_node_ptr` in the B-tree, proceed to Step 2.

Step 2. Based on the type of this node, consider six cases:

Case 1. `delete_key` is in the root node, which contains more than one key and is a leaf node.

Case 2. `delete_key` is in the root node, which contains more than one key and is not a leaf node.

Case 3. `delete_key` is in the root node, which contains only one key, and is not a leaf node.

Case 4. `delete_key` is in the root node, which contains only one key, and is a leaf node.

Case 5. `delete_key` is in the leaf node, which contains exactly N keys before deletion, so that after deletion, the node will have $(N - 1)$ keys, violating B-tree criterion.

Case 6. `delete_key` is in the leaf node, which contains at least $(N + 1)$ keys before deletion, so that after deletion, the node will have N keys, satisfying the B-tree criterion.

Step 3. To recover the B-tree property in Case 5 of step 4, borrow a key from a neighboring node considering the four cases:

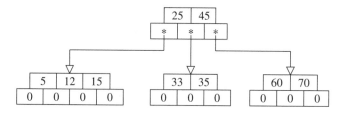

FIGURE 8.44. B-tree of order 2 before deletion of 25.

Case 5a. Borrow a key from the left neighboring node if it has at least $(N + 1)$ keys.

Case 5b. Borrow a key from the right neighboring node if it has at least $(N + 1)$ keys.

Case 5c. The left neighboring node has exactly N keys. Combine the node pointed to by `located_node_ptr` with the left neighboring node.

Case 5d. The right neighboring node has exactly N keys. Combine the node pointed to by `located_node_ptr` with the right neighboring node.

The tree now satisfies B-tree properties.

To illustrate these steps, first consider the B-tree of order 2 in Figure 8.45

In Case 1 of Step 2, the root node contains more than one key and is a leaf node. Simply delete the key by removing its entry from the node and by freeing up the memory space for the data element with `delete_key`.

In Case 2 of Step 2, the root node contains more than one key and is not a leaf node. Assume the key to be deleted is 25 in Figure 8.44. The root node contains keys 25 and 45. Since the key 25 has two nonempty subtrees, move the largest key 15 in the left subtree to the root to replace the key 25. After deletion of 25 from the root node, the B-tree of order 2 is in Figure 8.45.

In Case 3 of Step 2, the root node contains only one key and is not a leaf node. Consider the cases in Step 3. They are discussed later and are illustrated in Figure 8.47.

In Case 4 of Step 2, the root node contains only one key, and is a leaf node. Simply delete the B-tree node, and the tree becomes empty.

To illustrate Case 5c of Step 3, let us delete key 33 from the B-tree of order 2 in Figure 8.45. Since the node containing 33 has 2 keys, this node will have the key {35} after deletion, which violates the minimum criterion. To resolve this underflow state and to maintain ascending ordering among keys, we need to borrow one key from its left or right neighboring node.

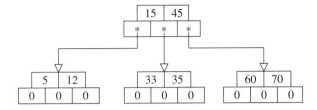

FIGURE 8.45. B-tree of order 2 after deletion of 25.

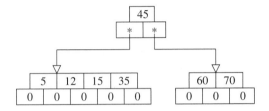

FIGURE 8.46. B-tree of order 2 after deletion of 33.

Since both neighboring nodes {5, 12} and {60, 70} have 2 keys each, borrowing one key from either of these neighbors will cause underflow in that neighbor. Thus, instead of borrowing a key, we combine the left neighbor (or the right neighbor) with this node {35}, which requires moving its parent key 15 down to the left subtree. The combined node is {5, 12, 15, 35}. After deleting 33, the B-tree of order 2 is shown in Figure 8.46.

To illustrate Case 3 of Step 2, the root node in Figure 8.46 contains 45, which is to be deleted. In this case, the left subtree node contains three keys 5, 12, 15, and 35, and the right subtree node contains two keys 60 and 70. Replacing the root key 45 by the smallest key 60 in the right subtree, will cause underflow in the right subtree node. Replacing the root key 45 by the largest key 35 in the left subtree will not cause any underflow in the left subtree node and maintain ordering and balance in the B-tree. Thus, in this case, there are three possible solutions:

- Replace the key to be deleted in the root node with the smallest key in the right subtree node.

- Replace the key to be deleted in the root node with the largest key in the left subtree node.

- Combine both left and right subtree nodes into a new root node when the left and right subtree nodes have N keys each.

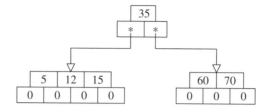

FIGURE 8.47. B-tree of order 2 after deletion of 45.

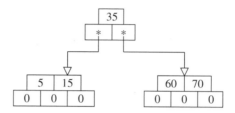

FIGURE 8.48. B-tree of order 2 after deletion of 12.

After deletion of the key 45 in the root node, the B-tree of order 2 in Figure 8.46 becomes the B-tree in Figure 8.47.

To illustrate Case 6 of Step 2, the key 12 in Figure 8.47 is to be deleted. Since the leaf node contains three keys 5, 12, and 15 before deletion of 12, it will contain two keys after deletion. The B-tree property remains unchanged. After deletion of the key 12 in the leaf node, the B-tree of order 2 in Figure 8.47 becomes the B-tree in Figure 8.48.

To illustrate Case 5d of Step 3, the key 15 in Figure 8.47 is to be deleted. Since the leaf node contains two keys 5 and 15 before deletion of 15, it will contain only one key after deletion, which causes an underflow. Since the right neighboring node contains exactly two keys 60 and 70, no keys can be borrowed from this node. Therefore, move the root node containing only one key 35 down to the left node, and combine the keys 5, 35, 60, and 70 into one node, which becomes the root and leaf node. After deletion of the key 15 in the leaf node, the B-tree of order 2 in Figure 8.48 becomes the B-tree in Figure 8.49.

The application for people database using B-tree object in Chapter 11 shows a C++ implementation of the delete operation for a B-tree object.

The main points for a B-tree of order N and with n number of data elements (keys) are summarized below.

- The B-tree remains balanced.

- The data elements in any node are ordered with respect to only one

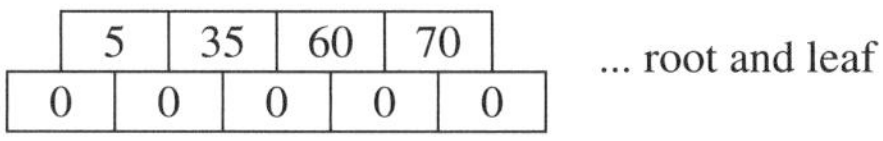

5	35	60	70	
0	0	0	0	0

... root and leaf

FIGURE 8.49. B-tree of order 2 after deletion of 15.

key.

- Duplicate keys are not allowed.

- The worst-case performance for the insert, delete, and search operations are $O(\log_2 n)$.

- Any node in a B-tree has at least N data elements (keys) and at most $2N$ data elements.

- Unlike the BST and AVL trees, the B-tree grows upward and outward.

- Splitting of a full node depends on the order N. Only splitting of a node causes increase in the height of a B-tree. Frequent splitting can be avoided by a large N.

- The height of a B-tree of order N with n data elements (keys) is $\log_N n$.

Other forms of a B-tree are B^*-tree, and the B^+-tree. In a B^+-tree with n data elements (keys), duplicate keys are allowed, and the worst-case performances of the insert, delete, and search operations are $O(\log_2 n)$. While the search operation is simple, the insert and delete operations are not.

8.11 Performance Analysis of Tree Operations

In this chapter, several forms of the tree object were discussed. The usage of these data structures depends on the applications and the operations we wish to perform in these applications. Thus, for the selection of an appropriate and efficient form of tree data structure, it is important to know at least the comparative-based worst-case performance of some key tree operations such as search, delete, and insert. The worst case occurs when the node to be searched or deleted is not in the tree or is at the leaf of the tree. Consider n nodes in the tree. Table 8.2 shows worst-case performances of operations for the trees.

To delete a data element specified by its index from an array tree will require only one comparison. However, the data element to be deleted is only specified by the key, the delete operation requires a search process,

Tree structure	Worst-case performance of		
	Search (random)	Delete (random)	Insert after a random element
Array binary tree	$O(n)$	$O(n)$	$O(n)$
Linked binary tree	$O(n)$	$O(n)$	$O(n)$
Binary search tree	$O(n)$ to $O(\log_2 n)$	$O(n)$ to $O(\log_2 n)$	$O(n)$ to $O(\log_2 n)$
Digital search tree (binary) (b-bit discrete keys)	$O(b)$	—	$O(b)$
Radix search trie (binary) (b-bit discrete keys)	$O(b)$	—	$O(b)$
AVL tree	$O(\log_2 n)$	$O(\log_2 n)$	$O(\log_2 n)$
B-tree	$O(\log_2 n)$	$O(\log_2 n)$	$O(\log_2 n)$
B^+-tree	$O(\log_2 n)$	$O(\log_2 n)$	$O(\log_2 n)$

TABLE 8.2. Performance of tree operations.

and the search does n number of comparisons when the target data element is not in the array binary tree. Therefore, the worst-case performances for the search and delete operations in an array tree of size n are $O(n)$.

For a degenerate BST with n nodes, the worst-case performances for search, delete, and insert are $O(n)$. For a nondegenerate BST with n nodes, the worst-case performances for search, delete, and insert are $O(\log_2 n)$.

Thus, the tree data structure is efficient and recommended for applications that frequently require random search, delete, and insert. Both AVL tree and B-tree are advantageous over BST because a BST may be degenerate, and AVL tree and B-tree can never be degenerate. Though the worst-case performances for search, delete, and insert in both AVL and B-trees are the same, a B-tree structure has an advantage over AVL tree because a B-tree is inherently balanced and an AVL tree requires a complex and time-consuming balancing.

The general tree data structure is used in applications for its own merits.

8.12   Exercises

1. For the `Binary_Tree` class in **Code 8.1**, implement and test the `public` member function that vertically prints a binary tree object, displaying the level number next to each node's data field. (Hint: see **Code 8.7**.)

2. For the `Binary_Tree` class in **Code 8.1**, implement and test the `public` member function that counts the number of leaf nodes in a binary tree object.

3. For the `Binary_Tree` class in **Code 8.1**, implement and test the `friend` function that checks the equality of two binary tree objects. The equality is characterized by the same structure and the same data fields of the corresponding nodes in two binary tree objects. Use the `overloaded` operator ==.

4. For the `Binary_Tree` class in **Code 8.1**, implement and test the `friend` function that copies one binary tree object into another. Use the `overloaded` operator =.

5. Write an algorithm for finding the parent of a node, identified by its key data, in a binary tree object.

6. For the `Binary_Tree` class in **Code 8.1**, implement and test the `public` member function for Exercise 8-5 using (a) a recursive method, and (b) a nonrecursive method.

7. Design an algorithm for inputting and building an ADT binary tree. Write and test an OOP that utilizes this algorithm.

8. Write and test an OOP that converts a binary tree into a general tree with child-sibling lists.

9. Design an algorithm for inputting and building an ADT general tree. Write and test an OOP that utilizes this algorithm.

10. Using postorder traversal, implement and test ~General_Tree() in **Code 8.3**.

11. For the `General_Tree` class in **Code 8.3**, implement and test a `public` member function that searches a general tree object for a node specified by a key `srch_key`.

12. Write and test an OOP for the *call tree* using a general tree as shown in Figure 8.11.

13. Write and test an OOP for the *descendant tree* using a general tree as shown in Figure 8.12. Include a menu-driven user interface for the search, display, modify, write to disk, read from disk, and quit operations. (Hint: Develop an user interface as a derived class of the `Tree` class.)

14. Write and test an OOP for the menu system using a general tree as shown in Figure 8.13. Include a menu-driven user interface for the search, display, modify, write to disk, read from disk, and quit

operations. (Hint: Develop an user interface as a derived class of the `Tree` class.)

15. Write and test an OOP for a file system using a general tree as shown in Figure 8.14. Assume that the data structure for a file, also called a *file control block*, includes variable file name, file size, file type (simple or directory), file owner's name, and file permissions (read, write, execute). Include a menu-driven user interface for the add, search, display, modify, write to disk, read from disk, and quit operations. The file name is used as the key. (Hint: Develop user interface as a derived class of the main tree class.)

16. Write and test an OOP for a system to maintain the database of employees of a university. Each employee's record consists of the attributes — name, address, phone number, job title, social security number, employee number, date of hire, marital status, current salary, and department name. Its user interface is menu driven providing support for the add, search, display, modify, write to disk, read from disk, and quit operations. The social security number is used as the key.

17. For the integer keys 55, 15, 35, 60, 25, 20, 40, build a pointer-based BST. Show that this BST is not the same BST as that shown in Figure 8.18.

18. For the given sets of integer keys (a) 13, 15, 12, 10, 14, 17, 16, 11, 17, 18, 16; (b) 15, 12, 10, 11, 14, 13, 11, 13, 12, 10, 17; (c) 16, 11, 12, 101, 19, 13, 18, 10, 70; (d) 120, 1000, 170, 180, 144, 99, 90, 20, 624, 88, build a BST in numerical ascending order. Show each manual step.

19. For each BST of Exercise 8-18, show the traces of (a) postorder, (b) preorder, and (c) inorder traversals.

20. Delete the node with integer key 14 from the BST in Exercise 8-18(a). Show the resulting tree.

21. Delete the node with integer key 15 from the BST in Exercise 8-18(b). Show the resulting tree.

22. Delete the node with integer key 99 from the BST in Exercise 8-18(c). Show the resulting tree.

23. Insert the integer key 100 into the BST of Exercise 8-18(a). Show the resulting tree.

24. Insert the integer key 16 into the BST for Exercise 8-18(b). Show the resulting tree.

25. Insert the integer key 115 into the BST for Exercise 8-18(a). Show the resulting tree.

26. Given the following sets of word keys or sentences, build a BST of words using alphabetical ascending order. Show each manual step.

    (a) {middle, bottle, puddle, little, apple, ripple, wiggle, jiggle, bubble, gobble}

    (b) {riddle, paddle, puzzle, dazzle, battle, rattle, giggle, juggle, saddle, silly}

    (c) {scales, fins, gills, midline, camouflage, fish, army, navy, heart, love, sincere, work}

    (d) "The quick brown fox jumps over the lazy dog."

    (e) "The choice of an efficient data structure is influenced by the application and the frequently used operations."

27. Show the (a) postorder, (b) preorder, and (c) inorder traces of each resulting BST from Exercise 8-26.

28. Delete the node with word key "jiggle" from the BST of Exercise 8-26(a). Show the resulting BST.

29. Delete node with word key "camouflage" from the BST of Exercise 8-26(c). Show the resulting BST.

30. Delete the node with word key "over" from the BST in Exercise 8-26(d). Show the resulting BST.

31. Delete the node with word key "application" from the BST in Exercise 8-26(e). Show the resulting BST.

32. Insert the word key `giggle` into the BST of Exercise 8-26(a).

33. Insert the word key `fins` into the BST of Exercise 8-26(b).

34. For the `Binary_Search_Tree` class in **Code 8.4**, implement and test the delete operation for a BST object.

35. For the `Binary_Search_Tree` class in **Code 8.4**, implement and test the retrieve operation for a BST object.

36. For the `Binary_Search_Tree` class in **Code 8.4**, implement and test a nonrecursive version of postorder traversal for a BST object.

37. For the `Binary_Search_Tree` class in **Code 8.4**, implement and test a nonrecursive version of preorder traversal for a BST object.

38. For the `Binary_Search_Tree` class in **Code 8.4**, implement and test a nonrecursive version of inorder traversal for a BST object.

39. For the `Binary_Search_Tree` class in **Code 8.4**, implement and test the nonrecursive version of `search_node_in_BST()` for a BST object.

40. Build an AVL tree for each set of integer keys in Exercise 8-18.

41. Delete node with integer key 14 from the AVL in Exercise 8-18(a). Show the AVL after deleting the key 14.

42. Delete node with integer key 15 from the AVL in Exercise 8-18(b). Show the AVL after deleting the key 15.

43. Delete the node with integer key 99 from the AVL tree in Exercise 8-18(c). Show the AVL after deleting the key 99.

44. Build an AVL tree for each set of word keys in Exercise 8-26.

45. Delete node with word key "jiggle" from the AVL in Exercise 8-26(a). Show the AVL after deleting the key "jiggle."

46. Delete node with word key "camouflage" from the AVL in Exercise 8-26(c). Show the resulting AVL tree.

47. Delete node with word key "over" from the AVL in Exercise 8-26(d). Show the resulting AVL tree.

48. Delete node with word key "application" from the AVL in Exercise 8-26(e). Show the resulting AVL tree.

49. For the `AVL_Tree` class in **Code 8.5**, the indentation problem occurs while printing an AVL tree object and the left child of the node above the leaf node is missing. Resolve this problem, and test.

50. For the `AVL_Tree` class in **Code 8.5**, the `public` member function `printlevel()` is recursive and implicitly uses a stack to print the AVL tree object vertically. To print the AVL tree object vertically, rewrite the associated functions that will use a queue.

51. For the `AVL_Tree` class in **Code 8.5**, implement the `public` member functions, `rotate_right()` and `rotate_left()`, and modify `add_node_into_AVL()` by incorporating these rotation functions. Test using the same data in **Code 8.5**.

52. For the `MRadix_Search_Trie` class, implement and test the destructor `~MRadix_Search_Trie()` in **Code 8.7**.

53. Build a B-tree of order N for each set of integer keys in Exercise 8-18 for the cases of (a) $N = 2$, (b) $N = 3$, and (c) $N = 4$.

54. Delete the node with integer key 14 from the B-tree of order 2 for the set in Exercise 8-18(a). Show the resulting B-tree.

55. Delete the node with integer key 15 from the B-tree of order 3 for the set in Exercise 8-18(b). Show the resulting B-tree.

56. Delete node with integer key 99 from the B-tree of order 4 for the set in Exercise 8-18(c). Show the resulting B-tree.

57. Build a B-tree of order N for each set of word keys in Exercise 8-26, for (a) $N = 2$ (b) $N = 3$, and (c) $N = 4$.

58. Delete node with word key "jiggle" from the B-tree of order 2 for the set in Exercise 8-26(a). Show the resulting B-tree.

59. Delete node with word key "camouflage" from the B-tree of order 3 for the set in Exercise 8-26(b). Show the resulting B-tree.

60. Delete node with word key "over" from the B-tree of order 4 for the set in Exercise 8-26(d). Show the resulting B-tree.

61. Delete the node for which the key is the word "application" from the B-tree of order 2 from Exercise 8-26(e). Show the resulting B-tree.

62. Write an algorithm to search a data object in the pure binary radix search trie of Figure 8.37. Implement and test a public member function of the MRadix_Search_Trie in **Code 8.7** using (a) a recursive method, and (b) a nonrecursive method.

63. Modify and test add_node_into_MRST() in **Code 8.7** such that identical keys are not ignored but may be stored in their respective leaf nodes. (Hint: Use a linked list.)

64. Implement and test an OOP for a discrete version of the 4-ary radix search trie of Section 8.9.4. Use the function extract_bit() (Hint: Examine 2 bits at a time.)

65. *Word dictionary application*: Write a routine extract_char() and apply it to the radix search trie above. Write a word dictionary application to use it.

66. *Expression tree*: An expression tree is useful in storing and evaluating infix algebraic expressions. An expression tree is a binary tree, which reads an infix expression from left to right. A parenthesis in the expression is used to specify a tight binding among operands and operators. The operators $+, -, *, \%, /$ are stored in root nodes, and the operands are in the leaf nodes. For an algebraic expression $(a - b) * c + d \% e$, the expression tree is:

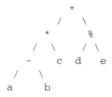

Write and test an OOP for evaluating an arithmetic expression using an expression tree object. The arithmetic expression contains integer or floating point operands, the operators +, -, *, %, /, and parentheses. The OOP must include methods for the following operations:

(a) Constructor and destructor. (b) Reads input infix-expression from a file. (c) Checks to see if the input expression has the correct infix form. (d) Builds an expression tree. (e) Prints the rooted tree in a vertical form. (f) Evaluates and prints the value. (g) Prints an infix expression using inorder traversal. (h) Prints a postfix expression using postorder traversal. (i) Prints a prefix expression using preorder traversal.

67. *Decision tree*: Like the binary search tree, a decision tree is useful for searching and sorting. Each node in a decision tree performs comparison of two keys and produces a decision of some sort. Based on the comparative value, the decision is taken to move to the left or the right branch of the node. The leaves of the decision tree provide the possible decisions (solutions) of the problem. One decision of the $n!$ permutations for n data elements (keys), is represented by each leaf. For example, for three distinct data keys x, y, and z, a decision tree is given below:

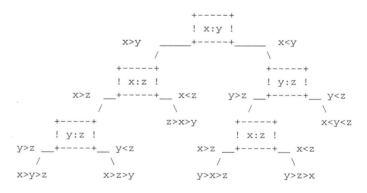

Implement and test an OOP for a decision tree. [Note that for a decision tree having $n!$ leaves, a sorting method using a decision tree makes $\log_2(n!)$ (i.e., $O(n \log_2 n)$) number of comparisons.]

68. Implement and test an OOP for a word dictionary based on a 26-ary radix search trie. Select 20 words beginning with the prefix "com" as the representable set of words.

69. Implement and test an OOP for a hybrid radix search trie version of the trie of Exercise 8-68. The trie should be 26-ary for the first two levels.

70. Implement and test an OOP for the trie of Exercise 8-68 using a BST object. Contrast the performance of these two structures.

71. Implement and test an OOP for a pure radix search trie for the people_1d database in Appendix C. Treat the keys as binary integers and use bit extraction and comparisons for branching. Show how to derive the data from the structure.

72. Implement and test an OOP for a Patricia trie for the people_1d database in Appendix C.

73. Implement and test an OOP for a Patricia tree for the people_1d database in Appendix C.

74. Implement and test an OOP for a parts inventory control database system (*PICDS*) using an AVL tree. The part's records are stored in an AVL tree with respect to the part number as the key. The record for each part contains part's number, part's name, part's description, part's quantity, part's price per unit, vendor's name, vendor's address, and vendor's phone. A duplicate parts record is not allowed. The PICDS has a menu-driven user interface supporting the following actions:

(a) Add a part to database.

(b) Delete a part from database.

(c) Modify a part in database.

(d) Show a part in database.

(e) Print all part numbers in database.

(f) Save database to disk.

(g) Read database from disk.

(h) Exit.

9

Multidimensional Search Trees and Search Tries

In Chapter 8, comparative-based search tree and digital-based radix search trie objects were introduced. All these structures were accessed on the basis of a single or *primary* key. That is, for a given set of data objects or records, each record contains a single element or attribute designated as *the* key upon which all insert, delete, and general query operations are based. All attributes of a record, aside from the designated key, are processed as *data*. In the present chapter, these concepts are extended to a treatment of search tree and search trie structures that provide for *multi-key access*.

9.1 Extending the Single-Key Model

Consider again the ADT BST introduced in Section 8.8. A balanced BST has been shown to support efficient (logarithmic) search and retrieval operations on a database of records for a designated search key. For the example of the `people_1d` database, the membership identification number serves as the underlying primary search key. Records retrieved on behalf of a target "member_id" contain the associated data attributes of name, age, income, occupation, and years of membership. However, *what if we wish to query the database on behalf of a non-key attribute or some combination of attributes?* In the context of the current example, let's say we wish to retrieve the records of all members of age 30 or those members between the ages of 25 and 35 with incomes in the range of $45,000 to $100,000.

With the BST in its present form, queries on behalf of such secondary keys amount to one or more exhaustive (linear) searches on an unordered list. When the BST is traversed as an unordered list, search pruning is defeated. In some situations exhaustive search may turn out to be acceptable: a query in the form of one or more exhaustive traversals of the tree that was expected to return a large percentage of the records within. On the other hand, if few records were expected to be returned from a vast database, then the performance of a brute force linear search is likely to be quite poor.

The process of searching a set of data objects (records) directly on behalf of a multiplicity of attributes (keys) is known as *associative search* or searching by *secondary* keys. While there are many approaches to be taken in the development of data structures and algorithms that support associative search, we choose to investigate several ADTs that have evolved as direct extensions of the tree and trie structures presented in Chapter 8.

9.2   Geometric Formulation of Associative Search

A convenient means of modeling associative access to data objects with multiple keys lies within a geometric framework. Such a framework is established with the adoption of a simple and intuitive abstraction that states that *data objects are points in a multi-attribute (multi-key) space.*

Within this framework a common class of data structures and algorithms may be applied to applications involving what are typically thought of as "traditional" record-oriented data objects as well as to applications involving data objects that are more readily thought of as geometric. Such structures and algorithms are categorically referred to as *point-access methods* (*PAMs*).

9.2.1   RECORDS AS POINTS IN KEY-SPACE

Data objects in the form of records with k keys are defined as points in a straightforward manner.

Definition 9.1 *A record is a* k-*tuple of keys* $(k_0, k_1, ...k_{d-1})$ *considered to be a point in a* k-*dimensional coordinate space called the attribute or key-space.*

Here, k is the *dimensionality* of the records, corresponding to the number of keys upon which the record may be searched on and thus the number of dimensions or coordinates that define the key-space. In geometric terms, the assignment of a coordinate system provides a one-to-one mapping between the points of the key-space and the set of all tuples of real numbers. As such, the coordinates of a point or record are Cartesian coordinates.

In Appendix C, the `people_2d` and `people_3d` databases are presented. These are multi-key versions of the `people_1d` database. While all three databases contain the same data, they differ in their specification of keys. In the context of the current discussion, `people_1d` records are seen as one-dimensional, while the records of the `people_2d` and `people_3d` databases are two- and three-dimensional, respectively. Each `people_2d` record contains a two-dimensional key that represents a point in the *age-income* key-space. Similarly, each `people_3d` record contains a three-dimensional key that represents a point in the three-dimensional *age-income-years* key-space.

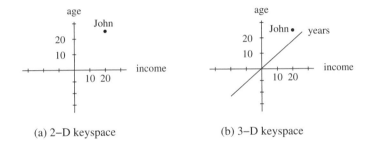

(a) 2–D keyspace   (b) 3–D keyspace

FIGURE 9.1. Plotting a record within a 2-d and a 3-d keyspace.

The two- and three-dimensional points corresponding to the record of John are plotted in Figure 9.1(a) and Figure 9.1(b), respectively. Figure 9.1(a) shows the *age* and *income* coordinates and the 2-tuple $(age, income) = (24, 20)$ while Figure 9.1(b) shows the *age*, *income*, and *years* coordinates and the 3-tuple $(age, income, years) = (24, 20, 2)$ corresponding to the record of John.

9.2.2 GEOMETRIC OBJECTS IN EUCLIDEAN SPACE

Beyond the field of traditional record-oriented database management systems (DBMS) has emerged a strong demand for methods for the management of geometric objects in multidimensional space. This demand has largely been driven by applications in the areas of computer graphics, computer-aided design (CAD), image processing, and geo-science information systems, all of which require efficient processing of large sets of geometric data. This rapidly growing and evolving area has become known as the discipline of *spatial data structures*.

The study of spatial data structures is intimately related to the field of *computational geometry*, which itself is best described as the study of algorithms for the solution of geometric problems. Critical to the solution of geometric problems is the availability of efficient data structures and access algorithms to geometric data. The works of Mehlhorn [Meh84] and Preparata and Shamos [Pre85] are valuable sources on the topic of multi-dimensional searching in the domain of computational geometry.

Several fundamental characteristics distinguish geometric data applications from those of the traditional record-oriented information processing variety:

- Spatial data typically represents geometric objects that are embedded in space. The space is usually some d-dimensional Euclidean space R^d, with a rectangular Cartesian system of coordinates, although other types of spaces and coordinate systems may exist.

- Geometric databases are not just large sets of records or points but include more complex geometric objects such as lines, rectangles, triangles, circles, and polygons.

- Access to spatial objects is a function of their location, size, shape, and overlap (extent) in space.

- Geometric search algorithms exploit the implicit structure of point-based objects; all objects are structurally interrelated by the metric structure of the embedding space in which the objects reside.

A spatial data structure provides an organization of geometric data objects in space. There are three major aspects of spatial organization to consider. First, a spatial data structure specifies a partitioning or decomposition of the entire data space into *cells*. Second, an indexing scheme provides a two-way mapping between any given region of the data space and the cells contained within that region. Alternately stated, an index maps the cells of the spatial decomposition to the regions in space occupied by a geometric object. Third, a scheme for representing geometric objects and positioning them in space must be specified.

Given a specific spatial region or neighborhood, a spatial data structure provides for efficient access to the data objects contained within that region. Spatial access can be broken down into two basic steps: *cell addressing* is the process of finding all the cells of a space partitioning that intersect or overlap the specified query region, and *data access* is the retrieval of all the objects contained within those cells.

The most simple case geometric object is the point, a zero-sized object with no shape or overlap. Points are usually stored and accessed solely by position. In an environment of point data, point-access methods (PAMs) are utilized for data search an retrieval.

In general, however, spatial data structures must be able to manage geometric objects of greater complexity. Extended geometric objects, such as lines, rectangles, triangles, circles, and polygons must be managed in terms of their size, shape, position, and overlap in space. Since such spatial objects have size, each may occupy several cells of partitioning and a scheme must be provided to handle this. Solutions for efficient access to extended spatial objects are referred to as *spatial-access methods* (*SAMs*). Thus, while a PAM provides for spatial access to sets of points, a SAM provides access to more complicated geometric objects (as well as points).

As an introduction to the subject, this book focuses on basic PAMs for geometric data. This strategy, however, does not preclude a discussion of SAMs, as it turns out that (1) extended geometric objects are commonly represented as sets of points, and (2) a majority of current SAMs are really just extensions to PAMs.

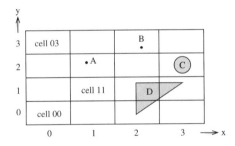

FIGURE 9.2. A 2-d (x-y) space and cell partitioning.

There are three common methods employed that convert point-access structures to spatial access structures. These are the techniques of *clipping*, *overlapping regions*, and *transformation*. With clipping, geometric objects are sliced or clipped along the boundaries of the spatial partitions of the data structure. The method of overlapping regions (alternately, overlapping cells) provides for objects that may overlap multiple spatial cells by including a reference to the object in each and every cell that it overlaps. The transformation technique maps extended spatial objects into points in a higher-dimensional space.

These concepts are illustrated with the aid of Figure 9.2. In this figure, a bounded two-dimensional x-y key-space is partitioned by a 4 × 4 *fixed grid* array of equal-sized (square) cells. Each cell may be considered a *bucket* for holding data objects. Cells are accessed as elements in a two-dimensional array.

In Figure 9.2 there are four data objects. Objects labeled A and B are simple points; objects A and B are retrieved by indexing cell[1][2] and cell[2][3], respectively. Object C is a circle represented as a collection of points; it is retrieved by accessing cell[3][2] in which it is fully contained. Object D is a triangle data object made up of three points. It, however, is not fully contained by a single cell. Its spatial extent overlaps cell[2][1], cell[2][0], and cell[3][1]. To handle this situation in a point-access structure, one might choose to clip the geometry of the triangle against the geometry of the three cells it overlaps, in much the same way a cookie cutter works. This would introduce new points at the intersections of the cell partitions and the triangle geometry. The final result would be three new objects, each contained within, and accessed from, their own cells. An alternate solution would be to include a reference to all the points making up the triangle in all cells overlapped by it. In other words, the data buckets of the three cells would each contain all three endpoints. Object D would then be retrieved by an access to any of these cells.

9.3   Types of Associative Search

Associative search problems typically involve operations such as finding the closest-point from a specified point, all points near a specified point, or all points within a specified range of points. The most commonly occurring types of associative searches fall into one of two broad categories — *region intersection queries* and *proximity queries*. For further information, refer to Orenstein [Ore82].

Region Intersection Queries

Given the complete set of data objects, an intersection type query is one that requests the retrieval of all data objects that *intersect a specified subset* of the complete set. Region intersection searches are among the most commonly exercised type of associative search. Three major types are listed in order of increasing complexity:

- *Exact match* queries, often referred to as *simple* or *point* queries, request the retrieval of a single data object whose k keys exactly match the k-key search target specification. If the data objects in the collection are not necessarily unique, the exact match search may return more than one item. In geometric terms, the search target of an exact match search is a k-dimensional point or k-tuple.

- *Partial match* queries search for all data objects whose keys match a specified subset of all possible keys. If a data object is completely identified by k keys, then a partial match would return all objects that match some target specification of p keys for $p < k$. Geometrically, the search target represents a $(k - p)$-dimensional hyperplane.

- *Range queries* are the same as partial match queries except that a range of values, as opposed to just a single value, may be specified for each key. An *orthogonal range* query specifies a range of values or each attribute. Geometrically, an orthogonal range search target represents a k-dimensional hyper-rectangular region; the k hyperplanes bounding the region are each orthogonal to a coordinate axis. Each range of values for a given attribute is an interval on a distinct coordinate axis. The Cartesian product of such intervals defines the hyper-rectangular region.

Proximity Queries

It is often the case that a search on a database is initiated with the intent of finding exactly what is being looked for (i.e., an exact match) or all items that fall within a specified range (i.e., a range query). However, in many situations, the exact match to the search target does not exist in the database and we may wish to settle for an item that is a *close* match. Problems of this nature are collectively referred to as proximity or *closest-point* searches. Proximity queries are based on a specified measure of dissimilarity or distance between data objects. A few of the most common proximity queries are listed as follows:

- Given a set of data objects, a *closest pair* query asks for the pair or some number of pairs of objects that are most alike for a given measure of dissimilarity. In geometric terms, the closest-pair query is a search for pairs of objects whose mutual distance is the smallest under a specified distance function.

- A *nearest neighbor* or *best match* query, on the other hand, specifies a target object and asks for one or more objects that are a best match with the target under a specified metric. For example, given a collection C of 100 points in k-dimensional space, a distance function D, and a target point P, a search for 10 points from C that have the smallest distance measure (under D) from point P is a best match search.

- Similarly, a *fixed-distance near neighbor* search is a query for all data objects within a fixed distance of a specified target object for a given distance function. Such a search is also referred to as a *bounded distance* query. In geometric terms, we typically speak in terms of a radial distance or radius. In a two-dimensional space, a fixed-radius near neighbor search represents a *circular range search* while in three dimensions it is a *spherical range search*. In general, a fixed-radius near neighbor search represents a search on a hyper-spherical range of the data space. This may be contrasted with the general case orthogonal range search, which represents a search on a hyper-rectangular range of the data space.

In conjunction with proximity searches, there are many types of dissimilarity measures or distance functions to be considered. The choice ultimately depends upon the nature of the application and the type of data involved.

For a given pair of records, a measure of dissimilarity or "distance" between them is a function of the dissimilarity of their keys. In geometric terms, keys correspond to the coordinates of points and *coordinate distance functions* define the one-dimensional distance between the coordinates of two points.

Metric distances, those that obey the property of triangle inequality (and $d(a, a) = 0$ and $d(a, b) = d(b, a)$), are among the most commonly employed, and among these, *Euclidean* distance is perhaps the most dominant. As stated above, the Euclidean plane and space is the domain of geometric applications and spatial data structures.

Other methods for computing (dis)similarity between data objects often involve a direct accounting or ranking of keys. For instance, given two objects A and B, the *Hamming distance function* $H(A, B)$ is defined as the number of keys for which the data objects A and B are different. Another approach is to specify a list of preference values for a given key and a ranking of preference lists among all of the target keys.

9.4 Examples of Associative Search

To illustrate several associative searches, consider two examples, one employing the `people_2d` database and the other employing `geometry_3d` database.

Example 1

The management of organization XYZ is conducting a survey of its membership. The database is comprised of the `people_2d` records. Each record contains a two-dimensional key that is the 2-tuple (age, income). In Figure 9.3, each record is plotted as a point in the *age-income* plane. Also shown are the geometries associated with the following example associative queries:

Query type	Query: Return name(s) for ...
Exact Match	$age = 35$, $income = 60$
Partial Match	$age = 65$
Range	$age = 22$, $20 \leq income <= 40$
Orthogonal Range	$20 \leq age \leq 40$, $30 \leq income \leq 60$
Polygonal Range	$30 \leq age \leq 60$, $income = income + 10 \times age$
Best Match	age and $income$ closest to John

The geometry of the exact match query is the point (35,60), and the search will return the name Steve. The partial match query asks for all records on the line $age = 65$ while the range query asks for all records on the segment of the line $age = 22$ bounded by incomes in the range of 20 to 40. Neither of these two queries will return any records. The orthogonal range query specifies a rectangular-shaped search region and for the given bounds and will return the records of Paul, Steve, Bob, and Jill. The polygonal query specifies a more general polygonal-shaped search region geometry, which is in this case a triangle. It will return the records of Jim and Peter.

Example 2

A computer graphics system processes geometric objects represented as collections of vertexes (points) defined in Euclidean 3-space with a three-

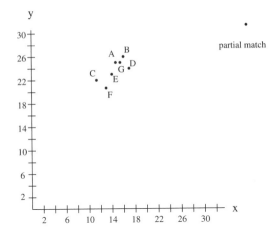

FIGURE 9.3. Associative queries on the people_2d database.

dimensional Cartesian coordinate system. A vertex is a 3-tuple (x,y,z) with associated attributes. Alternately, one may think of a vertex as a record containing 3 key attributes x,y,z, and data attributes, such as color and surface normal components. The geometry_3d database is an example of such a collection of data. Figure 9.4 shows the vertexes (points) of this database plotted in the x-y plane. Also illustrated is the geometry of the following example associative queries:

Query type	Query: Retrieve (draw) ...
Exact Match	Vertex at $(x, y, z) = (16.9, 24.1, 19.7)$
Partial Match	Vertexes on the line $y = 22.7$
Orthogonal Range	Vertexes within cube defined by
	$30.0 < x < 35.0, 30.0 < y < 35.0,$
	$30.0 < z < 35.0$
Fixed-Radius	Vertexes that are 4 units distance
Near Neighbor	away from vertex $I = (18.1, 21.2, 18.0)$
	Euclidean distance: $d^2 = x^2 + y^2 + z^2$
	(spherical range search)
Nearest Neighbor	Vertex that is the closest to
	the point $(x, y, z) = (18.1, 21.2, 18.0)$

The exact match query returns the vertex D since it exactly matches the target coordinate description. For the partial match search, the single vertex E is returned, as it is the only one on the specified line. The orthogonal range search specifies a cube region in the search space. However, no vertexes are returned, as none are contained within this cube. The fixed-

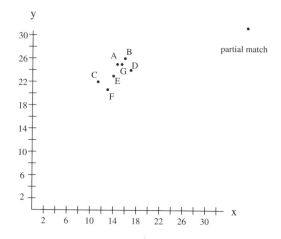

FIGURE 9.4. Associative queries on the geometry_3d database.

radius near neighbor query, on the other hand, specifies a search region corresponding to a sphere centered at vertex I and with radius 4.0. The search returns the vertex D.

9.5 Approaches to Associative Search

While many approaches exist for multi-key or multidimensional point access problems, no particular method is ideal for all applications. The process of choosing an appropriate method involves the nature of the data and the space-time requirements of the application.

Methods of associative search fall into two major categories: *hierarchical* and *non-hierarchical*. Among some of the most commonly employed techniques, multidimensional search trees and search tries are examples of hierarchical methods, while *inverted files*, *grid files*, and *multidimensional extendable hashing* are examples of non-hierarchical methods. The structure of Figure 9.2, above, is an example of a non-hierarchical data organization.

A full treatment of the subject of multidimensional search techniques is beyond the intent and scope of this book. Such an undertaking could easily fill an entire volume. Therefore, as stated earlier, search trees and search tries are chosen to be focused on, as they (1) are multidimensional extensions of the tree and trie structures introduced in Chapter 8 and (2) are very widely used. However, by focusing on tree and tries, it is not intended to imply that their methodology is necessarily superior to others. As pointed out above, each technique has its merits and drawbacks. The interested reader is encouraged to pursue numerous references on the subject. For instance, the work of Nievergelt, Hintenberger, and Sevcik [Nie84] is an excellent treatment of grid files and related techniques; for extendable hashing, the reader is referenced to the work of Fagin, Nievergelt, Pippenger, and Strong [RFS79]. For a comprehensive overview of multidimensional data structures, including an extensive bibliography on the subject, refer to the works of Samet [Sam89a], [Sam89b].

The inverted list was one of the first multi-key methods employed, making it, by default, the benchmark against which other newer methods are measured. In addition, because of its simplicity, it remains popular in some situations. For these reasons, we present a brief overview of the ADT inverted list.

9.5.1 ADT INVERTED LIST

If the data records of the `people_2d` database were organized as an unsorted list, as depicted in Figure 9.5(a), a request to retrieve a record based on a multiplicity of keys would involve a number of exhaustive sequential searches. More specifically, for a list of n records, each with k keys, the search time would be $O(n * k)$.

Figure 9.5(b) shows the ADT inverted list for the main sequential list of Figure 9.5(a). In actuality, an inverted list is a set of k lists, where k is the number of keys associated with each record. Each of these lists is a list of pointers to records in the main list, sorted to produce the associated key in ascending order. The resulting benefit of the inverted list(s) is that an efficient search can be made on any one key followed by $k - 1$ exhaustive searches on the remaining keys. For example, to perform an orthogonal range search to retrieve all records for $(25 \leq age \leq 50)$ and $(20 \leq income \leq 60)$, the following steps are taken:

Step 1. Search the sorted *age* inverted list and place a pointer to each record that falls within the specified age range in an auxiliary list. $(O(\log_2(n * k)))$

Step 2. Search the unsorted auxiliary list created in Step 1. Return all records with incomes within the specified range. $(O(n * k))$

For the given data, Step 1 produces an auxiliary list of records containing Bob, Jill, Steve, and Kathy, in that order. Step 2 yields the final result, returning the records of Jill, Bob, and Steve.

Property 9.1 *The average search time using an inverted list scheme can be shown to be* $O(n^{(1-1/k)})$.

The shortcoming of the inverted list method is that it is still a primary-key access method, as only a single selected key may be searched on efficiently. In addition, only one key is utilized at a time.

addr	Keys		attributes
	age	income	
&1	29	57	16, "Bob", "engineer", 3
&2	24	20	54 "John", "student", 2
&3	39	170	14, "Kathy", "doctor", 5
&4	51	95	63, "Peter", "sales", 1
&5	51	125	62, "Jim", "lawyer", 1
&6	22	4	48, "Nancy", "student", 2
&7	22	55	21, "Paul", "teacher", 5
&8	35	60	53, "Steve", "engineer", 1
&9	32	45	48, "Jill", "nurse", 4

age	income
&6 (Nancy)	&6 (Nancy)
&7 (Paul)	&2 (John)
&2 (John)	&9 (Jill)
&1 (Bob)	&7 (Paul)
&9 (Jill)	&1 (Bob)
&8 (Steve)	&8 (Steve)
&3 (Kathy)	&4 (Peter)
&4 (Peter)	&5 (Jim)
&5 (Jim)	&3 (Kathy)

(a) list of records   (b) inverted list(s)

FIGURE 9.5. ADT list and inverted list for people_2d database.

In sections that follow, structures that allow for symmetric direct multi-key access are investigated; that is, all keys are accessed with equal significance and efficiency.

9.6   Multidimensional Comparative-Based Search Trees

Single-dimensional comparative-based search trees generalize to multidimensional structures for support of associative search. Two popular approaches are the ADT K-trees and ADT kd-trees. Both of these types of structures support efficient point-access methods for a variety of associative queries.

9.6.1   K-Tree Objects

K-trees are a generalization of the single-key (single-dimensional) M-ary search tree. A K-tree object is specified by an ADT K-tree.

Definition 9.2 *An ADT* K-*tree is a multidimensional* M-*ary search tree (MMST) such that for a* k-*dimensional search space,* $M = K = 2^k$.

As a data comparative search tree, a K-tree stores data objects in both internal and leaf nodes. A hierarchical recursive subdivision of the k-dimensional search space is induced with the space partitions following the locality of the data. Each node in a K-tree contains $K = 2^k$ child pointers. The root node of the tree represents the entire, possibly semi-infinite, search space and each child of the root represents a K-*ant* of the parent space.

The K-tree handles any dimension space in a straightforward manner. Two of the most commonly occurring cases are for two and three dimensions. In two dimensions ($k = 2$, $K = 4$), a K-tree is a 4-ary tree with each node possessing 4 child pointers. In geometric terms, the search space (key-space) is a plane and the partitioning induced by the structure is a hierarchical subdivision of the search space into disjoint **quadrants**.

Definition 9.3 *A K-tree in two dimensions is called a* quadtree.

In three dimensions ($k = 3$, $K = 8$), each node of a K-tree has eight child pointers, each pointing to a disjoint cell or **octant** of the parent space.

Definition 9.4 *A K-tree in three dimensions is called an* octree.

The quadtree for the point data of the geometry_2d database is illustrated in Figure 9.6(a) along with a diagram of the corresponding partitioning (Figure 9.6(b)) of the x-y key-space. The quadtree in Figure 9.6 is assumed to be built in the insertion order of $(x, y) = \{$ (14.6, 25.0), (16.3, 26.5), (12.1, 22.0), (16.9, 24.1), (13.7, 22.7), (12.6, 20.8), (15.5, 24.4), (16.0, 22.4), (18.1, 21.2), (12.6, 20.8)$\}$, which corresponds to nodes $\{a, b, c, d, e, f, g, h, i, j\}$.

As an M-ary tree, one of the fundamental drawbacks of the ADT K-tree is its storage space requirements. In a standard implementation, each node of a k-dimensional K-tree requires 2^k child pointers. A tree of n records, each with k keys and A additional attributes, requires $(2^k + k + A) * n$ fields. As k increases, the amount of storage space required becomes prohibitive. In addition, as pointed out in the previous chapter, an M-ary tree can be wasteful on space, as many child pointers can go unused.

9.6.2   OOP IMPLEMENTATION OF QUADTREE

Code 9.1 is an OOP implementation of a pointer-based quadtree object for the people_2d database. The MultiDimen_Mary_Srch_Tree **class** defines quadtree objects. MMST_build() constructs the quadtree by calling MMST_insert_node() for each node. MMST_insert_node() recursively searches the tree for the appropriate position in which to insert the target key. This search is guided by the function find_direction(). Given a node and a vertex, this function determines which child K-ant of the node the vertex belongs in. The function is general purpose, as it can handle any number K. In this example, K = 4 and find_direction() returns the appropriate quadrant (4-ant), one of "northwest," "northeast," "southwest," and "southeast," denoted as NW, NE, SW, and SE, respectively. A node is inserted when a NULL pointer is reached. The function isSameKey() determines if the target key is equivalent to the key at any given node. The given implementation does not allow for identical keys, so

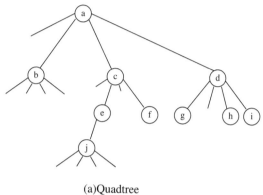

(a)Quadtree

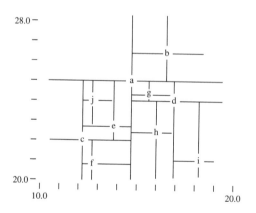

(b) Spatial partitioning

FIGURE 9.6. Quadtree and partitioning for geometry_2d database.

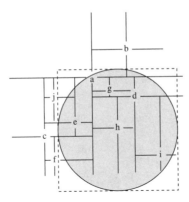

FIGURE 9.7. Circular range query on geometry_2d database.

the insertion process is aborted if isSameKey() determines that the key being inserted already exists in the tree.

The function MMST_proximitysearch() performs a circular range search. The geometry of this search is the shaded circle of radius 3.0 centered at node h, as depicted in Figure 9.7. The dissimilarity measure here is assumed to be Euclidean. The search is accomplished as a recursive two-step process. A square that corresponds to the bounding extent of the search circle is intersected with the tree at each node encountered. The bounds of this square are maintained in a two-dimensional range array that is initialized based on the given search center and radius. At each node, the direction of search is determined by this intersection; a search on a child is pruned if it is known that the region represented by the child does not intersect the search square. For all the nodes that do intersect the square, actual containment within the circle is determined by the function isInCircularRange().

In the current example in Figure 9.7, the circular range search in **Code 9.1** will return the vertexes A, E, D, G, and I. The vertex H is also returned, although this is optional, since it is the fixed-radius near neighbors of vertex H that are being asked for.

Code 9.1

```
//   Program: MMST_2D.c++
//   Purpose:
//     OOP implementation of a K-tree for geometry_2d database
//     (key1 = x, key2 = y coord.)
//     This example is for k = D = 2 (two-dimensional).
//     Thus K = 4 and the tree is a QUADTREE.
//     Children of a node appear in left to right order:
//         child 0 1 2 3  = SW NW SE NE
```

```
//
#include  <stdio.h>
const int MIN = 0;
const int MAX = 1;
const int D   = 2;  // 2-dimensional search keys
const int K   = 4;  // degree 4
const int M   = K;

class  Multi_Dimen_M_ary_Srch_Tree {
  private:
    typedef float  Keytype;
    struct DataObject {      // Geometry Vertex record
       Keytype  key[D];      // key[0] = x, key[1] = y
       unsigned long color;  // 3-component color
       char  label;
    };
    typedef struct MMST_NODE {
        DataObject    vertex_record;
        MMST_NODE     *child_ptr[M];
    } *MMST_PTR;
    MMST_PTR  root_ptr;
    void      init_MMST() { root_ptr = NULL; }
    int       find_direction(MMST_PTR, DataObject);
    int       isSameKey(Keytype *, Keytype *);
    int       isInCircularRange(Keytype *, Keytype *, Keytype);
  public:
    Multi_Dimen_M_ary_Srch_Tree() { root_ptr = NULL; }
    ~Multi_Dimen_M_ary_Srch_Tree();
    MMST_PTR  MMST_create_node();
    void      MMST_insert_node(MMST_PTR *, DataObject);
    void      MMST_build(DataObject *, int);
    void      MMST_PostOrder(MMST_PTR);
    void      MMST_proximitysearch(MMST_PTR , Keytype*,
              float , Keytype[D][2]);
    void      build_and_show_geom2D_as_MMST(void);
    MMST_PTR  get_root() { return  root_ptr; }
};
//   ---   Implement methods for "Multi_Dimen_M_ary_Srch_Tree"

Multi_Dimen_M_ary_Srch_Tree::~Multi_Dimen_M_ary_Srch_T ree()
{
   //  Left as an exercise
}
Multi_Dimen_M_ary_Srch_Tree::MMST_PTR
Multi_Dimen_M_ary_Srch_Tree::MMST_create_node()
{
    MMST_PTR new_ptr;

    if ((new_ptr = new MMST_NODE) == NULL) {
       printf("\n MMST_create_node: new failed.\n");
       return(NULL);
    } else {
       for (int i = 0; i < M; i++)
           new_ptr->child_ptr[i] = NULL;
```

```
            return (new_ptr);
    }
}

//  MMST_insert_node():
//     Inserts a node into a quadtree.
//     (Recursive implementation)
//
void Multi_Dimen_M_ary_Srch_Tree::MMST_insert_node
        (MMST_PTR *tree_ptr, DataObject vertex_record)
{
    MMST_PTR new_ptr;

    if (*tree_ptr == NULL) {
        new_ptr = MMST_create_node();
        new_ptr->vertex_record = vertex_record;
        *tree_ptr = new_ptr;
    }
    else {
      if (isSameKey((*tree_ptr)->vertex_record.key,
                    vertex_record.key))
          return;       // Key already exists
      else {
          int dir = find_direction(*tree_ptr, vertex_record);
          MMST_insert_node(&(*tree_ptr)->child_ptr[dir],
                           vertex_record);
      }
    }
}

//  MMST_build():
//     Build a MMST for vertex records in GEOMETRY_2D database
//
void Multi_Dimen_M_ary_Srch_Tree::MMST_build
                    (DataObject *vertex_records, int nobj)
{
    for (int i = 0; i < nobj; i++)
        MMST_insert_node(&root_ptr, vertex_records[i]);
}

//  MMST_proximitysearch():
//     Performs circular range search in a MMST.
//
void Multi_Dimen_M_ary_Srch_Tree::MMST_proximitysearch
    (MMST_PTR tree_ptr, Keytype *target,
     float r, Keytype range[][2])
{
    int i, dir[K];

    if (tree_ptr == NULL)
        return;
    if (isInCircularRange(tree_ptr->vertex_record.key,
                          target, r))
        printf(" Proximity search found: %c \n",
```

```
                        tree_ptr->vertex_record.label);
       for (i = 0; i < K; i++)
           dir[i] = 1;
       if (range[0][MIN] > tree_ptr->vertex_record.key[0])
           dir[1] = dir[0] = 0;
       if (range[0][MAX] <= tree_ptr->vertex_record.key[0])
           dir[3] = dir[2] = 0;
       if (range[1][MIN] > tree_ptr->vertex_record.key[1])
           dir[0] = dir[2] = 0;
       if (range[1][MAX] <= tree_ptr->vertex_record.key[1])
           dir[1] = dir[3] = 0;
       if (dir[0])
           MMST_proximitysearch(tree_ptr->child_ptr[0],
                                target, r, range);
       if (dir[1])
           MMST_proximitysearch(tree_ptr->child_ptr[1],
                                target, r, range);
       if (dir[2])
           MMST_proximitysearch(tree_ptr->child_ptr[2],
                                target, r, range);
       if (dir[3])
           MMST_proximitysearch(tree_ptr->child_ptr[3],
                                target, r, range);
}
//    For point P = (d0p,d1p) , find all nodes (d0n,d1n)
//    such that Euclidean distance r from P:
//        r^2 >= (d0p-d0n)^2 + (d1p-d1n)^2
//
int Multi_Dimen_M_ary_Srch_Tree::isInCircularRange
        (Keytype *key, Keytype *target, Keytype radius)
{
    Keytype   d, sum_sqrd = 0.0;

    for (int i = 0; i < D; i++) {
        d = target[i] - key[i];
        sum_sqrd += d * d;
    }
    if ((radius * radius) >= sum_sqrd)
        return (1);
    return (0);
}


//   MMST_PostOrder():
//    Print only the labels in each vertex's record
//    stored in ADT MMST.
void Multi_Dimen_M_ary_Srch_Tree::MMST_PostOrder
                              (MMST_PTR tree_ptr)
{
    if (tree_ptr != NULL) {
        for (int  i = 0; i < M; i++)
            MMST_PostOrder(tree_ptr->child_ptr[i]);
        printf(" %c ", tree_ptr->vertex_record.label);
    }
}
```

```
// isSameKey():
//   Given two D dimensional keys,
//   return 1 if same else return 0.
//
int Multi_Dimen_M_ary_Srch_Tree::isSameKey
                (Keytype *keyA, Keytype *keyB)
{
    for (int i = 0; i < D; i++)
        if (keyA[i] != keyB[i])
            return (0);
    return (1);
}


//  find_direction():
//     Returns K-ant in which to add a new node.
//
int Multi_Dimen_M_ary_Srch_Tree::find_direction
    (MMST_PTR tree_ptr,  DataObject vertex_record)
{
    int d = 0;

    for (int  i = 0; i < D; i++) {
      d = d << 1;
      if (vertex_record.key[i] > tree_ptr->vertex_record.key[i])
      d +=1;
    }
    return (d);
}


//  build_and_show_geom2D_as_MMST()
//   Demonstrate MMST for GEOMETRY_2D database
//   by building a QUADTREE for it.
//
void
Multi_Dimen_M_ary_Srch_Tree::build_and_show_geom2D_as _MMST()
{
    int      NumObj;
    float    radius;
    Keytype  range[D][2];    // D = 2
    Keytype  target[D];

    //  init_geom_db2(): Initialize GEOMETRY_2D
    //    database with 2 keys "x" and "y"
    //    in each vertex's record.
    static DataObject vertex_records[] = {
        { {14.6, 25.0}, 0xff0000, 'A'},  // Vertex A
        { {16.3, 26.5}, 0x333333, 'B'},  // Vertex B
        { {12.1, 22.0}, 0x202020, 'C'},  // Vertex C
        { {16.9, 24.1}, 0xffaacc, 'D'},  // Vertex D
        { {13.7, 22.7}, 0x00aacc, 'E'},  // Vertex E
        { {12.6, 20.8}, 0x00ff00, 'F'},  // Vertex F
        { {15.5, 24.4}, 0xff0000, 'G'},  // Vertex G
        { {16.0, 22.4}, 0xff0000, 'H'},  // Vertex H
```

```
            { {18.1, 21.2}, 0x0000ff, 'I'},  // Vertex I
            { {12.6, 20.8}, 0xffffff, 'J'}// Vertex J
        };
        NumObj = sizeof(vertex_records)/sizeof(vertex_records[0]);
        MMST_build(vertex_records, NumObj);
        printf(" The Quadtree shown by PostOrder traversal:\n");
        MMST_PostOrder(get_root());
        printf("\n");
        target[0] = 16.0;   // Vertex H, coord x
        target[1] = 22.4;   // Vertex H, coord y
        radius = 3.0;

        //   range[dimension][min/max]
        range[0][MIN] = target[0] - radius;
        range[0][MAX] = target[0] + radius;
        range[1][MIN] = target[1] - radius;
        range[1][MAX] = target[1] + radius;

        //   Perform circular range search for given center (target)
        //   and radius.
        MMST_proximitysearch(root_ptr, target, radius, range);
    }

// main():   Test driver OOP a Multi M-ary Search Tree
//           (MMST) object using the vertex records of
//           GEOMETRY_2D database in Appendix C.
//
void  main(void)
{
    //   Declare an object "mmstree_2D_obj"
    Multi_Dimen_M_ary_Srch_Tree  mmstree_2D_obj;
    printf("\n **   OOP IMPLEMENTATION OF %s ** \n %s \n",
      "MULTI-DIMENSIONAL SEARCH",
      "     TREE (QUADTREE) FOR GEOMETRY_2D DATABASE\n");
    mmstree_2D_obj.build_and_show_geom2D_as_MMST();
}
```

Code 9.1 for an OOP implementation of MMST for the geometry_2d database produces this output:

```
**   OOP IMPLEMENTATION OF MULTI-DIMENSIONAL SEARCH **
     TREE (QUADTREE) FOR geometry_2d DATABASE

The Quadtree shown by PostOrder traversal:
F   E   C   H   G   I   D   B   A
Proximity search found: A
Proximity search found: E
Proximity search found: D
Proximity search found: H
Proximity search found: G
Proximity search found: I
```

9.6.3 K-TREE BALANCE AND NODE DELETION

K-trees lack straightforward and efficient schemes for maintaining tree balance under dynamic conditions. Being a comparative-based tree, the balance of a K-tree is extremely sensitive to the order in which it is built and the effects of random insertions and deletions. Unfortunately, dynamic rebalancing techniques, such as the rotations technique employed by the AVL-tree, do not readily extend to their multidimensional cousins.

Node deletion is also difficult in a K-tree and is a problem under dynamic conditions. One compromise approach to node deletion is to mark nodes as "deleted" and subsequently reconstruct the tree whenever a static rebuild can be afforded.

The *pseudo quadtree* introduced by Overmars and van Leeuwen [Ove82] is a *non-homogeneous* variation of the standard quadtree, designed to facilitate node deletion and improve dynamic balance characteristics. A quadtree in non-homogeneous form distinguishes between internal nodes and leaf nodes such that internal nodes contain only a discriminating key and the leaf nodes (buckets) hold the data objects. While this facilitates rebalancing and deletion operations, the effectiveness of the pseudo-tree is somewhat limited. A non-homogeneous tree does have a useful advantage over its homogeneous counterpart for applications that will require secondary storage devices: only the tree structure of the internal nodes need be resident in local (main) memory while the external nodes or buckets containing the remainder of the data can sit on a secondary device such as disk storage.

An *optimized* K-tree takes a static approach to maintaining balance. A static rebalancing requires that all nodes be known ahead of time (a priori) and a complete rebuild of the tree be performed.

In summary, most known dynamic rebalancing schemes perform relatively poorly for K-trees; they are not ideally suited as dynamic structures. Also, excellent search performance can be achieved with a statically balanced K-tree, and thus, it is suitable for applications that require few updates on the database or can afford some intermittent global rebuilding.

9.6.4 KD-TREE OBJECTS

A *kd*-tree is a *multidimensional binary search tree* (MBST). As a binary tree object, it is a direct extension of the basic one-dimensional comparative-based binary search tree (BST) object introduced in Chapter 8. The *kd*-tree was developed as a means to improve on the space utilization deficiencies of the K-tree. This single data structure can handle a variety of associative (multidimensional) searches with efficient performance characteristics and storage requirements. The *kd*-tree can handle keys of any number of number of dimensions $k(k > 1)$, although they are most commonly applied as 2d-trees, 3d-trees, and 4d-trees.

The basic *kd*-tree differs from a BST in that at each level of the tree a different key value is utilized for branch decisions. The BST is a one-dimensional structure that bases branch decisions on *the* key while a *kd*-tree bases branch decisions on k keys for a k-dimensional search space. As with the single-dimensional BST, there is a single key per node, but in the multidimensional case, the key used varies from level to level. At any given level, one of k keys is selected and all the nodes on that level partition the search in the kth dimension. The dimension of the search space that the node subdivides is called the *discriminator* of the node and the value of the discriminating key represents the partition in that dimension. In a standard implementation, the discriminator of a node is typically assigned in a straightforward cyclical manner: Successive keys are cycled through repetitively and assigned to successive levels of the tree.

It follows that in one dimension, the 1d-tree is functionally equivalent to the BST. At each and every level of the tree, the node discriminator is the same.

The elegance of the *kd*-tree is exhibited in its simple divide-and-conquer strategy. Consider, for instance, a three-dimensional key-space described in terms of the spatial orientations `left`, `right`, `top`, `bottom`, `front`, and `back`, and a 3d-tree for representing points in that space. Assuming that the key to be discriminated on is selected as a direct cyclical function of tree level, the partitioning of the key-space and subsequent organization of the data may be described as follows:

Level 0 (root): Split space in the left-right orientation. With respect to the partition, place all points to left in left subtree, all points to right in right.

Level 1 nodes: Split space in the top-bottom orientation. With respect to the partition, place all points above in left subtree, all points below in right.

Level 2 nodes: Split space in the front-back orientation. With respect to the partition, place all points in front in left subtree, all points in back in right.

Repeat above steps cyclically.

The 3d-tree diagram for the `people_3d` database is shown in Figure 9.8. The tree was constructed by inserting the records in the random order: Bob, John, Kathy, Peter, Jim, Nancy, Paul, Steve, Jill. A pointer-based OOP implementation of this *kd*-tree object is presented below as **Code 9.2**.

Each record in the `people_3d` database contains three keys and is conveniently processed as a point in a three-dimensional key-space. The dimensions of the key-space or search are those of age, income, and years. Each record also contains three non-key attributes corresponding to the member_id, name, and occupation. A record is processed as a `DataObject`

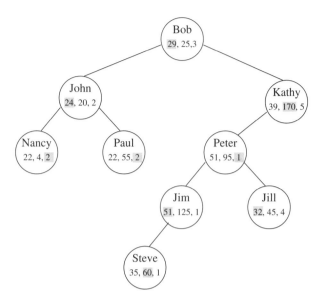

FIGURE 9.8. 3d-tree for people_3d database.

`struct` with four fields, as declared in `db3.h` (in Appendix C). The keys are declared as a three-dimensional array with indexes 0, 1, and 2 corresponding to age, income, and years, respectively.

A kd-tree node is processed as a `struct MBST_NODE` comprising three fields: a record of type `DataObject`, and two child pointers, `lo_ptr` and `hi_ptr`. This single `struct` can represent a node for any number of dimensions $k(k > 1)$. There is no need for an explicit field for the discriminator of a node since it can easily be a function of tree traversal. The OOP implementation in **Code 9.2** uses a cyclical discriminator that is a direct function of level. For a current discriminator d and a search-space dimensionality D, the discriminator for the next level is computed as $((d)+1)\,\%D$. Thus, starting at the root level 0, the successive discriminators are simply 0, 1, 2, 0, 1, ... and so on, for tree levels 0, 1, 2, 3, 4..., respectively.

The fundamental advantage of the kd-tree over the K-tree is its more efficient use of storage space. The kd-tree, as a binary search tree, requires only two child pointers per node, as opposed to 2^k for the K-tree. As a result, the percentage of child pointers likely to be utilized greatly increases. This observation is analogous to that made in Chapter 8 with regard to the space efficiency of a general M-ary tree versus that of a binary tree. In addition, since there are fewer child pointers at a kd-tree node, there are that many fewer key comparisons per node. A kd-tree requires 2 key comparisons at each node while a K-tree requires 2^k key comparisons per node. The kd-tree is also more flexible in that one basic structure can be applied to a problem of any number of dimensions. In practice, however, *kd*-trees of greater than 7 to 10 dimensions tend to be impractical.

9.6.5   OOP IMPLEMENTATION OF 3D-TREE

A pointer-based OOP implementation of a 3d-tree object is provided in **Code 9.2**.

Two *kd*-trees are built, one by random insertion and the other by a static median finding algorithm. Figure 9.8 illustrates the *kd*-tree for `people_3d` under random data insertion. `MBST_build_random()` accomplishes this.

Figure 9.9(a), below, shows the *kd*-tree for `people_3d` built by the function `MBST_build_balanced()`, using the median finding algorithm. At each level of the tree, the discriminator is chosen in the direct cyclical manner of a standard implementation. This is a static balancing method, as all the data are required a priori. At any given node, the `quickselect()` method is used to find the median of the existing set of data for the applicable discriminator. By inserting the median value as the root of the (sub)tree, we can ensure that each child of the node will contain a balanced number of children. The function is a variant of Quicksort; both partitioning schemes are the same, but `quickselect()` does not need to sort the entire file.

A rectangular range search on the balanced *kd*-tree is done by `MBST_rangesearch()`. Figure 9.9(b) depicts the rectangular "search box" geometry of the query. The range search amounts to a modified inorder traversal of the balanced tree. At each encountered node, the value of the point at the node is tested against the range of values for the box specified by the discriminator of the node. The ranges are stored in a two-dimensional array. If the tested range is found to be completely to the right or above the node's point, we proceed right, pruning the left child out. If the tested range is to the left or below the node's point, we proceed left, thereby pruning out the right child. Otherwise, both paths must be traversed. This process is recursively applied. When a root node is visited, `isInRange()` outputs the point at the node if it is contained.

`MBST_Sdelete_node()` is a static algorithm where nodes are marked as deleted but not removed until a complete rebuild of the tree is performed. `MBST_Ddelete_node()` implements a dynamic node deletion scheme, where a designated node is removed on the fly. Two node deletion functions are left as exercises for the reader.

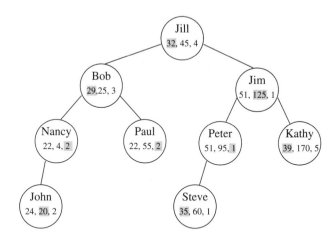

(a) Balanced kd−tree

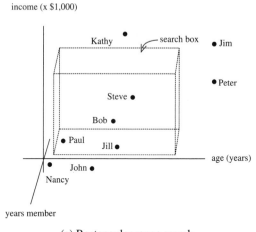

(a) Rectangular range search

FIGURE 9.9. Balanced *kd*-tree and rectangular range search.

Code 9.2

```
//   Program: MBST_3D.c++
//   Purpose:
//      OOP implementation of ADT K-D tree
//      (Multi-dimensional Binary Search Tree)
//      for PEOPLE_3D database.
//
#include  <stdio.h>

const int  MIN  = 0;
const int  MAX  = 1;
const int  INITIAL_DISC = 0;
#define    NEXTD(d)   ((d)+1)%D

const int  D = 3;   // three dimensional search keys

class  Multi_Dimen_Bin_Srch_Tree {
  private:
    typedef int Keytype;
    struct DataObject {  // member_record
        //  key[0] = age, key[1] = income (x $1000),
        //  key[2]= years member
        Keytype    key[D];
        int        id;          // member id
        char       *name;       // name
        char       *occupation; // occupation
    };
    typedef struct MBST_NODE {
        DataObject  record;
        MBST_NODE   *lo_ptr;     // "left"
        MBST_NODE   *hi_ptr;     // "right"
    } *MBST_PTR;

    MBST_PTR   root_ptr;
    void       init_MBST() { root_ptr = NULL; }
    Keytype    quickselect(Keytype*, int, int);
    Keytype    quickselect1(Keytype*, int, int, int);
    int        isInRange(Keytype*, Keytype[][2]);
    int        isSameKey(Keytype*, Keytype*);
    void       init_db3(void);    // [Exercise]
  public:
    Multi_Dimen_Bin_Srch_Tree() { root_ptr = NULL; }
    ~Multi_Dimen_Bin_Srch_Tree();
    MBST_PTR   MBST_create_node(DataObject);
    void       MBST_insert_node(MBST_PTR*, DataObject, int);
    void       MBST_Sdelete_node(MBST_PTR*, DataObject, int);
    void       MBST_Ddelete_node(MBST_PTR*, MBST_PTR, int);
    void       MBST_build_random(DataObject*, int);
    void       MBST_build_balanced (MBST_PTR*, DataObject*,
                                    int, int);
    void       MBST_PostOrder(MBST_PTR);
    MBST_PTR   MBST_search(MBST_PTR, DataObject );
    void       MBST_rangesearch(MBST_PTR, Keytype[][2], int);
```

```
      void       build_and_show_pepl3D_as_MBST(void);
      MBST_PTR  get_root() { return  root_ptr; }
};

// ---  Implement methods for "Multi_Dimen_Bin_Srch_Tree"
Multi_Dimen_Bin_Srch_Tree::~Multi_Dimen_Bin_Srch_Tree()
{
   //  Destructor:  Left as an exercise
}

//  quickselect():
//     Sort an array of keys using "Quick Select".
//
Multi_Dimen_Bin_Srch_Tree::Keytype
Multi_Dimen_Bin_Srch_Tree::quickselect
     (Keytype A[], int size, int m)
{
     return (quickselect1(A, 0, size - 1, m));
}

Multi_Dimen_Bin_Srch_Tree::Keytype
Multi_Dimen_Bin_Srch_Tree::quickselect1(Keytype *A,
        int first, int last, int median)
{
    int        i, j = 0;
    Keytype    pivot, tmp;

    if (first < last) {
       pivot = A[first];
       i = first;
       j = last;
       while (i < j) {
         while (A[i] <= pivot && i < last)  i += 1;
         while (A[j] >= pivot && j > first) j -= 1;
         if (i < j) {
            tmp = A[i];
            A[i] = A[j];
            A[j] = tmp;
         }
       }
       // swap A[first] and A[j]
       tmp = A[first];
       A[first] = A[j];
       A[j] = tmp;
       if (first + median - 1 < j)
           quickselect1(A, first, j - 1, median);
       if (first + median - 1 > j)
           quickselect1(A, j + 1, last, median - j);
    }
    return (A[j]);
}

Multi_Dimen_Bin_Srch_Tree::MBST_PTR
Multi_Dimen_Bin_Srch_Tree::MBST_create_node(DataObject record)
```

```
{
    MBST_PTR   new_ptr = new MBST_NODE;
    if (new_ptr == NULL) {
        printf("\n MBST_create_node: new failed.\n\n");
        return(NULL);
    } else {
        new_ptr->record = record;
        new_ptr->lo_ptr = NULL;
        new_ptr->hi_ptr = NULL;
        return (new_ptr);
    }
}


//   MBST_insert_node()
//     Inserts a node in an MBST (K-D tree).
//     (Recursive implementation)
//
void Multi_Dimen_Bin_Srch_Tree::
MBST_insert_node(MBST_PTR *tree_ptr, DataObject record,
                 int        disc)
{
    if (*tree_ptr == NULL) { // initially empty
        *tree_ptr = MBST_create_node(record);
    }
    else {
        if (isSameKey( (*tree_ptr)->record.key, record.key))
            return;                    //   key already exists
        else if ((*tree_ptr)->record.key[disc] >=
                              record.key[disc])
            MBST_insert_node(&(*tree_ptr)->lo_ptr, record,
                             NEXTD(disc));
        else
            MBST_insert_node(&(*tree_ptr)->hi_ptr,
                             record, NEXTD(disc));
    }
}


//   MBST_Sdelete_node():
//     Recursive version to delete a node in a kdtree.
//     A static deletion: mark nodes and rebuild at limit.
//
void  Multi_Dimen_Bin_Srch_Tree::MBST_Sdelete_node
      (MBST_PTR *tree_ptr, DataObject record, int disc)
{
   // Left as an Exercise
}


//   MBST_Ddelete_node():
//     Recursive version to delete a node in a kdtree.
//     A dynamic deletion: mark nodes and rebuild at limit.
//
void  Multi_Dimen_Bin_Srch_Tree::MBST_Ddelete_node
      (MBST_PTR *tree_ptr, MBST_PTR node_ptr, int disc)
{
```

```
  // (Exercise)
}

//  MBST_build_random():
//
void  Multi_Dimen_Bin_Srch_Tree::MBST_build_random
    (DataObject *records, int nobj)
{
    for (int i = 0; i < nobj; i++)
     MBST_insert_node(&root_ptr, records[i], INITIAL_DISC);
}

//  build_balanced():
//     Builds a balanced MBST. Uses selection sort to
//     find the median.
//
void Multi_Dimen_Bin_Srch_Tree::MBST_build_balanced
   (MBST_PTR *tree_ptr, DataObject *records, int nobj,
                    int disc)
{
    int        i, h, l, mw = 1;
    Keytype    *Keys;
    Keytype    medkey;
    DataObject *lo_records, *hi_records, median_record;
    int        mv   = nobj/2;
    int        lobj = mv;
    int        hobj = nobj - mv - 1;

    if (nobj == 0)
       return;

    // Allocate memory spaces for three arrays
    lo_records = new  DataObject [ nobj/2 + 1 ];
    hi_records = new  DataObject [ nobj/2 + 1 ];
    Keys = new Keytype [nobj];

    // get the keys for the current discriminator
    for (i = 0; i < nobj; i++)
       Keys[i] = records[i].key[disc];

    // get median key
    medkey = quickselect(Keys, nobj, mv + 1);
    for (i = 0, l = 0, h = 0; i < nobj; i++) {
        if (records[i].key[disc] > medkey)
          hi_records[h++] = records[i];
        else if ((records[i].key[disc] == medkey) &&
                  (mw == 1)) {
          median_record = records[i];
          mw = 0;
        }
        else lo_records[l++] = records[i];
    }
    *tree_ptr = MBST_create_node(median_record);
    MBST_build_balanced( &((*tree_ptr)->lo_ptr),
```

```
                          lo_records, lobj, NEXTD(disc));
        MBST_build_balanced( &((*tree_ptr)->hi_ptr),
                          hi_records, hobj, NEXTD(disc));
        // Release memory spaces, that are not needed.
        delete   lo_records;
        delete   hi_records;
        delete   [nobj]Keys;
    }


    //   MBST_search():
    //     Search for a k-dimensional key (point search)
    //
    Multi_Dimen_Bin_Srch_Tree::MBST_PTR
    Multi_Dimen_Bin_Srch_Tree::MBST_search
                  ( MBST_PTR tree_ptr, DataObject record)
    {
        int disc = INITIAL_DISC;

        while (tree_ptr != NULL) {
          if (isSameKey(tree_ptr->record.key, record.key))
            return (tree_ptr);
          if (tree_ptr->record.key[disc] >= record.key[disc])
            tree_ptr = tree_ptr->lo_ptr;
          else
            tree_ptr = tree_ptr->hi_ptr;
          disc = NEXTD(disc);
        }
        return (NULL);  // key not found or empty tree
    }


    //   isSameKey():
    //     Given two D-dimensional keys, check the keys
    //     are same. If so, return 1 if same else return 0
    //
    int  Multi_Dimen_Bin_Srch_Tree::isSameKey(Keytype *keyA,
                                                Keytype *keyB)
    {
        for (int i = 0; i < D; i++)
          if (keyA[i] != keyB[i])
              return (0);
        return (1);
    }


    //   isInRange():
    //     Given a D-dimensional key and a [D][2] range
    //     array, return 1 if WITHIN range else return 0.
    //
    int  Multi_Dimen_Bin_Srch_Tree::isInRange(Keytype *key,
                                                Keytype range[][2])
    {
        for (int i = 0; i < D; i++)
          if (!((key[i] >= range[i][MIN]) &&
              (key[i] <= range[i][MAX])))
              return(0);
```

```
    return(1);
}

//   MBST_PostOrder():
//    Perform postorder traversal of MBST.
//    (Recursive implementation)
//
void  Multi_Dimen_Bin_Srch_Tree::MBST_PostOrder
                              (MBST_PTR tree_ptr)
{
    if (tree_ptr != NULL) {
       MBST_PostOrder(tree_ptr->lo_ptr);
       MBST_PostOrder(tree_ptr->hi_ptr);
       printf(" %s ", tree_ptr->record.name);
    }
}

//   MBST_rangesearch():
//     Do orthogonal (RECTANGULAR) range search on
//     k-d tree. At each node, test the point against
//     the specified range for the discriminator
//     (dimension) for the node. The D-dimensional
//     "box" is specified as a [D][2] array, that is,
//     a D-dimensional array of lo/hi values
//     (Recursive Implementation)
//
//     Is this essentially an InOrder traversal, which
//     checks whether each encountered node is within
//     the D-dimensional box
//
void  Multi_Dimen_Bin_Srch_Tree::MBST_rangesearch
      (MBST_PTR tree_ptr, Keytype range[D][2], int disc)
{
    if (tree_ptr == NULL)
       return;    // tree is empty
    if (range[disc][MIN] <= tree_ptr->record.key[disc])
       MBST_rangesearch(tree_ptr->lo_ptr, range, NEXTD(disc));
    if (isInRange(tree_ptr->record.key, range))
     printf(" Range search found: %s\n", tree_ptr->record.name);
    if (range[disc][MAX] > tree_ptr->record.key[disc])
       MBST_rangesearch(tree_ptr->hi_ptr, range, NEXTD(disc));
}

//   build_and_show_pepl3D_as_MBST():
//    Demonstrate the use of a MBST for People_2D database.
//
void  Multi_Dimen_Bin_Srch_Tree::
            build_and_show_pepl3D_as_MBST(void)
{
    int       NumObj;
    Keytype   range[D][2];

    //   init_db3();
    //     Initialize PEOPLE_3D database with three search
```

```
    //      keys in each record. (See APPENDIX C)
    //
    static DataObject records[] = {
     { {29, 57, 3}, 16, "Bob", "engineer"},
     { {24, 20, 2}, 54, "John", "student"},
     { {39, 170, 5}, 14, "Kathy", "doctor"},
     { {51, 95, 1}, 63, "Peter", "sales"},
     { {39, 170, 5}, 14, "Kathy", "doctor"},//duplicate record
     { {51, 125, 1}, 62, "Jim", "lawyer"},
     { {22, 4, 2}, 48, "Nancy", "student"},
     { {22, 55, 5}, 21, "Paul", "teacher"},
     { {35, 60, 1}, 53, "Steve", "engineer"},
     { {32, 45, 4}, 48, "Jill", "nurse"}      // duplicate id
    };

    NumObj = sizeof(records)/sizeof(records[0]);

    range[0][MIN] = 20; range[0][MAX] = 100;
    range[1][MIN] = 45; range[1][MAX] = 150;
    range[2][MIN] = 2; range[2][MAX] = 6;

    MBST_build_random(records, NumObj);
    printf(" The K-D tree shown by PostOrder traversal:\n");
    MBST_PostOrder(get_root());
    printf("\n");

    MBST_rangesearch (get_root(), range, INITIAL_DISC);

    init_MBST();  // <== Causes memory leaks
    MBST_build_balanced(&root_ptr,
            records, NumObj, INITIAL_DISC);
    printf("\n After balanced version %s \n %s",
          "is built, the K-D tree shown",
          "by PostOrder traversal:\n");
    MBST_PostOrder(get_root());
    printf("\n");
}


// main():  Test driver for OOP implementation
//          of a (k-d tree) Multidimensional
//          Binary Search Tree (MBST) object.
//
void  main(void)
{
    // Declare an object "mbstree_3D_obj"
    Multi_Dimen_Bin_Srch_Tree  mbstree_3D_obj;

    printf("\n **  OOP IMPLEMENTATION OF %s ** \n %s \n",
      "MULTI-DIMENSIONAL",
      "      BST (K-D TREE) FOR PEOPLE_3D DATABASE\n");
    mbstree_3D_obj.build_and_show_pepl3D_as_MBST();
}
```

Code 9.2 for an OOP implementation of `people_3d` database using a MBST object produces this output:

```
 **   OOP IMPLEMENTATION OF MULTI-DIMENSIONAL  **
       BST (K-D TREE) FOR people_3d DATABASE

 The K-D tree shown by PostOrder traversal:
 Nancy   Paul   John   Steve   Jim  Jill   Peter   Kathy   Bob
 Range search found: Paul
 Range search found: Bob
 Range search found: Jill

 After balanced version is built, the K-D tree shown
 by PostOrder traversal:
  (null)   Nancy   (null)   Paul   John   (null)   Peter   (null)   Kathy
Bob
```

9.6.6 KD-TREE BALANCE AND NODE DELETION

As with K-trees, kd-trees lack straightforward and efficient schemes for dynamic node deletion and tree balancing. Like the binary search tree (BST), the shape of a randomly built kd-tree is highly dependent on the uniformity of the data and the randomness of its insertion. While statically balanced kd-trees perform well under worst-case conditions, kd-trees are susceptible to poor performance under the dynamic conditions of arbitrary sequences of insertions, deletions, and queries. Unfortunately, dynamic rebalancing schemes such as the AVL-tree for single-dimensional binary search tree do not readily extend to the multidimensional situation.

Several techniques have been proposed to address the issue of dynamic balancing of a kd-tree. Paralleling their work involving quadtrees, Overmars and van Leeuwen [Ove82] proposed the *pseudo kd-tree*. Vaishnavi [Vai84] presented a technique that follows on the AVL approach. Unfortunately, such dynamic balancing schemes are rather complex and provide limited results. Thus, kd-trees may perform poorly under the dynamics of nonrandom insertions of nonuniform data. Under such conditions, partial or global rebuilding operations are required.

One approach to static balancing of a kd-tree is to ensure that no child of a given node contains more than one half of the data objects below the current node. This scheme requires finding the median of the set of all possible keys at a given node corresponding to the discriminating dimension of the level. The tree is built by recursively inserting as the root of a subtree the data object that contains the median key. A perfectly balanced kd-tree can be built in $O(n \log n)$ time using this method. The function `MBST_build_balanced()` in **Code 9.2** is an implementation of such a static rebalancing scheme. The routine `quickselect()` employed is a variation of Quicksort that exploits the partitioning process of the latter to find median values in an array of key values.

A *kd*-tree with *adaptive partitioning* is another variant of the standard *kd*-tree that attempts to overcome tree imbalance by optimizing the method by which the node discriminators are chosen. Instead of cycling through the search dimensions as a function of level, only an adaptive partitioning scheme selects the discriminator for a level based on a statistical model. This differs from the algorithm of `kd_build_balanced()` above, in that it adaptively selects the discriminator at a node as well as the "best" value for the chosen discriminator. One model is to choose the key that has the largest spread of values about it. At a given level, inspect all the keys remaining to be inserted and choose as the discriminator the dimension for which the key's values have the best spread and for that dimension choose the median as the partition value. This is a static approach in that all the keys must be available in advance. Since the internal nodes do not necessarily contain actual key values, a non-homogeneous tree would result with all the data objects contained in the leaf nodes. Using this scheme it is possible to preprocess a perfectly balanced *kd*-tree with all the leaf nodes at the same level in $O(n \log n)$ time.

A static approach to node deletion can also be applied if the application can afford intermittent rebuilding of the entire tree. In such a scheme, nodes would retain an additional field so that they may be marked as deleted. At some interval, the tree is globally rebuilt with the tagged nodes removed (see Exercise 9-9).

9.7   Multidimensional Radix Search Tries

Single-dimensional digital-based radix search tries generalize to multidimensional structures for support of associative search. Two popular approaches are the ADT *K-tries* and ADT *kd-tries*, both of which provide efficient point-access methods for a variety of associative queries. These structures are the digital analogs of the comparative-based *K*-trees and *kd*-trees introduced in previous sections.

As radix search trie objects, the balance characteristics of the *K*-trie and *kd*-trie objects follow those of their single-dimensional cousins.

Property 9.2 *The shape (balance) of a* K-*trie or* kd-*trie is independent of key insertion order.*

There exists a unique trie for any given set of distinct keys (Property 8.3). The shape is sensitive to the spatial distribution of the data. Biased data can lead to degenerate tries with bad performance.

K-tries and *kd*-tries can provide reasonable worst-case performance without the dynamic balance complications of their comparative-based counterparts. They can provide very fast access to data, competitive with both comparative-based search trees and hashing methods. On the other hand, since multidimensional radix search tries cannot be rebalanced, their efficiency is dependent on well-behaved data. Additionally, some trie methods make very inefficient use of storage space.

A big advantage of K-tries and kd-tries, is that for well-behaved data (uniformly distributed, not clustered), they can maintain a balance under dynamic conditions on par with that of the statically balanced K-tree and kd-trees.

9.7.1 K-Trie Objects

K-tries are a generalization of the single-key (single-dimensional) M-ary radix search trie. A K-trie object is specified by an ADT K-trie.

Definition 9.5 *An ADT* K-*trie is a multidimensional* M-*ary radix search tree (*MMRST*) such that for a* k-*dimensional search space,* $M = K = 2^k$. *In its most general form, the* K-*trie is an* R^k-*trie for and radix* R. *(*$M = K = R^k$*)*

K-tries are the digital-analog of the comparative-based K-tree. These structures induce fixed radix partitions in a multidimensional key-space.

Figure 9.10(a) illustrates the quadtrie representation of the `people_2d` database. Its corresponding space partition diagram is given by Figure 9.10(b).

9.7.2 Kd-Trie Objects

A kd-trie object is specified by an ADT kd-trie.

Definition 9.6 *An ADT* kd-*trie is a multidimensional binary radix search trie (*MBRST*).*

As a binary trie, the kd-trie is a direct extension of the basic one-dimensional binary radix search trie (BRST) introduced in Chapter 8. Kd-tries are the digital-based analog of the comparative-based kd-trees.

The 2d-trie diagram for the `people_2d` database is shown in Figure 9.11(a). In this example, the income dimension was arbitrarily chosen as the discriminator at level 0 (root) of the trie. The discriminator is then selected in a direct cyclical fashion, while age at the next level and then back to income. The corresponding spatial partitioning is shown in Figure 9.11(b). The root space is bounded by income in the range of 0 to $200,000 and age in the range of 20 to 60 years. A rectangular mapping is adopted between the 2-dimensional representation of the data space and the spatial orientation of the children of the internal trie nodes. For income, all values less than the partition are placed in the left child of the partitioning node

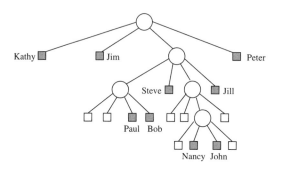

(a) Quadtrie

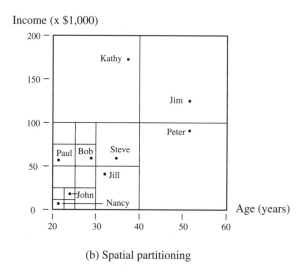

(b) Spatial partitioning

FIGURE 9.10. Quadtrie for the people_2d database.

and thus are below the partition while all those greater are placed in the right child and are above the partition. For age, all values less than the partition value are placed in the left child of the partitioning node and are drawn to the left of the partition while all those greater are placed in the right child and are drawn to the right of the partition. Other mappings are possible.

9.7.3   IMPLEMENTATION OF K-TRIE AND KD-TRIE

The OOP implementation of a region quadtrie object for an image processing application is presented in Section 12.1. The OOP implementation of the general case quadtrie object, as well as the general case *kd*-trie object, is left as an exercise.

9.7.4   COMPACT TRIE REPRESENTATIONS

Full pointer-based implementations of M-ary radix search tries require space allocation for M child pointers at each and every internal node. *Compact* or *compressed tries* are alternate representations that economize on space at the expense of being static structures. Compact tries exist in two general forms, *semi-pointered* and *pointer-less*.

A pointer-based trie may be represented in semi-pointered form in a straightforward manner. Consider again the pointer-based quadtrie of Figure 9.10(a) and its corresponding implementation of **Code 9.3**. With this implementation, each internal node contains an array of four child pointers. The quadtrie is converted to semi-pointered form by replacing the array of pointers with a single base pointer and a four-bit status word. The bits of the status word are assigned to the subtries of a node in a left-to-right order corresponding to the quadrants NW, NE, SW, and SE, respectively. A status bit is a "1" if the corresponding subtrie is not empty and zero otherwise. By storing each non-empty subtrie consecutively in memory, the address of the nth subtrie of a node is obtained by simply adding the number of "1" status bits up to and including the nth bit position of the status word to the base address of the node. For example, in Figure 9.10(a), the node that is the parent of the node containing Paul has a status word 0011, meaning that its NW and NE subtries are empty while the SW and SE subtries are occupied. If the parent has an integer address A, then its first and second non-null descendant subtries are located at A+1 and A+2, respectively.

A diagram of the semi-pointered quadtrie corresponding to the quadtrie of Figure 9.10(a) is given in Figure 9.12. In Figure 9.12, "&" is used to mean address of the variable.

A semi-pointered trie representation saves space by reducing the number of stored child pointers, whereas a pointerless trie representation attempts to realize a further savings by eliminating these pointers. While the former results in a pseudo-trie structure, a pointer-less representation is a list. Both

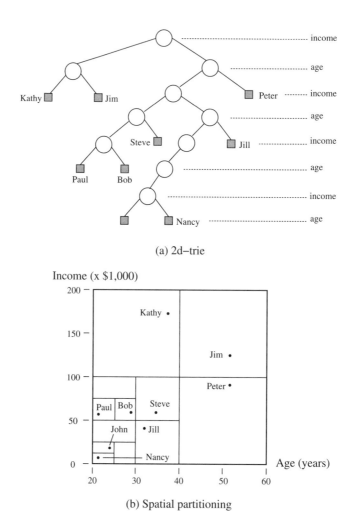

(a) 2d–trie

(b) Spatial partitioning

FIGURE 9.11. 2d-trie and partitioning for people_2d database.

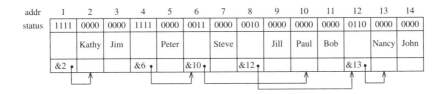

FIGURE 9.12. A semi-pointered quadtrie representation.

compact representations are static structures. Two common variations of pointer-less tries are discussed in Chapter 12.

9.8 Multidimensional Structures for External Search

The discussion of multidimensional data access structures to this point has, by default, assumed that the structures will reside in local (main) memory. However, this is not acceptable in the general case where large collections of data must be stored on, and accessed from, the disk. In Chapter 8, this issue was addressed for single-dimensional structures with the introduction of the B-tree object. In this section, the same issue will be briefly discussed in the context of a multidimensional search.

A fundamental approach to dealing with access of data on disk is to employ *bucket* or *grid cell* methods. The underlying concept is simple: large groups of data are stored in buckets corresponding to units of disk space and are accessed by efficient directories residing in local memory.

A fixed grid, such as the one presented in Section 9.2.2 (Figure 9.2) is perhaps the simplest of these schemes. Buckets correspond to the elements of the cell array and are accessed by simple array indexing. The grid file [Nie84] is a more advanced grid-based approach.

Non-homogeneous multidimensional trees may be used as directories to buckets of external data. The pseudo-quadtree introduced in Section 9.6.3 is an example. Its data are stored in its leaves while the internal branching structure serves as a fast directory.

Multidimensional tries also store data at their leaves (buckets), and thus are well suited for external search. The hierarchical branching structure of internal trie nodes can provide fast access (address computation) to the data buckets. In Chapter 12, Section 12.3, a bucket version of a quadtrie object is implemented for purposes other than external search. Nevertheless, this is the same type of structure.

Many multidimensional extensions to the ADT B-tree have been proposed. Among these are the *kB-tree* [GK80], the *k-d-b tree* [Rob81], and the *MBDT* [SO82].

Other interesting related structures include the *R-tree* [Gut84], the *BANG file* [Fre87], and *excell* [Tam81].

A more detailed discussion on this subject is beyond the intent and scope of this book, so the interested reader should consult the references.

9.9   Summary: A Taxonomy of Trees and Tries

In Figure 9.13, an overview of the trees and tries encountered in Chapter 8 and Chapter 9 is presented. At the highest level, all of these structures are distinguished as either data-comparative based or digital based. This distinction is one of search trees versus search tries. Figure 9.13 presents the ADT K-trees and K-tries and Figure 9.14 presents the ADT kd-trees and kd-tries.

9.10   Exercises

1. Write and test an OOP for the inverted list depicted in Figure 9.5.

2. For the K-tree of **Code 9.1**, write and test a `public` member function to perform a rectangular range search.

3. Modify the kd-tree of **Code 9.2** to employ a static rebalancing function employing adaptive partitioning. Propose and implement a statistical model for selecting discriminators.

4. Implement and test the method `MBST_Sdelete_node()` for **Code 9.2**. Add a field to the node description to serve as a node "node deleted" flag.

5. Implement and test the method `MBST_Ddelete_node()` for **Code 9.2**. This provides a dynamic node deletion capability (difficult problem).

6. Show that a kd-tree reduces to a binary search tree for $k = 1$ (one-dimensional).

7. Write and test the method `MBST_proximitysearch()` for the kd-tree of **Code 9.2**.

8. Modify the definition of a node for the kd-tree of **Code 9.2** such that it contains a discriminator field. Rewrite the given functions to take advantage of this.

9. In **Code 9.2**, modify given function to include a discriminator field as part of the node, and make use of it.

Comparison-Based Trees	Digital-Based Radix Tries
K-trees	K-tries
$\underline{2^k\text{-trees}}$ M-ary trees for $K = M = 2^k$	$\underline{R^k\text{-tries}}$ M-ary tries for $M = R^k$ for $M = R^k$
one-dimensional	
1-d Binary Search Tree (BST) $(k = 1;\ 2\text{-ary})$	(one-dimensional multi-way) 1-d Binary Radix Search Trie (BRST) $(R = 2; k = 1;\ 2\text{-ary})$ 1-d Quadtrie $(R = 4; k = 1;\ 4\text{-ary})$ 1-d Octrie $(R = 8;\ k = 1;\ 8\text{-ary})$ 1-d M-trie $(R = \text{M};\ k = 1;\ M\text{-ary})$
two-dimensional	
Quadtree $(k = 2;\ 4\text{-ary})$	2-d Quadtrie $(R = 2; k = 2;\ 4\text{-ary})$
three-dimensional	
Octree $(k = 3;\ 8\text{-ary})$	3-d Octrie $(R = 2; k = 3;\ 8\text{-ary})$
n-dimensional	
K-tree $(K = M = 2^n)$	n-d 2^n-trie $(R = 2; k = n; R^n\text{-ary})$

FIGURE 9.13. Taxonomy for K-trees and K-tries.

kd-Trees	kd-Tries
Multidimensional Binary Search Tree (MBST) (2^1-tree)	Multidimensional Binary Radix Search Trie (MBRST) (R^1-trie; $R = 2$)
one-dimensional	
Binary search tree (BST) (1-d-tree; $k = 1$)	Binary radix search trie (BRST) (1-d-trie; $k = 1$)
two-dimensional	
2-d-tree $k = 2$	2-d-trie $k = 2$
three-dimensional	
3-d-tree $k = 3$	3-d-trie $k = 3$
n-dimensional	
n-d-tree $k = n$	n-d-trie $k = n$

FIGURE 9.14. Taxonomy for kd-trees and kd-tries.

10. Write and test a version of **Code 9.2** that uses the median-based choice of discriminator as opposed to the standard cyclical method.

11. Implement and test an OOP for a pointer-based k-dimensional ADT K-trie.

12. Implement and test an OOP for a pointer-based k-dimensional ADT kd-trie.

13. Implement and test an OOP for a *bucket kd-trie*.

14. Implement and test an OOP for the semi-pointered quadtrie of Figure 9.11.

10

Graphs and Digraphs

For the list object, introduced in Chapter 5, it was shown that each data element contains at most one predecessor element and one successor element. Therefore, for any given data element or node in the list structure, we can talk in terms of a *next* element and a *previous* element.

In Chapter 8, these predecessor-successor relationships were relaxed with the introduction of the tree object. For the tree structure, a parent-child relationship was established such that any element or node in the structure, designated as the parent node, could contain some specified number of child nodes. This relationship, however, is one-way. That is, while any parent node may have a number of children, no child node may more than one parent.

In this chapter, the "one-way" restriction of the tree structure is relaxed with the introduction of the *graph* object. In a graph structure, a node or *vertex* may contain multiple predecessor nodes as well as multiple successor nodes.

Graph objects are widely used in the fields of computer science, chemistry, and mathematics. They are native to real world applications dealing with the general notion of connectivity or routing. These applications are wide and varied and range from the areas of computer network design and electronic circuit layout and verification to airline flight scheduling and social planning. For example, in the field of electronic circuit design, one may wish to query a system to ask if all the circuit connections are in place. In the area of airline routing, one may want to know what is the number of stops a plane must make between San Francisco and Washington, DC, and thus what the shortest flight path would be.

Many representations of graphs are possible. Three of the most commonly applied are

- *adjacency matrices,*

- *adjacency lists,* and

- *adjacency multilists.*

In this book we discuss only the first two types of representations.

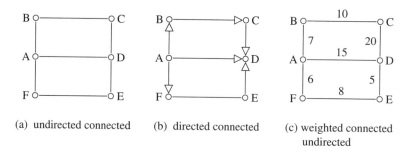

(a) undirected connected   (b) directed connected   (c) weighted connected
                                                          undirected

FIGURE 10.1. Three types of graphs.

10.1 Fundamental Definitions and Terminologies

Definition 10.1 *A graph* G *is defined to be a collection (union) of a set* V, *of vertices (or nodes), and a set* E, *of edges. Then for a finite* n,

$$G = \{V, E\}, \quad where \quad V = \{V_1, V_2, ..., V_n\}$$
$$E = \{E_{ij} = (V_i, V_j), 1 \le i \le n, 1 \le j \le n\}$$

An *edge*, or *arc*, defines the *connection* between two nodes, or vertices, say A and B, and is referred to as the pair *(A, B)* or *undirected* edge. If there is a direction, say from *initial* vertex A to *terminal* vertex B, the edge is called a *directed* edge, and is denoted by the ordered pair $< A, B >$. An arrow is used to denote the direction. A directed edge defines some ordering between the vertices. A *directed graph*, also referred to as a *digraph* or *network*, is a set of vertices and a set of directed edges. An *undirected* graph does not have any directed edges. Figures 10.1(a) and 10.1(b) show a undirected graph and a directed graph, respectively. In Figure 10.1(b), $< A, B >$ is a directed edge from the vertex A to vertex B.

Two vertices, A and B, are *adjacent* or *neighbors* if there exists an edge between them. If e denotes an undirected or directed edge between two vertices, A and B (A and B being terminal vertices in the case of a directed graph), the edge e is said to be *incident* with the vertices A and B.

A *cycle* or *loop* in a graph is a path in which the source and destination nodes are the same. An *acyclic* graph is one without any cycles (loops). An edge is a loop if it connects a vertex to itself. For a directed graph, a loop has the same initial and terminal vertices. The *degree* of a vertex A, $deg(A)$, in an undirected graph is the number of edges incident with the vertex A. A loop for a vertex A adds two to $deg(A)$.

In a directed graph, the *in-degree* of a vertex A is the number of directed edges terminating at A, and is denoted by $deg(A)$. In a directed graph, the *out-degree* of a vertex A is the number of directed edges with A as their initial vertex, and is denoted by $deg^+(A)$.

A vertex A is *isolated* or not connected if $deg(A) = 0$. A directed or undirected graph is *connected* if there is an edge between every pair of vertices. That is, a connected graph does not have any isolated vertexes. A graph is *unconnected* if it has at least one isolated vertex.

A directed or undirected graph is said to be *weighted* if there is a numerical value (e.g., cost, distance) associated with each (directed or undirected) edge. Figure 10.1(c) shows a weighted connected undirected graph. The weights for each edge are shown next to the edge. For example, the weight for the edge (A, D) is 15.

A *path* from a vertex A to a vertex B in a directed (undirected) graph is a sequence of one or more directed (undirected) edges from A to B; it is denoted by $p(A, B)$. A path of length m, from vertex A to vertex B, is a sequence of m vertices

$$v_0 = A, v_1, v_2, ..., v_m = B$$

where the undirected (directed) edges (v_i, v_{i+1}), for $i = 0, ..., (m-1)$, are in the graph; the number m represents the *hops* from A to B.

The *shortest path* from a vertex A to a vertex B in a weighted directed or undirected graph is the path with a minimum sum of weights of the edges in the path over all paths between A and B.

10.2   Graph Traversals

In the list data structure, the traversal always goes from the beginning data element of the list to the end of the list. Because of the special form of the stack and queue data structures, the traversal or visit of any random data element, except one or two data elements, is not allowed. In the binary tree data structure, the traversal uses one of the three most common methods — preorder, postorder, and inorder; these methods dictate the sequence in which the visits of the nodes are performed. A graph is a more general data structure of a tree in the sense that one vertex may have more than one adjacent vertex. This leads us to take extra care to avoid visiting a vertex multiple times. This becomes further complicated with the presence of loops. In order to avoid this problem, the key technique is to *tag* a vertex after it has been visited.

The graph traversal methods that are devised to avoid this problem, are

- *depth-first traversal (search)* (*DFS*), and

- *breadth-first traversal (search)* (*BFS*).

Unlike binary tree traversals, graph traversals are not unique, since a graph traversal can start at any vertex. Applications of graph traversals are found in such areas as determining the connection (arc) between two edges, building a *spanning tree* for a connected graph, and computing the shortest path between two given vertices in a weighted graph.

10.2.1 DEPTH-FIRST TRAVERSALS

The process of depth-first traversing a graph, also referred to as *backtracking*, is very similar to a preorder traversal of a binary tree. That is, the traversal moves away from a current vertex as soon as possible. For an undirected graph, assume that DFS starts its visit at a vertex A, which has the adjacent vertices A_i, for $i = 1, ..., p$. The start vertex A is visited. Then DFS moves to visit any unvisited adjacent vertex, say A_1, of A, and stores the remaining adjacent vertices A_i, for $i = 2, ..., p$, in a stack for a later visit if they remain unvisited. After all adjacent vertices of each adjacent vertex of A_1 are visited, DFS backs up to visit the remaining adjacent vertices $A_i (i = 2, ..., p)$ in the stack that have not been previously visited. The process continues until all vertices in the graph are visited. A recursive algorithm for *DFS* is given in terms of the following pseudo-code:

```
// Assume the visit flags for all vertices are
// initially set to FALSE.

Depth_First_Search (VERTEX A)
{
    Visit A;

    Set the visit flag for the vertex A to TRUE;

    For all adjacent vertices A (i = 1, ..., p) of A
                              i
        if (A  has not been previously visited)
             i
            Depth_First_Search(A );
                                i
}
```

To illustrate the DFS method, consider the undirected connected graph in Figure 10.2(a). A depth-first traversal of this graph starts at the vertex A. DFS visits A, sets its visit flag to FALSE, and prints A. Since the adjacent vertices of A are B and H, any one, say B, of these adjacent vertices is chosen for the next visit. Since the vertex B has not been previously visited, print B. Now consider the adjacent vertices A, C, G, F, H of B. Since A has been visited, select C for the next visit and keep the remaining neighbors of the vertex B for later visits. Visit C, and print C. Among the neighbors B, D, and F of the vertex C, the vertex B has been visited and so visit D by printing it. Among the neighbors of the vertex D, the vertices E and F have not been visited; visit E by printing it. Among the neighbors of the vertex E, visit the unvisited vertex F by printing it. Among the neighbors of the vertex F, visit the unvisited vertex G by printing it. Among the

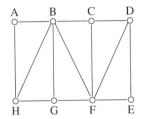

Vertex	Adjacent Vertices
A	B, H
B	A, C, G, F, H
C	B, D, F
D	C, E, F
E	D, F
F	B, C, D, E, G
G	B, F, H
H	A, B, G

(a) An undirected connected graph

(b) Graph vertices and their adjacent vertices

FIGURE 10.2. Illustration of DFS traversal.

neighbors of the vertex G, visit the unvisited vertex H by printing it. Since all the vertices of the undirected graph in Figure 10.2(a) are visited, the depth-first traversal visits the vertices in the sequence

$$A, B, C, D, E, F, G, H$$

Note that the sequence of visits would have been different if the neighbor H would have been chosen instead of the vertex B. This is why DFS does not produce a unique sequence of visits.

Note that DFS can also be applied for a directed graph.

10.2.2 BREADTH-FIRST TRAVERSALS

Breadth-first traversal (*BFS*) in a graph is very similar to the inorder traversal for binary trees. BFS visits a current vertex, say A, and all its adjacent vertices $A_i (i = 1, ..., p)$ if not visited previously, before visiting any adjacent vertices of $A_i (i = 1, ..., p)$.

Algorithm for Breadth-First Traversal

Assume BFS starts at vertex, A, which has p number of adjacent vertices. The steps of BFS are:

Step 1. Create and initialize queue object `Que_obj`.

Step 2. Initialize the queue object to be empty.

Step 3. For the set of n vertices, allocate an array object, `visit[ ]`, of size n.

Step 4. Initialize `visit[ ]` by setting all its b entries to FALSE.

Step 5. Set `visit[A]` to TRUE.

Step 6. Visit (e.g., print) the vertex A.

Step 7. Add the start vertex A to queue object, `Que_obj`.

Step 8. While "`Que_obj` is not empty", do steps 8.1 through 8.3.4.

Step 8.1. Remove the vertex at the head of `Que_obj`, and set it to `curr_start_vrtx`, (i.e.,

`curr_start_vrtx = Dequeue(Que_obj)`) (Note: In the first pass of the `while` loop, `curr_start_vrtx =` A)

Step 8.2. Get all vertices adjacent to `curr_start_vrtx`.

Step 8.3. For all vertices, say $A_i(i = 1, ..., p)$, adjacent to the current vertex `curr_start_vrtx`, do steps 8.3.1 through 8.3.4.

Step 8.3.1. If A_i has not been visited previously, (i.e., visit$[A_i] =$ FALSE), do steps 8.3.2 through 8.3.4.

Step 8.3.2. Visit$[A_i] =$ TRUE;

Step 8.3.3. Visit (e.g., print) A_i.

Step 8.3.4. Add the vertex A_i to `Que_obj` to visit its adjacent vertices.

Step 9. Deallocate and remove the queue object `Que_obj`.

Step 10. Deallocate and remove the array object `visit[ ]`.

Step 11. Return.

To illustrate the BFS method, consider the undirected connected graph in Figure 10.2(a). BFS starts at the vertex A. It visits A and all its adjacent vertices B and H. For the vertices A, B, and H, it sets their associated visit-status flag to FALSE, and prints them in the order A, B, H. Choosing the vertex B as the current vertex, BFS prints the unvisited adjacent vertices C, G, and F of the vertex B. Choosing the vertex C as the current vertex, BFS prints the unvisited adjacent vertex D of the vertex C. As before, BFS prints the unvisited adjacent vertex E of the vertex D. Since the adjacent vertices D and F of the current vertex E have been visited previously, BFS chooses the remaining adjacent vertex H of A as the current vertex. Since the vertex H and its adjacent vertices A, B and G have been visited previously, BFS stops. Thus, for the undirected connected graph in Figure 10.2(a), the breadth-first traversal visits the vertices in the sequence

A, B, H, C, G, F, D, E

Example Graph Object Methods

Instantiate and initialize a graph object.
Destroy (delete) a graph object.
Check if the set of graph vertices is empty.
Check if the set of graph edges is empty.
Check if two vertices are adjacent.
Build a graph object from a given set of vertices and edges.
Add a vertex in a graph object.
Search for a vertex specified by a single key.
Delete a vertex identified by a single search key value.
Update information of a given vertex in the graph.
Add an edge in a graph object.
Search for an edge specified by a key.
Delete an edge from a graph object.
Traverse a graph using depth-first traversal.
Traverse a graph using breadth-first traversal.
Print a graph object.
Determine attributes of a graph object.
Compute the shortest path between two given vertices.
Display the shortest path between two given vertices.

TABLE 10.1.

Note that the sequence of visits would have been different if the neighbor H would have been chosen instead of the vertex B. This is why BFS does not produce unique sequence of visits.

Note that BFS can also be applied for a directed graph.

10.3   Graph Objects

A *graph object* is specified by an ADT graph.

Definition 10.2 *An ADT graph is a data structure that contains a set of finite number of vertices and a set of finite number of edges, together with a set of operations that is used for defining, manipulating, and abstracting the vertices and edges.*

A set of possible methods on a graph object is shown in Table 10.1.

A vertex can be as simple as the types int, char, or a record with complex data types. The vertices and edges are the data elements of an ADT graph. These are internally represented using either (1) matrix or (2) pointers (linked lists). In either case, the internal representation of

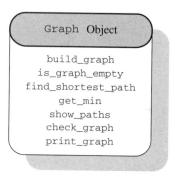

FIGURE 10.3. Graph object methods.

vertices and edges may change, but the operations (actions) on them will not change. This is the benefit of abstract data typing.

The same definition applies to both the ADT undirected graph and the ADT directed graph. For the ADT directed graph, the direction of edges must be kept in mind.

A *graph object* is an instance of a derived *implementation specific* class. The *base* class, from which the graph object is derived, is implementation unspecific; it provides a set of uniform methods (actions or interfaces) for a graph object, which are implemented in the derived class. For the current discussion, an abstract base class Graph is defined in the file bc_graph.h:

```
// bc_graph.h
//    Define abstract base class for graph objects.

class Graph {
  public:
    virtual int    build_graph(void) = 0;
    virtual int    is_graph_empty(void) = 0;
    virtual void   find_shortest_path(void) = 0;
    virtual int    get_min(void) = 0;
    virtual void   show_paths(KEY_TYPE src_vrtx,
                              KEY_TYPE dst_vrtx) = 0;
    virtual int    check_graph(void) = 0;
    virtual void   print_graph(void) = 0;
};
```

Figure 10.3 shows the Graph object and its publicly accessible members.

10.4   Implementations of a Graph

The data elements for an undirected or directed graph object are the set of vertices and the set of edges, and weights for an undirected and directed weighted graph object. There are several ways to structure these data elements. Among these structures are:

- An *adjacency matrix*.

- An array of pointers to singly or doubly linked lists of adjacent vertices (i.e., linked adjacency lists).

- A singly or doubly linked list of pointers to singly or doubly linked lists of adjacent vertices.

- An array of pointers to singly or doubly linked lists of edges (i.e., linked edge lists).

- A singly or doubly linked list of vertices and pointers to singly or doubly linked lists of edges.

For a graph with n vertices, the adjacency matrix is an n-by-n matrix, and an array is of size n. Since the size of an array or an adjacency matrix is static, these data structures are fixed and cannot grow or shrink during the program execution. The most ideal and efficient data structure for a graph that dynamically grows or shrinks, uses the linked lists (see the last category above).

In the following sections, graphs structured as an adjacency matrix and an array of pointers to linked adjacency lists will be discussed and implemented. The other approaches are left as exercises.

10.4.1 REPRESENTING A WEIGHTED UNDIRECTED OR DIRECTED GRAPH USING ADJACENCY MATRIX

The common method of representing a graph uses an *adjacency matrix*. The basic concept is to keep information on adjacent vertices in a two-dimensional array, called adjacency matrix. For a graph with n vertices, the adjacency matrix has n rows and n columns. The entries of the adjacency matrix depends on the type of graph — undirected or directed with or without weighted edges.

For an undirected, connected, and unweighted graph with n vertices, the adjacency matrix, Adj_Mat[ ][ ], is

$$Adj\_Mat[i][j] = \begin{bmatrix} 1 & \text{if vertex } A_i \text{ is adjacent to vertex } A_j \\ 0 & \text{if vertex } A_i \text{ is not adjacent to vertex } A_j \end{bmatrix}$$

This adjacency matrix is symmetric since a vertex A_i is adjacent to vertex A_j and vice versa for an undirected graph. Figure 10.4 shows an undirected, connected, and unweighted graph and its associated adjacency matrix.

For a directed, connected, and unweighted graph with n vertices, the adjacency matrix, Adj_Mat[ ][ ], is

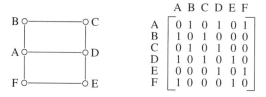

FIGURE 10.4. An undirected connected graph and its adjacency matrix.

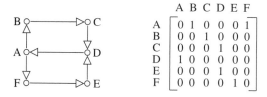

FIGURE 10.5. A directed connected graph and its adjacency matrix.

$$Adj\_Mat[i][j] = \begin{bmatrix} 1 & \text{if vertex } A_i \text{ is adjacent to vertex } A_j \\ 0 & \text{if vertex } A_i \text{ is not adjacent to vertex } A_j \end{bmatrix}$$

This adjacency matrix for a directed graph is not necessarily symmetric since a vertex A_i may be adjacent to vertex A_j (i.e., $< A_i, A_j >$ exists), but A_j may not be adjacent to A_i (i.e., $< A_j, A_i >$ does not exist).

Figure 10.5 shows a directed, connected, and unweighted graph and its associated adjacency matrix.

For an undirected, connected, and weighted graph with n vertices, the adjacency matrix, Adj_Mat[ ][ ], is

$$Adj\_Mat[i][j] = \begin{bmatrix} w_{ij} & \text{if vertex } A_i \text{ is adjacent to vertex } A_j \\ & \text{with edge weight } w_{ij} \\ 0 & \text{if vertex } A_i \text{ is not adjacent to vertex } A_j \end{bmatrix}$$

This adjacency matrix for an undirected and weighted graph is symmetric since a vertex A_i is adjacent to vertex A_j with weight w_{ij} edge (A_i, A_j), and vice versa. Figure 10.6 shows an undirected, connected, and weighted graph and its associated adjacency matrix.

For a directed, connected, and weighted graph with n vertices, the adjacency matrix, Adj_Mat[ ][ ], is

$$Adj\_Mat[i][j] = \begin{bmatrix} w_{ij} & \text{if vertex } A_i \text{ is adjacent to vertex } A_j \\ & \text{with edge weight } w_{ij} \\ INF & \text{if vertex } A_i \text{ is not adjacent to vertex } A_j \end{bmatrix}$$

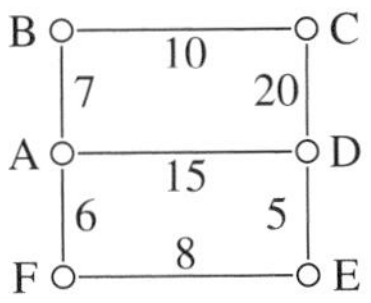

	A	B	C	D	E	F
A	0	7	0	15	0	6
B	7	0	10	0	0	0
C	0	10	0	20	0	0
D	15	0	20	0	5	0
E	0	0	0	5	0	8
F	6	0	0	0	8	0

FIGURE 10.6. An undirected connected weighted graph and its adjacency matrix.

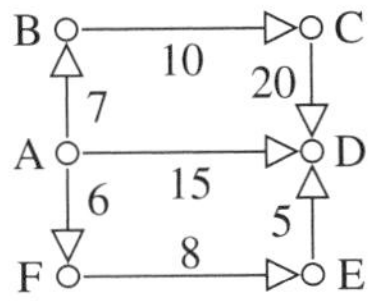

	A	B	C	D	E	F
A	0	7	0	15	0	6
B	0	0	10	0	0	0
C	0	0	0	20	0	0
D	0	0	0	0	0	0
E	0	0	0	5	0	0
F	6	0	0	0	8	0

FIGURE 10.7. A directed connected weighted graph and its adjacency matrix.

where "INF" means infinity or even a very large number to indicate that there is no weight or connection in that directed edge. This adjacency matrix for a directed and weighted graph is not necessarily symmetric since a vertex A_i may be adjacent to vertex A_j with weight w_{ij} edge $< A_i, A_j >$, and vice versa may not be true. Figure 10.7 shows a directed, connected, and weighted graph and its associated adjacency matrix using 0 for INF.

10.4.2 OOP IMPLEMENTATION OF A GRAPH USING ADJACENCY MATRIX

Figure 10.7 presents an abstract form of a directed, connected, and weighted graph with n vertices, and its adjacency matrix data structure. Keeping the adjacency matrix and OOP requirements in mind, the object is identified as digraph_obj, whose data (vertices, edges, weights, visit flags) and operations are directly derived from the definition of an ADT weighted digraph; the data are stored in the adjacency matrix. For the OOP characteristics of data-hiding, encapsulation, and methods for message passing, the implementation specific class Weighted_DiGraph is derived from the abstract base class Graph and is defined in the header file class_Weighted_DiGraph.h of **Code 10.1**:

```
class Weighted_DiGraph : private Graph {
  private:
    int  MAX_VERTEX;
    // adjacency matrix of the directed graph
    //   int WT_ADJACENCY_MATRIX[MAX_VERTEX +1][MAX_VERTEX +1];
```

```
    WEIGHT *WT_ADJACENCY_MATRIX;
    //  VERTEX structure of a vertex which contains
    //  the vertex's phase and shortest path.
    struct VERTEX {
        int    shortestpath;
        char   phase;
    };
    //  VERTEX VERTICES[MAX_VERTEX + 1];
    VERTEX *VERTICES;
    int   NUM_OF_VERTICES;
    //  For store & retrieve A[i][j]
    WEIGHT &adj_matrix (int i, int j)
    { return WT_ADJACENCY_MATRIX [i* (MAX_VERTEX + 1) + j]; }
    void   relax(int);
    void   init_digraph(void);
    void   init_digraph_vertices(void);
    int    check_digraph(void);
    int    create_directed_graph(void);
    void   Dijkstra_shortest_path(void);
  public:
    Weighted_DiGraph(int max_vrtx);
    ~Weighted_DiGraph();
    void   intro (void);
    int    build_graph(void) {return create_directed_graph();}
    int    is_graph_empty(void) { return 0;}
    void   find_shortest_path(void) {Dijkstra_shortest_path();}
    int    get_min(void);
    void   show_paths(KEY_TYPE src_vrtx, KEY_TYPE dst_vrtx);
    void   show_paths();
    int    check_graph(void) { return check_digraph();}
    void   print_graph(void) {printf("\nNot implemented\n");}
};
```

The Weighted_DiGraph class, illustrated in Figure 10.8, defines a type for weighted directed graph objects, digraph_obj, encompassing both data and operations. MAX_VERTEX, WT_ADJACENCY_MATRIX[][], VERTEX structure, VERTICES[ ], NUM_OF_VERTICES, and the function members adj_matrix() and relax() are made private for hiding and protecting them from possible corruption and misuse. Since some function members, e.g., Weighted_DiGraph() and ~Weighted_DiGraph(), are public, these are interfaces to the outside world in order to facilitate message passing between Weighted_DiGraph-type object and any object of the same or different type. That is, these public member functions are publicly accessible. The methods of the Weighted_DiGraph class are discussed in the following, and their implementations are shown in **Code 10.1**.

The OOP implementation of a weighted digraph object using an adjacency matrix representation and Dijkstra's shortest path algorithm is given in **Code 10.1**.

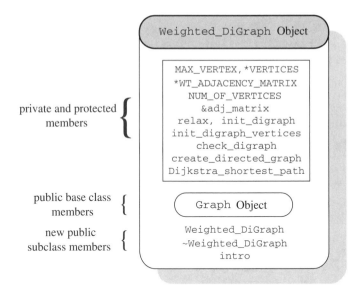

FIGURE 10.8. Weighted_DiGraph object.

10.4.3 METHODS OF Weighted_DiGraph CLASS

Weighted_DiGraph() is the constructor and publicly accessible member function of the class Weighted_DiGraph. It initializes MAX_VERTEX by its argument, max_vrtx. It allocates memory space for an object of the class Weighted_DiGraph using the new operator as follows. It allocates the array VERTICES[] of (MAX_VERTEX+1) number of vertices of type VERTEX, and an adjacency matrix WT_ADJACENCY_MATRIX[][] of (MAX_VERTEX+1) * (MAX_VERTEX+1) number of WEIGHT type elements. It is automatically called when an instance (object), digraph_obj, is declared in main().

~Weighted_DiGraph() is a publicly accessible member function of the class Weighted_DiGraph. It is the destructor for an object of type Weighted_DiGraph. It deallocates memory space for the entire array VERTICES[ ] of vertices, and WT_ADJACENCY_MATRIX[ ][ ], the adjacency matrix. It is implicitly called at the program exit.

The operation, create_directed_graph() of type int, is a public member function of the class Weighted_DiGraph. It accepts number of vertices and path lengths as weights, and builds a weighted adjacency matrix. It calls adj_matrix() to achieve this. It returns if it succeeds in building the weighted digraph, otherwise it returns 0.

The operation init_digraph() of type void is a private member function of the class Weighted_DiGraph. It initializes a weighted digraph

object by setting each entry (i.e., weight) of the weighted adjacency matrix
WT_ADJACENCY_MATRIX[ ] [ ] to 0. It calls adj_matrix() to achieve
this. Since the weighted digraph object does not have any vertices, edges, or
associated weights at the initial state, initialization is done in this manner.

Find_shortest_path() is a publicly accessible function of the class
Weighted_DiGraph. It calls this class's private member function
Dijkstra_shortest_path(). Dijkstra_shortest_path() asks a
user to input source and destination vertices, and determines shortest path
and distance between these vertices using Dijkstra's shortest path algorithm. This procedure calls get_min(), relax(), and show_paths().

The operation get_min() of type int is a public member function
of the class Weighted_DiGraph. It returns the index of VERTEX[ ] for
the vertex with the shortest path. It uses the linear search method from
the vertices that have FOUND phase attributes, that is, that are available
to be visited.

The operation relax() of type void is a private member function
of the class Weighted_DiGraph. It finds the vertex with the minimum
label value (i.e., shortest weight) among the vertices that are not in the
working set S. It updates the labels (i.e., shortestpath) of vertices that
are adjacent to the vertex with the currently minimum shortest path.

The operation show_paths() of type void is a public member function of the class Weighted_DiGraph. It shows the shortest path length
from a given source vertex to a destination vertex in a graph.

Main() is the test driver for an OOP implementation of the weighted digraph using adjacency matrix. It declares an object digraph_obj of type
Weighted_DiGraph with 100 vertices, which automatically calls the constructor Weighted_DiGraph(). Since main() is not a member function
of the Weighted_DiGraph class, it sends messages to the digraph_obj
object through the publicly accessible interface routines (methods). The
messages include providing instruction, building the weighted digraph object from inputs from keyboard, and determining the shortest path using
Dijkstra's algorithm.

Code 10.1

```
//   Program:   digraph.c++
//   Purpose:
//     Object-oriented implementation of a
//     directed graph using ADJACENCY MATRIX.
//     Also, implement Dijkstra's shortest path
//     algorithm.
//
#include <stdio.h>
#include <ctype.h>
#include <math.h>
#include <stdlib.h>
typedef  int KEY_TYPE;
```

```
#include "bc_graph.h"    //  For base class "Graph"
typedef   int  WEIGHT;  //  weight = arc length
const int HUGE_WEIGHT = 999999999;

// NOTFOUND is a phase of a vertex in the graph
//   where the vertex has not been found yet via
//   the relax() function
const int NOTFOUND = 0;
// FOUND is a phase of a vertex in the graph where
//    the vertex has been found but the shortest
//    path not yet determined
const int FOUND = 1;
// TAKEN is a phase of a vertex in the graph where
//    the vertex's shortest path has been found.
const int TAKEN = 2;
#define ERROR1   "ERROR, TOO MANY VERTICES FOR THIS CONFIG"
#define ERROR2   "ERROR, NEGATIVE LENGTHS"
#define ERROR3   "ERROR, INVALID SOURCE VERTEX"
#define ERROR4   "ERROR, INVALID DESTINATION VERTEX"
#include "class_Weighted_DiGraph.h"

//  ---  Implement methods for Digraph object  ---

Weighted_DiGraph::Weighted_DiGraph (int max_vrtx)
{
    MAX_VERTEX = max_vrtx;
    WT_ADJACENCY_MATRIX = new WEIGHT [(MAX_VERTEX + 1) *
                                      (MAX_VERTEX + 1)];
    VERTICES = new VERTEX [MAX_VERTEX + 1];
}

Weighted_DiGraph::~Weighted_DiGraph () // Destructor
{
    delete [] WT_ADJACENCY_MATRIX;
    delete [] VERTICES;
}

int Weighted_DiGraph::create_directed_graph (void)
{
    // answer to whether or not there
    // is a path between two vertices.
    char    answer[4];
    WEIGHT  new_wt;

    printf (" Enter number of vertices in graph ==> ");
    scanf ("%d", &NUM_OF_VERTICES);
    if (NUM_OF_VERTICES > MAX_VERTEX) {
        printf("%s \n", ERROR1);
        return (0);
    }
    if (NUM_OF_VERTICES < 1) // invalid input
        return (0);
    init_digraph();
    // enter path lengths
```

```
    printf("\n");
    for (int i = 1; i <= NUM_OF_VERTICES; i++) {
       for (int j = 1; j <= NUM_OF_VERTICES; j++) {
          printf("%s %d to vertex %d (Y/N) ==> ",
             " Is there a path from vertex",i,j);
          scanf("%s", answer);
          if ((answer[0] == 'y')
             (answer[0] == 'Y')) {
             printf(" Enter path length ==> ");
             // WT_ADJACENCY_MATRIX[i][j])= adj_matrix(i, j)
             scanf("%d", &new_wt);
             adj_matrix(i, j) = new_wt;
          }
       }
    }
    return (1);
}


//  Dijkstra_shortest_path():
//    Uses Dijkstra's algorithm to compute
//    the shortest path between the source
//    vertex (vertex) and destination vertex.
//
void Weighted_DiGraph::Dijkstra_shortest_path(void)
{
    int   source,        // source vertex
          destination,   // destination vertex
          min;           // index of vertex with shortest path
    // error = 1 if there is a negative path weight or
    //            impossible source and destination vertices.
    int error;
    // size = count of the number of vertexs that have
    //        had their shortest paths determined.
    int size;

    error = check_digraph();
    if (error) {
        printf(" %s \n", ERROR2);
        return;
    }
    error = 1;
    while (error) {
        printf("\n Enter the Source Vertex Number ==> ");
        scanf("%d", &source);
        if ((source >= 1) && (source <= NUM_OF_VERTICES))
                error = 0;
        else
                printf("%s \n", ERROR3);
    }
    error = 1;
    while (error) {
        printf("\n Enter the Destination Vertex Number ==> ");
        scanf("%d", &destination);
        if ((destination >= 1) &&
```

```
                (destination <= NUM_OF_VERTICES))
                    error = 0;
            else
                    printf(" %s \n", ERROR4);
    }
    // put all vertex phases to NOTFOUND and
    // shortestpath lengths to HUGE_WEIGHT
    init_digraph_vertices();
    VERTICES[source].shortestpath = 0;
    VERTICES[source].phase = FOUND;
    size = 0;

    while (size++ < NUM_OF_VERTICES) {
        // return vertex with minimum shortest path.
        min = get_min();
        // this vertex is no longer available, i.e., TAKEN.
        VERTICES[min].phase = TAKEN;
        // determine shortest paths from a given vertex.
        relax (min);
    }
    // show the shortest path from source to destination.
    show_paths (source, destination);
}

// init_digraph(): Initialize digraph.
//
void Weighted_DiGraph::init_digraph(void)
{
    int i, j;
    // initialize paths to length 0
    for (i = 1; i <= NUM_OF_VERTICES; i++)
        for (j = 1; j <= NUM_OF_VERTICES; j++)
            //   WT_ADJACENCY_MATRIX[i][j] = 0;
            adj_matrix(i, j) = 0;
}

// init_digraph_vertices(): Initialize vertices of digraph
//
void Weighted_DiGraph::init_digraph_vertices(void)
{
    // initialize phase and shortest path of vertices
    for (int i = 1; i <= NUM_OF_VERTICES; i++) {
        VERTICES[i].phase = NOTFOUND;
        VERTICES[i].shortestpath = HUGE_WEIGHT;
    }
}

// get_min():
//   Returns shortest path to an available vertex
int Weighted_DiGraph::get_min(void)
{
    int min = HUGE_WEIGHT,    // min path found so far
        index = 0;            // vertex index
    for (int i = 1; i <= NUM_OF_VERTICES; i++) {
```

```
            if (VERTICES[i].phase == FOUND) { // vertex is available
                if (VERTICES[i].shortestpath < min) {
                    // new minimum
        index = i;
        min = VERTICES[i].shortestpath;
                }
            }
        }
        return index;
}


// relax():
//    Determines shortest paths to vertices
//    reachable from a given vertex.
//
void Weighted_DiGraph::relax(int min)
{
    for (int i = 1; i <= NUM_OF_VERTICES; i++) {

        // WT_ADJACENCY_MATRIX[min][i] == adj_matrix(min, i)
        if (adj_matrix(min, i) &&
            (VERTICES[i].phase != TAKEN)) {
          // there is a path and the end vertex is available
          VERTICES[i].phase = FOUND;
          if ((VERTICES[min].shortestpath +
                adj_matrix(min, i)) <
                (VERTICES[i].shortestpath))
          // a shorter path then previously
          // found is available.
          // Store newly found shortest path.
          VERTICES[i].shortestpath = VERTICES[min].shortestpath +
                                     adj_matrix(min, i);
        }
    }
}


//   show_paths():
//     Shows shortest path length from a given
//     source vertex to a destination vertex in a graph
//
void
Weighted_DiGraph::show_paths(int source, int destination)
{
    // Check whether the destination vertex is
    // reachable from source.
    if (VERTICES[destination].shortestpath < HUGE_WEIGHT)
        printf("\n Shortest %s %d to %d = %d\n",
                "path from vertex", source, destination,
              VERTICES[destination].shortestpath);
    else  // vertex was not reachable from source
        printf("\nNo path available %s %d to %d\n",
                "from vertex", source, destination);
}
```

```
//   check_digraph()
//     Checks for negative path weights in
//     weighted digraph.
//
int  Weighted_DiGraph::check_digraph (void)
{
    int  i, j;
    for (i = 1; i <= NUM_OF_VERTICES; i++)
        for (j = 1; j <= NUM_OF_VERTICES; j++)
            // if (WT_ADJACENCY_MATRIX[i][j] < 0)
            if (adj_matrix(i, j) < 0)
                return 1;
    return 0;
}
// intro(): Prints introduction and limitation.
void Weighted_DiGraph::intro (void)
{
    printf ("\n *** OOP IMPLEMENTATION OF %s %s %s",
              "WEIGHTED DIGRAPH ***",
              "\n         USING ADJACENCY MATRIX AND",
              "\n            DIJKSTRAS SHORTEST PATH");
    printf ("\n\n %s %s %s %s %s %s \n\n",
      "This program will create a directed graph via",
      "\n inputs from the screen, determine the shortest",
      "\n path from a given source to a given destination,",
      "\n and output the shortest path length.",
      "\n\n NOTE: This program currently has a limitation",
      "\n         of no more than 100 vertices in the digraph.");
}

//   main():
//     Test driver for OOP implementation of a weighted
//     digraph object, and Dijkstra's shortest path algorithm.
//
void main(void)
{
    //  Declare an object with 100 vertices
    Weighted_DiGraph  digraph_obj(100);
    int success;

    digraph_obj.intro();
    success = digraph_obj.build_graph();
    if (success)
        digraph_obj.find_shortest_path();
}
```

Code 10.1 for an OOP implementation of a weighted digraph in Figure 10.13(a) using adjacency matrix produces this output:

```
*** OOP IMPLEMENTATION OF WEIGHTED DIGRAPH ***
      USING ADJACENCY MATRIX AND
      DIJKSTRAS SHORTEST PATH
```

This program will create a directed graph via
inputs from the screen, determine the shortest
path from a given source to a given destination,
and output the shortest path length.

NOTE: This program currently has a limitation
      of no more than 100 vertices in the digraph.

Enter number of vertices in graph ==> 6

Is there a path from vertex 1 to vertex 1 (Y/N) ==> n
Is there a path from vertex 1 to vertex 2 (Y/N) ==> y
Enter path length ==> 7
Is there a path from vertex 1 to vertex 3 (Y/N) ==> n
Is there a path from vertex 1 to vertex 4 (Y/N) ==> y
Enter path length ==> 1
Is there a path from vertex 1 to vertex 5 (Y/N) ==> n
Is there a path from vertex 1 to vertex 6 (Y/N) ==> n
Is there a path from vertex 2 to vertex 1 (Y/N) ==> n
Is there a path from vertex 2 to vertex 2 (Y/N) ==> n
Is there a path from vertex 2 to vertex 3 (Y/N) ==> y
Enter path length ==> 6
Is there a path from vertex 2 to vertex 4 (Y/N) ==> n
Is there a path from vertex 2 to vertex 5 (Y/N) ==> y
Enter path length ==> 8
Is there a path from vertex 2 to vertex 6 (Y/N) ==> n
Is there a path from vertex 3 to vertex 1 (Y/N) ==> n
Is there a path from vertex 3 to vertex 2 (Y/N) ==> n
Is there a path from vertex 3 to vertex 3 (Y/N) ==> n
Is there a path from vertex 3 to vertex 4 (Y/N) ==> n
Is there a path from vertex 3 to vertex 5 (Y/N) ==> n
Is there a path from vertex 3 to vertex 6 (Y/N) ==> y
Enter path length ==> 2
Is there a path from vertex 4 to vertex 1 (Y/N) ==> n
Is there a path from vertex 4 to vertex 2 (Y/N) ==> y
Enter path length ==> 4
Is there a path from vertex 4 to vertex 3 (Y/N) ==> n
Is there a path from vertex 4 to vertex 4 (Y/N) ==> n
Is there a path from vertex 4 to vertex 5 (Y/N) ==> y
Enter path length ==> 3
Is there a path from vertex 4 to vertex 6 (Y/N) ==> n
Is there a path from vertex 5 to vertex 1 (Y/N) ==> n
Is there a path from vertex 5 to vertex 2 (Y/N) ==> n
Is there a path from vertex 5 to vertex 3 (Y/N) ==> y
Enter path length ==> 9
Is there a path from vertex 5 to vertex 4 (Y/N) ==> n
Is there a path from vertex 5 to vertex 5 (Y/N) ==> n
Is there a path from vertex 5 to vertex 6 (Y/N) ==> y
Enter path length ==> 5
Is there a path from vertex 6 to vertex 1 (Y/N) ==> n
Is there a path from vertex 6 to vertex 2 (Y/N) ==> n
Is there a path from vertex 6 to vertex 3 (Y/N) ==> n
Is there a path from vertex 6 to vertex 4 (Y/N) ==> n

```
Is there a path from vertex 6 to vertex 5 (Y/N) ==> n
Is there a path from vertex 6 to vertex 6 (Y/N) ==> n

Enter the Source Vertex Number ==> 1

Enter the Destination Vertex Number ==> 6

Shortest path from vertex 1 to 6 = 9
```

10.4.4 OOP IMPLEMENTATION OF A GRAPH USING LINKED ADJACENCY LISTS

Figure 10.9 shows the abstract connected and weighted digraph of Figure 10.7, and its linked implementation using an array of 6 pointers to the singly linked list of adjacent vertices (i.e., adjacency lists).

Keeping the singly linked adjacency lists and OOP requirements in mind, the object is identified as lnk_wt_digraph_obj, whose data (vertices, edges, weights, visit flags) and operations are directly derived from the ADT definition of a weighted digraph; the vertices are stored in an array, and the adjacent vertices are stored in singly linked data structures. For the OOP characteristics – data-hiding, encapsulation, and methods for message passing – the Wt_DiGraph class is derived from the abstract base class Graph and is defined in the header file class_Wt_DiGraph.h of **Code 10.2**:

```
class Wt_DiGraph : private Graph {
  private:
    typedef char DATA_TYPE;
    typedef int  WEIGHT;
    typedef int  INDEX;

    typedef struct ADJACENT_VERTEX {
        KEY_TYPE            vrtx_key;
        WEIGHT              weight;
        ADJACENT_VERTEX     *next;
    } *ADJACENCY_LIST_PTR;

    typedef struct VERTEX {
        KEY_TYPE            vrtx_key;
        DATA_TYPE           data;
        WEIGHT              label;
        VISIT_FLAG          visited;
        int                 hops, path[20];
        ADJACENCY_LIST_PTR  adj_list_hd_ptr;
    } *VERTEX_PTR;

    //  VERTEX_ARY[MAX_VERTEX] :An array of vertices
    VERTEX_PTR     VERTEX_ARY;
    int            MAX_VERTEX;
    INDEX          TAIL;
```

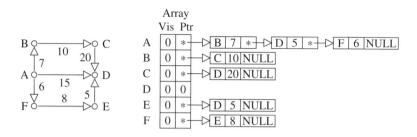

FIGURE 10.9. A directed connected weighted graph and its singly linked adjacency lists.

```
int    build_wt_digraph();
void   print_digraph(void);
public:
   Wt_DiGraph (int max_no_of_vertices);
   ~Wt_DiGraph();
   int    build_graph(void) {return build_wt_digraph();}
   int    is_graph_empty(void);
   void   find_shortest_path(void);
   int    get_min(void) {return 0;}      // Not implemented
   void   show_paths(int, int) {}        // Not implemented
   int    check_graph(void) {return 0;}  // Not implemented
   void   print_graph(void) { print_digraph(); }
   VERTEX_PTR    create_vertex();
   void   intro (void);
   void   add_vertex(KEY_TYPE, DATA_TYPE);
   INDEX  search_vertex(KEY_TYPE);
   void   add_adjacent_vrtx(KEY_TYPE, KEY_TYPE, WEIGHT);
   void   get_src_dst_vertices(
             KEY_TYPE *src_vrtx_key, KEY_TYPE *dst_vrtx_key);
};
```

The Wt_DiGraph class, illustrated in Figure 10.10, defines a type for a weighted directed graph object, lnk_wt_digraph_obj, encompassing both data and operations. The data members MAX_VERTEX, TAIL, VERTEX_ARY[ ], and VERTEX and ADJACENT_VERTEX structures are made private for hiding and protecting them from possible corruption and misuse. The function members Wt_DiGraph(), ~Wt_DiGraph(), and is_graph_empty() are public, and are therefore publicly accessible interfaces to the outside world in order to facilitate message passing between Wt_DiGraph-type object and any object of the same or different type.

The OOP implementation of a weighted digraph object using linked adjacency list representation and Dijkstra's shortest path algorithm is given in **Code 10.2**.

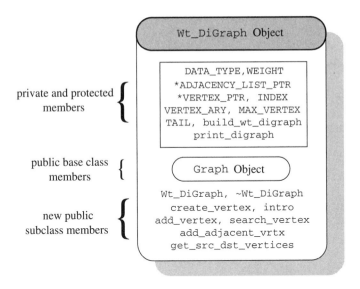

FIGURE 10.10. Wt_DiGraph object.

10.4.5 METHODS OF THE Wt_DiGraph CLASS

The operation Wt_DiGraph() is a public member function of the class
Wt_DiGraph. It is the constructor for an object of type Wt_DiGraph.
It initializes MAX_VERTEX by its argument, max_no_of_vertices. It
allocates memory space for a Wt_DiGraph type object using the new operator as follows. It allocates the array VERTEX_ARY[ ] of MAX_VERTEX
number of vertices of type VERTEX. It sets TAIL to -1 since initially the
object is empty. TAIL is a counter in VERTEX_ARY[ ] to indicate the last
vertex in the array. It is automatically called when an instance (object),
lnk_wt_digraph_obj, is declared in main().

~Wt_DiGraph() is a public member function of the Wt_DiGraph
class. It is the destructor for an object of type Wt_DiGraph. If the digraph is empty, it deallocates memory space for the entire vertex array
VERTEX_ARY[ ] of vertices. Otherwise, it iteratively frees up memory
spaces of each ADJACENT_VERTEX type element in each singly linked adjacency list, and then the vertex array of size MAX_VERTX. It is implicitly
called at the program exit.

The operation is_graph_empty() of type void is a public member
function of the Wt_DiGraph class. It compares TAIL with -1, and returns
1 if the digraph is empty; otherwise, it returns 0.

The operation create_vertex() of type VERTEX_PTR is a public
member function of the Wt_DiGraph class. It allocates memory space for

a new vertex of type VERTEX using the new operator. If allocation fails, it prints an error message and returns NULL pointer value.

The operation add_vertex() of type void is a public member function of the Wt_DiGraph class. It accepts two arguments, new_key and new_data. If TAIL counter has not reached the maximum MAX_VERTEX, it increments TAIL counter by 1. It sets the fields vrtx_key to new_key, data to new_data, label to 0, hops to 0, visited to FALSE, and adj_list_hd_ptr to NULL. The function now adds the new vertex in the location VERTEX_ARY[TAIL]. If the array of vertices is full, it prints a message.

The operation build_graph() of type void is a public member function of the Wt_DiGraph class. It accepts number of vertices and path lengths as weights. It builds an array of vertices by successively calling add_vertex(). It builds singly linked adjacency lists for each vertex by successively calling search_vertex() and add_adjacent_vrtx().

The operation print_digraph() of type void is a private member function of the Wt_DiGraph class. It prints the weighted digraph object as follows. It prints the key for each vertex in the array VERTEX_ARY[], and iteratively prints the keys of adjacent vertices in each associated singly linked adjacency list.

The operation search_vertex() of type INDEX is a public member function of the Wt_DiGraph class. It accepts the search key as the argument. Since the vertices are stored in an array VERTEX_ARY[ ], the functions use the linear search method. If the vertex is found, it returns the matching array index; otherwise, it returns -1.

The operation add_adjacent_vrtx() of type void is a public member function of the Wt_DiGraph class. It accepts three arguments, to_adjacent_key, adjacent_vrtx_key, and new_weight. It calls search_vertex() twice to search the vertices identified by the keys to_adjacent_key and adjacent_vrtx_key. If one of these vertices is not found, it prints a message and returns. Otherwise, it allocates memory space for ADJACENT_VERTEX type vertex. If the allocation fails, it returns. If the allocation succeeds, it sets the new vertex's vrtx_key to adjacent_vrtx_key, weight to new_weight, and next to NULL. Finally, it adds the new adjacent vertex at the head of the singly linked adjacent list for the vertex with key to_adjacent_key.

The operation find_shortest_path() of type void is a public member function of the Wt_DiGraph class. If the digraph is empty, it prints a message and returns. Otherwise, get_src_dst_vertices() is called, which asks the user to input source and destination vertices. It determines the shortest path and distance between these two vertices using Dijkstra's shortest path algorithm. It also prints the number of hops in the shortest path from the source vertex to the destination vertex.

Main() is the test driver for an OOP implementation of the weighted digraph using adjacency lists. It declares an object lnk_wt_digraph_obj of type Wt_DiGraph with 20 vertices, which automatically calls the constructor Wt_DiGraph(). Since main() is a client of the Wt_DiGraph class, it sends messages to the lnk_wt_digraph_obj object through the object's public methods intro(), build_graph(), print_graph(), and find_shortest_path(). The messages include providing instruction, building the weighted digraph object from inputs from keyboard, printing the digraph object, and determining the shortest path using Dijkstra's algorithm.

Code 10.2

```
//  Program: lnk_adj_digraph.c++
//  Purpose:
//    OOP implementation of a weighted digraph
//    using singly linked adjacency lists. Also,
//    implement Dijkstra's shortest path algorithm.
//
#include <stdio.h>
#include <stdlib.h>
#include <ctype.h>
typedef  int  KEY_TYPE;
#include "bc_graph.h" // For base class "Graph"
const int  HUGE_WEIGHT = 999999999; // for infinity
enum  VISIT_FLAG {TRUE, FALSE};
#include "class_Wt_DiGraph.h" // For derived class

//  Wt_DiGraph(): Constructor of Wt_DiGraph object
//
Wt_DiGraph::Wt_DiGraph(int max_no_of_vertices)
{
   MAX_VERTEX = max_no_of_vertices;
   VERTEX_ARY = new  VERTEX[MAX_VERTEX];
   TAIL = -1;  // array of vertices is empty
}

//  ~Wt_DiGraph(): Destructor of Wt_DiGraph object
//
Wt_DiGraph::~Wt_DiGraph()
{
   //  If nonempty digraph, delete each singly
   //  linked adjacency list
   if (!is_graph_empty()) {
     for (INDEX i = 0; i <= TAIL; i++) {
        ADJACENCY_LIST_PTR
          adjacency_ptr = VERTEX_ARY[i].adj_list_hd_ptr;
        while (adjacency_ptr != NULL) {
          ADJACENCY_LIST_PTR tmp_ptr = adjacency_ptr;
          adjacency_ptr = adjacency_ptr->next;
          delete  tmp_ptr;
        }
     }
   }
}
```

```
      delete  [] VERTEX_ARY;
}


//  is_graph_empty(): Check whether a digraph is empty.
//
int Wt_DiGraph::is_graph_empty(void)
{
   return (TAIL == -1);
}


//  create_vertex():
//     Create a new vertex of the Wt_DiGraph
//
Wt_DiGraph::VERTEX_PTR Wt_DiGraph::create_vertex()
{
   VERTEX_PTR  new_ptr;

   new_ptr = new  VERTEX;
   if (new_ptr  == NULL)
      printf("\n create_vertex: alloc failed \n");
   return (new_ptr);
}


// add_vertex():
//   Add the new vertex in Wt_DiGraph object.
//
void
Wt_DiGraph::add_vertex(KEY_TYPE new_key, DATA_TYPE new_data)
{
    // Is the vertex array full? If so, error msg
    if ((TAIL + 1) != MAX_VERTEX) {
       VERTEX_ARY[++TAIL].vrtx_key        = new_key;
       VERTEX_ARY[  TAIL].data            = new_data;
       VERTEX_ARY[  TAIL].label           = 0;
       VERTEX_ARY[  TAIL].hops            = 0;
       VERTEX_ARY[  TAIL].visited         = FALSE;
       VERTEX_ARY[  TAIL].adj_list_hd_ptr = NULL;
    }
    else
     printf ("\n add_vertex: Array of vertices is full\n");
}


//  build_wt_digraph():
//     Builds a number of Wt_DiGraph nodes
//     specified by user. Also creates edges
//     with weights corresponding to distances.
//
int Wt_DiGraph::build_wt_digraph(void)
{
   KEY_TYPE     key1, key2;
   int n_vertices, edge_weight,
         maxweight = HUGE_WEIGHT,
         vrtx_ary_index;
```

```
    printf("\n Enter number of vertices %s ",
           "in your Weighted DiGraph:");
    scanf("%d", &n_vertices);
    if (n_vertices > MAX_VERTEX) {
       printf ("\n build_wt_digraph: %s %d \n",
         "Number of vertices is more than max",
         MAX_VERTEX);
       return(0);
    }
    for (INDEX i = 0; i < n_vertices; i++) {
       add_vertex(i, i);
       printf("\n Vertex: %2d  has been created.", i);
    }
    printf("\n");
    for (i = 0; i < n_vertices; i++) {
      // checks for edges from each node
      key1  =  (KEY_TYPE) i;
      vrtx_ary_index = search_vertex(key1);

      for (INDEX j = 0; j < n_vertices; j++) {
        key2 = (KEY_TYPE) j;
        if (j != i) {
          printf(" Enter %s %2d to Vertex %2d:   ",
                   "distance from Vertex", i, j);
          // printf(" Else enter n/N for next vertex\n");
          if (scanf("%d", &edge_weight) == 1) {
             getchar();  // if there is an edge then insert it
             add_adjacent_vrtx (key1, key2, edge_weight);
             printf("%s: %2d  to  Vertex: %2d %s\n",
                    " Edge from Vertex", i ,j, "was created");
             if (maxweight < edge_weight)
               maxweight = edge_weight;
          }  // end of (scanf( ...))
          else {
            getchar();
            printf(" No new edge was created.\n");
          }
        }  // if j != i
      }  // for j < n_vertexs
    }    // for i < n_vertexs
  return(1);
}

// print_digraph():
//   Print weighted digraph by its vertices and
//   associated (singly linked) adjacency lists.
//
void Wt_DiGraph::print_digraph(void)
{
    ADJACENCY_LIST_PTR   adjacency_hd_ptr;

    printf("\n\n GRAPH VERTICES   ADJACENCY LISTS");
    printf("\n ==============   ===============\n");
```

```
    if (is_graph_empty()) {
       printf("\n Weighted digraph is empty");
       return;
    }
    for (INDEX i = 0; i <= TAIL; i++) {
       printf("      %d:              ",
      VERTEX_ARY[i].vrtx_key);
       adjacency_hd_ptr = VERTEX_ARY[i].adj_list_hd_ptr;
       while (adjacency_hd_ptr != NULL) {
          printf(" %d ->", adjacency_hd_ptr->vrtx_key);
          adjacency_hd_ptr = adjacency_hd_ptr->next;
       }
       printf(" NULL \n");
    }
}


//   search_vertex():
//     Search weighted digraph object for a vertex given
//     by its key, srch_key. Since vertices are stored
//     in an array, VERTEX_ARY[], do a linear search.
//
Wt_DiGraph::INDEX
Wt_DiGraph::search_vertex(KEY_TYPE srch_key)
{
    if (!is_graph_empty()) {
       for (INDEX i = 0; i <= TAIL; i++)
          if (srch_key == VERTEX_ARY[i].vrtx_key)
             return (i);
    }
    return (-1);  // not found
}


//   add_adjacent_vrtx():
//     Add a vertex adjacent to a given vertex in
//     beginning of its singly linked adjacency list.
//
void Wt_DiGraph::add_adjacent_vrtx(
    KEY_TYPE   to_adjacent_key,
    KEY_TYPE   adjacent_vrtx_key, WEIGHT new_weight)
{
    INDEX   vertex1;

    // Check both vertices in Wt_DiGraph object
    vertex1 = search_vertex (to_adjacent_key);
    if (vertex1 == -1) {
       printf("\n add_adjacent_vrtx: %s \n",
          "To-adjacent vertex not in graph");
       return;
    }
    if (search_vertex (adjacent_vrtx_key) == -1) {
       printf("\n add_adjacent_vrtx: %s \n",
          "Adjacent vertex not in graph");
       return;
    }
```

```
    // Allocate memory space
    ADJACENCY_LIST_PTR new_ptr = new ADJACENT_VERTEX;
    if (new_ptr == NULL)
        return;
    new_ptr->vrtx_key  = adjacent_vrtx_key;
    new_ptr->weight    = new_weight;
    new_ptr->next      = NULL;
    // Add it to the head of adjacency list
    new_ptr->next = VERTEX_ARY[vertex1].adj_list_hd_ptr;
    VERTEX_ARY[vertex1].adj_list_hd_ptr = new_ptr;
}


//  find_shortest_path():
//     Find the shortest path between two specified
//     source and destination vertices in a weighted
//     digraph using Dijkstra's algorithm.
void Wt_DiGraph::find_shortest_path(void)
{
    ADJACENCY_LIST_PTR   adjacency_ptr;
    VERTEX_PTR   end_ptr, min_label_vertex, tmp_vertex;
    WEIGHT       label, temp, shortest_dist = 0;
    INDEX        src_vrtx_index, dst_vrtx_index;
    KEY_TYPE     src_vrtx_key, dst_vrtx_key;

    if (is_graph_empty()) {
        printf("\n find_shortest_path: Empty graph\n");
        return;
    }
    get_src_dst_vertices(&src_vrtx_key, &dst_vrtx_key);
    for (INDEX i = 0; i <= TAIL; i++)
        // initialize label with dummy
        VERTEX_ARY[i].label  =  HUGE_WEIGHT;

    src_vrtx_index = search_vertex (src_vrtx_key);
    if (src_vrtx_index == -1) {
        printf("\n find_shortest_path: Source vertex %i %s",
               src_vrtx_key, "is not in graph");
        return;
    }
    dst_vrtx_index = search_vertex (dst_vrtx_key);
    if (dst_vrtx_index == -1) {
        printf("\n find_shortest_path: Dest vertex %i %s",
               dst_vrtx_key, "is not in graph");
        return;
    }
    end_ptr = &VERTEX_ARY[dst_vrtx_index];

    // initialize label of start vertex (A) with 0
    min_label_vertex = &VERTEX_ARY[src_vrtx_index];
    min_label_vertex->label = 0;

    min_label_vertex->path[min_label_vertex->hops] =
                        min_label_vertex->vrtx_key;
    while (min_label_vertex->vrtx_key != end_ptr->vrtx_key) {
```

```
          //  Loop till end vertex is reached
          temp = HUGE_WEIGHT;
          for (INDEX i = 0; i <= TAIL; i++) {
            //  finds vertex with minimum label
            //  not in working set S (see algorithm)
            if ((VERTEX_ARY[i].visited != TRUE) &&
                (temp > VERTEX_ARY[i].label)) {
              temp = VERTEX_ARY[i].label;
              min_label_vertex = &VERTEX_ARY[i];
            }
          }
          shortest_dist = min_label_vertex->label;
          adjacency_ptr = min_label_vertex->adj_list_hd_ptr;
          label =  min_label_vertex->label;
          while (adjacency_ptr !=  NULL) {
            //  calculate label value for vertices that
            //  have edges from the minimum label vertex

            tmp_vertex = &VERTEX_ARY[search_vertex (
                           adjacency_ptr->vrtx_key)];
            tmp_vertex->label = label + adjacency_ptr->weight;
            //  Keep shortest path information for each vertex
            //  starting from source vertex to it
      for (i = 0; i < min_label_vertex->hops; i++) {
        tmp_vertex->path[i] = min_label_vertex->path[i];
            }
            tmp_vertex->hops = min_label_vertex->hops;
            tmp_vertex->path[tmp_vertex->hops++] =
                           min_label_vertex->vrtx_key;
            // elist_ptr  =  elist_ptr->next;
            adjacency_ptr = adjacency_ptr->next;

          } //  end of while (adjacency_ptr !=  NULL)
          // takes this node out of the set for
          // consideration of next minimum label
          min_label_vertex->visited = TRUE;

        } //  end of while (min_label_vertex->vrtx_key ...)
        //  ---  Print shortest path
        printf("\n %s: %2d to Vertex: %2d is:  %d\n",
          "Shortest Distance from Vertex", src_vrtx_key,
                          dst_vrtx_key, shortest_dist);
        printf(" The Shortest Path is: ");
        for (i = 0; i < end_ptr->hops; i++)
          printf(" %d ->", end_ptr->path[i]);
        printf(" %d \n", end_ptr->vrtx_key);
        //  ---  Print  number of hops in shortest path
        printf(" %s: %2d to Vertex: %2d is:  %d\n",
              "Number of Hops from Vertex", src_vrtx_key,
              dst_vrtx_key, end_ptr->hops);
}

// get_src_dst_vertices():
```

```
void Wt_DiGraph::get_src_dst_vertices(
     KEY_TYPE *src_vrtx_key, KEY_TYPE *dst_vrtx_key)
{
    KEY_TYPE   vertex1, vertex2;
    int        num_vertices = 0;
    int        try1, again;

    do {
       printf("\n ** To quit enter q/Q **\n");
       printf(" ** To calculate shortest %s **\n\n",
               "path between two Vertices");
       printf(" Enter Source Vertex: ");
       try1 = 0;
       if (scanf("%d", &vertex1) != 1) {
          try1 = 1;
          exit (1);
       }
       // if ((vertex1 < 0)   (vertex1 >= num_vertices)) {
       if ((vertex1 < 0)   (vertex1 > TAIL)) {
        printf("\n Vertex ** %d  ** does not exist\n",
               vertex1);
         exit(1);
       }
       getchar();
       do {
         again = 0;
          printf(" Enter Destination Vertex: ");
          if (scanf("%d", &vertex2) != 1)
             again = 1;
          // if ((vertex2 < 0)   (vertex2 >= num_vertices)) {
          if ((vertex2 < 0)   (vertex2 > TAIL)) {
            printf("\n Vertex ** %d ** does not exist\n",
                    vertex2);
            exit (1);
          }
          getchar();
       } while (again);
    } while (try1);
    *src_vrtx_key = vertex1;
    *dst_vrtx_key = vertex2;
}

void  Wt_DiGraph::intro(void)
{
    printf ("\n *** OOP IMPLEMENTATION OF %s %s %s",
            "WEIGHTED DIGRAPH ***",
            "\n        USING LINKED ADJACENCY LIST AND",
            "\n           DIJKSTRAS SHORTEST PATH");
    printf("\n USAGE: \n %s",
            "\n    You will first be prompted for number of\n");
    printf("    vertices in Digraph, MAX = %d. %s \n",
            MAX_VERTEX, "These will be created");
    printf("%s %s %s %s %s %s",
       "   and then you will be prompted to create the\n",
```

```
     "    edges with corresponding distance, press n/N\n",
     "    for the next edge. The Weighted DiGraph will then\n",
     "    be printed in linearized form. And you will be\n",
     "    prompted for start vertex, and end vertex of\n",
     "    path wanted. This will be calculated and\n",
     "    printed in linearized form. \n");
}

//   main(): Test driver for weighted & directed graph object.
//
void main(void)
{
    Wt_DiGraph   lnk_wt_digraph_obj(20);

    lnk_wt_digraph_obj.intro();
    if (lnk_wt_digraph_obj.build_graph()) {
       lnk_wt_digraph_obj.print_graph();
       lnk_wt_digraph_obj.find_shortest_path();
    }
}
```

Code 10.2 for an OOP implementation of a weighted digraph in Figure 10.13(a) using linked adjacency lists produces this output:

```
*** OOP IMPLEMENTATION OF WEIGHTED DIGRAPH ***
      USING LINKED ADJACENCY LIST AND
DIJKSTRAS SHORTEST PATH
USAGE:
    You will first be prompted for number of
    vertices in Digraph, MAX = 20. These will be created
    and then you will be prompted to create the
    edges with corresponding distance, press n/N
    for the next edge. The Weighted DiGraph will then
    be printed in linearized form. And you will be
    prompted for start vertex, and end vertex of
    path wanted. This will be calculated and
    printed in linearized form.

Enter number of vertices in your Weighted DiGraph: 6

Vertex:  0  has been created.
Vertex:  1  has been created.
Vertex:  2  has been created.
Vertex:  3  has been created.
Vertex:  4  has been created.
Vertex:  5  has been created.
Enter distance from Vertex  0 to Vertex  1:   7
Edge from Vertex:  0  to  Vertex:  1 was created
Enter distance from Vertex  0 to Vertex  2:   n
No new edge was created.
Enter distance from Vertex  0 to Vertex  3:  1
```

```
Edge from Vertex:  0  to   Vertex:  3 was created
Enter distance from Vertex  0 to Vertex  4:  n
No new edge was created.
Enter distance from Vertex  0 to Vertex  5:  n
No new edge was created.
Enter distance from Vertex  1 to Vertex  0:  n
No new edge was created.
Enter distance from Vertex  1 to Vertex  2:  6
Edge from Vertex:  1  to   Vertex:  2 was created
Enter distance from Vertex  1 to Vertex  3:  n
No new edge was created.
Enter distance from Vertex  1 to Vertex  4:  8
Edge from Vertex:  1  to   Vertex:  4 was created
Enter distance from Vertex  1 to Vertex  5:  n
No new edge was created.
Enter distance from Vertex  2 to Vertex  0:  n
No new edge was created.
Enter distance from Vertex  2 to Vertex  1:  n
No new edge was created.
Enter distance from Vertex  2 to Vertex  3:  n
No new edge was created.
Enter distance from Vertex  2 to Vertex  4:  n
No new edge was created.
Enter distance from Vertex  2 to Vertex  5:  2
Edge from Vertex:  2  to   Vertex:  5 was created
Enter distance from Vertex  3 to Vertex  0:  n
No new edge was created.
Enter distance from Vertex  3 to Vertex  1:  4
Edge from Vertex:  3  to   Vertex:  1 was created
Enter distance from Vertex  3 to Vertex  2:  n
No new edge was created.
Enter distance from Vertex  3 to Vertex  4:  3
Edge from Vertex:  3  to   Vertex:  4 was created
Enter distance from Vertex  3 to Vertex  5:  n
No new edge was created.
Enter distance from Vertex  4 to Vertex  0:  n
No new edge was created.
Enter distance from Vertex  4 to Vertex  1:  n
No new edge was created.
Enter distance from Vertex  4 to Vertex  2:  9
Edge from Vertex:  4  to   Vertex:  2 was created
Enter distance from Vertex  4 to Vertex  3:  n
No new edge was created.
Enter distance from Vertex  4 to Vertex  5:  5
Edge from Vertex:  4  to   Vertex:  5 was created
Enter distance from Vertex  5 to Vertex  0:  n
No new edge was created.
Enter distance from Vertex  5 to Vertex  1:  n
No new edge was created.
Enter distance from Vertex  5 to Vertex  2:  n
No new edge was created.
Enter distance from Vertex  5 to Vertex  3:  n
No new edge was created.
Enter distance from Vertex  5 to Vertex  4:  n
```

```
No new edge was created.


GRAPH VERTICES    ADJACENCY LISTS
==============    ===============
           0:       3 -> 1 -> NULL
           1:       4 -> 2 -> NULL
           2:       5 -> NULL
           3:       4 -> 1 -> NULL
           4:       5 -> 2 -> NULL
           5:       NULL


** To quit enter q/Q **
** To calculate shortest path between two Vertices **

Enter Source Vertex: 0
Enter Destination Vertex: 5

Shortest Distance from Vertex:  0 to Vertex:  5 is:  9
The Shortest Path is:  0 -> 3 -> 4 -> 5
Number of Hops from Vertex:  0 to Vertex:  5 is:  3
```

10.5   Spanning Trees of a Graph

Spanning trees of a graph belong to one of the applications of graph traversals.

Definition 10.3 *A spanning tree of a graph is a subgraph that has all the nodes (vertices) and some edges sufficient to build a tree.*

A spanning tree of a graph G contains all the vertices of G and a minimum number of edges of G so that there is a path between any two vertices of G.

In a spanning tree, redundant paths between any two vertices in G are removed, and new edges are added, if necessary, in a spanning tree. A connected graph G has always a spanning tree. Also, a graph having a spanning tree is connected. However, a connected graph can have more than one spanning tree, because they can be built from any vertex of the graph. Two graph traversal methods categorize spanning trees — *depth-first spanning trees* and *breadth-first spanning trees*.

How these spanning trees are constructed for a given connected graph is discussed in the following sections.

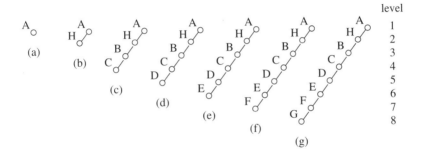

FIGURE 10.11. Traces of constructing a depth-first spanning tree for the graph of Figure 10.2(a)

10.5.1   CONSTRUCTING A SPANNING TREE USING DEPTH-FIRST TRAVERSALS

A spanning tree for a connected graph G is a depth-first spanning tree when it is constructed using the depth-first traversal. Any vertex of G is selected as the root, and the edges that are not previously visited during the depth-first traversal are successively added to form the rooted spanning tree. A "marking" flag is used to indicate that an incident edge has been visited, that is, has been already in the tree.

The algorithm is left as an exercise. The process of constructing a spanning tree is illustrated for the connected and undirected graph G in Figure 10.2(a), which uses depth-first traversal as follows.

The vertex A is arbitrarily selected as the root, which is the start vertex of depth-first traversal (DFS) of G. Figure 10.11 shows how progressively DFS constructs the depth-first spanning tree rooted at the vertex A.

Starting from the vertex A, DFS finds that the neighbors of vertex A are vertices B and H. Since B and H have not been previously visited and there are no edges between A and B or A and H, the DFS arbitrarily selects H as the next start vertex and adds the edge between vertex A and vertex H in level 2 of Figure 10.11(b). Since the vertex H has neighbors A, B, and G, and the edge (H, A) is already in the spanning tree, an edge (H, B) between H and the unvisited neighbor B is added as shown in Figure 10.11(c). Using the criterion "unvisited" vertex neighbor and the nonexistence of the corresponding edge in the current spanning tree, edges from neighbors of neighbors of B are successively added, which yields the spanning tree in Figure 10.11(f). At this stage, the vertex F is arrived at, which is the neighbor of E. DFS traversal selects the unvisited neighbor G of F as the next start vertex and adds an edge (F, G) in the spanning tree in Figure 10.11(g). Since the neighbors B, F, and H of vertex G have been previously visited, the "anchor" case is arrived at and does not add any edges in the spanning tree in Figure 10.11(g). Now we backtrack to vertex B, which is the remaining and unselected neighbor of the first start vertex A. Since vertex B has been previously visited and is in the current spanning tree, and since there are no more neighbors of vertex A, the construction process stops. The final depth-first spanning tree for the graph of Figure 10.2(a) is in Figure 10.11(g). Note the recursive nature of this construction process. Also, we could have gotten a different spanning tree if the neighbor B of the start vertex A was selected. In general, the depth-first spanning tree of a graph G is not unique since any vertex is arbitrarily chosen for depth-first traversal. However, the selection of a start vertex would have been strictly followed if there were any ordering requirement among vertices.

10.5.2   CONSTRUCTING A SPANNING TREE USING BREADTH-FIRST TRAVERSALS

A spanning tree for a connected graph G is a breadth-first spanning tree when it is constructed using the breadth-first traversal. Any vertex of G is selected as the root, and the edges that are not previously visited during the breadth-first traversal, are successively added to form the rooted spanning tree. A "marking" flag is used to indicate that an incident edge has been visited, that is, has been already in the tree, and a vertex is previously visited.

The algorithm and its implementation are left as exercises. The process of constructing a spanning tree for the connected and undirected graph G in Figure 10.2(a), which uses the breadth-first traversal (BFS), is illustrated as follows.

Vertex A is arbitrarily selected as the root, which is the start vertex of breadth-first traversal (BFS) of G. Figure 10.12 shows how progressively BFS constructs the breadth-first spanning tree rooted at the vertex A. Starting from the vertex A, the BFS finds that the root vertex A has unvisited neighbors B and H, and inserts vertices B and H as children and adds edges (A, B) and (A, H) in level 2 of Figure 10.12(b). The BFS stores the neighbors of B and H in the queue for later processing (i.e., visit). Since vertex B has neighbors C, G, and F that have not been previously visited, BFS adds edges (B, C), (B, G), and (B, F) in level 3 of Figure 10.12(c).

Since the neighbors A, B, and G of vertex H have been previously visited, the construction process skips adding any new edges for H. In level 4 of Figure 10.12(c), the edge (C, D) for the unvisited neighbor D of C and the edge (F, E) for the unvisited neighbor E of F are added. Since all the neighbors of vertices D and E in level 4 have been visited previously, the construction process using BFS stops. Thus, one breadth-first spanning tree for the connected graph in Figure 10.2(a) is shown in Figure 10.12(c). As in depth-first spanning trees, breadth-first spanning trees are not unique due to the same reasons.

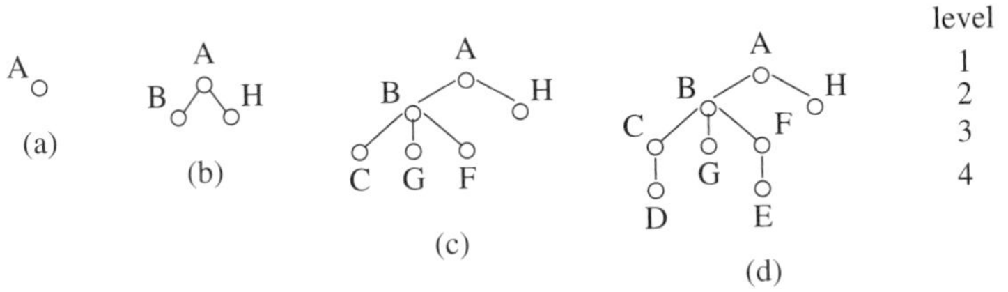

FIGURE 10.12. Traces of constructing a breadth-first spanning tree for the graph of Figure 10.2(a)

10.6 OOP Application: Determining the Shortest Path in a Weighted Digraph Using Dijkstra's Algorithm

In a computer network, the main requirement is the transfer of messages and data between two or more computers (or *nodes*). To perform this, a dynamic table of alive neighboring nodes in the network is maintained and used to determine the least hop (i.e., the path with the minimum sum of distances or costs of edges of this path) between the source and destination nodes in the network. Such a computer network is viewed in general as a weighted digraph where the distance or the cost of the communication line between two nodes is considered as the weight. An example is the airline system, where the problem is to determine the cheapest route (path) between two cities in order to minimize operating costs. In essence, the shortest-path problem is to determine a path between two nodes with a minimum sum of distances or costs in a weighted, connected, and undirected or directed graph. Dijkstra's algorithm is designed to solve this problem. The worst-case performance of Dijkstra's algorithm for a weighted, connected, and undirected or directed graph with n vertices is $O(n^2)$. In the following, the Dijkstra's algorithm will be discussed and illustrated for a weighted digraph as an application of graph objects. An implementation of the Dijkstra's shortest path algorithm for weighted digraph objects using an adjacency matrix representation was presented as **Code 10.1**. An of the same algorithm implemented with a linked adjacency list representation was presented as **Code 10.2**.

Dijkstra's Algorithm

Given a connected and weighted (undirected or directed) graph G with n vertices and all positive weights, $A = A_0, A_1, ..., A_{n-1} = Q$ and all positive weights, the goal is to determine the shortest path from the single-source (start) vertex A to the destination vertex Q. Dijkstra's algorithm starts out by setting a working set S of vertices of G. It assigns a label $L(A_k)$ to each vertex A_k of G. The label $L(A_k)$ means the weight of the shortest path from a source vertex, for example A, to the vertex A_k, where the start vertex A is in the path. Initially, the set S is empty, $L(A) = 0$, and the labels for all other vertices are set to infinity or a very large positive number. At each iteration, the algorithm selects a vertex, say A_k not in S such that $L(A_k)$ is the smallest among all vertices not in S; updates $L(A_k)$ by the current smallest label; adds A to S; updates the labels of all adjacent vertices, say A_j, of vertex A_k by the smaller of $L(A_j)$ and "$L(A_k) +$ weight(A_j, A_k)" or "$L(A_k) +$ weight$(< A_k, A_j >)$."

The iterative process stops when $A_k == Q$. $L(Q)$ is the minimum weight (distance or cost) of the shortest path from vertex A to vertex Q in the weighted graph G. Another version uses the working set S containing all vertices, and deletes the vertex from S at each iteration.

The steps of Dijkstra's algorithm are:

Step 1. (Initialization of weighted graph G)
$$V = A_0 = A_0, A_1, A_2, ..., A_{n-1} = Q$$
$$E = (A_i, A_j) \; or < A_i, A_j > \text{ for digraph, with}$$
$$w_{ij} = weights(A_i, A_j)$$

Step 2. (Initialization for Dijkstra algorithm.)

Step 2.1. Initialize working set S to empty; $S = .$

Step 2.2. Set $L(A) = 0$. For $k = 1, ..., (n - 1)$, set $L(A_k) = $ Infinity weight or a very large number (e.g., 9999999).

Step 3. (Iteration) While (destination vertex Q is not in S), do steps 3.1 through 3.5.

Step 3.1. Select the nearest vertex, say A_k, not in S, i.e., $L(A_k)$ is a minimum among all vertices not in S.

Step 3.2. Add A_k to S: $S = S \cup A_k$.

Step 3.3. If $A_k = Q$, return with $L(Q)$.

Step 3.4. For all adjacent vertices A_j of A_k that are not in S, update their label values by the smaller of $L(A_j)$ and "$L(A_k) +$ weight(A_k, A_k)" or "$L(A_k) +$ weight$(< A_k, A_j >)$." That is, $L(A_j) = $ minimum $(L(A_j), L(A_k) +$ weight$(A_j, A_k))$. (Note $L(A)$ is the current minimum weight of the shortest path from A to A_j.)

Step 3.5. Go to Step 3.

Step 4. $L(Q)$ is the weight of the shortest path from A to Q. The shortest path is determined.

Note that in Step 3.4, $L(A_j)$ is the current minimum weight of the shortest path from A to A_j.

`Dijkstra_shortest_path()` in **Code 10.1** implements Dijkstra's algorithm for a weighted digraph object, whose data are represented by an adjacency matrix. `Find_shortest_path()` in **Code 10.2** implements Dijkstra's algorithm for a weighted digraph, whose data are represented by singly linked adjacency lists.

To illustrate Dijkstra's algorithm, consider the weighted digraph in Figure 10.13(a), and source vertex A and destination vertex Q. For each iteration, the traces of Dijkstra's algorithm for determining the shortest path from A to Q are shown in Figures 10.13(b)–(f), in which asterisk (*) means the vertex is added to S, and the number and vertices in parentheses against each vertex mean the smallest label and corresponding path, respectively. "oo" means infinity label value. Figure 10.13(a) shows the initialization step. Figure 10.13(b) adds A to set S, and updates the labels of its neighbors B and D so that $L(B) = 7, L(D) = 1$. Since $L(D)$ is the minimum among all vertices not in S, the method takes the nearest vertex D in S and updates the labels of its neighbors B and E so that $L(B) = 5$ and $L(E) = 4$ (note $L(B)$ was 7 prior to this iteration) in Figure 10.13(c). In Figure 10.13(d), vertex B with minimum $L(B)$ is added to S, its neighbor's $L(C) = 11$, and $L(E)$ is already minimum. In Figure 10.13(e), vertex E with minimum $L(E)$ is added to S, its neighbor's $L(Q) = 9$, and $L(C)$ is already minimum. In Figure 10.13(f), vertex Q with minimum $L(Q)$ among the vertices C and Q is added to S, and it has no neighbors (considering directed edges out of Q). Since the vertex Q is the destination vertex and in S, the iteration stops. Note that vertex C was never added to S in this process. The final shortest path from A to Q in the weighted digraph of Figure 10.13(a) is (A, D, E) with the smallest weight, 9.

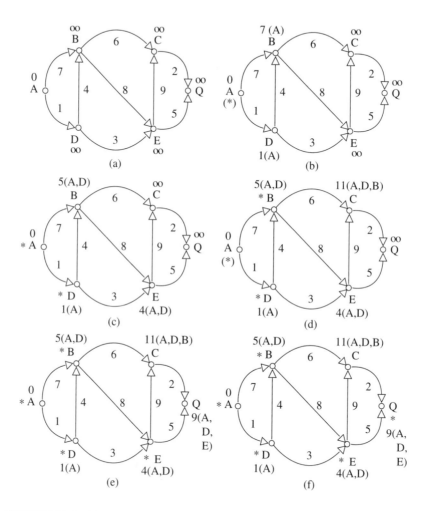

FIGURE 10.13. Traces of Dijkstra's algorithm for determining the shortest path from A to Q.

10.7   Exercises

1. Do a depth-first traversal of each of the following connected graphs.

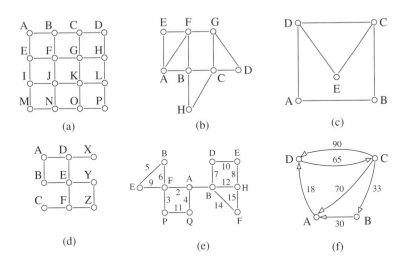

2. Do a breadth-first traversal of each of the connected graphs in Exercise 10-1.

3. Write an algorithm for constructing a depth-first spanning tree from a connected undirected graph.

4. Construct a depth-first spanning tree for each of the connected graphs in Exercise 10-1.

5. Write an algorithm for constructing a breadth-first spanning tree from a connected undirected graph.

6. Construct a breadth-first spanning tree for each of the connected graphs in Exercise 10-1.

7. Using Dijkstra's algorithm, compute the shortest path from vertex Z to vertex F in the weighted undirected connected graph (e) of Exercise 10-1. Show all traces of the iteration.

8. Using Dijkstra's algorithm, compute the shortest path from vertex A to vertex D in the weighted directed connected graph (f) of Exercise 10-1. Show all traces of the iteration.

9. For the connected and weighted digraph object using the adjacency matrix in **Code 10.1**, write and test a `public` member function of the `Weighted_DiGraph` class that deletes a specified vertex.

10. For the connected and weighted digraph object using the adjacency matrix in **Code 10.1**, write and test a `public` member function of the `Weighted_DiGraph` class that shows the number of hops in the shortest path from a given source vertex to a destination vertex.

11. For the connected and weighted digraph object using the adjacency matrix in **Code 10.1**, write and test a `public` member function of the `Weighted_DiGraph` class that performs depth-first traversal of the digraph object.

12. For the connected and weighted digraph object using the adjacency matrix in **Code 10.1**, write and test a `public` member function of the `Weighted_DiGraph` class that performs breadth-first traversal of the digraph object.

13. For the connected and weighted digraph object using the adjacency matrix in **Code 10.1**, write and test a `public` member function of the `Weighted_DiGraph` class that constructs a spanning tree using depth-first traversal of the digraph object. DFS starts from any vertex of the digraph object.

14. For the connected and weighted digraph object using the adjacency matrix in **Code 10.1**, write and test a `public` member function of the `Weighted_DiGraph` class that constructs a spanning tree using breadth-first traversal of the digraph object. BFS starts from any vertex of the digraph object.

15. For the connected and weighted digraph object using the adjacency matrix in **Code 10.2**, write and test a `public` member function of the `Wt_DiGraph` class that deletes a specified vertex.

16. For the connected and weighted digraph object using the adjacency matrix in **Code 10.2**, write and test a `public` member function of the `Wt_DiGraph` class that shows the number of hops in the shortest path from a given source vertex to a destination vertex.

17. For the connected and weighted digraph object using the adjacency matrix in **Code 10.2**, write and test a `public` member function of the `Wt_DiGraph` class that performs depth-first traversal of the digraph object.

18. For the connected and weighted ADT digraph using the adjacency matrix in **Code 10.2**, write and test a `public` member function of the `Wt_DiGraph` class that performs breadth-first traversal of the digraph object.

19. For the connected and weighted digraph object using the adjacency matrix in **Code 10.2**, write and test a `public` member function of

the Wt_DiGraph class that constructs a spanning tree using depth-first traversal of the digraph object. DFS starts from any vertex of the digraph object.

20. For the connected and weighted digraph object using the adjacency matrix in **Code 10.2**, write and test a public member function of the Wt_DiGraph class that constructs a spanning tree using breadth-first traversal of the digraph object. BFS starts from any vertex of the digraph object.

21. **Code 10.2** demonstrates the partial and dynamic implementation of a digraph. For complete dynamic implementation, both the list of vertices and the lists of adjacency vertices must be linked lists. When an undirected or directed and unweighted or weighted graph object is implemented using doubly linked list of vertices and doubly linked adjacency lists, write and test an OOP with the following actions:

(a) Constructor.

(b) Destructor.

(c) Create an undirected or directed and unweighted or weighted graph object.

(d) Print the object in (c).

(e) Perform DFS of the object in (c).

(f) Perform BFS of the object in (c).

(g) Construct a spanning tree using DFS of the object in (c).

(h) Construct a spanning tree using BFS of the object in (c).

(i) Determine the shortest path from a specified source vertex to a specified destination vertex. Use Dijkstra's shortest path algorithm.

(j) Display the shortest path from a specified source vertex to a specified destination vertex.

(k) Display the number of hops in the shortest path from a specified source vertex to a specified destination vertex.

(l) Determine the size of the graph object.

22. Redo Exercise 10-21 when an undirected or directed and unweighted or weighted graph object is implemented using one singly linked list of vertices and singly linked edge lists.

11

An Object-Oriented Database with B-Trees

A simple people database will be developed and implemented employing an array and B-tree objects. A B-tree is a useful and de facto standard data structure for external searching, and sorting, and database programming. The efficiency and usefulness of the B-tree lie in its important features – balanced, ordered multiple keys in a single node, grouping of keys, and its controlled growth. In this chapter, the simple object-oriented `people_1d` database is used to convey the basic ideas such that it can be adapted to any modification to suit an application. This application forms a B-tree object from an array of keys, and demonstrates the message-passing technique between a `people_1d` database object `pdb_obj` and a B-tree object `btree_obj`.

11.1   Specification of People Database System

As described in Chapter 1, a database is an organized set of a collective forms of related data called records and some basic operations such as entering a record, searching a record, sorting records by keys, and displaying a record.

The people database is a collection of records involving information about people and their memberships in an organization. Each record contains six attributes: member ID, name, occupation, age, income of member, and the years that the member has belonged in the organization. The record for each member in the people database is shown in Appendix C. It is specified as a structure containing the following field attributes:

Field name	Field description and type
Member ID	Membership number; integer
Name of member	String of variable length
Occupation	String of variable length
Age	Age of member; integer
Income	yearly gross (x $1000); integer
Years	number years member; integer

The "member ID" is used as the only key for searching and sorting of records in the database. Using this key, all records will be stored in a B-tree data structure. The specification of the `people_1d` database also includes an OOP implementation, a simple menu-driven user (operator) interface, which simply depends on a monochrome display terminal hardware, and provides the following operations:

```
** Objected Oriented People Database **
    People DataBase MAIN MENU

Add a member                  ..  a
Change a member record        ..  c
Show a member record          ..  d
Print entire database         ..  p
Store database on disk        ..  s
Restore database from disk ..  r
Exit from database            ..  e

Select menu (a, c, d, p, s, r, e):
```

11.2   OOP Implementation of Simple People Database Using B-Trees

In `peopl_db.c++` of Appendix C, each record is defined by the `struct` construct `DataObject`. Since the requirement specifies storing the records of the `people_1d` database in a B-tree of some order `BTREE_ORDER`, recall the abstract structure of a node for a B-tree of order n contains at least n keys or at most k_i $(i = 0, 1, ..., (2n-1))$ keys and p_i $(i = 0, ..., 2n)$ pointers to the children of keys, and is of the form:

p_0	k_0	p_1	k_1	...	p_{2n-1}	k_{2n-1}	p_{2n}

The keys are in ascending order, the pointer p_i $(i = 0, ..., (2n-1))$ points to a node child or left subtree that contains keys less than k_i. The pointer p_{2n} points to a node child or right subtree that contains keys greater than the key $k_{(2n-1)}$ in value. This is discussed in detail in Chapter 8.

For a quick illustration, the `people_1d` database is constructed as a B-tree of order 2 with "member ID" as the key, and the object is `btree_obj`. For the member records with the keys

$$16, 54, 14, 63, 62, 48, 21, 53$$

the keys are inserted into the leaf node with the ascending order 14, 16, 54, and 63. Since this B-tree node becomes full, the node is split when inserting

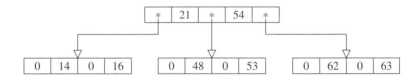

FIGURE 11.1. People database as a B-tree of order 2.

62. Figure 11.1 shows the final B-tree structure of the people_1d database containing all the keys. The number 0 means the NULL pointer value. **Code 11.1** uses these keys and produces the same B-tree structure.

Keeping an OOP-implementation requirements for the people_1d database in mind, we identify an object btree_obj whose data members are of type BTREE_NODE and are structured as a B-tree. The methods for this object are the menu operations and the operations identified for an ADT B-tree. To fulfill the requirement for data-hiding, encapsulation, and message-passing facilities of an OOP, the object's type B_Tree is defined by the class construct in the header file class_B_Tree.h as follows:

```
const int BTREE_ORDER  = 2;
const int MAX_RECORDS  = 2 * BTREE_ORDER;
typedef    int          INDEX;
typedef    People_Database::DataObject DATA_TYPE;

class B_Tree : private People_Database {
  private:
    typedef struct BTREE_NODE {
      DATA_TYPE    records[MAX_RECORDS];
      int          num_records;
      BTREE_NODE   *parent_ptr;
      BTREE_NODE   *child_ptr[MAX_RECORDS + 1];
    } *BTREE_PTR;
    BTREE_PTR  root_ptr;
    int        NOBJ;
    void       init_BTREE() { root_ptr = NULL; }
    int        locate_position_in_node (BTREE_PTR BTnode_ptr,
                       Keytype   search_key);
    void  find_key_in_btree (BTREE_PTR tree_ptr,
           Keytype   srch_key, BTREE_PTR *srch_BTnode_ptr,
           INDEX  *srch_index);
    DATA_TYPE divide_full_node (BTREE_PTR where_ptr,
                   BTREE_PTR   new_ptr,
                   BTREE_PTR   lft_childptr,
                   DATA_TYPE   new_record,
                   INDEX       index);
    void  add_key_in_node (BTREE_PTR    where_ptr,
           BTREE_PTR  lft_childptr, BTREE_PTR rgt_childptr,
```

```
                  DATA_TYPE new_record);
     void   read_str_input (char **str);
   public:
     B_Tree(int nobj);    //  Constructor
     ~B_Tree();           //  Destructor
     BTREE_PTR  get_root() { return (root_ptr); }
     void   add_key_in_btree    (DATA_TYPE   new_record);
     void   build_BTREE (DATA_TYPE *A);
     void   show_btree (void);
     void   wait_for_any_key (void);
     void   show_menu (void);
     void   do_menu (void);
     void   add_a_mem_into_db (void);
     void   change_a_mem_record (void);
     void   show_a_record (void);
     void   store_peopl_db_on_disk (void);
     void   restore_peopl_db_from_disk (void);
   };
```

Note that this class definition is generic enough that the `DataObject` structure and related menus can be easily modified to adapt to any other application that will use the B-tree data structure. Indeed, this will not require any changes in B-tree operations.

The abstract base class `Tree` in Chapter 8 is not used to derive the class `B_Tree` from it. The reasons are stated below:

- Show another way that defining a generic abstract base class is not a panacea — that is, the developer may choose to define a new abstract base class for an object that is more specialized in the application.

- It is decided to define a class `B_Tree` that does not inherit any data or methods from another base class.

- It could have also defined an abstract base class `B_tree` from which a family of B-tree subclasses can be derived.

11.2.1 METHODS OF THE B_Tree CLASS

`B_Tree()` is a `public` member function of the `B_Tree` class. It is the constructor for this class. Using the `new` operator, it dynamically allocates memory space for an object of the class `B_Tree`. It is automatically called when a class variable of type `B_Tree` is declared (e.g., in `main()`).

`~B_Tree()` is the destructor for the `B_Tree` class. This `public` member function is used to destroy or deallocate a `B_Tree` type object, and is implicitly called at the program exit. Its implementation is left as an exercise.

The operation `init_BTREE()` of type `void` is a `private` member function of the `B_Tree` class. It initializes the object `btree_obj` by setting its member `root_ptr` to NULL. It is declared `private` to ensure protection to a `B_Tree` type object. Otherwise, outside functions may inadvertently initialize an object of `B_Tree` type.

The operation `get_root()` of type `BTREE_PTR` is a public member function of the `B_Tree` class. It provides read-only access to the root pointer.

The operation `locate_pos_in_node()` of type `INDEX` is a public member function of the `B_Tree` class. It expects a `BTnode_ptr` of type `BTREE_PTR` as an argument. It assumes that `BTnode_ptr` is not `NULL`. Since the keys of records are stored in ascending order in a B-tree node, this function uses a linear search method, locating and returning the appropriate position (array index) in the array of keys in the B-tree node. It is called by `find_key_in_btree()` and `add_key_in_node()`.

`Find_key_in_btree()` of type `void` is a `private` member function of the `B_Tree` class. As arguments, it expects a `tree_ptr`, an address of `srch_BTnode_ptr` of type `BTREE_PTR`, a `srch_key` of type `Keytype`, and an address of `srch_index`. It is a recursive function. If the B-tree is empty, it simply returns. Otherwise, it checks to see whether `srch_key` is out of range, since the keys in a B-tree node are in ascending order. Using the standard linear search method, if it finds a match of the key, it respectively sets `srch_BTnode_ptr` and `srch_index` to the B-tree node and the array index where the search key is found. Otherwise, the function calls `locate_pos_in_node()` to locate the position in the B-tree node pointed to by `tree_ptr`, and proceeds to search it in its left child subtree if `srch_key` is less than the located record's key in the node. Otherwise, it proceeds to search it in its right child subtree by calling itself.

`Divide_full_node()` of type `DataObject` is a `private` member function of the `B_Tree` class. It expects the pointers `where_ptr`, `new_ptr`, and `lft_childptr` of type `BTREE_PTR`, `new_record` of type `DataObject`, and `index` of type `INDEX`. The pointer `where_ptr` points to the B-tree node where the new DataObject will be inserted. It divides the full node (i.e., number of keys/records is 2 `*` `BTREE_ORDER`), pointed to by `where_ptr`, into two B-tree nodes. To split a B-tree node, it computes the median key of the node pointed to by `where_ptr`. It copies all data records with keys less than the median key into the new node. It moves the data element with the median key to its parent node. If the parent is full, it continues the splitting process on the parent node. It is done in a "rippling" manner. The parent pointers in children are updated in this process. It is called by `add_key_in_node()`.

`Add_key_in_node()` of type `void` is a `private` member function of the `B_Tree` class. It adds a new record into a B-Tree object. If the B-tree object is empty, it creates a root node. The keys are stored in ascending order in a node. If a B-tree node becomes full (i.e., reaches `MAX_RECORDS`) before the addition of the new key, it calls `divide_full_node()` to split the full node into two B-tree nodes, and inserts the new record in the appropriate node; the median key is moved to its parent node. It

updates the root pointer if it creates a new root node. It is called by
`add_key_in_btree()`.

`Add_key_in_btree()` of type `void` is a `public` member function of
the `B_Tree` class. It expects a record, `new_record`, of type `DataObject`
as an argument. It calls `find_key_in_btree()` to check whether the
new record already exists. If the record already exists, it simply returns.
Otherwise, it iteratively finds the location of B-tree node, where the new
record is to be inserted. Finally, it calls `add_key_in_node()`.

To implement the menu-driven user interface on an ASCII terminal,
some methods are defined as `public` members of the `B_Tree` class. Alternatively, a separate class, `People_Menu`, containing these menu-related
methods, could have been defined as a derived class of the `B_Tree` class.
These methods are now described. This alternative technique is left as an
exercise.

The operation `show_menu()` of type `void` is a `public` member function of the `B_Tree` class. It is used to clear the screen, and to display the
database's menu options for the user.

The operation `add_a_mem_into_db()` of type `void` is a `public`
member function of the `B_Tree` class that is used to process the menu
option *Add a member*. It clears the display screen and asks the user to
input member-related information. Then it calls `add_key_in_btree()`,
which inserts the member's record in the B-tree structured `people_1d`
database.

The operation `change_a_mem_record()` of type `void` is a `public`
member function of the `B_Tree` class. It is used to process the menu
option "Change a member record." It clears the display screen. It asks
the user to input the member's key and member number. Then it calls
`find_key_in_btree()`, which searches the member's data by the specified key in the B-tree structured `people_1d` database. If the member is
not found in the database, it displays a message and returns. Otherwise,
the function gets the new information for the member from the user, and
changes the member's attribute fields.

The operation `show_a_record()` of type `void` is a `public` member function of the `B_Tree` class. It is used to process the menu option "Show a member record." It clears the display screen. It asks the
user to input member's key, the member identification number. It calls
`find_key_in_btree()`, which searches the member's data in the B-tree
of the `people_1d` database. If the member is not found in the database,
it displays a message and returns. Otherwise, the function displays the
member's information fields on the screen.

The operation `show_btree()` of type `void` is a `public` member function of the `B_Tree` class. It is used to process the menu option "Print entire
database." It is an iterative function. It vertically prints only the keys of
elements in the B-tree object.

`Store_peopl_db_on_disk()` of type `void` is a `public` member function of the `B_Tree` class. It is used to process the menu option "Store database on disk." If the database is empty, it displays an error message and returns. Otherwise, it attempts to open a file, `People.db`, on disk as a writable binary file. If the attempt fails, it displays an error message and returns. Otherwise, iteratively it prints all keys in the B-tree node followed by all children of each key. It calls the formatted block write function `fwrite()` to write each `DataObject` in the given file. Then the function closes this file and returns. Its recursive implementation is left as an exercise.

The operation `restore_peopl_db_from_disk()` of type `void` is a `public` member function of the `B_Tree` class. It is used to process the menu option "Restore database from disk." If the present B-tree structured database in the working buffer is not empty, it asks the user for confirmation before nullifying it. Otherwise, it attempts to open the file `People.db` for reading binary data. If the attempt fails, it displays an error message and returns. Otherwise, it reads `DataObject` record block by block using `fread()`, and calls `add_key_in_btree()`, which continues building the B-tree until the reading of all data records is complete. Then the function closes this file and returns.

The operation `do_menu()` of type `void` is a `public` member function of the `B_Tree` class. It asks for the user's selection from the terminal, and invokes the appropriate action to process the user's selection.

`Main()` is the test driver for an OOP implementation of the Parts Inventory Control System. It declares an object, `btree_obj`, of type `B_Tree`. Since main() is not a member of the `B_Tree` class, it sends messages to the object `btree_obj`. The messages include initializing the object, displaying menu, and processing the user's menu selection.

The OOP implementations of the above functions are given in **Code 11.1**.

11.3   Object-Oriented People Database Program

Code 11.1

```
//   Program:   Peopl_db_btree.c++
//   Purpose:
//      Object-Oriented implementation of a
//      PEOPLE_1D database (see Appendix C)
//      using B-trees. Database records are
//      stored in B-tree.
//   To compile using Borland's Turbo C++,
//      tcc -DMSDOS Peopl_db.cpp
//
#include <stdio.h>
```

```
#include <stdlib.h>
#include <math.h>
#include <ctype.h>
#include <string.h>
#include <iostream.h>

//  Define a macro for clearing show screen
#ifdef  MSDOS
#include  <conio.h>       //  For clrscr() call
#include  "peopl_1d.cpp" // See Appendix C
#define   CLEAR_SCREEN() (clrscr())
#else      // in Unix
#include  "peopl_1d.c++"  // Database in Appendix C
#define   CLEAR_SCREEN() (system("clear"))
#endif
const int YES = 1;
const int NO  = 0;
const int BTREE_ORDER  = 2;
const int MAX_RECORDS  = 2 * BTREE_ORDER;
typedef    int          INDEX;
typedef    People_Database::DataObject DATA_TYPE;


//  Define "B_Tree" class
class B_Tree : private People_Database {
  private:
    typedef struct BTREE_NODE {
      DATA_TYPE    records[MAX_RECORDS];
      int          num_records;
      BTREE_NODE   *parent_ptr;
      BTREE_NODE   *child_ptr[MAX_RECORDS + 1];
    } *BTREE_PTR;
    BTREE_PTR  root_ptr;
    int        NOBJ;
    void       init_BTREE() { root_ptr = NULL; }
    int    locate_position_in_node (BTREE_PTR BTnode_ptr,
                   Keytype   search_key);
    void   find_key_in_btree (BTREE_PTR tree_ptr,
           Keytype   srch_key, BTREE_PTR *srch_BTnode_ptr,
           INDEX   *srch_index);
    DATA_TYPE divide_full_node (BTREE_PTR where_ptr,
              BTREE_PTR    new_ptr,
              BTREE_PTR    lft_childptr,
              DATA_TYPE   new_record,
              INDEX        index);
    void   add_key_in_node (BTREE_PTR      where_ptr,
           BTREE_PTR  lft_childptr, BTREE_PTR rgt_childptr,
           DATA_TYPE new_record);
    void   read_str_input (char **str);
  public:
    B_Tree(int nobj);  //  Constructor
    ~B_Tree();          //  Destructor
    BTREE_PTR  get_root() { return (root_ptr); }
    void  add_key_in_btree   (DATA_TYPE   new_record);
    void  build_BTREE (DATA_TYPE *A);
```

```
    void  show_btree (void);
    void  wait_for_any_key (void);
    void  show_menu (void);
    void  do_menu (void);
    void  add_a_mem_into_db (void);
    void  change_a_mem_record (void);
    void  show_a_record (void);
    void  store_peopl_db_on_disk (void);
    void  restore_peopl_db_from_disk (void);
};


//  B_Tree():
//    Construct B-Tree object from People_Database
//
B_Tree::B_Tree(int nobj): People_Database(nobj)
{
   NOBJ = nobj;   // From People_Database
   init_BTREE();
}


//  ~B_Tree():
//    Destroy memory spaces for a B-Tree object
//
B_Tree::~B_Tree()
{
   //  Destructor: It is left as an exercise.
}


//  locate_position_in_node():
//    The keys of records are stored in an
//    ascending ordered array in a B-tree node. It
//    locates the appropriate position (array index)
//    in the array of keys in the B-tree node.
//    It assumes: BTnode_ptr is not NULL.
//
INDEX B_Tree::locate_position_in_node (BTREE_PTR BTnode_ptr,
                                Keytype srch_key)
{
   INDEX i, no_of_keys = BTnode_ptr->num_records;

   for (i = 0; i < no_of_keys; i++)
     if (srch_key < BTnode_ptr->records[i].key)
       return (i);
   return (no_of_keys);
}


//  find_key_in_btree():
//    Find a record identified by a key, srch_key,
//    in a B-tree. If found, it returns pointer
//    to the B-tree node, srch_BTnode_ptr, and
//    the array index, srch_index, in the node
//    (keys are stored in an array). If not found,
//    srch_BTnode_ptr = NULL, & srch_index = -1.
//    (Recursive implementation) (Its iterative
```

```
//     implementation is left as an exercise)
//
void B_Tree::find_key_in_btree (BTREE_PTR tree_ptr,
     Keytype srch_key, BTREE_PTR  *srch_BTnode_ptr,
     INDEX *srch_index)
{
   *srch_BTnode_ptr = NULL;
   *srch_index     = -1;

   if (tree_ptr != NULL) { // nonempty tree
     // Get no of keys in the node
     int no_of_keys = tree_ptr->num_records;
     //  Since the keys in a B-tree node are in
     //  ascending order, check if out of range.

     if (((srch_key < tree_ptr->records[0].key) &&
          (tree_ptr->child_ptr[0] == NULL))
         ((srch_key > tree_ptr->records[no_of_keys-1].key) &&
          (tree_ptr->child_ptr[no_of_keys] == NULL))) {
       return;  // not found
     }
     for (INDEX position = 0; position < no_of_keys;
          position++) {
      if (srch_key == tree_ptr->records[position].key) {
       *srch_BTnode_ptr = tree_ptr;
       *srch_index      = position;  // location in node
       return;
      }
     }
     // Locate the position in the node
     position = locate_position_in_node(tree_ptr,
                                  srch_key);
     if ((srch_key < tree_ptr->records[position].key) &&
         (tree_ptr->child_ptr[position] != NULL))
        // Search it in its left child subtree
        find_key_in_btree (tree_ptr->child_ptr[position],
            srch_key, srch_BTnode_ptr, srch_index);

     if ((srch_key > tree_ptr->records[position-1].key)
         && (tree_ptr->child_ptr[position] != NULL))
        // Search it in its right child subtree
        find_key_in_btree (tree_ptr->child_ptr[position],
            srch_key, srch_BTnode_ptr, srch_index);
   }
   // Record with the given key is not found.
}


//  divide_full_node():
//    It is called by add_key_in_node(). It divides a
//    full node. This code is credited to
//    Sengupta and Edwards [1991].
//
DATA_TYPE    B_Tree::divide_full_node(
   BTREE_PTR where_ptr, BTREE_PTR new_ptr,
```

```
   BTREE_PTR lft_childptr, DATA_TYPE new_record,
   INDEX index)
{
  int        i = 0, j = 0,
             mid_element_inserted = NO;
  DATA_TYPE    mid_element;

  //  build new/left node and insert new record
  //  if appropriate
  //
  while (i < BTREE_ORDER) {
    if (mid_element_inserted == NO && j == index) {
      new_ptr->records[i] = new_record;
      new_ptr->child_ptr[i] = lft_childptr;
      ++i;
      mid_element_inserted = YES;
    }
    else {
      new_ptr->records[i] =
                    where_ptr->records[j];
      new_ptr->child_ptr[i] =
                    where_ptr->child_ptr[j];
      ++i;
      ++j;
    }
}

//  establish middle record and use new record
//  if appropriate
//
if (mid_element_inserted == NO && j == index) {
  mid_element = new_record;
  new_ptr->child_ptr[i] = lft_childptr;
  mid_element_inserted = YES;
}
else {
  mid_element = where_ptr->records[j];
  new_ptr->child_ptr[i] =
               where_ptr->child_ptr[j];
  ++j;
}

//  update parent pointers in children if required
if (new_ptr->child_ptr[0] != NULL)
  for (i = 0; i <= BTREE_ORDER; i++)
    new_ptr->child_ptr[i]->parent_ptr = new_ptr;
//
//  update existing/right node and insert new
//  record if appropriate
//
i = 0;
while (i < BTREE_ORDER) {
  if (mid_element_inserted == NO && j == index) {
    where_ptr->records[i] = new_record;
```

```
      where_ptr->child_ptr[i] = lft_childptr;
        ++i;
        mid_element_inserted = YES;
      }
      else {
        where_ptr->records[i] =
                    where_ptr->records[j];
        where_ptr->child_ptr[i] =
                    where_ptr->child_ptr[j];
        ++i;
        ++j;
      }
    }
    where_ptr->child_ptr[i] =
                  where_ptr->child_ptr[j];

    //  update parent pointers in children if required
    if (where_ptr->child_ptr[0] != NULL)
      for (i = 0; i <= BTREE_ORDER; i++)
        where_ptr->child_ptr[i]->parent_ptr = where_ptr;

    return (mid_element);
  }


  //  add_key_in_node():
  //    Add a new record into a B-Tree object.
  //    If the B-tree is empty, it creates a root node.
  //    Keys are stored in ascending order in a node.
  //    If a B-tree node becomes full (i.e., MAX_RECORDS)
  //    before the addition of the new key, the full node
  //    is divided (split) into two B-tree nodes, and
  //    new record is inserted in the appropriate node;
  //    the median key is moved to its parent node.
  //    It updates root pointer if it creates a new root
  //    node. It is called by add_key_in_btree().
  //    This code is credited to Sengupta and Edwards [SE91].
  //
  void   B_Tree::add_key_in_node (
    BTREE_PTR   where_ptr, BTREE_PTR   lft_childptr,
    BTREE_PTR   rgt_childptr, DATA_TYPE   new_record)
  {
    BTREE_PTR    new_ptr;
    DATA_TYPE   mid_element;
    INDEX        index, i, no_of_keys;

    //  if node does not exist, create new root node
    if (where_ptr == NULL) {
      new_ptr = new BTREE_NODE;
      new_ptr->records[0] = new_record;
      new_ptr->child_ptr[0] = lft_childptr;
      new_ptr->child_ptr[1] = rgt_childptr;
      new_ptr->parent_ptr = NULL;
      if (lft_childptr != NULL && rgt_childptr != NULL) {
        lft_childptr->parent_ptr  = new_ptr;
```

```
            rgt_childptr->parent_ptr = new_ptr;
        }
        new_ptr->num_records = 1;
        root_ptr = new_ptr;
        return;
    }

    index = locate_position_in_node (where_ptr, new_record.key);
    if (where_ptr->num_records < MAX_RECORDS) {
      //  insert new element
      no_of_keys = where_ptr->num_records;
      //  move right most child pointer
      where_ptr->child_ptr[no_of_keys+1] =
                      where_ptr->child_ptr[no_of_keys];
      //
      //  move elements and left children to make
      //  room for the new record
      //
      for (i = no_of_keys; i > index; i--) {
        where_ptr->records[i] =
                      where_ptr->records[i-1];
        where_ptr->child_ptr[i] =
                      where_ptr->child_ptr[i-1];
      }
      where_ptr->records[index] = new_record;
      where_ptr->child_ptr[index] = lft_childptr;
      where_ptr->child_ptr[index+1] = rgt_childptr;
      where_ptr->num_records += 1;
    }
    else {  //  divide B-tree node into two
      new_ptr = new BTREE_NODE;
      new_ptr->parent_ptr = where_ptr->parent_ptr;
      new_ptr->num_records = BTREE_ORDER;
      where_ptr->num_records = BTREE_ORDER;
      mid_element = divide_full_node (where_ptr,
                      new_ptr, lft_childptr,
                      new_record, index);
      add_key_in_node (where_ptr->parent_ptr,
          new_ptr, where_ptr, mid_element);
    }  // end 'else'
}

// add_key_in_btree ():
//    Add a new member record to a B-Tree.
//    Inserting a duplicate key is not allowed.
//    This code is credited to Sengupta and Edwards [SE91].
//
void B_Tree::add_key_in_btree (DATA_TYPE new_record)
{
    BTREE_PTR    BTnode_ptr;
    INDEX        index, i, no_of_keys;

    //  see if the record already exists
    find_key_in_btree (root_ptr, new_record.key,
```

```
                              &BTnode_ptr, &index);
      if (BTnode_ptr != NULL) {
        printf(" add_key_in_btree: Insertion of %s\n",
               "duplicate key not allowed");
        return;   // the record already exists
      }
      //  find node where new record is to be inserted
      BTnode_ptr = root_ptr;
      while (BTnode_ptr != NULL) {
        no_of_keys = BTnode_ptr->num_records;
        i = 0;
        while (i < no_of_keys &&
          new_record.key > BTnode_ptr->records[i].key)
             ++i;
        if (BTnode_ptr->child_ptr[i] != NULL)
          BTnode_ptr = BTnode_ptr->child_ptr[i];
        else
          break;
      }
      add_key_in_node (BTnode_ptr, NULL, NULL, new_record);
    }


    // build_BTREE():
    //    Build a people database using a B-tree object
    //    from an array of records, by successively
    //    calling   add_key_in_btree().
    //
    void  B_Tree::build_BTREE(DATA_TYPE *record)
    {
       for (int j = 0; j < NOBJ; j++)
          add_key_in_btree(record[j]);
    }


    //   show_menu():
    //     Show menus as a menu-driven interface
    //     to users of people database.
    //
    void   B_Tree::show_menu (void)
    {
      CLEAR_SCREEN();
      printf ("\n ** Objected Oriented People Database **");
      printf ("\n         People DataBase MAIN MENU\n");
      printf ("%s %s %s %s %s %s %s",
          "\n Add a member               ..  a",
          "\n Change a member record     ..  c",
          "\n Show a member record       ..  d",
          "\n Print entire database      ..  p",
          "\n Store database on disk      ..  s",
          "\n Restore database from disk ..  r",
          "\n Exit from database          ..  e");
    }


    //   do_menu():
    //     Get the correct choice number from 1 to 5.
```

```
//      Transfer control to the corresponding function.
//
void  B_Tree::do_menu(void)
{
   char   selection;

   printf("\n\n Select menu (a, c, d, p, s, r, e): ");
#ifdef MSDOS
   switch (getche()) {
#else
   fflush(stdout);
   cin >> selection;
   switch (selection) {
#endif
      case 'a':
      case 'A':
            add_a_mem_into_db (); break;
      case 'c':
      case 'C':
            change_a_mem_record (); break;
      case 'd':
      case 'D':
            //  Find member record in people_db & show.
            show_a_record (); break;
      case 'p':
      case 'P':
            show_btree ();
            wait_for_any_key(); break;
      case 's':
      case 'S':
            store_peopl_db_on_disk (); break;
      case 'r':
      case 'R':
            restore_peopl_db_from_disk (); break;
      case 'e':       // Exit
      case 'E':
            printf("\n Exiting from database ...\n");
            exit (0);
      default:
            printf("\n Unknown choice !!!");
            wait_for_any_key(); break;
   }
}

//  read_str_input():
//     Get a character string from console.
//
void  B_Tree::read_str_input (char **str)
{
   char  *input_str = new char [256];

   gets (input_str);
   if (input_str[0] != '\0') {
      // Allocate memory space for variable  string
```

```
      *str = new char [strlen(input_str) + 1];
      strcpy (*str, input_str);
    }
    delete  input_str;
}


//  wait_for_any_key ():
//    Wait for any key to be pressed.
//
void    B_Tree::wait_for_any_key (void)
{
  printf ("\n\n To continue, depress <Enter> ...");
#ifdef  MSDOS
  if (getch () == 0)
    getch ();
#else
    getchar ();   // in Unix
#endif
}

//  add_a_mem_into_db ():
//    Add a record into a B-Tree.
//
void    B_Tree::add_a_mem_into_db (void)
{
  DATA_TYPE  new_record;
  char   *input_str = new char [256];

  CLEAR_SCREEN ();
  printf ("\n Add a Member into People Database");
  printf ("\n -------------------------------");
  printf ("\n Member Id <integer>:  ");
  gets (input_str);
  new_record.key = atoi (input_str);
  printf ("\n Member Id:  %d\n", new_record.key);
  printf (" Member Name:  ");
  read_str_input (&new_record.name);
  printf (" Member Occupation:  ");
  read_str_input (&new_record.occupation);
  printf (" Member Age:  ");
  gets (input_str);
  new_record.age = atoi (input_str);
  printf (" Member Income (x $1000):  ");
  gets (input_str);
  new_record.income = atoi (input_str);
  printf (" Years of Membership:  ");
  gets (input_str);
  new_record.years = atoi (input_str);

  add_key_in_btree (new_record);
  delete  input_str;   // release unwanted space
  return;
}
```

```
//  change_a_mem_record():
//   Change or update a record in a B-Tree.
//
void  B_Tree::change_a_mem_record (void)
{
  BTREE_PTR    BTnode_ptr;
  int          loc_in_node;
  char         *input_str = new char [256];

  CLEAR_SCREEN();
  printf ("\n Change a Member Record in Database");
  printf ("\n ----------------------------\n");
  printf ("\n Member Id <integer>:   ");
  gets (input_str);

  find_key_in_btree (root_ptr, atoi(input_str),
        &BTnode_ptr, &loc_in_node);
  if (BTnode_ptr == NULL) {
    printf ("\n Member Id %i %s",
        atoi(input_str), "is not in Database");
    wait_for_any_key ();
    return;
  }
  printf ("\n Change Member Id %d",
            BTnode_ptr->records[loc_in_node].key);
  printf ("\n Hit <Enter> if you do not %s",
          "want to change");
  printf ("\n ------------------------%s",
          "-------------");
  printf ("\n Member Name [%s]: ",
      BTnode_ptr->records[loc_in_node].name);
  read_str_input (&BTnode_ptr->records[loc_in_node].name);
  printf (" Member Occupation [%s]: ",
    BTnode_ptr->records[loc_in_node].occupation);
  read_str_input(&BTnode_ptr->records[loc_in_node].occupation );
  printf (" Member Age   [%i]: ",
    BTnode_ptr->records[loc_in_node].age);
  gets (input_str);
  if (input_str[0] != '\0')
    BTnode_ptr->records[loc_in_node].age = atoi (input_str);
  printf (" Member Income  [$%d]: ",
   BTnode_ptr->records[loc_in_node].income * 1000);
  gets (input_str);
  if (input_str[0] != '\0')
      BTnode_ptr->records[loc_in_node].income =
                                    atoi (input_str);
  printf (" Years of Membership  [%d]: ",
      BTnode_ptr->records[loc_in_node].years);
  gets (input_str);
  if (input_str[0] != '\0')
      BTnode_ptr->records[loc_in_node].years =
                            atoi (input_str);
}
```

```
//   show_a_record():
//      Show a record in a B-Tree.
//
void    B_Tree::show_a_record (void)
{
  BTREE_PTR    BTnode_ptr;
  int          loc_in_node;
  char         *input = new char[256];

  CLEAR_SCREEN();
  printf ("\n Show a Member in Database");
  printf ("\n ------------------------");
  printf ("\n Member Id <integer>: ");
  gets (input);
  find_key_in_btree (root_ptr, atoi(input), &BTnode_ptr,
                     &loc_in_node);
  if (BTnode_ptr == NULL) {
    printf ("\n Member Id %i %s ",
            atoi(input), "is not in People Database");
    wait_for_any_key ();
    return;
  }
  printf ("\n Member Name:  %s",
      BTnode_ptr->records[loc_in_node].name);
  printf ("\n Member Occupation: %s",
      BTnode_ptr->records[loc_in_node].occupation);
  printf ("\n Member Age:   %i",
      BTnode_ptr->records[loc_in_node].age);
  printf ("\n Member Income:  %i",
      BTnode_ptr->records[loc_in_node].income * 1000);
  printf ("\n Years of Membership:  %i",
      BTnode_ptr->records[loc_in_node].years);
  delete  input;
  wait_for_any_key ();
  return;
}


//   show_btree():
//      Show each record's key in a B-tree format:
//      root node, followed by leftmost child, ...,
//      rightmost child. (Iterative method)
//
void    B_Tree::show_btree (void)
{
  BTREE_PTR  BTnode_ptr = root_ptr, advance_ptr;

  printf("\n ==  B-Tree Display of %s == \n",
         "Database Records");
  if (BTnode_ptr != NULL) {
    // Print all records in the B-tree node
    // pointed to by 'BTnode_ptr'
    for (int k = 0; k < BTnode_ptr->num_records; k++)
      printf (" %d ", BTnode_ptr->records[k].key);
    printf ("\n");
```

```
   for (int i = 0; i <= BTnode_ptr->num_records; i++) {
    advance_ptr = BTnode_ptr->child_ptr[i];

    while (advance_ptr != NULL) {
       // Print all records in each child node
       // pointed to by 'BTnode_ptr->child_ptr[i]'

       for (int k = 0; k < advance_ptr->num_records; k++)
          printf (" %d ", advance_ptr->records[k].key);
       printf ("\n");
      advance_ptr = advance_ptr->child_ptr[i];
    }
  }
 }
 else
    printf ("\n B-Tree for People database is empty\n");
}

//  store_peopl_db_on_disk ():
//    Store each record of people database in the
//    B-tree by block-by-block writes in a file on
//    disk.  (Iterative method)
//
void   B_Tree::store_peopl_db_on_disk (void)
{
  FILE        *db_file_ptr;
  BTREE_PTR  BTnode_ptr = root_ptr,
             advance_ptr;

  if (root_ptr == NULL) { // empty B-tree database
    printf ("\n store_peopl_db_on_disk: Empty database\n");
    wait_for_any_key();
    return;
  }
  db_file_ptr = fopen ("People.db", "wb");
  if (db_file_ptr == NULL) {
    printf ("\n store_peopl_db_on_disk: People %s \n",
            "database cannot be opened.");
    wait_for_any_key();
    return;
  }
  if (BTnode_ptr != NULL) {
    // Write all records in the B-tree node
    // pointed to by 'BTnode_ptr'
    for (int k = 0; k < BTnode_ptr->num_records; k++)
      fwrite (&BTnode_ptr->records[k],
            sizeof (BTnode_ptr->records[k]),
            1, db_file_ptr);

    for (int i = 0; i <= BTnode_ptr->num_records; i++) {
      advance_ptr = BTnode_ptr->child_ptr[i];

      while (advance_ptr != NULL) {
```

```
                // Write all records in each child node
                // pointed to by 'BTnode_ptr->child_ptr[i]'

                for (int k = 0; k < advance_ptr->num_records; k++)
                  fwrite (&advance_ptr->records[k],
                      sizeof (advance_ptr->records[k]),
                      1, db_file_ptr);
                advance_ptr = advance_ptr->child_ptr[i];
            }
        }
    }
    fclose (db_file_ptr);
    printf("\n Successfully stored People database.\n");
}


//  restore_peopl_db_from_disk ():
//     Restore people database stored as a B-tree
//     and in file "People,db" on disk. It simply
//     returns if the database is empty.
//
void    B_Tree::restore_peopl_db_from_disk (void)
{
    FILE        *db_file_ptr;
    DATA_TYPE   new_record;

    if (root_ptr != NULL) {
        CLEAR_SCREEN();
        printf ("\n Working Database is not %s \n %s",
          "empty.", "Are you sure to overwrite it (y/n)? ");
        char confirm = getchar();
        if (confirm == 'N'   confirm == 'n')
            return;
    }
    //  Overwriting present database tree is confirmed.
    if ((db_file_ptr = fopen ("People.db", "rb")) == NULL) {
        printf ("\n ERROR:  Cannot open database file.");
        wait_for_any_key ();
        return;
    }
    init_BTREE();   // Start from empty B-tree
    while (fread (&new_record, sizeof (new_record),
            1, db_file_ptr) == 1)
        add_key_in_btree (new_record);
    fclose (db_file_ptr);
}


//  main():
//     Main test driver for People Database
//     implemented as a B-Tree with OBJECT-
//     ORIENTED PROGRAMMING approach.
//
void  main (void)
{
    int  REPEATED = 1;
```

```
        // See Appendix C for "People_Database".
        // Declare "People_Database" object with size=10
        People_Database pdb_obj(10);
        pdb_obj.build_initial_db();
        B_Tree   btree_obj(10); // No. of DataObjects = 10
        printf("\n OBJECT-ORIENTED PEOPLE %s \n %s \n",
            "DATABASE", "          USING B-TREE \n");
        // ** Building B-tree of order 2
        printf ("\n Building initial people database ...\n");
        btree_obj.build_BTREE(pdb_obj.get_db());
        printf("\n Saving People database ...\n");
        btree_obj.store_peopl_db_on_disk();
        btree_obj.show_btree();
        btree_obj.wait_for_any_key();
        while (REPEATED) {    // infinite loop until "e"
            btree_obj.show_menu();
            btree_obj.do_menu();
        }
    }
}
```

Code 11.1 for an OOP implementation of the `people_1d` database using B-tree objects produces this output:

```
OBJECT-ORIENTED PEOPLE DATABASE
        USING B-TREE


Building initial people database ...
add_key_in_btree: Insertion of duplicate key not allowed
add_key_in_btree: Insertion of duplicate key not allowed

Saving People database ...

==  B-Tree Display of Database Records ==
21  54
14  16
48  53
62  63


To continue, depress <Enter> ...

** Objected Oriented People Database **
      People DataBase MAIN MENU

Add a member                 ..  a
Change a member record       ..  c
Show a member record         ..  d
Print entire database        ..  p
Store database on disk       ..  s
```

```
Restore database from disk ..  r
Exit from database           ..  e

Select menu (a, c, d, p, s, r, e): a

Add a Member into People Database
--------------------------------
Member Id <integer>:  50

Member Id:  50
Member Name:  Feliciano Sunga
Member Occupation:  Accountant
Member Age:  42
Member Income (x $1000):  45
Years of Membership:  10

** Objected Oriented People Database **
      People DataBase MAIN MENU

Add a member                 ..  a
Change a member record    ..  c
Show a member record      ..  d
Print entire database     ..  p
Store database on disk    ..  s
Restore database from disk ..  r
Exit from database           ..  e

Select menu (a, c, d, p, s, r, e): p
==  B-Tree Display of Database Records ==
21  54
14  16
48  50  53
62  63


To continue, depress <Enter> ...

** Objected Oriented People Database **
      People DataBase MAIN MENU

Add a member                 ..  a
Change a member record    ..  c
Show a member record      ..  d
Print entire database     ..  p
Store database on disk    ..  s
Restore database from disk ..  r
Exit from database           ..  e

Select menu (a, c, d, p, s, r, e): c
Change a Member Record in Database
--------------------------------

Member Id <integer>:  50
```

```
Change Member Id 50
Hit <Enter> if you do not want to change
------------------------------------
Member Name [Feliciano Sunga]:
Member Occupation [Accountant]:
Member Age   [42]: 40
Member Income  [$45000]: 47
Years of Membership  [10]:

Select menu (a, c, d, p, s, r, e): p
Show a Member in Database
------------------------
Member Id <integer>: 50

Member Name:  Feliciano Sunga
Member Occupation:  Accountant
Member Age:  40
Member Income:  47000
Years of Membership:  10

To continue, depress <Enter> ...

** Objected Oriented People Database **
      People DataBase MAIN MENU

Add a member                .. a
Change a member record      .. c
Show a member record        .. d
Print entire database       .. p
Store database on disk      .. s
Restore database from disk .. r
Exit from database          .. e

Select menu (a, c, d, p, s, r, e): a

Add a Member into People Database
---------------------------------
Member Id <integer>:  45

Member Id:  45
Member Name:  Joseph Fota
Member Occupation:  Software Engineer
Member Age:  28
Member Income (x $1000):  40
Years of Membership:  8

** Objected Oriented People Database **
      People DataBase MAIN MENU

Add a member                .. a
Change a member record      .. c
Show a member record        .. d
Print entire database       .. p
Store database on disk      .. s
```

```
Restore database from disk ..  r
Exit from database           ..  e

Select menu (a, c, d, p, s, r, e): p

==  B-Tree Display of Database Records ==
21   54
14   16
45   48   50   53
62   63



To continue, depress <Enter> ...

Add a member                 ..  a
Change a member record       ..  c
Show a member record         ..  d
Print entire database        ..  p
Store database on disk       ..  s
Restore database from disk ..  r
Exit from database           ..  e

Select menu (a, c, d, p, s, r, e): a

Add a Member into People Database
-------------------------------
Member Id <integer>:  35

Member Id:  35
Member Name:  Mary Anderson
Member Occupation:  Musician
Member Age:  49
Member Income (x $1000):  100
Years of Membership:  15


** Objected Oriented People Database **
        People DataBase MAIN MENU

Add a member                 ..  a
Change a member record       ..  c
Show a member record         ..  d
Print entire database        ..  p
Store database on disk       ..  s
Restore database from disk ..  r
Exit from database           ..  e

Select menu (a, c, d, p, s, r, e): p

==  B-Tree Display of Database Records ==
21   48   54
14   16
35   45
50   53
```

```
62   63


To continue, depress <Enter> ...


** Objected Oriented People Database **
      People DataBase MAIN MENU

Add a member                  ..  a
Change a member record        ..  c
Show a member record          ..  d
Print entire database         ..  p
Store database on disk        ..  s
Restore database from disk ..  r
Exit from database            ..  e

Select menu (a, c, d, p, s, r, e): e

Exiting from database ...
```

Note that the right child node of the node with 21 contains four keys —
45, 48, 50, and 53. While adding the member record with key 35, the same
node is located for the key to be inserted into, but this node being full, it
is split into two halves, and the median key 48 is moved to the root node.
The root node now contains data records with keys 21, 48, and 54.

11.4   Limitations of Implementation

The known limitations of the object-oriented people database that arose
from the implementation in **Code 11.1**, are:

- The delete operation of a record is not implemented.

- The operation `restore_peopl_db_from_disk()` restores the database
  from disk. After getting confirmation from the user, it simply calls
  `init_BTREE()` to nullify the existing nonempty database. This causes
  memory leaks. Before restoring the database, it should deallocate the
  existing nonempty database. This is left as an exercise. In a single-
  user environment, this is acceptable, but in a multi-user environment,
  the problem is very complex; mutual exclusion must be implemented
  before overwriting the working buffer.

- A member record is not inserted in the B-tree if it already exists.

- The member type `DataObject` is so generic that this OOP can be
  easily modified or enhanced to adapt to any database application
  other than for people by redefining the `DataObject` structure.

11.5 Exercises

1. Write and test the destructor ~B_Tree() in **Code 11.1**.

2. Write and test an iterative version of find_key_in_btree(), which is a public member function in **Code 11.1**.

3. Write and test a recursive version of show_btree(), which is a public member function in **Code 11.1**.

4. Write and test a recursive version of store_peopl_db_on_disk(), which is a public member function in **Code 11.1**.

5. Write and test a public member function of the B_Tree class in **Code 11.1**, which deletes a specified key from a B-tree object. (Hint: Need to write supporting functions for "combine," "borrow," and "replace" keys.) Add and test a "delete" menu in the menu system.

6. *Memory Leaks*: The operation restore_peopl_db_from_dsk() in **Code 11.1** restores the people database from disk. After getting confirmation from the user, it simply calls init_BTREE() to nullify the existing and working nonempty database. However, this causes *memory leaks*. Before restoring the database, it should deallocate the existing nonempty database. To this effect, modify and test the public member function restore_peopl_db_from_disk() of the B_Tree class.

7. In **Code 11.1**, modify and test the class B_Tree and the constructor B_Tree(), such that one may specify the order for an object of the B_Tree class. For example, in main(), declare objects with orders 3 and 4:

```
B_Tree  b_tree_obj1(3);  // BTREE_ORDER = 3
B_Tree  b_tree_obj2(4);  // BTREE_ORDER = 4
```

Display and analyze the structures of B-tree objects b_tree_obj1 and b_tree_obj2 for the same set of keys:

$$\{15, 12, 10, 11, 14, 13, 11, 13, 12, 10, 17\}.$$

8. *Project*: Redo Exercise 8-68 for a parts inventory control database using a B-tree object.

12

Applications in Image Processing, Computer Graphics, and Computer-Aided Design

This chapter illustrates the use of multidimensional search tree and search trie objects for applications in image processing, computer-aided design (CAD), and computer graphics. Four applications are presented, two employing comparative-based multidimensional search trees and two employing digital-based multidimensional search tries. All four are applications of spatial data structures.

12.1   2-D Digital Image Compression with a Quadtrie Object

Applications such as those in the areas of office automation (OA), computer imaging and graphics, and geographic information systems often require the management of large image-files.

An array representation is the most simple and most flexible image format. Typically, a digital image is treated as a two-dimensional array of picture elements or *pixels*. A *run* is a sequence of identically valued pixels. An image processed as a sequence of runs is said to be in *raster* format.

Figure 12.1(a) depicts the graphic of an "arrow" in the form of a binary digital image with an 8×8 pixel resolution – the image is a square containing a total of 64 individual picture elements. Each pixel of the image array may take on a value of either 0 or 1. In the context of the current discussion, we will assign the color black to a pixel value of 0 and the color white to a pixel value of 1. The corresponding displayed image, shown in Figure 12.1(b), is said to be a *bitmap image*, as each element of the stored image maps directly to a pixel of the display image array.

For many applications concerned with large digital images, it is often desirable and/or necessary to employ encoding or compression techniques that improve on the efficiency of image storage and transmission. Among the most commonly employed image coding or compression techniques are:

- *runlength coding,*

<table>
<tr><td>0</td><td>0</td><td>0</td><td>1</td><td>1</td><td>0</td><td>0</td><td>0</td></tr>
<tr><td>0</td><td>0</td><td>1</td><td>1</td><td>1</td><td>1</td><td>0</td><td>0</td></tr>
<tr><td>0</td><td>1</td><td>1</td><td>1</td><td>1</td><td>1</td><td>1</td><td>0</td></tr>
<tr><td>1</td><td>1</td><td>1</td><td>1</td><td>1</td><td>1</td><td>1</td><td>1</td></tr>
<tr><td>0</td><td>0</td><td>1</td><td>1</td><td>1</td><td>1</td><td>0</td><td>0</td></tr>
<tr><td>0</td><td>0</td><td>1</td><td>1</td><td>1</td><td>1</td><td>0</td><td>0</td></tr>
<tr><td>0</td><td>0</td><td>1</td><td>1</td><td>1</td><td>1</td><td>0</td><td>0</td></tr>
<tr><td>0</td><td>0</td><td>1</td><td>1</td><td>1</td><td>1</td><td>0</td><td>0</td></tr>
</table>

323
242
161
080
242
242
242
242

(a) stored array   (b) bitmap display   (c) runlength code

FIGURE 12.1. A binary image array and bitmap display.

- *hierarchical coding,*

- *transform coding,*

- *pulse code modulation (PCM),*

- *predictive coding,*

- *interpolative coding,* and

- *statistical coding.*

Runlength coding is one of the simplest, most effective, and widely employed image compression techniques. The basic idea behind this method is the compaction of long runs of image data by replacing each run of repeat information with one instance of the information and a count of how many times it repeats. Thus, for example, in Figure 12.1, the third run of the image (run 2, since the first is labeled as run 0) has a runlength encoding given as

$$1\backslash 0\backslash 6\backslash 1\backslash 1\backslash 1\backslash 0$$

where the backslash character is employed as a means of delimiting the count from the data. This particular encoding indicates that the run of the image under consideration contains one 0 followed by six 1's followed by one 0. Since this is a binary image, it is possible to realize a further reduction by encoding just the run counts. This involves choosing the polarity of the data for the first count and alternating it for each successive count. Thus, assuming that a run always begins with a 0 valued pixel, the runlength code for the previous example is given as 161. Reversing the polarity, the runlength code would be 0161. Figure 12.1 shows the runlength codes for the "arrow" image using the former polarity.

Runlength encoding and decoding of a raster image is the model commonly employed for image compression and decompression in *facsimile* (FAX) transmission systems. While highly efficient, the runlength model possesses two limiting characteristics:

- the runlength coding strips most of the original image structure, leaving the resulting image difficult to manipulate, and

- the image is not complete until each and every row has been processed.

Hierarchical coding schemes tend to be a bit less efficient than the runlength model but retain a higher degree of original image structure. Such coding schemes are advantageous in situations where the amount of data required (i.e., image detail) is variable. Applications in the field of satellite image processing, for example, can exploit *progressive image transmission* to terminate the transmission of a hierarchical digital image when enough data have been received to produce the desired level of image detail.

A digital image array represented as a *region quadtrie* object is one effective means of producing a hierarchical data encoding. Image compression is realized with such a structure through the exploitation of *spatial coherence* and *aggregation*. A region quadtrie recursively subdivides a bounded image array into four equal-sized quadrants. If a resulting (sub)array is not homogeneous, that is, if all the pixels within the (sub)array are not of the same "color," then it is further subdivided. This recursive splitting continues until each region is homogeneous or a maximum resolution (level) is reached.

Property 12.1 *When a digital image is encoded into a region quadtrie, the leaves of the resulting trie object represent a hierarchy of all disjoint homogeneous quadrants of the original digital image. The root of the trie object corresponds to the whole image, while a leaf at the maximum level of subdivision corresponds to a pixel. All intermediate leaves represent quadrants of the image that contain pixels of the same color aggregated into a common block.*

It is this process of combining spatially coherent blocks of pixels that leads to image compression.

The region quadtrie representation of the arrow image is shown in Figure 12.2. The corresponding partitioning of the image-space induced by the quadtrie is shown in Figure 12.3(a). This example is not intended to serve as the most efficient means of compressing the simple binary imagery of the arrow. (A direct storage of the bits of the image into contiguous bytes of memory would be far simpler and efficient.) Our goal is to demonstrate the use of the quadtrie structure and to point out the feature of progressive refinement that hierachical encoding schemes may take advantage of.

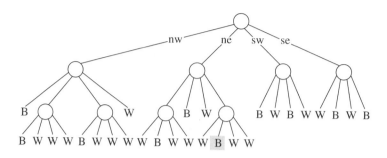

FIGURE 12.2. Region quadtrie for arrow image.

One of the simplest means for building a pointer-based region quadtrie from an array of data is to first construct a pure (complete) quadtrie for the data set and then traverse the entire trie, recursively folding leaf nodes into their parent node if all four children of the parent are of the same color. While this method is feasible, it is not necessarily practical. Its fundamental limitation is the need for storage space to hold the fully populated pure trie.

An alternate to this "top-down" approach is to visit the pixels in an order known as a *Morton order* or *z-order*, as depicted in Figure 12.3(b). The z-order is a convenient mapping of the two-dimensional addressing of the array into a one-dimensional (linear) address. This addressing facilitates a "bottom-up" build of the quadtrie. Given that the children of a quadtrie node are arranged in the order northwest (NW), northeast (NE), southwest (SW), and southeast (SE), the z-order is equivalent to a postorder traversal of the leaf nodes of a complete quadtrie. By following this order, the trie can be constructed in such a manner that no node is created until it represents a homogeneous region.

Code 12.1 is an implementation that constructs a pointer-based region quadtrie from the "arrow" image array of Figure 12.1(a). It is based on a z-order traversal described above and is algorithmically the same as that described by Samet [Same80].

Since a quadtrie encoding of an image realizes its space savings by exploiting spatial coherence and aggregation, the less spatial coherence, the less efficient the quadtrie. In the worst case, as with a "checkerboard" image, there may be no aggregation possible. The quadtrie would end up as a complete or pure trie, where each leaf is at the maximum level and contains a unique pixel. Such a quadtrie encoding would require more storage space and be less accessible than a straight array representation.

While a quadtrie encoding is capable of image compression, it is possible to obtain further compaction by implementing the trie in compact form. Thus, instead of the fully pointered quadtrie, as depicted in Figure 12.2,

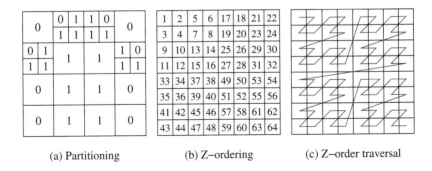

FIGURE 12.3. Region quadtrie partitioning and indexing.

one may choose a semi-pointered or pointerless implementation. As shown in Section 8.9, such compact tries can realize a savings in storage space at the expense of being static structures.

Pointerless tries are lists, and as such, are inefficient at random access. For applications involving digital image compression, transmission, and display, such structures can realize a savings in image storage space while facilitating sequential access. Thus, pointerless tries are a useful means for efficiently storing and displaying static digital images. They commonly exist in one of two forms, *treecodes* and *leafcodes*.

A treecode is a list of all nodes in the trie (tree) encountered under a specified traversal of the entire trie. The traversal is usually preorder (depth-first), and treecodes implemented as such are also known as *depth-first (DF) expressions*. The resulting treecode is a list or string of the node types encountered. If we label internal non-homogeneous nodes as GRAY (G), white homogeneous leaf nodes as WHITE (W), and black homogeneous leaf nodes as BLACK (B), then the treecode corresponding to the region quadtrie of Figure 12.2 is given as

GGBGBWWWGBWWWWGGWBWWBWGWBWWGBWBWGWBWB

The implementation of routines to convert from a M-ary trie object to a treecode and back is straightforward and is left as an exercise.

While a treecode is a list of all nodes, a leafcode is a list of just leaf nodes. In a treecode, each leaf node is represented by three fields: level, a *locational code*, and data. The locational code is a concatenation of base-M (or base-$(M + 1)$, depending on the implementation) numbers or *direction codes* that locate the leaf along a path from the root of the trie to the specified level. A trie in the form of a leafcode is commonly referred to as a *linear trie*. Depending on the implementation, the level field may or may not be necessary.

The function BlackCodes() of **Code 12.1** converts the quadtrie of Figure 12.2 into a leafcode representation. Further compaction is realized by storing only the black nodes in the structure. The white nodes are derivable. The children of a node are assumed to appear in the order NW, NE, SW, SE and are assigned the directional codes 0, 1, 2, and 3, respectively. The locational code of a leaf node is a base-4 (base-M, M = 4) number derived by concatenating the locational codes encountered as the path from the root of the trie to the leaf is traversed. For example, for the leaf node in Figure 12.2 at level 3 that is shaded has a locational code given by the directions <NE,SE,NE> corresponding to the base-4 number <131> or the number 29 in base-10. Thus, the output of BlackCodes() yields 3:29 (level:code) for this black node.

It turns out that if we sort the location codes into ascending order, then the leaves will be accessed in a breadth-first order. This, in turn, is the basis of progressive image refinement.

Property 12.2 *Nodes closer to the root of the trie will be accessed and displayed prior to those at deeper levels. Given the hierarchy of the data in the quadtrie, this results in a coarse image closer to the root and successive refinement as the deeper leaves are filled in.*

Code 12.1

```
// Program:   image.c++
// Purpose:
//    OOP implementation of IMAGE Processing
//    using a QUADTRIE object. It produces a
//    region quadtrie for an image array of size:
//        2^MAX_LEVELS*2^MAX_LEVELS.
//
//    x,y is the location of the SE most pixel of
//    the current subarray of the image.
//
#include  <stdio.h>
const int NW = 0;      // North West
const int NE = 1;      // North East
const int SW = 2;      // South West
const int SE = 3;      // South East
const int BL = 0;      // black
const int WH = 1;      // white
const int GR = 2;      // grey

class  Region_Quadtrie {
  private:
    int      MAX_LEVELS; // e.g., = 3
    int      Size;       // Size = 2^MAX_LEVELS
    typedef struct Pixel {
```

```
        int color;
    } *PIX_PTR;
    typedef struct RQTnode {
        Pixel pixel;
        RQTnode *parent_ptr;
        RQTnode *child[4];
    } *RQTnode_PTR;

    typedef PIX_PTR ImageArray[8][8];
    ImageArray Image;
    RQTnode_PTR root_ptr;
    int   power(int, int);
    int   isLeaf(RQTnode_PTR);
  public:
    Region_Quadtrie(int max_levels);
    ~Region_Quadtrie();

    RQTnode_PTR get_root() {return root_ptr;}
    RQTnode_PTR RQT_create_node(RQTnode_PTR, int, int);
    RQTnode_PTR search_regions(int, int , int, int*);
    void        build_region_quadtrie(void);
    void        RQT_PostOrder(RQTnode_PTR);
    void        BlackCodes(RQTnode_PTR, int, int);
    void        print_image(void);
    void        build_initial_image (void);
};

// --- Implement methods for "Region_Quadtrie"
Region_Quadtrie::Region_Quadtrie (int max_levels)
{
    root_ptr    = NULL;
    MAX_LEVELS  = max_levels;
    Size = power(2, MAX_LEVELS);
}

Region_Quadtrie::~Region_Quadtrie()
{
    // This "Destructor" is left as an exercise
}

Region_Quadtrie::RQTnode_PTR
Region_Quadtrie::search_regions(int csize,
                  int x, int y, int *color)
{
    static int dx[] = {1, 0, 1, 0};
    static int dy[] = {1, 1, 0, 0};
    int i, colors[4];
    RQTnode_PTR inode_ptr, ptrs[4];

    if (csize == 1) {  // at a SE pixel
      *color = Image[y-1][x-1]->color;
      return (NULL);
    }
    else {
```

```
    csize = csize/2;
    for (i = NW; i <= SE; i++)
       // check all children
      ptrs[i] = search_regions(csize, x-csize*dx[i],
                          y-csize*dy[i], &(colors[i]));
      if ((colors[NW] != GR ) &&
          (colors[NW] == colors[SW]) &&
          (colors[NW]==colors[SE]) &&
          (colors[NW] == colors[NE]) ) {
          *color = colors[NW];
          return (NULL);
      }
      else {
        // create an INTERNAL GRAY node
        inode_ptr = RQT_create_node(NULL, NULL, GR);
        for (i = NW; i <= SE; i++) {
           if (ptrs[i] == NULL)
           ptrs[i] = RQT_create_node(inode_ptr, i, colors[i]);
           else {
              inode_ptr->child[i] = ptrs[i];
              ptrs[i]->parent_ptr = inode_ptr;
           }
        }
        *color = GR;
        return(inode_ptr);
      }
   }
}


Region_Quadtrie::RQTnode_PTR
Region_Quadtrie::RQT_create_node
     (RQTnode_PTR root_ptr, int dir, int color)
{
    RQTnode_PTR new_ptr = new RQTnode;

    if (new_ptr == NULL) {
        printf("\n RQT_create_node: malloc failed.\n");
        return (NULL);
    }
    if (root_ptr != NULL)
        root_ptr->child[dir] = new_ptr;
    new_ptr->parent_ptr = root_ptr;
    new_ptr->pixel.color = color;

    for (int i = NW; i <= SE; i++)
        new_ptr->child[i] = NULL;
    return (new_ptr);
}


void Region_Quadtrie::build_region_quadtrie (void)
{
    int         color;
    RQTnode_PTR trie_ptr;
```

```
    trie_ptr = search_regions(Size, Size, Size, &color);
    if (trie_ptr == NULL)
      // create homogeneous (all W or B) node
      root_ptr = RQT_create_node(NULL, NULL, color);
    else
      root_ptr = trie_ptr;
}

void Region_Quadtrie::RQT_PostOrder (RQTnode_PTR trie_ptr)
{
    if (trie_ptr != NULL) {
      RQT_PostOrder(trie_ptr->child[NW]);
      RQT_PostOrder(trie_ptr->child[NE]);
      RQT_PostOrder(trie_ptr->child[SW]);
      RQT_PostOrder(trie_ptr->child[SE]);

      // print only leaf nodes
      if (isLeaf(trie_ptr))
        if (trie_ptr->pixel.color == BL)
          printf(" B");
        else if (trie_ptr->pixel.color == WH)
          printf(" W");
    }
}

int Region_Quadtrie::isLeaf (RQTnode_PTR trie_ptr)
{
    if ((trie_ptr->child[NW] == NULL) &&
        (trie_ptr->child[NE]== NULL)  &&
        (trie_ptr->child[SW]== NULL)  &&
        (trie_ptr->child[SW]== NULL))
      return (1);
    else
      return (0);
}

void Region_Quadtrie::print_image (void)
{
    printf("Image Array:\n");
    printf("------------\n");
    for (int y = 0; y < Size; y++) {
        for (int x = 0; x < Size; x++)
            printf("%d ", Image[y][x]->color);
        printf("\n");
    }
}

int Region_Quadtrie::power(int a, int b)
{
    int i, pw = 1;

    if (b == 0) return (pw);
    for (i = 0; i < b; i++) pw = pw * a;
    return (pw);
```

```
    }

    void Region_Quadtrie::BlackCodes (RQTnode_PTR trie_ptr,
                int code, int level)
    {
        int p = power(4, level), L = level+1;
        int Cnw, Cne, Csw, Cse;
        Cnw = Cne = Csw = Cse = code;

        if (trie_ptr != NULL) {
          BlackCodes(trie_ptr->child[NW], Cnw += p*NW, L);
          BlackCodes(trie_ptr->child[NE], Cne += p*NE, L);
          BlackCodes(trie_ptr->child[SW], Csw += p*SW, L);
          BlackCodes(trie_ptr->child[SE], Cse += p*SE, L);

          // print only BLACK leaf location codes
          if (isLeaf(trie_ptr) && (trie_ptr->pixel.color == BL))
            printf("%d:%d ", level, code);
        }
    }

    void Region_Quadtrie::build_initial_image (void)
    {
        Pixel *pix_ptr;

        // allocate array of pixels
        for (int i = 0; i < Size; i++) {
           for (int j = 0; j < Size; j++) {
              if ((pix_ptr = new Pixel) == NULL) {
                 printf("\n create pixel: malloc failed.\n");
                 //  return (NULL);
                 return;
              }
              Image[i][j] = pix_ptr;
           }
        }
        // build image array (arrow)
        for (i = 0; i < 3; i++)
           Image[0][i]->color = BL;   // BLack
        for (i = 5; i < 8; i++)
           Image[0][i]->color = BL;
        for (i = 0; i < 2; i++)
           Image[1][i]->color = BL;
        for (i = 6; i < 8; i++)
           Image[1][i]->color = BL;
        for (i = 0; i < 1; i++)
           Image[2][i]->color = BL;
        for (i = 7; i < 8; i++)
           Image[2][i]->color = BL;
        for (i = 0; i < 2; i++) {
           Image[4][i]->color = BL;
           Image[5][i]->color = BL;
           Image[6][i]->color = BL;
           Image[7][i]->color = BL;
```

```
        }
        for (i = 6; i < 8; i++) {
            Image[4][i]->color = BL;
            Image[5][i]->color = BL;
            Image[6][i]->color = BL;
            Image[7][i]->color = BL;
        }
        for (i = 3; i < 5; i++)
            Image[0][i]->color = WH;   // WHite
        for (i = 2; i < 6; i++)
            Image[1][i]->color = WH;
        for (i = 1; i < 7; i++)
            Image[2][i]->color = WH;
        for (i = 0; i < 8; i++)
            Image[3][i]->color = WH;
        for (i = 2; i < 6; i++) {
            Image[4][i]->color = WH;
            Image[5][i]->color = WH;
            Image[6][i]->color = WH;
            Image[7][i]->color = WH;
        }
}


//  main():  Test driver for OOP implementation of Image
//           processing using ADT Quadtrie data structure
void  main(void)
{
    //  Declare an object with MAX_LEVELS = 3
    Region_Quadtrie  image_quadtrie_obj(3);

    printf("\n ** OOP IMPLEMENTATION OF %s ** %s\n",
        "IMAGE PROCESSING", "\n                USING QUADTRIE");
    image_quadtrie_obj.build_initial_image ();
    image_quadtrie_obj.print_image ();
    printf("\n");
    image_quadtrie_obj.build_region_quadtrie();
    printf("Leaf nodes of image region quadtrie (postorder)\n");
    printf("----------------------------------------------\n");
    image_quadtrie_obj.RQT_PostOrder
            (image_quadtrie_obj.get_root());
    printf("\n\n");
    printf("Black leaf location codes (level:code)\n");
    printf("------------------------------------\n");
    image_quadtrie_obj.BlackCodes
            (image_quadtrie_obj.get_root(), 0, 0);
    printf("\n");
}
```

Code 12.1 produces this output:

```
                    USING QUADTRIE
    Image Array:
    ------------
    0 0 0 1 1 1 0 0 0
    0 0 1 1 1 1 0 0
    0 1 1 1 1 1 1 0
    1 1 1 1 1 1 1 1
    0 0 1 1 1 1 0 0
    0 0 1 1 1 1 0 0
    0 0 1 1 1 1 0 0
    0 0 1 1 1 1 0 0


    Leaf nodes of quadtrie (postorder)
    ----------------------------------
    B  B  W  W  W  B  W  W  W  W  W  B  W  W  B  W  W  W  B  W  W  B  W  B  W  W  B  W  B


    Black leaf codes (level:code)
    ----------------------------------
    2:0  3:4  3:8  3:17  2:5  3:29  2:2  2:10  2:7  2:15
```

12.2   Computer-Aided VLSI Design Verification with a 4D-Tree Object

The design of *very large-scale integrated (VLSI) circuits* is a computation-ally demanding application that involves the processing of very collections of rectangles. Such an application is impossible without a digital computer and data structures that facilitate query operations on a geometric database of this nature.

An integrated circuit design is usually developed as a series of layers or *masks*. Crucial to the success of a design is the verification that the geometries of each mask layout meet the governing design rules. One common design rule query is the search for all rectangles that do not possess a minimal specified clearance from all other rectangles.

It is shown here how a *4D*-tree object (*kd*-tree, $k = 4$) may be applied to reduce the number of rectangle-to-rectangle comparisons required to perform a minimal clearance design rule check on a layout of rectangles. The algorithm described here is attributed to Lauther [Lau78].

A rectangle is described by its four extremal x-y coordinates, x_min, y_min, x_max, y_max. These coordinates are treated as the keys of a rectangle data record. At any level L in a 4D-tree, the discriminating key of a rectangle R is derived as a modulus four function of the level, denoted by the notation disc(Lmod4,R). The following four equalities describe the boundry of rectangle R:

$$x\_min(R) \quad = \quad disc(0, R); \tag{12.1}$$

$$y\_min(R) = disc(1, R); \tag{12.2}$$
$$x\_max(R) = -disc(2, R); \tag{12.3}$$
$$y\_max(R) = -disc(3, R); \tag{12.4}$$

Consider two rectangles, A and B. In order for rectangle A to intersect rectangle B, all four of the following inequalities must hold:

$$x\_min(A) \leq x\_max(B); \tag{12.5}$$
$$y\_min(A) \leq y\_max(B); \tag{12.6}$$
$$-x\_max(A) \leq -x\_min(B); \tag{12.7}$$
$$-y\_max(A) \leq -y\_min(B); \tag{12.8}$$

To take into account rectangle-to-rectangle clearance, we bloat the geometry of one rectangle by a clearance distance c. The inequalities given by equations 12.6 through 12.8 are conveniently restated in terms of discriminators and a clearance factor c:

$$disc(0, A) \leq -disc(2, B) + c; \tag{12.9}$$
$$disc(1, A) \leq -disc(3, B) + c; \tag{12.10}$$
$$disc(2, A) \leq -disc(0, B) + c; \tag{12.11}$$
$$disc(3, A) \leq -disc(1, B) + c; \tag{12.12}$$

If any of the conditions stated in equations 12.6 through 12.8 are violated, then rectangles A and B do not intersect. Furthermore, if any of the conditions stated in equations 12.10 through 12.12 are violated, then rectangles A and B not only do not intersect but are separated by the specified minimal clearance.

A trivial layout of eight rectangles, labeled a through h, is illustrated in Figure 12.4. The geometric bounds corresponding to a bloating of the rectangles a and e by one unit is shown in dashed lines. If all rectangles are supposed to be separated by the minimal clearance, then a design rule check should reveal two violations: the overlap of rectangles g and f and the lack of minimal clearance between rectangles d and e.

Algorithmically, the 4D-tree based rule checker is comprised of a tree preprocessing phase followed by a traversal phase. During the preprocessing phase, a height-balanced kd-tree is built using a median-finding algorithm. The balanced 4D-tree for the data of Figure 12.4 is shown in Figure 12.5.

Once the tree is built, a search based on a modified inorder traversal finds all violating rectangles. An outline of the method is:

Step 1. Traverse the left subtree if it is not empty.

Step 2. Process the root node (N_r); for the rectangle (R_{root}) associated with the root node:

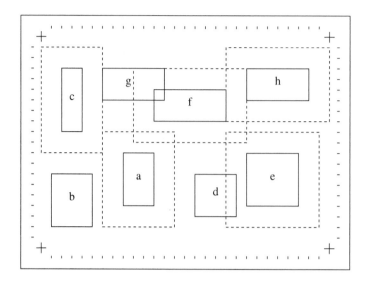

FIGURE 12.4. A simple layout of rectangles.

(a) Test R_{root} against all the remaining unprocessed nodes. These are simply the inorder successors of N_r.

(b) If a successor node (N_s) is encountered with discriminator d such that

```
disc(d, Ns) > - disc((d + 2)%4, Nr) + c
```

then all successors of N_r that are in the right subtree of N_s need not be examined.

Step 3. Traverse the right subtree if it is not empty.

Search pruning is evidenced by Step 2(b), above. As a result of the geometric sorting accomplished by the tree build, all nodes in the right subtree of a node N_s that meet the indicated condition may be rejected, as it is guaranteed that each will violate one of the conditions necessary for intersection. As an example, consider for the data of Figure 12.4, a search with node b as the root node N_r and node f as the current search node N_s. Inequalities 2(a) and 2(b) do not hold in this case and thus it is determined that N_r and N_s do not intersect. The remaining inorder successors of f to be examined are nodes d, e, and h, all in the right subtree of f. Yet, we know from testing condition 2(a) that $disc(0, f) > -disc(2, b)$. By definition, it is also known that all nodes, N, in the right subtree of f must have $disc(0, N) > disc(0, f)$. Therefore, the nodes d, e, and h can be ignored as it known that condition 2(a) must fail between them and node b. This

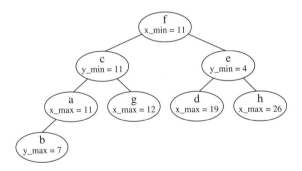

FIGURE 12.5. Balanced 4D-tree for rectangle data.

pruning action demonstrates the benefit of a 4D-tree implementation over an exhaustive search in which every rectangle is checked against all others.

A pointer-based implementation of a 4D-tree for the design-rule verification algorithm described here is given below as **Code 12.2**. The function `FourDT_build_balanced()` builds a height-balanced 4D-tree. This routine is analogous to the `MBST_build_balanced()` routine given in **Code 9.1** of Chapter 9. Both utilize the same `quickselect()` median-finding algorithm. The function `FourDT_rule_search()` implements the modified inorder tree traversal on the preprocessed tree, employing the routine `rectangles_intersect()` to find all sets of rectangles that either overlap or violate a specified one unit clearance.

Code 12.2

```
// Program:  kdtree_VLSI.c++
// Purpose:
//    OOP implementation of a VLSI database using a
//    4d-tree ( kd-tree, k = 4) data structure.
//    For rectangles, labeled a through e (Figure 12-3)
//    correspond to rectangles 0 through 7, respectively.
//
#include <stdio.h>
#ifdef   MSDOS
#include <alloc.h>
#include "peopl_db.cpp"
#else
#include <malloc.h>
#include "peopl_db.c++"  // See Appendix C;
#endif

const int X     = 0; const int Y    = 1;
const int XMIN  = 0; const int YMIN  = 1;
const int XMAX  = 2; const int YMAX  = 3;
const int INITIAL_DISC = 0;
```

```
#define NEXTD(d)((d)+1)%D

const int  D = 4;        // four-dimensional k-d tree
const int  NUMOBJ = 8; // in People database
typedef int Keytype;
typedef Keytype Key4[D];

class VLSI_4DTree {
  private:

    struct Rectangle {
    Key4    key;    // key[0] = x_min, key[1] = y_min
    int     rid;    // key[2] = x_max, key[3] = y_max
    };

    typedef struct FourDT_node {  // kdnode
      Rectangle    rectangle;
      FourDT_node  *lo_ptr;    // "left"
      FourDT_node  *hi_ptr;    // "right"
    } *FourDT_PTR;

    FourDT_PTR  root_ptr;
    void        init_VLSI_4DTree() { root_ptr = NULL; }
    Keytype     quickselect(Keytype *, int, int);
    Keytype     quickselect1(Keytype *, int, int, int);
  public:
    VLSI_4DTree() { root_ptr = NULL; } // Constructor
    ~VLSI_4DTree();                          // Destructor

    void    FourDT_rule_search
                    (FourDT_PTR, FourDT_PTR, int, int);
    FourDT_PTR    FourDT_build_balanced
                    (FourDT_PTR, int, int);
    void    check_inorder_successors
                    (FourDT_PTR, Rectangle, int, int);
    int     rectangles_intersect
                    (Rectangle, Rectangle, int);
    void    rectlist_insert(Rectangle, FourDT_PTR *);
    FourDT_PTR    create_FourDTnode(Rectangle);
    void    FourDT_InOrder(FourDT_PTR);
    void    build_initial_VLSI_4Dtree(void);
    FourDT_PTR get_root() { return root_ptr; }
};

// ---  Implement methods for "VLSI_4DTree" class

VLSI_4DTree::~VLSI_4DTree()
{
    // Destructor:  Left as an exercise
}


VLSI_4DTree::FourDT_PTR VLSI_4DTree::create_FourDTnode
                                      (Rectangle r)
```

```
{
  FourDT_PTR new_ptr = new FourDT_node;

  if (new_ptr == NULL) {
    printf("\n create_FourDTnode: alloc failed.\n");
    return (NULL);
  }
  new_ptr->rectangle = r;
  new_ptr->lo_ptr = NULL;
  new_ptr->hi_ptr = NULL;
  return (new_ptr);
}

void VLSI_4DTree::rectlist_insert
                (Rectangle  rect, FourDT_PTR *head)
{
  FourDT_PTR new_ptr;

  new_ptr = create_FourDTnode (rect);
  new_ptr->hi_ptr = *head;    // use hi as "next"
  *head = new_ptr;
}

//  FourDT_build_balanced():
//    Build balanced. Uses quickselect() to find
//    the median key values. (Recursive method)
//
VLSI_4DTree::FourDT_PTR
  VLSI_4DTree::FourDT_build_balanced(FourDT_PTR rootlist_ptr,
                                     int nobj, int disc)
{
  int          i, hi, lo, flag = 1;
  Keytype      *keys, curr_key, med_key;
  FourDT_PTR   rtlist_ptr,   lolist_ptr = NULL;
  FourDT_PTR   med_node_ptr, hilist_ptr = NULL;

  if ((rtlist_ptr = rootlist_ptr) == NULL)
    return (NULL);
  keys = (Keytype *) malloc(nobj * sizeof(Keytype));

  // get the keys for the current discriminator
  for (i = 0; i < nobj; i++) {
    keys[i] = rtlist_ptr->rectangle.key[disc];
    rtlist_ptr = rtlist_ptr->hi_ptr;
  }
  // find median index and key
  med_key = quickselect(keys, nobj, nobj/2);

  for (i = 0, lo = 0, hi = 0; i < nobj; i++) {
    curr_key = rootlist_ptr->rectangle.key[disc];

    if (curr_key > med_key) {       // put in hi list
      rectlist_insert
              (rootlist_ptr->rectangle, &hilist_ptr);
```

```
      hi++;
    }
    else if ((curr_key == med_key) && flag) {
      med_node_ptr = rootlist_ptr; flag = 0;
    } else {        // put in lo list
        rectlist_insert
               (rootlist_ptr->rectangle, &lolist_ptr);
        lo++;
    }
    rootlist_ptr = rootlist_ptr->hi_ptr;
  }
  med_node_ptr->lo_ptr = FourDT_build_balanced
                        (lolist_ptr, lo, NEXTD(disc));
  med_node_ptr->hi_ptr = FourDT_build_balanced
                        (hilist_ptr, hi, NEXTD(disc));
  return (med_node_ptr);
}


int VLSI_4DTree::rectangles_intersect
          (Rectangle A, Rectangle B, int clearance)
{
  if ((A.key[XMIN] <= (B.key[XMAX] + clearance)) &&
      (A.key[YMIN] <= (B.key[YMAX] + clearance)) &&
      (-A.key[XMAX] <= (-B.key[XMIN] + clearance)) &&
      (-A.key[YMAX] <= (-B.key[YMIN] + clearance)) )
    return (1);
  else return (0);
}


//  FourDT_rule_search():
//     Recursive search in a 4D-tree
//
void VLSI_4DTree::FourDT_rule_search
  (FourDT_PTR root_ptr,FourDT_PTR tree_ptr,int C,int d)
{
  Rectangle node_root;

  if (tree_ptr != NULL) {
    FourDT_rule_search
          (root_ptr, tree_ptr->lo_ptr, C, NEXTD(d));
    node_root = tree_ptr->rectangle;
    check_inorder_successors(root_ptr,node_root,C,d);
    FourDT_rule_search
          (root_ptr, tree_ptr->hi_ptr, C, NEXTD(d));
  }
}


void VLSI_4DTree::check_inorder_successors
      (FourDT_PTR tree_ptr, Rectangle Nr, int C, int d)
{
  if ((tree_ptr != NULL) &&
      (tree_ptr->rectangle.rid != Nr.rid) ) {
    check_inorder_successors
                (tree_ptr->lo_ptr, Nr, C, NEXTD(d));
```

```
    if (tree_ptr->rectangle.rid != Nr.rid) {
      if (rectangles_intersect
                (tree_ptr->rectangle, Nr, C))
        printf(" design violation: rectangles %d and %d\n",
                tree_ptr->rectangle.rid, Nr.rid);
      if (tree_ptr->rectangle.key[d] >
                      (Nr.key[(d+2)%4] + C))    return;
      }
      check_inorder_successors
              (tree_ptr->hi_ptr, Nr, C, NEXTD(d));
  }
}


void VLSI_4DTree::FourDT_InOrder
                            (FourDT_PTR tree_ptr)
{
  if (tree_ptr != NULL) {
    FourDT_InOrder(tree_ptr->lo_ptr);
    printf(" %d\n ", tree_ptr->rectangle.rid);
    FourDT_InOrder(tree_ptr->hi_ptr);
  }
}


Keytype VLSI_4DTree::quickselect
          (Keytype array[], int size, int m)
{
  return(quickselect1(array, 0, size - 1, m));
}


Keytype VLSI_4DTree::quickselect1
    (Keytype *array, int lower, int upper, int med)
{
  int      j,k;
  Keytype amem, tmp;

  if (lower < upper) {
    amem = array[lower];
    j = lower; k = upper;
    while (j < k) {
      while (array[j] <= amem && j < upper) j+=1;
      while (array[k] >= amem && k > lower) k-=1;
      if (j < k) {
        tmp = array[j];
        array[j] = array[k];
        array[k] = tmp;
      }
    }
    // swap A[lower] and A[k]
    tmp = array[lower];
    array[lower] = array[k];
    array[k] = tmp;
    if (upper <= med) lower = k+1;
    if (upper >= med) upper = k-1;
  }
```

```
    return(array[med]);
}

//  build_initial_VLSI_4Dtree():
//
void VLSI_4DTree::build_initial_VLSI_4Dtree(void)
{
    Keytype      range[D][2];
    FourDT_PTR   rlist_ptr = NULL;

    // {x_min, y_min, x_max, y_max}
    static Key4 keys[] = {
                    {8,  4,  11, 9},       // a
                    {1,  2,  5,  7},       // b
                    {2,  11, 4,  17},      // c
                    {15, 3,  19, 7},       // d
                    {20, 4,  25, 9},       // e
                    {11, 12, 18, 15},      // f
                    {6,  14, 12, 17},      // g
                    {20, 14, 26, 17} };    // h

    Rectangle rectangles[NUMOBJ];

    init_VLSI_4DTree();
    for (int i = 0; i < NUMOBJ; i++) {
      rectangles[i].rid = i;
      for (int j = 0; j < D; j++)
        rectangles[i].key[j] = keys[i][j];
      rectlist_insert(rectangles[i], &rlist_ptr);
    }
    root_ptr = FourDT_build_balanced
                (rlist_ptr, NUMOBJ, INITIAL_DISC);
}

// main():   OOP VLSI Design using 4-D tree.
//
void main(void)
{
    //  Declare a VLSI_4DTree type object
    VLSI_4DTree   VLSI_4dtree_obj;
    int           Clearance = 1;

    printf ("\n ** OOP IMPLEMENTATION %s **\n %s \n\n",
        "OF VLSI DESIGN", "                USING 4D-TREE");
    VLSI_4dtree_obj.build_initial_VLSI_4Dtree();
    printf(" Design rule verification summary:\n");
    printf(" -------------------------------\n");
    VLSI_4dtree_obj.FourDT_rule_search
            (VLSI_4dtree_obj.get_root(),
             VLSI_4dtree_obj.get_root(), Clearance, 0);
}
```

Code 12.2 produces this output:

```
** OOP IMPLEMENTATION OF VLSI DESIGN **
            USING 4D-TREE

Design rule verification summary:
---------------------------------
design violation: rectangles 5 and  6
design violation: rectangles 3 and  4
```

12.3 3-D Ray-Tracing Acceleration with an Octrie Object

In the field of computer graphics, one popular method employed for producing highly realistic 2-*D* images of a 3-*D* synthetic world is *ray-tracing*. This technique is a digital simulation of the physical process of how a camera captures a scene on film.

Figure 12.6 depicts the basic configuration of such a simulation. A *synthetic camera* is modeled as a viewpoint (E) and an image "film" in the form of 2-*D* array of pixels. Light *rays* emitting from various sources are traced through the scene, reflecting from object to object, finally arriving at the viewpoint. The "value" of a light ray is recorded at the pixel intersected on the image array. As a matter of practicality, this process is usually executed in reverse. By starting at the viewpoint, the simulation can be focused on the *primary* rays of interest, which are those from the viewpoint through each pixel of the image array. Such a process is known as *backward ray-tracing*.

Image synthesis by ray tracing is algorithmically straightforward but computationally expensive. In order to render an image of reasonable resolution and quality, a substantial number of primary and multiply reflected rays need to be considered. Our goal in this section is to show how to reduce the amount of computation required. While the above description is basic, a more detailed discussion of the physical or mathematical intricacies of the ray tracing process does not serve our purpose.

The cost of ray tracing is dominated by the sheer number of ray-object intersection calculations required. Consider the solution for a single pixel on the image film, starting with the primary ray emanating from the viewpoint and passing through this pixel. The first task is to determine the first (if any) object hit by the ray. The brute force approach of a *naive* ray tracer amounts to intersecting the ray with each and every object in the environment and selecting the intersection closest to the origin of the

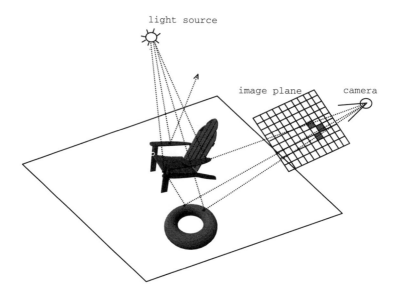

FIGURE 12.6. Tracing light rays.

ray. Such an exhaustive search is costly in an environment comprised of many geometric objects. Once the appropriate intersection is found, the effect of the collision with the surface of the object is recorded, the ray is reflected/refracted about the surface, and the trace continues in a recursive manner until the ray either exits the environment or some specified termination condition is reached. This process is repeated for each and every pixel in the image plane.

One way to reduce the number of ray-object intersection tests is to organize the objects in the environment into a hierarchical data structure. The most commonly employed data structuring techniques fall into two major categories:

- *object subdivision*, and

- *space subdivision*.

A *hierarchical extent tree* is an example of object subdivision — it is an object-based search tree that organizes objects into a hierarchy of *bounding volumes*, clustering objects together and recording the space they occupy. The basic idea behind a hierarchy of bounding volumes is that if a ray does not intersect a given parent volume it cannot intersect the child volumes (and their associated objects) within. These volumes and objects are effectively pruned from the search.

An *octrie* object, on the other hand, is an example of space subdivision — it is a space-based search trie that subdivides the environment into a hierarchy of disjoint volume elements or *voxels*, the 3-*D* analog of a pixel, and records how the objects occupy these subregions of space. Each ray is subsequently "walked" through the array of voxels in the direction of its propagation and is tested against the objects contained in each encountered region, a process often referred to as *space tracing*.

A ray-tracer implemented using an octrie object is presented as **Code 12.3**. The whole environment, corresponding to the root voxel, is defined as a cube, 200 units on a side, and contains a group of three spheres, each described in terms of its center and radius. The octrie is built as a preprocessing stage by OCTRIE_build(), which calls OCTRIE_insert_obj() for each sphere object. OCTRIE_insert_obj() is a recursive routine that inserts a sphere object at the appropriate leaf node (voxel) in the trie. The number of spheres that may occupy a leaf voxel is specified by a bucket size. If an object arrives at a full bucket and the maximum level has not been reached, then the voxel is further subdivided. The function sphere_in_voxel() is called by the object insertion routine to determine if a given sphere is contained within a given voxel. This is done by comparing the distance between the center of the sphere and the center of the voxel with the combined distances of the radius of the sphere and the distance from the center of the voxel to any corner of the voxel. This routine is an approximation, as it will always accurately determine that a sphere is not contained (fully or partially) while it may accept a sphere that is actually outside. This will not lead to an error but may precipitate some unnecessary intersection calculations.

The trie build is a preprocess step and the trie is static once it is completed. The function sphere_in_voxel() takes a ray and steps it through the 3-*D* voxel array, returning the coordinates of the intersection point with the first object hit (if any). At any given voxel, the function ray_intersects_sphere() intersects the ray with all spheres contained within the voxel. If there is no intersection then the "next" cell in the forward direction of the ray is located by OCTRIE_next_voxel(). The next cell is located by first finding the point at which the ray exits the current voxel. This is accomplished by intersect_ray_voxel(), although the implementation given here does not take into account the special case of a ray exiting a corner or an edge. OCTRIE_point_in_next_voxel() then steps a small distance from the exit point in a direction away from the exit face to obtain a point in the next voxel. The step size is chosen as half the length of a side of the smallest possible voxel, a distance that guarantees that we do not step beyond one neighboring voxel. Given a point in the next voxel, OCTRIE_voxel_search() searches from the root of the trie to determine the leaf that contains this point. The process proceeds from voxel to voxel until an intersection is located or the bounds of the environment are reached. Since voxels are disjoint, the first intersection found is known to be reliable.

Note that **Code 12.3** fires a single ray and finds an intersection within the environment, but it does not reflect that ray (and thus does not recurse). A good exercise would be to modify the code to reflect an incident ray recursively.

Code 12.3

```
//   Program:  octrie_ray.c++
//   Purpose:
//     OOP implementation of 3-D Ray-Tracing
//     Acceleration with an Octrie_Ray
//
#include <stdio.h>
#include <math.h>
#ifdef    MSDOS
#include <alloc.h>
#define   SQRT(x) (sqrt(x))
typedef   double  Coord[3];
#else
#include <malloc.h>
#define   SQRT(x) (fsqrt(x))
typedef   float  Coord[3];
#endif
const int ERROR= NULL;
const int INTERNAL = 0;
const int LEAF= 1;
const int X= 0;
const int Y= 1;
const int Z= 2;
const int LEFT= 1;
const int RIGHT= 2;
const int TOP= 3;
const int BOTTOM= 4;
const int FRONT= 5;
const int BACK= 6;
const int BUCKET_SIZE = 2;
const int MAX_LEVELS  = 10;

class Octrie_Ray {
  private:
    typedef int Nodetype;
    struct Voxel {  // define type Voxel
       Coord Lcoord;
       Coord Hcoord;
    };
    struct Ray {  // define type Ray
       Coord origin;
       Coord dir;
    };
    struct Sphere {  // define type Sphere
       char  *label;
       Coord center;
       float radius;
    };
```

```
    typedef struct OCTRIE_dummy {
       Nodetype     type;
    } *OCTRIE_PTR;

    typedef struct OCTRIE_InternalNode {
       Nodetype     type;
       OCTRIE_dummy  *child[8];
    } *IPTR;

    typedef struct OCTRIE_LeafNode {
       Nodetype     type;
       int          nobj;    // number of objects held by node
       Sphere *objptr[BUCKET_SIZE]; // array of ptrs to spheres
    } *LEAF_PTR;

    OCTRIE_PTR root_ptr;
    float RootMin[3], RootMid[3], RootMax[3];

  public:
    Octrie_Ray()  { root_ptr = NULL; }  // Constructor
    ~Octrie_Ray();                        // Destructor
    OCTRIE_PTR OCTRIE_create_node(Nodetype);
    OCTRIE_PTR OCTRIE_insert_obj(Sphere*,
                         OCTRIE_PTR, Voxel);
    void       build_OCTRIE(Sphere*, int, Voxel);
    void       build_ray_and_show (void);
    Sphere*    OCTRIE_raytrace(OCTRIE_PTR, Ray,
                            Voxel, Coord);
    LEAF_PTR   OCTRIE_next_voxel(OCTRIE_PTR, Ray,
                            Voxel, Voxel*);
    LEAF_PTR   OCTRIE_voxel_search(OCTRIE_PTR,
                            Coord, Voxel*);
    Coord*     OCTRIE_point_in_next_voxel(Coord,
                            int, float);
    int        intersect_ray_voxel(Ray, Voxel, Coord*,
                            Coord*, int*, int*);
    int        sphere_in_voxel(Voxel, Sphere*);
    int        ray_intersects_sphere(Sphere*, Ray,
                            Coord);
    unsigned   find_direction(Coord, float*, float*,
                               float*);
    int        normalize(Coord);
    void       OCTRIE_PostOrder(OCTRIE_PTR);
    OCTRIE_PTR get_root() { return root_ptr; }
};
// --- Globals
float Step;
Octrie_Ray::Voxel
  root_voxel = { {0., 0., 0.},  // ENVIRONMENT BOUNDS
                 {200., 200., 200.}};

// --- Implement methods of "Octrie_Ray" class

Octrie_Ray::~Octrie_Ray()  // Destructor
```

```
{
    // Left as an exercise
}

Octrie_Ray::OCTRIE_PTR
Octrie_Ray::OCTRIE_create_node(Nodetype type)
{
    OCTRIE_PTR new_ptr;

    if (type == LEAF) {
      if ((new_ptr = (OCTRIE_PTR)malloc(sizeof(OCTRIE_LeafNode)))
                       == NULL) {
            printf("\n create_node: malloc failed \n\n");
            return (NULL);
        }
        ((LEAF_PTR)new_ptr)->type = type;
        ((LEAF_PTR)new_ptr)->nobj = 0;
        printf("Creating LEAF node\n");
        return (new_ptr);
    }
    else {
        if ((new_ptr = (OCTRIE_PTR)malloc(
                       sizeof(OCTRIE_InternalNode)))== NULL) {
            printf("\n create_node: malloc failed \n\n");
            return (NULL);
        }
        for (int i = 0; i < 8; i++)
            ((IPTR)new_ptr)->child[i] = NULL;
        ((IPTR)new_ptr)->type = type;
        printf("Creating INTERNAL node\n");
        return ((OCTRIE_PTR)new_ptr);
    }
}

//  build_OCTRIE():
//     Build an octrie of nobj objects.
void Octrie_Ray::build_OCTRIE(Sphere *obj, int nobj, Voxel V)
{
    for (int i = 0; i < nobj; i++)
        root_ptr = OCTRIE_insert_obj(&(obj[i]),
                                         root_ptr, V);
}

//  OCTRIE_insert_obj():
//     Recursively insert a sphere into the octrie.
//
Octrie_Ray::OCTRIE_PTR
Octrie_Ray::OCTRIE_insert_obj(Sphere *Nsp,
                     OCTRIE_PTR root_ptr, Voxel vox)
{
    Coord       min, mid, max;
    Voxel       subvox[8];
    OCTRIE_PTR  new_ptr;
```

```
max[X] = vox.Hcoord[X]; min[X] = vox.Lcoord[X];
max[Y] = vox.Hcoord[Y]; min[Y] = vox.Lcoord[Y];
max[Z] = vox.Hcoord[Z]; min[Z] = vox.Lcoord[Z];

// mid[X,Y,Z] is the center of the current voxel
for (int i = 0; i < 3; i++)
    mid[i] = min[i] + (max[i]-min[i])/2.;

//************************
// CASE 1: at a null node *
//************************
if (root_ptr == NULL) {
    if (sphere_in_voxel(vox, Nsp)) {
        new_ptr = OCTRIE_create_node(LEAF);
        ((LEAF_PTR)new_ptr)->objptr[0] = Nsp;
        ((LEAF_PTR)new_ptr)->nobj = 1;
        return ((OCTRIE_PTR)new_ptr);
    }
 return(root_ptr);
}
//************************
// CASE 2: at a LEAF node *
//************************
//
//   (a) if numobjs for current leaf < BUCKET_SIZE,
//       add NEWOBJ  to list for leaf.
//   (b) else need to split, create INTERNAL node(s)
//

// note: may want to free() redundant nodes

if (root_ptr->type == LEAF) {
    int n = ((LEAF_PTR)root_ptr)->nobj; // #obj at leaf

    // if below bucket capacity and
    // sphere is in voxel, insert here
    if ((n < BUCKET_SIZE) &&
         sphere_in_voxel(vox, Nsp) ) {
        ((LEAF_PTR)root_ptr)->objptr[n] = Nsp;
        ((LEAF_PTR)root_ptr)->nobj += 1;
        return (root_ptr);
    }
    else {
      // otherwise, create an internal node.
      // Recursively insert existing objects
      // into children. Then recursively insert
      // the new object.

      new_ptr = OCTRIE_create_node(INTERNAL);
      for (i = 0; i < n; i++)
        OCTRIE_insert_obj(((LEAF_PTR)root_ptr)->objptr[i],
                                          new_ptr, vox);

      // insert the NEW object @ the new internal node
```

```
              root_ptr = OCTRIE_insert_obj(Nsp, new_ptr, vox);
         }
    }
    else {

         //*****************************
         // CASE 3: at an INTERNAL node *
         //*****************************
         // Insert NEW object in all applicable directions

         subvox[0].Lcoord[X] = min[X];
         subvox[0].Lcoord[Y] = min[Y];
         subvox[0].Lcoord[Z] = min[Z];    // DFL
         subvox[0].Hcoord[X] = mid[X];
         subvox[0].Hcoord[Y] = mid[Y];
         subvox[0].Hcoord[Z] = mid[Z];
         subvox[1].Lcoord[X] = min[X];
         subvox[1].Lcoord[Y] = min[Y];
         subvox[1].Lcoord[Z] = mid[Z];    // DBL
         subvox[1].Hcoord[X] = mid[X];
         subvox[1].Hcoord[Y] = mid[Y];
         subvox[1].Lcoord[Z] = max[Z];
         subvox[2].Lcoord[X] = mid[X];
         subvox[2].Lcoord[Y] = min[Y];
         subvox[2].Lcoord[Z] = min[Z];    // DFR
         subvox[2].Hcoord[X] = max[X];
         subvox[2].Hcoord[Y] = mid[Y];
         subvox[2].Lcoord[Z] = mid[Z];
         subvox[3].Lcoord[X] = mid[X];
         subvox[3].Lcoord[Y] = min[Y];
         subvox[3].Lcoord[Z] = mid[Z];    // DBR
         subvox[3].Hcoord[X] = max[X];
         subvox[3].Hcoord[Y] = mid[Y];
         subvox[3].Lcoord[Z] = max[Z];
         subvox[4].Lcoord[X] = min[X];
         subvox[4].Lcoord[Y] = mid[Y];
         subvox[4].Lcoord[Z] = min[Z];    // UFL
         subvox[4].Hcoord[X] = mid[X];
         subvox[4].Hcoord[Y] = max[Y];
         subvox[4].Lcoord[Z] = mid[Z];
         subvox[5].Lcoord[X] = min[X];
         subvox[5].Lcoord[Y] = mid[Y];
         subvox[5].Lcoord[Z] = mid[Z];    // UBL
         subvox[5].Hcoord[X] = mid[X];
         subvox[5].Hcoord[Y] = max[Y];
         subvox[5].Lcoord[Z] = max[Z];
         subvox[6].Lcoord[X] = mid[X];
         subvox[6].Lcoord[Y] = mid[Y];
         subvox[6].Lcoord[Z] = min[Z];    // UFR
         subvox[6].Hcoord[X] = max[X];
         subvox[6].Hcoord[Y] = max[Y];
         subvox[6].Lcoord[Z] = mid[Z];
         subvox[7].Lcoord[X] = mid[X];
         subvox[7].Lcoord[Y] = mid[Y];
```

```
        subvox[7].Lcoord[Z] = mid[Z];    // UBR
        subvox[7].Hcoord[X] = max[X];
        subvox[7].Hcoord[Y] = max[Y];
        subvox[7].Lcoord[Z] = max[Z];

        for (i = 0; i < 8; i++) {
          if (sphere_in_voxel(subvox[i], Nsp))
            ((IPTR)root_ptr)->child[i] =
                OCTRIE_insert_obj(Nsp,
                    ((IPTR)root_ptr)->child[i], subvox[i]);
        }
    }
    return(root_ptr);
}


//  OCTRIE_raytrace():
//    Given an environment of geometric objects encoded
//    into an octrie and a directed ray.  Trace the ray
//    through the environment. Computes the first
//    intersection in the path of the ray. Returns pointer
//    to sphere (and hit coord) if there is a hit, else
//    returns NULL (ray exits environment without a hit).
//
Octrie_Ray::Sphere*
Octrie_Ray::OCTRIE_raytrace(OCTRIE_PTR root_ptr, Ray ray,
                      Voxel rootvox, Coord hit)
{
    LEAF_PTR leafptr;
    Voxel CurrVox;

    CurrVox = rootvox;
    leafptr = OCTRIE_voxel_search(root_ptr, ray.origin, &CurrVox);

    while (leafptr != NULL) {
      int n = leafptr->nobj;
      for (int i = 0; i < n; i++)
        if (ray_intersects_sphere(leafptr->objptr[i], ray, hit))
            return (leafptr->objptr[i]);
    leafptr = OCTRIE_next_voxel(root_ptr, ray, CurrVox, &CurrVox);
    }
    return (NULL);
}

// sphere_in_voxel():
//    Routine to test if a given sphere occupies (partial or
//    full) a specified 3d box.
//    Used by octrie build routine to determine voxel occupancy.
//
int  Octrie_Ray::sphere_in_voxel(Voxel v, Sphere *sphere)
{
    float radsqr = 0., radsqr_vox = 0.;
    Coord min, max, mid;

    max[X] = v.Hcoord[X]; min[X] = v.Lcoord[X];
```

```
    max[Y] = v.Hcoord[Y]; min[Y] = v.Lcoord[Y];
    max[Z] = v.Hcoord[Z]; min[Z] = v.Lcoord[Z];

    for (int i = X; i <= Z; i++) {
        // mid[X,Y,Z] is the center of the current voxel
        mid[i] = min[i] + (max[i]-min[i])/2.;
        radsqr_vox += (min[i]-mid[i]) * (min[i] - mid[i]);
        radsqr += (mid[i] - sphere->center[i]) * (mid[i] -
                    sphere->center[i]);
    }
    if (radsqr > radsqr_vox + sphere->radius)  // outside
        return (0);
    else
        return (1);
}


//  OCTRIE_voxel_search():
//    Given a ptr to an octrie and a target point (x,y,z).
//    Search for a leaf node that contains the coord.
//    Return a ptr to such node (and the bounds of the
//    corresponding voxel). Return NULL if not found.
//    (Nonrecursive implementation)
//
Octrie_Ray::LEAF_PTR
Octrie_Ray::OCTRIE_voxel_search(OCTRIE_PTR root_ptr,
                            Coord pt, Voxel *vox)
{
    float voxmin[3], voxmid[3], voxmax[3];
    OCTRIE_PTR node_ptr = root_ptr;

    for (int i = X; i <= Z; i++) {
        voxmin[i] = RootMin[i];
        voxmid[i] = RootMid[i];
        voxmax[i] = RootMax[i];
    }
    while (node_ptr->type != LEAF) {
        int d = find_direction(pt, voxmin, voxmax, voxmid);
        node_ptr = ((IPTR)node_ptr)->child[d];
    }
    for (i = X; i <= Z; i++) {
        vox->Lcoord[i] = voxmin[i];
        vox->Hcoord[i] = voxmax[i];
    }
    return ((LEAF_PTR)node_ptr);
}


//  find_direction():
//    order of voxels (0-8) = (LBF,LBB,LTF,LTB,
//                             RBF,RBB,RTF,RTB)
//
unsigned Octrie_Ray::find_direction(Coord pt, float *min,
                                    float *mid, float *max)
{
    unsigned d = 0;
```

```
    for (int i = X; i < Z; i++) {
        d = d << 1;
        if (pt[i] > mid[i] ) {
            min[i] = mid[i];
            d++;
        }
        else max[i] = mid[i];
    }
    return (d);
}


// intersect_ray_voxel():
//    Algorithm credited to Glassner [Glas89].
//    Returns side of exit intersection
//
int Octrie_Ray::intersect_ray_voxel(Ray ray, Voxel vox,
                    Coord *ienter, Coord *iexit,
                    int *inface, int *outface)
{
    int     i, Enter_vox, Exit_vox, in = 0, out = 0;
    float   inv_d, min, max;
    float   dlo, dhi, CurrNear, CurrFar;

    static int face[3][2] = {{LEFT, RIGHT}, {BOTTOM, TOP},
                            {FRONT, BACK}};

    // if ray is parallel to any plane, reject ray.
    for (i = X; i <= Z; i++) {
        if (ray.dir[i] == 0)
            if ((vox.Lcoord[i] > ray.dir[i])
                (vox.Hcoord[i] < ray.dir[i])) return (0);
    }
    for (i = X; i <= Z; i++) {
        inv_d = 1./ray.dir[i];
        dlo = inv_d * (vox.Lcoord[X]-ray.origin[i]);
        dhi = inv_d * (vox.Hcoord[X]-ray.origin[i]);

        if (dlo > dhi) {
            min = dhi; max = dlo;
            Enter_vox = face[i][1]; Exit_vox = face[i][0];
        }
        else {
            min = dlo; max = dhi;
            Enter_vox = face[i][0]; Exit_vox = face[i][1];
        }
        if (i == X) { CurrNear =  min; CurrFar = max; }
        else {
            if (CurrNear < min) {
              CurrNear = min; Enter_vox = in;
            }
            if (CurrFar > max) {
              CurrFar = max; Exit_vox = out;
            }
```

```
        }
        if ((CurrNear > CurrFar)   (CurrFar < 0.))
            return (0);

        for (i = X; i <= Z; i++) {
            *ienter[i] = CurrNear * (ray.origin[i] + ray.dir[i]);
            *iexit[i] =  CurrFar * (ray.origin[i] + ray.dir[i]);
        }
        *inface = in; *outface = out;
        return (out);
    }
}


//   OCTRIE_next_voxel():
//     Given  a voxel and a directed ray (parametric)
//     Return a pointer to a leaf node corresponding to the
//     next voxel pierced by ray or NULL if out of bounds.
//     Finds the exit point of ray with current voxel.
//     Determines point that is "Step" dist away from exit
//     face into the "next" voxel.
//     Searches octrie from root for leaf node containing
//     the point in the next voxel.
//
Octrie_Ray::LEAF_PTR
Octrie_Ray::OCTRIE_next_voxel(OCTRIE_PTR root_ptr,
                              Ray ray, Voxel cvox, Voxel *nvox)
{
    int inface, outface;
    Coord in, out, *nextcoord;

 // intersect_ray_voxel(ray, cvox, &in, &out, &inface, &outface);
    intersect_ray_voxel(ray, cvox, (Coord *)in, (Coord *)out,
                        &inface, &outface);
    nextcoord = OCTRIE_point_in_next_voxel(out, outface, Step);
    if (nextcoord == NULL)
        return (NULL);
    return (OCTRIE_voxel_search(root_ptr, *nextcoord, nvox));
}


//   OCTRIE_point_in_next_voxel():
//     Given a point of exit, face of exit, and
//     an incremental distance.
//     Return a pointer to a point in next voxel.
//     Return null if next point exits environment.
//
Coord* Octrie_Ray::OCTRIE_point_in_next_voxel
                        (Coord pexit, int face, float d)
{
    switch (face) {
        case LEFT:
            pexit[X] = pexit[X] - d;
            return (pexit[X] <= root_voxel.Lcoord[X]) ?
                    (NULL) : (Coord *)(&pexit);
        case RIGHT:
```

```
                pexit[X] = pexit[X] + d;
                return (pexit[X] >= root_voxel.Hcoord[X]) ?
                        (NULL) : (Coord *)(&pexit);
            case BOTTOM:
                pexit[Y] = pexit[Y] - d;
                return (pexit[X] <= root_voxel.Lcoord[Y]) ?
                        (NULL) : (Coord *)(&pexit);
            case TOP:
                pexit[Y] = pexit[Y] + d;
                return (pexit[Y] >= root_voxel.Hcoord[Y]) ?
                        (NULL) : (Coord *)(&pexit);
            case FRONT:
                pexit[Z] = pexit[Z] - d;
                return (pexit[Z] <= root_voxel.Lcoord[Z]) ?
                        (NULL) : (Coord *)(&pexit);
            case BACK:
                pexit[Z] = pexit[Z] + d;
                return (pexit[Z] >= root_voxel.Hcoord[Z]) ?
                        (NULL) : (Coord *)(&pexit);
            default:
                return ((Coord *)&pexit);
    }
}


int Octrie_Ray::normalize(Coord vect)
{
    float mag = SQRT (vect[X] * vect[X] + vect[Y]*vect[Y] +
                      vect[Z] * vect[Z]);
    if (mag == 0)
       return (ERROR);   // divide by zero
    mag = 1./mag;
    vect[X] = vect[X] * mag;
    vect[Y] = vect[Y] * mag;
    vect[Z] = vect[Z] * mag;
    return (1);
}


//   ray_intersects_sphere():
//     Given a sphere and a directed ray (parametric)
//     Return 1 if ray intersects sphere, else return 0.
//
int Octrie_Ray::ray_intersects_sphere(Sphere *sphere,
                                      Ray ray, Coord Ipoint)
{
    Coord RaytoCenterVect;
    float radsqrd, dist, dsqrd;
    float RaytoCenterSqrd = 0, RaytoPoint = 0;

    radsqrd = (sphere->radius * sphere->radius);
    for (int i = X; i <= Z; i++) {
       RaytoCenterVect[i] = sphere->center[i] - ray.origin[i];
       RaytoPoint += RaytoCenterVect[i] * ray.dir[i];
       RaytoCenterSqrd += RaytoCenterVect[i] * RaytoCenterVect[i];
    }
```

```
    dsqrd = radsqrd - (RaytoCenterSqrd - (RaytoPoint*RaytoPoint));

    if (dsqrd < 0.) return (0); // ray does not intersect sphere

    dist = SQRT(dsqrd);
    for (i = X; i <= Z; i++)
        Ipoint[i] = ray.origin[i]+(RaytoPoint-dist)*ray.dir[i];
    return (1);
}


// OCTRIE_PostOrder():
//    Traverse the octrie in PostOrder. Print all "label"
//    attributes for each LEAF node record. Print "I" for
//    each INTERNAL node encountered. (Recursive method)
//
void Octrie_Ray::OCTRIE_PostOrder(OCTRIE_PTR node_ptr)
{
    int  i, n;
    if (node_ptr ==  NULL) {
        printf("x");
        return;
    }
    if (node_ptr->type != LEAF) {
        for (i = 0; i < 8; i++) {
        printf("@");
            OCTRIE_PostOrder(((IPTR)node_ptr)->child[i]);
        }
        printf(" I ");
    }
    else {
        n = ((LEAF_PTR)node_ptr)->nobj;
        for (i = 0; i < n; i++)
         printf(" %s ", ((LEAF_PTR)node_ptr)->objptr[i]->label);
    }
}


// build_initial_ray():

void  Octrie_Ray::build_ray_and_show (void)
{
    Sphere Objs[3];
    Ray ray;
    Coord hit;

    // mid[X,Y,Z] is the center of the current voxel
    for (int i = X; i <= Z; i++) {
        RootMin[i] = root_voxel.Lcoord[i];
        RootMax[i] = root_voxel.Hcoord[i];
        RootMid[i] = root_voxel.Lcoord[i] +
                    (root_voxel.Hcoord[i] -
                     root_voxel.Lcoord[i])/2.;
    }
    // Define initial SPHERES
    Objs[0].center[X] = 30.; Objs[0].center[Y] = 10.;
```

```
    Objs[0].center[Z] = 50.;
    Objs[0].radius = 40.; Objs[0].label = "A";
    Objs[1].center[X] = 150.; Objs[1].center[Y] = 150.;
    Objs[1].center[Z] = 10.;
    Objs[1].radius = 2.; Objs[1].label = "B";
    Objs[2].center[X] = 12.; Objs[2].center[Y] = 175.;
    Objs[2].center[Z] = 100.;
    Objs[2].radius = 3.; Objs[2].label = "C";

    // Define initial RAYS
    ray.origin[X] = 5.; ray.origin[Y] = 5.;
    ray.origin[Z] = 5.;
    ray.dir[X] = 1.; ray.dir[Y] = 2.; ray.dir[Z] = 4.;

    // normalize the ray direction vector
    normalize(ray.dir);

    int NumObj = sizeof(Objs)/sizeof(Objs[0]);
    printf("NUMBER OF OBJECTS = %d\n", NumObj);
    Step = (root_voxel.Hcoord[X] - root_voxel.Lcoord[X])
                / ((MAX_LEVELS + 1) * 2.);
    build_OCTRIE(Objs, NumObj, root_voxel);

    printf("The OCTRIE after PostOrder traversal:\n");
    OCTRIE_PostOrder(get_root());
    printf("\n");

    if (OCTRIE_raytrace(get_root(),
            ray, root_voxel, hit) == NULL)
        printf("NO OBJECT HIT\n");
    else
      printf("HIT = %f %f %f\n", hit[X], hit[Y], hit[Z]);
}

// main():  Test driver for OOP implementation of
//          3-D Ray-Tracing Acceleration with an ADT Octrie
//
void main(void)
{
    //  Declare an object of "Octrie_Ray" class
    Octrie_Ray  octrie_ray_obj;

    octrie_ray_obj.build_ray_and_show ();
}
```

The octrie-based ray-tracing accelerator of **Code 12.3** produces the following output:

```
NUMBER OF OBJECTS = 3
The OCTRIE when traversed by PostOrder():
@ A @ A @x@x@ C @ C @ B @ B  I
```

HIT = 7.914973 10.829947 16.659893

12.4   3-D Hidden Surface Removal with a BSP Tree Object

In a 3-*D* computer graphics system, a fundamental step in the rendering of realistic synthetic images is the removal of portions of objects from the image screen that are partially or fully occluded by other objects in the scene. This process is commonly referred to as *hidden surface removal*. In practice, solutions to this visibility problem might be more accurately described as hidden surface replacement, where pixels in the *frame buffer* (image storage array) are overwritten or replaced if not visible.

One solution to the hidden surface removal problem is to sort all surfaces relative to their depth from some viewer and then draw them in an order determined by the position of that viewer. In doing so, surfaces that are not visible to the eye are drawn first and then covered-up by those in front of them. We show here how a *binary space partition (BSP) tree* object, a special-case variant of the *kd*-tree object, may be utilized to accomplish object priority sorting to support hidden surface removal.

The BSP tree and the standard *kd*-tree are alike in that both are multi-dimensional comparative-based binary search trees. They differ in the way they partition the search space. As we have seen, the *kd*-tree is a rectilinear structure; in 3-space, the partitioning planes introduced are all orthogonal to the axis of the coordinate system and each other, resulting in disjoint rectangular regions. For the BSP tree, this restriction is relaxed; partition planes need not be orthogonal, resulting in a partitioning of the search space into arbitrarily shaped disjoint convex regions. The BSP tree is further characterized as follows:

- The root node of the entire tree represents the entire search space.

- At each node the search space is subdivided into two half spaces. In a three-dimensional database of polygons, the partitioning geometry is the plane that embeds the polygon associated with the node and is described by its plane equation $(ax + by + cz + d) = 0$. (In two dimensions the partition is a line that embeds the node's line segment geometry and is given by $(ax + by + c = 0)$.)

- To establish orientation, we label the sides of each partitioning plane as *front* or *back*. The front side is the one whose equation is of the form $(ax + by + cz + d) \geq 0$. We let this be the *left* child in the binary search tree. The back side is the one whose equation is of the form

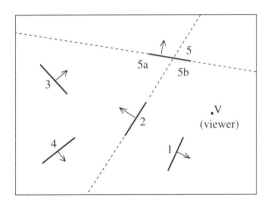

FIGURE 12.7. A set of polygons and a viewpoint V (top view).

$(ax + by + cz + d) < 0$. We let this be the *right* child in the binary search tree.

- With the database processed as a list of polygons, the tree is built by recursively choosing a root polygon from the list on which to partition space. At each node, a polygon from the corresponding (sub)list is selected as the root of the (sub)tree and the (sub)list is split into a front list and a back list. Processing continues until all lists are exhausted.

- Upon insertion, all geometry that crosses the partition of the current selected root node must be clipped into two pieces and placed into the appropriate back or front subtrees. The creation of new geometry is referred to as *fragmentation*. The choice of root polygons greatly influences the amount of fragmentation that will occur and thus the size of the tree.

As an example, consider the set of five polygons depicted in Figure 12.7. To make it easier to visualize what is going on, we have drawn the polygons as a set of line segments; think of this as a "top view" of the geometry. Each line segment is identified by a numeric label and the front side of each is indicated by an arrow. A viewer position V is indicated. For the line segments labeled as 2 and 5, a dashed line is drawn to show the full extent of partitioning. Figure 12.8(a) shows the resulting BSP tree after the first recursion when segment 2 is selected as the root of the tree. Figure 12.8(b) shows the final BSP tree with segment 2 as the root of the first level of recursion and segments 3 and 1 as the roots of the second level of recursion. Notice here the fragmentation caused by segment 2, as it has split segment 5 into two new segments, 5a and 5b. An alternate tree is depicted

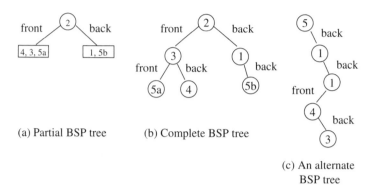

(a) Partial BSP tree   (b) Complete BSP tree

(c) An alternate
BSP tree

FIGURE 12.8. BSP tree construction.

in Figure 12.8(c), for which segment 5 was chosen as the first level root. No fragmentation occurs in this case and thus a smaller tree is realized.

Once built, the BSP tree contains the database sorted in such a manner that a simple symmetric traversal will output polygons in a correct *back-to-front* or *front-to-back* spatial ordering relative to any arbitrary viewpoint. One of the most commonly employed BSP tree rendering algorithms is a back-to-front method called the *painter's algorithm*. This is a modified inorder traversal rendering method that will "paint" an image of a scene from any specified point of view with hidden surfaces removed. At each node in the tree, it is determined which side of the partition the viewer resides in and this determines which subtree is traversed first. Polygons are painted on the output screen as they are encountered; polygons may overlap previously drawn polygons according to the visibility sort encoded into the BSP tree structure.

Painter's Algorithm (Recursive)

> At each node:
>
> - Determine which side of the associated partition the viewpoint is located.
> - Traverse the subtree of the "other side" of this partition.
> - Render the root node geometry.
> - Traverse the side of the partition that the viewpoint resides in (determined in the first step, above).

To illustrate the painter's algorithm, consider traversing the BSP tree of Figure 12.8(b) from the vantage point of the given viewer *V*.

- V is on the back side of partition 2 so traverse the front side (left child).

- V is on the front side of partition 3 so traverse the back side (right child).

- Render segment 4, render segment 3, render segment 5a.

- Traverse the back side of partition 2 (right child).

- Traverse the back side of partition 1 (right child).

- Render segment 5b, render segment 1.

The image generation time with a BSP tree is dependent on the height of the tree traversed. As indicated above, one of the major problems with a BSP tree is growth of the tree due to an explosion of object fragmentation. This potentially could lead to a doubling or tripling in the size of the original database. While it is almost impossible to avoid fragmentation, it can be minimized by wisely choosing the root polygon for splitting lists. In an *optimal BSP tree* construction algorithm, heuristics are used to choose the root polygon at a given node that will result in the least amount of fragmentation.

Another solution to the hidden surface problem is the *z-buffer* algorithm. While the BSP tree is a structure built in the *object-space* of the database, a z-buffer operates in the *image-space* of the frame buffer. The z-buffer does not rely on an explicit sort. The basis of the z-buffer algorithm is that at each pixel in the image, the depth or "z" value from the viewer to the corresponding point on the most recently drawn surface is saved. For each successive surface, if the depth value for the pixel is less than that in the z-buffer, the current pixel obscures the existing one and replaces it.

The z-buffer is a simple and elegant solution that has become the most common approach to the hidden surface removal in high performance computer graphics systems. The BSP approach, on the other hand, produces a sort of the database, and is useful in applications that require a sort.

A pointer-based BSP tree is presented in **Code 12.4**. The recursive function BSPT_build() builds the tree as described above. A polygon is defined in terms of a structure containing an integer ID, the coefficients of its embedding plane, and a list of vertices.

At any given node, side_PolyToPoly() determines on which side the polygon being inserted resides relative to the partition induced by the node. For simplicity, we have chosen a database that does not contain polygons that intersect each other. This allows us to avoid actually clipping geometry, but in a more realistic scenario fragmentation will occur, requiring the routine split_polygon() to slice up geometry.

With the tree built, the routine `BSPT_inorder()` performs a painter's algorithm traversal. For the given example, an output of polygons in back-to-front order is produced for the three independent viewpoints, E1, E2, and E3.

Code 12.4

```
//   Program:  bsptree.c++
//   Purpose:
//      OOP implementation of 3-D Hidden Surface Removal
//      with a BSP Tree object.
//
#include  <stdio.h>

const int FRONT = 1;
const int BACK  = 2;
const int SPLIT = 0;
const int EYE   = 0;
const int POLY  = 1;

const int X     = 0;
const int Y     = 1;
const int Z     = 2;
const int A     = 0;
const int B     = 1;
const int C     = 2;
const int D     = 3;

class  Hidden_Surf_Rem_BSPTree {
  private:
    typedef float Vertex[3];
    typedef float Coeff[4];
    typedef Vertex Point;

    struct V_node {        // singly linked list
       Vertex    vertex;   // of vertices
       V_node    *next;
    };
    struct Polygon {
        int     pid;
        Coeff   coeff;
        V_node  *vlist;   // list of vertices
    };
    struct P_node {        // singly linked list
        Polygon  poly;     // polygon nodes
        P_node   *next;
    };
    typedef struct BSPT_NODE {
        Polygon    poly;
        BSPT_NODE  *front_ptr;
        BSPT_NODE  *back_ptr;
    } *BSPT_PTR;
```

```
    BSPT_PTR root_ptr;   // root of the tree
    int      NUM_POLYS;  // number of polygons
    void     init_BSPtree() { root_ptr = NULL; }
  public:
    Hidden_Surf_Rem_BSPTree(int num_polygons);
    ~Hidden_Surf_Rem_BSPTree();

    BSPT_PTR  get_root() { return root_ptr; }
    BSPT_PTR  BSPT_build(BSPT_PTR);
    void      BSPT_inorder(Vertex, BSPT_PTR);
    V_node*   create_vnode(Vertex);
    P_node*   create_pnode(Polygon);
    BSPT_PTR  create_treenode(Polygon);
    void      vtxlist_insert(Vertex, V_node**);
    void      polylist_insert(Polygon poly, BSPT_PTR*);
    BSPT_PTR  bsp_select_root(BSPT_PTR);
    void      split_polygon(BSPT_PTR, BSPT_PTR, Polygon*,
                            Polygon*);
    int       side_PolyToPoly(Polygon, Polygon);
    int       side_PointToPoly(Vertex, Polygon);
    void      render(Polygon);
    void      show_initial_hddn_surf(void);
};


// ---  Implement methods for "Hidden_Surf_Rem_BSPTree"

Hidden_Surf_Rem_BSPTree::Hidden_Surf_Rem_BSPTree
                                (int num_polygons)
{
   NUM_POLYS = num_polygons; // NUM_POLYS = 8
   init_BSPtree();
}


Hidden_Surf_Rem_BSPTree::~Hidden_Surf_Rem_BSPTree()
{
  // Destructor:  Left as an exercise
}


// BSPT_build():
//   Build a BSP tree from a list of polygons.
//   (Recursive function)
//
Hidden_Surf_Rem_BSPTree::BSPT_PTR
Hidden_Surf_Rem_BSPTree::BSPT_build(BSPT_PTR rlist_ptr)
{
    int       side;
    Polygon   front, back;
    BSPT_PTR  rnode_ptr;
    BSPT_PTR  blist_ptr = NULL;
    BSPT_PTR  flist_ptr = NULL;

    if (rlist_ptr == NULL)
       return (NULL);
    rnode_ptr = bsp_select_root(rlist_ptr);
```

```
      while (rlist_ptr) {
        if (rlist_ptr->poly.pid != rnode_ptr->poly.pid) {
          side = side_PolyToPoly(rnode_ptr->poly,
                       rlist_ptr->poly);
          if (side == FRONT)
             polylist_insert(rlist_ptr->poly, &flist_ptr);
          else if (side == BACK)
             polylist_insert(rlist_ptr->poly, &blist_ptr);
          else {
             split_polygon(rnode_ptr, rlist_ptr, &front, &back);
             polylist_insert(back, &blist_ptr);
             polylist_insert(front, &flist_ptr);
          }
        }
        // front_ptr is "next" pointer
        rlist_ptr = rlist_ptr->front_ptr;
      }
      rnode_ptr->front_ptr = flist_ptr;
      rnode_ptr->back_ptr  = blist_ptr;

      BSPT_build (flist_ptr);
      BSPT_build (blist_ptr);

      return(rnode_ptr);
}


//   BSPT_inorder():
//     Traverse BSP tree in InOrder method.
//
void Hidden_Surf_Rem_BSPTree::BSPT_inorder(Point eye,
                                  BSPT_PTR root_ptr)
{
      if (root_ptr == NULL)
         return;

      if (side_PointToPoly(eye, root_ptr->poly) == FRONT ) {
         BSPT_inorder(eye, root_ptr->back_ptr);
         render(root_ptr->poly);
         BSPT_inorder(eye, root_ptr->front_ptr);
      }
      else {
         BSPT_inorder(eye, root_ptr->front_ptr);
         render(root_ptr->poly);
         BSPT_inorder(eye, root_ptr->back_ptr);
      }
}


//   create_vnode(): Create vertex node of type V_node.
//
Hidden_Surf_Rem_BSPTree::V_node*
Hidden_Surf_Rem_BSPTree::create_vnode(Vertex v)
{
      V_node *new_ptr;
```

```
        if ((new_ptr = new V_node) == NULL) {
            printf("\n create_vnode: new failed. \n");
            return (NULL);
        }
        for (int i = X; i <= Z; i++)
            new_ptr->vertex[i] = v[i];
        new_ptr->next = NULL;
        return (new_ptr);
}


// create_treenode():
//    Allocate BSP tree node.
Hidden_Surf_Rem_BSPTree::BSPT_PTR
Hidden_Surf_Rem_BSPTree::create_treenode(Polygon p)
{
    BSPT_PTR new_ptr;

    if ((new_ptr = new BSPT_NODE) == NULL) {
        printf("\n create_treenode: new failed.\n");
        return (NULL);
    }
    new_ptr->poly = p;
    new_ptr->front_ptr = NULL;
    new_ptr->back_ptr = NULL;
    return (new_ptr);
}


void Hidden_Surf_Rem_BSPTree::polylist_insert(Polygon poly,
                                              BSPT_PTR *head)
{
    BSPT_PTR  new_ptr = create_treenode(poly);
    new_ptr->front_ptr = *head;  // used front_ptr as "next"
    *head = new_ptr;
}


// vtxlist_insert():
//    Insert a vertex in singly linked list of vertices.
//
void Hidden_Surf_Rem_BSPTree::vtxlist_insert(Vertex vtx,
                                             V_node **head)
{
    V_node  *new_ptr = create_vnode(vtx);
    new_ptr->next = *head;
    *head = new_ptr;
}


int Hidden_Surf_Rem_BSPTree::side_PointToPoly(Point pt,
                                              Polygon proot)
{
    float ca = proot.coeff[A], cb = proot.coeff[B],
          cc = proot.coeff[C], cd = proot.coeff[D];

    if ((ca * pt[X] + cb * pt[Y] + cc * pt[Z] + cd) < 0)
```

```
        return (BACK);
    else
        return (FRONT);
}


int Hidden_Surf_Rem_BSPTree::side_PolyToPoly(Polygon proot,
                                                Polygon ptest)
{
    float db;

    int    init = 1, side, curr_side;
    V_node *vptr = ptest.vlist;
    float ca = proot.coeff[A], cb = proot.coeff[B],
          cc = proot.coeff[C], cd = proot.coeff[D];

    while (vptr != NULL) {
        db = (ca * vptr->vertex[X] + cb * vptr->vertex[Y] +
              cc * vptr->vertex[Z] + cd);
        if (db < 0.0)
            curr_side = BACK;
        else
            curr_side = FRONT;

        if (init) {
            side = curr_side;
            init = 0;
        }
        else if (curr_side != side)
            return (SPLIT);
        vptr = vptr->next;
    }
    return (side);
}


void Hidden_Surf_Rem_BSPTree::render(Polygon p)
{
    printf(" %d: ", p.pid);
}


void  Hidden_Surf_Rem_BSPTree::split_polygon(BSPT_PTR root,
              BSPT_PTR list, Polygon *front, Polygon *back)
{
    printf("SPLIT\n"); // Left as an exercise
}


Hidden_Surf_Rem_BSPTree::BSPT_PTR
Hidden_Surf_Rem_BSPTree::bsp_select_root(BSPT_PTR plist)
{
    // Just returns given node pointer.
    // Exercise: code other schemes
    return (plist);
}


void Hidden_Surf_Rem_BSPTree::show_initial_hddn_surf(void)
```

```
{
    BSPT_PTR      plist_ptr = NULL;

    //  V_node        *v_head[NUM_POLYS];
    V_node      *v_head[8];
    //  Polygon      Polys[NUM_POLYS];
    Polygon     Polys[8];

    static Vertex polys[] = {
      {10.,7.5,15.}, {15.,7.5,10.}, {13.,12.5,12.},
      {11.,3.5,7.}, {15.,2.5,6.}, {13.,9.,7.},
      {9.,5.1,19.}, {20.,5.5,16.}, {15.,0.,16.},
      {3.,0.5,14.}, {4.,0.5,8.}, {4.,5.5,12.},
      {13.,10.,15.},{17.,10.,13.},{15.,12.,14},
      {6.,10.,7.}, {7.,10.,4.}, {7.,12.,6.},
      {1.,10.,7.}, {3.,10.1,4.}, {3.,15.,5.},
      {7.,7.0,16.}, {8.,7.5,13.}, {8.,8.5,14.} };

    static Coeff Co[] = {
      {25.000000, 0.000000, 25.000000, -625.000000},
      {5.500000, -2.000000, 24.000000, -221.500000},
      {-16.500000, 15.000000, -58.500000, 1183.500000},
      {30.000000, -4.000000, 5.000000, -158.000000},
      {4.000000, 0.000000, 8.000000, -172.000000},
      {6.000000, -2.000000, 2.000000 ,-30.000000},
      {4.799995, -2.000000, 9.799997, -63.399994},
      {3.500000, -1.000000, 1.000000, -33.500000} };

    static Point Eye_1 = {6., 8., 10.};
    static Point Eye_2 = {14., 5., 4.};
    static Point Eye_3 = {15., 10., 12.};

    for (int i = 0; i < NUM_POLYS; i++) {
     v_head[i] = NULL;
     for (int j = 0; j < 3; j++)
       vtxlist_insert(polys[3 * i + j], &v_head[i]);

     Polys[i].pid = i;
     Polys[i].coeff[0] = Co[i][0]; Polys[i].coeff[1] = Co[i][1];
     Polys[i].coeff[2] = Co[i][2]; Polys[i].coeff[3] = Co[i][3];
     Polys[i].vlist = v_head[i];
     polylist_insert(Polys[i], &plist_ptr);
    }
    root_ptr = BSPT_build (plist_ptr);
    printf(" BSP tree traversed by modified %s \n",
           "inorder [painter's algorithm]");
    printf(" ----------------------------%s",
           "---------------------------");
    printf("\n Polygons rendered from [Eye_1]: ");
    BSPT_inorder(Eye_1, root_ptr);
    printf("\n Polygons rendered from [Eye_2]: ");
    BSPT_inorder(Eye_2, root_ptr);
    printf("\n Polygons rendered from [Eye_3]: ");
    BSPT_inorder(Eye_3, root_ptr);
```

```
        printf("\n");
    }

    //  main():  Test driver for OOP implementation of 3-D
    //             Hidden Surface Removal with a BSP Tree.
    void main(void)
    {
        // Declare an object with NUM_POLYS = 8
        Hidden_Surf_Rem_BSPTree  polygn_bsp_tree_obj(8);

        printf ("\n ** OOP IMPLEMENTATION OF %s **\n %s \n",
                "3-D HIDDEN SURFACE REMOVAL",
                "                         USING BSP TREE");
        polygn_bsp_tree_obj.show_initial_hddn_surf();
    }
```

The BSP-based hidden surface remover of **Code 12.4** produces the following output:

```
** OOP IMPLEMENTATION OF 3-D HIDDEN SURFACE REMOVAL **
                      USING BSP TREE
BSP tree traversed by modified inorder [painter's algorithm]
-------------------------------------------------------------
Polygons rendered from [Eye_1]:  2:  4:  0:  1:  7:  6:  3:  5:
Polygons rendered from [Eye_2]:  6:  3:  5:  7:  2:  4:  0:  1:
Polygons rendered from [Eye_3]:  6:  3:  5:  7:  1:  0:  2:  4:
```

12.5   Exercises

1. Implement a function that will convert a quadtrie object from a tree representation to a treecode representation. Implement a function to convert the treecode back into a tree representation.

2. Write a function that will convert the raster representation of the image array of Figure 12.1(a) to a pointer-based region quadtrie.

3. Write a function print_regiontrie() that "displays" the image encoded in the pointer-based region quadtrie of 12.2. The output should be in the same format as that produced by the function print_image() of **Code 12.1**.

4. Write a function print_lineartrie() that "displays" an image encoded as a linear quadtrie.

5. Write a function to convert a list of leafcodes back into an explicit pointer-based trie.

6. Write an OOP implementation of a region quadtrie object to represent an 8×8 pixel image array of a checkerboard. Show that these data degenerate into a pure or complete trie. Compare the space utilization with that of an array representation.

7. Write and test destructor ~VLSI_4DTree() for the VLSI design application of **Code 12.2**.

8. Show how the linear quadtrie can be represented by a base-5 leafcode and no explicit level.

9. Write and test a version that implements inorder traversals for a linear quadtrie as an iterative procedure with an explicit stack.

10. Modify **Code 12.4** to handle arbitrary polygons. Note that rectangle as xy-min/max specifies a bounding box. The overlap of bounding boxes is a necessary but not sufficient condition for the polygons that they contain to overlap.

11. Implement the ray tracing accelerator of **Code 12.3** as a *kd*-trie object instead of the octrie object.

12. Implement the public member function split_polygon() and modify the given database of **Code 12.4** such that fragmentation of objects will occur.

13. For the BSP tree of **Code 12.4**, implement other versions of the public member function bsp_select_root() for selecting an optimum root node (other than the first encountered as shown in **Code 12.4**). This is an *optimal BSP tree*.

14. Write and test the destructor ~Hidden_Surf_Rem_BSPTree() in **Code 12.4**.

Appendix A

C++ Fundamentals

A.1 C++ Key Words

auto	enum	operator	template
break	extern	overload	this
case	float	private	typedef
char	for	protected	union
class	free	public	unsigned
continue	friend	register	virtual
const	goto	return	void
default	if	sizeof	while
delete	inline	short	
do	int	static	
double	long	struct	
else	new	switch	

A.2 C++ Special Characters

+	-	*	/	%	+=	-=	*=	/=	%=
++	--	**	[	]	(	)	{	}	;
/*	*/	,	!=	>	<	==	>=	<=	!
&&		&		^	~		<<	>>	<<=	>>=
:	::	&=	=	^=	?	\t	\n	\r	\b
//	[]	~	()	->	->*	!=			

A.3 Allowed Overloaded Operators in C++

+	-	*	/	%	+=	-=	*=	/=	%=
++	--	~	[]	()	,	!=	>	<	==
&&		&	^	^=	<<	>>	>>=	<<=	&=
>=	<=		=	!	!=	[]	()	'	->
->*	new	delete							

A.4 C++ Built-in Data Types

char	signed char	unsigned char
double		
float		

```
int             signed int           unsigned int
long            signed long          unsigned long
long int        signed long int      unsigned long int
short
signed
unsigned
```

A.5 Statement Formats of Some C++ Keywords

```
Format                                      Description
==================================================================

class  <class_name> :                       'class' to define the type
  <access_specifier> <base_class> {         of objects. It encompasses
 private:                                    data and functions. The
  <mem_type>   <mem_id>;                     format without ":" is
  ...                                        used to define the base
  friend  <function_name>;                   class.
  friend  <class_name>;
 protected:
  <mem_type>   <mem_id>;
  ...
 public:
  <mem_type>   <mem_id>;
  <type>       <method_name>;
  operator     <op_name>;
};

do {                                        The statements are executed
    <statement_1>; ...                      first, and then the condition
} while <condtion>;                         is checked.

for (<initializer>; <condition>;            The statements within 'for'
    <increment>) {                          loop are executed till the
    <statement_1>; ...                      condition is true.
}

if (<condtion>) {                           If condition is true, execute
    <statement_1>; ...                      statements 'statement_1', ...,
} else {                                    otherwise excute statements
    <statement_2>; ...                      'statement_2', ....
}

overload  <function_name>(<args>);          A function is declared as
                                            an overloded function.

struct <struct_name> {                      Structure (record) with
  <mem_type>   <mem_id>;                     several distint members.
  ...
};

switch (<value>) {                          Based on 'value', appropriate
```

```
  case <value_1>:                        statements are executed.
    <statement_1>; ...
    break;
  case <value_2>:
    <statement_1>; ...
    break;
  default:
    <statement_1>; ...
    break;
}

while (<condtion>) {                  The statements within 'while'
    <statement_1>; ...                loop are executed till the
}                                     condition is true.
```

A.6   A Sample C++ Program

```c
#include <stdio.h>
void main(int argc, char  *argv[])
{
    int first_term = 3, common_diff = 2, next_term;

    printf("\n Arithmetic Progression is: \n");
    for (int i = 0; i < 10; i++) {
       next_term = first_term + common_diff * i;
       printf(" %d,", next_term);
    }
    printf("\n");
}
```

A.7   C++ Preprocessor Directives

These lines must start from column 1.

```
#define  <id>  "<string>"

#define  <id>  (<id_1>, ..., <id_n>) "<string>"
```

```
#if  <expression>        If expression is true, statements
  <statement_1>; ...     statement_1, ... are executed;
#else                    otherwise, statement_2, ... are
  <statement_2>; ...     executed.
#endif
```

```
#ifdef  <expression>     This means if the expression is
  <statement_1>; ...     defined, statements statement_1,
#else                    ... are executed; otherwise,
  <statement_2>; ...     statement_2, ...  are executed.
#endif
```

```
#include "file_name"       Include file from local directory
#include <file_name>       Include file from defined directory
                           (must specify "<" and ">")

#ifndef <expression>       If "expression" is not defined,
  <statement_1>; ...       statements statement_1, ... are
#else                      executed; otherwise, statement_2,
  <statement_2>; ...       ... are executed.
#endif

#undef <id>                Remove the defined status of
                           identifier.
```

A.8   Creating Executables for C++ Programs

Assuming Borland International's C++ compiler on IBM PC or compatible computer running MS-DOS, do the following steps:

```
Step 1.   Create <PROG_1>.CPP using an editor, ("cpp" extension
          is required.)
Step 2.   TCC -D<flag> <PROG_1>.CPP  /I A:INCLUDE /I B:INCLUDE
Step 3.   <PROG_1>.EXE is the created executable in the current
          directory.
```

Assuming AT&T's C++ compiler on a computer running UNIX operating system, do the following steps:

```
Step 1.   Create <PROG_1>.c++ using an editor, ("c++" extension
          is required.)
Step 2.   CC -D<flag> <PROG_1>.c++ -o <PROG_1>
Step 3.   <PROG_1> is the created executable in the current
          directory.
```

Appendix B

Assorted Library Functions for Handling Strings

The following is a cross-reference of some string-handling library functions used throughout this book. These functions come with the C++ compiler and are declared in the header file `<string.h>`.

```
STRING-HANDLING FUNCTION         DESCRIPTION
===========================================================
char *strcat (char *s1,          Appends string s2 to the end of
       const char *s2)           s1, updates s1, and returns s1.

char *strncat (char *s1,         Appends first n characters of
   const char *s2, int n)        string s2, updates s1, and
                                 returns s1.

char *strdup (const char *s1)    Allocates memory space,
                                 duplicates s1, and returns the
                                 duplicate string.

int strcmp (const char *s1,      Lexicographically compares
       const char *s2)           string s1 with string s2,
                                 returns an
                                     integer < 0 if s1 < s2, or
                                     integer = 0 if s1 = s2, or
                                     integer > 0 if s1 > s2.

int strncmp (const char *s1,     Lexicographically compares first
       const char *s2, int n)    n characters of both strings s1
                                 and s2; returns the same result
                                 as strcmp().

char *strcpy (char *s1,          Copies string s2 to s1,
       const char *s2)           updates and returns s1.

char *strncpy (char *s1,         Copies first n characters of
       const char *s2, int n)    string s2 to s1, updates and
                                 returns s1.

int strlen (const char *s)       Returns the number of characters
                                 in string s; does not include
                                 the terminating null character.
```

```
char *strchr (const char *s,    Searches for the given character
                    int ch)     'ch' in string s. If found,
                                it returns a pointer to the first
                                occurrence of 'ch' in s; a NULL
                                pointer is returned otherwise.

char *strstr (const char *s1,   Searches for first occurrence
              const char *s2)   of string s2 (without the null
                                character) in string s1.
                                If found, it returns a
                                character-type pointer to it,
                                or a NULL pointer otherwise.
```

Appendix C

Example Databases

C.1 PEOPLE and GEOMETRY Databases

There are two example databases, named PEOPLE and GEOMETRY, used this book for illustration and implementation of data structures.. Section 1.5 (Chapter 1) outlines their content. The following sections show the complete databases pictorially and give the corresponding header file code included by the example program to access them.

C.1.1 PEOPLE_1D

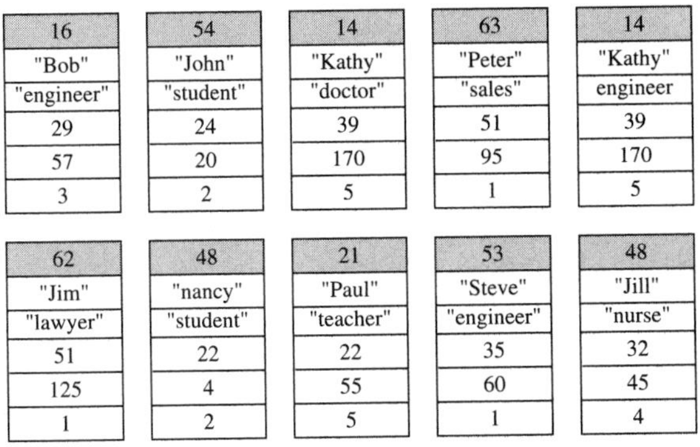

16	54	14	63	14
"Bob"	"John"	"Kathy"	"Peter"	"Kathy"
"engineer"	"student"	"doctor"	"sales"	engineer
29	24	39	51	39
57	20	170	95	170
3	2	5	1	5

62	48	21	53	48
"Jim"	"nancy"	"Paul"	"Steve"	"Jill"
"lawyer"	"student"	"teacher"	"engineer"	"nurse"
51	22	22	35	32
125	4	55	60	45
1	2	5	1	4

FIGURE C.1. People_1d records.

Code AC.1

```
// Program: people_db.c++
//          PEOPLE_1D database with one attribute
//          "member id" as one key.
//
typedef int  Nodetype;
class People_Database {
  private:
    typedef int  Keytype;
    struct  DataObject {     // Member record
```

```
        Keytype key;          // member id
        char    *name;        // name
        char    *occupation;
        int     age;          // age
        int     income;       // yearly gross (x $1000)
        int     years;        // number years member
      };
      DataObject *people_db;
      int        NUMOBJ;
   public:
      People_Database(int numobj);
    ~ People_Database();
      void  build_initial_db(void);
      DataObject *get_db() {return people_db;}
};

People_Database::People_Database(int numobj)
{
   // Allocate an array of given 'numobj'
   people_db = new DataObject[ NUMOBJ = numobj ];
}
People_Database::~People_Database()
{
   delete [NUMOBJ] people_db;
}

// ---  Initial setup of People database  ---
void People_Database::build_initial_db(void)
{
   people_db[0].key = 16;
   people_db[0].name = "Bob";
   people_db[0].occupation = "engineer";
   people_db[0].age = 29;
   people_db[0].income = 57;
   people_db[0].years = 3;

   people_db[1].key = 54;
   people_db[1].name = "John";
   people_db[1].occupation = "student";
   people_db[1].age = 24;
   people_db[1].income = 20;
   people_db[1].years = 2;

   people_db[2].key = 14;
   people_db[2].name = "Kathy";
   people_db[2].occupation = "doctor";
   people_db[2].age = 39;
   people_db[2].income = 170;
   people_db[2].years = 5;

   people_db[3].key = 63;
   people_db[3].name = "Peter";
   people_db[3].occupation = "sales";
   people_db[3].age = 51;
```

```
people_db[3].income = 95;
people_db[3].years = 1;

people_db[4].key = 14;      // duplicate record - ERROR
people_db[4].name = "Kathy";
people_db[4].occupation = "doctor";
people_db[4].age = 39;
people_db[4].income = 170;
people_db[4].years = 5;

people_db[5].key = 62;
people_db[5].name = "Jim";
people_db[5].occupation = "lawyer";
people_db[5].age = 51;
people_db[5].income = 125;
people_db[5].years = 1;

people_db[6].key = 48;
people_db[6].name = "Nancy";
people_db[6].occupation = "student";
people_db[6].age = 22;
people_db[6].income = 4;
people_db[6].years = 2;

people_db[7].key = 21;
people_db[7].name = "Paul";
people_db[7].occupation = "teacher";
people_db[7].age = 22;
people_db[7].income = 55;
people_db[7].years = 5;

people_db[8].key = 53;
people_db[8].name = "Steve";
people_db[8].occupation = "engineer";
people_db[8].years = 35;
people_db[8].income = 60;
people_db[8].years = 1;

people_db[9].key = 48;   // duplicate id - ERROR
people_db[9].name = "Jill";
people_db[9].occupation = "nurse";
people_db[9].age = 32;
people_db[9].income = 45;
people_db[9].years = 4;
}
```

C.1.2   PEOPLE_2D

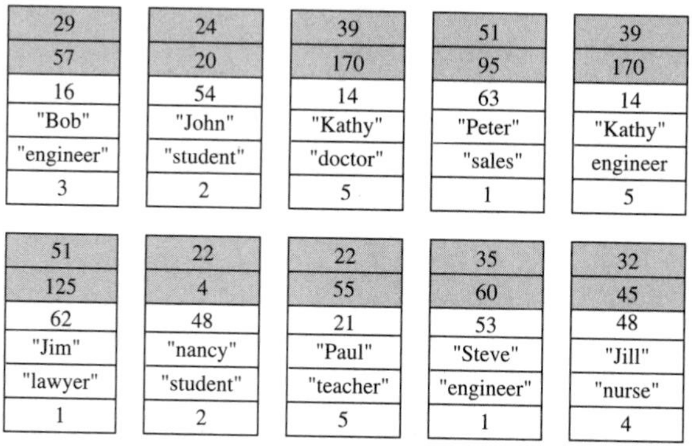

29
57
16
"Bob"
"engineer"
3

24
20
54
"John"
"student"
2

39
170
14
"Kathy"
"doctor"
5

51
95
63
"Peter"
"sales"
1

39
170
14
"Kathy"
engineer
5

51
125
62
"Jim"
"lawyer"
1

22
4
48
"nancy"
"student"
2

22
55
21
"Paul"
"teacher"
5

35
60
53
"Steve"
"engineer"
1

32
45
48
"Jill"
"nurse"
4

FIGURE C.2. People_2d records.

Code AC.2

```
// Program: db2.h
//
//          PEOPLE_2D database with two attributes
//          "age" and "income" as two keys.
//
const int D = 2;          // 2-dimensional key
struct DataObject {       // member_record
   Keytype key[D];        // key[0]=age, key[1]=income (x $1000)
   int  id;               // member id
   char *name;            // name
   char *occupation;      // occupation
   int years;             // number years member
};


// ==========================================
// Program:  init_db2.h
// ==========================================
static DataObject records[] = {
   { {29, 57}, 16, "Bob", "engineer", 3},
   { {24, 20}, 54, "John", "student", 2},
   { {39, 170}, 14, "Kathy", "doctor", 5},
   { {51, 95}, 63, "Peter", "sales", 1},
   { {39, 170}, 14, "Kathy", "doctor", 5}, // duplicate record
   { {51, 125}, 62, "Jim", "lawyer", 1},
   { {22, 4}, 48, "Nancy", "student", 2},
   { {22, 55}, 21, "Paul", "teacher", 5},
   { {35, 60}, 53, "Steve", "engineer", 1},
   { {32, 45}, 48, "Jill", "nurse", 4}     // duplicate id
};
```

C.1.3 PEOPLE_3D

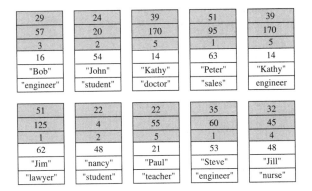

FIGURE C.3. People_3d records.

Code AC.3

```
// Program:  db3.h   (for PEOPLE_3D)
//     (3 dimensional, 1-key defines 1-dimension)
//
#define D   3   // 3-d key
typedef int Keytype;
struct DataObject {   // member_record
    // key[0]=age, key[1]=income (x $1000),
    // key[2]= years member
    Keytype key[D];
    int    id;          // member id
    char   *name;       // name
    char   *occupation; // occupation
};
// =======================================
// Program:  init_db3.h
// =======================================

static DataObject records[] = {
    { {29, 57, 3}, 16, "Bob", "engineer"},
    { {24, 20, 2}, 54, "John", "student"},
    { {39, 170, 5}, 14, "Kathy", "doctor"},
    { {51, 95, 1}, 63, "Peter", "sales"},
    { {39, 170, 5}, 14, "Kathy", "doctor"}, // duplicate record
    { {51, 125, 1}, 62, "Jim", "lawyer"},
    { {22, 4, 2}, 48, "Nancy", "student"},
    { {22, 55, 5}, 21, "Paul", "teacher"},
    { {35, 60, 1}, 53, "Steve", "engineer"},
    { {32, 45, 4}, 48, "Jill", "nurse"}     // duplicate id
};
```

C.1.4   GEOMETRY_2D

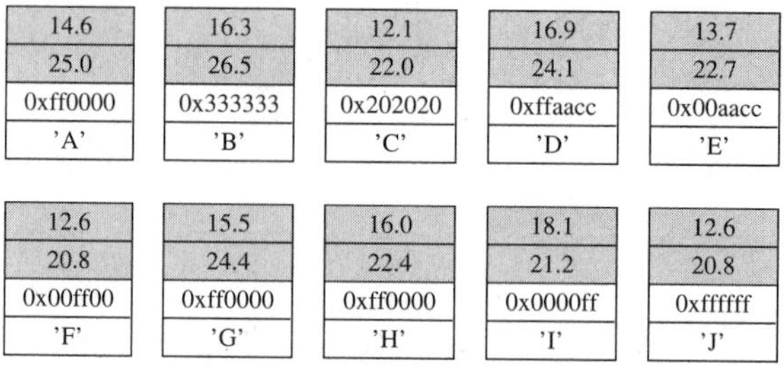

14.6	16.3	12.1	16.9	13.7
25.0	26.5	22.0	24.1	22.7
0xff0000	0x333333	0x202020	0xffaacc	0x00aacc
'A'	'B'	'C'	'D'	'E'

12.6	15.5	16.0	18.1	12.6
20.8	24.4	22.4	21.2	20.8
0x00ff00	0xff0000	0xff0000	0x0000ff	0xffffff
'F'	'G'	'H'	'I'	'J'

FIGURE C.4. Geometry_2d records.

Code AC.4

```
// Program:  db_geo2.h
//           For GEOMETRY_2D database with two keys "x" & "y"
//
const int D = 2;            // 2-dimensional key
struct DataObject {         // vertex
   Keytype    key[D];       // key[0] = x, key[1] = y
   unsigned   long color;   // 3-component color
   char       label;
};


// ==========================================
// Program:  init_db2.h
// ==========================================

static DataObject vertex_records[] = {
   { {14.6, 25.0}, 0xff0000, 'A'},   // Vertex A
   { {16.3, 26.5}, 0x333333, 'B'},   // Vertex B
   { {12.1, 22.0}, 0x202020, 'C'},   // Vertex C
   { {16.9, 24.1}, 0xffaacc, 'D'},   // Vertex D
   { {13.7, 22.7}, 0x00aacc, 'E'},   // Vertex E
   { {12.6, 20.8}, 0x00ff00, 'F'},   // Vertex F
   { {15.5, 24.4}, 0xff0000, 'G'},   // Vertex G
   { {16.0, 22.4}, 0xff0000, 'H'},   // Vertex H
   { {18.1, 21.2}, 0x0000ff, 'I'},   // Vertex I
   { {12.6, 20.8}, 0xffffff, 'J'}    // Vertex J
};
```

C.1.5 GEOMETRY_3D

14.6	16.3	12.1	16.9	13.7
25.0	26.5	22.0	24.1	22.7
10.0	11.6	12.0	19.7	14.3
0xff0000	0x333333	0x202020	0xffaacc	0x00aacc
'A'	'B'	'C'	'D'	'E'

12.6	15.5	16.0	18.1	12.6
20.8	24.4	22.4	21.2	20.8
10.5	15.0	12.0	18.0	10.9
0x00ff00	0xff0000	0xff0000	0x0000ff	0xffffff
'F'	'G'	'H'	'I'	'J'

FIGURE C.5. Geometry_3d records.

Code AC.5

```
// Program:  db_geo3.h
//           For GEOMETRY_3D database with keys
//           "x", "y", and "z"
//
const int D = 3;        // 3-dimensional key

struct DataObject {    // vertex
   Keytype   key[D];    // key[0]=x, key[1]=y, key[2]=z
   unsigned long color; // 3-component color
   char      label;
};


// ========================================
// Program:  init_db3.h
// ========================================

static DataObject vertexes[] = {
   { {14.6, 25.0, 10.0}, 0xff0000, 'A'}, // Vertex A
   { {16.3, 26.5, 11.6}, 0x333333, 'B'}, // Vertex B
   { {12.1, 22.0, 12.0}, 0x202020, 'C'}, // Vertex C
   { {16.9, 24.1, 19.7}, 0xffaacc, 'D'}, // Vertex D
   { {13.7, 22.7, 14.3}, 0x00aacc, 'E'}, // Vertex E
   { {12.6, 20.8, 10.5}, 0x00ff00, 'F'}, // Vertex F
   { {15.5, 25.4, 15.0}, 0xff0000, 'G'}, // Vertex G
   { {16.0, 22.4, 12.0}, 0xff0000, 'H'}, // Vertex H
   { {18.1, 21.2, 18.0}, 0x0000ff, 'I'}, // Vertex I
   { {12.6, 20.8, 10.9}, 0xffffff, 'J'}  // Vertex J
};
```

References

[Ade62]   Landis E. M. Akademii D. Adel'son-Vel'skii, G. M. *Nauk SSSR 146;English translation in Soviet Mathematics (Providence)*, 3:1259–1263, 1962.

[Atk86]   et al. Atkinson, M. Min-max heaps and generalized priority queues. *Comm. ACM*, 29(10):996–1000, October 1986.

[ATT89]   ATT. *UNIX System V AT&T C++ Language System Release 2.0 -Product Reference Manual*. AT&T, 1989.

[ATT91]   ATT. *C++ Language System Release 3.0 -Product Reference Manual*. AT&T & UNIX System Laboratories, Inc., 1991.

[Bay71]   R. Bayer. Binary b-trees for virtual memory. In *Proc. 1971 ACM SIGFIDET Workshop*, pages 219–235, ACM, 1971.

[Bay72]   R. Bayer. Symmetric binary b-trees: data structure and maintenance algorithms. *Acta Informatica*, 1(4):290–306, 1972.

[Boo91]   G. Booch. *Object Oriented Design With Applications*. The Benjamin/Cummings Publishing Company, Inc., 1991.

[BW88]   H. J. Boehm and M. Weiser. Garbage collection in an uncooperative environment. *Software–Practice and Experience*, 18(9):807–820, 1988.

[Dei90]   H. M. Deitel. *An Introduction to Operating Systems*. Addison-Wesley Publishing Company, Inc., 1990.

[Fre60]   E. Fredkin. Trie memory. *Comm. of ACM*, 490–499, 1960.

[Fre87]   M. Freeston. The bang file: a new kind of grid file. In *Proc. ACM SIGMOD Int. Conf. on Management of Data*, pages 260–269, 1987.

[GK80]   R. H. Guting and H. P. Kriegel. Multidimensional b-tree: an efficient dynamic file structure for exact match. In *Proceedings of the Tenth Gesellschaft fur Informatik Conference*, pages 375–388, 1980.

[Gla89] A. S. Glassner. *An Introduction to Ray Tracing.* Academic Press, 1989.

[Gut84] A. Guttman. R-trees: a dynamic index structure for spatial searching. In *Proceedings SIGMOD*, 1984.

[Hoa62] C. A. R. Hoare. Quicksort. *The Computer Journal*, 5:10–15, 1962.

[Hol87] A. I. Holub. *C Companion.* Prentice-Hall, Englewood Cliffs, New Jersey, USA, 1987.

[Knu73] D. Knuth. *The Art of Computer Programming: Sorting and Searching.* Addison-Wesley, 1973.

[Laf91] R. Lafore. *Object-oriented Programming in Turbo C++.* Waite Group Press, 1991.

[Lau78] U. Lauther. 4-dimensional binary search trees as a means to speed up associative searches in design rule verification of integrated circuits. *Journal of Design Automation and Fault-Tolerant Computing*, 2(3):241–247, 1978.

[LZ74] B. Liskov and S. Zilles. Programming with abstract data types. *ACM Sigplan Notices*, 9(4):50–59, 1974.

[Meh84] K. Mehlhorn. *Data Structures and Algorithms 3: Multi-dimensional Searching and Computational Geometry.* Springer-Verlag, 1984.

[Mey88] B. Meyer. *Object-Oriented Software Construction.* Prentice-Hall, New York, USA, 1988.

[Moo66] R. E. Moore. *Interval Analysis.* Prentice-Hal, New Jersey, USA, 1966.

[Mor68] D.R. Morrison. Patricia - practical algorithm to retrieve information coded in alphanumeric. *ACM*, 15(4):514–534, October 1968.

[Nie84] Hinterberger H. Sevcik K. C. Nievergelt, J. The grid file: an adaptable, symmetric multikey file structure. *ACM Trans. on Database Systems*, 9(1):38–71, March 1984.

[Ore82] Jack Orenstein. Multidimensional tries used for associative searching. *Information Processing Letters*, 14(4):150–157, 1982.

[Ove82] Leeuwen J. V. Overmars, M. H. Dynamic multi-dimensional data structures based on quad- and d-d trees. *Acta Informatica*, 17:267–285, 1982.

[Pre85]   Shamos M. I. Preparata, F. P. *Computational Geometry.* Springer-Verlag, 1985.

[Ram89]   M. W. Ramakrishna. Practical performance of bloom filters and parallel free-text searching. *Comm. ACM*, 32(10), 1989.

[RFS79]   N. Pippenger R. Fagin, J.Nievergelt and H.R. Strong. Extendible hashing - a fast access method for dynamic files. *ACM Trans. on Database Systems*, 4(3):315–344, September 1979.

[Rob81]   J. T. Robinson. The k-d-b tree: a search structure for large multidimensional dynamic indexes. In *Proc. ACM SIGMOD Conf.*, 1981.

[Sam89a] H. Samet. *Applications of Spatial Data Structures.* Addison-Wesley, 1989.

[Sam89b] H. Samet. *The Design and Analysis of Spatial Data Structures.* Addison-Wesley, 1989.

[SE91]   S. Sengupta and P. Edwards. *Data Strucures in ANSI C.* Academic Press, San Diego, California, USA, 1991.

[Sed77]   R. Sedgewick. The analysis of quicksort programs. *Acta Informatica*, 7:327–355, 1977.

[She59]   D. L. Shell. A high speed sorting procedure. *Comm. ACM*, 2(7), July 1959.

[SO82]   P. Scheuerman and M. Ouksel. Multidimensional b-trees for associative searching in database systems. *Information Systems*, 7(2):123–137, 1982.

[Str89]   B. Stroustrup. Parameterized types in C++. *Journal of Object-Oriented Programming*, 1(5):5–16, 1989.

[Str91]   B. Stroustrup. *The C++ Programming Language, Second edition.* Addison Wesley, 1991.

[Tam81]   M. Tamminen. The excell method for efficient geometric access to data. *Acta Polytechnica Scandinavica - Mathematics and Computer Science Series*, 34, 1981.

[Vai84]   V. K. Vaishnavi. Multidimensional height-balanced trees. *IEEE Transactions on Computers*, 33(4):334–343, April 1984.

[WF90]   K. Weiskamp and B. Flamig. *The Complete C++ Primer.* Academic Press, 1990.

Index